PS

1

LOVE AND DEATH IN THE AMERICAN NOVEL

Leslie A. Fiedler (signature)

BY LESLIE A. FIEDLER

The Last Jew in America

Back to China

Waiting for the End

The Second Stone

Pull Down Vanity

No! in Thunder

An End to Innocence

STEIN AND DAY / *Publishers* / New York

LOVE AND DEATH IN THE AMERICAN NOVEL

Revised Edition, 1966

PREFACE

TO THE SECOND EDITION

REREADING *Love and Death in the American Novel* ten years after the moment at which I first began to set it down, I have been delighted and astonished to discover that I still believe what it says. The voice which speaks in its pages I no longer recognize as quite my own, but I find it a sympathetic one—for all its exclamatory and insistent tone. Like others, I have now grown so used to what was new and daring in its theses once, that I am sometimes annoyed at how hard it presses or how pleased it seems with its own insights. "But we all accept these contentions," I am tempted to cry. "This is where we now begin." Yet for old times' sake, I have not willingly surrendered more than a few exclamation points, strategic capitalizations, or italicized words.

In preparing a new edition I have, therefore, not tampered with the language or the style of the original, only everywhere pruned and condensed, out of a sense that the first version was somehow too thickly allusive, with too many asides, too intent on overwhelming the sceptical to suit the needs of readers a decade later.

I have, moreover, worked back into the main body of the text certain detailed analyses of *The Scarlet Letter, Moby Dick,* and *Huckleberry Finn,* originally consigned to a kind of appendix called "Accommodation and Transcendence." I have done this first of all because I believe that is where they best fit, but also because I have a hunch that some readers of the earlier edition never reached them at all—and they are of critical importance to the total meaning of my book.

That book as now revised seems to me a more shapely and for that reason a clearer one—one in which, for instance, the balance between psychological and sociological insights essential to my approach is more readily perceived; and the relation of both to the books I best love more cogently exposed. And especially, 1 hope, even the most casual reader will be able this time around to recognize the sense in which *Love and Death* can be read not as a conventional scholarly book—or an eccentric one—but a kind of gothic novel (complete with touches of black humor) whose subject is the American experience as recorded in our classic fiction. Our most serious as well as our funniest writers have found the gothic mode an apt one for telling the truth about the quality of our life; and I should, therefore, have been ashamed not to try to use it for my own purposes.

Despite all these safeguards, however, I discover that my excisions and re-arrangements have given a new pattern and rhythm and pace to a statement unaltered in substance and only slightly modified in tone.. If *Love and Death* is a more spare and elegant book this time around, it is because it can afford to be a less forensic, even a less formidable one.

It has survived into a new literary era and will, I trust, continue to flourish in a new cultural climate, which, indeed it may have helped to create. The year 1960 is not very far behind us; but certain kinds of criticism still practiced and admired then—the last examples of the new genteel tradition, with its emphasis on textual analysis, its contempt for general ideas, and its fear ol popular culture—now strike us as irrelevant and remote. It is my sense of the continuing relevance and immediacy of this study which has impelled me to recast and re-issue it. It is my hope that to new readers and old, it will seem still as lively and in the best sense of the word, as vulgar as ever.

LESLIE A. FIEDLER
Buffalo, New York
January, 1966

PREFACE

TO THE FIRST EDITION

THE CAUTIOUS READER, approaching a book as thick and complex as this, has every right to expect some prefatory word from the author about what he is after, what he thinks he has done; and the author (if he is I, at least) is delighted to explain himself, to welcome the kind of audience he has all along desired, and to warn off the unsympathetic. This is not, in the customarily accepted sense of the word, an academic or scholarly book, though it is indebted throughout to works of scholarship. The lack of footnotes and formal bibliography will advise the wary that I have sought everywhere the kind of validity which depends not on faithfulness to "fact' but on insight and sensitivity to nuance. I do not mean, of course, that I have despised accuracy (within the limits of my approach and temperament I have sought it) but that I have tried to produce a literary rather than a scientific work, a labor of love rather than one of patience.

I have not, however, written what is most often meant these days by a "critical" study, mere textual analysis, ahistorical, anti-biographical: the kind of guide for courses in higher remedial reading which an age of lapsing literacy perhaps demands, but which it is somewhat craven to supply. There are, to be sure, many full-scale readings of novels included in these pages: lengthy analyses of *Moby Dick, The Scarlet Letter,* and *Huckleberry Finn,* and shorter ones of books ranging from *Edgar Huntly* and *The Last of the Mohicans* through *Uncle Tom's Cabin* and *The Monks of Monk Hall* to *The Victim.* But nowhere is it suggested that such résumés are the key to the essential work of art, whatever that catch phrase may still mean; and they are everywhere embedded in a context of more general or theoretical explications.

The experience of a work of art is, as everyone seems willing to grant without pondering the implications, unique and untranslatable; to suggest that one has captured it in an analysis is, therefore, to falsify and mislead. The best criticism can hope to do is to set the work in as many illuminating contexts as possible: the context of the genre to which it belongs, of the whole body of work of its author, of the life of that author and of his times. In this sense, it becomes clear that the "text" is merely one of the contexts of a piece of literature, its lexical or verbal one, no more or less important than the sociological, psychological, historical, anthropological or generic. The contextual critic desires only to *locate* the work of art, to point toward the place where his contextual circles overlap, the place in which the work exists in all its ambiguity and plenitude.

Ideally, of course, an object of critical attention should be set in *all* its relevant contexts; but this is the never-completed communal task of criticism as a continuing institution, and no one critic is able to do more than a small part of the whole job. With both the goals and limitations of contextual criticism in mind, I have attempted in the present study to emphasize the neglected contexts of American fiction, largely depth-psychological and anthropological, but sociological and formal as well. Certain other approaches and insights, well-established in textbooks and in the classroom, I have not touched on at all, assuming them to exist in the minds of anyone who would be led to read this book. My own contributions I consider not as alternative to standard ways of reading but as complementary to them; I find no greater pleasure than in reminding myself that my interpretations are as partial as those which bore me the most. I trust that in the end my own insights will, without themselves coming to seem dishearteningly satisfactory, make more established ways of understanding our fiction appear pat and inadequate.

Nothing (I know, as all writers suspect and any teacher is aware) will drive some readers back from the certainties of textbook explanations to the difficulties of the work of art itself; but others, less resolutely insensitive, will, I hope, be troubled enough by suggestions of new possibilities in old works, so that (whether ultimately they accept my views or not) they will never again be able

to half-read *Huckleberry Finn* or *The Last of the Mohicans* in the
the state of torpor they have taken for cultural security. American
literature is distinguished by the number of dangerous and disturbing books in its canon—and American scholarship by its ability to
conceal this fact. To redeem our great books from the commentaries on them is one of the chief functions of this study.

I have, in general, tried to demonstrate that the American novel
has a character and fate different from the novel in France, Germany, even Russia. That there are resemblances, too, the very use
of the common term for the genre makes evident; but such resemblances are not my primary concern. In order to make clear the
divergence of our own novelistic tradition from the continental ones
(and of our own life from life in Europe), I have found it useful to
concentrate on the themes of love and death as treated by our
major writers—and especially on the duplicity with which those
themes are handled in the United States. My treatment is, therefore, thematic rather than strictly historical, selective rather than
exhaustive. Though the time span covered in my essay extends
from 1789 to 1959, I have not pretended to deal with all the remembered novelists of those years. Particularly in the more recent
period, I have ignored certain fictionists, highly regarded in some
quarters, who do not share what I believe to be the major concerns
of our tradition. I have not, however, failed to treat any writer
whom I consider to be of first rank merely because he has had the
ill grace to be un-symptomatic or eccentric; in no case have I deliberately sacrificed considerations of value to the pursuit of my
themes. Nonetheless, certain partisan readers will doubtless resent
the passing mention or the total silence accorded such novelists as
William Dean Howells, Sinclair Lewis, John Dos Passos, or
Thomas Wolfe. I can only hope that they will find appropriate
compensation in my concern with figures often scanted despite
their real merits: William Hill Brown, George Lippard, Oliver
Wendell Holmes, Nathanael West, and Wright Morris.

My desire to define what is peculiarly American in our books has
made it necessary for me to approach our literature from a com-
paratist point of view; and I have not hesitated to include rather
detailed readings of books by Samuel Richardson, Walter Scott,
and M. G. Lewis, books which provided prototypes for our own
earliest attempts in the various sub-forms of the novel. To discuss
literature in the United States without reference to contemporary
developments in Europe, seems to me as futile as discussing it

without a consideration of the way in which the very concept of literature and the theme of love were re-born together in the West at the end of the Middle Ages. That such a consideration demands certain general theories about art and the human mind has stimulated rather than dismayed me; and the forewarned reader should be no more dismayed when he comes upon a rather full examination of the rise of courtly-love poetry at the end of the eleventh century, or of the novel and the Sentimental Love Religion in the mid-eighteenth.

I have learned painfully that without such a pre-discussion before him, any but the most sophisticated reader is likely to misunderstand some of my specific observations on our literature and ourselves—my theory, for instance, about the relationship between sentimental life in America and the archetypal image, found in our favorite books, in which a white and a colored American male flee from civilization into each other's arms. Certainly, my earliest formulation of this theory in "Come Back to the Raft Ag'in, Huck Honey" has met with a shocked and, I suspect, partly willful incomprehension. I have been accused of impiety, grossness, a contempt for the classics of childhood, even of a disturbing influence on private lives. I trust that the full development of my contentions in these pages will obviate at least the simpler kinds of misunderstanding, and that my additional comments on the importance in our literature of brother-sister incest and necrophilia will not stir up new protests of a similar kind.

I do not relish the role of a private eye making courtroom revelations, but it is one into which some of our writers have, not without malice, forced the critic. Walt Whitman, who finally gives so much away, makes this point clear:

> For it is not for what I have put into it that I have written this
>   book,
> Nor is it by reading it you will acquire it . . .
> For all is useless without that which you may guess at many
>   times and not hit, that which I hinted at . . .

The failure of the American fictionist to deal with adult heterosexual love and his consequent obsession with death, incest and innocent homosexuality are not merely matters of historical interest or literary relevance. They affect the lives we lead from day to day and influence the writers in whom the consciousness of our plight is given clarity and form. Paul Bowles, writing highbrow terror-fiction in the middle of the twentieth century, cannot escape the limitations that plagued Charles Brockden Brown at the beginning of the eighteenth; and Saul Bellow, composing a homoerotic *Tarzan of the Apes* in *Henderson the Rain King,* is back on the raft with Mark Twain. There is a pattern imposed both by the writers of our past and the very conditions of life in the United States from which no American novelist can escape, no matter what philosophy he consciously adopts or what theme he thinks he pursues. In Parts One and Two of this study, I have traced in some detail the emergence and development of this pattern; and in Part Three, I have tried to show how our three greatest novelists, each once and once only, made of the pattern they could not evade literature of the first excellence.

Though this is finally a very personal book, in which I attempt to say with my own voice out of my own face (all masks abandoned) what I have found to be some major meanings of our literature and our culture, it does not spring to life unbegotten, unaffiliated and unsponsored. In one sense, it has been essentially present from the moment that I read aloud to two of my sons (then five and seven) for their first time *Huckleberry Finn,* and saw all at once what it has taken me so long to get down. In another, it has taken shape slowly through a lifetime of reading and seven years or more of concentrated labor. My first obligation, then, is to Mark Twain and to my children; my second, much harder to document, to all the texts on which I comment, to hundreds of critical and scholarly books, most of which I do not mention—as well as to certain fugitive remarks and by-the-way observations, sowed by friends and enemies in conversations I no longer quite remember.

Four major sources of indebtedness I feel moved to acknowledge here, though in all four I have so grossly adapted, so shamelessly distorted certain original insights that their authors may well find my acknowledgments presumptuous, even offensive. The first is C. S. Lewis, whose *The Allegory of Love* taught me at the age of eighteen the sense in which love is an invention and the poets its inventors. His book has left me ever since wrestling with the problem of the psychic break-through that at the same moment introduced into a patriarchal world the worship of women and into a Christian one the cult of art. Other insights into this problem I have found in Denis de Rougement—and in the Provençal poets with whom both the latter and Lewis deal; but my introduction to a fertile and fascinating area I owe primarily to *The Allegory of Love*.

Similarly, certain Marxian critics had made clear to me before I was twenty what otherwise might have remained too obvious for me to see: that the class-relations of a culture help determine the shape of its deepest communal fantasies, the obsessive concerns of its literature. Without clues from such analysts, I do not think I could have understood, for instance, the genesis of the radical shift in the nature of the villain as portrayed in European and American gothic fiction—and the ideological revolution which that shift projects. Yet the substitution of the Indian for the Inquisitor, the symbol of untamed nature for that of corrupt civilization, as horror and threat, bodies forth certain essential meanings of Poe and Hawthorne, and underlies certain intolerable contradictions in Melville and Twain. In light of my debt to Marxist thought, it seems fair enough that the first statement of one of the key notions of this book should have appeared in *Partisan Review,* American heir—for a while at least—to the Marxian critical approach.

To Freud and his followers, and also to Carl Jung, I owe a similar debt. Readers familiar with orthodox Freudianism and Jungian revisionism will recognize the sources of much of my basic vocabulary; I cannot imagine myself beginning the kind of investigation I have undertaken without the concepts of the conscious and the unconscious, the Oedipus complex, the archetypes, etc. Only my awareness of how syncretically I have yoked together and how cavalierly I have transformed my borrowings prevents my making more specific acknowledgments. Quite appropriately, I was able to develop some of the leading arguments in this book in the Freud Memorial Lecture for 1956, given before the Philadelphia Association for Psychoanalysis, for which opportunity I owe thanks especially to Dr. Paul Sloane and Robert Waelder.

Of all the literary critics who have written about American books, the one who has seemed to me closest to the truth, even at those points where I finally disagree with him, and who has brought to his subject an appropriate passion and style, is, of course, D. H. Lawrence. His *Studies in Classic American Literature* attempted for the first time the kind of explication which does not betray the complexity or perilousness of its theme; and in the pages of that little book I found confirmation of my own suspicions that it is duplicity and outrageousness which determine the quality of those American books ordinarily consigned to the children's shelf in the library. Only Melville himself, in his published remarks on Hawthorne, more precisely identified the nature of the American novel.

Such acknowledgments as these, however, only begin to indicate the sources on which I have drawn for a book that was not wholly written in the privacy of my study, but which found its shape in the classroom and on the lecture platform. Especially fruitful were: my classes at what is now the Indiana School of Letters in 1952 and 1954; my lectures in Rome, Bologna, and Venice as a Fulbright Fellow between the fall of 1951 and the summer of 1953; my platform appearances before college and professional groups all up and down the United States in the last five or six years; and especially the Christian Gauss Seminars at Princeton in 1957, during which I worked out almost all of Part Three of this study.* I cannot enumerate all of those to whom I am grateful for making these occasions possible and lively (I do not even remember the name of the figure who remains most vivid in my mind—the questioner at one lecture, so appalled by the enormity of what I had to say about the relationship of Queequeg and Ishmael, that he accused me of having stolen his raincoat!), but I should like to name a few: Mario Praz, Agostino Lombardo, Carlo Izzo, Gabriele Baldini, John Crowe Ransom, James Cox, R. P. Blackmur, and E. B. O. Borgerhoff. Easiest to forget and hardest to thank, because they have provided the very atmosphere in which I live, are my colleagues and students at Montana State University—who have sustained me by their affection and trust for nearly twenty years. All the others will forgive me, I know, if I name only H. G. Merriam and Edmund Freeman.

My deepest debt goes back beyond any of these to the time during which I was a graduate student of William Ellery Leonard, a great and, I hope, unforgotten teacher, as well as a rebel, poet, translator, and essayist. It was he who first not merely told but showed me—showed in the rich, tragic quality of his own being as well as by the excitement that he engendered in the classroom— that literature is more than what one learns to read in schools and libraries, more even than a grace of life; that it is the record of those elusive moments at which life is alone fully itself, fulfilled in

---

* All the content of Part Three of the first edition has been incorporated in other sections in the present edition.

consciousness and form. No one who has been his student can regard literary criticism as anything less than an act of total moral engagement, in which tact, patience, insolence, and piety consort strangely but satisfactorily together; nor can anyone who once listened to him believe that the truth one tries to tell about literature is finally different from the truth one tries to tell about the indignities and rewards of being the kind of man one is—an American, let's say, in the second half of the twentieth century, learning to read his country's books.

LESLIE A. FIEDLER

Missoula, Montana
13 October 1959

CONTENTS

PART TWO: ACHIEVEMENT
AND FRUSTRATION

LOVE AND

DEATH

IN THE

AMERICAN

NOVEL

PART ONE

PROTOTYPES AND EARLY ADAPTATIONS

1

THE NOVEL AND

AMERICA

BETWEEN THE NOVEL and America there are peculiar and intimate connections. A new literary form and a new society, their beginnings coincide with the beginnings of the modern era and, indeed, help to define it. We are living not only in the Age of America but also in the Age of the Novel, at a moment when the literature of a country without a first-rate verse epic or a memorable verse tragedy has become the model of half the world.

We have known for a long time, of course, that our national literary reputation depends largely upon the achievement of our novelists. The classical poetic genres revived by the Renaissance had lost their relevance to contemporary life before America entered the cultural scene; and even the lyric has provided us with occasions for few, and limited, triumphs. Not only in the United States, though pre-eminently there, literature has become for most readers quite simply prose fiction; and our endemic fantasy of writing "the Great American Novel" is only a local instance of a more general obsession. The notions of greatness once associated with the heroic poem have been transferred to the novel; and the shift is a part of that "Americanization of culture" which some European intellectuals continue ritually to deplore.

But is there, as certain continental critics have insisted, an "American novel," a specific sub-variety of the form? If we turn to these critics for a definition, we come on such terms as "neo-realist," "hard-boiled," "naive," and "anti-traditional"—terms derived from a standard view of America as an "anti-culture," an

23

eternally maintained preserve of primitivism. This view (notoriously exemplified by André Gide) ends by finding in Dashiell Hammett the same values as in William Faulkner, and is more a symptom of European cultural malaise than a useful critical distinction. It is tempting to insist on the pat rebuttal that, far from being an anti-culture, we are merely a branch of Western culture; and that there is no "American novel," only local variants of standard European kinds of fiction: American sentimental, American gothic, American historical romance, etc. Certainly no single subgenre of the novel was invented in the United States. Yet the peculiarities of our variants seem more interesting and important than their resemblances to the parent forms.

There is a real sense in which our prose fiction is immediately distinguishable from that of Europe, though this is a fact that is difficult for Americans to confess. In this sense, our novels seem not primitive, perhaps, but innocent, unfallen in a disturbing way, almost juvenile. The great works of American fiction are notoriously at home in the children's section of the library, their level of sentimentality precisely that of a pre-adolescent. This is part of what we mean when we talk about the incapacity of the American novelist to develop; in a compulsive way he returns to a limited world of experience, usually associated with his childhood, writing the same book over and over again until he lapses into silence or self-parody.

Merely finding a language, learning to talk in a land where there are no conventions of conversation, no special class idioms and no dialogue between classes, no continuing literary language—this exhausts the American writer. He is forever *beginning*, saying for the first time (without real tradition there can never be a second time) what it is like to stand alone before nature, or in a city as appallingly lonely as any virgin forest. He faces, moreover, another problem, which has resulted in a failure of feeling and imagination perceptible at the heart of even our most notable works. Our great novelists, though experts on indignity and assault, on loneliness and terror, tend to avoid treating the passionate encounter of a man and woman, which we expect at the center of a novel. Indeed, they rather shy away from permitting in their fictions the presence of any full-fledged, mature women, giving us instead monsters of virtue or bitchery, symbols of the rejection or fear of sexuality.

To be sure, the theme of "love" in so simple a sense is by no means necessary to all works of art. In the *Iliad,* for instance, and in much Greek tragedy, it is conspicuously absent; and in the heroic literature of the Middle Ages, it is peripheral where it exists at all. The *"belle Aude"* of the *Chanson de Roland* is a supernumerary, and the only female we remember from *Beowulf* is a terror emerging from the darkness at the bottom of the waters. The world of the epic is a world of war, and its reigning sentimental relationship is the loyalty of comrades in arms; but by the eighteenth century the notion of a heroic poem without romance had come to seem intolerable. The last pseudo-epics of the baroque had been obsessed with the subject of love, and the rococo had continued to elaborate that theme. Shakespeare himself appeared to the English Augustans too little concerned with the "reigning passion" to be quite interesting without revision. Why, after all, should Cordelia not survive to marry Edgar, they demanded of themselves—and they rewrote *King Lear* to prove that she should.

The novel, however, was precisely the product of the sentimentalizing taste of the eighteenth century; and a continuing tradition of prose fiction did not begin until the love affair of Lovelace and Clarissa (a demythicized Don Juan and a secularized goddess of Christian love) had been imagined. The subject par excellence of the novel is love or, more precisely—in its beginnings at least—seduction and marriage; and in France, Italy, Germany, and Russia, even in England, spiritually so close to America, love in one form or another has remained the novel's central theme, as necessary and as expected as battle in Homer or revenge in the Renaissance drama. But our great Romantic *Unroman,* our typical anti-novel, is the womanless *Moby Dick.*

Where is our *Madame Bovary,* our *Anna Karenina,* our *Pride and Prejudice* or *Vanity Fair?* Among our classic novels, at least those before Henry James, who stands so oddly between our own traditions and the European ones we rejected or recast, the best attempt at dealing with love is *The Scarlet Letter,* in which the physical consummation of adultery has occurred and all passion burned away before the novel proper begins. For the rest, there are *Moby Dick* and *Huckleberry Finn, The Last of the Mohicans, The Red Badge of Courage,* the stories of Edgar Allan Poe—books that turn from society to nature or nightmare out of a desperate need to avoid the facts of wooing, marriage, and child-bearing.

The figure of Rip Van Winkle presides over the birth of the

American imagination; and it is fitting that our first successful homegrown legend should memorialize, however playfully, the flight of the dreamer from the drab duties of home and town toward the good companions and the magic keg of Holland's gin. Ever since, the typical male protagonist of our fiction has been a man on the run, harried into the forest and out to sea, down the river or into combat—anywhere to avoid "civilization," which is to say, the confrontation of a man and woman which leads to the fall to sex, marriage, and responsibility.

Rip's world is not only asexual, however, it is terrible: a world of fear and loneliness, a haunted world; and the American novel is pre-eminently a novel of terror. To "light out for the territory" or seek refuge in the forest seems easy and tempting from the vantage point of a chafing and restrictive home; but civilization once disavowed and Christianity disowned, the bulwark of woman left behind, the wanderer feels himself without protection, more motherless child than free man. To be sure, there is a substitute for wife or mother presumably waiting in the green heart of nature: the natural man, the good companion, pagan and un-ashamed—Queequeg or Chingachgook or Nigger Jim. But the figure of the natural man is ambiguous, a dream and a nightmare at once. The other face of Chingachgook is Injun Joe, the killer in the graveyard and the haunter of caves; Nigger Jim is also the Babo of Melville's "Benito Cereno," the humble servant whose name means "papa" holding the razor to his master's throat; and finally the dark-skinned companion becomes the "Black Man," which is a traditional American name for the Devil himself.

The enemy of society on the run toward "freedom" is also the pariah in flight from his guilt, the guilt of that very flight; and new phantoms arise to haunt him at every step. American literature likes to pretend, of course, that its bugaboos are all finally jokes: the headless horseman a hoax, every manifestation of the super-natural capable of rational explanation on the last page—but we are never quite convinced. *Huckleberry Finn,* that euphoric boys' book, begins with its protagonist holding off at gun point his father driven half mad by the D.T.'s and ends (after a lynching, a dis-interment, and a series of violent deaths relieved by such humor-ous incidents as soaking a dog in kerosene and setting him on fire) with the revelation of that father's sordid death. Nothing is spared; Pap, horrible enough in life, is found murdered brutally, aban-doned to float down the river in a decaying house scrawled with obscenities. But it is all "humor," of course, a last desperate attempt to convince us of the innocence of violence, the good clean fun of horror. Our literature as a whole at times seems a chamber of horrors disguised as an amusement park "fun house," where we pay to play at terror and are confronted in the innermost chamber with a series of inter-reflecting mirrors which present us with a thousand versions of our own face.

In our most enduring books, the cheapjack machinery of the gothic novel is called on to represent the hidden blackness of the human soul and human society. No wonder our authors mock themselves as they use such devices; no wonder Mistress Hibbins in *The Scarlet Letter* and Fedallah in *Moby Dick* are treated half jocularly, half melodramatically, though each represents in his book the Faustian pact, the bargain with the Devil, which our authors have always felt as the essence of the American experience. However shoddily or ironically treated, horror is essential to our literature. It is not merely a matter of terror filling the vacuum left by the suppression of sex in our novels, of Thanatos standing in for Eros. Through these gothic images are projected certain obsessive concerns of our national life: the ambiguity of our relationship with Indian and Negro, the ambiguity of our encounter with nature, the guilt of the revolutionist who feels himself a parricide—and, not least of all, the uneasiness of the writer who cannot help believing that the very act of composing a book is Satanic revolt. "Hell-fired," Hawthorne called *The Scarlet Letter,* and Melville thought his own *Moby Dick* a "wicked book."

The American writer inhabits a country at once the dream of Europe and a fact of history; he lives on the last horizon of an endlessly retreating vision of innocence—on the "frontier," which is to say, the margin where the theory of original goodness and the fact of original sin come face to face. To express this "blackness ten times black" and to live by it in a society in which, since the decline of orthodox Puritanism, optimism has become the chief effective religion, is a complex and difficult task.

It was to the novel that the American writer turned most naturally, as the only *popular* form of sufficient magnitude for his vision. He was, perhaps, not sufficiently sophisticated to realize that such learned forms as epic and tragedy had already outlived their usefulness; but, working out of a cultural background at best sketchy and unsure, he felt insecure before them. His obligations urged him in the direction of tragedy, but traditional verse tragedy was forbidden him; indeed, a chief technical problem for American novelists has been the adaptation of nontragic forms to tragic ends. How could the dark vision of the American—his obsession with violence and his embarrassment before love—be expressed in the sentimental novel of analysis as developed by Samuel Richardson or the historical romance as practiced by Sir Walter Scott? These sub-genres of fiction, invented to satisfy the emotional needs of a merchant class in search of dignity or a Tory squirearchy consumed by nostalgia, could only by the most desperate expedients be tailored to fit American necessities. Throughout their writing lives, such writers as Charles Brockden Brown and James Fenimore Cooper devoted (with varying degrees of self-consciousness) all their ingenuity to this task, yet neither Brown nor Cooper finally proved capable of achieving high art; and the literary types invented by both have fallen since into the hands of mere entertainers—that is, novelists able and willing to attempt anything *except* the projection of the dark vision of America we have been describing. The Fielding novel, on the other hand, the pseudo-Shakespearean "comic epic" with its broad canvas, its emphasis upon reversals and recognitions, and its robust masculine senti-mentality, turned out, oddly enough, to have no relevance to the American scene; in the United States it has remained an exotic, eternally being discovered by the widest audience and raised to best-sellerdom in its latest imported form, but seldom home-produced for home consumption.

It is the gothic form that has been most fruitful in the hands of our best writers: the gothic *symbolically* understood, its machinery and décor translated into metaphors for a terror psychological, social, and metaphysical. Yet even treated as symbols, the machinery and décor of the gothic have continued to seem vulgar and contrived; symbolic gothicism threatens always to dissolve into its components, abstract morality and shoddy theater. A recurrent problem of our fiction has been the need of our novelists to find a mode of projecting their conflicts which would contain all the dusky horror of gothic romance and yet be palatable to discriminating readers, palatable first of all to themselves.

Such a mode can, of course, not be subsumed among any of those called "realism." Our fiction is essentially and at its best nonrealistic, even anti-realistic; long before *symbolisme* had been invented in France and exported to America, there was a full-fledged native tradition of symbolism. That tradition was born of the profound contradictions of our national life and sustained by the inheritance from Puritanism of a "typical" (even allegorical) way of regarding the sensible world—not as an ultimate reality but as a system of signs to be deciphered. For too long, historians of American fiction have mistakenly tried to impose on the course of a brief literary history a notion of artistic "progress" imported from France or, more precisely perhaps, from certain French literary critics.

But the moment at which Flaubert was dreaming *Madame Bovary* was the moment when Melville was finding *Moby Dick,* and considered as a "realistic" novel the latter is a scandalous botch. To speak of a counter-tradition to the novel, of the tradition of "the romance" as a force in our literature, is merely to repeat the rationalizations of our writers themselves; it is certainly to fail to be *specific* enough for real understanding. Our fiction is not merely in flight from the physical data of the actual world, in search of a (sexless and dim) Ideal; from Charles Brockden Brown to William Faulkner or Eudora Welty, Paul Bowles or John Hawkes, it is, bewilderingly and embarrassingly, a gothic fiction, nonrealistic and negative, sadist and melodramatic—a literature of darkness and the grotesque in a land of light and affirmation.

Moreover—and the final paradox is necessary to the full complexity of the case—our classic literature is a literature of horror for boys. Truly shocking, frankly obscene authors we do not possess; Edgar Allan Poe is our closest approximation, a child playing at what Baudelaire was to live. A Baudelaire, a Marquis de Sade, a "Monk" Lewis, even a John Cleland was inconceivable in the United States.* Our flowers of evil are culled for the small girl's bouquet, our novels of terror (*Moby Dick, The Scarlet Letter, Huckleberry Finn,* the tales of Poe) are placed on the approved

---

* In recent years the situation appears to have altered radically—perhaps, in part, because the taste of boys has changed, as the "latency period," which Freud thought immutable, tends to be abolished. At any rate, the line between "pornography" and respectable literature has blurred; and certain traditional themes of American literature—the love of white and colored males, for instance, and the vilification of women—are rendered with explicit sexual detail. Indeed, such detail becomes required rather than forbidden as American puritanism learns to stand on its head. It is a long way from James Fenimore Cooper to James Baldwin, or from Herman Melville to Norman Mailer; but even if our dreams have become more frankly erotic, the American *eros* has not really changed. We continue to dream the female dead, and ourselves in the arms of our dusky male lovers.

book lists of Parents' Committees who nervously fuss over the latest comic books. If such censors do not flinch at necrophilia or shudder over the book whose secret motto is "I baptise you not in the name of the Father . . . but of the Devil," or fear the juvenile whose hero at his greatest moment cries out, "All right, I'll *go* to Hell," it is only another irony of life in a land where the writers believe in hell and the official guardians of morality do not.

Yet our authors are as responsible as the P.T.A.'s for the confusion about the true nature of their books; though they may have whispered their secret to friends, or confessed it in private letters, · in their actual works they assumed what camouflage prudence dictated. They *wanted* to be misunderstood. *Huckleberry Finn* is only the supreme instance of a subterfuge typical of our classic novelists. To this very day, it is heresy in some quarters to insist that this is not finally the jolliest, the *cleanest* of books; Twain's ironical warning to significance hunters, posted just before the title page, is taken quite literally, and the irreverent critic who explicates the book's levels of terror and evasion is regarded as a busybody and scandalmonger. Why, one is driven to ask, why the distortion and why the ignorance?

Perhaps the whole odd shape of American fiction arises simply (as simplifying Europeans are always ready to assure us) because there is no real sexuality in American life and therefore there cannot very well be any in American art. What we cannot achieve in our relations with each other it would be vain to ask our writers to portray or even our critics to miss. Certainly many of our novelists have themselves believed, or pretended to believe, this. Through *The Scarlet Letter,* there is a constant mournful undercurrent, a series of asides in which Hawthorne deplores the sexual diminution of American women. Mark Twain in *1601* somewhat similarly contrasts the vigor of Elizabethan Englishwomen with their American descendants; contrasting the sexual utopia of pre-colonial England with a fallen America where the men copulate "but once in seven yeeres"; and his pornographic sketch ends on the comic-pathetic image of an old man's impotent lust that "would not stand again." Such pseudo-nostalgia cannot be taken too seriously, however; it may, indeed, be the projection of mere personal weakness and fantasy. Certainly, outside their books, Hawthorne and Twain seem to have fled rather than sought the imaginary full-breasted, fully sexed woman from whom American ladies had presumably declined. Both married, late in life, pale hypochondriac spinsters, intellectual invalids—as if to assert publicly that they sought in marriage not sex but culture.

Such considerations leave us trapped in the chicken-egg dilemma. How can one say whether the quality of passion in American life suffers because of a failure of the writer's imagination or vice versa? What is called "love" in literature is a rationalization, a way of coming to terms with the relationship between man and woman that does justice, on the one hand, to certain biological drives and, on the other, to certain generally accepted conventions of tenderness and courtesy; and literature, expressing and defining those conventions, tends to influence "real life" more than such life influences it. For better or for worse and for whatever reasons, the American novel is different from its European prototypes, and one of its essential differences arises from its chary treatment of woman and of sex.

To write, then, about the American novel is to write about the fate of certain European genres in a world of alien experience. It is not only a world where courtship and marriage have suffered a profound change, but also one in the process of losing the traditional distinctions of class; a world without a significant history or a substantial past; a world which had left behind the terror of Europe not for the innocence it dreamed of, but for new and special guilts associated with the rape of nature and the exploitation of dark-skinned people; a world doomed to play out the imaginary childhood of Europe. The American novel is only *finally* American; its appearance is an event in the history of the European spirit—as, indeed, is the very invention of America itself.

II

Though it is necessary, in understanding the fate of the American novel, to understand what European prototypes were available when American literature began, as well as which ones flourished and which ones disappeared on our soil, it is even more important to understand the meaning of that moment in the mid-eighteenth century which gave birth to Jeffersonian democracy and Richardsonian sentimentality alike: to the myth of revolution and the myth of seduction. When Charles Brockden Brown, the first professional American author, sent a copy of his *Wieland* to Thomas Jefferson in 1798, he must, beneath his modest disclaimers, have

had some sense of his and the President's kinship as revolutionaries. "I am therefore obliged to hope," Brown wrote, "that . . .
the train of eloquent and judicious reasoning . . . will be regarded
by Thomas Jefferson with as much respect as . . . me." But if
Jefferson ever found the time to read Brown's novel, he left no
record; we know only that he expressed general approval of
"works of the imagination" as being able, more than history, to
"possess virtue in the best and vice in the worst forms possible."
It is a chillingly rational approach to art and a perhaps sufficient
indication of the hopelessness of Brown's attempting in those
sensible years to live by his writing.

Yet despite the fact that no professional novelist of real seriousness was to find a supporting public in America for twenty-five or
thirty years more, Brown's instincts had not deceived him. He and
Jefferson *were* engaged in a common enterprise; the novel and
America did not come into existence at the same time by accident. They are the two great inventions of the bourgeois, Protestant mind at the moment when it stood, on the one hand, between
Rationalism and Sentimentalism, and on the other, between the
drive for economic power and the need for cultural autonomy.
The series of events which includes the American and the French
Revolutions, the invention of the novel, the rise of modern psychology, and the triumph of the lyric in poetry, adds up to a
psychic revolution as well as a social one. This revolution, viewed
as an overturning of ideas and artistic forms, has traditionally been
called "Romantic"; but the term is paralyzingly narrow, defining
too little too precisely, and leading to further pointless distinctions
between Romanticism proper, pre-Romanticism, *Sturm und Drang,*
Sentimentalism, *Symbolisme,* etc. It seems preferable to call the
whole continuing, complex event simply "the Break-through," thus
emphasizing the dramatic entry of a new voice into the dialogue
of Western man with his various selves.

The Break-through is characterized not only by the separation
of psychology from philosophy, the displacement of the traditional
leading genres by the personal lyric and analytic prose fiction
(with the consequent subordination of plot to character); it is
also marked by the promulgation of a theory of revolution as a
good in itself and, most notably perhaps, by a new concept of
inwardness. One is almost tempted to say, by the invention of a
new kind of self, a new level of mind; for what has been happening since the eighteenth century seems more like the development

of a new organ than the mere finding of a new way to describe old experience.

It was Diderot who represented a first real awareness that man is *double* to the final depths of his soul, the prey of conflicting psyches both equally himself. The conflict had, of course, always been felt, but had traditionally been described as occurring between man and devil, or flesh and spirit; that the parties to the dispute are both man and spirit was a revolutionary suggestion. In his demi-novel, *Rameau's Nephew,* Diderot projected the conflicting divisions within man's mind as the philosopher and the parasite, the rationalist and the underground man, debating endlessly the cause of the head versus that of the gut. And in his pornographic *Bijoux Indiscrets,* he proposed another version of the same dialogue: the enchanted (and indiscreet) genitals speak the truth which the mouth will not avow, thus comprising an allegorical defense of pornography in the guise of a pornographic work. In the same year in which Richardson's sentimental novel *Clarissa* was published, John Cleland's long-lived dirty book *The Memoirs of Fanny Hill* was making a stir. Pornography and obscenity are, indeed, hallmarks of the age of the Break-through. Not only pious novels but titillating ones show the emergence of the underground emotions (of what the period itself euphemistically called "the heart") into high culture. Quite as influential as Diderot (or Richardson or Rousseau) in the *bouleversement* of the eighteenth century is the Marquis de Sade, who stands almost emblematically at the crossroads of depth psychology and revolution.

Not only did de Sade shed new light on the ambivalence of the inner mind, revealing the true darkness and terror implicit in the drive which the neo-classical age (revolting against Christian notions of sin) had been content to celebrate as simple "pleasure" or polite "gallantry"; he may even have caused that symbolic storming of an almost empty prison with which the Fernch Revolution begins. Himself a prisoner in the *Tour de la liberté* of the Bastille, de Sade, through an improvised loudspeaker made of a tube and funnel, screamed to bystanders to rescue his fellow inmates who were having their throats cut—and scattered handwritten leaflets complaining about jail conditions to the crowd he attracted. On July 3, 1789, he was finally transferred elsewhere to insure "the safety of the building," but not before he had started to write *Justine, or the Misfortunes of Virtue,* that perverse offshoot of the Richardsonian novel, and had thus begun to create the first example of revolutionary pornography.

In the Marquis de Sade, the Break-through found its most stringent and spectacular spokesman: the condemned man judging his judges, the pervert mocking the normal, the advocate of destruction and death sneering at the defenders of love and life; but his *reductio* follows logically enough from assumptions shared by Jefferson and Rousseau, Richardson and Saint-Just. Whatever has been suspect, outcast, and denied is postulated as the source of good. Before the Break-through, no one, Christian or Humanist, had doubted the inferiority of passion to reason, of impulse to law; and though it is possible sophistically to justify all eighteenth-century reversals by quoting the verse which says the last shall be the first, Christianity is dead from the moment such a justification is made. The Break-through is profoundly anti-Christian though it is not always willing to appear so. There is a brief age of transition when the Enlightenment and Sentimentalism exist side by side, when it is still possible to pretend that true reason and true feeling, the urgings of passion and the dictates of virtue are identical—and that all are alike manifestations of the orthodox God. But Sentimentalism yields quickly to the full Romantic revolt; in a matter of months, Don Juan, enemy of Heaven and the family, has been transformed from villain to hero; and before the process is finished, audiences have learned to weep for Shylock rather than laugh him from the stage. The legendary rebels and outcasts, Prometheus and Cain, Judas and the Wandering Jew, Faust and Lucifer himself are one by one redeemed. The parricide becomes an object of veneration and tourists (among them that good American abroad, Herman Melville) carry home as an icon Guido's picture of Beatrice Cenci, slayer of her father!

The process is continuous and nearly universal. Even the values of language change: "gothic" passes from a term of contempt to one of description and then of praise, while "baroque" makes more slowly the same transition; meanwhile terms once used honorifically to describe desired traits—"condescension," for example—become indicators of disapproval. The child is glorified over the man, the peasant over the courtier, the dark man over the white, the rude ballad over the polished sonnet, the weeper over the thinker, colony over mother country; the commoner over the king—nature over culture. At first, all this is a game: the ladies of the court in pastoral dress swing high into the air to show their legs with a self-consciousness quite unlike the abandon of children to which they are pretending. But in a little while, Jean-Jacques Rousseau has fainted on the road to Vincennes and awakened to find his waistcoat soaked with tears; and it is suddenly all in earnest. Whatever was down is now up, as the undermind heaves up out of the darkness; barricades are erected and the novel becomes the reigning form; the Jew walks openly out of the ghetto, and otherwise sensible men hang on their walls pictures of trees and cattle. The conjunctions are comic in their unexpectedness and variety.

It is hard to say what was cause and what effect in the complex upheaval; everything seems the symptom of everything else. Yet deep within the nexus of causes (gods must die for new genres to be born) was that "death of God" that has not yet ceased to trouble our peace. Somewhere near the beginning of the eighteenth century, Christianity (more precisely, perhaps, that desperate compromise of the late Middle Ages and early Renaissance, Christian Humanism) began to wear out. It was not merely, or even primarily, a matter of the destruction of the political and social power of one Church or another, much less of the lapse of economic control by the priests. The divisions within Christendom surely contributed to the final collapse, but they are perhaps better regarded as manifestations than as causes of the insecurity over dogma that was at work deep within. Institutionalized Christianity at any rate began to crumble when its mythology no longer proved capable of controlling and revivifying the imagination of Europe.

The darker motive forces of the psyche refused any longer to accept the names and ranks by which they had been demeaned for almost two thousand years; once worshiped as "gods," they had been made demons by fiat, but now they stirred again in discontent. Especially the Great Mother—cast down by the most patriarchal of all religions (to the Hebrews, she was Lilith, the bride of darkness), ambiguously redeemed as the Blessed Virgin and denied once more by a Hebraizing Protestantism—clamored to be honored once more. The very distinction between God and Devil, on which the psychic balance of Europe had for so long been staked, was threatened. It did not matter that some people (chiefly women) continued to go to church, or even that there were revivals within the framework of surviving sects; fewer and fewer men lived by the legends of the church, and the images of saints represented not living myths but "mythology" in a literary sense.

The effect of the growing awareness (an awareness, to be sure, at first shared by only a handful of advanced thinkers) of this cosmic catastrophe was double: a sense of exhilaration and a spasm of terror, to which correspond the two initial and overlapping stages of the Break-through. There was first of all the conviction of the Age of Reason and its spokesmen, the *philosophes,* gravediggers of the Christian God, that they—and all of mankind— were at last *free,* free of the superstition and ignorance so long sponsored by the priests for their own selfish ends. Those demons into which the early Christian apologists had translated the gods of antiquity seemed to the *philosophes* idle inventions of the Church itself: bugaboos to scare the pious into unquestioning subservience. Even the Christian God seemed to them such a contrivance, demonic and irrational. In the imagined universe presided over by their own "Author of Creation," there could be no place for mystery or blackness. Once *"l'infâme,"* the scandalous Church, had been crushed, all monsters would be eliminated forever, and man could take up his long, baffled march toward perfection in a sweet, sunlit, orderly world. Just such a vision, however modified by circumstance, moved the Deist intellectuals who founded America, especially that Thomas Jefferson to whom C. B. Brown, himself a follower of the *philosophes,* proffered his gothic novel.

Insofar as America is legendary, a fact of the imagination as well as one of history, it has been shaped by the ideals of the Age of Reason. To be sure, the European mind had dreamed for centuries before the Enlightenment of an absolute West: Atlantis, Ultima Thule, the Western Isles—a place of refuge beyond the seas, to which the hero retreats to await rebirth, a source of new life in the direction of the setting sun which seems to stand for death. Dante, however, on the very brink of an age which was to turn the dream into the actualities of exploration, had prophetically sent to destruction in the West, Ulysses, the archetypal explorer. The direction of his westward journey through the great sea is identified with the sinister left hand; and Ulysses himself comes to stand for man's refusal to accept the simple limits of traditional duty; "not the sweetness of having a son, nor the pious claim of an old father, nor the licit love that should have made Penelope rejoice could quench in me the burning to become familiar with the vice of men and men's valor." It is a fitting enough epigraph to represent that lust for experience which made America. There is, indeed, something blasphemous in the very act by which America was established, a gesture of defiance that began with the symbolic breaching of the pillars of Hercules, long considered the divine signs of limit.

To be sure, the poets of later Catholicism made an effort to recast the dream of America in terms viable for their Counter-Reformation imaginations, to forge a myth that would subserve new political exigencies. It is, however, the Enlightenment's vision of America rather than that of the Church that was written into our documents and has become the substance of our deepest sense of ourselves and our destiny. If North America had remained Latin, the story might have been different; but Jefferson himself presided over the purchase of the Louisiana Territory, which settled that question once and for all. History sometimes provides suitable symbolic occasions, and surely one of them is the scene that finds Jefferson and Napoleon, twin heirs of the Age of Reason, preparing the way for Lewis and Clark, that is to say, for the first actors in our own drama of a perpetually retreating West. Napoleon, it must be remembered, was the sponsor of the painter David and Jefferson the planner of Monticello; good neo-classicists both, they place the American myth firmly in the classicizing, neo-Roman tradition of the late eighteenth century. The New World is, of course, in one sense an older one than Europe, a preserve of the primitive, last refuge of antique virtue; indeed, the writers and artists of the Empire period could never quite tell the difference between Americans, red or white, and the inhabitants of the Roman Republic. The face of Washington, as rendered in bronze by Houdon, is that of the noblest Roman of them all, or, in Byron's phrase (already a cliché), "the Cincinnatus of the West."

But America is not exclusively the product of Reason—not even in the area of legend. Behind its neo-classical façade, ours is a nation sustained by a sentimental and Romantic dream, the dream of an escape from culture and a renewal of youth. Beside the *philosophes,* with whom he seemed at first to accord so well that they scarcely knew he was their profoundest enemy, stands Rousseau. It is his compelling vision of a society uncompromised by culture that has left the deepest impress on the American mind. The heirs of Rousseau are Chateaubriand and Cooper, after whom the world of togas and marble brows and antique heroism is replaced by the sylvan scene, across which the melancholy refugee plods in search of the mysterious Niagara, or where Natty Bumppo, buckskinned savior, leans on his long rifle and listens for the sound of a cracking twig. The bronze face of a bewigged Washington gives way to the image of young Abe splitting logs in a Kentucky clearing.

The dream of the Republic is quite a different thing from that of the Revolution. The vision of blood and fire as ritual purification, the need to cast down what is up, to degrade the immemorial images of authority, to impose equality as the ultimate orthodoxy—these came from the *Encyclopédie,* perhaps, as abstract ideas; but the spirit in which they were lived was that of full-blown Romanticism. The Revolution of 1789 (for which ours was an ideological dress rehearsal) may have set up David as its official interpreter, but it left the world to Delacroix; and though it enthroned Reason as its goddess, it prepared for a more unruly Muse.

In Sentimentalism, the Age of Reason dissolves in a debauch of tearfulness; sensibility, seduction, and suicide haunt its art even before ghosts and graveyards take over—strange images of darkness to usher in an era of freedom from fear. And beneath them lurks the realization that the "tyranny of superstition," far from being the fabrication of a Machiavellian priesthood, was a projection of a profound inner insecurity and guilt, a hidden world of nightmare not abolished by manifestos or restrained by barricades. The final horrors, as modern society has come to realize, are neither gods nor demons, but intimate aspects of our own minds.

2

THE NOVEL'S AUDIENCE
AND THE SENTIMENTAL
LOVE RELIGION

IT SHOULD BE QUITE CLEAR at this point that the word "novel" is being used here not to mean any long prose fiction, but to designate specifically the "modern" or "bourgeois" novel, that is to say, the kind of book first written in the second quarter of the eighteenth century by men like Richardson or Prévost or Marivaux. Such a definition excludes not only the long fictions of the Hellenistic period, but also the Mannerist proto-novels of the later sixteenth century as the *Arcadia,* Lyly's *Euphues,* even so great a work as *Don Quixote.* Though the latter, unlike most prose fictions contemporary with it, is still read for pleasure, and though its influence is occasionally felt still in modern fiction, it institutes no continuing tradition, but stands looking backward toward those romances of chivalry which it was intended to mock. Similarly, baroque fictions like the *Cléopatre* of La Calprenède or Mlle. de Scudéry's *Le Grand Cyrus* remain outside the main line of descent; meant to dazzle with their richness an aristocratic audience and dedicated to the revival of courtly love, they seemed alien to the class of readers for whom the modern novel was produced. Even Madame de Lafayette's subtle and subdued attack on *l'amour courtois,* in her *Princesse de Clèves,* does not break out of the limits of the courtly baroque; and a character in a Richardson novel typically found her heroine "silly."

When the novel proper was finally born, it pretended—at least in the hands of Richardson and his followers—to serve verisimilitude first of all: to deal with the truth of daily existence. In the language of eighteenth-century genre criticism, it was classified not as legend or epic (despite Fielding's attempt to justify his own practice in epic terms) but as "fictional history." The Richardsonian novel has a mythology to be sure, but it is an unavowed, a secret one, rediscovered in the depths of the human heart, at the center of what the Marquis de Sade described as "nature's maze," where the monstrous and the heroic eternally abide. Even the gothic novel seeks its "magic and phantasmagoria" not so much in traditional story as in contemporary nightmare—projecting the same terrors which Richardson treated in terms of psychological motivation and social conflict.

The turning of the modern novel from mythology to psychology, from a body of communal story to the mind of the individual is an enterprise typical of our times. Indeed, only in the sub-mind of a dreaming man can we discover images common to everyone in our multifarious culture; and these images, though not traditional mythology, are myth in the profoundest sense of the word. The novel has, in the course of its search for inwardness, managed to save the mythic in an age of prose and science. This Diderot, Encyclopedist and advocate of reason, perceived in reading *Clarissa,* greatest of the novels of the high priest of sentimentalism, Samuel Richardson. Of Richardson, Diderot observes: "It is he who carries the torch to the back of the cave. . . . He blows upon the glorious phantom who presents himself at the entrance of the cave; and the hideous Moor whom he was masking reveals himself." Surely, "the hideous Moor" is a striking symbol of the demonic in ourselves, which the Enlightenment inadvertently discovered in its quest for light.

Born in a time of rationalism, the novel breaks through the rational, representing one facet of that strange revolt against the Enlightenment bred within the Enlightenment itself. "The Dream of Reason breeds monsters," Goya inscribed as a rubric on his *Caprichos,* and precisely those monsters the bourgeois novel describes. But the novel not only attacks the sovereignty of reason, it challenges the primacy of ideas. On the one hand, it opposes to the idea the fact, and moves in the direction of realism; on the other hand it holds up against the idea feeling, and tends toward sentimentalism.

The irrational essence of the novel is revealed by the very nature of its form, a form without a theory. It was born by accident, as it were, out of an odd mating of allegory with the plot structure of sensational drama, and of the letter book with prose history or scandalmongering. It is a genre that still defies an Aristotelian definition, a kind contrived when all the kinds had already been classified and arranged, an unforeseen and disruptive stranger. Its very name was used in earlier times as a term of deprecation, as if the genre were essentially disreputable. For traditional critics in the eighteenth century, it appeared to be essentially sub-literature and any attempt to distinguish between serious fiction and trash seemed to them as absurd as a similar distinction among comic books would seem now.

It was not until the appearance of *Madame Bovary* in France, or James's *The Art of Fiction* in England, that the novel seemed even discussable as art; until then (and to some degree to this very day), prose fiction was left in the hands of improvisors and amateurs, who were expected to proffer their untidiness and lack of self-consciousness as their very credentials.

Called for by no one in authority, condemned with equal fervor by critics and clergy, why did this hybrid form come into existence at all? And how has it managed, against all prevision, to replace the traditional poetic forms as the reigning genre of the West? It is well known that the novel succeeded, in the first instance, because it managed to satisfy a new group of readers, to whose cultural aspirations and spiritual needs it responded with peculiar aptness. This new audience was middle-class, Protestant, and urban, which is to say, uncertain of its status and alienated from older folk literature. It was the first body of readers in Europe to stand outside the gentlemanly value-system invented in the Renaissance and sponsored by court, salon, and school, the first "mass public." The Bible should have supplied this public with all the "literature" it needed; but its members lived at a time when for all but the most devout religion no longer dominated the imagination, having become observance only rather than life itself. At this group—not at its devoted center, but its less pious periphery—the novel was aimed.

The new group of readers was a large one, the largest in history, and it grew steadily on into the nineteenth century until it had established publishing as the first mass-production industry in the world; but its members were imperfectly educated—progressively less well educated, some would argue, the larger their number grew. Before the rise of the bourgeoisie, literacy was not considered something valuable in itself, but merely one of a desirable set of skills, values, and traditions. When a man learned to read at all, he acquired, with the mechanical art of spelling out words, certain standards; but with the final victories of the new class, literacy became a political demand and a sign of status, like suffrage or the right to carry weapons. As a crowning privilege, a final token of recognition, the bourgeoisie asked to enter into the culture of the ruling classes, to be permitted to read and write on the highest levels. In the Augustan literature of England, one finds the first fruits of this privilege in a literature in which common sense and a respect for antiquity exist side by side.

But traditional literature, even in its accommodated Augustan form, did not satisfy the hunger of the majority of the new social group; and certainly the masculine wit of eighteenth-century verse and essay seemed more at home in the coffee house than in the boudoir, where the middle classes tended to believe books were properly to be consumed. The merchant was unwilling to spend much of his time (which he never forgot was money) on the trivialities of art; such pursuits seemed to him more proper for the female members of his family—for his wife or, more particularly, his daughter, not yet burdened with the cares of running a household. The moment at which the novel took hold coincides with the moment of the sexual division of labor which left business to the male, the arts to the female—thus laying up for the future the perils of Bovaryism, on the one hand, and on the other, the dictatorship of "what the young girl wants" or, perhaps better, what her father thinks she *should* want. In light of the novel's predominantly feminine audience, it is scarcely surprising that its ideal theme should be love and marriage, and that its ideal protagonist should be a woman—no grand lady, but some girl, passionate and pure, and known only by her first name: Clarissa, Pamela, Charlotte, Emma, Julie.

Traditional literature in verse was certainly not attractive to them. It was, quite simply, too difficult—not only in diction and metaphor, but also, perhaps especially, in its involvement with codes and conventions belonging to a life alien and incomprehensible to them. The concept of honor, for instance, and the adulterous codes of courtly love, were strange and abhorrent to the bourgeois mind. It was to take much time and a long growth in self-confidence before any spokesman for the new group dared commit to print such a wholesale condemnation of "aristocratic literature" as that Tolstoy (himself an aristocrat!) expressed in

What is Art? But his apparent paradoxes had long been common-places of the middle-class Protestant mind, which had in the interim been carrying on an underground warfare against high culture, with the best-selling novel as a chief weapon. The novel, though it is many other things and has been captured for their own purposes by serious artists, was the first of a series of inventions devised by mass culture for giving the illusion of reading while requiring, less and less rigorously, its practice—a series that has come by now to include the book digest, the picture magazine, the comic-book, movies, television, etc.

As practical men, the new middle classes found literature frivolous; as pious ones, they found it idolatrous; as class-conscious citizens, they felt it too committed to court and salon. Yet they could not live without it; a lust for images of their own lives, projections of their own dreams and nightmares moved them obscurely. They demanded a form that would be really their own, a mass-produced commodity to be bought or rented in the market-place like other goods, a thick and substantial item to be placed on the table with other evidences of their wealth and taste. The novel is the first large-scale example of "mass art." It is quite different from "folk art," with its hand-made appearance and its air of knowing its place, for folk art is rooted in the country and in agriculture; it changes slowly and almost imperceptibly, its chief appeal being its resemblance to what has come before. "Mass art," on the other hand, is urban art, changing with the rapid changes of fashion, and seeming as much the product of new advances in technique as of any profound shift in the imagination. Like other mass-produced products, it tends to drive out of existence craft objects, which cannot survive the class structures which demand them and the class-consciousness which defines their consumers. Just as the spectacular rise of the novel is inconceivable without the perfection of printing, its final victory is inconceivable without the invention of the circulating library; mass-produced, it is also mass-circulated like any commodity in an expanding mercantile economy.

Not intended for recitation or performance in the fields or at the courts like verse, not intended for public production like drama, the novel belongs to an era when literature came to be thought of as something enjoyed in loneliness. The family reading aloud in the patriarchal parlor for a time challenged but could not really destroy the concept of reading as a retreat to privacy—in the closet, the boudoir, the toilet, last of refuges, the point is the same. Literature, which had originally served to enhance the sense of community, bringing shoulder to shoulder a representative audience, before the storyteller or at the open-air tragic festival, now served only to make possible the simultaneous solitude of thousands of readers. Mass production and lonely consumption—these are the hallmarks of a new age. The process that had begun with the move into an indoor, darkened theater reached its climax in the novel, that private theater in the innermost darkness of the individual mind.

The form of the novel was, however, not only determined by the conception of art as a commodity for private consumption; it was a result also of the hypocrisy of the bourgeoisie in the presence of art, and is for this reason the art form least like art. Prose was, of course, less suspect than verse to the "no-nonsense" middle-class mind; and the novel from its beginnings was intended to seem closer to the chronicles and news accounts which its readers trusted than to poetry which they feared. The novel is fiction pretending to be truth, the marvelous pretending to be the probable. One can scarcely open an early example of the genre without finding in the body of the work a condemnation of "novels," i.e., all *other* novels, and on the title page the claim "founded in truth" or "a tale of truth." It is well to remember that the "realism" that distinguishes the novel from the start is rooted in this kind of double-dealing.

Though the novel marks the entrance of the libido onto the stage of European art, in it the libido enters with eyes cast down and hands clasped—in the white garments of a maiden. Richardson speaks in the same breath of himself as an artistic innovator and religious reformer, boasting that he has helped establish "A new species of writing, that might possibly turn young people into a source of reading different from the pomp and parade of Romance writing, and dismissing the improbable and marvelous with which novels generally abound, might tend to promote the cause of religion and virtue." "The improbable and marvelous" are not, of course, necessarily opposed to "religion and virtue"; in the seventeenth century they were, indeed, exploited in behalf of such ends by the more lavish artist-propagandists of the Counter-Reformation. The novel is, however, essentially a Protestant genre, and begins, in effect, by removing the gilded crosses, the polychrome marbles, and the stained glass from the house of fiction. It is, perhaps, better to think of Richardson's stylistic reform as "puritan" rather than "realistic" in any modern sense of the world. For him, mere faithfulness to the world of appearances must be defended in terms of its usefulness in promoting true piety as defined by scripture.

But there is still to be examined a third level of duplicity in the novel: beyond its representing the marvelous as the ordinary and passionate impulse as Christian piety, it also represents entertainment pretending to be a sermon (or alternately, a sermon pretending to be entertainment). "To promote the cause of religion and virtue," Richardson designated as the end of fiction, and his followers took up the same strain: "to inspire the FEMALE MIND with a principle of SELF COMPLACENCY and to promote the ECONOMY of HUMAN LIFE", to "win the mind to Sentiment and Truth." On its most obvious level, the novel was a kind of conduct book for the daughters of the bourgeoisie, aimed at teaching obedience to parents and wariness before potential seducers; and dedicated therefore to the same brand of poetic justice as that advocated by Thomas Jefferson. Not only did the bourgeois novelist seek to "present virtue in the best & vice in the worst forms possible"; he was also dedicated to showing vice punished and virtue rewarded as they are uncomfortably not in history.

The earliest novelists (particularly in America) were eternally aware of the voices from pulpit and press that cried out against the novel as "one great engine in the hands of the fiend of darkness," a charge whose validity they were willing to grant for all fiction but their own; and they strove to silence their critics by embodying in their work the practical morality of the class they served. Over and over they expressed the conviction of their readers that success is, if not salvation itself, at least its sign; and that virtue must be rewarded here and now, certainly in the final chapters of a book. But beside virtue and truth, the early novel enshrines "sentiment"; beside Christianity, it honors the Sentimental Love Religion, which was hopelessly confused in its pages with orthodoxy.

Though the novel merely seemed to serve the thin, rigid Protestantism that threatened it, it paid allegiance in fact to that secret religion of the bourgeoisie in which tears are considered a truer service of God than prayers, the Pure Young Girl replaces Christ as the savior, marriage becomes the equivalent of bliss eternal, and the Seducer is the only Devil. The Sentimental Love Religion demands of its adherents that they be unaware of the implications of their faith; and there are, therefore, no official scriptures of the new religion. Not even half-playfully formulated as were the conventions of courtly love by Andreas Capellanus, the codes of sentimental love were set forth only implicitly in the stereotyped characters and plots demanded of the novelists of the age. In this respect, they were much like our own latter-day romantic myths, which persist unexamined and only half-recognized in ladies' magazines and popular movies. The presence of such unconfessed dogmas and their appropriate mythologies is manifested chiefly in the extraordinary success of certain books—books which pretend to be novels, but are in fact secret scriptures. Best-sellers are by and large holy books, and the age of the best-seller is an age unable to confess its true religion except in terms of commodity fiction.

Certain elements of the underground faith of the eighteenth century have come to seem to us absurd; but we live still in the Age of the Novel (and of the cinema which is its child), so that no matter how vulgarized the sentimental myth may have become, no matter how smugly we snicker at it, we are somehow still its victims and beneficiaries. Certainly, there is no one in our world to whom the phrase "They lived happily ever after" is meaningless or unclear; for us the "happy ending" is defined once and for all: after many trials, the sacred marriage! Our secure sense of what happiness means in this context has nothing to do with what we *know* about divorce statistics or the possibilities of successful adjustment in marriage; it is a mythological rather than a factual statement.

The mythology it represents is, however, far from eternal. To Augustine or Dante, Sophocles or Plato, to the author of *Beowulf* or of the *Chanson de Roland,* the tag "they lived happily ever after" would by no means have had the meaning it has for us. Plato would not even have identified the "they" as male and female; while neither he nor Augustine would have conceived ultimate bliss as a joining of flesh with flesh, no matter how fully sanctified by ritual and custom. Even for Dante, real happiness would have meant the final turning of the lover and the beloved from each other to God, from the creature to the Creator. The belief in love between man and woman as the supreme happiness is neither a classical concept nor a Christian one; it finds certain parallels in the New Comedy of Menander or Plautus and Terence and in the Alexandrian romances; but the concept of the Pure Maiden is strange to the earlier prototypes—and one would have thought that the coming of Christianity (with its basic view of woman as temptress) would have discouraged rather than fostered such sentimental idolatry.

II

What, then, is the source of the convention of sentimental love? To be understood at all, it must be seen as part of a continuous process whose end is not yet in sight. It stands between the codes of courtly love, on the one hand, and recent Romantic defenses of passion as the end of life, on the other. Though in its eighteenth-century sentimental form it postulates marriage as salvation, this is only a parochial development (Protestant, chiefly Anglo-Saxon) of a larger theory of love between the sexes as the fountainhead of virtue and joy. There are two major moments in the process: the Catholic, aristocratic, Mediterranean moment and the Protestant, bourgeois, Atlantic moment. Both are associated with the birth of new, apparently secular literary forms, which are in fact the disguised scriptures of unofficial religions. The wave that begins in Provence in the waning years of the eleventh century and turns from the sacred language of Latin to the vernacular re-invents the lyric and regards the *canzone* as the great literary form. The second wave, which starts somewhere just before the middle of the eighteenth century in England, disavows traditional verse forms in favor of prose and elevates the novel to the supreme place among literary genres.

Both represent the inruption of the female principle into a patriarchal world, a revenge of the (officially rejected) Great Mother. Certainly in each, there is a symbolic installation of Woman, half in play, half in ritual earnest, in positions of reverence and power quite out of accord with her actual status—or her theoretical place according to Christian orthodoxy. It is striking that the characteristic modern literary forms (as opposed to those genres archaeologically revived from the study of the ancients) begin only in conjunction with such revivals of the dethroned Aphrodite, who is also the Muse of antiquity; and conversely, that such inruptions of the female principle demand a break with traditional forms and language. Though Adelbert the Archbishop of Tours could write in Latin to Adele, the daughter of William the Conqueror: "He is useless and vile who confounds your worth with other mortals. For sure you will always be the first of the other Goddesses," he is only indulging in a Humanist exercise. It was not the language of the Church and the revival of learning but the mother tongue that was necessary to produce *amour courtois,* as prose was necessary (when women ceased to respond to verse) to the birth of the Sentimental Love Religion.

No genuine archetypal figure from the mythologies of the past ever dies, no matter how reviled and bedeviled; thrust down as divinity, it will emerge as sentiment or hysteria or madness. In primitive Christianity, however, as in the Judaism of the Old Testament, the Great Mother had been viewed as abomination, the idol of the Canaanites. She persists only as the Bride of Darkness, the flesh of the sow, the whore of Babylon; and even Mother Eve is conceived of primarily as the source through which evil entered the world.

The huge, warm, enveloping darkness of unconscious life, the blind source of passion and reproduction and death, takes form as the triple Goddess and is worshiped in the ancient world by men content to be eternal sons. The Lord of Hosts of Christian and Jew represents an utterly different principle, one who can never be enthroned side by side with the Mother, as in Greece after the defeat of the matriarchy, but who insists upon reigning by himself, in a splendor so lonely and abstract that the ancient world thought him no god at all—merely *nothing!* Without some rebellion against the female blackness, there can be, of course, no civilization, no science, no law, no proper consciousness at all; but denied utterly, that blackness returns as nightmare or as art, in the witch cult or in Romantic literature to undermine everything built in its despite.

With the rebirth of secular literature in Provence there appears a strange new concept of sexual passion *—not as the (simple but rather degrading) pleasure it seemed to Ovid, nor as the madness of middle-aged mothers it seemed to Euripides, nor as the terrible burning it seemed to St. Paul, but as the supreme end of life: the subject par excellence of art, the pivot of polite society, the school of virtue. The center of courtly love is the convention of the inferiority of the lover to his mistress—or, more properly, to the Mistress, that physically undefined, faceless and history-less goddess, cruel, remote, and desirable. In a society where, by law and

---

* Certain academic types have in our time attempted to demonstrate that courtly love never existed at all. But there have always been such blasphemers, for whom the myth by which Dante and Chaucer and Spenser lived and dreamed has seemed an insufficient and unreliable truth.

custom, women were disposed of at the will of their fathers and husbands, where it would have been considered a lack of manliness not to rape an unprotected lower-class female, and where the Church insisted upon the submission of wives to husbands and preached the essential unchastity of all women—in such a society, the lover pretended the most abject humility before an idealized beloved, submitted to her most outrageous whims without regard to dignity and in the teeth of reason.

There may have been, as some of the earlier writers on the subject suggest, a social basis for this astonishing pose, i.e., the situation, not uncommon in Provence, in which landless knights dependent for their very existence on the idle lady of the castle played out in verse and song endless, humble flirtations. But William of Poitou, with whom courtly love poetry as we know it begins, was a king, not a dependent knight. He is a strange double-faced figure: the author of phallic poems full of male arrogance ("and so I screwed them eighteen times so hard I broke my belt and armor") and contempt for women, and, at the same time, the first of the poets of domnei—the service of ladies. The relationship of lover to lady is expressed in feudal terms (as, indeed, the relationship of man to God was contemporaneously expressed) because this was for the time the natural language of subordination. The lover is his beloved's "man"; he owes her "service"; she is even sometimes addressed as *"midons,"* not "my lady" but, literally, "my lord."

That final epithet strikes, however, a disconcerting note, poses problems not easily explicable even in terms of feudal usage. If on the one hand the code of courtly love blurs oddly into heresy, the last major flare-up of Manichaean dualism in Europe, on the other, it even more strangely merges with homosexuality. Indeed, one senses from the start in the verse of courtly love a desire to mitigate by ritualized and elegant foreplay a final consummation felt as brutal, or else a desire to avoid entirely any degrading conjunction with female flesh. It is wrong, I think, to believe with Denis de Rougemont (in his *Love in the Western World*) that the troubadours were secret sharers in the Albigensian heresy; they were heretics of another order—not secret but *unconscious* self-castrators. For surely their exaggerated worship of the lady unmanned them successfully enough to have pleased any of the world-denying Cathari among the Albigensians.

In any case, the service of love, beginning with an abject surrender of the will to an arbitrary lady, passes readily into an abysmal sort of masochism, and ends with the appearance of certain symptoms which would nowadays be taken to indicate a break-down, and which would once have been read as signs of demonic possession: sleeplessness, hot flashes and chills, loss of appetite and a consequent wasting away, obsessive preoccupation with the beloved, inability to perform ordinary duties or even to keep one's clothing in repair, melancholy, anxiety spells, etc., etc. No wonder some students of the literature are tempted to read these symptoms as encoded ritual, to protest that so much torment so solemnly endured cannot be caused by the mere issue of sleeping with a woman, while others have insisted that the lover is not in love with the lady at all, but with suffering itself—ultimately with death.

There is a kind of truth in both these contentions. It is not prob-able that the poets of Provence (however close their personal ties to the Albigensian heretics) were writing about the forbidden religion taught by the Cathari; though there may have been an occasional secret believer who *used* the praise of Woman as a screen for his beliefs. The religion of the poets of courtly love is no more the Albigensian heresy than it is Christianity, despite the figures they borrowed from the ritual of the latter creed, their habit of referring to "martyrs" and "saints" and "relics" of love. Indeed, trifling with sacred terminology is a kind of blasphemy which be-comes balder and balder, culminating in the pornographers of the eighteenth century, one of whom describes the male orgasm as "a sacrifice poured out upon the altar of Nature." The God of the troubadours is not the *Amor* of fearful aspect that they borrowed from classic mythology; he is only another sort of window-dress-ing. Their deity is the lady, the female principle, the White God-dess, never really deposed in the Mediterranean basin, though for a thousand years driven underground.

The dissatisfaction with the overwhelming paternalism of feudal Christianity, which led to the specifically religious protest of Albi-gensianism, also lay behind the aesthetic revolution of the trouba-dours. Courtly love developed in a society no longer content with pious asceticism and simple-minded codes of combat loyalty, but unwilling to submit to the money values of the wealthy merchants just then flourishing in southern France. Against the worship of money the poets of Provence quite freely inveigh; against the ideals of the Church they do not dare to speak candidly, though Christ as well as mammon is inimical to the world they dream. What they desire is a secular utopia of "courtesy," where the free dialogue between male and female is endlessly varied with pretty compliments and parlor games and songs. They invoke the Great Goddess primarily as a Muse, a civilizing Muse who will preside over the rebirth of the lyric and the reform of manners. But even the manners to which they aspire deny the orthodox belief that "the extinction of humanity would be preferable to propagating it by sexual intercourse" or that "the man who loves his own wife too passionately is an adulterer."

The Christianity which promulgated such harsh doctrines had quite simply failed to make possible an accord between man's passionate impulses and his ego-ideals. The celibacy of the clergy was notoriously more theoretical than actual; and the lay Christian seemed doomed forever to shuttle between riots of self-indulgence and orgies of maudlin repentance. A new concept of salvation was demanded that would take into account the dark surge of sexual desire: the helplessness of the male before the female and the serpent to whom she listens. Salvation according to the female principle is called *"joia,"* an ambiguous term meaning both the simple pleasure of physical consummation (what the Italians even now call *"piacere"*) and the satisfaction of loving, with or without consummation. The love mythology of Europe is attracted, on the one hand, to this ideal of love as the *gai saber,* the education of the soul to courtesy through joy; but on the other is drawn toward the *Liebestod,* the sense that only death is the true *princesse lointaine,* the absolute Bride. Love as joy and love as death; from its very beginnings courtly love looks in both directions.

The themes of self-punishment and self-destruction are inseparable (in the West at least) from the worship of the Female, who represents the dissolution of consciousness as well as poetic vision, the blackness of extinction as well as that of ecstasy. "The horseleech's two daughters: give and give." Submission to the Mother, moreover, is felt as a betrayal of the Father, as the priests of Christianity are only too willing to remind the poets, who, more often than not, end by recanting all their lovely praises of love when the church bell tolls them home. The conviction of guilt associated with the new concept of love is projected in its adulterous form, with the strategic substitution of the secondary triangle husband-wife-lover for the primary one father-mother-son. The sense of Oedipal guilt is surely one source of the taboo of silence; this is the secret that cannot be told, but which is forever betrayed by the *trichador,* the dark double of the lover who exposes him to the husband-father, who is also the Christian God. Poor husband, he is the surrogate for all the self-reproach of a poet leaving the ortho-dox ego-system of the Church for the plunge into the unconscious! Yet he is a real husband, too, for courtly love is life as well as myth; and the archetype becomes the mere poetry of the seducer, the poetry finally bedroom farce.

In the mythicized life of the troubadour Guillem de Cabestanh, we can read in archetypal form the nightmare of the lover, his guilt-ridden fantasy of the punishment which is a final ecstasy, and which he desires as much as he fears: "and he [the husband] killed him [the lover]; and had his heart drawn out of his body and his head cut off . . . and he had the heart roasted and seasoned with pepper and had it given to his wife [the beloved] to eat. And when the lady had eaten it, Raimons de Castel Rossillo said to her, 'Do you know what you have eaten?' and she said, 'No. Except that it was a most tasty and delicious dish' . . . and he told her it was the heart of El Guillem de Cabestanh . . . and when she came to herself she said, 'My lord, you have indeed given me so fine a dish that I shall never eat another . . .' and so she died."

In our society, at any rate, the archetypes of the Love Religion in its first phase are all adulterous: Paolo and Francesca, Tristan and Iseult, Lancelot and Guinevere. Indeed, the love of the trou-badours is as naturally adulterous as the songs that express it are vernacular; it is to an alliance without benefit of clergy with a woman and not a girl that they aspire. One must be wary of the troubadours' own explanations of why marriage is the enemy of love; they serve to conceal the fact that the beloved *must* be mar-ried—but to someone other than her lover; she must, in short, be like a mother: remote, superior, unattainable, or at least attainable only with the sense of breaking the deepest taboo. No wonder the lover desires almost as much not to possess her as to possess her: "He knows little or nothing of *dompnei* [the Woman cult] who desires to have his *donz* [master-mistress] completely."

To comprehend the power of courtly love, the unforeseen effect this pass-time for idle courtiers has had on the soul of the West, is to become aware of the sense in which it is a true counter-religion to Christianity. Between its elevation of the lady to a kind of God-head and the Christian teaching that such adulation is idolatry or worse there can be no compromise. Certain latter-day Christian apologists (notably Charles Williams) have tried to redeem in mystical terms the identification of love of woman and love of

God; and such apologists certainly had forerunners as early as Botticelli, who represented Venus rising from the sea in terms of an iconography previously used only for the baptism of Christ— thus equating *amor* and *caritas,* passion and charity. More typical, however, are the words of Andreas Capellanus, who in the final pages of his handbook for the courts of love recanted in classic form: "No man through any good deeds can please God so long as he serves in the service of love." This is the irreconcilable Christian answer to the assertion of the troubadour Bernard de Ventadour: *"nuls om ses amor re no vau."* No man is worth anything without love!

Insofar as courtly love represented a general break-through of the mother image into the under-mind of Europe, the Catholic Church was able to deal with it in its immemorial way, absorbing it into the cult of the Virgin. Ben Jonson once remarked of Donne's *Anniversarie,* "that it said of a mortal woman what should only have been said of the Blessed Virgin"; and the criticism suggests the solution: to substitute the Virgin for the secular madonna of the typical love poem. After all, Mariolatry and courtly love are both aspects of the same psychic revolution, that resurgence of the Female which, toward the close of the Middle Ages, left its impress everywhere, even on the chessboard, where the queen appears for the first time as the all-powerful piece. It was certainly less difficult for the Church to assimilate the courtly Woman cult to the adoration of the Virgin than it had been to syncretize the scriptural legends of the Mother of God with the folktales which attributed to her the role of Aphrodite. In the *Golden Legend* itself, Mary figures as the Great Goddess, lying in bed beside unworthy husbands while their wives steal out to their lovers, or presiding over the births of illegitimate children.

Insofar, however, as courtly love attempted to celebrate the love of man and woman as a source of grace, a rival to the love of God, it was attacked bitterly by the Church; and what poet pledged to courtly values could doubt, so long as he remained a Christian, that his soul was in jeopardy? What could he do? On the one hand, he could live as most men have in the last two thousand years, by compartmentalizing his allegiances. Even as in our time men can serve money or the state, pushing off repentance to a deathbed scene, so then some served Woman until the failure of animal vigor left them nothing but the pleasures of recantation. Others tried to have it both ways at once by idealizing, which is to say, de-carnalizing love; but this was likely to leave them with the conflict compounded rather than resolved. The idealized codes of love demanded the pure worship of the mistress; the flesh required sexual satisfaction; the love of God demanded the renunciation of both. The love of another man's wife remained adulterous whether consummated in the flesh or not; and superadding a pseudo-religious note merely complicated the original sin with an overlay of idolatry. What began in the self-consciousness of the poets as a playful parody of Christianity, ends as a full-fledged counter-religion, complete with ritual and metaphysics.

It was the Italians who completed the "sanctification" of passion. From Frederic II of Sicily, who learned from the Arabs to keep a harem and from the Provençals to sing the praise of women, the tradition was carried on to the *Vita Nuova* of Dante, where what had already been transformed from passion to art becomes theology. For every man, Dante suggests, there is somewhere a woman who is his personal mediator, a "miraculous" avenue to salvation. The name "Beatrice" provides tempting opportunities for puns on "she who beatifies"; and Dante cannot resist extending his quibbles until he has hinted that Beatrice is, in some mystical sense, Christ! At this point the Inquisition moved in to expurgate his little book. Beyond the mystical symbolism of the *Vita Nuova* lies the allegory of the *Comedy,* which makes of Beatrice Divine Theology, and the game is saved: not an actual woman but only that for which she stands is the source of salvation. It is a solution which leaves unresolved the contradiction with which it began; leaves to the soul of the West an institutionalized schizophrenia. So Petrarch, who followed Dante, after a lifetime of singing his passion can only disavow it in his old age. *"Vergogna e 'l frutto!"* Shame is the fruit!

In the Catholic south of Europe, the conflict of maternal and paternal, of lust and order, has *never* been resolved—only (somewhat cynically) compromised. The nominal victory has been awarded God the Father, but he remains invisible, while everywhere the Virgin with the Babe in her lap looks complacently down. The orthodox Trinity of Father, Son, and Holy Ghost has yielded in art and the popular imagination to the baroque trinity, derived ultimately from Venus, Vulcan, and Cupid, and still, despite the new names of Mary, Joseph, and Jesus, what it always was: an archetypal representation of cuckold, mother, and son, the last degradation of fatherhood. But the seventeenth century, which saw the triumph of the baroque trinity, witnessed also the last literary revival of courtly love, from which (progressively debased but still living) has been derived the cynical ritual of upper-class adultery.

Yet however vulgarized, the tradition of domnei has served in the South to maintain that sense of the reality and power of passion which gives to Mediterranean literature a dimension lacking in the North. In a world where the smallest boy screams "Horns!" as a conventional insult, the comedy of cuckoldry can never die; and where such comedy exists, its darker tragic counterpart is always waiting to be reborn. Indeed, from Stendhal to Flaubert, from Constant to Balzac and Zola, adulterous love defined the theme of the novel for the Mediterranean world. A critic like Denis de Rougement, brought up on continental fiction, can say almost without thinking what to an American is unthinkable: "To go by literature, adultery would seem to be the most notable occupation of both Europe and America. Few are the novels that fail to allude to it." One remembers William Dean Howells, realistic American novelist, who in forty novels did not treat adultery once; but this serves only to emphasize the truth of de Rougemont's contention for Europe.

On the other hand, where the Marian, Catholic tradition existed alone, the novel as a form never attained first importance. The heroic figure of the seducer, the pathetic figure of the seduced, and the comic figure of the deceived husband found their natural embodiment on the stage, especially in opera, which functioned as the novel of a resolutely illiterate South. The Don Juan archetype, in which we see the ambivalence of the European mind toward the courtly lover at the moment when his courtesy had come to seem merely the wiles of a seducer, was treated worthily by a novelist only once, and then by an Englishman, who calls him Lovelace and pretends he is not a myth at all. In Italy, the bourgeois novel came late and in imitation of foreign examples; in Spain its beginnings were even further delayed and less noteworthy; in Greece it has scarcely come into existence in our time. Though there has been a handful of first-rate novelists in the world of the Great Mother, there is no tradition of the novel, and few works that live in the imagination of Europe as great examples.

III

It was on the religious marches of Europe, where mother-directed Catholicism and father-centered Protestantism met, in France, Germany, and England, that the novel especially flourished; Rousseau moves typically back and forth between the two worlds of Catholicism and Protestantism, though finally his *sensibility* is as Protestant as that of Richardson or Goethe, the other founding fathers of the form. Committed to the Northern rejection of the Virgin, such men sought with special urgency to smuggle the mother principle back into their cultures. They were thus specially qualified to satisfy the secret hunger of the puritanical bourgeoisie, which demanded bootlegged madonnas; it was the function of the early novel to supply them. Here is another source of guilt, added to the original conflicts which underlie the origins of love in Europe. No wonder the early novelists carried forward in the new genre the theme of the *Liebestod* rather than of the *gai saber*. Tristan is their legendary hero rather than Don Juan, the sufferer rather than the seducer, whose sword serves as a barrier between him and his beloved rather than a weapon with which he hews his way to her side.

By the time of Rousseau's *Julie,* the pattern is set and in Goethe's *Werther* it inflames the imagination of the world: tears as the only orgasm possible to the languishing lover whose beloved is cut off from him by marriage or betrothment, disease or class or color—or, finally, by an incestuous degree of relationship. How many early novels (including the first one ever published in America) end with the discovery by the hero that the mistress for whom he has sighed is his sister! In the full flush of romantic candor, the long-kept secret is almost revealed in its nakedness; the desired bride is the sister, first surrogate for the mother—and the enemy is the father.

If, on the one hand, the triangle of wife-husband-lover becomes that of sister-father-brother, translated down toward its Oedipal base, on the other hand, it is interpreted upward into metaphysical abstractions. The forbidden bride becomes the Indeterminate, the Impossible itself; and it becomes difficult to know whether the lover is pursuing his sister or the horizon. In either case, however, the only consummation is death. "The grave's a fine and private place," the poet Andrew Marvell had naively observed, "but none, I think, do there embrace." He is, of course, egregiously wrong; in a score of sentimental novels (as well as in the tales of that supereminent necrophile Poe) the grave proves the only marriage bed; and the dust of those who cannot on earth embrace without guilt mingles innocently there. For death which punishes also forgives, which seems to sunder really joins. It is the night side of the Great Mother herself—a terrifying (but delicious) name for the lapsing of male consciousness into the female unknowing, from which it fell originally to pain and division and endless desire.

This tension out of which the European novel develops depends upon a delicate balance of Catholic and Protestant, aristocratic and bourgeois, North and South, which threatens to dissolve on the one side into Latin "gallantry," on the other, into Anglo-Saxon sentimentality. In one case, the suffering servitor becomes Don Juan; in the other, the *donna angelicata* becomes the Angel in the House; in one instance, *joia* becomes *piacere,* in the other it is converted into ever-after happiness. The beginning of the latter trend first became noticeable toward the end of the sixteenth century, when there appeared in England two simultaneous though quite opposed attempts to resolve the contradictions between courtly love and Christianity. The first is expressed in the *Sonnets* of Shakespeare (summarily in sonnet 144), the other in Spenser's *Faerie Queene* (especially in Books III and IV).

The Shakespearean solution was so extraordinary, so alien to officially accepted codes of bourgeois society, that it has scarcely been recognized at all. The resistance to the meaning of these "sugared" poems began as indifference (more than thirty years passed between the first and second editions), and developed with their growing popularity into outright expurgation, until in the seventeenth century certain embarrassingly male pronouns were quietly changed to the appropriate female forms, thus disguising the eccentric point of the sequence. A few lines from sonnet 144, however, put that point succinctly:

> Two loves I have, of comfort and despair,
> Which like two spirits do suggest me still;
> The better angel is a man right fair,
> The worser spirit a woman colour'd ill.
> To win me soon to hell, my female evil
> Tempteth my better angel from my side . . .

The theory of two loves, one angelic, the other diabolic, is at least a new way of stating the old problem, especially when these drives are directed respectively toward a fair youth (loved as purely as any Italian poet of the sweet new style longed for his lady) and the black woman (lusted after in self-hatred and disgust). But this means that sentimental salvation is attributed to the male, passionate damnation to the female. Shakespeare has used the form of the sonnet sequence, ordinarily dedicated to the service of ladies, to disavow domnei; and so successful is his subterfuge that men in willful ignorance have continued for generations to read to their mistresses Shakespeare's anti-feminist praises of the youth, for these are truly love poems of great tenderness. This obvious fact modern critics have tended to disregard in their concern with establishing the fact that Shakespeare did not actually have physical relations with boys. Apparently, such critics are not discomfited by the notion that the poet slept with women and considered it filthy, while chastely embracing an idealized male lover.

For Shakespeare himself, however, the system of two loves was not a satisfactory compromise, since the two loves tend to fall together; the youth desired as a symbol of innocent love, himself lusts for the female symbol of concupiscence, and there remains only the terrible cry, as old as Christianity itself: "Th' expense of spirit in a waste of shame/Is lust in action." The fable of the *Sonnets* describes the fate of the youth as he falls into the power of the Lady who "would corrupt my saint to be a devil." But the seed of corruption was already in him, already in the chaste relationship between him and the poet. There is no pure masculine principle, no male immune to the sinfulness represented by the Female; the fair youth having had a mother is tainted with evil from birth. Only the "man not born of woman," the motherless man, can break out of the trap of sin. The same kind of scholar who finds the *Sonnets* morally unexceptionable is shocked by, tries to expurgate as clearly un-Shakespearean, the speech in *Cymbeline* in which Posthumus Leonatus declares:

> Is there no way for men to be, but women
> Must be half-workers? We are all bastards,
> And that most venerable man which I
> Did call my father was I know not where
> When I was stamp'd . . .
>   Could I find out

> The woman's part in me! For there's no motion
> That tends to vice in man but I affirm
> It is the woman's part. . . .

It is all of a piece, however: the dream of a pure, homoerotic love and the sense of panic before the terrible Female. Shakespeare's mind is possessed by the witch-stepmother figures out of Germanic legend; in *The Tempest,* his nearly final statement and one of his few original plays, the only mother evoked is that devil's dam, Sycorax, the "blue-eyed witch." Set against her is the *anima* figure of Miranda, daughter of the father, pledged to virginity as long as the play lasts, and permitted to marry in a union blessed by Circe but untainted by the intervention of Aphrodite or Eros:

> I met her Deity
> Cutting the clouds toward Paphos, and her son
> Dove-drawn with her. Here thought they to have done
> Some wanton charm upon this man and maid . . .
>   but in vain.
> Mars' hot minion is returned again;
> Her waspish-headed son has broke his arrows,
> Swears he will shoot no more . . .

It is the Protestant White Goddess who presides over Shakespeare's nearly sexless romance, the Great Mother stripped of her Satanic and aphrodisiac aspects.

Here his solution most nearly coincides with the Puritan synthesis of the *Faerie Queen.* Where the Mother of God is rejected as an image, the notion of love sanctified by marriage, of the wife as a secular madonna, takes over the special authority. It seems only natural to us (so fully are we the heirs of the Spenserian synthesis) that the passion which leads to virtue and *gentilesse* be felt by a man for a maiden and that it be sealed by marriage. June is for us a month as sacred as was May to the sighing, adulterous lovers of Provence, and the twin symbols of June, sentimentalized on a thousand cards of congratulation, are the bridal bouquet and the white veil symbolizing virginity. We must remember, however, that for medieval orthodoxy marriage did not make sex a holy thing; not until the sixteenth century was the marriage ceremony officially declared a sacrament. To marry rather than burn, to wed for the sake of progeny and companionship, these were standard and acceptable notions; but to identify the feeling which leads to and persists in marriage with the ennobling passion sung by the troubadours, this was a revolutionary step.

When the "virgin knight" Britomart in Book III of the *Faerie Queen* rescues Amorest from "the house of Busyrane,/Where Loves spoiles are exprest" and where an altar is erected to Dan Cupid *"Victor of the Gods,"* the end of courtly love is at hand. It is the British Protestant who first learns of that catastrophe; but the news soon spreads to the rest of the bourgeois world. The lover may kneel still before his mistress, but he kneels not to pledge himself to humility and secrecy, but to ask her hand, that is, to become not her servant but her master. The courtly conviction that love cannot exist in marriage is denied; and though the trappings of courtly service (plus the courtly belief in love as the fountainhead of virtue) persist, *amour courtois* is dead. It is instructive to compare the sentimental eroticism of Spenser's Northern romantic epic with the ironical sensuality of Ariosto's Southern *Orlando Furioso,* so closely linked to the former in form and versification. Ariosto's Angelica, who inspires no thought but rape even in the mind of the most ascetic and ancient monk, is also a product of the break-up of courtly love; but she marks the point at which domnei is modified by civilized laughter into the sensuality of the gentleman, while Spenser's Amoret memorializes the troubled search for a love that is also chastity, for an order of passion amenable to law.

Henceforth, in Anglo-Saxondom at least, the beloved who was the Muse of Europe's reborn lyric will be a respectable woman! Yet to make art of married bliss has proved impossible. In verse, the cult of the Wife ends up in so dull a piece of sentimentality as Coventry Patmore's *Angel in the House;* and even in the novel it produces at best the mild, Biedermeier effects of, say, the domestic scenes in *David Copperfield.* Quite early, the bourgeois sentimental novelists discovered that their proper subject was not marriage itself but what leads up to it: courtship, or its travesty, seduction. This subject Spenser was too learned to discover; he succeeded no more than Shakespeare in inventing abiding images for the new concept of love he foreshadowed.

He arrived on the scene too early, before the class whose aspirations he anticipated was securely enough placed to demand an art of its own. Between the values Spenser advocates and the form he employs, there is a deep contradiction. He looks backward—he is an archaizer not only in language—to the traditions of the metrical romance, an aristocratic amusement, intended for those idle and well-read enough to play with Arthurian or Carolingian mythology. Besides, Spenser's personal predilections were modified by the official cult of the Queen, that Gloriana-worship which, under Elizabeth I, usurped the traditions of domnei for political ends. For England, the Great Goddess had been made flesh. How different it was some two hundred and fifty years later, when Victoria assumed the throne but rejected the role of Gloriana in favor of that of the modest wife—and how poor Dickens howled through the streets of London, driven by her marriage into a frenzy that was only half play-acting. Between the late sixteenth and the early nineteenth century, a sentimental revolution had occurred, which Spenser could foresee but not begin, a revolution carried out in modest silence by the literary form that had in the meantime dethroned poetry—the modern or bourgeois novel.

3

RICHARDSON AND THE
TRAGEDY OF SEDUCTION

THE NOVEL PROPER could not be launched until some author imagined a prose narrative in which the Seducer and the Pure Maiden were brought face to face in a ritual combat destined to end in marriage or death; the form and its mythology were born together, in the works of Samuel Richardson, a melancholy and pious printer, who in 1740 became the first modern novelist almost by mistake. He wrote three large, tearful novels before he was through, *Pamela, Clarissa,* and *Sir Charles Grandison*—the first still read, at least in schools, but condescendingly (did not Fielding laugh it from the scene with *Shamela* and *Joseph Andrews?*), the other two now left to gather dust in libraries, though all Europe once wept over *Clarissa;* and Jane Austen, who could not bear the tragic tone of the greater work, learned her craft from *Grandison. Autres temps, autres moeurs.*

Pamela is the comedy of sentimental love, *Clarissa* the tragedy; *Grandison* is an afterword that added little new. It is *Clarissa* that counts for our purpose, not only because it is superior to its predecessor and successor—it is a study of the ambiguities of motivation unequaled until Proust—but because it is a product of mythopoeic power as well as art. In *Clarissa,* the mythology of the Sentimental Love Religion, the bourgeois *Liebestod* is defined once and for all; and the bare outline of its plot, its mythos, at least, should be familiar to anyone interested in the history of the novel.

Clarissa Harlowe is a dutiful daughter, the glory of her family, at once submissive and strong-willed, pious and intelligent, modest and beautiful. Harried by almost inexplicable hostility, by the hatred of a jealous brother (who wants to ruin her) and the bullying of a tyrannical father (who wants to marry her off to a wealthy, ugly old man), she is driven into the hands of Lovelace, who desires only to seduce her. Lovelace is a Machiavelli of the boudoir, a Don Juan who turns monomaniac before the unconquerable virtue of Clarissa, who loves him deeply but will not surrender to him on his terms. Lovelace is driven not by lust but by a desire for power and by perverted principle, for he is an "emancipated man" of his time, a rationalist and free-thinker who opposes marriage on theoretical grounds. He is also an aristocrat, handsome, courageous, endowed with all the charms of a disappearing class. Indeed, Richardson rendered so faithfully the strength of Lovelace's appeal that his hero-villain won the hearts of lady readers more completely than he could ever win Clarissa's.

The chief action of the book concerns Lovelace's attempts to reduce Clarissa to submission after she has fallen under his control. He subjects her to one indignity after another, finally tricking her into living in a brothel unawares, but he cannot sway her will; at last, in desperation he drugs and rapes her. That this is no victory he is painfully aware (Clarissa is not so sure; scrupulous beyond all reason, she suspects her deepest self of some secret complicity), for he desires the submission not of her body but her soul, and when he can gain her assent in no other way offers to marry her. His proposal Clarissa (staunchly backed by Richardson, despite a flood of letters from readers urging him to relent) will not accept, though she loves him still. Instead, she proceeds to die slowly and stubbornly of a broken heart, meanwhile designing and ordering her coffin and writing appropriate verses. Too late, her family repents, and at the end Lovelace is killed in a duel by his closest friend—not, however, before having a vision of Clarissa in heaven and himself in hell.

Practically everyone who knows the name of Richardson knows the meager plot of *Pamela:* how the virtuous lower class girl resists the advances of her employer's son and finally compels him to marry her. It is the first success story of the female bourgeois world, at once practical, prurient, and edifying—a thoroughgoing piece of *almost* unconscious duplicity, though quite charming all the same. The "almost" is the secret of Richardson's deepest appeal: he knows really what Pamela is after all along, knows her for the female Ben Franklin that she is, though he does not quite know how he knows it; this happy state of quasi-insight (he never falsifies the hidden motivations of his protagonists) he shares with his heroines and the readers who identify with them. *Clarissa* is, however, no second *Pamela;* for Richardson had the unexpected integrity to resist rewriting the successful formula he himself had invented. The piety and pornography remain in his second book (one is a reward for enduring the other), but the morality has matured, survived the temptation of the happy ending. The reformed rake as repentant husband now strikes Richardson as a pretty doubtful kind of reward for virtue; and the acceptance of such a husband as pretty doubtful virtue. His insight into the complexities of the female mind has become terrifyingly acute; it takes an equally acute critic (Dr. Johnson was one!) to realize, for instance, that Clarissa, for all her undoubted goodness, somehow never *quite* manages to tell the *exact* truth. At this point, Richardson has truly carried the torch to the back of the cave.

Yet this book, equally impressive as myth and psychology, is unfortunately impossibly long and consequently (in a world grown even more indolent than harried) almost unread. C. F. McIntyre, translator and editor of Baudelaire's poems, could not in 1947 identify Lovelace; in explicating *"Danse macabre,"* he took the name for that of the Cavalier poet and ended in bewilderment. Similarly, a living authority on the American novel has written of *Clarissa* (with whose influence on our own books he had had to come to terms) that "it showed the sad end of a girl who failed to resist a man's blandishments before she got his wedding ring" and describes that heroine as "wicked"! The flippant tone is that required in some quarters of a sophisticated modern writing about the sentimental novel, and can be forgiven; but the critic's ignorance of the novel itself is unpardonable.

Against such latter-day misrepresentations, it must be insisted that Richardson succeeded in creating a heroine capable of satisfying the moral standards of almost everyone in his time from the most advanced Encyclopedist to the most philistine member of the middle class. Far from finding his *Clarissa* "wicked," all but the sternest of fathers exonerated it of any part in causing "female depravity"; and we even read of quite pious Christians permitting their daughters to read only "The Holy Bible and *Clarissa Harlowe.*" The novelist's more ardent female admirers described Richardson's printing press as an "altar" from which "hallowed incense" wafted forth, and referred to the pages of his books as "virgin sheets" that "no prostitution stains."

These seem oddly reverential terms for one who was, after all, secretly (perhaps even from himself) preparing that revolution of passion that was to reach its climax in Romanticism. Among the immediate heirs of Richardson were Rousseau and Goethe, not to mention Choderlos de Laclos and the Marquis de Sade. Yet there is something just all the same in the religious metaphors, for *Clarissa* was the first sacred book of the bourgeoisie, and if the church bells were tolled throughout England to signalize its heroine's death it is because that death was more than a literary event. Like the myth of the Crucifixion, the myth of Clarissa's immolation represents archetypally that victory which can only be wrung from defeat and which lifts up the heart in exultation above merely human notions of success and failure. But her story functions on other levels besides the final religious one; it manages, indeed, to symbolize all the chief aspirations of an entire class, aspirations of which its fable was in some cases their first consciousness. What Tristan had been for the aristocrat in love, Clarissa was for the bourgeoisie—a symbol of the self to which ordinary men in the midst of ordinary experience vainly aspire. Like a true archetype, she has not ceased to move us even now that we have ceased to read the work that first bodied her forth.

I I

Perhaps even more clearly than Clarissa, Lovelace is an archetypal figure: just as Hamlet signifies finally only "hamletism" or Don Quixote "the quixotic," so Lovelace represents a complex that only his name fully defines. Baudelaire used that name without a capital in his *"Danse macabre,"* and defending the use of the lower case his French editor insisted, *"En somme, Lovelace est preseque un substantif de convention."* It is tempting to identify him simply as Don Juan, from whom, to be sure, he is somehow derived. Certainly, like the older archetype, Lovelace embodies contempt for religion, aristocratic charm, and an absolute, almost magical, ability to compel love; and like his predecessor, he is swordsman and libertine—dangerous thoughts in his head, a naked blade in his hand. The deaths of both figures are caused, at one remove or another, by duels, in that conflict of honor that is the traditional prerogative of the aristocrat in combat, just as seduction is his privilege in the area of passion. Both are caricatures of the courtly lover, whom they portray as a glib but essentially brutal sexual aggressor.

Don Juan, however, is essentially the impenitent; he can be damned but not persuaded, punished but not defeated. And the instrument of his damnation is the figure of the Father, that stone papa who stands for the patristic Church he has challenged. From Tirsa de Molina to Molière, Don Juan is unequivocally condemned, at least in the conscious judgments of the playwrights who evoke him; but he is the sole hero of the dramas through which he moves, and becomes easily (a mere change in acting technique will do the trick) the sympathetic rebel beloved by the Romantics. Lovelace, on the other hand, though equally courageous, equally irresistible in love, meets an opponent who is stronger than God—stronger, that is, than any religious scruple the seventeenth century had been able to set in the way of the principle of sexual conquest. The women who surround Don Juan in his legendary career blend into one another and the darkness out of which he emerges. Donna Ana, Donna Iñez, Donna Elvira, even taken together with all their wifely claims and oaths of holy chastity, do not add up to one Clarissa: a female principle equal and opposite to the male force of Don Juan. His legend projects the naked encounter of father and son (the women mere occasions), of the alienated individual and the society he defies. There is no mother figure to balance either, no symbol of nature or feeling strong enough to function as a principle of grace in a world completely given over to power and pleasure.

In the story of Lovelace, however, there is portrayed the meeting of an irresistible force and an immovable obstacle, that is to say, of Lovelace and Clarissa. Clarissa stands for a power not yet even conceived by the mind of seventeenth-century Italy or Spain, a power before which Lovelace can no longer function as the universal lover (with his vain mathematical boast: *mille e tre!*) but is transformed into the monogamous Seducer, the seducer who has found his life's work in a single woman. But monogamy, with whatever dishonorable intentions, leads finally to submission to the lady and repentance before her, if not before the God in whose name she speaks. It is tempting, indeed, to say that there is no God (certainly, no God the Father!) in the world of Richardson where His name is so often invoked. In his Manichaean world, there are only man and woman in eternal conflict; for the divine principle has been subsumed in the female even as the diabolic has been in the male.

Clarissa is, then, simply woman, but she is disconcertingly sexless in her bourgeois form—no symbol of insatiable passion or teeming fertility, but a savior, a mediator. She is the Persecuted Maiden, a projection of male guilt before the female treated as a mere sexual object; and she flees through two hundred years of fiction, hounded by father and lover, brother and fiancé: the heroine of all her sex, who applaud her example but are powerless to help her in her hour of need. She is feeling without passion, and her love climax is tears. She is a Protestant virgin, proper to a society that destroyed the splendid images of the Mother of God, but she is also the product of anti-metaphysical Sentimentalism, which found it easier to believe that the human could achieve divinity than that the divine could descend into the human. It is as Pure Maiden that she offers salvation, and upon her maintenance of that purity depends not only her own eternal bliss but that of the male who attempts to destroy it. Even more specifically she is the bourgeois Maiden, whose virginity is the emblem of the ethical purity of her class, the soul of a world whose body is money; and upon her triumph and fall the fate of that class symbolically depends.

Clarissa is, indeed, indistinguishable from her virginity. But that virginity, unlike the chastity advocated by the early Church, is not in itself an end, a supreme good; it is the sign that she has been tried and found worthy of fulfillment in marriage. If Clarissa as a maiden is the type of the savior, marriage is the symbol for the salvation she promises. Marriage alone, "marriage with a Good Woman," can save the depraved male; but such a marriage is of no effect unless woman brings intact to her wedding day the magic of her maidenhead. In a society where morality comes to be associated more and more exclusively with sexual continence, where being good is equated with being chaste, where love is happiness and marriage the fulfillment of love, there is a natural demand for "purity" in its most physical sense—for the unruptured hymen.

This is why in the bourgeois mind purity is associated only with the female; for the maidenhead of the male is too abstract to be believed in. It is not merely that only in a girl is virginity a fact provable in court; it is also that, for the middle-class mind, only femaleness has anything symbolically to do with purity. The final form of Protestantism is Puritanism, whose basic mode of perception is allegorical and to which the sexes are therefore emblems of salvation and damnation. To the mid-eighteenth-century bourgeois, the male is *per se* the tempter, and the female *per se* the savior; it is as simple as that.

Wherever, in any case, a sentimental world-view is substituted for a rationalist one, the male principle comes to seek the dark one, the female the light. Where, on the other hand, law is considered superior to impulse, reason to feeling, the symbolic Fall stories project a female tempter, or, at the very least, portray woman as the gate through which evil comes into the world. "The woman gave me and I did eat." The period of the male tempter is comparatively short in Europe, though long enough to have produced the Faust-Gretchen story as its supreme manifestation. Soon, however, the European writer and the American alike learn to distinguish between feminine and female, to split Woman into Dark Lady and Fair Maiden, savior and tempter, between whom the helpless male is eternally torn. The vampire who began as a male ghoul soon becomes the female "vamp" and the man her victim; but for a while at least, woman plays in the literature of the West the single role of victim-savior.

It must be noted finally that Clarissa represents not only the archetype become a fictional character, but also the fictional character projected as a moral paradigm. Life itself was required to provide examples no longer permitted to be painted on church windows. In the bourgeois world, particularly in its Anglo-Saxon reaches, every woman was expected to seem if not to be Clarissa; it was a burden, indeed, not cast off until the battles of the feminists had been fought and won. The imposition of the Clarissa-image on the young girl represents an insidious form of enslavement; all the idealizations of the female from the earliest days of courtly love had been in fact devices to deprive her of freedom and self-determination, but this last represents the final attempt to imprison woman within a myth of Woman. The demand that every woman act out the allegorical role of Womanhood is like the contemporary pressure on all Negroes to play The Negro; and the Clarissa image, when degraded from archetype to stereotype, is analogous to the current image of Uncle Tom.

Clarissa cannot exist without Lovelace any more than he without her; without him, she is a thematic abstraction awaiting a drama to embody it, a figure of speech in a sermon; without her he is only

Don Juan in the world of the bourgeoisie, that is to say, Lord Byron before the fact. Once mutually defined, their futures differ greatly; for Lovelace stands at the end of a tradition, Clarissa at the beginning.* From her descend directly Goethe's Charlotte and Gretchen, the Julie of Rousseau, Diderot's *La Religieuse,* the Justine of the Marquis de Sade, Melville's Lucy and Hawthorne's Hilda, even the Daisy Miller of Henry James. But Lovelace is quickly degraded into the stock villain of popular fiction and drama; it is hard to think of any later incarnation which approaches in scope or subtlety the vision of Richardson (perhaps the Valmont of *Les Liaisons Dangereuses*). Typically, he is converted into the masturbatory fantasy figure of bourgeois ladies: from the Montraville of Mrs. Rowson's *Charlotte Temple* to the Noel Airman of Herman Wouk's *Marjorie Morningstar.* In the gothic novel, he leads a somewhat more complex life, becoming the Byronic hero with burning eyes and a secret shame, and he is even improbably converted, via the Saint-Preux of Rousseau and the Young Werther of Goethe, into the image of the guilty artist in the middle-class world.

In the original Richardsonian forms, however, Lovelace and Clarissa are defined by their fatal encounter, that is to say, by the archetypal act of Seduction. In this relationship they stand alone; the characters who surround them, in Richardson's novel and in other early workings of the theme, serve only to maneuver them into isolation. Much later, when the myth has been completely profaned, deliberately burlesqued in comic strips and unwittingly parodied in movies, when Clarissa has become Belinda and Lovelace Rudolph Razzeltine, a third character is added: the blond, moose-jawed, clean-living Hairbreadth Harry, who arrives in the nick of time to snatch Belinda from the revolving saw or the approaching train. This is a perversion of the legend, necessitated by the habit (particularly strong in nineteenth-century America) of thinking of Woman as weakness rather than strength, thus standing the Clarissa-archetype on its head. The original point was, of course, that Clarissa needed the intervention of no hero to save either herself or Lovelace; for she was conceived as spirit, and spirit as the only force capable of defeating evil. But evil par excellence was seduction, that "fate worse than death" whose conventional description now cues only the undergraduate's guffaw. The

---

* Though sociologically defined as belonging to just about the same level of society, they are mythologically presented as aristocrat and *bourgeoise.*

melodramatic phrases, "Unhand me, you villain" and "At last you are in my power," whose very success made them ridiculous, are, it must be admitted, the invention of Richardson, who in two books created once and for all the standard language of the drama of seduction: comically in *Pamela,* in which the seducer fails; tragically in *Clarissa,* in which to one degree or another the seducer succeeds.

Seduction is at best a slippery concept, applying as it does to an act halfway between legitimate persuasion and rape, to which moral indignation can respond but which the law cannot define. Implicit in it is a belief in the weakness of women in the hands of men that directly contradicts the heroic feminist myth which emerges from its literature. Several generations of insistence upon the equality of the sexes has made the term all but meaningless to many moderns; and our "sexual emancipation" has made it hard for us to share the pity and horror with which a whole society once contemplated the Fallen Woman. The plaintive lines of Goldsmith, which reflect faithfully the sentimentality of Richardson,

> When lovely woman stoops to folly,
> And finds too late that men betray,
> What charm can soothe her melancholy?
> What art can wash her tears away?
>
> The only art her guilt to cover,
> To hide her shame from ev'ry eye,
> To give repentance to her lover,
> And wring his bosom is—to die.

become the rueful travesty of T. S. Eliot:

> When lovely woman stoops to folly and
> Paces about her room again, alone,
> She smooths her hair with automatic hand,
> And puts a record on the gramophone.

The old notions of seduction and virginity are not yet dead, however, on a less sophisticated level; until a very few years before the writing of Eliot's *The Waste Land,* in which Lovelace has become "the young man carbuncular" and Clarissa "the typist home at teatime," *Charlotte Temple,* a novel of seduction written in

1791, was being reprinted and widely sold in the United States; while in 1955, the revived seduction theme in all its pristine naïveté could make of *Marjorie Morningstar* a best-seller and of its protagonist a national heroine.

Behind the seduction theme lies the bourgeois redefinition of all morality in terms of sexual purity. If the Pure Maiden is the savior, alone capable of converting male rationality (which threatens to become free-thinking) to faith, and male sexuality (which threatens to become animal aggression) to tenderness, and if marriage is the holy state itself, then seduction is truly blasphemy: the denial of the savior and of salvation. Even worse, it is the sin of Judas, "betrayal with a kiss"!

The theme of seduction stands for more than blasphemy, however; it also represents a view of the sexual encounter as a battle. It is, indeed, as Denis de Rougement has observed, a special accomplishment of the modern age to have made of war a passion; and the same age has made of passion a war. The head-on collision of Pamela and Mr. B. or of Clarissa and Lovelace represents, perhaps first of all, the notion of love as the war of the sexes: an almost irreconcilable struggle between the male, who desires sexual satisfaction without marriage, and the female, who desires marriage if not without sex, at least with as little of it as possible. But this struggle is carried on in a world where all the socially powerful (i.e., the men) are arrayed solidly on one side, and all the socially powerless (i.e., the women) attempt to unite on the other —though, indeed, they cannot prevent occasional defections to the side of power.

Superficially, the literary war of the sexes reflects a psychological fact of bourgeois self-consciousness, institutionalized in bourgeois life; symbolically, it stands for a more complex sociological phenomenon: for class war in eighteenth-century England. Part of the appeal of the seduction novel rested surely on its presentation of the conflict of aristocracy and bourgeoisie within the confines of the boudoir. Typically, the Lovelace character is a nobleman, the girl he attempts to seduce of humbler stock. Sometimes, like Clarissa, she is rich and bourgeois, occasionally she is poor; and the seducer is sometimes given anti-democratic speeches, in which he scorns the notion of a marriage that will bring him neither profit or distinction. Against such cold class-consciousness and self-seeking are balanced the arguments of sentimentality: that it is the quality of the soul which counts, that the truest nobility is piety, etc., etc. In this sense, the novel is the long-delayed answer of the lower classes to the courtly *pastourelle,* the love debate of shepherdesses and nobleman, which ends typically with a tumbling in the grass. It is a protest, democratic and sentimental at once, against the courtly love codes and the sexual tyranny which they disguised. It rejects alike the conviction that love must be adulterous and the off-hand assumption that the lord of the manor has a right to take whatever girl of inferior rank is pleasing to him. On the one hand, the bourgeois novel insists that the pre-marital period is the proper time for love and legitimate marriage its only proper consummation; on the other, it asserts the sexual rights of its daughters as persons, capable of consent or refusal. But its protest against seduction is metaphorical as well as literal; through Richardson a whole class cries: We will be raped and bamboozled no more!

There is moreover an even deeper level at which the war of the sexes and classes is understood to represent a psychological division in the soul of man itself—and the conflict of ideologies which arises from this division. Lovelace and Clarissa are, as we have seen, the male principle and the female, Devil and savior, aristocracy and bourgeoisie; but they are also the head and the heart—what we would call now super-ego and (in somewhat expurgated form) id. Lovelace is above all things an intellectual—*philosophe* and libertine, Clarissa essentially a believer, however agile at apologetics—a sentimental Christian; Lovelace, that is to say, is a parody of the Enlightenment itself, Clarissa the idealization of all that lies beyond mere rationalism.* Richardson as a champion of the heart over the head, a secret enemy of Reason, is the philistines' Rousseau, the Jean-Jacques of the timid bourgeoisie. Like his French opposite number, he exacts from his reader the supreme tribute of tears. The triumphant fall of Clarissa, by releasing pity and melting the heart, becomes the instrument of salvation it recommends. Whoever weeps is saved; and all Europe wept at Clary's end, felt itself redeemed by self-knowledge as well as sympathy.

Yet though *Clarissa* is a sacred book and a treasure house of symbols dear to the rising bourgeoisie, it is by no means a book only valuable as scripture and symbol. It achieves its mythic reso-

---

* We must not be deceived by how well Clarissa talks; it is her feelings that count. She is a rationalizer of her heart's promptings, not a heartless rationalist.

nance without sacrificing verisimilitude, without ceasing to be a scrupulous portrayal of contemporary manners and modes of consciousness. Its very epistolary form, the presentation through letters not of action itself but of response to action, is not merely an amateur's way out, as some critics have thought, but the analyst's way in, a way of rendering inwardness with extraordinary immediacy. Indeed, after abandoning the letter convention, the novel did not achieve comparable subtlety and directness in the presentation of thought until the invention of stream-of-consciousness in the twentieth century. The creation of "character" in the full modern sense, that is, of fictional actors at once complexly motivated and consistent, highly individualized and typical—this is the essential achievement of Richardson's art.

To one brought up inside the view of the English novel that was universally accepted at the beginning of the present century, Richardson is hard to appreciate. Was his reputation not almost immediately deflated by the irony of Fielding? Did not readers move with relief from the fetid atmosphere of his airless boudoirs to the broad open-air vistas of the pseudo-Shakespearean novel of masculine protest? Did not ingenious plotting and fast action, good theater, replace the tedious revelation of the dark underside of the souls of young girls? Of course they did not; for the novel must continue to carry the torch to the back of the cave (whatever else it does in addition) or surrender its birthright, its essential function. Parody destroys nothing; it is only a reluctant and shamefaced way of honoring an example one is ashamed to acknowledge, and, for one too proud to attempt so popular a form as the novel without tongue in cheek, a way of becoming a novelist.

4

THE BOURGEOIS

SENTIMENTAL NOVEL

AND THE

FEMALE AUDIENCE

FIELDING, especially since the rejection of gentility has become an important touchstone in the academic world of the United States and new notions of sexual freedom have prevailed, has come to seem the true, tough-minded ancestor of "honest" fiction, the preferred father of the novel. The legendary contest with which modern fiction is supposed to have begun is the struggle between Pamela and Joseph Andrews, in which the sentimental sister is mocked to silence by her comic brother and the way is cleared for Tom Jones.

The preference of contemporary American critics for the Good Bad Boys of Fielding over the Good Good Girls of Richardson is a phenomenon some of whose causes will be made clear in the following discussion; but the critics' personal inclination is not of first importance. Nor does it matter in a total view of the American novel that to most of Europe, Fielding has always seemed of lesser importance than Richardson. Even Dr. Johnson's view of the matter can be shrugged aside as aberrant. After all, he was a man given over to prejudice and invective, one with the temerity to call Fielding a "blockhead," in the very interchange in which he insists, "Sir, there is more knowledge of the heart in one letter of Richardson's than in all *Tom Jones*." But the student of American letters must come to terms with the earliest American reactions to the author of *Clarissa*.

In 1790, Enos Hitchcock wrote, "His Clarissa has been considered by good judges, as the most finished model of female excellence which has ever been offered for their imitation," and Charles Brockden Brown puts into the mouth (or rather, in good Richardsonian fashion, onto the tip of the pen) of his heroine the following pledge of allegiance: "I am a disciple of that religion and philosophy of which the effects are to be seen in Clarissa. O best of men!" Though *Tom Jones* had to wait fifty-four years for an American edition, *Pamela* was published in Philadelphia only four years after its appearance in England. (The latter was the first book printed in America, naturally enough by Benjamin Franklin, who, though no friend of sentimental love—"use venery," he coolly recommended, "for health and offspring"—knew something about business.) The British fleet during the Revolution brought in *Clarissa* in eight-volume sets, and by 1800 there were twenty native imprints of Richardson in the United States, even illustrated and abridged versions of *Clarissa* and *Grandison,* "for the Instruction and Amusement of Children"!

For better or for worse, the values of the Sentimental Love Religion, inextricably bound up with the example of Richardson, entered into the American novel at the moment of its creation. There is scarcely a nineteenth-century book written by an American, whether avowedly in the analytical school that derives from *Pamela,* or in the gothic tradition out of Ann Radcliffe and "Monk" Lewis, or in the line of the historical romance as defined by Scott, which does not accept the standards of that code. These are the three chief strains of our earliest fiction, and, whatever other differences may separate them, they are at one in espousing "that religion and philosophy of which the effects are to be seen in Clarissa."

It is not enough, however, simply to say that Sentimentalism triumphed everywhere in our fiction; it must also be added that it proved almost everywhere a *blight,* a universal influence which was also a universal calamity. The Pure Young Maiden who derives from Clarissa and pre-empts the place of the heroine in our classic books is almost invariably a dull and embarrassing figure, a monster of virtue, her derivation a vulgarization and a falling off. The scarcely distinguishable ingenues of Cooper, the incredible Lucy over whom Melville drivels in *Pierre* (so shamelessly that his admirers have tried ever since to persuade themselves he was engaging in burlesque), Hawthorne's pale Priscilla and unbearably dovelike Hilda: these are the scandals of our literature. Indeed, it was their awareness of the inadequacy of such female characters (and their inability to imagine others) that led many of our authors to that strategy of evasion, that flight from society to nature, from the world of women to the haunts of womanless men, which sets our novel apart from that of the rest of the Western world.

Why did the Richardsonian example, elsewhere so fertile, prove so sterile in the United States? A tradition capable of supplying the love story for Part I of *Faust,* for *I Promessi Sposi,* or even for *The Heart of Midlothian* might well have been expected to inform works of equal merit in America. Why does the relationship of Heinrich and Gretchen (like that of Clarissa and Lovelace) still possess the imagination of the West, breeding new works of art, while that of Lucy and Pierre seems irrelevant and a little comic? The beginning of an explanation can be found in the fact that there is no real tradition of gallantry in America, no debased aristocratic codes of love against which the bourgeois belief can define itself; and consequently the tension and urgency which make dramatic the works of Richardson and Rousseau and Goethe are lacking. It is impossible to contrast domestic virtues with courtly ones in a country where there has never been a court, so that the essential Richardsonian conflict, which is also the dialectic of the form, is inevitably lost.

It is true, of course, that Richardson himself formally rejected adultery as a subject; and the struggle over the virtue of Clarissa has been moved from the arena of marriage to that of maidenhood. Yet where the figure of Don Juan persists, no matter in what disguise, the theme of adultery hides underground, as it were, awaiting a resurrection. In the novels of Richardson's most faithful followers, in the *Nouvelle Héloïse* of Rousseau or Goethe's *Werther,* published within twenty-five years of *Clarissa,* the old courtly theme reasserts itself: adultery, consummated or unconsummated, comes to stand beside seduction at the sentimental heart of these fictions; and when seduction itself loses not only its appeal but its very meaning, the European novel reverts completely to the oldest theme of Western secular literature. "Society requires that women have husbands," Denis de Rougemont remarks, "but in novels it is found necessary that they have lovers."

Not so in American fiction during its classical period, where except for Hawthorne's odd example, no major book confronts that major theme until the time of Henry James. Similarly, there existed in America no body of pornographic literature. But this cuts our bourgeois literature off from the device of borrowing the brutality and frankness of pornography on the grounds that opposing forces, in order to meet, even on a moral battleground, must adopt similar strategies. There is a real sense in which the novels of Richardson, at their Hogarthian strongest and most appealing, are "dirty books." It is no accident that *Fanny Hill*, that masterpiece of British pornography published in the same year as *Clarissa*, itself adopted—however cursorily—the letter form of *Pamela;* or that Diderot was the author of the *Bijoux Indiscrets*, an extended smutty joke, or that in his most Richardsonian novel, *La Religieuse*, he pursued sexual titillation even in the midst of moralizing and tears. Implicit in Diderot—and, though quite differently, also in Rousseau—are the seeds of the infamous *Justine*, the book the Marquis de Sade would never quite confess he had written, and of *Les Liaisons Dangereuses*, last of the great epistolary novels, which defined a delicate line between obscenity and art, inconceivable to the American mind.

The American novelist, then, was deprived of the privilege of defining his own middle-class values against a surviving tradition of gallantry or *gauloiserie*. Only in Puritanism could he discover an antithesis to his sentimental world-view, a source of tension to protect him from moral flaccidity. But before the novel proper was invented, Puritanism had begun to decay; indeed, the Sentimental Love Religion was itself, as we have seen, a by-product of the softening of Protestant rigor; and novels could not even have been printed if the church of the Pilgrims had not first relinquished its social control. The printing press came first to America, like so much else, in the service of God, and the first book published on our soil was *The Whole Book of Psalmes Faithfully Translated into English Metre*.

But the century that elapsed between the publication of the *Bay Psalm Book* in 1640 and that of the American edition of *Pamela* in 1744 saw the break-up of the political power of Puritanism in America, and the consequent slow transformation of Calvinist dogma into sentimental piety. By 1688, it was clear that no new settlement could restore the power destroyed by the Restoration of the Stuarts; and the hysterical hunt for a conspiracy of witches represents the loss of nerve among the elders of the church, a desperate attempt to identify some visible enemy who could be blamed for what time and history had done to their dream. The vision of a Protestant Commonwealth in the New World compromised and dissipated, they could find nothing better to do than hang old women and dogs. Worse, however, was to come; for in the final years of the eighteenth century and the first decades of the nineteenth (at precisely the moment when the American novel was being born), the old church was forced to endure a double-barreled attack. From without and within Calvinist doctrine was assailed: by the Deists who deserted the places of worship and by the "liberal Christians" (who were to call themselves in the end "Unitarians") who attempted to take them over. By the time the first American novel appeared, in the critical year of 1789, Calvinism was doomed, on the one hand, to be dissipated among a hundred frantic, life-denying sects, and on the other, to be gradually sapped away by "liberalism." The father-centered, ascetic, intellectual faith upon which America had been founded survived, by the time of William Hill Brown, the first native novelist, chiefly in the form of secularized feelings of guilt.

To those guilt-feelings the American novel paid tribute by attempting to justify its existence on moral grounds—declaring itself the servant of religion and especially the keeper of the consciences and the virginity of young girls. The original Puritan impulse had represented an extreme revulsion from Mariolatry, an absolute refusal to give the female principle its due. As late as Hawthorne (though perhaps later for him than for others not so obsessed with the Puritan past), the image for the ancestral faith is a paternal image: "Grave, bearded, sable-cloaked and steeple-crowned . . . with his Bible and his sword . . . ," and that image Hawthorne mythicized for us all in *The Scarlet Letter*.

By the time of Mark Twain, however, even the claims of the old faith are asserted only by women; it is woman who has become the guardian of morality and the embodiment of conscience, whether in the palatable form of the widow Douglas, "dismal regular and decent . . . in all her ways," yet able to "talk about Providence in a way to make a body's mouth water" and much given to weeping over "poor lost lambs"; or the more forbidding shape of Miss Watson, "a tolerable slim old maid with goggles on," addicted to telling squirming small boys "all about the bad place." "Crying" religion or "pecking" religion, Calvinist or sentimental, religion is thought of as exemplified by mother or aunt, the Puritan image of the bearded Progenitor gone once and for all.

The American had finally denied too many fathers to survive except as the fatherless man. The fatherland abandoned, the Pope rejected, the bishops denied, the king overthrown—only the mother remained as symbol of an authority that was one with love. What the original, archetypal American experience established as a pattern, the experience of the immigrant generations somehow repeats; for better or worse, the children of Slavic peasants, of German revolutionaries and Jewish scholars are become alike heirs of a handful of Englishmen who settled New England. "The individual rejection of the European father . . . every second-generation American had to perform . . . ," Geoffrey Gorer writes in *The American People;* "the making of an American demanded that the father should be rejected both as a model and as a source of authority. Father never knows best." The symbolic vacuum left by the deposition of the Father is filled by the figure of woman, as Maiden and Mother; and America remains still the only Christian country in which a major religious denomination was founded by a woman.

The American novel is both beneficiary and cause of this symbolic shift of allegiance. Its salvationist myths meet head-on the older Pauline notions of the female as tempter and marriage as a necessary evil. In the strongholds of Calvinism, it was taught that copulation of husband and wife on the Lord's day is especially sinful, which is to say, that the rite of marriage does not transform the sexual act into a sacramental one. Indeed, the distrust of sexuality is not denied by the sentimental code itself, which only combined it uneasily with a sense that not the lonely saint but the married man is the truest friend of God. The Sentimental Love Religion, which simultaneously disowns sex and glorifies woman, could not triumph until the traditional association of the fear of passion with a contempt for the female had fallen apart.

The myth of the Fall in the Garden was interpreted by the Puritan allegorist as it had been interpreted by Milton: once reason (represented by the male) has been lulled to sleep, feeling (represented by the female) is easily subverted by evil, and in turn easily subverts reason itself. This is, of course, almost precisely opposed to the deepest meaning of the sentimental myth of the Seducer and the Maiden; for that archetype projects the image not of passion seducing intellect, but of the head attempting to lead the heart astray. The anti-intellectualism of the sentimental code, its theory that simple feeling is closer to God's truth than educated intelligence, could exist only in the decline of Puritanism and is, indeed, a symptom of that decline.

More, however, is involved than this. The Sentimental Love Religion challenges the fundamental Calvinist belief in natural depravity; for it teaches that women, woman in general and some women in particular, are absolutely pure; and that their merely human purity can do Christ's work in the world: redeem corrupted souls from sin.

In America, especially, the use of women as symbols of piety and purity led to an unfortunate series of misunderstandings.* With no counter-tradition, cynical or idealizing, to challenge it, the sentimental view came to be accepted as quite *literally* true, was imposed upon actual woman as a required role and responded to by men as if it were a fact of life rather than of fancy. Even Hawthorne, who attempted valiantly to restore the anti-sentimental insights of Calvinism to secular thinking, stumbled here. Of his Hilda in *The Marble Faun,* whom he seems always on the tantalizing verge of turning into the Blessed Virgin, he remarks through his mouthpiece, the artist Kenyon: "Her womanhood is of the ethereal type, and incompatible with any shadow of darkness or evil." This comment Miriam, herself a nonethereal type, glosses further: "You are right . . . there are women of that ethereal type as you term it, and Hilda is one of them. She would die of her first wrong-doing—supposing for a moment that she would be capable of doing wrong."

One has only to imagine the incredulity of St. Paul or Augustine, Calvin or Cotton Mather before such a statement to realize how revolutionary it is in its implications. Any cynical phrase taken at random out of Rabelais is far closer to orthodox opinion on the subject: "When I say, *womankind,* I speak of a sex so frail, so variable, so changeable, so futile, inconstant and imperfect, that, in my opinion, *Nature* . . . did in a manner . . . stray exceedingly from that excellence of providential judgment by which she had created and formed all other things, when she built, framed and made up the woman."

Richardson himself did not for all his bland moralizing portray his heroines as so exempt from all sinfulness. Pamela is gifted with the sharpest of eyes for the main chance, and Clarissa, pattern of excellence that she is, has her weaknesses. It is not Puri-

---

* Even female Indians were regarded as dusky Pamelas. And it would be a shame not to mention in this connection the name of Pocahontas, who has been the inspiration of so many bad sentimental novels—as well as of so many debunking male travesties, culminating in John Barth's *The Sot-weed Factor* (1960).

tanism, which however pharisaical was not given to self-deceit, which creates the illusory image of female perfection, but the genteel oposition which sought to humanize the earlier faith. The very force which permits the appearance of the novel and welcomes its tearful philanthropy leads to a falsification of life (at least on the side of women) which emasculates the form. Whatever his opinion of sexual passion, no Puritan denied or was afraid to describe its omnipresence and power. And even as late as 1803, it was possible to devote one of the chief commencement addresses at Harvard to the subject of Seduction, a topic which by the end of the century had become taboo on all public occasions, and is, indeed, not even treated in the novels of a "realist" like William Dean Howells.

No Puritan divine would have been shocked as Thoreau was at the appearance of phallic forms in nature, for he would have expected no better. And none would have thought that the way to deal with sex was to ignore it, or to ban from literature the words by which it is customarily described; but the genteel impulse, confusing civilization and bowdlerization, chose to speak of dying as "passing over," of pregnancy as an "interesting condition," and of copulation not at all. Richardsonian Sentimentalism was degraded step by step to genteel sentimentalism, as the novel of seduction was deprived of its now unmentionable theme.

The Seducer was first demoted to the unworthy wooer, pressing his insulting suit, and then was eliminated completely, while the Clarissa character was reduced in age from maturity to early adolescence to childhood—so that her virtue might be tested and proved without the intrusion of sex. At the close of the eighteenth century, an abridged Clarissa was considered quite suitable fare for children; at the beginning of the nineteenth century, grown women felt safe from possible offense only with a juvenile: thrilled sedately as Ellen Ware faced down the insolent dry-goods salesman in Susan Warner's *The Wide, Wide World,* that child's book which became one of the great adult best-sellers of our history. The movement which produced so strange a development was the movement of warm-hearted reform that nurtured abolition, prohibition, anti-vivisection, and vegetarianism; that drove Mama to the Chautauqua lecture and Papa outdoors to smoke; that delivered pious America from the threat of damnation and the fear of the seducer. It was in short what its best friend and severest critic, Mark Twain, called "civilization."

II

Before the sentimental novel came to America, it had already been transformed by the heirs of Richardson in England; and it is through those heirs that the master was approached in the United States. Like all provincial literatures, the American began with a cultural lag, emulating long-lapsed styles of the center. It was not until 1789, nearly fifty years after the publication of *Pamela,* that our first home-grown sentimental novel appeared. The year 1789 marked the close of a long dull period of recapitulation in the literature of Europe; there was a sense that the masters had all departed, leaving no worthy successors. Fielding had died in 1754, Richardson in 1761, Sterne in 1770, and Smollett in 1771. The year of Richardson's death had seen the appearance of Rousseau's *Nouvelle Héloïse,* and Smollett's death had coincided with the publication of *Werther.*

On the continent as well as in England, the work of the great ground-breakers was over; and everywhere there was a sense that the old lines of development would have to be given a new turn or abandoned altogether. To be sure, a "new" literature was beginning in England at almost the same moment that the sentimental novel was being reborn in America. The main body of work of Mrs. Radcliffe began to appear in 1789, a series of novels which, with *The Monk* of M. G. Lewis, was to succeed in creating the "modern novel" of the declining eighteenth century —the gothic romance. This form, however, was not to reach America for another decade. Our first authors looked for examples to the continuing tradition of Richardson, and what they found was not particularly exciting.

The intended audience for Richardsonian fiction had been from the beginning largely if not exclusively feminine. The protagonists of his books had been, indeed, females in whom his readers could find a glorified image of themselves; but when women became the chief authors as well as the chief characters of the novel, a real change took place. Never before had there been an art form in whose production women played so predominant a part (except, perhaps, the late baroque romances of France), and whose modes and values they so decisively influenced that later male authors had (like Melville in *Pierre*) to imitate them in order to bid for their audiences. Before his death, Smollett had been driven to cry out that "that branch of business is now engrossed by female authors who publish merely for the propagation of virtue. . . ." "Merely for the propagation of virtue," he ironically defines their goal; but his metaphors, "branch of the business," "engrossed" indicate the other goal of such writers.

One essential contradiction of Puritanism, at least, survived to haunt the lady purveyors of genteel, sentimental fiction: the mutually incompatible injunctions to be "one deadhearted to the world" and to "bestir yourself for profit!" At any rate, the manufacture of novels is the first business in the modern world into which women were permitted to enter in large numbers, and in which, competing on an equal footing with males, they achieved financial success. If the birth of the novel is in one sense an episode in the rise of the bourgeoisie and in another an incident in the genteel reform of manners, it is also a critical moment in the emancipation of woman.

America was no exception in the trend toward female authorship; indeed, before the publication of Cooper's *Precaution* in 1820, one-third of all our novels had been written by women— and within that third were to be found almost all the early bestsellers. Past the middle of the same century, Hawthorne is still deploring the "d——d mob of scribbling women," who have pre-empted the audience for novels; while the books of Susanna Rowson, Harriet Beecher Stowe, and Susan Warner remain to this day the most popular American fiction of all time, rivaled only by such later products of female authors as *Gone With the Wind* and *Peyton Place*. It is difficult in the early stages to distinguish between the work of the British lady-epigones and the American ones; indeed, the authors sometimes moved back and forth between the old country and the new with an ease which distresses the classifier. Mrs. Susanna Rowson, author of the most reprinted of all American books, *Charlotte Temple,* was born in England and wrote her first three novels there; *Charlotte* itself was published in London three years before its appearance in New York. For the English, however, Mrs. Rowson is a minor figure in the decline of the Richardsonian novel, a belated supernumerary of the rank of the Miss Minifies or Mrs. Woodfins; for us, she is a pioneer! To be sure, such third-rate sentimentalists made some difference in the history of English taste—but for America they made *all* the difference.

What, then, was the nature of their achievement? What did the

Sentimental Love Religion and the novel of analysis become in their hands? It must be said first of all that the sentimental novel of analysis, once firmly in the hands of genteel females, ceased to be analytic at all. To observers as different in taste and ambitions (though all male!) as Diderot, the Marquis de Sade, and Dr. Johnson, it was clear from the start that the abiding value of Richardson's work lay in his knowledge of the intricacies of the female mind (or, as it was called then, the "heart"), and in his invention of a technique for rendering in all their complexity and evanescence moments of choice or equivocation within that "heart." Neither inwardness nor character, however, interested the scribbling ladies at all. They sought, however unconsciously, the mythical beneath the psychological—and rendered the myth in sub-literary or pre-literary form, degraded it to the stereotype. They preserved the letter form of Richardson's fiction with no feeling for what that device was intended to do: to redeem the novel's action from the historical past for the dramatic present. For them, it was simply the way novels were put together.

Integrated into carefully differentiated letters, rendered always through an actor in his story, Richardson's prosiest sermons have a point and an aesthetic function. They serve to define character and milieu with a truth quite independent of their own validity in terms of ethical systems. But introduced into third-person narrative, or only perfunctorily assigned to some interpolated mouthpiece of the author, they remain interesting only so long as they strike the reader as fresh or significant. Plot is, of course, another matter. Richardson is certainly no greater contriver of plots, but he does possess extraordinary mythopoeic powers—so that, though there is perfect justice in Samuel Johnson's rejoinder to one who found Richardson "very tedious": "Why, Sir, if you were to read Richardson for the story, your impatience would be so much fretted that you would hang yourself," there is much more to be said. It was, at any rate, precisely "the story" that the female Richardsonians sought to extricate and recreate, for they were aware, as Johnson was not, that even the bare bones of the seduction archetype had an import for the whole community beyond that of literature. The appeal of the seduction mythos is, however, limited in time; only for a little while was it able to appeal to an audience which included the learned as well as the scarcely literate. Yet even in reduced straits, it retains some vestige of its legendary power, and can at any moment achieve an unforeseen popular success.

The natural ease of Richardson's style concealed its technical virtuosity and led his imitators to believe, on the one hand, that anyone who could write letters could string them together into a book; and, on the other, to feel that artlessness was itself a Richardsonian quality: a natural adjunct of piety and a guarantee of the "truth" as well as the moral usefulness of a work which no sentimental Christian would concede was merely art. The lady Richardsonians were moreover not only the enemies of psychology and technique; they were also the sworn foes of candor. Though they clung for a long time to the seduction theme itself (they could think of no other core for a novel equally sure-fire in its appeal) and consequently never became quite pure enough to satisfy their even more genteel descendants, they expurgated the treatment of the encounter at the heart of their fiction, until they almost seemed to be writing in code. Richardson himself is not guiltless of euphemism in dealing with rape or devirgination or even childbirth, but he is able to write scenes such as that of the death of the bawd, Mrs. Sinclair ("Behold her, then, spreading the whole troubled bed with her huge quaggy carcase: her mill-post arms held up . . . her livid lips parched and working violently . . . her wide mouth . . . splitting her face, as it were two parts; and her huge tongue hideously rolling in it . . . her bellows-shaped and various coloured breasts ascending by turns to her chin, and descending out of sight, with the violence of her gaspings") with a forthrightness and vigor lost to his tradition after its capture by women.

As early as *The Hapless Orphan* (1793), American novelists were attempting to find sentimental substitutes for the struggle with the seducer; and before the process begun in the declining years of the eighteenth century was through, the treatment of seduction had been surrendered to literary radicals and semi-pornographers. *Charlotte Temple* itself, that first American monument to expurgated Richardsonianism, came at last to be thought of as a "dirty book," and was peddled in working-class districts (slightly amended and dressed in lurid covers) to young girls in search of literary titillation. It was a long way, however, from the first expurgations of the seduction theme to its final casting out; and before that rejection could be accomplished the genteel revolution had to run its full course.

Even more critical, perhaps, than the flight from art and candor, is the rejection of tragedy in the second-generation sentimental novel. The success of his attempt at a tragedy of seduction, in

Clarissa, is attested by the impossibility of summarizing the latter book in any pat formula. We have already noticed how misleading a modern, off-hand attempt to sum up its effect can be. Whatever *Clarissa* is, it is not an account of "the sad end of a girl who failed to resist a man's blandishments." For Richardson, the effects of violation are real and irrecoverable; Clarissa's devirgination has taken away her *mana* as Maiden-savior, and she is for him, a creature of his time, as "ruined" as if she had consented. She triumphs only (the Kierkegaardian terms suggest themselves inevitably) "by virtue of the absurd," because her creator has rejected for her the "aesthetic" solution of a "happy ending." The outward form of her victory is death.

Such a tragic conclusion (whose complexities, indeed, I have only begun to suggest) not only baffled Richardson's readers, who bombarded him with requests to relent and restore Clary to life and Lovelace, but shocked even Fielding, one of whose objections to Richardson was to his stubbornly dark vision of life; while so great a writer as Jane Austen could not, as we have noticed, accommodate to her world of wit and dialectic the grimness of *Clarissa.* If such distinguished, genial spirits faltered before the inexorable doom of Clarissa, no wonder the unintellectual imitators of Richardson were incapable of responding to the complex moral dilemma and the desperate triumph of this heroine. They wanted virtue rewarded and vice punished—virtue triumphant in indignity was for them a concept as dangerous as it was difficult.

Not that at first they avoided all "sad" endings; far from it! They had been taught by Sterne as well as by Richardson the lesson (which Goethe and Rousseau each expounded after his own taste) that only he who weeps is saved. It was a reigning doctrine in an age which saw sensibility compound sentimentality and which took tears for the truest testimony of good faith. Never had the lust of ladies for a "good cry" found such sage apologists. But the sentimental ending is not inevitably a tragic one; and for the pathos of *Clarissa* the followers of Richardson substituted a lesser pathos. Their novels, when they did not deal with the success of a worthy girl, complied in fact with the formula misread into their master: "the sad end of a girl who failed to resist a man's blandishments."

The seduced maiden, in such fictions, finds herself pregnant and abandoned by her lover, who has meanwhile fallen in love with a good woman and married. He is more often shown as negligent than cruel (the soft hearts of the genteel Richardsonians mitigating

Lovelace himself), sometimes even the victim of the deceits of a trusted friend. He finally discovers the plight of his abandoned love, but before he can arrive with help the traduced girl has found peace in suicide or has died giving birth under the most miserable of conditions—usually to a little girl. Not uncommonly, the author pleads at this point for understanding and sympathy toward the seducer's victim, pointing out that some humble life of usefulness might still remain for the ruined girl, but such authors scarcely ever can bring themselves to let her live, thus surrendering the tearful climax. Her death, however, is never proffered as the absolute end; there is always a hint that her suffering has redeemed her in the eyes of a benevolent Maker (the harsh, Puritan God had been deposed before such novels began to appear) and that her tears will be wiped away in heaven.

For those who did not find motive enough for tears in such suicides or childbed deaths, there was in reserve the child left by the dying mother to the protection of some kind female benefactor (always conveniently out of town at the critical moment). A not unusual fate for such illegitimate girls was to fall in love with the legitimate sons of their reformed fathers, learning only at the very altar the truth which condemned them to a single, melancholy, and useful life or a death by brain fever. Such flirtations with incest, however, betray the influence of the French novelist Prévost, and are the fruits of a hunger for "unnatural" sensationalism which goes beyond the decent bourgeois limits of Richardsonian pathos.

It took scores of years to persuade the great, genteel audience, male and female alike, that the "happy ending" was preferable to the tearful close. The death of Little Eva surely sold as many copies of *Uncle Tom's Cabin* as the fatal whipping of the pious slave; and Dickens could with the death of Little Nell stir up a public orgy of weeping in which we find it hard to believe. As the thrill of seduction was expurgated from popular fiction and the threat of rape removed, death was more and more demanded; the titillation provided once by peering through the keyhole at the nubile maiden struggling for her honor was, somewhat perversely, replaced by the ambiguous pleasure of standing over the snow-white deathbed of the virgin child.

Finally, melancholy becomes contraband in the polite world of woman's books, permitted when bootlegged in small amounts, but frowned on as "morbid" when overwhelmingly present. When the sentimental novel of seduction is reborn in the twentieth century as *Marjorie Morningstar,* Herman Wouk grants to his seduced heroine the happy ending of marriage—though he is still deeply enough committed to the genteel mystique of virginity to make it clear that her husband only accepts her as something maimed. Cheerfulness may at long last become obligatory in popular American fiction, but it has to fight hard against the allure of tearful melodrama, that *ersatz* of tragedy striving always to recapture the somber thrill that shook all of Europe when Clarissa died.

A further distortion of the Richardsonian prototype attempted to transform the seduction theme into a feminist attack upon the male, a symbolic castration of the oppressing sex. There had been present in Richardson from the first, of course, a view of the sexual encounter as warfare between man and woman, with the male in the role of the enemy. In his novels, however, the identification of the male with evil had been determined by the Sentimentalist's need to make the negative principle the "head," i.e., the intellectualism of the male. He felt obligated, moreover, in his portrayal of the class struggle to make the representative of the bourgeoisie a woman, since he would have regarded the marriage of an upper-class woman to a man from the lower classes—a duchess, let us say, to a footman—as degrading and a little ridiculous. To Englishmen, it has always seemed necessary only to change the sexes in the *Pamela* story in order to turn it into parody; and no one but a sentimental rebel and outsider like Rousseau dared treat seriously the aspiration of a Saint-Preux for his aristocratic pupil-mistress. But Richardson, too, within his own cautious limits, was a revolutionary, his books the manifesto of a class struggling for dignity as well as power. In America, his class-determined fable had to be adapted to the needs of a society quite different from the one which had bred it. What was an American bourgeoisie to make of the opposition to Don Juanism so essential to the Sentimental Love Religion, or the sense in which virtue was identified with the social demands of a rising mercantile class? The scrupulosity with which Richardson in his novels balanced bourgeois-domestic virtues against courtly-gallant ones (not only in the persons of Pamela and Mr. B., but even in Clarissa and Lovelace, whose social origins are so much alike) was wasted on the reader who inhabited a world in which there were nothing but bourgeois-domestic values.

In America, therefore, which possessed no hereditary aristocracy and whose shifting class distinctions took no hold on the popular imagination, the class-war meanings of the sentimental novel are lost. This fact Oliver Wendell Holmes quite clearly saw and registered in the opening pages of his own sentimental novel *Elsie Venner:* "There is nothing in New England corresponding at all to the feudal aristocracies of the Old World. Whether it be owing to the stock from which we were derived . . . or the abrogation of the technical 'law of honor,' which draws a sharp line between the personally responsible class of 'gentlemen' and the unnamed multitude who are not expected to risk their lives for an abstraction— whatever be the cause, we have no such aristocracy here as that which grew up out of the military systems of the Middle Ages." Take the sword out of the hand of Lovelace-Don Juan and an essential part of his meaning has disappeared.

To be sure, there was some attempt in the United States to interlace the seduction story with reflections on the relations of rich and poor, and especially on the desire of young men to marry for money; but such moralizing seems perfunctory in the hands of all but such socialist novelists as George Lippard (who wrote in the mid-nineteenth century one of the most eccentric of all anti-seduction novels, *The Monks of Monk Hall*) or Theodore Dreiser (who made of the sentimental heroine the protagonist of books otherwise brutally realistic). It was a long time, however, before socialism penetrated deep enough into the American mind to make a modern version of the class-struggle novel possible; and meanwhile generation after generation of female sentimentalists contented themselves with portraying good Revolutionary colonial girls defending their honor against swaggering Redcoats, or Confederate lasses fighting the same fight against dashing Union officers, or last of all, the country girl upholding her honor against the city slicker. In this sense, the farmer's daughter and the traveling salesman of a thousand dirty jokes represent a last degradation (though a strange persistence, too) of the archetypal figures of Clarissa and Lovelace.

Such versions of the sexual conflict remain peripheral in our early novels, however; the center is elsewhere. In popular fiction produced in America by and for females, the seduction fable comes chiefly to stand for the war between the sexes and the defeat of the seducer (in such books he is finally conquered whether or not he initially prevails) as a symbol of the emasculation of American men. The Satanism of Lovelace is interpreted as standing for nothing more than the nature of maleness itself; while the divinity of Clarissa comes more than ever to signify the essential goodness of

women as such. Granted both such pat symbolism and the obligation to poetic justice, and it is clear that the sentimental novel in
the United States must end with the downfall of the male. From
Charlotte Temple to the latest daytime serial on radio or TV, the
legend of a moral struggle ending in the moral dominance of
woman informs the literature which makes the mass mind of
America. In this country the only class war is between the sexes!

Tearful extravaganzas in which the female is portrayed as pure
sentiment, the male as naked phallus proliferated endlessly. In the
end, even that intelligence for which the Lovelace figure originally
stood is travestied in favor of woman's "finer feelings"; though the
male is allowed still to spout "ideas," those ideas are revealed as
irrelevant to life and good sense, the babble of a bookish child. It
is easy enough, in a way, to understand why women should have
propagated and welcomed this mythical account of the qualities of
the sexes and of their relationship. What is baffling is why men,
too, should have accepted this travesty on their nature and role in
life; but they did, in fact, accept it, even repeating in their own
books the formulas of feminist sentimentality. Perhaps it seemed to
them, on one level of consciousness or another, a symbolic restitution for the injustices they had no intention of reforming—rather
like the wealthy Victorian's self-satisfied weeping over the plight
of the poor.

In the end, male and female arrived at a mutual pact, based on
guilt and resentment, to castrate father: to make him seem a
spoiled child rather than a sexual aggressor. The acceptance by the
male of the female image of him first as seducer and blackguard,
then (in America) as Bad Boy, follows naturally upon the female's
acceptance of the male's image of her as sexless savior and (in
America) eternal Mama; and perhaps, after all, the former travesty
is a revenge for the latter one, rather than for the social indignities
visited upon woman.

Whatever the social reality, in fiction certainly, instances of male
humiliation are endlessly multiplied. The first popular American
image of the Seducer, our own Lovelace, was Mrs. Rowson's
Montraville, who betrayed Charlotte Temple, and whom we meet
for the last time in *Lucy Temple* (also known as *Charlotte's
Daughter; or the Three Orphans*), "sunk upon the shoulder of his
wife, pale and almost lifeless" and learn "that he sometimes la-
bored under slight fits of insanity . . . indeed it is only by powerful
opiates that he obtains any, and by them alone the smallest exhila-

ration of spirits." Not merely as a seducer but as a father (in wedlock and out) Montraville is punished, forced to watch his children on the verge of an incestuous catastrophe bred by his sin and cowardice. Mrs. Rowson leaves her readers in no doubt as to the cause of the degradation of her seducer. "All blighted," she explains, "by once yielding to the impulse of guilty passions."

Hawthorne himself, so oppressed by the "female scribblers," was not averse to taking a leaf from their book. Dimmesdale moves through the final pages of *The Scarlet Letter* like one half dead, "his movements resembling the wavering effort of an infant with its mother's arms in view. . . ." And those "mother's arms" do in fact await him, stretched out by Hester whom he traduced. The pattern of Mrs. Rowson is repeated once more in *The Blithedale Romance.* "As they approached me," Hawthorne writes of his archetypal couple, "I observed in Hollingsworth's face a depressed and melancholy look, that seemed habitual; the powerfully built man showed a self-distrustful weakness, and a child-like or childish tendency to press closer, and closer still, to the side of the slender woman whose arm was within his." The ending is the same on the level of best-selling pseudo-piety: "scarcely a man," "infant," "child-like or childish," "sunk upon the shoulder of his wife." And the wife hovers over the broken male, not only with what Hawthorne describes as a "protective and watchful quality" —but also what he is acute and disingenuous enough to call a "veiled happiness." Hawthorne had begun by describing her as "as perilously situated as the maiden whom, in the old classical myths, people used to expose to a dragon": but she has triumphed over the dragon-father—her weakness is stronger than his strength. And she smiles now at being able to support what she has already unmanned. She has made of the resolutely masculine rebel against domestic conformity a dependent child.

Hollingsworth is, however, no seducer, but an advocate of reform, what Hawthorne calls "that steel engine of the Devil's contrivance, a philanthropist." He is, in short, what we would call a radical and an "intellectual," the dreamer of a utopian society incapable of loving his individual fellow men. He is only half the total (villainous) male principle of *The Blithedale Romance;* his alter ego is the dark and utterly damned hypnotist Westervelt, who also has tried to seduce the will of the veiled maiden, Priscilla. Together they add up to the original "libertine," free thinker, *and* trifler with women, the Don Juan archetype who survives unsplit though debased in more orthodox female fiction: as, for instance, the Baron de Launa, the "illuminated" (i.e., enlightened) Baron of Mrs. Sarah Sayward Barell Keating Wood, who published in 1800 a gothic-sentimental farrago called *Julia and the Illuminated Baron.*

Mrs. Wood is the prototype of the early American lady novelist in many senses, but in none more so than in her desire to have the best of all possible worlds. Eager to espouse the cause of women, she goes out of her way to introduce into her fictional action the actual living poetess, Mrs. Morton, "the darling of the muses"; but she is careful to make it clear that the female writer should not be a refugee from traditional female duties. At least of herself she asserts that "not one social, or one domestic duty, have ever been sacrificed or postponed by her pen." Desiring all the romantic associations of the European scene and having a declared "aversion to introducing living characters," Mrs. Wood sets her scene in France and Spain. Yet she cannot resist bringing one of her protagonists back to America to meet Mrs. Morton and to be rescued by the slaves of the "illustrious Washington." Most typically of all, she insists upon making her villain at once a nobleman (to trade on all the good bourgeois prejudice against a corrupt hereditary nobility) and a member of the Illuminati, that is, a secret Jacobin plotter (to take advantage of the genteel conservative reversion from the excesses of the French Revolution). The Baron de Launa is a fascinating transitional figure, a sort of composite bugaboo of middle-class timidity: half Don Juan and half Robespierre, a projection of the blackness of the past and of the threat of the future. The verse on the title page of Mrs. Wood's novel makes it quite clear that her chief fear is of the revolutionary conspirator; the aristocrat is a vestigial ghost.

> This volume to the reader's eye displays
> Th' infernal conduct of abandoned man;
> When French philosophy infects his ways,
> And pours contempt on Heav'n's eternal plan;
> Reversing order, truth, and ev'ry good,
> And whelming the world with ruin's awful flood.

The final effect of the kidnaping of the sentimental form and fable by women writers in a relatively classless society was to define in America from the very beginning an *anti-literature:* bourgeois, timid, not quite literate—and to identify this *ersatz* art with the values and aspirations of women. There is, after all, another distinction among social groups in America, logically separable from that of male and female, with which it tends to be confused, and that is the division between the "intellectual" and the unlettered or practical man in the street together with his home-loving wife. It is the "Brahmin caste," defined by Oliver Wendell Holmes as a "harmless, inoffensive, untitled aristocracy," which seems to the female novelists not at all harmless or inoffensive, but rather the prime source of villainy and seduction. From the Sanford of Mrs. Foster's *The Coquette* (reputed to have been drawn from the real-life character of Pierrepont Edwards) to Hawthorne's Dimmesdale, the traducers of women in our literature have tended to be drawn from Holmes's "race of scholars . . . in which aptitude for learning . . . [is] congenital and hereditary." Similar tendencies toward a timid, best-selling literature existed elsewhere, but were counterbalanced by great mediating figures like Rousseau or Goethe, who tickled at once the most genteel ladies and the Encyclopedists themselves—thus keeping together almost to the verge of our time the two audiences whose sundering has finally wounded literature everywhere.

In America, however, the late start of the novel and the lack of distinguished figures in its early years helped create simultaneously the genteel, sentimental, quasi-literate, female audience (female in sensibility whatever the nominal sex of the readers who composed it) and a product which satisfied it. *Against* this audience and in competition with the writing which satisfied it, our best fictionists from Charles Brockden Brown to Edgar Allan Poe to Hawthorne and Melville have felt it necessary to struggle for their integrity and their livelihoods. Though the interruption of the Scott-Cooper tradition of the novel serves later to conceal the fact for a little while, this profound split has always influenced the shape of our literature and is one still felt by practicing authors as an essential and crippling aspect of their situation. For better or for worse, the best-seller was invented in America (the flagrantly *bad* best-seller) before the serious successful novel.

III

Mrs. Rowson's *Charlotte Temple* is a book scarcely *written* at all, only in the most perfunctory manner told; yet it is the first book by an American to move American readers, and certain historians of the American novel, not themselves critics or readers of criticism, have praised it absurdly for its "basic sincerity and power," or its "simple vividness." To be sure, the popularity of *Charlotte* poses a real problem. Why a book which barely climbs above the lower limits of literacy, and which handles, without psychological acuteness or dramatic power, a handful of stereotyped characters in a situation already hopelessly banal by 1790, should have had more than two hundred editions and have survived among certain readers for a hundred and fifty years is a question that cannot be ignored. It is tempting to say that popular taste given the choice between a better and a worse book will inevitably choose the worse; but this is an anti-sentimental simplification no more helpful than its sentimental opposite number. Only certain bad books succeed, apparently not by the simple virtue of their badness, but because of the theme they have chosen to handle badly.

Mrs. Rowson's book apparently comprises something that is not literature, though it is published in the guise of literature. It is apparent at least that the appeal of *Charlotte* is based not upon form or characterization or insight or beauty of language, not even upon the simplest skills of composition, but upon the bare bones of plot, on what its readers would call quite simply "the story." That story, which it is almost impossible to retell without improving, represents in its essential form the myth or archetype of seduction as adapted to the needs of the American female audience. To Mrs. Rowson we must be grateful for having separated the archetype from its literary or pseudo-literary envelope, for having, as the scientists say, "isolated" it.

To be sure, there are some literary pretensions in Mrs. Rowson's approach—a certain self-consciousness which makes her pause occasionally to address the critic over the shoulder of the servant girl who is her ideal reader. "I hope, Sir," she remarks, addressing naturally the *male* caviler, "your prejudices are now removed in regard to the probability of my story? Oh, they are. Well, then, with your leave I will proceed." But her intended literary devices are most often as naively transparent as the pseudo-quotation from Shakespeare on her title page: "She was her parents' only joy/ They had but one—one darling child." This poor, limping verse she attributes hopefully to *Romeo and Juliet;* but though she was an actress and became a teacher, she has misremembered or simply faked.

Occasionally, she strives for a kind of Biedermeier decoration, visualizing a scene in terms of the most sentimental genre painting of her day: "we will have some cows, and you shall be queen of the dairy; in the morning, while I look after my garden, you shall take a basket on your arm, and sally forth to feed your poultry; and as they flutter round you in token of humble gratitude, your father shall smoke his pipe in a woodbine alcove. . . ." But aside from the old man with his pipe and the humbly grateful hens, nothing is visualized in the book. It is morality not art at which Mrs. Rowson consciously aims; and she desires, as she tells us disarmingly if ungrammatically, nothing more than to convince her readers "that I have not wrote a line that conveys a wrong idea to the head." She is, indeed, almost openly anti-literary in a defensive way, hinting that "trifling performances" like her own are to be preferred to "the most elegant, finished piece of literature whose tendency might deprave the heart or mislead the understanding." Her book at least is firmly committed to the notion "that vice, however prosperous in the beginning, in the end leads only to misery and shame."

There is no duplicity in *Charlotte Temple,* or at least, only the unwitting duplicity of the best-seller which confuses the wish with the fact, and presents the dreams of its readers as an account of real actions in the real world. It is a book no one could have faked, even its tender lingering over the details of vice which it presumably hates arising from an essential artlessness. As even its title declares, Mrs. Rowson's novel (called *Charlotte* in the English edition of 1791, *Charlotte Temple* in America in 1794) is completely a woman's book—a tale in which female suffering is portrayed from a female point of view in order to stir female sympathy; while vice and virtue are judged by female standards. Mrs. Rowson, who was in her life governess, lady novelist, actress, playwright, songwriter, and head of a girls' school, who had been forced by her husband's failure to make herself a career and forge by her own hard work a shield of respectability, stood unequivocally on the woman's side in that war of the sexes whose existence she would not for a moment have denied. Her title declares her allegiance, her conviction that she is one of the girls. The single first name (returning to the tradition of *Pamela*) suffices to describe what the book is about; and there is no ambitious subtitle to lead us up metaphysical blind alleys—only the conventional boast "A Tale of Truth." The facts related do, indeed, seem to be derived from the real-life experiences of a certain Charlotte Stanley, but Richardson had invented that person's life before she managed to live it.

The action of *Charlotte Temple* begins in England and passes to America, making England the place of Charlotte's innocence and the United States that of her repentance, with the ocean between the scene of her deflowering. She is buried in an American grave, where, her fall redeemed by death, she becomes an American Magdalene, a saint of love. Meanwhile, her seducer, who vainly offers his bosom and his sword to Charlotte's father at that very grave, returns to England. Mrs. Rowson, herself an immigrant, manages thus to tie together the fable of seduction and the story of immigration into the United States, creating a kind of sentimental myth of the relationship of the two countries—and thereby insuring the success of her book on this side of the water. Certainly, it was a failure in England, living its incredible posthumous life only here.

Charlotte is betrayed not only by the British officer, Montraville, but also by her French teacher, Mlle. La Rue, who persuades her to elope with her lover and actually runs away to America with her. Mlle. La Rue, who projects all the American fear of Latin perfidy, plays the Juliette to Charlotte's Justine: the one represents virtue traduced and defeated, the other vice cherished and rewarded; though, indeed, just before the book ends Mlle. La Rue is given—rather perfunctorily—her just deserts. Charlotte, after her sin, is overwhelmed with remorse and hounded by disaster. Cast off by Montraville, who marries a wealthy woman, deprived even of the conscience money he sends her by his companion Belcour, who thinks poverty will force her to become his mistress, and vilified as faithless by Belcour when he fails in his suit, Charlotte endures unremitting misery. Mlle. La Rue, on the other hand, profits by her calculated vice, finally marrying a prosperous and credulous merchant and living the life of comfortable, respectable New York society.

It is to her old teacher and false advisor that Charlotte turns in the most absurd of all the book's bathetic scenes, only to be forced out into the wintry storm, pregnant and destitute. "Here on my knees I conjure you to save me from perishing in the street. . . . O, for charity's sweet sake, this night let me be sheltered from the winter's piercing cold." But Mlle. La Rue, now Mrs. Crayton, is merciless. "Take her away . . . she will really frighten me into hysterics; take her away, I say, this instant." Charlotte finds shelter in the house of a servant of Mrs. Crayton, kinder than his mistress, but dies after bearing her child in a bare and drafty hovel. Her father arrives from England in time to witness her death and hear her plea that he protect her child; "She raised her eyes to heaven —and then closed them forever." There remains nothing more but the duel at the graveside between Montraville and his false friend, Belcour, in which the latter is killed; and, almost as an after-thought, the coming of Mlle. La Rue as a dying beggar to the door of Charlotte's parents.

It is the Richardsonian story as it has descended through the female line in its most banal form. In Mrs. Rowson's version, how-ever, it succeeded in projecting once and for all the American woman's image of herself as the long-suffering martyr of love—the inevitable victim of male brutality and lust. Not for nothing is Charlotte called "Temple"; she represents a cult object, a center of worship—and on her (supposed) tomb, the floral tribute of gen-erations of girls expressed their adoration of the Great Goddess whom they could venerate only if they believed her a "real" woman like themselves.

It is the nature of American scriptures to be vulgarizations of the holy texts from which they take their cues; and just as *The Book of Mormon* caricatures the Bible unawares, so *Charlotte Temple* is an unwitting travesty of *Clarissa Harlowe*. The sacred power is still there, but the subtlety and passion, the style and distinction have gone. What was mythic literature has become sub-literate myth.

Mrs. Rowson, who had little sense, of course, of the scriptural character of her best-selling book, tried to continue it in a sequel, as if it were an ordinary novel. *Lucy Temple,* however, lacked the archetypal appeal of the earlier volume; though (as we have noted earlier) it establishes the prototype of the repentant seducer, re-duced to trembling dependence and near idiocy. *Lucy Temple* deals with the fortunes of three unprotected girls, one of whom is seduced, tricked into a false marriage, stripped of all her posses-sions, while another marries a country parson who has come into considerable wealth. It is with the third orphan (Charlotte's daugh-ter, Lucy!) that the book is chiefly concerned, for her life exempli-fies the continuing evil bred by seduction. Lucy learns almost too late that her husband-to-be is her brother, legitimate son of the officer who had betrayed and abandoned Charlotte. The revelation comes to her in a moment of philanthropic indulgence, when to celebrate her coming wedding she has given a feast and distributed a hundred guineas to sixty of "the most respected poor" of the parish. The theme of brother-sister incest haunts the early American novel on its lower levels of literacy as well as on the higher—· a nightmare from which our writers do not choose to awaken too soon, since it is one their readers are willing to pay to share.

Mrs. Rowson was too pious, however, to grant either her audience or herself a sentimental orgy of death; her Lucy makes a "perfect recovery," while her lover, instead of committing suicide, takes himself off to India. "She regarded him," Mrs. Rowson informs us, "as devoted to his country, herself as set apart for the holy cause of humanity." That "holy cause" she serves by becoming a teacher of "female children," and presiding as high priestess over a school-house indistinguishable from a temple: "a specimen —one might almost say, a model of Ionic architecture . . . with chaste white pillars and modest walls. . . ."

IV

The sentimental legend of seduction could not, in any case, be laughed out of existence. Not only did the editions of *Charlotte Temple* dizzyingly, incredibly proliferate, but other examples quickly appeared, some from the fertile pen of Mrs. Rowson herself, some from those of others. Hannah Foster's *The Coquette,* for instance, published in 1797, fictionalized a contemporary scandal (which may have involved Aaron Burr or, at least, the son of Jonathan Edwards) with only the most perfunctory attempt at disguise. The heroine, called in real life Elizabeth Whitman, is known in this book as Eliza Wharton; but her "real life" sentimental mishaps, like those of many well-read young ladies at the end of the eighteenth century, fall only too patly into the stereotypes of seduction derived from Richardson. Indeed, events can never provide for the imagination new sentimental plots, since sentiment is first imagined and only then lived. In society as well as in literature, the archetypal encounter of Lovelace and Clarissa was reported over and over—or at least imposed itself upon life in the perceiving mind—until that encounter, and its actors, had become stereotypes from which no American author could entirely escape.

Charles Brockden Brown, whose anti-bourgeois novels we shall examine in detail later, submitted to Richardson as enthusiastically as any of his female contemporaries. In a sketch for a sentimental novel which he abandoned, the so-called "Correspondence with Henrietta G." (taken by some critics—so confused do sentimental life and sentimental literature become—to be an actual exchange of letters entered in his journal), he entrusts what are surely his sentiments to one of his fictional correspondents: "I am a disciple of that religion and philosophy of which the effects are to be seen in the conduct of Clarissa. O best of men! Most eloquent of writers! It is from thy immortal production that I have imbibed the love of virtue; of moral harmony and beauty. From thee also have I gathered critical instruction and learned to speak and write. . . ."

In his last two novels, Brown made a valiant attempt to redeem Richardson from his genteel imitators, to create, by casting aside the seduction theme, a Richardsonian novel of sentimental analysis in a domestic setting, stripped of tragic and melodramatic elements alike. Had he succeeded, he might have become our own improbable Jane Austen, from whose similar attempt there developed in England the psychological-domestic novel of love and marriage that leads through George Eliot to Henry James. But Brown lacked the wit and irony as well as the talent for structure of Jane Austen —so that, aiming at modesty, he created dullness; and avoiding the spectacular, he fell into the inane. Certainly, what quiet triumphs his books achieved went unnoticed in his own day.

Clara Howard and *Jane Talbot,* both of which appeared in 1801, indicate by their very titles Brown's desire to return to the woman-centered novel with which Richardson began. His earlier books, all of which had failed to win popularity, are called by the names of their male protagonists: *Wieland, Arthur Mervyn, Ormond,* and *Edgar Huntly;* and the experience with which they deal is filtered through the perceptions of those protagonists. The later books, however, portray a world of female interests regarded through female eyes, perhaps partly as a bid for the alluring female audience that had already made Mrs. Rowson's fortune. In *Clara Howard,* the epistolary method of Richardson is used to tell the unspectacular tale of the difficulties that lie in the way of Clara's marriage to Philip Stanley, who is engaged (without love) to another woman. It is not a question of whom he will marry, but of who (both women are bolder than he) will marry him. Stanley's first love has disappeared, and Clara, though she is fond of him, dutifully sends him out to search for her.

Such minor misfortunes as slander, fraud, disease, and especially mental anguish befall all three members of this conscientious triangle before their problems are resolved (the lost Mary found engaged to someone else, etc.) and the wedding with which the book must end can take place. The plot is trivial, perfunctory both in its development and resolution, the study of the "heart" (particularly of the motives of a woman emotionally unwilling to part with the man she is morally unable to accept) everything. For the seduction archetype, Brown has substituted the more ancient New Comedy archetype of boy-gets-girl-loses-girl-gets-girl; but he is handicapped by his own lack of belief in the kind of romantic love which alone can justify that standard plot. Quite early in life, he had gone on record as deploring the fact that "the languishing and sighing lover is an object to which the errors of mankind have annexed a certain degree of importance"; and must have been embarrassed to find himself the author of a novel whose sub-title is "The Enthusiasm of Love."

Brown seems further to have been unaware that the New Comedy plot, being a comic version of the Oedipus conflict, demands that the initial check to love come from parental opposition, preferably the intervention of an unsympathetic father, whom the son can finally defeat in taking possession of the contested girl. The competing self-sacrifice of two women in love with the same man is hardly a satisfactory substitute. The popular mind demanded then, as it demands now, a villain, whether father or seducer, some dark projection of id or super-ego to be symbolically defeated; but Brown's book had no villain at all.

Brown had earlier employed seducers in his books; fathers scarcely exist at all in his work. His world (a little like that of Mark Twain) is one of mothers and sisters; mamas in particular are everywhere, even the sweethearts of his rather childlike, dependent men being addressed on occasion as "my dear mama"; but papas are at a premium. In *Jane Talbot,* however, there is at least the dramatic tension provided by the Bad Mother, Jane's adopted mother, Mrs. Fielder, who has forced her into one loveless marriage, and, even after the death of Jane's first husband, refuses to let her marry her first love, Henry Colden.

Colden, who, like many of Brown's young men, thinks of marriage as a way of finding a mother and a source of income at once, would not consider marrying Jane if she were disinherited; and so her mother's opposition is critical. "I cannot labor for bread," he tells Jane with astonishing candor, "I cannot work to live. . . . Hence it is, that if by marriage you should become wholly dependent on me it could never take place." But Colden's principles include others beside the resolve not to "labor for bread." He is, indeed, a committed radical, a follower of Godwin; and Mrs. Fielder rejects him as a prospective son-in-law because she believes him to be "the advocate of suicide; a scoffer at promises; the despiser of revelation, of Providence and a future state; an opponent of marriage, and . . . one who denied (shocking!) that anything but mere habit and positive law stood in the way of marriage, nay, of intercourse without marriage, between brother and sister, parent and child."

Here is Lovelace returned to life ("an opponent of marriage"), with Werther ("the advocate of suicide"), Chesterfield ("a scoffer at promises") and Diderot ("one who denied, etc., etc.") thrown in to complete the composite portrait of a villainous "libertine." To be sure, Colden only *appears* to be such a villain; but at least he provides momentarily a defining opposite to Jane, with his shadow sets off the whiteness of her virtue. Without a Lovelace there can be no Clarissa; and without Colden, Jane would have seemed as incomplete as Clara Howard. It is no tragic opposition, however, which they provide one another, but rather an educational one. Each learns from the other: Jane to make her piety more rational, Henry to make his rationalism more pious. But the exchange is by no means equal, Colden being much overmatched in moral energy by Jane Talbot. He is only a *theoretical* seducer, in need of money, an adolescent libertine, whose maturity is indistinguishable from his defeat, which is to say, his marriage. Converted at last to a belief in the "Divine Parent and Judge," he goes like a happy victim to the altar. So denatured a version of the clash between the Pure Maiden (Jane is not even a virgin) and the libertine (Henry is doubtless more virgin than she) provides no archetypal thrill, no drama deeper than words.

Earlier, in *Ormond: or The Secret Witness* (1799), Brown had created a more vivid and convincing Lovelace figure. Ormond is not really, despite the title, the central character of the story—though he comes closer than any male protagonist in Brown to being the equal of the woman he confronts. Constantia Dudley is the name of the non-Christian Clarissa to whom he acts the Lovelace, a woman who, Brown tells us, "formed her estimate of good and evil on nothing but terrestrial and visible consequences." It is perhaps the anti-clerical nature of this middle-class Great Goddess that made her so favorite a figure for Shelley, though there is something chilling about her reasonable approach to problems of matrimony. "To marry in extreme youth," she has told herself, "would be proof of pernicious and opprobrious temerity"; and one scarcely wonders at such cool wisdom from the daughter of a father who, "instead of familiarizing her with the amorous effusions of Petrarch and Racine . . . made her thoroughly conversant with Tacitus and Milton."

The softer and more romantic qualities of womanhood are reflected by the other female characters with whom Constantia is surrounded, especially by Helena Cleves, type of the sentimental, soft-headed woman made to be seduced. Through this gallery of females strides Ormond, armed and fully phallic; he has just returned from a military career which has ended on the barricades in France and possesses as a mistress the soft Helena, who commits suicide when he deserts her to woo Constantia. Toward him, as a projection of himself, Brown has all the ambivalence of a Goethe or Rousseau contemplating the Artist-Seducer; for Brown is aware that the principles which inspire Ormond are the revolutionary, enlightened ones which moved his own youthful enthusiasm. In Ormond, however, they have gone wrong, the Dream of Reason turned monstrous: "considerations of justice and pity were made, by a fatal perverseness of reasoning, champions and bulwarks of his most atrocious mistakes."

Ormond is, indeed, the mirror image of Henry Colden, Colden seen in reverse: at first, apparently an attractive though fanatically radical young man, he is revealed at last as a rapist and murderer. Colden, on the other hand, begins by seeming a thoroughgoing scoundrel, but turns out to be no more than the headstrong exponent of abstract nonconformism. For the latter, there is the reward of marriage and financial security, salvation by the female; for the former, death at the hands of his beloved, destruction by the female. In her father's neo-classic retreat at Perth Amboy, as chaste in its marble dress as the "temple" of Mrs. Rowson's *Lucy,* Constantia stabs Ormond with her penknife, swoons beside him and the bloody body of a man he has killed, preparing for her rape.

Ormond is surely the most passionate of Brown's books, but there is little erotic passion displayed between the men and women in it. Ormond pursues Constantia out of some dark need to symbolize in her violation his triumph over the female principle; while she is drawn to him largely by a curiosity much like his own. The book's sole marriage, offered as a sop to sentimental readers, perhaps, joins Constantia's friend, Sophia, through whom the story is chiefly told, to a certain Courtland. But for Courtland we are scarcely prepared; he remains a strangely unintegrated character, left over, apparently, from an incomplete work, *Jessica,* and used to give to the volume the slight note of conventional good cheer with which it closes. The tone with which Sophia describes the affection that leads to their marriage is oddly cool:

> Sufficient opportunity was afforded us, in an unrestrained and domestic intercourse of three months, . . . to gain a knowledge of each other. There was that conformity of tastes and views between us which could scarcely fail, at an age and in a situation like ours, to give birth to tenderness. . . . He had offered to be my companion [on a voyage to America], but this offer my regard to his interest obliged me to decline; but I was willing to compensate him for this denial, as well as to gratify my own heart, by an immediate marriage.

No sooner has she married him, however, than she leaves him in Europe while she sets sail for the United States in search of her beloved Constantia. How different the tone in which their reunion after long absence is described:

> I could not bear to withdraw my eyes from her countenance. If they wandered for a moment, I fell into doubt and perplexity, and again fixed them upon her, to assure myself of her existence.
>
> The succeeding three days were spent in a state of dizziness and intoxication. The ordinary functions of nature were disturbed. The appetite for sleep and for food were confounded and lost amidst the impetuosities of a master-passion. . . . I would not part from her side, but ate and slept, walked and mused and read, with my arm locked in hers, and with her breath fanning my cheek. . . .
>
> O precious inebriation of the heart! O pre-eminent love! . . . surely thy sanction is divine, thy boon is happiness!

Which seems an ecstatic rhapsody on passion, which the description of friendship? What were contemporary readers to make of such a perverse reversal of the expected terms of affection? Certainly, they were not looking for such homoerotic tenderness at the sentimental climax of a story of seduction. Love between the Pure Maiden and the most brutal Seducer they could understand and respond to, but not that between the Maiden and an old girl friend.

Surely they could not have interpreted their girlish reunion as a grand passion, purest form of the "precious inebriation of the heart." Like a more recent critic, the contemporary reader must have murmured to himself at the point where Sophia departs in the midst of her own honeymoon: "this circumstance is an added argument in favor of what has already been said that Brown did not understand the workings of the human mind. . . ." And that reader would have concluded with another commentator, "Love and friendship . . . are excluded from his bosom." For better or worse, the buyers of best-sellers had no need of Brown; everything that they meant by love had been defined for them by the clichés of female Richardsonianism, which had passed into their very lives and their own patterns of courtship and marriage.

In this light, Brown's failure at dealing with the love between men and women seems as symptomatic as the successes in the market-place of Mrs. Rowson's sentimental travesties—so deeply had the formulae of degraded Richardsonianism impressed themselves on the American imagination, that in the United States, well up into the twentieth century, no novelists, however committed and talented, could treat the relations of the sexes without falling prey to their influence. Only by bypassing normal heterosexual love as a subject could such writers preserve themselves from sentimentality and falsehood. Brown had failed in his direct attempt to recapture passion from the "female scribblers"; but in other works, he adapted to America the uses of terror, discovered a rival passion which could fill the vacuum left by the failure of love. He is the father of American gothic, and the initiator—as we shall see in Chapter 6—of a truly fertile line of development for the serious novel in the United States.

5

THE BEGINNINGS OF THE
ANTI-BOURGEOIS
SENTIMENTAL NOVEL
IN AMERICA

NOT ONLY THE FEMALE SCRIBBLER recreated the seducer in the image of the intellectual and the artist; for quite opposite reasons, certain anti-bourgeois novelists had made the same transformation, in books which asked the reader to identify not with the female victim but with her male betrayer—thus introducing a note of moral ambiguity baffling to the simple-minded sentimentalist. Such novels provided models and prototypes for writers of fiction eager to break out of the trap of female Richardsonianism. Oddly enough, it was Richardson himself who provided hints for such writers. Like his eminent contemporary and fellow carrier of the torch to the back of the cave, Mesmer, Richardson founded two traditions at once: from the former via Phineas Quimby there evolved the Christian Science of Mrs. Eddy and via Charcot the psychoanalysis of Sigmund Freud; from the latter via Mrs. Rowson came *The Wide, Wide World* and via Rousseau Proust's *Remembrance of Things Past*.

By the time Mrs. Trollope made her well-advertised visit, the names of Rousseau and of Voltaire may have been indeed, as she reports, known to Americans "more as dirty words than as great names," but this certainly was not the case in the earliest days of our history. Before any native novelists had appeared, Rousseau's fiction was immensely popular with our readers, his chief novel, translated in England as the *New Eloisa*, becoming between 1761, when it was published, and 1764, when Horace Walpole's *The*

Castle of Otranto appeared to supplant it, the most widely read novel in the colonies.

Goethe was even more widely read. His *Werther* had to wait for American publication only five years after the successful British edition of 1779; and thus appeared in the United States well before the first American novel, William Hill Brown's Werther-like *The Power of Sympathy.* The hero of that book is found dead at the action's end, a suicide, "a letter . . . unsealed upon the table, and *The Sorrows of Werther . . .* lying by its side." Indeed, by the time Brown's book was in circulation, there had been seven American editions of *Werther;* and a series of poems and dramas on the theme, as well as adaptations and apocryphal continuations, had tried to take advantage of its popular appeal.

It is hard to distinguish the influence of Richardson himself on the "masculine" Rousseau-Goethe strain within the sentimental novel from that of his near-contemporary, the French novelist Prévost; and students of the matter have debated acrimoniously their relative weight in the development of what can only be called the anti-bourgeois novel. The bulk of the Abbé Prévost's important work had already been done before the appearance of *Pamela; The Man of Quality* was completed by 1731, *Cleveland* by 1739, *Le Doyen de Killerine* by 1740, and English editions had appeared almost simultaneously. Indeed, Richardson himself reached the continent chiefly in the translation made by Prévost (Rousseau, for instance, knew *Clarissa* only in Prévost's French), a translation in which Prévost admits that he "changed or suppressed" what he found unsuitable for the genius of his own tongue.

Even more importantly, perhaps, Prévost in his earlier novels had discovered, almost invented, England as a fact of the French imagination and consequently of the imagination of Europe. This imaginary Protestant (in fact a Benedictine, who, after various sentimental and ideological difficulties, settled back into the monastery), after some years of exile in England, peopled his works almost exclusively with Protestant characters and returned almost compulsively to his semi-mythicized English scene, the Protestant homeland. The sensibility that produced the novel is as we have seen essentially a Protestant one, and Prévost is its interpreter to Catholic Europe. If the triumph of the novel on the continent in the mid-eighteenth century meant also that England became the second fatherland of European intellectuals, the credit must go to A. F. Prévost d'Exiles, who continued in his periodical, *Le pour et le contre,* the task he had begun in his books: to prepare Europe for the impact of Richardson.

Prévost was the lesser writer in many ways, the author of untidy, sprawling books whose development is dependent on the passionate whim of their picaresque protagonists, and which wander, therefore, quite in the manner of the obsolescent romances, over the face of a largely legendary world. That Prévost calls his settings "England" or "America" rather than Arcadia makes finally little difference. He achieved one minor success, by the way as it were, in *Manon Lescaut,* originally an appendix to *The Man of Quality;* but he hit upon neither the bourgeois setting nor the seduction theme, which were necessary to give life to the modern novel. In addition, he lacked the sharp focus of the epistolary form, primitive examples of which existed in European literature but which did not become the prevailing novelistic form until Richardson arrived on the scene.

In organization and narrative technique, certainly, the *Werther* of Goethe, like the *Nouvelle Héloïse* of Rousseau, depends directly on the model provided by *Clarissa,* whose superiority to his own work Prévost frankly acknowledges in the introductory note to his translation. When the full impact of Prévost was felt, it contributed in both England and France to a reversion to that "improbable and marvelous" which Richardson had abjured, to the rebirth of the romance in the revolutionary, sadist, highbrow form of the gothic novel; but where it existed balanced against the domestic and puritanical realism of Richardson, it helped to produce the anti-bourgeois sentimental novel of Goethe and Rousseau.

From Richardson, both Goethe and Rousseau learned the basic lesson that the subject of the novel is the "human heart," which is to say, the psyche in all its complexities and dark self-deceits, but especially in the moment of love. In them, the novel remains both psychological and erotic, dedicated not to the unwinding of an action replete with sharp reversals and recognitions, but to the exploration of a moral choice. The setting remains ordinary bourgeois life, for them "provincial" life, a world remote from the court and the great centers. Richardson could conceive without difficulty a simple domestic scene in the midst of London; his continental successors felt the need of a bucolic background, defined with that compromise between pastoral and genteelly realistic which came to be called Biedermeier. In both, there is the desire still to avoid all extravagances of action, to relate ordinary occurrences, which offer their readers, in a language as simple and un-distinguished as their own, "tableaus of the objects that surround them, of duties within their grasps, of the pleasures of their own conditions. . . ."

In their search for the normal and the insipid, they go beyond their master himself. Rousseau puts it quite bluntly in the mouth of an interlocutor in his second preface: "As for interest, it is for everybody, it is nothing. Not an evil action, not a wicked man making the good ones tremble; events so natural, so simple, that they are too much so; nothing unforeseen, no *coup de théâtre;* everything is expected well in advance, everything happens as expected." This is not really, of course, the whole story; for the underplaying of action is made up for by an overplaying of feel-ing, an exploitation of sentiment and sensibility that approaches the pathological; and over the whole account, for all its domesticity, hangs the shadow of suicide, the allure of death felt as a final, dark titillation. Death of course belongs to the Clarissa archetype from the beginning. She is "absolute for death" from the point of her violation on; and her elaborate preparations for a pious and decorous end become almost obscene. Rousseau, however, taking a cue from Prévost, turns death from the hope of the ruined virgin into the secret longing of the melancholy protagonist, the male hero.

The whole drift of the anti-bourgeois tradition is in the direction of substituting a male mind for the female one at the center of the novel. Rousseau represents a transitional phase; he calls his book still, in the proper Richardsonian way, by the simple first name of his heroine, *Julie, ou la Nouvelle Héloïse.* This is only proper, for it is she who keeps the action moving forward and who, in her death, only somewhat less orthodox than Clarissa's, "edifies a pastor and converts an atheist." Rousseau is using his fable, after all, to plead a fundamentally feminist case, and thus to win for himself the feminine audience. Young girls, to be sure, he warns off in an introductory note, or at least pretends to; but to experi-enced ladies he promises to demonstrate, what they are, of course, already more than willing to believe, that "the cause of their un-ruliness is less in themselves than in our evil institutions," prima-rily in forced marriages dictated by "the avarice and vanity of parents."

Yet Saint-Preux is regarded with a particular tenderness and re-mains the mouthpiece of his author, as Lovelace is *not,* of course, the mouthpiece of Richardson; for Rousseau is bound to his seducer by an evident autobiographical tie, which is by no means the link binding the earlier novelist to his unequivocal villain. Already in Rousseau's fiction, Lovelace has been crossed with those melancholy outcasts into whom Prévost projected his own plight: Cleveland or Patrice; and though the inherited Don Juan figure does not cease to be a seducer (at least in intent), he blurs into the exiled, sensitive soul. Juan and Faust melt into a single romanticized figure, the exponent of freedom and death. On the one hand, such protagonists are thought of as being accursed, possessed by the *mal anglais,* the longing for self-destruction; on the other hand, they are considered *chosen* out of mankind for a terrible privilege. "I do not pretend that all of mankind should immolate itself by general agreement nor make a vast sepulchre of the world," writes Rousseau through his surrogate Saint-Preux. "There are those unfortunates too privileged to follow the common way, and for whom despair and bitter sufferings are the passport of Nature."

But suicide remains incidental in *Julie,* a rejected temptation; and the novel's male protagonist cannot really hold the center of the stage. Julie, whom he seduces but is forbidden to marry because of their difference in rank and fortune, becomes in the second part of the book a full-fledged Clarissa-character. She is Clarissa as housewife and mother, all the more Clarissa for attaining the age and status from which the violation of Lovelace cut off her prototype; for Julie's devirgination does not send her quite to the grave. She is married by Wolmar, *philosophe* and atheist, who invites her former lover back into their household as a tutor for their children, deliberately planning this improbable *ménage à trois* to discover whether or not his wife's virtue has survived her first fall. In this icily contrived ordeal, Julie triumphs; the passion of Saint-Preux, still smoldering despite a therapeutic trip around the world, is turned into holy adoration; and when she finally attains for herself that death which Saint-Preux has longed for but failed to claim through suicide, she begins the conversion of her husband to a belief in God and the immortality of the soul.

Trying to rescue one of her children who has fallen into the water, Julie contracts pneumonia, and dies in the midst of pious discourses. Her death, however, is the goal to which she has all along aspired, her release to a world where she will be able to await a guiltless embrace with her first lover; and when she has finally died, her sanctification is complete. A veil of gold embroidered with pearls is thrown over her already decaying face by her friend Claire, and so veiled she is put into the earth. The last word and the last tear belong to her friend rather than to her lover, as her sanctified end seals her into the pantheon of female saviors. Saint-Preux, having failed to achieve the death that redeems his mistress (though he sought it once by kissing her suppurating hand in an attempt to share her smallpox), must live on with her children and her husband, to complete the works of piety and salvation she has begun.

Werther is at last granted the accolade of death which Saint-Preux could not wrest from Julie, who had inherited it by matriarchal right from Clarissa herself; but he gives up in return for that reward even the brief physical consummation which the French lover had attained with his mistress. Though he wears the very uniform of Saint-Preux, buff and blue, and celebrates the same religion of sensibility, Goethe's protagonist is denied not only marriage but any carnal union on earth; for him death becomes finally, what it is in the process of becoming in *La Nouvelle Héloïse,* the only bridal bed. "Yes, Charlotte, thou art mine," he writes before his death by his own hand, to the woman who has (sanely enough) chosen his rival Albert, the practical man over the visionary. "I only go before thee to my father—to thy father . . . then will I claim thee as my own, and in the presence of the Eternal be united with thee from everlasting to everlasting!"

In the *Nouvelle Héloïse,* it is Julie who confides to a last letter a similarly dangerous sentiment: "Shall my soul exist without you? Without you, what bliss shall I taste? No, I do not leave you, I go to wait for you. The virtue which separates us on earth shall join us in our heavenly home." Clarissa could not even conceive of, much less accept, the extraordinary doctrine of sanctified posthumous adultery which informs both *Julie* and *Werther.* In the two later works, the *Liebestod* theme as well as the concept of the grand passion as necessarily adulterous return again into the consciousness of Europe, from the repressed depths of the collective mind where they had bided ever since the death of the codes of courtly love. In Rousseau and Goethe, the Tristan and Isolde story stirs again, blends with the Clarissa-Lovelace archetype.

Had Charlotte married Werther, Goethe makes clear without explicit statement, she would have turned him into an Albert (but this, not long before, was called "saving him"); rejecting him as a lover, without casting him off completely, she drives him toward death. To make the point clear, she is shown as actually sending him the pistols with which he will eventually destroy himself, even dusting them off like a good little housewife! She knows really at this point that Werther must die, and, however hesitantly, accepts the only climax which can preserve the (technical) integrity of her marriage and the innocence of her extra-marital relation. Her complicity in this regard Werther recognizes and hails: "Your hands have grasped these pistols . . . you have wiped them for me! . . . those hands from which I have long earnestly wished to receive my fate!" Here is the final twist—not a travesty but a sentimental reversal—of the theme of the redeeming Maiden. Woman who was the angel of redemption becomes the angel of death; but for Werther, death *is* redemption, the only salvation he can use.

By the time *Werther* was written the anti-bourgeois sentimental novel had become, in its most extreme form, the anti-type, the mirror image of the bourgeois sentimental novel. The two types are not, however, always clearly separated; they share the same thematic material and, can, indeed, cohabit within the covers of the same book, as in the case Rousseau's *Nouvelle Héloïse,* the first part of which belongs to the anti-bourgeois kind, though the second part subscribes to bourgeois orthodoxy. The traditions employ a common setting and a common technique; they both relate domestic events against a bourgeois, Protestant family background; both dedicate themselves to the commonplace; and both use the letter form of narration. In each, changes are rung on the expected topics of seduction, suicide, sentiment, and (occasionally) incest; and appropriately enough, reverence is paid to Richardson, though there is for each a different Richardson.

For the anti-bourgeois writer, incest, which Richardson himself completely avoided but which most even of his pious followers took up out of Prévost and the very air of the declining eighteenth century, became more than an added spice or even (as for the genteel moralists) a dramatic testimony to the continuing ill effects of seduction upon succeeding generations. For them it became, especially in terms of brother-sister incest, a challenge to the most sacred of bourgeois taboos. Unwitting attractions of this kind, the "power of sympathy" which drew together children of the same father unaware of their kinship, they took as a sign of the "triumph of nature" over social conventions and attempts at concealment; while the deliberate turning to the sister as preferred mistress they interpreted as a revolutionary gesture of contempt for middle-class custom and law. Those thinkers who had fallen under the spell of the Encyclopedists took a cue from Diderot in the *Supplement to the Voyages of Bougainville,* contending that any ban on a sexual union between brother and sister was irrational and maddening. The advocacy of mother-incest was avoided, not so much because—as Diderot cynically observed—no sane man of twenty would prefer a woman of forty to a girl of eighteen, but because it was *too* audacious, challenged the rule of the father too brutally.

Insofar as the anti-bourgeois novel took up the cause of passion against prudence, of nature against "habit and positive law," it was led to defend such unions. The threat of the father to the daughter (a favorite theme of Prévost, who likes to identify father and seducer) came to stand for the tyranny of the past, the blighting restraint exercised by inherited authority, while the joining of brother and sister, in however ambiguous an alliance, against the corrupt parent became the very symbol of justified revolution—and, indeed, a give-away of the Oedipal aspects of all eighteenth-century revolutionary thought. In light of this, it is easy to understand why the story of the Cenci and the image of the father-slaying Beatrice Cenci in particular haunt the Romantic imagination which gradually disengages itself from the sentimental one. Before full Romanticism emerges, however, the incest motif will have broken out of the shell of the sentimental-domestic tradition altogether. There is in it something too outrageous, too atrocious to be contained in a genre that disavows the improbable; and we shall see how it finds freer expression in the gothic tradition which makes the outrageous its *raison d'être.*

Suicide is, as a symbol of protest, more manageable within the limits of Richardsonian sensibility, more at home in the context of familiar realism and observation of contemporary manners. Death, even in a form as shocking to Christian orthodoxy as self-murder, offends the bourgeois mind less than sex. In an argument between Werther and Albert the challenge which killing oneself posed for bourgeois morality is dramatically summed up. For Werther, suicide is the noblest of all actions, a revolutionary gesture; for Albert, a man who would shoot himself is quite simply "the worst of lunatics." Werther demands that at the very least suicide be treated as *problematic;* Albert apparently feels that to yield even so far would mean giving away the belief in the goodness and reasonableness of life. Albert, however, is the bourgeois embodiment of Reason (beyond him lies only the final travesty of Flaubert's Homais), the natural enemy of the anti-bourgeois man of feeling. Imperceptibly, the sentimental plea to understand the poor, seduced, and abandoned girl who seeks death when there is no other way out ("Her lover," says Werther, commenting on just such a case, "is faithless, perjured!—he forsakes her . . . dark envelops her—. . . . Thus blinded . . . she plunges into the merciless deep, and sinks to rise no more!") blends into a defense of the deliberate rebel not only against the tyranny of convention, but against maturity, responsibility, life itself. ("In this picture, Albert, is portrayed the history of many men. . . .")

The defense of suicide may seem to Albert an act of madness, but it is inevitable corollary to the worship of feeling, to the religion of sentiment of which Richardson is the high priest. Some historians of the novel have distinguished between the two kinds of novels here classified as bourgeois and anti-bourgeois in terms of "sentiment" and "sensibility"; they attribute to the direct influence of Richardson the novel of sentiment but credit to the example of Prévost and Sterne the rise of the novel of sensibility. Those terms fade into each other, however, for they describe degrees in the cult of feeling: a resolve, on the one hand, to exploit emotion for its own sake, and on the other, to do so out of a sense that true goodness is to be found primarily there. For both Richardson and Sterne to weep was to be saved, and it was Richardson who insisted, "Sensibility is the principal glory of human nature." Yet tears do become for some writers not a kind of wordless prayer but a prelude to an abandonment (in despite of conventional morality) to the promptings of passion.

"A flood of tears," Goethe writes, "streamed from the eyes of Charlotte. . . . Werther threw down the paper, grasped her hand, and bedewed it with his tears. Charlotte . . . held her handkerchief to her eyes—their agitation was mutual and extreme . . . the sorrow she felt almost deprived her of the use of reason: she affectionately folded her hands in his, pressed them to her bosom . . . her glowing cheek sank on his . . . they were insensible to everything but mutual love." Richardson's conviction that true feeling is more akin to religious devotion than to animal impulse has been oddly transformed via Rousseau into the assumption which underlies this scene: the belief that passion justifies all, or at least dissolves all resistance to believing that it does. No longer is the religion of feeling sustained by the Bible and the "virgin pages" of *Clarissa* alone;

there has flowed into it not only the *Schwärmerei* of Jean-Jacques Rousseau but also that mystique of the natural and the primitive derived by the eighteenth century from the pages of Homer, *Ossian,* and Shakespeare and from the newly recovered folk ballads. Once grant to Richardson that the "goodness of the Heart" is "much preferable to the Head alone," and the way is open to the shameless glorification of the heart alone over the head: to a celebration of passion as superior to all institutions—state, church, the marriage ceremony itself.

The Pure Maiden of Richardson survives relatively unchanged in the period of readjustment between Richardson and Goethe; she is only debased a little, not destroyed—becomes Gretchen, which is to say a symbol of piety still, though weak and simple and utterly passive. Her lover meanwhile has become Faust, Goethe's Faust, which is to say a portrait of the artist as an unconventional young man. The pathos of the seduction story remains all the same; the traduced and deserted girl still compels the sympathy of the rebel, even as she has that of the bourgeois woman. The seducer himself, however, has become a man of the heart rather than of the head; and the fabulous encounter which in the images of Lovelace and Clarissa had symbolized the conflict of pious feeling with cynical reason, stands now for the clash of feeling with feeling—a timid sensibility confronting a bolder one. Saint-Preux is given an aristocratic name, evoking at once the departed glories of feudalism and the Church, but he is an aristocrat only in terms of an utterly new set of standards, an aristocrat of the spirit, ennobled by sensibility alone. Werther is the heir to his title, a Don Juan who, forced to drop his sword, has picked up instead the pen, the painter's brush—the tear-stained copy of *Ossian.*

Reason meanwhile has been split off, committed to a third character without an exact prototype in the original Richardsonian fable: the dull and philistine suitor (blending with the comic figure of the unwanted old man Soames who woos Clary at her family's behest), finally the husband, as the Clarissa-Lovelace archetype reverts to the mythic pattern of courtly love (where it does not more daringly set up a love-conflict of father-sister-brother), to the first European triangle of husband-wife-poet lover.

Yet the actors in this triangle have changed profoundly between the twelfth century and the early nineteenth. No longer is the husband a cruel tyrant forcing his unfaithful wife to eat the heart of her beloved; now he is pre-eminently the man of Reason: Rousseau's coolly understanding *philosophe,* Wolmar, or Goethe's patient and only too level-headed bourgeois, Albert. Meanwhile, the courtly lover, neurotically swooning and pining away, has been turned into the figure of the anti-bourgeois artist caught between bravado and self-hatred. Goethe provides in his life's work a whole gallery of such perfunctorily disguised self-portraits, from the completely slimy Weislinger in *Götz von Berlichingen* through the equivocal Werther to the essentially heroic Faust of Part I.

As the novel becomes in the hands of the anti-bourgeois writer more lyrical and more autobiographical than the Richardsonian prototype, seduction and adultery (unconsummated in life but fulfilled in the grave) turn into symbols not of a struggle between established and rising classes, but between the exceptional individual and conventional society. In this struggle, the woman comes to stand both for the seducer's reward and his temptation to compromise; while the seducer himself is more and more closely identified with the author, a projection of his self-pity and self-loathing. The self-conscious artist of the new age feels himself at once of the middle class and estranged from it, the son of a bourgeois committed to oppose everything in which the bourgeoisie believes. By the very act of becoming a writer, he has (he cannot help feeling) betrayed his father, abandoned the male world of consciousness and action for a dark flirtation with the unconscious, out of which he has emerged as from the womb of his mother. The girls who symbolize this betrayal of the paternal principle must be, less equivocally even than Clarissa, images of the Great Mother; they must be discovered first by their lovers like Charlotte surrounded by "six lovely children," at last like Julie on her deathbed reaching out to her children; or even seen in the midst of life as the living symbol of eternal motherhood, like Hawthorne's Hester, half avatar, half travesty of "that sacred image of sinless motherhood, whose infant was to redeem the world."

No wonder that the seducer-artist, secret lover of his forbidden Mother and eternally unsure that what seems for him life-fulfillment is not also sin and death, is doomed to impotence and despair. Out of the odd mating of Richardson's debased Don Juan and Prévost's melancholy exile, Cleveland, was born the archetype of the Outsider, the alienated artist, which was to persist in the mind of the West well into our own time. Variously figured forth in literature, the myth becomes flesh, passes from art to life in the shape of those great "dandies" Poe and Byron and Baudelaire.

With the figure of the seducer as intellectual invented by bourgeois women to terrify themselves and declare their contempt for culture, the rebellious artist identifies himself in perverse pride; and his role has ever after been confused, in his own mind and that of the society he battles, with the role of the fictional figure he emulates. Thanks to the sentimental novel, the artist came quite soon to be thought of not as one who makes things, a man with a talent or a skill, but as one who feels them, a quivering sensibility; and it has been possible for a long time to conceive of a poet who has never written a poem—only developed the life style proper to one who aspires to writing poetry.

This is the heritage bequeathed by the age of sensibility to that of Romanticism, this image of the *poète maudit,* the taboo figure whose blessing is his curse, the sensitive young man too good for a world he never made. In 1850, he is called Ishmael, in 1940 Shem the Penman; but he does not die. He cannot, for he is the projection of everyone in the modern world, artist or not. Where the last great communal myth system begins to collapse and the individual finds himself unprotected against the inruption of the id, unsure of his relationship to the ego-ideals left him by the past, he becomes aware of himself as everywhere alone. Only the artist, however, dares to confess this fact even to himself; and thus, especially when he is young, he is likely to think of himself as alone in the loneliness which is actually his bond with the rest of the world. Particularly in America, where a nation of rootless men confronts not the vestiges of older cultures, but the wilderness, this loneliness is most deeply felt and (by many) most hysterically denied. And here the artist, sole aristocrat in a world that has denied the aristocratic principle, must play out against great odds the role of Werther and Don Juan, the part of Faust.

II

Advertised as the first American novel, *The Power of Sympathy: or, The Triumph of Nature,* which appeared in Boston in 1789, represents a serious bid to enter the lists of literature. The strategies (and presumably the motives) of the author are a little confusing: the title page declares his book no mere fiction but an account "founded on truth," while the pair of couplets immediately below insist that the book's aim is to "win the Mind to Sentiment and Truth"; and the elegant dedication that follows more specifically explains that the author's intent is "to represent the specious CAUSES, and to expose the fatal CONSEQUENCE of SEDUCTION" for the benefit of "the young ladies of United Columbia."

Yet the work was published anonymously, as if the writer were not quite convinced that he was engaged in an honorable enterprise; and the frontispiece has nothing to do with the main story, illustrating neither "the power of sympathy" or "nature" triumphant, but portraying the climax of a rather unconvincingly interpolated episode based on a contemporary scandal involving adultery and suicide. The bow to piety and truth combines oddly with the attempt to cash in on current notoriety afflicting a respectable family; and the sanctimonious dedication turns disturbingly into an appeal to the most light-headed of all novel-readers, though apparently the chief consumers of the form, "the young Ladies," or, as the author describes them elsewhere, the "tender youth." The one young lady who appears in the book, however, a "Miss" of fourteen much worried about the dictates of taste "in the centre of politeness and fashion," affects to despise the kind of sentimental book in which she is a character. "The bettermost genii," she asserts, "never read any sentimental books—so you see sentiment is out of date."

The author of *The Power of Sympathy,* who is believed now to have been William Hill Brown, had a strong sense of writing an old-fashioned book, one without chic or current appeal. "Why my dear . . . ," the same young lady insists further, "I abominate everything that is sentimental—it is so unfashionable too." Oppressed, on the one hand, by a feeling that he is out of date in his literary ambitions, Brown is plagued, on the other, by a distrust of the very form of the novel—or at least by a sense that he must pretend to distrust that form. He comments in one place on the "many fine girls ruined by reading novels," though he hastens to make clear that he means specifically novels "not regulated by the chaste principles of true friendship, rational love and connubial duty." But there is, alas, little enough of such friendship, love, or duty in his book; only much talk about them.

There is a thick sententiousness about the book, borrowed from Richardson and outdoing the master in this one regard; but Richardson's name is not invoked in defense of sentiment. The much less respectable Sterne is instead called upon to testify and is in return defended. "Alas! poor *Yorick,*" Brown writes. "May thy pages never be soiled by the fingers of prejudice." Even the most solid and respectable of his male characters, called with obvious aptness "Worthy," blasts the "anti-sentimentalists" who object to Sterne. "Eyes have *they,*" he thunders in Biblical terms, "but they see not—ears have *they,* but they hear not. . . ." Brown's own exclamatory style, all dashes, italics, and exclamation marks, is derived from the master invoked—though it has survived to our own day chiefly in the letters of schoolgirls. Brown, indeed, seems convinced that the future of the sentimental literature he loves, a literature which defends the "man of sense" (needless to say, "sense" here means "sensibility" and not reason) against the "Chesterfieldian" coxcomb, depends upon female writers as well as readers; and he issues a plea for more American novels "from the pens of ladies." In part, perhaps, because of this feminist plea, he was for a long time thought to be a woman, a certain Mrs. Morton, poet and sister to the dying lady in the scandalous frontispiece of his book.

At the heart of Brown's book, there presides the figure of the wise and widowed Mrs. Holmes, a "serious sentimentalist," flanked by an even more prolix and pious sage, her father-in-law, with whom she dispenses *"Mentor*-like lessons of instruction" to the novel's other characters. "The idiosyncratic feature of the American conscience," Geoffrey Gorer aptly remarks, "is that it is predominantly feminine. . . . Duty and Right Conduct become feminine figures." Mr. Gorer goes on to note (and it is worth pausing to take account of such future developments at the point where the super-ego in female form first enters our fiction) that "the fact that the rules for moral conduct are felt to emanate from a feminine source is a source of considerable confusion to American men. They tend to resent such interference in their own behavior, and yet are unable to ignore it, since the insistent maternal conscience is a part of their personality. . . . A second result . . . is that . . . modesty, politeness, neatness, cleanliness—come to be regarded as concessions to feminine demands, and . . . as such they are sloughed off—with relief but not without guilt—whenever a suitable occasion presents itself . . . the stag poker game, the fishing trip, the convention. . . ."

The semi-mythicized figure of Mrs. Holmes is set, appropriately enough, in a semi-mythicized rococo landscape, the first Great Good Place of our literature: the "dear groves" of *Belleview.* It is here in the midst of nature, that she conducts her "amiable conversations"—and it is for the natural world as opposed to the heartless social world of the city that Belleview stands. But Brown's is a neo-classical, a sentimental Nature, a world in which the contrary demands of Nature and Reason are served at once—the equivalent in terms of landscape of the concept of "rational love," or of the blend of "sentiment and truth" invoked in the superscription of the book. The lady of such a place can be neither illiterate or a prude. If, on the one hand, Mrs. Holmes advises her female correspondents to pretend deafness to any remarks directed against the clergy, she advocates the same reception for slurs cast on "Mechanicks." She is a democrat as well as a convinced churchgoer, and a defender of women's rights as well as a spokesman for their duties. She speaks out in favor of the "learned lady," and she defends such semi-respectable writers as Sterne and La Rochefoucauld. She even joins boldly in an attack on "poetic justice" in literature, protesting the invariable rewarding of the innocent as a false representation of life—and recommends the cynical maxims of the French philosopher as a proper antidote. She is in no grim sense a Puritan, but subscribes to her father-in-law's advocacy of charity for fallen women and to his belief in a God ever ready to forgive those who weep. Hers is a world not completely set against passion, though aware of its dangers, but rather one committed to the notion that "Love softens and refines the manners—mends the heart—makes us better men—gives the fainthearted strength. . . ."

Even this sentimental-enlightened view of life, in which Reason and Nature correspond as in an elegant dance, is finally brought into question, for it proves incapable of coming to terms with the revelation of seduction and the threat of incest or with the fact of suicide. Into the very heart of the Garden intrude death and deflowering; and from the Garden itself, from the very hands of Mrs. Holmes, comes the news that precipitates the black climax of the book. Seduction for Brown finally becomes the symbol of the uncontrollable demonic element in life, which lays waste the civilized but natural haven of Belleview. The book opens under the aegis of Mrs. Holmes, but closes under the influence of Werther. In its early pages, the "serious sentimentalist" has quoted the optimistic injunction of Goethe: "REVERENCE THYSELF!"; in the final pages, the hero, turning to literature for comfort, opens a book and reads the following words: "the time of my fading is near, and the blast that shall scatter my leaves. Tomorrow shall the traveller come, he that saw me in my beauty shall come; his eyes shall search the field, but they will not find me." The quotation is from *Ossian,* but surely the book in which Harrington found it was *The Sorrows of Young Werther;* for it is while reading these final verses in his own translation, that Werther is overcome by a prescience of his doom and flings himself at the feet of Charlotte, "insensible to everything but mutual love." Certainly, when Harrington is dead, that dangerous book is found by his side.

Like Werther, too, he condemns society as a conspiracy against the individual. "I despise its opinion—*Independency of spirit* is my motto—I think for myself." And he is led to reject its value and codes as entirely conventional. Finally, he consigns to God and the kingdom of Heaven, quite in the manner of Goethe and Rousseau, the task of righting the wrongs perpetrated in their names by society on earth. Suicide itself, Harrington hopes, can be redeemed by the sentimental baptism of tears. "Let tears of sorrow blot out my guilt from the book of thy wrath," he prays hopefully, and foresees himself not only ultimately forgiven but joined to the woman forbidden him on earth. "In heaven—there alone is happiness—there shall I meet her—there our love will not be a crime. . . ."

It is not, however, adultery, achieved or unconsummated, which the American writer is justifying in terms so like those of his European forerunners; this time it is unconsummated incest, and the villain is (in good American style) not the husband but the father. The Oedipus triangle based on the family romance may be translated from father-mother-son to husband-wife-lover in its European forms, courtly and anti-bourgeois sentimental; but in America it more dangerously takes the form father-sister-brother— though that form can be connected back through the generations with the familiar seduction theme in its "safe" Richardsonian version. Incest may be the secret horror toward which *The Power of Sympathy* tends, but seduction is its more openly elaborated motif.

From the dedication "to the young Ladies of United Columbia . . . to expose the fatal CONSEQUENCES of SEDUCTION," through the preface which repeats it almost word for word, to the body of the book, the theme is worked out in an exhausting series of variations. We learn that seduction "opens the door to a train of miseries," that "there is no human vice of so black a die . . . or which causes a more general calamity." It becomes at last the very image of original sin, and each of the two volumes, into which the book was originally divided, contains an allegory in which the terror of seduction is projected in religious terms. Four times the theme of sexual violation is taken up in *The Power of Sympathy,* first in "the story of Miss Whitman,'" a quite factual account of the famous seduction later worked by Hannah Foster into *The Coquette.* William Hill Brown entrusts to a paragraph spoken by old Mr. Holmes and to a long footnote of his own this tale of a woman betrayed by too much reading and a plausible love. Once pregnant, she tries in vain to buy herself a husband, then produces a dead child and herself dies of puerperal fever. Brown's account is eked out by an extract from one of Miss Whitman's letters and her own verse Elegy, in which, presumably at the point of death, she invokes her faithless lover under the ironic name of Fidelio. That same name in its female form is bestowed on another example of "the fatal CONSEQUENCES of SEDUCTION." Fidelia is a mad peasant girl dressed in flowing white, out of Shakespeare by way of Goethe, who had been "carried off by a ruffian" a few days before her intended marriage. Her true lover had committed suicide in despair, leaving her to a life of Ophelia-like insanity. Obviously a European peasant, she wanders quite improbably on the outskirts of Belleview, the sacred domain of Mrs. Holmes, casting a shadow even on that refuge.

The name of Ophelia, denied her closest counterpart in the novel, is reserved for the lady whose death graces the frontispiece, beneath which are inscribed her last words, "O Fatal! Fatal Poison!" Hers is not a conventional seduction story at all, but rather one of adultery. It is with her brother-in-law that Ophelia falls in love, while living in her sister's house; and their affair ("incestuous," Brown calls it) is revealed by "symptoms which rendered it necessary for Ophelia to remove into the country." The brother-in-law, who had promised to get a divorce and marry the dishonored Ophelia, is so annoyed by the interference of Ophelia's father that his love turns to hate, and Ophelia in despair drinks poison and dies. The story is awkwardly introduced and remains the only subplot not linked somehow to Belleview, which is the book's real center. It would be possible to believe it quite simply prompted by a desire to boost sales by exploiting fresh gossip, though in actuality it backfired, causing the partial suppression of the book; but it does at least foreshadow the subthemes of incest and suicide, and especially "the severe use of paternal power," elsewhere so important in the scheme of the novel.

The main plot begins with young Harrington playing the typical role of the seducer. He has seen a girl called Harriot and he desires her; but his father has forbidden an early marriage, and he is, in any case, "not such a Republican," he confides to his friend Worthy, "as to marry a poor girl. . . ." He has even prepared arguments to overwhelm her virtue, but never quite gets around to urging her to "obey the dictates of nature," for he is really more moralist than "amoroso." With astonishing speed he is converted to more democratic attitudes and to a decision to marry when confronted with "the dignity of *conscious* virtue" in Harriot, who, though penniless and ignorant of her own origins, is able to reverence herself in precisely the manner recommended by Mrs. Holmes.

There is, however, a second turn in the logic of the plot; for no sooner has Harrington been converted from would-be seducer to conventional suitor than the voice of Mrs. Holmes is raised in warning: "I HAVE A TALE TO UNFOLD!" Harrington is about to marry his sister! Harriot is the daughter of a certain Marcia Fawcett and Harrington's father, the fruit of her mother's fall from virtue; and it was to Belleview that her mother had come to die, when cast off by the older Harrington for the sake of the woman he married. Though the betrayed woman had won the love and charity of the senior Mr. Holmes, the forgiveness of God was another matter: He had pursued her sin (or was it the sin of her seducer?) even to the second generation, bringing to the verge of an incestuous union two sensitive creatures who could not accept life without each other. Faced with this consequence of the sin of others, Harriot goes into a rapid decline and dies (her passion still alive despite the knowledge that her lover is her brother), while Harrington commits suicide. The more liberal Christian or sentimental theories of forgiveness crumble before the mystery of the endless effects of iniquity; and the happy theory that love "mends the heart and makes us better men" buckles before the puzzle of the incest taboo and the unwillingness of passion to accept its limits.

The Power of Sympathy: or, The Triumph of Nature becomes finally (or rather, wants to, *tries* to become) what its title declares it: more a psychological, even a metaphysical essay than a lurid story told to shock and amuse. Like *Werther* itself, Brown's book threatens to turn into a study of the ambiguity of Nature; and like Goethe's later *Wahlverwandschaften,* whose title almost translates its own, it studies the strange, sometimes fatal attractions which move us beyond the power of will to resist or reason to control. In the first volume of *The Power of Sympathy,* the term Nature is used quite simply to describe a realm of peace and pleasure, symbolized by Belleview in all its rural charm. "Nature is everywhere liberal in dispensing her beauties and her variety—and I pity those who look round and declare they see neither," Mrs. Holmes writes.

Even into the earlier portions of Part II, the same view persists; Harrington can conceive of no higher name for his God than the good Deist term "Author of Nature." "Author of Nature!" he cries out in ecstasy. "From thee . . . floweth this tide of affection and SYMPATHY!" Here, on the same optimistic note, enters the second key term of the work; yet within three pages, Mrs. Holmes is writing, "Great God! of what materials hast thou compounded the hearts of thy creatures; Admire, o my friend! the operation of NATURE—and the power of SYMPATHY!—" For the lovers, who are brother and sister, have been fatally attracted to each other by the very force that makes their union impossible, by "the link of Nature." Indeed, the terrible climax of their double death is described as "the triumph of Nature," and Harrington is called "the dupe of Nature." But God, after all, is "the Author of Nature"—and the book trembles on the verge of blasphemy.

If Nature has brought Harrington and Harriot to their impasse and Nature is the handmaiden of God, in what sense is it possible to blame them for whatever they may do? The ideal represented by Mrs. Holmes's garden, the utopian dream of "rational love" proves to be an illusion; love and reason only accidentally coincide; the head and the heart are by no means always allies. "The head and the heart are at variance, but when Nature pleads, how feeble is the voice of Reason. . . ." "Allied by birth, and in mind . . . ," Harriot writes to her lover-brother, "the sympathy which bound our souls together, at first sight, is less extraordinary. . . . Shall we strive to oppose the *link of nature* that draws us to each other?"

With the temerity of passion, she ends using the very argument of Nature to justify incest which Harrington finally had not dared plead to justify simple fornication. The temptation to believe her argument and act on it, Harriot's death conveniently removes from them both; but another peril remains. "Reason is taken from the helm of life—" writes Worthy, Harrington's confidant, "and Nature—helpless, debilitated Nature . . . splits upon the rocks. . . ." What, then, is Brown's attitude to the suicide of Harrington, left to the mercy of what his friend calls "helpless, debilitated Nature"? Harrington's father has prophetically beheld him in a vision in hell among the other self-murderers; but Harrington himself foresees an ascension to Heaven as a reward for his long suffering and looks forward to a reunion with Harriot there. "Sympathy unites whom Fate divides," "in death they sleep undivided," we are told; but does the common burial signify an eternal union in heaven, where their "love will be no crime"?

The book finally equivocates in a way not untypical of the later American novel, hanging onto not the best but the worst of two possible worlds: the smugness of liberal gentility and the factitious sensationalism of anti-bourgeois sentimentality. When read at all, *The Power of Sympathy* has seemed to the respectable a suspect work, described, for instance, in a history of the novel published in 1952 as "a morbid, nasty book." At the same time, it has struck others as merely "a good domestic story calculated to impart unmistakeable impressions to the young." Its fundamental seriousness is the one quality both descriptions fail to take into account; but that seriousness cannot be ignored without falsifying the book altogether, for it is a literate book according to the standards of its own time, and an ambitious one.

It is, however, marred by an annoying thinness of realization throughout; Brown could not or would not take the pains to specify solidly the reactions of his characters, though he had in the letter form he borrowed from Richardson an admirable instrument for detailed psychological analysis. His people not only float in a scarcely defined space (he is interested in settings only when they are symbolic like the summerhouse of Mrs. Holmes), they act out of scarcely defined personalities. What bulk his novel finally possesses is attained not by working out the implications of action, motive, or theme but by working in extra sub-plots and extended homilies. Our earliest books are astonishingly slim in a time when Europe abounded with examples of the thick book, as if the mere effort of imagining a creative work on this side of the ocean exhausted the energy of the author; and the scant realization of *The Power of Sympathy* cannot, therefore, have been the cause of its unpopularity. Certainly it attracted little attention. What the partially effective efforts at suppression by the Apthorp family (relatives of "Ophelia") had begun, public indifference completed. The novel seems to have been mentioned in print only seven times from the date of its publication to 1850; and what recognition it has now is almost completely a function of the impulse toward exhaustive scholarship rather than of renewed critical interest.

Even less well read and remembered is Brown's *Ira and Isabella,* in which he returned once more to the theme of incest. This time he produced neither a tragedy of incest, like his own *The Power of Sympathy,* nor a *comédie larmoyante,* like Mrs. Rowson's *Lucy,* but a howling travesty—endowed with a "happy ending" capable of dissolving in laughter the whole obsessive concern with "the fatal CONSEQUENCES of SEDUCTION." One hopes the burlesque is deliberate, but it is hard to be sure. At any rate, in *Ira and Isabella,* the protagonists, who learn that their intended marriage cannot take place because Isabella is the illegitimate daughter of Ira's father, then discover that Ira, too, is illegitimate, not the son of that presumed father at all; and bastards both, they are blissfully united.

Though William Hill Brown's second book is an equivocal travesty and his first the mere skeleton of a novel, he remains a considerable figure. *The Power of Sympathy* may be finally only a sketch, but it is the sketch of a serious book; and it is probable that its failure is more the product of its virtues than of its faults. A mere accident of history determined that the first American novel be (despite its equivocations and uncertainty) fundamentally anti-bourgeois; the necessities of American character, particularly that of the largest reading public, made it impossible that from such a book a successful literature could take its cue.

6

CHARLES BROCKDEN BROWN
AND THE INVENTION
OF THE AMERICAN GOTHIC

THE GOTHIC, WHOSE EXAMPLE spurred on those serious American writers whom the example of the sentimental had only galled, is a sub-genre of the novel, invented in England, though it was adapted in Germany quite early by writers like E. T. A. Hoffmann, and reached our own novelists in both its British and German forms. Its first practitioner was Horace Walpole, who published, on Christmas Eve of 1764, *The Castle of Otranto*. Toward this improbable account of flight and pursuit in a pseudo-medieval setting and toward its hero-villain Manfred, Walpole's attitude was double. On the one hand, he concealed his authorship behind an Italian pen name and shrugged off the whole enterprise by remarking that "it is not everybody in this country may play the fool with impunity"; on the other, he boasted in a foreword of having freed "great resources of fancy" that had been unfortunately "dammed up by common life."

All the major themes and symbols of the gothic were present in Walpole's book, but it did not prove capable of starting a new fashion in fiction; the European imagination was not yet ready for it, would not be ready until that imagination had been modified by the Revolution and the Terror. Before 1789, *The Castle of Otranto* seemed merely a sport, the eccentric product of a literary antiquarian; after 1790, it was revealed as the lonely forerunner of an attempt at creating "the modern novel"—a term used by the Marquis de Sade (surely for the first time) in his *Idées sur les romans* to characterize the gothic romance. It was through the works

126

not of Walpole but of two other English novelists that the gothic became the prevailing European mode in the years when William Hill Brown and Mrs. Rowson were still trying in the United States to revive the sentimental.

Just as the Richardsonian novel soon became the contested heritage of two conflicting parties, philistine and anti-bourgeois, so the gothic novel was fought for. But even as the sentimental novel seems essentially genteel, and is only exploited against the grain for anti-philistine ends, so the gothic romance is fundamentally anti-bourgeois and can only with difficulty be adapted to the needs of the sentimental middle classes. Nonetheless, it was a "female scribbler," Ann Radcliffe, celebrated by her bourgeois admirers as the "Shakespeare of the Romance writers," who first managed to make a success of gothic fiction. Her books, which appeared between 1789 and 1797, are all much alike, variations on the archetypal theme which she found in Walpole and made her own.

Through a dream landscape, usually called by the name of some actual Italian place, a girl flees in terror and alone amid crumbling castles, antique dungeons, and ghosts who are never really ghosts. She nearly escapes her terrible persecutors, who seek her out of lust and greed, but is caught; escapes again and is caught; escapes once more and is caught (the middle of Mrs. Radcliffe's books seem in their compulsive repetitiveness a self-duplicating nightmare from which it is impossible to wake); finally breaks free altogether and is married to the virtuous lover who has all along worked (and suffered equally with her) to save her. In the end, all the ghosts that have terrorized her are explained as wax-works or living men in disguise, the supernatural appearances that have made her enemies seem more than human revealed as mere mechanical devices, etc.

Mrs. Radcliffe's most successful version of her single theme is found in *The Italian,* which appeared in 1797; and, indeed, it is Italy, the Mediterranean South with its overtones of papistry and lust, that is the true ghost, never quite exorcized by the fables of the more genteel gothicists. That symbolic Italy represents only one of their debts to Restoration drama, from whose stock of sensational effects the gothic novelists rifled whatever seemed to them of use. If the gothic romance seems in certain regards more theatrical than the sentimental novel, whose beginnings after all were model letter books for the uncultured, this is because many of its devices were to begin with stage properties, and Walpole himself the author of *The Mysterious Mother* as well as *The Castle of Otranto*—in Byron's words, of "the last tragedy" as well as the "first Romance" of European literature. The basic fable of the gothic novel, however, at least as defined by Mrs. Radcliffe, seems actually derived from such books as *Clarissa.* Schedoni, the sinister male protagonist of *The Italian,* pursues his victim, just as Lovelace once pursued Clarissa; and at the center of the story appears that girl on the run, the Persecuted Maiden who, under one name or another, had been fleeing violation ever since Angelica took off at high speed through the pages of *Orlando Furioso.* There are, nonetheless, notable differences between the Richardsonian and Radcliffean treatments of the pursuit of the Maiden.

First of all, there is the matter of setting. The flight of Clarissa, however mythic in its implications, takes place in society—in a real, contemporaneous world of fashion, friends, parents, parties, and business. The flight of the gothic heroine is out of the known world into a dark region of make-believe, past the magical landscapes of a legendary Italy, along the shadowy corridors of the haunted castle, which is to say, through a world of ancestral and infantile fears projected in dreams. The sentimental heroine confronts the dangers of the present, that is, of life as recorded in the newspaper; the gothic heroine evades the perils of the past, that is, of life as recorded in history.

There is, moreover, a question of tone and emphasis. However melodramatic or even tragic the implications of the sentimental fable, its intent is to reveal the power of light and redemption, to insist that virtue if not invariably successful is at least always triumphant. The gothic fable, on the other hand, though it may (in its more genteel examples) permit the happy ending, is committed to portraying the power of darkness. Perhaps another way to say this is that the fully developed gothic centers not in the heroine (the persecuted principle of salvation) but in the villain (the persecuting principle of damnation). The villain-hero is, indeed, an invention of the gothic form, while his temptation and suffering, the beauty and terror of his bondage to evil are among its major themes.

Finally, there is the matter of the archetypal function of the basic gothic story; for such a function it must have or it could not have persisted as it did. The Clarissa-Lovelace archetype expresses, as we have seen, the sense of their own innocence possessed by the classes for whom the novel was produced. The myth of *The Castle of Otranto,* on the other hand, projects a sense of guilt and anxiety, the guilt of the Break-through, as dimly perceived by the bourgeoisie—and especially by the intellectuals who were its sons. "What is this secret sin; this untold tale, that art cannot extract, nor penance cleanse?" asks the question quoted from Walpole's *The Mysterious Mother* by Mrs. Radcliffe in *The Italian.* The answer in the original play is incest—incest of brother and sister-daughter bred out of an original incest of mother and son—the breach of the primal taboo and the offense against the father! In more general terms, the guilt which underlies the gothic and motivates its plots is the guilt of the revolutionary haunted by the (paternal) past which he has been striving to destroy; and the fear that possesses the gothic and motivates its tone is the fear that in destroying the old ego-ideals of Church and State, the West has opened a way for the inruption of darkness: for insanity and the disintegration of the self. Through the pages of the gothic romance, the soul of Europe flees its own darker impulses.

These deeper implications are barely perceptible in the gently spooky fiction of Mrs. Radcliffe, in which terror is allayed by the final pages, all inruptions of the irrational rationally explained away. Indeed, so polite does horror become in her novels, that it seems to a modern palate insipid. But in the single volume of another gothic fictionist, the Walpolean fable takes on a significance that evaded Mrs. Radcliffe's total body of work; and all its absurdity, its outrageous violence is released. That writer is the *enfant terrible* Matthew Gregory Lewis, who at the age of twenty wrote in three weeks the four hundred pages of *The Monk,* by which name he insisted on being called forever after ("a two-fold barbarity, Madam"). It is a fantastic, amusing, horrifying book, this shrill *tour de force* produced at top speed by an English boy to support his deserted mother. Actually composed in Weimar, it benefits perhaps by approaching the tradition of *The Castle of Otranto* as developed in German horror fiction rather than in the novels of English gentlewomen.

At any rate, the appearance of *The Monk* in 1796 made its author a showpiece at all the literary parties of that London season, though it also shocked the official guardians of morality so deeply that for perhaps a hundred years it remained bootleg reading. "A romance, which if a parent saw it in the hands of a son or daughter, he might reasonably turn pale," one of its shocked readers called it; "a poison for youth and a provocative for the debau-

chés." One considerate bookseller was reported to have underlined
all "the worst parts for a sixteen year old subscriber, so that she
might skip them!" And it was, perhaps, in a similarly marked copy
that Byron browsed among its more scandalous passages, emerging with the horrified (and somewhat improbable) comment that
they represented the "philtered ideas of a jaded voluptuary." The
book seems inoffensive enough nowadays, though occasionally
melodramatic to the point of howling absurdity; but it was obviously intended to offend and disturb the right-minded bourgeoisie,
which in its own day rose satisfactorily to the bait.

A summary of its double plot gives some sense of the provocative nature of the novel, though shorn of the sensationally emphatic
style, much of its force (and a little of its ridiculousness) is lost.
The sub-plot is conventionally Radcliffean, dealing with two lovers,
Agnes and Raymond, who are separated in the midst of complications involving, among other horrors, the bleeding ghost of a nun.
Agnes is first imprisoned in a nunnery, then denounced by Ambrosio (the hero-villain of the main plot) and condemned to perpetual
incarceration among rotting corpses in the vaults beneath the convent. She is, however, rescued in time for a reunion with her lover
by a search party which discovers, at a critical moment of his villainy, Ambrosio and his Satanic mistress, Matilda.

Ambrosio, "Abbot of the Capuchins," is first presented as a
much-admired preacher, an ostensible saint; but he is readily
enough corrupted by the woman Matilda, who gains access to his
cell disguised as a young novice; indeed, by the time she appears
Ambrosio has already been inflamed by contemplating her portrait
in the guise of the Virgin. Soon after they have become lovers,
Ambrosio wearies of her and begins to dream of possessing Antonia, fifteen-year-old daughter of Elvira, a noble lady to whom he
is confessor. With the aid of Matilda, who calls up the Devil to
further his plans, he gets into the bedroom of Antonia, but is interrupted as he assaults her by Elvira, whom he kills.

He gives a sleeping potion to the terrified girl, who is taken for
dead and consigned to a tomb, where he at last successfully rapes
her among the rotting dead. When she screams, he murders her,
fearing discovery; but he is captured all the same by the soldiers
of the Inquisition, from whose prison he manages to escape by
selling his soul to the Devil. He is, however, immediately transported by demons to the top of a mountain peak, from which, after
being told that Elvira (whom he murdered) was his mother and

Antonia (whom he violated, then killed) his sister, he is cast to his terrified death.

By the time Lewis is through with this sadist farrago, the major symbols of the gothic have been established, and the major meanings of the form made clear. In general, those symbols and meanings depend on an awareness of the spiritual isolation of the individual in a society where all communal systems of value have collapsed or have been turned into meaningless clichés. There is a basic ambivalence in the attitude of the gothic writers to the alienation which they perceive. On the one hand, their fiction projects a fear of the solitude which is the price of freedom; and on the other hand, an almost hysterical attack on all institutions which might inhibit that freedom or mitigate the solitude it breeds. Chief of the gothic symbols is, of course, the Maiden in flight—understood in the spirit of *The Monk* as representing the uprooted soul of the artist, the spirit of the man who has lost his moral home. Not the violation or death which sets such a flight in motion, but the flight itself figures forth the essential meaning of the anti-bourgeois gothic, for which the girl on the run and her pursuer become only alternate versions of the same plight. Neither can come to rest before the other—for each is the projection of his opposite—*anima* and *animus,* actors in a drama which depends on both for its significance. Reinforcing the meaning of the haunted victim and the haunted persecutor (each the other's obsession) is the haunted countryside, and especially the haunted castle or abbey which rises in its midst, and in whose dark passages and cavernous apartments the chase reaches its climax. Symbols of authority, secular or ecclesiastic, in ruin—memorials to a decaying past—such crumbling edifices project the world of collapsed ego-ideals through which eighteenth-century man was groping his proud and terrified way. If he permitted himself a certain relish in the contemplation of those ruins, this was because they were safely cast down, and he could indulge in nostalgia without risk. If he was terrified of them, dreamed supernatural enemies lurking in their shadows, it was because he suspected that the past, even dead, *especially* dead, could continue to work harm. Even as late as Henry James, an American writer deeply influenced by gothic modes was able to imagine the *malaria,* the miasma which arises from decaying ruins, striking down Daisy Miller as she romantically stands at midnight in the Coliseum.

One of the most popular middlebrow derivatives of the gothic romance is the ghost story; and, indeed, from the start ghosts arise everywhere in the gothic's pages: pale symbols (parodies of the immortal soul in which men had begun to lose faith) of what persists after death. In the eighteenth century, the experience of rationalism had made it easier to believe that a noxious influence, an after-image which chilled the blood, outlasted physical decay, than that some integrating principle of good eternally survived. Similarly, the Devil lived on in the imagination after the death of God, men who would not have gone to church celebrating black masses or finding in the tale of terror some vestigial religious awe. Children of an age which had killed kings and bishops, cast down the holy places of their fathers, found it hard to convince themselves that specters did not walk with rattling chains, or that ancestral pictures did not bleed.

Beneath the haunted castle lies the dungeon keep: the womb from whose darkness the ego first emerged, the tomb to which it knows it must return at last. Beneath the crumbling shell of paternal authority, lies the maternal blackness, imagined by the gothic writer as a prison, a torture chamber—from which the cries of the kidnaped *anima* cannot even be heard. The upper and the lower levels of the ruined castle or abbey represent the contradictory fears at the heart of gothic terror: the dread of the super-ego, whose splendid battlements have been battered but not quite cast down —and of the id, whose buried darkness abounds in dark visions no stormer of the castle had even touched.

Most variously developed of all the gothic symbols is the Shadow, the villain who pursues the Maiden and presides over turrets and dungeon keep alike. He is apt to take the shape (in a genre which, like the sentimental novel, is both Protestant and bourgeois) of the devious Inquisitor, the concupiscent priest, the corrupt nobleman—or, with almost equal appropriateness, the depraved abbess or the lascivious lady of the manor. And yet there is a sense in which the evil principle is mythically male, the female at best an accessory; for deep in the middle-class mind persist the equations of the Sentimental Love Religion.

Certainly, it is the Shadow projected as male which most impresses itself upon the imagination, becomes standard to the form; and the hero-villain of the tale of terror turns out to be a descendant of Lovelace, after all, though of a Lovelace regarded with tenderness rather than contempt. Like his sentimental prototype, the Manfred figure stands for the *animus,* that masculine archetype in which the feminine psyche projects all it has denied. But he is the *animus* regarded as forgivable victim of passion and circumstance, as admirable sufferer. His brow furrowed, his face frozen in the grimace of pain, his eyes burning with repressed fury, his mind tormented with unspeakable blasphemies (ancestor of Byron's Giaour, of Ahab, Heathcliffe, Rochester, and a thousand other "ungodly, godlike" men), he is proposed as another symbol of alienation twinned with the Maiden he pursues, a jailer no less lonely than his prisoner.

To define this aspect of the gothic hero-villain, the Lovelace archetype is blended with that of the Wandering Jew, Ahasuerus or Cartaphilus doomed to stalk the earth in hopeless pain until the Second Coming; but especially he is fused with the image of Faust. Don Juan and Faust alike are former villains of the orthodox mind made heroes in an age of unorthodoxy, Promethean or Satanic figures; and both come to stand for the lonely individual (the writer himself!) challenging the mores of bourgeois society, making patent to all men the ill-kept secret that the codes by which they live are archaic survivals without point or power.

Often the two archetypes are blended in a single literary character, as in the lover-scientist Goethe calls by the name of Faust. But there is a real difference between the rebel whose life style is cued by passion and the one whose life style is compounded out of pride and terror—between the seducer and the black magician. Faust challenges the limitations set upon experience not in the name of pleasure but of knowledge; he seeks not to taste life without restraint but to control it fully; and his essential crime (or glory!) is, therefore, not seduction but the Satanic bargain: to sell one's soul to the Devil. But what does it mean to sell one's soul? The symbol is immensely complex, its significances multiple; they can be summed up, however, in the single phrase *to choose to be damned,* whatever damnation is. Not to fall into error out of a passionate loss of self-control, not even to choose to sin at a risk of damnation; but to commit oneself to it with absolute certainty for "as long as forever is."

Damnation itself means various things to men of varying belief: a commitment to the vagaries of the unconscious; an abandonment of the comforts of social life—of marriage and the family, wealth and recognition; a rejection of all bonds of love and sympathy, of humanity itself; a deliberate plunge into insanity; and acceptance of eternal torment for the soul. When Huck Finn cries out, "All

right, I'll *go* to Hell," and Ahab, "From hell's heart I stab at thee!";
when Hester Prynne tears off her scarlet letter, they are Faustian
heroes. Anyone who, in full consciousness, surrenders the hope of
heaven (what everyone says heaven is) for the endurance of hell
(what everyone knows hell to be) has entered into a pact with
Satan; and the very act, therefore, of writing a gothic novel rather
than a sentimental one, of devoting a long fiction to terror rather
than love, is itself a Faustian commitment. The gothic novel was
not fully itself until it had discovered and made its center the diabolic bargain; this is as essential to its total significance as seduction to the Richardsonian novel.

The primary meaning of the gothic romance, then, lies in its substitution of terror for love as a central theme of fiction. The titillation of sex denied, it offers its readers a vicarious participation in
a flirtation with death—approach and retreat, approach and retreat, the fatal orgasm eternally mounting and eternally checked.
More than that, however, the gothic is the product of an implicit
aesthetic that replaces the classic concept of nothing-in-excess with
the revolutionary doctrine that nothing succeeds like excess. Aristotle's guides for achieving the tragic without falling into "the
abominable" are stood on their heads, "the abominable" itself
being made the touchstone of effective art. Dedicated to producing
nausea, to transcending the limits of taste and endurance, the
gothic novelist is driven to seek more and more atrocious crimes to
satisfy the hunger for "too-much" on which he trades.

It is not enough that his protagonist commit rape; he must commit it upon his mother or sister; and if he himself is a cleric,
pledged to celibacy, his victim a nun, dedicated to God, all the
better! Similarly, if he commits murder, it must be his father who
is his victim; and the crime must take place in darkness, among the
decaying bodies of his ancestors, on hallowed ground. It is as if
such romancers were pursuing some ideal of absolute atrocity
which they cannot quite flog their reluctant imaginations into conceiving. For the abominable, to be truly effective, must remain literally unspeakable; and where—as in the case of *The Monk*—it
has adapted itself to the censor and the mode, become respectable
and chic, it ends by seeming ridiculous. The abominable as an
absolute leads to either sickness or silliness, betraying the man who
is obsessed by the horror he evokes or the one who plays at it
merely to shock and succeed.

Some would say, indeed, that the whole tradition of the gothic is a pathological symptom rather than a proper literary movement, a reversion to the childish game of scaring oneself in the dark, or a plunge into sadist fantasy, masturbatory horror. For Wordsworth, for instance, heir of the genteel sentimentality of the eighteenth century, gothic sensationalism seemed merely a response (compounding the ill to which it responded) to the decay of sensibility in an industrialized and brutalized world—in which men had grown so callous that only shock treatments of increasing intensity could move them to react. Yet there is more than this even to *The Monk*. If Lewis writes in one sense what he must and in another what he hopes will sell, he also writes for a more conscious and respectable end: to shake the philistines out of their self-satisfied torpor. *Épater la bourgeoisie:* this is the secret slogan of the tale of terror; and it remains into our own time a not-so-secret slogan of much highbrow literature, particularly of such spectacular bourgeois-baiting movements as Dada, Surrealism, and Pop Art.

When the Beatniks emerge from their own retreats, bearded and blue-shaded and bagel in hand, to mock the "squares" of San Francisco with the monstrous disorder of life as they imagine and live it, they are playing the latest version of the game invented by "Monk" Lewis. Despite its early adoption by Mrs. Radcliffe, the gothic is an avant-garde genre, perhaps the first avant-garde art in the modern sense of the term. A pursuit, half serious enterprise, half fashionable vice, of the intellectuals of the end of the eighteenth century, it remained highbrow enough to tempt the Shelleys and Byron, for instance, to try their hands at it. The popular success of *Frankenstein,* perpetuated still in movies and known in its essence to children in the street, has obscured the fact that it was launched as an advanced book; and that it belongs to a kind, one of whose functions was to shock the bourgeoisie into an awareness of what a chamber of horrors its own smugly regarded world really was.

But the gothic represents also an attempt to redeem "the improbable and marvelous," the stuff of the fancy which Richardson had presumably banned from the new novel. It was, in short, an anti-realistic protest, a rebellion of the imagination against confining fiction to an analysis of contemporary manners and modes. It is not, on the other hand, a reactionary literary movement; for the fantastic world to which it turns is altogether different from the fictional setting of the baroque proto-novel, against whose "pomp and pageantry" Richardson had revolted. The tone of the *Astrée*, for instance, is nostalgic, its fables devised to feed the pastoral reveries of an upper class turned toward the past. The gothic reassertion of *"sortilège et fantasmagorie,"* on the other hand, is sinister and disturbing, more like a nightmare than a dream; and its fables represent the hopes and fears of a group of intellectuals turned toward the future at a moment of revolutionary readjustment.

The Marquis de Sade in his essay on the "new novel" (as important for an understanding of the gothic as Diderot's *Éloge de Richardson* for an understanding of the sentimental) points out precisely what is at stake. Such books, he explains, are "the inevitable fruit of the revolutionary shocks felt by all of Europe. . . . For those who knew all the miseries with which scoundrels can oppress men, the novel became as hard to write as it was monotonous to read. . . . It was necessary to call hell to the rescue . . . and to find in the world of nightmare" images adequate to "the history of man in this Iron Age."

The key words are "nightmare" and "hell," revealing how consciously, on the one hand, some gothic writers turned to the night side of life, the irrational world of sleep, for themes and symbols appropriate to the terrors bred by the Age of Reason; and how, on the other hand, they saw their own role as Satanic, their kind of literature as a kind of half-playful black mass, an evocation of the Evil One, in whom, of course they were no longer prepared to confess believing. Gothicism is the Satanism of those to whom (officially at least) Satan has become a figure of speech. And yet the gothic writers insist upon using the traditional terminology for the diabolic, betraying a certain vestigial doubt (even perhaps hope) that there may be in the old legends a kind of truth.

Beside the good old word "hell," however, is placed the newer word "history," equally important to an understanding of the form; for behind the gothic lies a theory of history, a particular sense of the past. The tale of terror is a kind of historical novel which existed before the historical novel (the invention of Walter Scott) came into being. The Richardsonian novel of contemporary life had discovered the present for fiction, made time a medium in which characters moved. The social meanings of the Lovelace-Clarissa story assume a clear-cut conception of a differing Then and Now. Richardson claimed for his own province the Now, in which a servant could marry her employer's son; but by implication he has already defined a Then, in which that son would have taken such a girl whenever he desired her and on whatever terms his own whim prompted. This Then, the gothic novel claimed for its province, making of the past an essential subject of fiction for the first time. Shakespeare had, to be sure, written historical plays; but how ahistorical they, in fact, were: assuming a past indistinguishable from the present in all things (in costume, in speech, in moral attitudes) except for certain recorded events which happened to have happened then instead of now.

The gothic felt for the first time the *pastness* of the past; and though it did not, like the later novels of Manzoni and Scott, attempt with scholarly accuracy to document that difference, it tried to give some sense of it: the sense of something lapsed or outlived or irremediably changed. It is no accident that Horace Walpole was an "antiquary," a researcher into ancient modes and styles, who lived in a reconstructed "gothic" villa. The very adjective, which gave to both the home he designed and the fictional tradition he founded a name, implies a certain attitude toward the past. Originally "gothic" was a thoroughly pejorative word, applied not only to whatever belonged in fact to rude "medieval" times, i.e., any period before the sixteenth century, but also to any surviving mode of speech or behavior considered unworthy of enlightened modernity. Dueling, for instance, is referred to by one eighteenth-century critic as a "gothic custom," while another makes a fictional character condemn "husband" as a "gothic word." Rousseau, on the other hand, modestly describes his own novel, *La Nouvelle Héloïse,* as "gothic," meaning presumably that it possesses a certain antique simplicity and an unsophisticated style.

By and large, however, the writers of gothic novels looked on the "gothic" times with which they dealt (and by which, despite themselves, they were fascinated) as corrupt and detestable. Their vision of that past was bitterly critical, and they evoked the olden days not to sentimentalize but to condemn them. Most gothicists were not only avant-garde in their literary aspirations, but radical in their politics; they were, that is to say, anti-aristocratic, anti-Catholic, anti-nostalgic. They liked to think that if their work abounded in ghosts, omens, portents and signs, this was not because they themselves were superstitious, but because they were engaged in exposing "that superstition which debilitates the mind, that ignorance which propagates error, and that dread of invisible agency which makes inquiry criminal." Beneath the spectacular events of the tale of terror, the melodramatic psychology and theatrical horror, rings the cry, *"Écrasez l'infâme!"* The spirit of Voltaire broods over the haunted castle; and ghosts squeak eerily that they do not exist.

Yet the authors of gothic novels, followers of Voltaire though they were and exponents of the Enlightenment, were plagued by a hunger for the inexplicable, a need of the marvelous which they could neither confess nor escape. At a moment when everywhere rationalism had triumphed in theory and madness reigned in fact, they were especially baffled; and they ended by compounding the hypocrisy of their times with a corresponding hypocrisy of their own. In the name of optimism, they exploited melancholy; in the name of light, they paid tribute to darkness; in the name of history, they yielded themselves up to fancy.

Their attitude toward Catholicism is a case in point. Like most other classic forms of the novel, the gothic romance is Protestant in its ethos; indeed, it is the most blatantly anti-Catholic of all, projecting in its fables a consistent image of the Church as the Enemy; we have already noticed how standard and expected were the characters of the depraved monk, the suborned Inquisitor, the malicious abbess. Yet the gothic imagination feeds on what its principles abhor, the ritual and glitter, the politics and pageantry of the Roman Church. The ideal of celibacy and its abuses particularly intrigue the more prurient gothic fictionists, as do the mysteries of the confessional, where for ages—into the ear of God knows what lustful priest—was whispered "this secret sin, this untold tale," which they had made the subject of their art. Sixty years after *The Monk,* Nathaniel Hawthorne was still playing fast and loose with Catholicism, sending his Puritan protagonists into the very heart of Saint Peter's, into the confessional booth itself—only to withdraw them at the last possible moment, resolutely anti-Papist after all. The conversion of Hawthorne's own daughter to Catholicism and her entry into a convent mark a final consummation (achieved by history in despite of art) of the gothicists' long, absurd flirtation with the Church they presumably abhorred.

The contradictions between the liberal uses and demonic implications, the enlightened principles and reactionary nostalgia of the tale of terror by no means exhaust the ambiguities at its heart. A further conflict arises out of an attempt to solve the earlier ones by passing off the machinery of horror essential to the form as mere "play," "good theater," which demands not credence but the simplest suspension of adult disbelief. Far from satisfying the gothic writers, this device leaves them with the annoying sense that the kind of novel they produce presumably for high-minded ends is really no more than a lowbrow amusement, a literary vice (like the detective story and science fiction which are its heirs). Why, they are driven to ask themselves, do they indulge in the child's game of make-believe unless to titillate their own jaded sensations and those of their readers? But to *play* with horror, no matter what one's declared intent, is to pander to the lowest, darkest impulses of the mind.

Certain devices are built into the gothic from the start to help resolve its contradictions. There is, for instance, the convention of treating magic as science and thus reclaiming it for respectability in the Age of Reason; the magician Faust in his black robes becomes the scientist in his white coat (Dr. Frankenstein is a transitional figure on the way), and no good reader of newspapers cavils at him as improbable or outmoded. At first the sciences favored by the gothic romancers are those of the gothic past, astrology and alchemy; and such ancient symbolical dreams as the universal solvent and the elixir of life (in the works of Hawthorne, for instance, and those of E. T. A. Hoffmann) possess the imagination. Later, these are replaced or reinforced by the bourgeois pseudo-sciences of mesmerism, phrenology, ventrilocution (in the novels of Charles Brockden Brown and, once more, those of Hawthorne); and finally, in our own age, they are largely abandoned for popularized versions of modern physics.

Much more important in the early stages of the gothic was the convention of the "explained supernatural," invented first by Mrs. Radcliffe to assure her readers that nothing was really wrong with God's good world, though it might for a time seem so in the pages of her latest romance. Some anti-bourgeois, avant-garde gothicists found it convenient, too, to pretend that there were at last no ghosts, only wax images behind translucent black curtains; for they were, after all, as committed to an optimistic view of life by their rationalism as any lady entertainer of the bourgeoisie by her sentimental Christianity. The device of the explained supernatural is as useful for the reader as for the writer, enabling him to get his thrills and keep his self-respect; but it does more than that. It embodies in the very technique of fiction a view of the world which insists that though fear is real, its causes are delusive; that daylight reveals to us the essential goodness of a universe to which the shadows of night had given a false aspect of evil.

Like other self-protective devices of the gothic, the explained supernatural poses new problems as it solves old ones, leaving some readers at least with the sense of having been shamefully hoaxed, betrayed into responding with pity and terror to a mere bag of tricks. What is the point of horror that is not in some sense real? Only Hawthorne, of all writers who insist on casting a new light in their final pages on what they have all along presented in quite another, manages to leave us satisfied and unashamed; for he developed in his novels and tales a method of "alternative explanations" that permits us at the end of an action to throw back over it the interpretation that suits our temperament best. He gives us the choice of many readings: magical, mechanical, psychological; and even allows us not to make a choice at all, but like him to endure them all, to emerge from his story not with some assured insight into the causes of human depravity but only with a confirmed sense of the ambiguity of life.

Implicit in the gothic novel from the beginning is a final way of redeeming it that is precisely opposite in its implications to the device of the explained supernatural, a way of proving not that its terror is less true than it seems but more true. There *is* a place in men's lives where pictures do in fact bleed, ghosts gibber and shriek, maidens run forever through mysterious landscapes from nameless foes; that place is, of course, the world of dreams and of the repressed guilts and fears that motivate them. This world the dogmatic optimism and shallow psychology of the Age of Reason had denied; and yet this world it is the final, perhaps the essential, purpose of the gothic romance to assert.

The point was to find a means for expressing it; and that task was improbably entrusted to the gothic novel, whether its authors were aware of it or not. For that purpose they had to contrive a vocabulary of symbol and myth capable of bootlegging past the guardians of Reason perceptions of the irrationality of experience and life itself. The half-playful, half-pathological evocation of half-believed-in monsters remained for almost a hundred years the West's chief method for dealing with the night-time impulses of the psyche. What was essentially psychology and symbolism pretended, even sometimes to itself, to be horror pornography.

From the time of Richardson, the chief end of the novel had

been made clear: "to carry the torch to the back of the cave," to reveal the "hideous Moor" who lurks in its furthest reaches. The methods of Richardson are analytic, psychological; but the terms which occur to Diderot to explain them are melodramatic and symbolic—in short, "gothic." In *Clarissa,* the "cave" of the heart is concealed beneath the exterior actions of a girl and a man living ordinary lives in contemporary society; while the "hideous Moor" is no more than the sum total of the unconfessed, ambiguous motives prompting those actions, for which of course the actors give quite other, more laudable explanations. One can imagine, however, a kind of fiction in which the depths of the mind are represented in the text itself as a cave before whose mouth a bewildered girl stands paralyzed with fright; while the hideous Moor in fact leaps from its darkness, his black skin glistering, his white eyeballs bulging, his sinewy arms reached out to clasp and destroy. In such projective or symbolic fiction, character, setting, and incident alike are "true," not in their own right but as they symbolize in outward terms an inward reality.

In the history of the novel, the two modes, analytic and projective, have both flourished, the analytic developing through Flaubert and James to Virginia Woolf, Proust, and Joyce, the projective moving on through Poe and the Surrealists to a modern climax in Kafka. In many writers, however (in Melville for instance, and Dostoevski, in Dickens and Balzac and Faulkner), projective and analytic modes are mingled often confusedly; for such authors are the heirs of a confusion at the heart of the gothic about its own method and meaning. Precisely because the early practitioners of the tale of terror were only half aware of the symbolic nature of the genre, they did not know what kind of credence to ask for their protagonists—presenting them sometimes as fully motivated characters in the analytic sense, and at others, as mere projections of unconscious guilt or fear. Such an heir of the gothicists, for instance, as Melville was betrayed into giving to his symbolic Captain Ahab (who stands for "sultanic" hybris, i.e., for one aspect of the mind) a mind of his own; though the Parsee, who plays Satan to Ahab's Faust, is treated as a simple projection with an inner logic rather than a psychology.

Particularly in the tradition of the American novel, this confusion of modes and levels of credibility becomes a vexing problem; because of all the fiction of the West, our own is most deeply influenced by the gothic, is almost essentially a gothic one. In general, the European gothic reaches the level of important art only in poetry or drama, not in fiction; in America quite the opposite is the case.

Certainly the three novels granted by general consensus to be our greatest works are gothic in theme and atmosphere alike. It is not merely a question of certain trappings of terror: the delirious visions of Huck's father, the body dragged at midnight from the grave, the signs and portents of impending disaster discovered in howling dogs and slaughtered snakes, the ghostly visions through the fog of *Huckleberry Finn;* or the Spirit-Spout, the silent rising from the deep of the Great White Squid, the Saint Elmo's fire, the eerie Parsee who appears out of no place with his "tiger-like" crew, the baptism in pagan blood of *Moby Dick;* the Indian warlocks and Puritan witches, the yellow ruff and the memories of Anne Turner, the Black Man and his book, the letter A written in the heavens of *The Scarlet Letter.* Even more importantly, in each book, the Faustian bargain stands at the focus of action: Hester and Dimmesdale alike symbolically inscribe themselves as the Black Man's followers; Ahab, having entered into some unspeakable pact with Fedallah, strikes from hell's heart at the whale; Huck resolves to go to hell rather than restore a slave to his rightful owner. The Yankee skipper, the seduced woman, the motherless boy all play the role of Faust in our fiction, sometimes openly and in terror, sometimes secretly and as if it were a joke.

Not only in their major books, but elsewhere, too, our greatest writers sought out gothic themes: Melville most notably in *Pierre,* Hawthorne in *The Marble Faun,* Twain in *Tom Sawyer Detective* and *Pudd'nhead Wilson;* while the tale of terror in a thousand forms, as the story of slavery and black revolt, of Indian warfare, of urban violence, of quiet despair in the world of the freak and the invert and the maimed persists as a reigning genre among minor novelists, too. From Edgar Poe to Truman Capote, from Brockden Brown through George Lippard to Paul Bowles and Carson McCullers, from *The Monster* of Stephen Crane to *The Cannibal* of

John Hawkes, the images of alienation, flight, and abysmal fear possess our fiction. Until the gothic had been discovered, the serious American novel could not begin; and as long as that novel lasts, the gothic cannot die.

But why, one is driven to ask, *why* has the tale of terror so special an appeal to Americans? Surely its success must be derived in part from the failure of love in our fiction. Our novelists, deprived of the subject that sustained Stendhal or Constant, Flaubert or Proust, that seemed indeed to them *the* subject of the novel, turned to fables of loneliness and terror.

Moreover, in the United States, certain special guilts awaited projection in the gothic form. A dream of innocence had sent Europeans across the ocean to build a new society immune to the compounded evil of the past from which no one in Europe could ever feel himself free. But the slaughter of the Indians, who would not yield their lands to the carriers of utopia, and the abominations of the slave trade, in which the black man, rum, and money were inextricably entwined in a knot of guilt, provided new evidence that evil did not remain with the world that had been left behind.

How could one tell where the American dream ended and the Faustian nightmare began; they held in common the hope of breaking through all limits and restraints, of reaching a place of total freedom where one could with impunity deny the Fall, live as if innocence rather than guilt were the birthright of all men. In Huck's blithe assertion, "All right, I'll *go* to Hell," is betrayed a significant undermeaning of the Faustian *amor fati,* at least in its "boyish" American form: the secret belief that damnation is not all it is cracked up to be. In a strange way, the naturalized Faust legend becomes in the United States a way of denying hell in the act of seeming to accept it, of suggesting that it is merely a scary word, a bugaboo, a forbidding description of freedom itself! At any rate, Americans from the beginning responded passionately to the myth itself; even in the 1680's, before the invention of the main tradition of the novel, one Boston bookseller sold in the Colonies sixty-six copies of *The History of the Damnable Life and Deserved Death of Dr. John Faustus.* It was, needless to say, a record unapproached in those times by any other "light literature."

When the gothic novel appeared, then, it was greeted with great enthusiasm by Americans, who passed quite quickly from importing and reading its prototypes to attempting to emulate them. In this case, only ten years elapsed between the publication of the novels of Mrs. Radcliffe and Lewis and the first American gothic romances. Yet the gothic mode proved difficult to adapt to the demands of the American audience and the deeper meanings of American experience, for the generation of Jefferson was pledged to be done with ghosts and shadows, committed to live a life of yea-saying in a sunlit, neo-classical world. From the bourgeois ladies to the Deist intellectuals, the country was united in a disavowal of the "morbid" and the "nasty." No wonder the American pioneer in gothic fiction, despite the acclaim he won abroad, was driven first to abandon the gothic for the sentimental, then to give up novel writing completely.

If it had been only a matter of finding a reading public for the gothic, the situation would not have been really critical—only unprofitable; but there were other problems. The gothic, after all, had been invented to deal with the past and with history from a typically Protestant and enlightened point of view; but what could one do with the form in a country which, however Protestant and enlightened, had (certainly at the end of the eighteenth century!) neither a proper past nor a history? It was easy enough for the American writer to borrow certain elements, both of cast and setting, from the tale of terror; the Maiden in flight, for instance, was readily adaptable, and the hero-villain viable at least as a visual image—his burning eyes and furrowed brow transplanted themselves without difficulty. But what was to be done about the social status of such hero-villains? With what native classes or groups could they be identified? Traditionally aristocrats, monks, servants of the Inquisition, members of secret societies like the Illuminati, how could they be convincingly introduced on the American scene?

Similarly, it was not hard to provide the American equivalents of the moors, hills, and forests through which the bedeviled maidens of the gothic romances were accustomed to flee. But what of the haunted castle, the ruined abbey, the dungeons of the Inquisition? In America, such crumbling piles, architecturally and symbolically so satisfying to the eighteenth-century reader and writer, are more than a little improbable. Yet on them, not only the atmosphere, but an important part of the meaning of the tale of terror depended. An early American gothicist like the I. Mitchell who in 1811 published *The Asylum; or, Alonzo and Melissa* was able to imagine a gothic country house on Long Island; but such a structure in such a place remains not merely unconvincing but meaningless. The haunted castle of the European gothic is an apt symbol for a particular body of attitudes toward the past which was a chief concern of the genre. The counterpart of such a castle fifty miles from New York City has lost all point.

The problem of the gothic romance in this regard is analogous to that of the sentimental novel. Both had arisen out of a need of the bourgeoisie, fighting for cultural autonomy in a class society, to find archetypal characters and situations to embody their conflict with the older ruling classes. Just as the sentimental archetype had projected the struggle of the middle classes with established secular power, portrayed as a menace to their purity, so the gothic projected the struggle of those classes with ecclesiastical authority, portrayed as a threat to their freedom. In America, which possesses neither inherited aristocratic privilege nor an established Church, the anti-aristocratic impulse of the seduction theme is, as we have said, translated into feminism and anti-intellectualism; while the impatience with the past implicit in the gothic fable undergoes an even more complex metamorphosis. Charles Brockden Brown, single-handed and almost unsustained, solved the key problems of adaptation, and though by no means a popular success, determined, through his influence on Poe and Hawthorne, the future of the gothic novel in America.

If Brown deserved no other credit, he should be remembered at least as the inventor of the American writer, for he not only lived that role but turned it into a myth, later developed by almost everyone who wrote about his career. That he tried the impossible and that he failed; that he had disavowed his own art before his untimely death of tuberculosis at the age of thirty-nine; that he hardened from a wild disciple of the Enlightenment, a flagrant Godwinian ("Godwin came and all was light!") into a pious conservative; that he drew his inspiration from loneliness and male companionship, and that he ceased to be a creative writer when he married; that over his whole frantic, doomed career, the blight of melancholy presides. In a sense, Brown invented Edgar Allan Poe —all, that is to say, that the American writer came to seem to the mind of Europe and the sensibility of Romanticism—before Poe had ever written a line. Actually the latter poet was one year old when Brown died.

From the beginning, at any rate, it has been hard to describe Charles Brockden Brown without seeming to compose a poem on a symbolic subject. The portrait painter Sully, who saw him just before his death, has left the following account:

It was in the month of November,—our Indian summer,—when the air is full of smoke. Passing a window one day I was caught by the sight of a man, with remarkable physiognomy, writing at a table in a dark room. The sun shone directly upon his head. I shall never forget it. The dead leaves were falling then. It was Charles Brockden Brown.

If this seems less the product of observation than of Romantic fancy, it is no more fanciful than Brown's own description of himself to his dearest friend, Elihu Hubbard Smith, as "The child of passion and inconstancy, the slave of desires that cannot be justified . . ."; and it is considerably more restrained and faithful to fact than the account of his death, wracked by poverty and disease, imagined half a century later by his fellow Philadelphian and gothic heir, George Lippard. "The Heart Broken" is the title of Lippard's piece, by which he hoped, apparently, to do for Brown what Baudelaire was to do for Poe; but Lippard was unable to preserve the image of Brown as the victim of American philistinism after he had ceased to seem a figure of first literary importance.

To this very day, however, it is hard to rescue the man from the myth, to discover, for instance, even so simple a matter of record (one would assume) as what Brown looked like. According to one standard biography his hair was straight and "black as death," his complexion pale, sallow, and strange, accented by the "melancholy, broken-hearted look of his eyes." Another account describes him as "short and dumpy, with light eyes and hair inclining to be sandy, while the expression on his face reflected ill health rather than intellect. . . . Yet vividly in his countenance glowed the light of benevolence." Which is the truer portrait, the legendary delineation of what he hoped to seem or the more scholarly account with its overtone of debunking? Which is the *real* Charles Brockden Brown, the Brown who proved capable of bringing the American novel to birth?

The established facts of his brief career give some clues to the answer. He was born in Philadelphia in 1771 (the year in which Goethe published *Götz von Berlichingen*), and lived all his life in that city and in New York. He came from Quaker stock, which may have had some influence on his meditative habits, otherwise encouraged by his frail constitution and life-long sickliness. He is reported to have been a prodigy and to have received from the start a schooling worthy of his talents; but he was, despite the

praise that later came to his work, much of it from the best qualified sources, irremediably melancholy. Intellectual energy and
gloom complemented each other in his personality. Though he
never ceased proposing to himself the most ambitious cultural
schemes, he complained (or boasted—the tone is ambiguous) that
he was incapable not only of real happiness but even of the "lively
apprehension of misfortune."

What especially plagued him at the start was a conflict between
the commitment to a career in the law, into which his family had
urged him, and his own literary schemes, which he dreamed would
distinguish both him and his country. At the age of sixteen, for
example, he had already laid out plans for glorifying America (and
Charles Brockden Brown!) with three epics, on Columbus, Pizzaro,
and Cortez. New and radical ideas, derived ultimately from the
Encyclopedists and more directly from Godwin and Mary Wollstonecraft, tilted the balance against his proposed career as a lawyer; and put him into even sharper opposition to the society in
which he lived. To promulgate notions of social justice and to write
novels, to revolutionize American life and to achieve literary fame:
this double ambition he came to feel as a single impulse, not unlike
certain young radical writers in the United States of the 1930's.
The literary form which eminently suited both such political allegiances and such literary aspirations was at the moment he began
to write (the 1790's were almost gone) the "new novel," which is
to say, the gothic romance in its doctrinaire Godwinian form. "To
equal *Caleb Williams*" was the best Brown could hope for himself.

If there was a contradiction between the dream of a rational
Commonwealth and the hectic exploitation of horror in the gothic,
Brown did not feel it. His friend Smith, more consistent advocate
of the Enlightenment, might admonish him, "The man of Truth,
Charles, the pupil of Reason has no mysteries," but Brown could
turn with equanimity from the works of Diderot to *The Horrid
Mysteries* of the Marquis of Grosse. As a writer, he proposed both
to produce books with a "moral tendency" (enlightened, of
course) and to "ravish the souls" of his readers with "roaring passions." The essential human passion to which he hoped to appeal
in his examination of society, as well as by his exploration of terror, was curiosity: that curiosity of the sentimentalizing eighteenth
century, clues to which the Marquis de Sade was convinced he had
discovered in Richardson. "If you tell me," Brockden Brown once
wrote, "that you are one of those who would rather travel into the

mind of a ploughman than the interior of Africa, I confess myself of your way of thinking."

After publishing a dialogue on woman's rights called *Alcuin*— a preliminary concession to his doctrinal commitments—Brown plunged into a feverish bout of creative activity which saw the publication within two years (from September of 1798 to November of 1799) of his four best novels, *Wieland, Ormond, Arthur Mervyn* (Part I), and *Edgar Huntly;* and which left him with the uncompleted fragments of as many more. *Wieland,* which many readers value above all the rest, he completed within a month. This frantic outburst of energy seems to have been cued by two events, one internal, one external: first, his abandonment of the law and his decision to stake everything on his talent as a writer; and second, the death of his friend Elihu Hubbard Smith, who fell victim to yellow fever just as *Wieland* was coming off the press.

Brown had already lived through one epidemic in Philadelphia in 1793, but it was his second experience with the pestilence in the New York epidemic of 1798 that took possession of his imagination. Images of this disaster crept into the pages of *Ormond* and *Arthur Mervyn,* becoming for Brown symbols of all that is monstrous and inexplicable in life. Like Defoe before him and Manzoni and Camus afterward, he found in the plight of the city under a plague an archetypal representation of man's fate. For Brown, moreover, the general calamity was given added poignancy by the death of his friend, who, being a doctor, had not been able to flee its ravages. Despite the fact that he stayed with Smith throughout, actually falling ill himself though not critically, Brown apparently felt guilt as well as dismay at his friend's early death. He may even have suspected (who knows?) that he had infected Smith, carried the principle of infection which destroyed him.

It is possible that the character of Sarsefield, who appears first in *Ormond,* then in *Edgar Huntly,* with no explanation of the duplication, and who represents in each case the protagonist's closest friend, may play in the dreamlike plots of those two books the role of Smith. In *Ormond,* Sarsefield is slain by Turks, and is revenged in the best Achilles-Patroclus fashion by Ormond, who gallops from the field, five bloody heads of his opponents dangling from his saddle. In *Edgar Huntly,* the fantasy becomes even more ambiguously sinister, with Edgar shooting once at Sarsefield, Sarsefield once at him, though they are bound to each other by mutual love and the special bond between protector and protégé.

Brown's first four completed novels, combining as they do the appeals of the gothic and the sentimental, and written with a vigor unprecedented in American fiction, might have been expected to win a substantial audience for their author; but though they were critically well received, they didn't sell. The records show much praise, but no second printings. Partly in despair at not achieving popular success, partly out of a loss of faith in the radical principles which had been his motive force, Brown began to disengage himself from his commitment to fiction. As early as 1799, he had become the editor of a new magazine, and gradually the journalist, the man of letters took over from the poet, the mythopoeic writer. The process passed through two stages: first, a disavowal of the tale of terror, with its melancholy and pursuit of the outrageous; then a total rejection of the novel. The year 1800 saw the completion of the second part of *Arthur Mervyn* and the exhaustion of Brown's first spasm of creative energy. At this point he made a public pledge to abandon "the doleful tone and assume a cheery one," to substitute "moral causes and daily incidents in the place of the prodigious and the singular"—that is, to leave the gothic and take up the domestic sentimental.

But there had already been an undeclared shift in his attitudes between *Wieland* and *Ormond* on the one hand and *Edgar Huntly* and *Arthur Mervyn* on the other. The character of Carwin in *Wieland* (further developed in an unfinished work called *Carwin the Biloquist*) combines, in the style of Goethe, qualities of Don Juan and Faust. Carwin at one point declares to Clara, the suffering heroine of *Wieland* whom he stalks with Lovelace-like single-mindedness through the novel, "Even if I execute my purpose, what injury is done. Your prejudices will call it by that name, but it merits it not." He is the Richardsonian seducer, refusing even to grant that the dishonor which he threatens is real; all his formidable talents, even the mysterious gift of ventriloquism (which Brown calls "biloquism") are devoted to separating Clara from her true lover, maneuvering her into a position where she will have no protection against his assault.

Carwin, however, does not *look* like Don Juan: "His cheeks were pallid and lank, his eyes sunken, his forehead overshadowed by coarse, straggling hairs . . . his chin discoloured by a tetter. . . . And yet his forehead . . . his eyes lustrously black, and possessing, in the midst of haggardness, a radiance inexpressibly serene and potent . . . served to betoken a mind of the highest order. . . ." It is the face, of course, of the gothic hero-villain, of Mrs. Radcliffe's Schedoni or M. G. Lewis' Ambrosio: the ravaged aspect and hypnotic eye of one driven by a Faustian "thirst of knowledge," which was "augmented as it was supplied with gratification." "Curiosity," a Godwinian term, is the name Brown prefers for the Faustian lust to know; and Carwin even pleads in self-defense, after his activities have helped push Wieland, the brother of Clara, over the edge of religious insanity, that his "only crime was curiosity."

On this plea, Brown seems quite willing to acquit his hero-villain of any final guilt; for "curiosity" was his own reigning passion and Carwin is the projection of himself: insatiable seeker and man of many voices. "To excite and baffle curiosity," Brown once wrote about his own purpose as a novelist, "without shocking belief, is the end to be contemplated." In the end, Carwin is permitted to leave the pages of *Wieland* unpunished, though without any rewards—to take up once more his role of Wandering Jew, a tabooed figure incapable of finding rest or love. The true villain of the piece is not the doctrinaire revolutionary, the skeptical Carwin, but the religious fanatic, the believing Christian, Wieland, who ends by murdering his wife and threatening the life of his sister.

Through Wieland, Brown manages to project at once his distrust of religiosity and his obsession with the destructive aspects of the brother-sister relationship. *Geschwisterinzest* is everywhere in our literature (from William Hill Brown to Hawthorne, from Poe to William Faulkner) associated with death; only Brockden Brown, however, is willing to portray it as naked aggression. The tender alliance of brother and sister, so beloved of the Romantics, becomes in his works a brutal conflict; his brothers rob, cheat, and harry their sisters, yet are bound to them so closely that (as in *Edgar Huntly*) each feels his own life and death mysteriously linked to the fate of the other. At the climax of *Wieland,* Clara, threatened with death by her now maniacal brother, seems forced to choose between her own life and his. Brown relents a little, however, managing (through the intervention, this time beneficent, of Carwin) to contrive a resolution in which Wieland, taking up the knife Clara has dropped, stabs himself. The weapon is the sister's, but the hand which wields it the brother's own.

In *Ormond,* to whose sentimental aspects we have alluded earlier, the deed that is only threatened in the earlier book occurs. The Persecuted Maiden strikes back in self-defense; Constantia, Brown's second version of the Clarissa character he first sketched as Clara, kills her attacker, Ormond. Constantia, however, is not the sister of Ormond; and he is, therefore, permitted—the censor taken off guard—to approach her not in madness but in simple lust. Nevertheless, a point is made of Constantia's extraordinary resemblance to the actual sister of Ormond, as if to alert us to the fact that we are being presented with a case of attempted incest and fratricide once removed, though neither of these crimes, of course, could be proved in court.

There is, however, another significance to the murder of Ormond by Constantia, and this meaning Brown establishes with satisfactory clarity. By permitting his new Clarissa (however churchless he makes her out of respect to Godwin or Mary Wollstonecraft) to stab Lovelace-Faust, he symbolically disowns whatever in himself corresponds to the "curiosity," dedication to passion, and contempt for ordinary morality symbolized by the latter figure. After this, neither the Seducer nor the Faustian man is permitted to occupy the center of Brown's fiction; and even the love-combat of brother and sister is pushed to the periphery. He abandoned *Carwin the Biloquist* in mid-course and turned to *Arthur Mervyn* with its new kind of hero.

The yellow fever epidemic determines this unconfessed dividing line in his work: on the one hand, breaking up the group of New York intellectuals of which Smith had been the leading figure; and on the other hand, suggesting a new image for human misery, which cast doubt on man's ability to cope with it successfully. "The evils of pestilence by which this city has lately been afflicted will probably form an era in its history," Brown writes in the preface to *Arthur Mervyn*. "The schemes of reformation and improvement to which they will give birth, or, if no efforts of human wisdom can avail to avert the periodical calamity, the change in manners and population . . . will be, in the highest degree, memorable." The key phrase, of course, is "if no efforts of human wisdom can avail," reflecting the first shadow of the doubt which will eventually black out in the heart of Brown his youthful faith in "schemes of reformation and improvement."

From this point forward, at any rate, Brown's protagonists are dependent boys in search of motherly wives, rather than phallic aggressors in quest of virgins to sully. Victimized by cruel masters, images of the Bad Father, such protagonists wander about the world buffeted and misunderstood, until some understanding female, rich and mature and sexually experienced, provides them a haven. In them, "curiosity" still prevails, but it is no longer the fanatic passion of a Faust to know everything, only the nagging need of an ignorant boy to discover the adult secrets of the locked chamber, the forbidden room, the sealed chest. The Bluebeard myth replaces that of the Satanic bargain; and "curiosity" leads not to selling one's soul to the Devil, but to braving the taboo imposed by a cruel and irrational master. Having peeped through the keyhole at the forbidden mysteries, the curious boy is thenceforth persecuted, not for his guilt, but because of his knowledge of another's.

Finally, however, he is forgiven or rescued and adopted into marriage. So Arthur Mervyn is taken in hand by Mrs. Achsa Fielding ("she is six years older than you . . . she has been a wife and a mother already"), after a final nightmare in which he imagines the dead husband-father arising to shoot him through the heart. "My heart had nothing in it but reverence and admiration," he cries, protesting the innocence of his affection; but some guilt (some buried sense of the incest taboo broken) haunts him all the same. "Was she not the substitute of my lost mama? Would I not have clasped that beloved shade?"

The fact that Arthur Mervyn finally prefers the maternal widow, Mrs. Fielding, to Eliza Hadwin, a girl of fifteen, just the "age of delicate fervor, of inartificial love," infuriated Shelley, who, for all his admiration of Brown, could never forgive him for marrying off his hero to a sedate and wealthy Jewess instead of a poor "peasant-girl." There is, indeed, something symbolic in the choice at which Shelley, granted his point of view, had a right to rebel. For as surely as the death of Ormond had signified Brown's rejection of the demonic, his abandonment of Eliza represented his turning away from a Romantic commitment to art to an acceptance of the responsibilities of bourgeois life.

Clara Howard and *Jane Talbot,* those attempts at creating a sentimental novel without seduction, mark (as we have noticed) an effort at winning the great female audience; but more than that, they are further steps toward silence. In them, even the Bluebeard archetype has been surrendered and with it all desire to titillate curiosity or stir the darker passions. Brown is ready for the final disavowals, the surrender of his remaining liberal views ("From visionary schemes of Utopian systems of government and manners," his first biographer wrote, "Mr. Brown, like many others, became a sober recorder of things as they are") and of his career as an author ("Book-making, as you observe," Brown commented to his brother in 1800, "is the dullest of all trades, and the utmost any American can look for, in his native country, is to be reimbursed his unavoidable expenses").

With this brother and another, he went into the commission-merchant business; and, to set a final seal upon his capitulation, in 1804 married. But failure dogged his business efforts, compelling him at one point to sell "pots and pans over the counter," and tuberculosis brought suffering to his private life. What creative energies he had left, he devoted in these final years to *The Literary Magazine and American Register,* a periodical pledged always to keep in mind that "Christian piety is the highest excellence of human beings" and committed to printing material "free from sensuality and voluptuousness," which, "whether seconded or not by genius and knowledge, will . . . aim at the promotion of public and private virtues." Of his fiction, which came to seem to him as much an error as his early political activity, he wrote in 1803:

> I am far from wishing, however, that my reader should judge of my exertions by my former ones. I have written much, but take much blame to myself . . . and . . . no praise for any thing. I should enjoy a larger share of my own respect, at the present moment, if nothing had ever flowed from my pen, the production of which could be traced to me.

Myth (perhaps acted out by Brown himself as fact) has it that his last attempt at a tragedy he burned, keeping the ashes in a snuff-box on his desk until his death of tuberculosis in 1810.

III

Brown's achievement as a novelist is hard to assess. On only one thing do recent writers who discuss him agree, that his reputation is still moot and that it is somehow important for us now to come to terms with him. Brown remains in an odd way a living writer, because of the polemical tone which a discussion of his work necessarily still assumes. To define his rank and status involves an attempt at redefining the whole tradition of the American novel. Where he is placed depends upon, and in turn determines, the total shape of the literary hierarchy in which he is situated. A conventional "enlightened" attitude toward his work is expressed by

Parrington, who believed that though Brockden Brown was possessed of considerable technical skill, his example was "unfortunate" in so far as it represented an adaptation to American uses of the "blood-pudding school" of England. For Parrington, Brown's most admirable feature was his Godwinian politics, which led him to challenge the belief (held by "gentlemen who profited by social wrong") that injustice was "inherent in human nature"; and to insist that the source of that wrong "be sought in institutions rather than in the nature of man." The early American public, however —or at least so Parrington believed—ignored Brown's social theories in favor of his "gross Romanticism," so that his final influence was chiefly harmful.

More recently, George Snell has argued quite oppositely that although Brown is technically inept (Snell finds *Edgar Huntly,* for instance, "utterly incredible"), he was the founder of the "demonic, macabre, apocalyptic" school, which flourishes throughout the history of our literature and reaches a climax in Faulkner's *Absalom, Absalom!* It is certainly true, at any rate, that Cooper borrowed shamelessly from Brown; that Poe, who profited by his example, apparently esteemed him highly; and that Hawthorne not only placed him in his Hall of Fantasy (along with Homer, Shakespeare, Fielding, and Scott) but more generally observed that "no American writer enjoys a more classic reputation on this side of the water." Among his more eminent admirers who had gone on record by that time were Shelley (who ranked his gothic romances with Schiller's *Robbers* and Goethe's *Faust*), Keats, Hazlitt, and Godwin himself, who had returned Brown's admiration with enthusiasm on his own part. Certainly, it is utterly false to say, with a recent Parringtonian critic, that Brown is "liked only by the Professors who are taken in easily by the 'hollow men' of literature."

The problem is somewhat more complex than that. Those who find it difficult to take Brown seriously are, on the one hand, "realists" and, on the other, "formalists." Brown inevitably seems an incompetent and irrelevant writer to anyone who reads the history of our novel as a melodrama with a happy dénouement in which a virtuous but harried realistic tradition, after resisting the blandishments of fantasy, romance, and allegory, was recognized as the true heir to the patrimony. Brown, however, is an anti-realist in almost all respects, moving his irresolute and inconsistent protagonists through a time and space carelessly defined and bearing only a fitful, largely accidental resemblance to the facts of history or geography.

No more is Brown a formalist. He proves, indeed, especially disappointing to the critic who believes, or pretends to, that the novel is at best a skillful and sophisticated arrangement of words, a pleasantly intricate web of sensibility, which is judged good or bad in terms of how complex and various, though finally unified, is its abstract pattern. Brown is a writer careless to the point of shamelessness. He is likely to introduce a character into the action and let him wander about for pages before telling the reader where he comes from, what he is after, or even what his name is. Brown's resolutions are willful, hasty, often a little absurd, depending on broad coincidences hard to credit. Since he wrote four of his novels (plus the fragments of others) at the same time, he sometimes switches incidents or characters or simply names back and forth among them in a bewildering way. Often he will detach an episode for independent expansion or use elsewhere, leaving quite inexplicable vestiges in the original book. He is especially fond of attaching almost identical incidents to different characters in the same book, or of suggesting confusing resemblances between unrelated people without ever troubling to justify or exploit those deliberately planted resemblances.

The world through which his characters move is given local names (Philadelphia, for instance, or New York or Perth Amboy), but his scenes have little in common with the places they presumably represent. Only when he describes something monstrous and extraordinary like a city under a pestilence, do his descriptions approach the "reality" of the realists. Only when the real world itself, that is to say, comes to seem a symbolic nightmare does it accommodate itself to the sensibility and dreamlike style of Brown. That is why the set-piece of the anthologies, exempted from blame by his severest critics, is the description of the yellow fever epidemic in *Arthur Mervyn*.

For better or worse, then, Brown established in the American novel a tradition of dealing with the exaggerated and the grotesque, not as they are verifiable in any external landscape or sociological observation of manners and men, but as they correspond in quality to our deepest fears and guilts as projected in our dreams or lived through in "extreme situations." Realistic milieu and consistent character alike are dissolved in such projective fictions, giving way to the symbolic landscape and the symbolic action, which are the hallmarks of the mythopoeic novel. Simply to acknowledge the existence and importance of such a tradition is embarrassing to some readers; for it means, on the one hand, a questioning of the sufficiency of realism, which justifies art by correlating it with science; and on the other, it suggests a disturbing relationship between our highest art and such lowbrow forms of horror pornography as the detective story, the pulp thriller, and the Superman comic book, all of which are also heirs of the gothic.

To understand more specifically, however, the role of Brown in the definition of the American novel, it is necessary to look closely at *Edgar Huntly,* the most successful and characteristic of his gothic romances. *Wieland,* usually preferred to it, is convincing only here and there, being the victim of confusions that Brown could not assimilate (as he did those of *Edgar Huntly*) to the meanings of his story. The plot of the latter book can be summarized with relative simplicity, for a book of Brown. Searching for the murderer of Waldegrave, brother of his fiancée, Huntly discovers Clithero Edny who, beneath the elm under which Waldegrave had been murdered, comes at midnight to dig a pit in which he sits and sobs. Clithero is, it turns out, sleepwalking, tormented by various guilts which do *not* include that for the murder of which Huntly has suspected him. Rather he has (back in Ireland) killed the brother of his protector, Mrs. Lorimer, in a misguided effort at preserving her from that brother's irrational malice. Mrs. Lorimer, however, feels that she is doomed by her protégé's act, since she believes her own life tied by mystic bonds to that of her brother, who was her twin. In anguish over her delusion and the guilt which it imputes to him, Clithero goes mad and attempts to kill his mistress, thus helping to spare her the painful anticipation of her end.

Having told this improbable story to Huntly, Clithero disappears into the Pennsylvania wilderness, through which Huntly (prey of curiosity still) attempts to track him down, only to fall prey to somnambulism himself and to wake one day at the bottom of a pit. As Huntly at this stage of the novel has almost blurred into his alter ego Clithero, so the hole dug by the obsessed Irishman has mysteriously become the vast trap in which Huntly finds himself, confronted with a panther, a tomahawk mysteriously close to hand. The panther killed, then eaten raw and his flesh vomited up again (the whole episode comes to seem a rite of initiation which will prepare Huntly for later demands on his manhood), Huntly succeeds in finding a way out. He is led, however, through subterranean passages to a cave in which Indians hold captive a girl—strange to the main action of the story and quite unintegrated into what follows.

Huntly delivers her from the Indians, but is wounded in the struggle and left for dead; he is reborn again, however (surely he is the most often reborn of heroes), and begins a wilderness trek in which he shoots at and is shot at by unrecognized friends. Absolutely alone at last, with even those who love him turned unwitting foes, he nevertheless manages to return to civilization, where he learns that Waldegrave has been murdered by Indians, perhaps the very ones involved in his own adventure. This information when it comes seems utterly anticlimactic, irrelevant to what has become the real theme of the book. More important for the resolution is the further information that Sarsefield, Huntly's own benefactor, had been the first lover of Mrs. Lorimer. They are married, her husband having meanwhile died as well as her brother, who had hated Sarsefield; but Clithero reappears once more, frightening Mrs. Sarsefield into a miscarriage. He flees again and finally drowns himself to avoid being committed as insane, leaving Huntly free to complete their identification by wooing the daughter of Mrs. Lorimer, with whom Clithero had been in love.

It is a charmingly, a maddeningly disorganized book, not so much written as dreamed, but it convinces the reader, once he has been caught up in the fable, of its most utter improbabilities; for its magic is not the hocus-pocus of make-believe, but the irrational reality of the id. "The miracles of poetry, the transitions of enchantment," Edgar Huntly boasts, "are beggarly and mean compared with those I had experienced. Passage into new forms, overleaping the bars of time and space, reversal of the laws of inanimate and intelligent existence had been mine to perform and witness." Yet all these "perils and wonders" Brown has managed to present without invoking specifically supernatural agencies; not a breach of natural law, justifiable in terms of necromancy or sorcery, but only human madness and especially somnambulism, diseases explicable by medical science, lie at the root of the "marvelous" in *Edgar Huntly*.

Brown's novel is an initiation story, the account of a young man who begins by looking for guilt in others and ends finding it in himself; who starts out in search of answers but is finally satisfied with having defined a deeper riddle than those he attempted to solve. "What light has burst upon my knowledge of myself and mankind . . . ," Edgar Huntly cries. "How . . . enormous the transition from uncertainty to knowledge. . . ." But what has he learned really at the close of this odd murder mystery? That the Indians killed his friend is a piece of information which does not thrill the reader and could not have stirred him to so ecstatic a response. It is more general wisdom that Huntly acquires, discovering that "the crime originated in those limitations which nature has imposed on human faculties." This applies not only to the crime of Clithero of which it is specifically said; it is applicable to all human evil. "How little cognizance have men over the actions and motives of each other. How total is our blindness in regard to our own performances." Any man may wake to find himself at the bottom of a pit. *We are all sleepwalkers!*

But if we walk in our sleep, we also run in our dreams. Life is a nightmare through which we pursue or are pursued in a wilderness where the unexpected and the absurd, the irrelevance of what comes before to what comes after are the basic facts of existence. In *Edgar Huntly,* for instance, the boundaries between person and person are abrogated; people are always turning into each other. Clithero raises his hand to kill Mrs. Lorimer and discovers he is really assaulting his beloved, Clarice. Huntly comes upon a total stranger, a sleepwalker, only to find that he is a sleepwalker, too, and to end under the protection of the same foster-mother, engaged to the same sister-bride.

In this world of transformation, not only do unlikes turn into likes, but things themselves become their own opposites. The best motives lead to the worst ends: attempting to protect Mrs. Lorimer, Clithero kills her brother, almost kills her. The dead prove to be alive; Sarsefield, protector of Huntly, and Wiatte, brother of Mrs. Lorimer, "start to life at the same moment"; while Huntly, as we have seen, is himself apparently dead twice, rises twice to life. Friends become enemies, the protector the destroyer; Sarsefield almost kills Edgar even as Edgar tries to kill him. Through such an unstable world one must flee continually from foes known and unknown: from the lunatic and the brother inexplicably dedicated to evil, from the panther and the Indian and the unwittingly hostile friend—finally, from the principle of destruction in the very self. The image of flight with which the gothic began is in *Edgar Huntly* raised to its highest power, revealed as the image of life itself.

Brown, however, seems to have thought of *Edgar Huntly* as performing in the first instance a specifically American task. In a prefatory note, he speaks not only of his resolve to employ for the ends of wonder pathology rather than black magic, "to exhibit a series of adventures . . . connected with one of the most common and wonderful diseases of the human frame," but also of his desire to naturalize gothic terror by presenting it in terms of an action "growing out of the condition of our country." "New springs of action," he insists, "and new motives to curiosity should operate . . . ," since the institutions of our society "differ essentially from Europe." There is a little chauvinism in his plea, a little of the provincial's eagerness to strike a bold cultural pose; but there is also a sense of how unviable (as we have already observed) are the myths and meanings of the European gothic romance in a classless, historyless country. Had some early writer as self-consciously considered the problem of seduction in our literature, the role of love in American fiction might have been far different.

"One merit the writer may at least claim," Brown continues in the preface to *Edgar Huntly,* "that of calling forth the passions and engaging the sympathy of the reader, by means hitherto unemployed by preceding authors. Puerile superstition, and exploded manners; Gothic castles and chimeras, are the materials usually employed for this end. The incidents of Indian hostility,* and the perils of the western wilderness are far more suitable; and, for a native of America to overlook these, would admit of no apology." There is something so natural, so inevitable about Brown's proposed substitutions of American for European symbols that it is hard to appreciate, after the fact, how revolutionary a leap of the imagination his project demanded. The very success of his adaptive devices makes it hard to appreciate them yet testifies to how deeply they responded to our imaginative and mythic needs.

For the corrupt Inquisitor and the lustful nobleman, he has

---

* It is worth noting at this date when the Indian character is making such a spectacular comeback in serious fiction (in such books as Ken Kesey's *One Flew over the Cuckoo's Nest,* for instance) that the archetypal colored man of the American imagination is the redskin. Mythologically speaking, the Negro is a late comer to our literature, who has had to be adapted to the already existing image of the original Noble Savage. Our greatest Negro characters, including Nigger Jim, are, at their most moving moments, red men in blackface.

substituted the Indian, who broods over the perils of Brown's fictional world in an absolute dumbness that intensifies his terror. Brown's aboriginal shadows do not even speak. They merely threaten by their very presence, their "gigantic forms," "huge limbs," and "fantastic ornaments" representing visually the threat they embody. "I never looked upon or called up the image of a savage," Edgar Huntly says, "without shuddering." There is some sense in Brown of the historic "Indian problem," of the appropriation of their lands by white colonists and their futile dreams of revenge; but "Queen Mab," the spokesman for their cause, though prepared for at some length, does not finally appear in the book. It is not the Indian as social victim that appeals to Brown's imagination, but the Indian as projection of natural evil and the id; his red men are therefore treated essentially as animals, living extensions of the threat of the wilderness, like the panthers with whom they are associated.

For the haunted castle and the dungeon, Brown substitutes the haunted forest (in which nothing is what it seems) and the cave, the natural pit or abyss from which man struggles against great odds to emerge. These are ancient, almost instinctive symbols, the *selva oscura* going back to Dante and beyond, while the cave as a metaphor for the mysteries of the human heart is perhaps as old as literature itself. Brown tries quite consciously to identify the pit in which Edgar Huntly awakes with the terrible womb-tomb dungeons of Mrs. Radcliffe and Monk Lewis. "Methought I was the victim," Huntly says at the moment he becomes aware of where he is, "of some tyrant who had thrust me into a dungeon."

It should be noticed that the shift from the ruined castle of the European prototypes to the forest and cave of Brown involves a shift not just in the manner of saying what the author is after. *The change of myth involves a profound change of meaning.* In the American gothic, that is to say, the heathen, unredeemed wilderness and not the decaying monuments of a dying class, nature and not society becomes the symbol of evil. Similarly not the aristocrat but the Indian, not the dandified courtier but the savage colored man is postulated as the embodiment of villainy. Our novel of terror, that is to say (even before its founder has consciously shifted his political allegiances), is well on the way to becoming a Calvinist exposé of natural human corruption rather than an enlightened attack on a debased ruling class or entrenched superstition. The European gothic identified blackness with the super-ego and was therefore revolutionary in its implications; the American gothic (at least as it followed the example of Brown) identified evil with the id and was therefore conservative at its deepest level of implication, whatever the intent of its authors.

In so far, then, as our response to these natural symbols is determined by the native gothic tradition, we are conditioned to regard them, and the life of the unconscious for which they stand, as destructive. There is, however, a counter-tradition, Rousseauistic perhaps in its origins, for which forest, cave, and savage, Nature itself, and the instinctive aspects of the psyche they represent are read as beneficent, taken to symbolize a principle of salvation. The dialogue between these two views has continued, basically unresolved, in American life and art until our own time. But it could not even begin until the attitudes of Rousseau had been translated into an American language of myth and symbol, just as the attitudes of the gothic were so translated by Brown. This second great act of translation was achieved in James Fenimore Cooper's naturalization of the historical romance, to an examination of which we must turn next.

JAMES FENIMORE COOPER

AND

THE HISTORICAL ROMANCE

THE HISTORICAL ROMANCE shares with the gothic a concern with the past and desire to restore to prose fiction "the improbable and marvelous," which the sentimental novel of contemporary life had disavowed. It can be argued, as a matter of fact, that the historical romance is nothing more than a development—more masculine, more "scientific," and more genteel—of the middle-brow or Radcliffean branch of the tale of terror. One gothic sub-tradition, that is to say, is assumed into black Romanticism (which culminates in the *Fleurs du mal*), the other into white (which reaches a climax with Wordsworth's *Prelude*).

Like black or anti-bourgeois Romanticism, the white or philis-tine variety is based on a belief in the superiority of feeling to to intellect, the heart to the head; though for it, the heart is care-fully distinguished from the viscera or the genitals, whose existence is scarcely admitted at all. The white Romantic is as concerned as his more melancholy opposite number with the picturesque and the exotic, with whatever is different from everyday middle-class life; and like him, he seeks in ballad material, fairy tales, and folk epic a source of strength not readily available to the sophis-ticated writer in a complex society. For the white Romantic, however, the primitive remains something clean and heroic, im-mune to the darkness and the demonic; Homer not *Ossian* is his model, and he identifies the Homeric with the cheerful and hope-ful note required in his own work. To him melancholy is treason, the true faith an acceptance of the universe, which he confuses a little with the bourgeois culture of his own time. If he has any reservations about the world he lives in, they lead him toward nostalgia rather than rebellion.

White Romanticism is, then, closely related to the genteel Sentimentalism we have already had occasion to notice. Both, certainly, have a peculiar affinity for the middle-class, Anglo-Saxon mind, and both reject tragedy and sexual passion. The historical romance is, therefore, not merely a "male" counterpart to the Richardsonian ladies' novel, it is also a predestined best-seller; and, indeed, its most eminent producers were, like the "female scribblers" with whom they competed, merchant-authors, no less sensitive to the demands of the market-place than to those of art. For their mass audience, these entrepreneurs of fiction preserved such popular aspects of the gothic romance as the harried heroine and the motif of flight, sensing that Europe was not yet ready (if it ever would be) to let the Persecuted Maiden come to rest. In Scott, not only does she run still but the hero runs, too: side by side with his beloved, or toward her, or away—it scarcely matters, so long as they are both in motion. Indeed, one of Scott's favorite names for the novelist is the "master of motion."

Flight in the historical novel is, however, no longer archetypal in its implications. Hero and heroine flee not projections of their feared inner selves but real enemies, genuine conspiracies, external dangers. Action itself becomes the end, the evasion of ennui sought through a constant change of tempo and place. Though certain landscapes of the white Romantic fictionists come to have symbolic overtones, they are chiefly prized as examples of hitherto unexploited settings, glimpses of the unknown. Vicarious tourism draws the reader on, as he pursues the breathless hero to the mountain fastnesses of Scotland or the shores of Lake Otsego, to which in a little while he will come in person, guidebook in hand. The historical Romance (and its companion form, the Romantic narrative poem as practiced by Byron) represents the sight-seeing of the middle classes before cheap and speedy transportation had made it possible for them to do it in the flesh. The devotees of the genre are, unlike Brockden Brown's ideal reader, more interested in penetrating the interior of Africa than that of a ploughman's mind. It is precisely Africa they want, mapped, documented, and in detail; and it is Africa they get.

The Cook's tour of the historical romance extends, moreover, not only through space but time. Even as such fiction discovers

geography for the middlebrow imagination, it discovers history—
real history as distinguished from legend or myth. The gothicists
had plunged already into the "dark backward and abysm of time,"
but the haunted castle was a work of the imagination, not archae-
ology, and its inhabitants truer to the memories of nightmare than
to the findings of anthropology. The writers of the historical
romance, however, were pledged "to represent, by means of an
invented action, the state of mankind in a past, historic epoch"
(the definition is Manzoni's); and they felt more and more the
need to shore up their vision of how life had been at a certain moment with documents, statistics, and quotations out of the record.
That is why the novels of both Manzoni and Scott are eked out
with appendices that contain the raw fruits of their research, testi-
monies to their skill as historians and to the 'truth" which underlies
their fictions.

It is a thoroughly absurd idea, the notion that the truth of a
work of art is capable of documentary proof; and it becomes eventually an excuse for throwing overboard the elementary principles
of inner consistency, psychological conviction, and faithfulness to
the quality of experience, upon which the authority of a novel
really depends. Yet it was Scott himself who set all the West on
this false scent, being, for all his Romantic commitments, enough
the bourgeois of his time to believe in "positive science" and "positive truth." If we read him still, it is because he created a myth of
the past which cannot (whether we respond to it still with enthusiasm or not) ever die; but he prided himself on being the exponent
of a science of the past, naively convinced that it was his understanding of an earlier epoch that was immortal.

The myth of the past of which Scott is the master builder is
quite different from that created by the tale of terror, for the latter
is sentimentally radical, the former nostalgically conservative. The
young Charles Brockden Brown takes off from Diderot and the
assumptions of the Age of Reason, the middle-aged Sir Walter
Scott leads into the Oxford Movement and the revival of Catholicism. Cardinal Newman thought so, at least, observing that Scott
had served "by his words, in prose and verse, to prepare men for
some closer and more practical approximation to Catholic truth."
It would have surprised Scott (certainly a good Protestant in his
own eyes) to realize that his glorification of the past, his flirtation
with medievalism, his celebration of a glamour which had passed
away—commercially viable attitudes, all of them—could develop

into ideological forces leading to dramatic apostasies and strange conversions. He seemed sometimes merely to play at his own conservatism, acting the Jacobite much as Fenimore Cooper did the Tory—in part, because he was sure nothing could really come of it; and he found the safest of thrills in pledging allegiance to a cause securely lost! The historical romance is by definition not serious; indeed, the unconscious longing of the gothic romancers for the past they consciously vilify is a more genuine tribute than the *Ivanhoe* kind of pageant celebration.

Scott would not, of course, have wanted to leave Abbotsford for a medieval castle or a Highland hide-away, any more than Cooper would have wanted to abandon his Westchester County home or his Paris hotel for a wigwam; they felt free to create fantasies of flight from civilized comfort to primitive simplicity because they were sure that no one would believe them any more than they believed themselves. That is one advantage of being a businessman writing for other businessmen and their wives. They did not, however, defend their falsifications of the past in such frank terms; Cooper, for instance, was accustomed to present his own versions of the *beau idéal* of frontier life as if they were history; and only when driven to the wall would he admit the legendary quality (he preferred to think of it as "idealization") of his books. The super-myth of the theoretically anti-mythic historical romance is that its myth is History.

The early historical romance represents, in general, the tribute that philistinism pays to the instinctive, the civilized to the "natural," the moderate to the outrageous; for the past which it celebrates is characterized not only by its distance in time but by its presumable freedom from restraint and prudence, its absurd commitment to honor and courage. The "heroism" of the heroic age celebrated by the historical romances turns out to mean nothing more than the sum total of its differences from settled bourgeois life in the second and third decades of the nineteenth century.

Rob Roy or Natty Bumppo, Robin Hood or Chingachgook project the bourgeois's own slight margin of resentment against the safe, commercial way of life he has desired, and for which, indeed, he would fight. The white Romantic's outlaw or Indian is neither a demonic nor a disturbing figure by the time he has been naturalized in popular literature, though his prototype, appearing on the outskirts of the city, would have been hunted down by posse or police. Such tame Outsiders represent the impulsive and the irrational only as a passing temptation (appealing chiefly to unsettled youth) not as a profound threat; and when the historical romancer follows his creations into the wildwood, everyone knows that he is only kidding; that he is, in fact, sitting in a warm, well-furnished study, worrying—between bouts of composition—about his copyrights or income tax.

The Faust of the gothicists can find no place in such anti-demonic fables, with their reluctance to face the ambiguous or the problematic. Robin Hood or Daniel Boone move into the mythic center; the unsophisticated rebel-victim or half-civilized refugee from society. The historical romance permits no hero-villains. The hero is the man who receives the rewards (comes into the inheritance, marries the girl he loves, wins the approval of the reader); and the man who receives the rewards is the hero—life is as simple as that. The villain, conversely, is the one who is baffled and exposed, frustrated in his schemes and revealed as devoid of honor, finally rejected by the reader. He may even be a seducer, if his actual crime is delicately enough suggested, and if his victim is a lower-class girl. Even Scott, his reputation already established, was forced to expurgate an upper-class seduction from *St. Ronan's Well.*

The essential fable of the historical romance (more stereotype, perhaps, then archetype) ritually assures its readers of the triumph of good over evil—and to make this point with sufficient clarity, there can be no confusion between virtue and vice. Initially confused about his own ambitions or the true identity and character of those who surround him, often himself maligned and misrepresented, the hero is forced to flee—usually into the midst of some famous historic conflict just then conveniently approaching its climax. The heroine meanwhile has been abducted or is off on some private evasion of her own, for reasons only revealed in the final pages. The two are kept apart as long as possible, but are finally joined by the intervention of either some noble figure out of history or some notorious outlaw fresh from the greenwood (if possible, of both). By the same agency, their problems are resolved, their enemies discomfited, all confusions cleared up. The good is revealed as good—and triumphant; the evil as evil—and defeated. There is no suggestion that good and evil may be bound to each other by any link but chance, or that the confusions of life may be rooted in moral ambiguity rather than in temporary ignorance or deliberate deceit.

The historical novelists provide many satisfactions and delights:

comedy and intrigue, adventure and conflict and suspense. At their best, they are masters of pace, compelling the reader's breathless commitment to the unfolding of an action, and masters of illusion, convincing the reader that it terribly matters whether a ninny of a boy and a pale shadow of a girl end up in each other's arms. They are skilled at the evocation of a scene, especially in a natural setting, and at transition from scene to scene; they can even make plausible the development of less complicated varieties of hatred and love. But they are powerless to suggest the complexities of human motivation, the discrepancy between will and action, the immense possibilities of self-deceit, the "mystery of iniquity." The novel moved toward the nineteenth century as the potential heir to the tragic view of life, with which the stage seemed no longer able to come to terms; but the historical romance refused to fulfill the obligation that possibility imposed; it had no means for confessing that the tragic is real.

Twice in the history of the English novel, tragic prototypes had appeared, and twice they had been rejected, before the second decade of the nineteenth century was over. The example of *Clarissa* proved viable only on the continent; in England itself, it was, as we have seen, debased and bowdlerized by the genteel female novelists, who, with uncanny precision, initiated everything in it that was false or readily falsified. The gothic strain, which in America had fed the fancy of C. B. Brown and was to inspire Poe, and which in Germany had become an essential ingredient of the First Part of *Faust,* progressed in England no further than the extravagances of *The Monk*. The tragic elements of the Faustian theme, implicit from the first, remained undeveloped or travestied, until they were utterly rejected by the genteel male novelists who founded the historical romance. These founding fathers turned back, not inappropriately, to the example of Fielding, who had at the very start of the bourgeois novel provided (first in *Joseph Andrews,* then more spectacularly in *Tom Jones*) an anti-tragic alternative to Richardsonianism.

Fielding's example cues first of all a literature of masculine protest, an attempt to rescue prose fiction from the bourgeois ladies, who were in fact Richardson's chief, though by no means only, readers. For the heroine, Fielding proposed to substitute the hero; for the boudoir, the out-of-doors; for an obsessive concern with seduction and marriage, a more varied interest in social relations of all kinds; for what he took to be Richardson's hypocritical prurience, an easy tolerance of promiscuity and a general candor in dealing with sex. Fielding, however, went further than this, identifying as feminine—and therefore to be avoided—not only conventional Christian piety, but sensibility itself, and, indeed, any analytic concern with the "heart." The fear of not seeming manly enough haunts him everywhere, inhibiting reflection and delicacy and subtlety alike; and leading to that exaggerated heartiness, bluffness, and downright crudity of manner, required in a society where the male has continually to prove that he is one of the boys.

The conventional womanly tearfulness of the sentimental novel Fielding did not clearly distinguish from its underlying tragic view of existence, rejecting both in favor of a presumably more masculine comic view of life. His comedy depends upon a fundamental assumption that goodheartedness—a quality apparently to be found almost universally in personable, wild young men—will prove a sufficient defense against malice and misfortune; and that there is a principle of simple justice at work in the world. "Comic epic" is the term Fielding himself preferred for his work; and by "epic" he apparently intended to suggest both the rich, rolling expansiveness of his fictional world, and his narrative method, which (allowing for auctorical asides) aims rather at spinning a yarn than analyzing motives. Fielding's method is in fact more dramatic than epic, as befits one who began as a dramatist, and Shakespeare is his model rather than Homer; though his, it must be understood, was a far different "Shakespeare" from the one we have inherited from the later Romantics.

Through the later eighteenth and earlier nineteenth centuries, the illusion of the pseudo-Shakespearean novel lured on writers and critics alike, the name of Shakespeare being rather promiscuously bestowed on novelists of varying abilities and types. With the coming of Scott, however, the title was bestowed, as it were, finally; and the other contenders retired from the field. But what did the title *mean*? There were, to be sure, certain attributes of Shakespearean drama directly translated into the novel of masculine protest: the sense of swarming life, for instance, and the broad social range of the dramatis personae, with characters high and low carefully distinguished by levels of speech; and in these respects Scott was Shakespearean above all the rest. But essentially the word "Shakespeare" was used as an honorific to make popular writers seem of more than current interest, to redeem the best-seller for literature. It described especially the writer who was "healthy," which is to say, unaware of or unwilling to admit the importance of the problematical and the demonic.

Broad bawdry, turbulent action, horseplay and honest male sentiment—these come to be the hallmarks of pseudo-Shakespearean art. That these characteristics inadequately represent the Shakespeare we think we read is beside the point; they are the essential characteristics of the Anglo-Saxon, male middlebrow—and Shakespeare is the one artist about whom he considers it manly to have no doubts.

The pseudo-Shakespearean novel is, however, not merely middlebrow; it is also theatrical. An age which, for a while, had to content itself with reading plays, was tempted into writing fiction as if it were stage drama for closet reading, into shifting the center of interest from character to plot, from analysis to action. The limitations of inwardness imposed by the conventions of the stage, against which the greatest dramatists have always struggled, were welcomed by the exponents of anti-sensibility as a principle of the novel. Those larger-than-life gestures, so necessary in the theater, where the distance between spectator and actor cannot be varied or controlled, were transplanted into prose fiction. More specifically, New Comedy in its late domestic, sentimental form became the model for the structure of the novel. The rigid, theatrical plot, with its clearly marked reversals and recognitions, imposed on prose narrative its mechanical patterns; the revelation (of true parentage, of innocence or guilt, of concealed identity) with its attendant moment of surprise and relaxed tension, came to be thought of as the point of the novel—which had, at this point, utterly forgotten its torch-carrying function.

But the New-Comic love affair replaced the love-combat between seducer and virgin, hero-villain and terrified fugitive. Henceforward love in middle-class fiction would mean almost exclusively the adventure of a featureless juvenile and ingenue, separated by purely external circumstances and united at the close to no one's real surprise; and from Scott through Dickens, even the most serious British novelists found themselves absurdly committed to investing scores of pages, thousands of words in a theme which might have little to do with their essential plots or their own views of life. This tribute paid, however, they were granted a surprising degree of freedom in the remainder of their books, providing always that nothing elsewhere cancelled out the possibility of the final embrace or cast doubt on its importance in the eternal scheme of things.

The pseudo-Shakespearean novel had from the first inhibited inwardness and tragedy; but at the moment that it was bred with the Romantic myth of the past to produce the historical romance, it was further expurgated. Gentility had spread insidiously from the female audience to the male, forbidding, on the one hand, the candor and sexual horseplay of Fielding, and, on the other, the horror-pornography of the tale of terror. The historical romance is the "cleanest" of all sub-genres of the novel thus far, the creation of a self-conscious attempt to redeem fiction at once for respectability and masculinity. The acclaim which greeted Scott is surely due in part to a sense in the bourgeois community that the novel in his hands at long last had become fully acceptable, not merely "pure" but patriotic, too. Opening Scott's last volume, one could look forward to communing with a "healthy" soul engaged in an examination of the historic past which had helped determine contemporary society, and finding in it heroic and eccentric types able to make one glad to be alive.

II

Though attempts to write fiction based on historic events and involving historic characters had been made well before the beginning of the nineteenth century, the historical romance as we have defined it is the invention of one man, Sir Walter Scott; and the genre did not exist until the appearance of his *Waverley* in 1814. Before he became a novelist, Scott had collaborated in the publication of a collection of Border ballads, *The Minstrelsy of the Scottish Border,* and had written poems of his own, derived in theme and manner from those ballads. Some of them were included in the *Minstrelsy* itself; and it is hard, indeed, to tell where his editorial reconstructions end and his own pieces begin. Scott started his career as a writer by adapting, almost counterfeiting the folk literature of an earlier age—out of motives both antiquarian and patriotic, motives which persist into his later fiction and help give it its typical form.

Cues for such a nationalist, historical approach to literature, Scott had found earlier in the work of German poets like Bürger, whose "Lenore" he had translated, and Goethe, whose *Götz von Berlichingen* he had also put into English. In German *Sturm und Drang,* he had come upon the exploitation of terror as well as the mystique of the folk and the quest for a native tradition; and to such terror he had pledged himself as a young man, decorating his room with a skull and striking all the proper gothic poses. His interest in German culture had led to a meeting with "Monk" Lewis, to whose *Tales of Wonder* he contributed some of his early verse. The titles of the two anthologies to which the young Scott entrusted his first work mark the double inspiration with which he began: the evocation of wonder and the revival of minstrelsy. Had he become a novelist at this stage, he might have been a full-blown gothic romancer.

Indeed, he appends to *Waverley* two fragmentary ventures into prose fiction, the first of which is the Walpoleian *Thomas the Rhymer,* and the second *The Lord of Ennerdale,* a novel in the manner of Mrs. Radcliffe. In the General Preface to the *Waverley Novels,* Scott describes his first attempt: "I had nourished the ambitious desire of composing a tale of chivalry, which was to be in the style of the Castle of Otranto, with plenty of Border characters, and supernatural incident." But that "ambitious desire" had remained unfulfilled for fifteen years; and the book, which might have been published in the same year as *Edgar Huntly,* managed to see the light as a "curious" fragment, representing outlived aspirations, thirteen years after Brockden Brown had given up fiction and four years after his death. It must be remembered that Scott began as a middle-aged novelist; born in the same year as Brown, he did not publish his first romance until he was forty-three!

Not only Scott but the world he lived in had lost its youthful fire in the years between the French Revolution and the rise and fall of Napoleon; both he and it were ready for the voice of moderation, weary of shrillness and horror. Yet Scott never surrendered completely his own taste for the gothic; he acted as the literary sponsor of Maturin, perhaps the most talented of all purely gothic authors in England, and defended *Frankenstein* against other bourgeois critics. In only two of his novels does Scott manage to dispense with the supernatural, disavowing the use of all portents, ghosts, witches, and prophecies; and so self-conscious is he about the gesture, that he goes out of his way to boast of eschewing "the mystic, and the magical." "The mystic, and the magical" an audience brought up on the tale of terror demanded, and Scott strove to please, without permitting the gothic to dominate his plots or cast its dismal pall over the "healthy" vigor of which he was proud.

The trappings of the gothic seemed to him part of the popular author's stock in trade; the meanings of the gothic were alien to him.

Only once did Scott produce a book of sheer terror, an essentially gothic tale in which love and death are blended to produce the authentic sadist shudder; but this novel was rather the creation of his illness than of his will. In such pain from a gallstone attack that he could not even write, Scott dictated *The Bride of Lammermoor,* a novel of which he later remarked that "he did not recollect a single incident, character or conversation." After he had, with some trepidation, read it through, he found it "monstrous, gross and grotesque," but (fortunately, he thought) comical, too. "Still the worst of it," he commented, "made me laugh, and I trusted the good-natured public would not be less indulgent." To take horror too seriously, he felt, was to confuse life with delirium, to become like Coleridge too murky and opaque, or like C. B. Brown unhealthy. Scott did, indeed, believe Brown to have possessed "wonderful powers," but to have wasted them on the gothic mode, which was old-fashioned and not even "wholesome."

Scott's fundamental conception of the function of the novel was too modest to sustain the Faustian pose; his one "hell-fired" book he, quite unlike Hawthorne, regarded not as a triumph but as a mistake. That the novel might "instruct the youthful mind" or even "sometimes awaken the better feelings and sympathies," he was prepared to grant; but basically he thought fiction "a mere elegance, a luxury contrived for the amusement of polished life." The novelist was for him not prophet or oracle or teacher, only an elegant entertainer, a puppet master; and the outcome of the plots he contrived had nothing finally to do with the values by which men lived: "whether the Devil flies away with Punch, or Punch strangles the Devil, forms no real argument as to the comparative power of either one or the other, but only indicates the especial pleasure of the master of motion."

The real point is that Scott was an amateur, a novelist not because this seemed an important vocation, but because authorship was one of the things that befell him in a busy life, and because by it he had won fame and even wealth. The writing of fiction, which he first attempted before the turn of the century, he put aside until 1805, when he made a start on the book that was finally to appear as *Waverley.* But this romance of 1745 he decided, on the advice of a friend, to leave incomplete, like his earlier efforts. He was unwilling, he tells us, to risk the reputation he had built up as a poet (particularly for *The Lady of the Lake*) by throwing on the market an untried commodity bearing the name of the old firm. One day, however, searching for some fishing tackle, Scott found his abandoned manuscript among the lines and flies! The year was 1814 and his poetry beginning to run a poor second to Byron's, so that the discovery seemed to him a sign, an indication of a new way to woo his old audience. For a while he continued to produce both verse and prose until the failure of "The Lord of the Isles" convinced him that his poetry was no longer commercially viable. "Well, well, James . . . ," he told his publisher, "since one line has failed, we must stick to something else."

From that point on, he was a novelist, though for a long time only by way of an avocation. Quite as importantly in his own eyes, he was a lawyer, sheriff, sportsman, and antiquarian, and most importantly of all, the Laird of Abbotsford. Only financial disaster made him a writer of novels before all else, driving him to produce between his forty-third and sixty-first years more than twenty-five books. He wrote at immense speed and under the terrible pressure of a need to owe no one anything, until his body buckled under the strain; yet he earned in some quarters more contempt than pity. "Wretched trash," Coleridge wrote in 1827 of the books Scott had been publishing just before that year, and added coldly that Scott's collapse was the proper reward for an "attempt to unite the Poet and the Worldling."

Certainly, there is more than a little truth in the final charge. Into Scott's work went not only the lawyer's respect for institutions and precedents, but also the entrepreneur's view of business as the high chivalry of the modern world; while his view of himself as an amateur did not preclude him from making money out of his books, but only from taking himself seriously as an artist. And though the personal bitterness of a Coleridge (who thought of Scott as his literary heir turned philistine) now seems irrelevant, his more general view still prevails among some critics; E. M. Forster, for instance, after telling us that Scott has "neither artistic detachment nor passion" ("he only has a temperate heart and gentlemanly feelings, and an intelligent affection for the countryside"), goes on to say: "And his integrity—that is worse than nothing, for it was a purely moral and commercial integrity . . . he never dreamt that another sort of loyalty exists."

Yet it is not fair to say merely that Scott is the creator of the male middlebrow audience and of the "healthy" best-seller; for besides a "temperate heart," "gentlemanly feeling," etc., he possesses mythopoeic powers to an extraordinary degree. It is hard—and a little discomfiting—for critics to remember that the novel may function on the level of myth as well as that of literature. As an artist, Scott is deficient in moral intelligence, clumsy in style, inadequate in characterization (except for the flat "clown," who passes from Shakespeare through him to the contemporary stage), untidy in form; as a maker of legends, however, he possesses authenticity and greatness. It is this nonliterary greatness which enabled him to stir the imagination of Europe and make the past of Scotland seem the mythic past of a whole continent. There is something a little absurd about Italian sopranos and tenors shrilling romantic phrases at each other in the cardboard Highlands of *Lucia di Lammermoor;* and the Russian court ladies who came draped in tartans on a pilgrimage to Abbotsford are ridiculous enough. Nevertheless both anomalies represent the awareness of half the world that Scott's genteel projections of lost causes and lapsed allegiances along the Border respond to a psychic need felt in Italy and Russia as well as in the British Isles.

The classic formulation of Scott's white Romantic myth is to be found in *Rob Roy,* whose seeds are already in *Waverley.* In his introductory note to the latter book, Scott tells us that it was the product of improvisation, a romance which had largely written itself:

> The whole adventures of Waverley, in his movements up and down the country with the highland cateran Bean Lean, are managed without skill. It suited me best, however, the road I wanted to travel, and permitted me to introduce some description of scenery and manners. . . .

Though couched as an apology, this is actually a summary of the essential archetypes of the Scott plot. The "movements up and down the country" represent the motif of flight and pursuit; the "scenery" stands for the mythicized Highland landscape; and the "highland cateran Bean Lean" is typical of those id-figures who emerge from the primitive wilderness and project the irresponsible yearnings of Scott's finally responsible protagonists. Even more important in *Waverley,* though not mentioned here, is the more beneficent spokesman for life outside the law, Fergus McIvor. Waverley himself typifies those young men whom Scott, in a review of his own work, called "amiable and very insipid," one of whom in each of his books represents the author and his ideal reader. The true heart of the adventures of such a young man, which is what most of Scott's fables boil down to, is not the love interest (in *Waverley* the choice between those symbolic posies, the wild Flora and the domesticated Rose) but the *road* which leads across the Border from England to the Lowlands and the Highlands, winding back and forth through space and time between "a civilized age and country" and one more "favourable for romance."

In *Rob Roy,* Scott is more than usually conscious of this purpose, and for that reason calls his book for once (he informs us at the suggestion of his publisher) by the name of the Highland character who embodies the theme of cultural contrast on which he trades. "It is this strong contrast," he writes in an introduction, "betwixt the civilized and cultivated mode of life on one side of the Highland line, and the wild and lawless adventures which were habitually undertaken and achieved by one who dwelt on the opposite side of that ideal boundary, which creates the interest attached to his name." Scott's sentence is neither elegant nor entirely lucid, but it makes its main point, defining symbolically "the Highland line," "that ideal boundary," across which a young man, this time English and called Frank Osbaldistone, shuttles in search of himself, and indicating why the title of the book is the name of a character whose affairs occupy so small a proportion of its total bulk.

Scott is somehow aware that the nominal themes of the book do not represent its deepest source of appeal. The question of whether Frank will save his father's threatened business, outwit the villain Rashleigh and marry Diana Vernon are mere *plot* concerns, as conclusively foregone as the outcome of the events of 1715, which provide the historical background for the action. What is really at stake throughout is the question of where the final allegiance of Frank will go: to his father (whose point of view is seconded by "the Bailie") or to Rob Roy. In the Bailie and Rob are projected the two paternal images which divided the soul of the Scottish author proud of his double descent: from the lowlander, the prudent, middle-class merchant, pledged to profits, security, Protestantism, and the English King; and from the wild Highland brigand, dedicated to honor, mad adventure, Catholicism, and the Jacobite cause. On an even deeper level, they represent the principles of obedience and subversion, the controlled life of the super-ego and the impulsive life of the id. The darker aspects of the latter way of life are projected by the villain Rashleigh, stock Seducer and gothic persecutor, who possesses all the characteristics of Rob Roy (he, too, is a Jacobite, an enemy of the state, a disturber of the peace) except honor; and they are displayed in harsher colors, too, in Helen McGregor, wife of Rob, a black Hecate figure, blood-stained, fanatic, and immune to mercy.

Whatever these two represent in its demonic form, Rob embodies in all its allure; he is the very spirit of risk and of the wilderness which he inhabits, a natural man and embodiment of the romantic North. He is a thoroughly mythical character (for all of Scott's attempts to prove his historical truth through most of an introduction, five appendices and a "Post-script"), linked backward through his name, with its overtone of despoiling the king, to Robin Hood and Robin Goodfellow—those greenwood gods of the folk. Both analogies were surely in Scott's mind, for he mentions the former semi-mythic character by name, attributing the fame of Rob Roy to his having played "such pranks in the beginning of the 18th century, as are usually ascribed to Robin Hood. . . ." And the word "pranks" seems more reminiscent of Robin Goodfellow himself than of the quasi-historical namesake. Rob Roy is not merely on another side from Frank Osbaldistone's father; he is in another world, belongs to another race. Scott describes him as possessing the "wild virtues . . . and unrestrained license of an American Indian," and characterizes his ideas of morality as "those of an Arab chief. . . ."

Rob Roy is more than a greenwood spirit and Noble Savage, however; he is in a real sense the Muse of young Frank, the embodiment in life of all that the Romantic writer seeks in art. At one place in *Rob Roy,* Scott makes the point that there is a "natural taste" which belongs to mountaineers, and that Highlanders in particular possess feelings "allied with the romantic and poetical." Frank was at twenty (he tells his own story backward in the novel, from the viewpoint of a successful middle-aged man) convinced that he was a poet, impatient with everything except "literature and manly exercises." From the lofty vantage of his art, he especially looked down on business. The sense in which the businessman could be understood as an "ambitious conqueror," or in which "he resembled a sailor whose confidence rises on the eve of tempest or battle" Frank could not then perceive. No more could

he understand his father's (and Scott's) belief that commerce con-
nects "nation with nation, relieves the wants, and contributes to
the wealth of all."

To that father, who felt obliged to despise poets not only as a
businessman but also as a member of a dissenting sect, Frank
seemed merely to insist on idling away his life like a boy when he
should have been earning a living like a man. Scott stacks the
cards against poor Frank and against the cause of art as well by
attributing to Frank an absurd poem and an incompetent translation of *Orlando Furioso*. The latter effort, merely mentioned in
Chapter II at the point of Frank's break with his father, is actually
read aloud to Diana Vernon in Chapter XVI, at the climax of the
action. Far from greeting it with sympathy or praise, Diana makes
it the occasion for a tirade against Frank for wasting his time on
verse when he should be concerned with his father's property as
well as his and hers. Turning on him in the name of mercantile
and bourgeois notions of morality, she is, ironically enough, described by Scott as "resembling one of those heroines of the age
of chivalry."

Over and over again the blunt, philistine point is hammered
home: not poetry but business is the end of life and, indeed, the
chivalry of the modern world. Frank, however, learns this dispirit-
ing lesson almost too late for it to be of any use, having first left
his father's home and counting house in pride and obduracy. "But
it was too late . . . and Heaven had decreed that my sin should be
my punishment, though not to the extent which my transgression
merited." From this point on, he is plunged into a series of adventures which threaten to bring ruin to the family firm, poverty and
even death to him; but the original sin, it should be noted, the first
Fall of the bourgeois-Protestant world is *the refusal to go into the
father's business*. Not even for so dire a transgression, however,
does Scott permit the truly tragic to enter his fictional world. Frank
escapes (sinner though he is) the devious plots of the enemies of
his father and his kind, largely through the aid of Rob Roy, the
Highland rebel who loves him as a son yet must yield him up at
the end to Lowland prudence and accommodation.

The demands of the happy ending require that Frank be recon-
ciled with his father and give up both poetry and Rob Roy, who
is last seen "astride a rock with his long gun, waving tartans, and
the single plume in his cap." But the same exigencies also require
that in return for Frank's sacrifice of his "inclinations" to the

needs of the firm, old Mr. Osbaldistone permit him to marry Diana
Vernon, a Roman Catholic and daughter of a leading Jacobite.
Diana is, indeed, an alter ego of Rob himself, another spirit of the
wildwood, whose first appearance is as a huntress (like the goddess
whom her name recalls), riding a jet-black horse, her own jet-
black hair streaming in the wind. "Wild gaiety" and "romance" are
the association she evokes in the mind of Frank; while for Andrew
Fairservice, comic version of the dissenting Lowland viewpoint, she
is the essence of paganism itself: "a daft queen they ca' Diana
Vernon (weel I wot they might ca' her Diana of the Ephesians,
for she's little better than a heathen—better? she's waur. . . .)"

Yet she is not the Great Dark Goddess she seems, only the Good
Bad Girl, that stock character of popular fiction, who despite
appearances and circumstances, proves virtuous in the end. Did
she not dissuade Frank from the pursuit of poetry, sending him
back to protect his father's interests? Everyone is permitted to have
his cake and eat it, too, in the imaginary world of Scott. Symbolic
figures representing irreconcilable allegiances seal their parting with
a kiss, the Bailie and the outlaw (kinsmen, of course) embracing
each other and promising mutual service, each in his kind. Frank
has had to give up the art of literature, though he married an embodiment of the "romantic." But Scott can practice the art his hero
surrenders, for he knows how to make it not the rival but the co-
adjutor of commerce. Thus his readers are permitted at one and
the some time to despise literature and to enjoy a novel, aware
that it is "a mere elegance, a luxury contrived for the amusement
of polished life."

In terms of the fable itself, Rob Roy, surrogate for the primitive
and the poetical, has been dismissed to his Highland fastness, left
to eke out his remaining days in a struggle for a lost cause, and to
be no more a protector and a guide but only a bitter-sweet memory. It is his own youth which the bourgeois artist is dismissing,
though he confuses it with the youth of his society. Yet finally the
name of Rob Roy names the book and sells it ("the germ of popularity," Scott calls his title); and he is invoked in its final words:
"Old Andrew Fairservice used to say, that 'There were many
things ower bad for blessing, and ower gude for banning, like ROB
ROY.' " It is the final tribute of the white Romantic to the world of
untamed nature and the id, which he can bring himself neither to
live by nor disown; and the Rob Roy-Robin Hood archetype projects this ambivalence. The bourgeois world could not afford to let

so apt a symbol of its divided heart die out of the literature while that division lived on; and in America in particular it throve especially, both in the form Scott gave it and in the adaptation of James Fenimore Cooper.

III

Cooper is eminent among the followers of Scott; only Manzoni rivals him, and Manzoni was limited by the fact that the sole Noble Savages of his world were peasants. But Cooper was in a favorable position for taking up the master's suggestion that Robin Hood and the Indian are one; and he ended by creating a middlebrow image of the primitive as heroic which displaced even the Highlander in the mind of the West. Cooper's red men had an initial advantage in their dusky skins, for in the dreams of Caucasians forbidden impulses are typically projected in dark-skinned figures. Moreover, his primitives resemble more closely than the wild clansmen of Scott the version of the Noble Savage proposed by the rudimentary anthropology of the Encyclopedists, which already existed in the imagination and awaited only a fable, an archetype as apt as Scott's, to become a staple of the bourgeois novel.

That fable was created in a series of five novels by James Fenimore Cooper, who had learned from Scott to invest his projections of the primitive with the pathos of the lost cause, and to play out his action on the "ideal boundary" between two cultures, one "civilized and cultivated," the other "wild and lawless." The American name for that "ideal boundary" is, of course, the "frontier"; and on a continent which provided almost limitless possibilities for moving such a frontier westward, there was not one "Highland line" but many. For Scott's romantic North, Cooper substituted his own romantic West and the end is not yet in sight. It is taking no final credit from Cooper, justly irked throughout his life at being tagged "the American Scott," to say that he learned much from (not imitated!) the author of *Rob Roy,* any more than it is uncomplimentary for him to insist that he is indebted to Brockden Brown for the suggestion that "the incidents of Indian hostility, and the perils of the Western wilderness are far more suitable" for the American writer than "castles and chimeras."

Merely to have conceived of joining the materials of Brown to the modes of Scott, of blending the American highbrow and the

European middlebrow, is a creative act; to have by that act re-deemed the American past for the imagination is an even greater achievement; yet Cooper performed, as we shall see, more even than this. Unlike Scott, Cooper was not willing to be a mass enter-tainer of polite society; his books were to him weapons in a battle against the abuses of society. With a courage unsurpassed by any American writer since, he engaged in a quarrel with his own coun-try and people, his own time and place, marked by all the ferocity of baffled love. Yet like Scott, he desired deeply, too, to be a *suc-cess,* commercially as well as critically. "A good, wholesome, prof-itable and continued pecuniary support," he wrote, "is the applause talent most craves." Indeed, before excoriating the mass American audience, Cooper had won it; so that he found himself in the al-most unparalleled position of being listened to by those who really represented all he most detested in American life.

Finally (though not before supporting himself by his pen for twenty years), Cooper managed to lose the public he roundly abused yet expected to sympathize with him and subsidize his at-tacks. Most of his books (he wrote some forty-five, fiction and non-fiction) have not survived the fluctuations of his reputation or the issues which prompted them. His talent for invective and his moral intelligence were greater than his psychological insight or poetic skill, and his collected works are monumental in their cumu-lative dullness. Particularly unreadable are the novels of his later years, when his invective had turned to hysteria and his intelligence was stifled by his piety. To the student of ideas, he is endlessly fascinating; and a history of his times could be (and, indeed, has been) mined from the body of his fiction. But to the reader of novels he is, except for a handful of books, a tantalizing, an ulti-mately disappointing case.

He himself foresaw his fate, writing in 1850, "If anything from the pen of this writer . . . is at all to outlive himself, it is, unques-tionably, the series of 'The Leather-Stocking Tales.' " But this does not quite manage to state the whole irony of the situation. Out of his immense production, the bulk of it serious to the point of di-dactic deadliness, the handful of books still read with pleasure by any number of Americans are entertainments, the most Scott-like of all his romances. Moreover, we read them in large print and embellished with pictures, remember them, if at all, as children's books, exciting and incredibly boring by turns. And to realize that in all likelihood *The Last of the Mohicans* has been throughout the world the most widely read of all American novels only chills us the more.

It is true that in the past eminent European novelists like Balzac and D. H. Lawrence have been moved to exclaim over certain works of Cooper, "beautiful . . . grand . . . a masterpiece . . ." or "a crescendo of beauty"; and Melville himself once said in formal tribute, "The man, though dead, is still as living to me as ever. . . . He was a great, robust-souled man, all whose merits are not yet fully appreciated." But Lawrence's enthusiasm was directed to the Leatherstocking Tales, Balzac's to *The Pathfinder* in particular; and, indeed, around these few books whatever vital controversy still rages is centered. Twain's famous attack, "Fenimore Cooper's Literary Offenses," like Lawrence's great defense in *Studies in Classic American Literature,* is based on that handful of texts; while in Melville's short eulogy the disquieting note is struck, ". . . his works are among the earliest I remember, as in my boyhood producing a vivid and awakening power upon my mind." "As in my boyhood"—there is the fatal phrase. Let us not avoid it, but take it as a clue to the very essence of Cooper's appeal.

In what novels of his survive, Cooper is a writer for children, more specifically for boys. In this respect his Leatherstocking Tales share a single fate with the first two parts of *Gulliver's Travels, Robinson Crusoe,* at least some of the romances of his master Scott —particularly, perhaps, *Ivanhoe*—and such books of Dickens as *Oliver Twist,* as well as Stevenson's *Treasure Island* and *David Balfour.* All of these books (the examples which occur are inevitably Anglo-Saxon) have certain characteristics in common; all of them have male protagonists, adult or juvenile; all involve adventure and isolation plus an escape at one point or another, or a flight from society to an island, a woods, the underworld, a mountain fastness—some place at least where mothers do not come; most all of them involve, too, a male companion, who is the spirit of the alien place, and who is presented with varying degrees of ambiguity as helpmate and threat: Friday, Alan Breck Stewart, Long John Silver, Fagin, Robin Hood. The relation between the protagonists takes various forms: servant and master, foster-father (good or bad) and foster-son, lover and beloved. It is always opposed, at least implicitly, to the "stickier" and more sentimental kinds of relationships involving women, whether that of mother and child, husband and wife, or passionate wooer and mistress. When endearments are permitted between such male pairs (as between Oliver and Fagin, for instance, or Long John Silver and Jim Hawkins), they are typically presented as blandishments concealing a threat; for such love always threatens to develop into sexuality and sexuality would turn the pure anti-female romance into the travesty of inversion and would frighten off the child reader.

Found here and there in British literature, scarcely at all in other traditions, this "boyish" theme recurs with especial regularity in American fiction, most notably in the two greatest novels ever written in the United States, *Moby Dick* and *Huckleberry Finn,* but elsewhere, of course, in Twain and Melville, as well as in Dana, Stephen Crane, Henry James, Hemingway, Faulkner, and Sherwood Anderson, among others. There is obviously something in the American character that responds to its appeal—or perhaps, conversely, the theme itself through our great books has served to create in its own image what we call the American character.

It is Cooper who first dreams the American version of this theme, converting a peripheral European archetype into the central myth of our culture. The consignment of his work, then, to the world of children is not, in a child-centered world, a sign of failure but of success; and precisely because he is the first writer in the United States of boys' books, he is the first truly American writer to have appeared. To understand the Leatherstocking series is, therefore, to understand the most deeply underlying image of ourselves; and to begin that understanding we must examine the career of James Fenimore Cooper, try to see clearly his actual relationship to the wilderness which he made the setting of his most successful books. There is some difficulty in dealing with the life of a man, who, though he lived much in the public eye, guarded many details of his existence from public scrutiny. He rather despised Scott for having taken pains to provide his biographer with documents and information, and forbade his own family to permit the publication of any authorized life. Yet in his novels and in the press, in his letters and his non-fiction, the record has been made.

IV

He was born in 1789, the year of the publication of *The Power of Sympathy,* in Burlington, New Jersey, but moved as an infant to the town which now bears his name, near Lake Otsego in New York state. His childhood home was on the edge of the forest in space, on the further margin of Indian-fighting days in time. The actual savages had long since departed westward and the real woodsmen had followed them; but a semi-Christianized, usually drunken stray of an Indian could occasionally be seen on the streets of his home town, or some old trapper, bewildered and offended by the inroads of civilization. It is important to realize how close Cooper was to and how far from the material he was to make his own. It is perhaps this particular degree of remoteness which determines the oddly abstract existence of the forest in his work—as if he had never walked through it (or on the other hand certainly not *studied* it) but only dreamed it. Cooper can, when he wants to, reel off lists of native American trees; but ordinarily his characters flee or pursue through woods which contain not oaks or beeches or maples, only unnamed archetypal trees, the tree-ish, conceptual trees children draw.

The simple fact seems to have been that Cooper had no especial affection for the American woods, in particular, or the American landscape in general, any more than he had for the American weather or seasons, about which he complains in his later, non-mythical books. Only the symbolic or, as he might have said, the "ideal" forest appealed to him; of the actual one, which he made but did not find romantic, he remarks in *Wyandotté,* "There is a wide-spread error on the subject of American scenery . . . the world has come to attach to it an idea of grandeur, a word that is in nearly every case misapplied. The scenery of that portion of the American continent which has fallen to the share of the Anglo-Saxon race very seldom rises to a scale that merits this term. . . ." Cooper, in any case, after a long career of mythicizing that landscape, declared his preference for the "sublimity of the Alps," the "wild grandeur" of the Italian lakes, the "noble witchery" of the Mediterranean coast.

Cooper's own family was made up of well-to-do landowners, men who by wise investments and speculation had grown rich on the lands opened up by the pioneers—and which had, of course, been first of all robbed from the Indians. Apparently, no direct connection of Cooper had acquired his land by force rather than purchase, and he did not, therefore, have the appropriator's need to vilify the expropriated, or the inherited guilt (of a Hawthorne, for instance) which plagues the descendants of such appropriators. Indeed, as economic depression depleted his own financial resources (like Scott he ended by writing under financial pressures), and as agitation began against the old patroon system, Cooper began to feel himself one of the dispossessed. It was easy for him to identify himself, too, in terms of his distinguished ancestors, great white chiefs all of them, with the ancestral nobility of the Indian tribes— and to identify the agitators calling for the breaking up of inherited estates with the crude squatters and despoilers who had first driven the red man from forest and plain.

It must be remembered that Cooper asks of his reader not sympathy for the Indian people in general but for the Indian chief, the aristocrat at the end of his line. He is the most class-conscious of all American writers (to him Scott seemed not gentleman enough!), class-conscious the way only a provincial New York aristocrat could be; and his Jacksonianism was based on agrarian sympathies and especially a violent opposition to Whiggery: the philosophy of the new mercantile middle class. In his works, the American Revolution is presented as an unfortunate incident in the lives of men bound together by class interests, who divide temporarily in their allegiances but return again to their estates and their customary social intercourse after the war. He even goes out of his way to be kind to George III; and, indeed, until later experiences soured him, was mildly Anglophile in a typically upper-class way, even pretending to be English when he wrote his first book—though that device, indeed, may have been a cynical one, prompted by what he knew of the general public's provincial unwillingness to admire native efforts in the arts.

Cooper's religious affiliations reflect both his class position and his sense of continuity with Anglo-Saxon tradition; unlike that unchurched Universalist (trained by Moravians) Natty Bumppo, he was an Anglican, though he was not confirmed until the very end of his life. He had been a warden of Christ Church in Cooperstown long before he received his confirmation from his wife's brother, an Episcopal bishop. With Natty, Cooper shared an immunity to Calvinism and its vestigial influences rare among American writers; between them, they represent the beginning of an anti-Puritan strain in our literature that sustains the credo of original innocence. There are, to be sure, occasional Puritans among the characters of Cooper's books, but they are cruelly caricatured (the Reverend Meek Wolfe in *The Wept of Wish-ton-Wish* is a typical example, his name in itself a summary of Cooper's views), and the author rejects them without a trace of real ambivalence.

The residual secular Puritanism which gives to the anti-Puritanism of Hawthorne or the anti-Presbyterianism of Melville its special complexity and depth is totally lacking in Cooper. It is perhaps because the doctrine of original sin has lost for him, with the loss of its Calvinist underpinnings, all effective force that his novels fail finally to achieve a tragic dimension. Melville writing on Hawthorne was to observe that the "blackness, ten times black" against which tragedy is defined in American writers derives from vestiges of New England theology, and there is real truth in the observation. Certainly Cooper, lacking that religious background, lacks also the philosophical denseness and moral richness of the greatest American fiction of the nineteenth century. There is nothing in his basic attitudes to counter the sentimental piety of genteel Protestantism except a certain eighteenth-century faith in progress and civilization; but this does not set up a tension favorable to serious art. Evil is finally as unreal to Cooper as to that oddly Whiggish Tory, Scott.

What chiefly determined the shape of his career, however, was his marriage, a happy and apparently placid one, to the daughter of a rich and distinguished family. To Susan De Lancey he surrendered the direction of his domestic life, making her his social arbiter in a way typically American. His submission (whatever reservations he had were buried deep and could express themselves only in literature) he granted cheerfully to his wife and four daughters, following whose whims and needs he changed his home to a place closer to the city, then plunged into a seven years' tour of Europe in search of the refinements of civilization. When his family finances collapsed, he wrote furiously for thirty years to provide his wife and daughters with the comforts he thought of as the proper tribute of the male to the superior virtue of the female.

The notion of the sacredness of womanhood and the sanctity of every member of the sex, the supreme creed of the female sentimentalists, he accepted as literal truth, ritually portraying all upper-class, white, Anglo-Saxon women as without sin. If he ever groaned beneath the weight of this intolerable burden of an eternally confessed moral inferiority, he never groaned openly and would have been appalled to think his wooden ingenues were in fact his revenge upon the sex; just as his dream of an idyllic union with the red man was his inner escape from a world of blameless, sexless females. Only the Indian in him, which is to say the unconscious, is allowed to blaspheme against the pale-face virgin. Whittal, the half-wit pseudo-savage of *The Wept of Wish-ton-Wish,* says of Faith, the blue-eyed, blue-veined, blondest of all possible Snow Maidens,

" 'tis a woman of the pale-faces, and, I warrant me, one that will never be satisfied till she hath all the furs of America on her back, and all the venison of the woods in her kitchen. . . ."

After his marriage, Cooper was apparently set to live the eventless, busy life of a gentleman, but two events, one a national disaster, the other a casual challenge, turned him into a writer. In 1820, at the age of thirty, he wrote his first book, *Persuasion,* apparently in order to win a bet from his wife, who had taken him up on a casual remark that he could produce a book as good as the piece of female fiction she had annoyed him by praising. Yet his first book is no burlesque (as were Fielding's and Cervantes' under somewhat similar circumstances), not an anti-novel at all, but a quite serious, somewhat plodding, Jane Austen-ish study of the problem of marriage—indistinguishable, one imagines, from the novel he had begun by emulating.

Scott had started his career as a writer by trying to counterfeit the folk style of the Border ballads; Cooper began his imitating an English gentlewoman entertaining and edifying her peers. It is disconcerting to find him impersonating a female (as late as 1823 he was continuing in this vein, publishing two short stories under the name of "Jane Morgan"), but even more so to discover him betraying the American's provincial hunger for counterfeiting European civilization. Cooper was soon forced, however, both by his own sense of the inadequacy of his first venture and by the critics' adverse comments on his failure to use the native scene, to an even more devious act of dissimulation. In *The Spy* he produced an American imitation of the kind of book written by Europeans for whom the United States is a symbol of primitivism and anti-culture. Here, indeed, is the secret of his success on the continent, for he is above all others the kind of "American romancer" Europeans dream and need; or at least, in a few of his many books, he managed to seem so. For Americans his appeal is somewhat more complicated. To his earliest native readers, his evocation of a way of life not so far from theirs in time (in *The Spy* he recounted events not fifty years past), or even in its quality, provided an illusion of remoteness. The indulgence in nostalgia for past simplicity is a final assurance of present sophistication.

At any rate, *The Spy,* which appeared in 1821 and was immediately successful, is the most Scott-like of all Cooper's novels, based on historical documents throughout, even Harvey Birch, the protagonist referred to by the title, being derived from an actual prototype. More importantly, Cooper has chosen the American Revolution as a setting because it provides just such an "ideal boundary" as Scott loved, across which the protagonists (a young Loyalist officer in disguise plays the role of the pursued juvenile, though his sister is the genteel heroine and is married off to a major in the Colonial forces) move between safety and danger, as well as between competing ways of life and codes of behavior. Most striking of all is the resemblance of Cooper's paired mysterious figures, upper-class and lower, Washington and Harvey Birch, to their counterparts in Scott's *Ivanhoe,* Richard Coeur de Lion and Robin Hood.

Yet *The Spy* fails to capture the archetypal appeal of its model. It is as moving as *Ivanhoe,* perhaps, on the mythical level, but cannot approach in this respect those Scott fictions which make the Highlands and Highlanders their theme. Cooper's fated Highlands is the forest, his predestined wild Highlander the Indian and the woodsman, his inevitable "ideal boundary" the frontier. These are all pre-existing concepts ready to live the life of legends in the American mind, awaiting only the word that will release them; that word Cooper finally speaks, though almost inadvertently, in *The Pioneers,* which was published in 1823. Reaching back in search of his own beginnings and those of his family, he discovers beneath that half-remembered, half-invented world one even more archaic: the childhood of America, which does not indeed really exist until he first embodies it.

The Pioneers was the first written of the Leatherstocking Tales; and though Leatherstocking himself is kept firmly in his place (he is a standard lower-class comic character, allowed to compete in pathos but not in importance with the provincial aristocrats who are Cooper's mythicization of his own family) and the Noble Savage appears only as the lost and drunken Old John Mohegan, the presence of these two characters was enough to assure the novel's success. Great analytic or poetic works, depending for their acceptance on an intimacy with language and structure which may seem at a first reading strange or even obscure, often have to wait long for their popularity; but the mythic work is likely to be greeted by instant acclaim. Certainly, the American public responded with enthusiasm to the first authentic romance by the dreamer of its national dream, for 3,500 copies of *The Pioneers* sold before noon of the day of publication.

Cooper was committed for the rest of his life to the promulgation of a myth; and though toward the end of his career, he came to understand the sense in which this was his essential function, for a long time he remained confused. The myth-maker and the man of letters were uneasily combined in him, and both were joined, after the collapse of his fortune prevented his living out a gentlemanly life of leisure, by the businessman, the canny exploiter of his own talent. He was an irascible man, driven by internal demons as well as external need, and he maintained the most difficult sort of relationship with his public, storming at his readers, scolding his critics, hysterically defending his own most trivial private activities in thick pseudo-fictions. What baffled him most, however, beneath all the minor contretemps in which he invested so much energy, was the contrast between his ability, as a half-conscious framer of legends, to satisfy deeply the mass audience, and his inability, as a fully conscious moralist and polemical social critic, to win its approval.

After *The Pioneers,* at any rate, he knew that he was destined to spend the rest of his life as an author of one sort or another; and, having moved to the suburbs of New York City (not only for his daughters' sake, but also to be closer to his publishers) he set about writing a sea story, which was to beat Scott at his own game. Proud of his own knowledge of seamanship and a little contemptuous of Scott's, he fell into Scott's own trap of identifying the truth of a novel with the faithfulness to fact of its details. If Cooper never managed to write a romance of the sea as satisfactory as his romances of the forest, it was because he knew the sea too well, approached it not as a dreamer but as an expert. Nevertheless, in *The Pilot* (and in at least one other of his several tales of the sea, *The Red Rover*), he produced one of the few books of his that can still be read with pleasure by the casual reader. The appearance of *The Last of the Mohicans* in 1826, however, marked his final discovery of his true vein; and from this point on, the true history of Fenimore Cooper becomes the fictional history of Natty Bumppo.

As Cooper moved in his imagination deeper and deeper into the American wilderness, he was in fact withdrawing farther and farther from it. His fancy continued on a pious pilgrimage westward —across the Mississippi to the Great Plains, even as he and his family made a cultural pilgrimage eastward—across the Atlantic to France and Italy. He finished *The Prairie,* most Western in its setting of all the Leatherstocking Tales, in Paris in 1827. It was presumably the end of the series (which Cooper was never to finish; actually, he wrote two more novels for it in the '40's and planned a third just before his death), for in it, Natty, having penetrated the territory of the Pawnee and the Sioux, dies, an old man, facing into the sunset. From 1826 to 1833, the Coopers remained in Europe, chiefly around the fashionable center of Paris; though Italy, with its indolence and gentle pride, seems to have pleased Fenimore Cooper best. It was not yet common in those days to speak of expatriation; and, indeed, Cooper left the United States not as one going into exile but as befitted his class and literary reputation, with a nominal consular post. Even when he had resigned this position, he continued to act the part of an unpaid but official representative of his country. In the midst of attending receptions, visiting celebrities, seeing sights and being lionized, he managed to find time for writing, for he depended upon the sale of his books to foot the bill.

He had been warned before he left that any American who stayed abroad more than five years ran the risk of never returning, and he stayed for seven and a half—in spirit never did go home again. He and America had drifted apart in the period of his absence; and though while abroad he had defended American culture against European attacks, he himself joined the assault on his return. Like many Americans in Europe, he had confused the nostalgic memory of his country with its fact, and coming back, he found it guilty of betraying both the memory and his defense of it based on the memory. He had already begun to fall into disfavor even before his return, for quite nonliterary reasons, his odd combination of Tory principles and democratic action proving especially infuriating to the Whigs; and he compounded the animosity after his repatriation. He had apparently toyed with the idea of giving up writing in 1833, but the seeming triumph of the "dollar-dollar set" depressed him, as did the disappearance of the older ruling classes of which he considered himself a member. "Where is the Gentry?" he cried, and lashed out at the financiers who had taken its place. Unfortunately, he was a man with little sense of proportion, and his larger quarrel with his country was soon almost lost in a petty quarrel with his fellow townsmen over picnicking rights on his Lake Otsego property. Certainly, this picayune issue bulks too large in his *Home as Found,* published in 1838, which otherwise might have formulated the first major statement in our fiction of the Europe-America theme.

For better or worse, Cooper plunged into a round of libel suits, statements to the press, endless wrangles about everything from the accuracy of his own naval history to women's property rights, the jury system, and universal suffrage. First of all American writers to take on the role of public accuser and nay-sayer, he still found time to complete his mythical account of that American past which he felt his enemies betrayed. In *The Pathfinder,* which appeared in 1840, and *The Deerslayer,* which came out a year later, Cooper turned back from the end of Natty Bumppo's life to his youth, to a time as distant as possible from the contemporary era which so irked him. Meanwhile, he had become more and more religious, committing himself, when all visible institutions failed his hopes (despite his increasing bitterness, neither hopelessness nor tragic acceptance were possible for him), to a pious trust in Providence. In *Oak Openings,* which was published in 1848 and which represents, therefore, his very latest thought, Cooper denied in the name of his newly confirmed faith the demonic, pre-Christian voice of the New World, which had spoken through him in his mythic books.

In the words of a converted Indian, once Scalping Peter and at the end just Pete, Cooper rejects the "Injin" in himself. " 'Tell me you make a book,' he said. 'In dat book tell trut! You see me poor old Injin. . . . I was great chief but we was children . . . t'ink tomahawk and warpath and rifle bess t'ings in whole world. . . . Stranger, love God. B'lieve his Blessed Son, who pray for dem dat kill Him. Injin don't do dat. Injin not strong enough to do such a t'ing. . . . I have spoken. Let dem dat read your book understand.' " After such a declaration, Cooper could not really return again to the Great Serpent or Long Rifle who had stood so long beside him, could not be as a child with the children of his pagan imagination. Just past sixty, he weakened quite suddenly and without previous warning, and in a little over a year he was dead. Daniel Webster was called upon to deliver an official eulogy at the memorial services, to render the thanks of a nation to the first maker of its myths; but he spoke out of ignorance of Cooper's works—a last, not untypical indignity: "As far as I am acquainted with the writings of Mr. Cooper, they uphold good sentiments, sustain good morals, and maintain just taste."

Though obviously spoken at a venture, these words do, alas, characterize much of Cooper's work; for they are intended to describe the sort of literature a gentleman might write, and Cooper was, whenever he wrote self-consciously, above all things a gentleman. Only his intelligence is slighted by Webster's summary, and the mythopoeic power which, in a handful of books, delivered him from the limitations of his class and his time. That handful of books we must be content (taking Cooper's own word for it) to consider the sole *living* part of his achievement. That he naturalized the sea story to the new world or first realized how shipboard society could be used to portray microcosmically a whole culture; even that he invented, in Eve Effingham, James's American girl before the fact, are matters of *historical* interest only.

Yet it is well to remember that Cooper invented not only the "Western," the prototype of all cowboy-and-Indian romances, the first embodiment of the ritual drama played out to this day in television fantasies called *Gunsmoke* or *Wyatt Earp,* but that he is also the first American author to project an alternative formulation of the theme which, in Hawthorne and Henry James, Fitzgerald and Hemingway, is played out in terms of a confrontation of Europe and America. This Europe and this America are, however, no more facts of geography than Cooper's Indians and whites are facts of ethnography; the place-names stand for corruption and innocence, sophistication and naïveté, aesthetics and morality.

The gentlemanly Cooper not only dreamed Tom Mix and Gary Cooper before the nineteenth century was half over; he also projected Lambert Strether, and all the other ambassadors without portfolio who, like Cooper himself, go to Paris to discover America and their own souls. Yet though the America-Europe theme and the Indian-white archetype go back to a common Romantic source, the former, in an odd way, turns the latter on its head. What does the damage is the suggestion that not naïveté and simple virtue but sophistication and elegance are lost with the passage of time and the march of progress. In the end, the study of the American abroad debouches into ambiguities which baffle popular understanding even as they shock popular morality. The "ambassadorial" novel can never like the Western win the mass audience; it must function as art rather than myth, depend on craftsmanship rather than intuition. It is for this reason that Cooper, who never solved the problems of language or form, could only project and not construct successful fictions on the Jamesian theme; books like *Home as Found* remain theoretical, concepts rather than realizations. Cooper had, alas, all the qualifications for a great American writer except the simple ability to write.

The Western, on the other hand, requires no "writing," for it is truly mythic, a substantial part of its meaning contained in the bare plot, transcending the limitations of language and surviving even in children's cut editions, television or movie versions and comic books. Precisely because the Leatherstocking Tales are the world's first Westerns, they have come to possess the imagination of the world—which is a satisfactory enough joke on the most self-consciously civilized and gentlemanly of all our writers, *"le grand écrivain Américain,"* whose image of himself so infuriated the ungentlemanly D. H. Lawrence. It no longer really matters whether one has actually read Cooper's books or not; he is possessed by them all the same, and just as Dumas in nineteenth-century France could call a work *Les Mohicans de Paris,* Bernard Malamud in twentieth-century America can entitle a story "The Last Mohican." Neither has to doubt that he will be understood, for the title of Cooper's romance has become a part of the common symbolic language of the western world.

V

Two mythic figures have detached themselves from the texts of Cooper's books and have entered the free domain of our dreams: Natty Bumppo, the hunter and enemy of cities; and Chingachgook, nature's nobleman and Vanishing American. But these two between them postulate a third myth, an archetypal relationship which also haunts the American psyche: two lonely men, one dark-skinned, one white, bend together over a carefully guarded fire in the virgin heart of the American wilderness; they have forsaken all others for the sake of the austere, almost inarticulate, but unquestioned love which binds them to each other and to the world of nature which they have preferred to civilization. To understand these figures and their relationship, we must first understand the order of the genesis of their myth: the sequence of the novels in which they appear, both as Cooper wrote them and in terms of the dates of their actions.

Though *The Pioneers* appeared in 1823, it is set in 1793, when Natty is over seventy; and though *The Deerslayer,* the last of the novels to be published, came out in 1841, the events it describes belong to the years between 1740 and 1745, when Natty is not yet twenty-five. Between the first and last written of the Leatherstocking Tales, the protagonist grows backward in time from old age to youth, from experience to innocence, from a world which Cooper could still, though barely, remember (in 1793, he would have been four years old) to an era before his father was born, a completely imaginary past. But Natty also moves through time from a moment when the United States had won its independence and had established a Constitution to a period when its separate existence had not yet been imagined.

But it is not quite as simple as all that; for if, on the one hand, Cooper between 1823 and 1840 re-imagined Leatherstocking from an "old and helpless man" to a youth not yet initiated into a career of killing, on the other hand, by 1827 he had also moved him *forward* some ten years, converting him from a pathetic-comic oldster with one tooth, haunting the margins of the settlements he despises—to a magnificent old patriarch who has come to die in ultimate loneliness in the ultimate West. After *The Pioneers,* that is to say, there are two separate pairs of books: one pair, *The Last of the Mohicans* and *The Prairie,* appearing in 1826 and 1827, the other, *The Pathfinder* and *The Deerslayer,* being published in 1840 and 1841. In the first book of each pair, Natty is placed in middle life (in *The Last of the Mohicans,* he is just the age of his author at the moment of writing the book); then he is either pushed forward into a mythical old age, or back to a legendary youth. In each of the later books of the pairs, he stands on the verge of a critical transition: in *The Deerslayer,* he is initiated into manhood; in *The Prairie,* inducted through death into whatever lies beyond. Each romance celebrates, as it were, a *rite de passage.*

In both cases, Natty is transfigured by a confrontation with death; in one, with that of his first victim, in the other, with his own. But in both, he is mythicized, transformed from the mundane reality of *The Pioneers* to another order of being. In that first novel, he is an old outcast, by turns noble and absurd, the kind of peripheral character who in a play by Shakespeare would have talked in prose. In Cooper, he talks by fits and starts a semi-comic American dialect which sets him off from the gentle characters who talk like an English novel for ladies. Natty is an ambiguous type at this stage, a kind of cross between Huck Finn and his Pap, alternately fleeing and defying the law for dubious reasons, and in the end, "lighting out for the Territory." Attending him and reinforcing his meanings is Old John Mohegan (the *first* last of the Mohicans), an Indian as old as he or older, who has been converted both to the white man's religion and the white man's fire-water. Twin symbols of dispossession, of all that cannot survive the inevitable and desirable (providential, says pious Mr. Cooper) march of civilization, they are not only doomed, but degraded. Yet the one is capable of setting out once more to pursue the retreating West, and the other of destroying himself in a symbolic holocaust. In that flight and from those ashes, they are reborn, stripped by youth or age of their accidental comic attributes (the dripping nose, the rags, the lone tooth-stump) until they are revealed in all their mythic purity: the Christian Noble Savage and the pagan Noble Savage, confronting each other across the "ideal boundary," the fleeting historical moment at which, both harried by the civilization that will ultimately destroy them, they meet. In the end, one is a little paganized, the other a little Christianized—their respective nobilities both augmented in the process.

Natty is an oddly elusive character, almost anonymous. He apparently shuns his baptismal name and is finally buried under a mere initial. Almost as if he were an Indian, he earns not inherits his name, and is known variously as Deerslayer, Hawkeye, Pathfinder, Long Rifle, Leatherstocking, the Trapper. He is overtly pious, meek, chaste (of course!), sententious—often a bore, a Protestant Noble Savage, worshiping in the Universalist Church of the Woods; and yet he is also a dangerous symbol of Cooper's secret protest against the gentle tyranny of home and woman. A white man, who knows the "gifts" of his color and will not take a scalp or be rude to a lady, a man without caste, who knows his place and recognizes all officers and gentlemen as his superiors, he is still a law unto himself: judge and executioner, the man with the gun, the killer—however reluctant. He is the prototype of all pioneers, trappers, cowboys, and other innocently destructive children of nature, which is to say, of the Westerner, quick on the draw and immune to guilt.

In some ways, Leatherstocking seems a Faust in buckskins. Faustian man, however, knows even as he acts that he is damned; that his enterprise is ambiguous at the very least, and that he must pay in suffering for the freedom he demands. Though he defines himself by denying the Calvinist or Catholic theology of his world, the Faustian man needs that theology to create the tensions of his life; he is a blasphemer, and blasphemy is the sign of the secret though tormented believer. The Westerner, on the other hand, knows that what he does is blessed; that God and nature are one; that man, even in solitude, is good. Faust without sin is Natty Bumppo.

And the Devil who is his companion, when genteel Christianity has denied the ultimate reality of the demonic, is Chingachgook, the Great Serpent, as he is called by one to whom the Serpent is no longer the eternal Adversary. The Indian represents to Cooper whatever in the American psyche has been starved to death, whatever genteel Anglo-Saxondom has most ferociously repressed, whatever he himself had stifled to be worthy of his wife and daughters; but the Indian also stands for himself, which is to say, for a people dispossessed in the name of a God they do not know and whose claims they will not grant. The charge of General Lewis Cass and other literal-minded critics of Cooper that his Indians have "no living prototypes in our forest," that they are "of the school of Mr. Heckewelder and not of the school of nature," is quite beside the point, though no more than Cooper deserves for his own insistence on the historical truth of his "narratives."

Cooper tells precisely the same sort of truth about the Indian that Mrs. Stowe was to tell about the Negro; in each it is guilt that speaks, the guilt of a whole community. Cooper's own boyhood was passed after the last Indian inruptions into his part of the world were over, after the Anglo-Saxons had triumphed not only over the savages but over their allies, the French, too—dark aliens who had once unleashed the primitive terror. Yet when he was a child, the nightmare of the red uprising still haunted his home town, and at one point the militia was organized to stand off a raid that never materialized. It is a little like the Southerners' uneasy dream of the black insurrection, almost as much a wish as a fear. To exorcise that self-punishing bad dream, Cooper returns, through the long story it took him nearly twenty years to tell, to the good dream which is its complement and antidote: the dream of primeval innocence and the companionship of red man and white. Ironically enough, he situates that dream in a time when the Indian menace was still real, had not yet been transformed from a daylight threat to a nighttime shadow troubling the *yengsees'* sleep.

Though the Leatherstocking romances are, first of all, entertainments, they are also propitiatory offerings. There is in all of them, at one point or another, a reflection of Cooper's quarrel with himself (with the "Indian" deep within him): the sound of an inner voice explaining, justifying, endlessly hashing over the appropriation of the land, on which Cooper's own wealth and status so directly depended. His first means of coming to terms with his guilt-feelings is by identifying himself with the injured party, dissociating himself from the exploiters. In reading his romances, the American boy becomes for a little while the Indian, the trapper; and returning later to his memories or to the books themselves, finds it easy to think of himself as somehow really expropriated and dispossessed, driven from the Great Good Place of the wilderness by pressures of maturity and conformism.

However seriously Cooper may have wanted to be taken on the level of ethnology or political history, he could not avoid projecting in the "natural man" and the "natural scene" a myth, an archetypal embodiment of psychological truth, which was opposite in all its implication to that of Charles Brockden Brown. As the latter is responsible for giving to the gothic myth its standard American form, so Cooper is responsible for the naturalization of the Rousseauistic myth. In each, the dark-skinned savage is used to represent the unconscious mind, what the age itself liked to call the "heart," and between the two is created a total picture of the ambivalence of the American sentimentalist toward the id and its promptings. From the beginnings of our literature, the question has been posed: Is the "natural" a source of spontaneous goodness, instinctive nobility, untutored piety? Or is it the breeding ground of a black, demonic, destructive force hostile to our salvation? Or is it the common spring of two conflicting impulses, one positive, one negative?

Needless to say, the American mind has wavered on the subject, not only in instances of author combating author, but often in terms of a single author arguing with himself, one impulse of his own mind evoking the counter-impulse. In Melville's *Moby Dick,* for instance, the sinister natural figure of Fedallah is set against the virtuous natural figure of Queequeg, while in the works of Twain, Nigger Jim confronts Injun Joe, the dark-skinned protector contrasted with the dark-skinned aggressor. Even in Mrs. Stowe, the primitive piety of Uncle Tom is balanced by the unredeemed natural mischief of the demonic Topsy. Cooper seems at first glance committed to a single side, or at least, so it is easy to remember him. We perhaps recall the eulogy of the good forest in *The Deerslayer,* spoken by Natty, who has just refused like a proper American to marry the Fallen Woman, Judith Hutter. And we recall by way of contrast the haunted black forest of Brown, think perhaps of what Hawthorne is to say later of the "dark inscrutable forest," "where the wildness of her nature [Hester Prynne's] might assimilate itself with a people alien from the law. . . ." Hawthorne can imagine the Faustian man in the American woods, but cannot conceive of the innocent Westerner.

There are, therefore, no Noble Savages in Hawthorne, any more than there are in Brown, no dusky Apollos, no wildwood gentlemen—only warlocks and bestial assassins, demi-devils and demi-brutes. But there are in Cooper himself counter-Indians, as it were, savages almost as ignoble as any of theirs. Bland and un-Puritan as he was, Cooper was forced still to admit that even in the wilderness there was violence and terror, even in the natural something dangerous to the progress of mankind. Certainly he was prepared to grant the reality of the bad Indian, deriving from a clue in Heckewelder, the Moravian missionary whose study of Indian life had so influenced him, his famous theory of the Two Tribes: Mohegan and Mingo, Pawnee and Sioux. Sometimes there is a suggestion that bad Indians are the product of interbreeding; the Mingoes, for instance, are less pure of blood than the Mohicans. Cooper certainly shares, and to some extent has helped perpetuate, the popular American belief that the breed is hopelessly evil. Yet there is a counter-suggestion in his work that the bad Indian is a false Indian, not really an Indian at all: and in *The Redskins* he makes a distinction (indicated in his subtitle, "Indian and Injin") between real redskins, who respect property and ancestral rights, and leveling white men, disguised as savages to hide their depredations against the landholders. In any case, Cooper manages to propagate both aspects of the American ambivalence toward the Indians: the Easterner's or missionary's sentimentalizing of the Vanishing American, and the Westerner's or Indian fighter's cynical contempt for the savage. Cooper's bad Indians, it must be understood, are neither the unredeemed pagans of Hawthorne nor the undeveloped animals of Brockden Brown; they are Elizabethan stage villains.

Throughout *The Last of the Mohicans,* there are chapter headings which identify the villain of that book with Shylock, Cooper's bad Indian with Shakespeare's Machiavel. But the key passage ("Cursed be my tribe/If I forgive him . . .") suggests the further identification of the whole Indian people with that other exiled race, the Jews. The worst the Indian does, Cooper implies by the comparison, is an act of vengeance for compounded ancient wrongs; and the malice of the bad Indian demands as complicated a response as that of Shylock. However sanctioned by Providence, the European persecution of the pagan Indian has bred monsters, just as the earlier European exclusion of the "perfidious Jew" had created usurers. It is a stroke of genius, this uniting of the images of the usurer and the scalper (of the rejected super-ego and the offended id), each with a knife in his hand, each dedicated to a terrible revenge. Yet in *The Last of the Mohicans,* the point is made in appended quotations rather than in the story itself, as if Cooper were not quite ready to let it become a central theme.

He takes it up again, however, this time more centrally, in one of the strangest of his books, that pious last testament to which we have already alluded, *The Oak Openings.* In this novel, Cooper writes for the last time a romance of Indian life (the date is 1812, the setting Michigan); but he is interested no longer in pursuit and escape. This time he is concerned with the problem of conversion: the conversion to Christianity of the Indian, Scalping Peter, whose dreams of an Indian uprising help bring about the murder of Parson Amen, a missionary to the red men. Parson Amen begins as a comic character, like David Gamut in *The Last of the Mohicans,* a weaponless man in a world of weapon-bearers, utterly ignorant of the conditions of life in the world he enters or of the elementary skills required for survival in it. He is revealed finally as a Holy Fool, however, his failure to come to terms with a world of violence his greatest virtue; and even his madness assumes in the course of the book the semblance of symbolic truth. He believes obsessively that the Indians are the Lost Tribes of Israel, and this provides at first numerous occasions for Cooper's typically heavy-handed humor.

But out of the misunderstandings that arise between him and the baffled Indians, to whom he insists on preaching this disconcerting doctrine, arise certain key questions on which the meanings of the novel depend: Are the Indians, indeed, lost—and is their casting away a mystery like that of the Jews? Or is it the *yengsees,* the whites, who are, as the Indians assert in rebuttal, really lost—turned toward the setting rather than the rising sun which points the way to their proper home? After all, the English are the "Jews" who have betrayed not only Christ but their Indian brethren; while the Indians are, in their own eyes at least, guiltless of that primeval crime, the Crucifixion, which has cursed the

Christian world with the evil spirits of rootlessness and aggression. Yet in the course of Cooper's fable, the Indians commit precisely the sin against a redeemer of which they have declared themselves innocent: they kill the missionary even as he prays for them, forgives them; and the hapless Peter, their conscience (though, like his namesake, not bold enough in the moment of crisis), ends repentant, asking forgiveness of the whites.

It is a dazzling piece of sleight-of-hand, which solves the problem of white guilt (from which Cooper began) by insisting on the deeper guilt of the Indian, who not only fails to *practice* forgiveness, but will not even pretend to honor it. Not with arms can the Indian avenge his expropriation (Peter, who preaches the great Indian revolt, ends by saving the whites from those he has inflamed), only with prayer accept it. In return, the repentant redskin is granted the privilege of being told by some ineffectual, pale-face maiden that the Indians have in fact a better right to America than the whites, or of being assured by a half-mad preacher that he and his people are, like the Jews, chosen. "They have been, and are still, the chosen people of the Great Spirit, and will one day be received back to his favor. Would that I were one of them, only enlightened by the words of the New Testament!"

If the good-bad Indian come to wisdom sounds a little like Uncle Tom, it is because Cooper and Mrs. Stowe were genteel sentimentalists together, the one no more capable than the other of tragic ambivalence or radical protest.

The Uncle Tom resolution of the Indian problem only comes, however, when Cooper has exhausted the vein of the Leatherstocking Tales. In that series itself, Cooper never combines a good Indian and a bad in a single skin, for this would make him human and require that he be treated as a psychological entity instead of an allegory; he is content to display projections of the beneficent and malevolent primitive in action side by side, portraying the one as the ally of Natty Bumppo, the other as his foe. The happy ending assures us that the principle of natural evil goes inevitably down to defeat and death; while the pathetic ending, with which it is intertwined, reminds us that the principle of natural good also (though more heroically) perishes from our world. The primitive, good or evil, Cooper never lets us forget is past history and a present dream.

Read against the factual background of Cooper's own life as

well as the lives of most of his readers, the Leatherstocking romances seem the simplest kind of wish-fulfillment fantasies. D. H. Lawrence, in his immensely illuminating study of Cooper, lists the obvious contrasts between reality and myth set up in the series: The Wigwam vs. My Hotel—Chingachgook vs. My Wife—Natty Bumppo vs. My Humble Self; and he underlines the particular pathos of the final contrast by quoting from one of Cooper's letters describing his social activities in Europe: "In short, we were at the table two counts, one monsignore, an English Lord, an ambassador and my humble *self*." It all seems pat enough, this turning from (a relished yet somehow resented) real life in society to a dream life in nature: a kind of Walter Mitty story with Walter Mitty offstage as author—and therefore a Walter Mitty story told without irony. But it is more complex than this; for deeply implicated in the boyish reverie that turns the harried husband and breadwinner into the man in the woods with a gun, modest and potent at once, are disturbing sexual overtones, which combine with and are reinforced by an uneasy ambivalence toward the problem of race relations.

VI

In order to see clearly what is involved, we will have to look more closely at *The Last of the Mohicans*. It was not Cooper's own favorite in the series (he preferred *The Deerslayer*), but it has always been the world's, because in it there is defined almost perfectly the basic myth of Leatherstocking. Not merely are elements scattered through the other four romances here gathered together: the good Indian and the bad, the dark Maiden and the fair, the genteel lover and the stern, tender-hearted father, the comic tenderfoot and the noble red patriarch; these elements are presented in their pure essences. Natty is nowhere more super-eminently his sententious, cool, resourceful self, Chingachgook nowhere more noble or terrifyingly at home in the woods (and his archetypal meanings are here reinforced by Uncas, Cooper's third mythical character, who makes here his only appearance); while Magua is so essentially the bad Indian, "reptile," "fury," "Devil," and Shylock in one, that beside him Cooper's other villains seem scarcely to exist. Cora and Alice (the names themselves are almost mythical), the passionate brunette and the sinless blonde, make once and for all the pattern of female Dark and Light that is to become the standard form in which American writers project their ambivalence toward women.

No chases are more thrilling and absurd, no movements into danger less credibly motivated, no rescues more hair-raisingly ridiculous, no climaxes more operatic than those of *The Last of the Mohicans.* The scenery is almost totally abstract, archetypal; among unnamed trees, two women and their protectors flee before a sinister purusit, twice resumed, which takes them to the mythic cave of Charles Brockden Brown, behind a rocky waterfall worthy of Scott, and eventually onto the bosom of a wooded lake (Cooper's very own!), the image of which haunts our dreams but can never be discovered by picnicker or fisherman. And in all the magic woods (sometimes more like those of Shakespeare's *A Midsummer Night's Dream* than any native forest), no mosquito bites, no ant crawls; the charmed underbrush itself relents and will not tear the clothes or mar the looks of the two girls who without soap or comb or brush must maintain their symbolic beauty, light and dark, unblemished. Were one of the actors once to sweat or belch or retire to the bushes to relieve himself, the spell would be broken; we would know that all of them were merely flesh. But nothing gives the game away. The Indians talk like mythic Celts out of *Ossian,* the gentry like Fenimore Cooper remembering the genteel British novel, Natty himself like an improbable blend of stage provincial, backwoods preacher, and instinctive sage. The novel is so all of a piece that reality does not intrude.

The "history" of the French and Indian Wars, into which the fable is set, belongs in our minds to the pre-history of America, an archaic world in which anything is possible; and for all his occasional concern to get the facts right, his title-page vaunt that he is writing a historical "narrative," Cooper cannot persuade us that the victims of the historic massacre described at the center of his book really bleed. It is a dream "dreamt among the trees," a Midsummer Night's dream. From the play of that name, indeed, Cooper derives almost as many chapter headings as he does from *The Merchant of Venice;* and truly *The Last of the Mohicans,* too, presents us with a world subject to magical transformations. Not only does the threat of death turn in an instant to the promise of life, the darkest danger to the most glorious delivery; but men are changed into beavers, bears revealed as men.

The reader's problem is finally how to take the romance at all seriously, to find in it more than amusement, a Midsummer Night's entertainment. "The 'pure' adventure story is deliberately superficial," James Grossman tells us in an otherwise insightful book on Cooper; "It has no serious concern with the outside world which it uses as a decoration and aid to action." Yet it is incredible that a book which has moved the world for more than a hundred years should have "no serious concern" with that world. The so-called literature of escape is always at its depths religious, a ritual statement of what its audience prays the world might be or even hopes it is. If Cooper, for once, had not planted explicit meanings in his fable, such meanings might well have been implicit in the theme he imagined. But there is evidence that he was attempting quite consciously to grapple, in the midst of scenes of adventure, with a serious subject, indicated by the quotation (from *The Merchant of Venice,* once more) on the title page: "Mislike me not for my complexion. . . ." *

It is an odd (and ambitious) novel that tries to be at once the dark Shakespearean comedy and the light, a farcical presentation of metamorphosis and romantic love—and a somewhat melancholy, bitter-sweet examination of the problems of race and color. Yet this is precisely what Cooper has tried; and it is misleading for Grossman to insist that *"The Last of the Mohicans* uses race as a painter might use coloring arbitrarily for effect." It should be remembered that *The Last of the Mohicans* (1826) was written just after *Lionel Lincoln* (1825) and was followed by *The Prairie* (1827), *The Red Rover* (1828), and *The Wept of Wish-ton-Wish* (1829). These books frame the beginning, in 1826, of Cooper's seven-year expatriation, and bear directly on certain feelings stirred up in him by the desire to leave, for a while at least, his own country. The novels in this group revolve in large part around two themes: the relations of white America to white Europe, and those of white America to red America. More profoundly, they are concerned with the sense of guilt felt by Americans over the Revolution against the mother country and the expropriation of the Indians.

Lionel Lincoln is one of the darkest of Cooper's books, the nearest thing perhaps to a true gothic romance that he ever pro-

---

* The line is, of course, spoken in Shakespeare by a Moor, i.e., a Black Man—and here Cooper anticipates the mythological adaptation, so important in later American books, of the Negro character to the myth of the Indian.

duced. Against a background of mysterious events, it tells the story of Lionel, an officer in the British Army though a native of America, who is nearly converted to the Colonial cause. At the last minute, however, he discovers that the wise old patriot who had nearly convinced him is an escaped lunatic—for whom authority means the keeper, and freedom an opportunity to indulge his delusions. Whatever Cooper's conscious opinions of the justice of the American War of Independence, his unconscious doubts are here clearly enough portrayed! And they are further illuminated by his ambivalence toward the protagonist of *The Red Rover,* a Revolutionary pirate who has taken to a career of crime because the commander of a British ship on which he was serving had insulted America. Buccaneer and madman, these are the images which occur to him for the revolutionist, the founding father or first fighter for the Republic. But his quest for the beginnings of the American character takes him back beyond the period of our Revolutionary War, back to the conflict of *yengsee* and Indian, to the original struggle for the American land. In *The Last of the Mohicans,* he seemed to find the moment he sought in the French and Indian War; and in *The Prairie,* which he completed in Europe, he killed off Natty Bumppo, as if to indicate that he was through with the theme.

Cooper had, however, stirred up in *The Last of the Mohicans* and ignored in *The Prairie* a problem more complicated even than that of the struggle for a continent—the question of the relations between men of different races in the New World; and to that problem he returned in *The Wept of Wish-ton-Wish,* which is his attempt to deal nonmythically (i.e., without the presence of Natty Bumppo) with the problem of miscegenation, in terms of the question: Has the flight from Europe and the expropriation of the Indians bound white man and red in such an inextricable knot of mutual interest and guilt that they must eventually blend into one (accursed!) race?

In *The Wept* an Indian boy, Conanchet, captured by whites, is recaptured by an Indian raiding party, who take along with him a girl child of the family which has kept him in captivity. When they are both grown, he makes the white girl, who presumably loves him, his squaw; but when he discovers that her parents are still alive he surrenders her to them, and gives himself up to his Indian enemies, dying by the hand of Uncas, remote ancestor of the handsome young brave of *The Last of the Mohicans.* It is

Conanchet, however, who plays the true Uncas role in this novel, being described as "the last sachem of the broken and dispersed tribes of the Narragansett."

The contrast of color between him and his wife, whom he calls Narra-mattah, Cooper emphasizes with all the ambivalent relish of one savoring the nightmare of miscegenation, never letting us forget that it is a "dark glittering eye" and "dark visage" which daily approached the "golden hair and azure eyes" of the kidnaped pale maiden. There is something close to obscenity in his lingering descriptions of Narra-mattah's white, white skin with its "delicate tracery of veins." Conanchet, who shares Cooper's primitive horror of the mixing of blood, finally turns away his beloved white squaw with her papoose, "an offspring with an Indian cross of blood." "Conanchet is a tall and straight hemlock," he firmly tells the clinging, protesting woman, "and the father of Narra-mattah is a tree of the clearing, that bears red fruit. The Great Spirit was angry when they grew together. . . . Let the mind . . . forget the dream among the trees." He can be persuaded only to grant her the hope of reunion in heaven, a sop for her sentimental unwillingness to accept the terrible boundary between race and race: "they say that one just man died for all color. . . . If this be true he [Conanchet] will look for his woman and boy in the happy hunting-grounds."

Conanchet is good Indian enough to disavow the mingling of alien bloods and the mixture of cultures, Christian and pagan, for which it stands. His foil in the book is the imaginary bad Indian, Whittal-Nipset, a half-wit white boy, who has also been captured by the Indians and has emerged from his stay among them convinced that he is a redskin warrior: "Whittal is a warrior on his path. . . . Nipset hath a mother in her wigwam. . . ." Not only does he parody the hope of acculturation elsewhere favorably embodied in Natty Bumppo, but he travesties, too, the Indian case against the white world, elsewhere nobly presented by patriarchs like Tamenund or pled with heroic malice by such villains as Magua. In the mouth of the pseudo-Nipset, all the charges of the Indians, their boasts of virtue and long-suffering become absurdities, the fantasies of a deranged child. Like the half-idiot boy in *Lionel Lincoln,* who seconds the patriotic escaped madman, Whittal caricatures cruelly whatever he advocates; and the dream of "going native," the dream "dreamt among the trees," which Cooper himself to some degree has sponsored, is here finally denied. There is no escaping the march of civilization or the obligation of one's innate "gifts." In any case, *The Wept of Wish-ton-Wish* must be read as the first anti-miscegenation novel in our literature; and *The Last of the Mohicans* must be re-read in its light. Miscegenation is the secret theme of the world's favorite story of adventure, the secret theme of the Leatherstocking Tales as a whole.

The plot of *The Last of the Mohicans* is essentially the New-Comic fable which Scott had made standard in the historical romance, decorated with American-gothic trimmings out of Charles Brockden Brown. Against a background of Indian terror, there are played out an abduction, a rescue, a final duel (involving the death of the villain), and a plighted troth to indicate the restoration of order and innocence. Everything, however, has been strangely doubled, so that the novel finally contains *two* full romantic plots, separated by the "historic" description of the massacre at Fort Henry, "a Narrative of 1757." A pair of girls, Cora and Alice Munro, attempt (for reasons never made quite convincing) to join their father, the commanding colonel at Fort William Henry, though that stronghold is being besieged by Montcalm and his Indian allies. They are provided with one heroic escort, Major Heyward; and are accompanied by one comic traveling companion, a wandering psalmist called David Gamut. Gamut is typical of those Cooper figures, whose final avatar is Parson Amen, representing the absurdity and pathos in the wilderness of men who will not touch a gun but take quite literally the Christian injunction to return good for evil. "Praised be God," David Gamut says, "I have never had occasion to meddle with murderous implements." On the way to the fort the girls and their escort are betrayed to their enemies by a treacherous Indian guide, Magua, but are rescued by Natty, Chingachgook, and Uncas. The massacre intervenes; the two girls are again captured by Magua, are once more rescued by Natty and company; and, after various complications, are finally delivered by a struggle in which one girl, one good Indian, and several bad Indians die.

It all seems fair enough—two plots, two chases, and two deliveries being just twice as good as one; and, in any case, it all fits quite nicely the required two-volume form in which Cooper's novels appeared. But there is a deeper duplicity at stake. Why, for instance, two girls? They are paired off, light against dark, for what one might call with Mr. Grossman "decorative" purposes, just as in Rousseau and even in Richardson, before him, there had been, for contrast and balance, a female companion to the heroine. But the relationship of Cooper's two girls is so close (they have a father in common) and their appearances so strikingly different, that one suspects the author of some deeper intention. Alice, the "most juvenile" of the "two females," has a "dazzling complexion, fair golden hair and bright blue eyes." The developing action shows, too, that she is not gifted with the firmness of her sister Cora, whose "tresses . . . were shiny and black like the plumage of a raven," while "her complexion was not brown, but it rather appeared charged with the color of the rich blood, that seemed ready to burst its bounds." Yet Cora, for all her bursting blood, envies the more pallid Alice. "She is fair! Oh surpassingly fair!" Cora sighs. "Her soul is pure and spotless as her skin."

The point is clear: one is "spotless," which is to say, sexless; the other charged with blood and ready to break through all bounds: a passionate woman, who appeals to the instinctual Indians and who in turn responds to their dark, primitive beauty. "Who that looks at this creature of nature," she exclaims in admiration, beholding Uncas, "remembers the shade of his skin"; or again, this time of Magua, "Shall we distrust a man because his manners are not our manners and that his skin is dark?" Yet "noble, melancholy" Cora is not merely a woman capable of stirring and responding to passion. She is corrupted woman, stained even before birth with the blackness of the primitive and passional, her mother having been "a lady . . . descended, remotely, from that unfortunate class . . . so basely enslaved. . . ." (Cooper cannot bring himself to say the word "Negro"!) She represents, in short—though rather in what she is, than what she does—all that early nineteenth-century male gentility privately lusted for in a female, but publicly denied, would not marry.

It is for this reason that Major Heyward will not have Cora; though we know that she loves him and suspect that he responds a little. He was, after all, to confound matters even further, "born at the south, where those unfortunate beings are considered of a race inferior. . . ." Major Heyward will not, however, admit the charge of Cora's father, "You scorn to mingle the blood of the Heywards with one so degraded," preferring to attribute his reluctance to the power exerted on him by "the sweetness, the beauty, the witchery" of the Snow Maiden, Alice. She is, conveniently enough, no daughter of a dark-skinned mother, but fit offspring of the Scottish "suffering angel," who had waited in her cold North for twenty years in perfect celibacy, until her husband's first wife had died. When Heyward proposes at last to the pure Alice, she responds, not with the proud warmth of Cora, but trembles and almost faints as is "common to her sex."

Not only is the ingenue doubled in *The Last of the Mohicans,* but doubled, too, are the savages, good Indian and bad, Uncas and Magua, paired lovers of Cora. How much these two are alike and yet how different they are! Uncas leaps into sight at one critical moment, "fresh and bloodstained" from his heroic efforts, while Magua (whom Cora has first beheld with pity and admiration as well as horror) holds up his "reeking hand" to boast, "It is real but comes from white veins." The redskin killer as deliverer and aggressor, they are both finally destroyed by their love for the "noble, melancholy" maiden; though Uncas is first advanced by that love on the evolutionary scale "centuries ahead" of his race, while Magua is degraded by it almost to an animal level. Cooper will not attribute the threat of rape even to Magua, taking pains to deny that Indians ever practice such a crime, though he will not permit himself to use the word. He portrays Magua as proposing only a loveless, a forced marriage. "Let the daughter of the English chief follow and live in his wigwam forever," and, at the baffled climax, threatening her with death: "Woman, choose; the wigwam or the knife of Le Subtil."

In the end, the two dark lovers of the dark Cora struggle to destroy each other. She is killed by a follower of Magua; that follower in turn killed by Uncas, who is stabbed to death by Magua. It is Natty Bumppo who finally shoots the bad Indian, hanging to a cliff in vain attempt at escape. Though Cooper's own contemporaries urged him to let Cora and Uncas be joined in marriage, his horror of miscegenation led him to forbid even the not-quite white offspring of one unnatural marriage to enter into another alliance that crossed race lines. The last of the Mohicans is portrayed as the last, the Vanishing American shown to have vanished because (so Cooper at least believed) the color line is eternal and God-given. It is a fantastically ahistorical note.

At the funeral of Cora, the Indian girls who strew her body with flowers sing of her union in the Happy Hunting Grounds with the gallant warrior who had preferred her because "she was of a

blood purer and richer than the rest of her nation." But Natty
will not permit their pious hope, shaking his head "like one who
knew the error of their simple creed"; and when Colonel Munro,
broken by his bereavement, urges the Scout to tell the female
mourners that "the time shall not be distant when we may assemble around His throne without distinction of sex, rank or color,"
he refuses. " 'To tell them this,' he said, 'would be to tell them
that the snows come not in the winter, or that the sun shines
fiercest when the trees are stripped of their leaves.' " Even beyond
death, the ferocity of Cooper's dread of miscegenation will not
yield. With Magua he seems to believe (though his relative rank-
ing of the races would have been different) that the Great Spirit
has made men of different colors as unlike as the different species
of the animal world: the Negroes black as bears and condemned
to work forever like the beavers; the whites pale as ermine and
destined to be traders, though also dogs to their women and wolves
to their slaves; the Indians redder and brighter than the sun,
chosen to represent the image of God and to live a fully human
life.

It is clear finally that the doubling of the women and Indians
in Cooper's novel not only reflects his ambivalence toward the instinctual life in sex and nature, but also permits him to double the
plots and themes which they embody. In one fable, the bad Indian
and the soldier struggle for the Maid without Spot, who is at last
won by the hero and married; in the other, the good Indian and
the bad contest the possession of the Dark Lady, to whom the
victor is united only in a *Liebestod*. In the world of Grace, true
happiness is possible; but in the world of Nature, all lies under a
curse. "Cursed be my tribe/if I forgive him . . ." says Shylock-
Magua; but cursed also is the tribe which does not forgive—which
is to say, all imperfect mankind. Civilization and submission, however incomplete, to Christianity mitigate the curse, which is therefore virulently effective only on the dark-skinned and primitive
peoples of the world. Various characters in *The Last of the Mohicans* speak variously of the curse. For Munro, it is slavery itself:
"a curse entailed upon Scotland by her unnatural union with a
foreign and trading people"—miscegenation between the Scottish
noble savages and the mercantile pale-faces to their south! For
Cora, the curse is a mystery. To the ancient Indian, Tamenund,
she declares, with "burning" blushes, "Like thee and thine, venerable chief . . . the curse of my ancestors has fallen heavily on their

child"; but when asked why grace has been shown to the whites and only rigorous justice to the colored peoples, her sole answer is an evasion: "but why—it is not permitted to inquire." In his own final words, Tamenund can only echo her, "Men of the Lenape! . . . the face of the Manitou is behind a cloud! . . . You see him not; yet his judgments are before you." It is a tautology with which we are left: one is cursed for not being white by the fact of not being white.

VII

There is real tragic potential in the theme of miscegenation as a curse and punishment for a curse, potential to be realized in the fiction of William Faulkner; but neither in *The Last of the Mohicans* nor *The Wept of Wish-ton-Wish* does Cooper succeed in releasing its power either as poetry or action. The New-Comic theme is even more perfunctorily handled, a gesture by Cooper to the *Zeitgeist* rather than a concession to his own deepest needs. We are aware of the implicit tragic theme as a somber undertone, of the nominal New-Comic theme chiefly as an annoyance; but there is a third theme, not yet fully explicated, on which the life of the novel in the world's imagination largely depends. The third theme is closely linked, of course, to the extraneous hero, Natty Bumppo. In the earliest novel in which he appeared, Natty was scarcely integrated into the main plot and therefore posed no difficult questions; but once he had been promoted from his status as a supernumerary, moved to the center of the continuing series, he became an embarrassment. In an age of Romance, what can one do with the hero who, *in essence and by definition, cannot get the girl?*

In order to answer this, it is necessary to understand first of all *why* Natty can never marry; and it is doubtful whether Cooper himself ever consciously or clearly saw this, though instinctively he remained faithful to the limitation, the uncomprehended taboo. In *The Prairie,* as in *The Last of the Mohicans,* Natty is the deliverer, the rescuer, the man who arrives in the nick of time— but only to deliver the ingenue into the arms of someone else, a stuffy and genteel young man of the proper station in life to marry the kind of young lady Cooper considers worthy of being a heroine. It is partly his class origins which make it impossible for Natty, after he has killed Magua, to be rewarded with Alice.

"Now, I come of a humble stock," he says, knowing his own place in the scale of things like all "good" men in Cooper, "though we have white gifts and a white natur'." But even when Cooper goes out of his way to provide Natty with girls of his own caste—Mabel Dunham, the Sergeant's daughter in *The Pathfinder*, or Judith Hutter, the bastard foster-daughter of Floating Tom in *The Deerslayer*—Natty cannot take the final step. Either, as in the former case, we are told that the girl he loves loves someone else; or, as in the latter, that the girl loves him, but is too "stained" for his native nobility, the fallen daughter of a fallen mother, betrayed by aspirations above her station to the officer-seducers of the nearby garrison.

The truth is that Natty is barred from marriage and the family by a prior commitment to a lonely life in a state of nature. "Moral hermaphrodite" that he is (the term is Balzac's), he can only enter into an abstract and fruitless union with the wilderness itself; his true Bride is, as he tries to tell Judith Hutter, the forest, or more precisely the Spirit that inhabits it: "She's in the forest, Judith—hanging from the boughs of the trees in a soft rain. . . ." And when asked if he has ever found it pleasant to listen to a girl's laughter, he answers, "Lord bless you, gal—to me there is no music so sweet as the sighing of the wind in the treetops and the rippling of a stream . . . unless, indeed, it be the open mouth of a certain hound, when I'm on the trail of a fat buck." An obvious choice for Natty would seem to be an Indian girl, brought up to the world he loves and, in a sense, its very personification; but Natty is, as we have begun to see, a fanatical exponent of racial purity. Magua may speak of him (he intends a grudging compliment) as "one whose skin is neither red nor pale," but Natty insists with almost maddening repetitiousness throughout *The Last of the Mohicans* that he is "a white man without a cross," that the has "no taint of Indian blood." "I am white," he is still maintaining in *The Deerslayer*, "have a white heart, and can't in reason, love a red-skinned maiden," though he is willing to grant when pressed that he is "a little red-skin in feelin's and habits." When he is offered an Indian bride in that later book, she is old and ugly, the whole episode a degrading travesty, monstrous enough to justify Deerslayer's comment, "I've known them that would prefer death to such a captivity."

The entire incident represents an attempt not only to caricature Indian-white relations but to parody marriage itself, as the word "captivity" reveals. The union with a squaw means to Natty not only the mingling into an unthinkable hybrid of gifts intended by God to be distinct; it also stands for the loss of freedom involved in any permanent connection with a woman, red or white. It would have meant in short a kind of *emasculation,* since the virility of Natty is not genital but heroic and cannot survive in the marriage bed any more than beside the hearth. Insofar as Natty projected the marginal discontent of Cooper (and his America) with the kind of life which in the main he loved, he was doomed to remain unattached to Woman, who symbolized that life. "I may never marry," Natty says at one point, "most likely Providence [which is to say, James Fenimore Cooper], in putting me up here in the woods, has intended I should live single and without a lodge of my own."

Yet there is a relationship which symbolically joins the white man to nature and his own unconscious, without a sacrifice of his "gifts"; and binds him in life-long loyalty to a help-meet, without the sacrifice of his freedom. This is the pure marriage of males— sexless and holy, a kind of counter-matrimony, in which the white refugee from society and the dark-skinned primitive are joined till death do them part. Natty himself in *The Last of the Mohicans* contrasts the love which links him to Uncas (and his father, the Sagamore) with the sentiment which has sent Heyward in pursuit of Alice: "I have heard . . . that there is a feeling in youth which binds man to woman closer than the father is to the son— It may be so. I have seldom been where women of my color dwell; but such may be the gifts of nature in the settlements." It is an odd enough notion that tender heterosexual love is a possession only of men in settlements, and that in its place the forest breeds an equally tender passion between males who "winters and summers, nights and days, have . . . roved the wilderness in company, eating of the same dish, one sleeping while the other watched. . . ." Uncas, to be sure, dies at the end of the action, but Chingachgook is left; and it is with him that Natty shares a common grief even as Uncas and Cora share a common death, Major Heyward and Alice a common marriage bed. "No, no," cries Hawkeye, gazing yearningly at the rigid features of his friend, who has been bewailing his loneliness, "no, Sagamore, not alone. The gifts of our colors may be different, but God hath so placed us as to journey in the same path. I have no kin, and I may also say, like you, no people. . . . The boy has left us for a time; but Sagamore, you are not alone."

The man without a cross and almost without a country clasps hands with the dispossessed savage, who has outlived his race—expropriator and expropriated, united by their tears; and we learn not only that they will remain faithful until Chingachgook has leaped into the flames (this we have known since the first romance of the series), but also that not even death will part the twain. The union in heaven that Natty will not grant the man and woman—between whom passion made the bar eternal—he grants himself and his Indian friends, for they yearn to join not flesh but souls. "Depend on it, boy, whether there be one heaven or two, there is a path in the other world by which honest men may come together again," he says in *The Last of the Mohicans;* and in the later *Deerslayer,* he makes an even stronger case. "But of all doctrines, Sarpent," he insists, "that which disturbs me . . . most, is the one that teaches us to think a pale-face goes to one heaven and a red-skin to another; it may separate in death them which lived much together, and loved each other well in life."

Yet the passion that joins male to male in Cooper is not in its implications as innocent as he wants to think. Why, if there is no sense of a lurking danger in such a relation, has he made the beloved Chingachgook not merely dusky (a natural sign of the forbidden), but marked him with a death's head for a totem, and called him the Great Serpent. The "sarpent," who is the special enemy of woman, is also, and by the same token, the symbol of temptation; and of this Cooper is dimly aware. "Now I'm naturally avarse to sarpents and I hate even the word," Natty remarks, "On account of a certain sarpent at the creation of the 'arth, that outwitted the first woman; yet, ever since Chingachgook earned the title he bears, why the sound is as pleasant to me as the whistle of the whip-poor-will of a calm evening." The clue is here, the revelation that the very end of the pure love of male for male is to *outwit* woman, that is, to keep her from trapping the male through marriage into civilization and Christianity. The wilderness Eros is, in short, not merely an anti-cultural, but an anti-Christian, a Satanic Eros; and yet it is proffered by Cooper (barring such an occasional slip as we have just examined) and accepted by his readers as innocent. To believe this one must become as a boy, to whom neither sex nor violence is real, and to whom mother is the secret enemy, to be evaded even as she is loved.

That is why Cooper is so fond of presenting his anti-female alliance of outcast and savage in an atmosphere of make-believe, of "playing Indians." Even in *The Wept of Wish-ton-Wish,* for instance, there is a mock-marriage of Indian and white used to underline by contrast the horror of the real mating of Conanchet and Narra-mattah. That pure union joins "the last of the Narragansetts" to Submission, a mysterious white man, who declares of himself: "Though of white blood and of Christian origins, I can almost say that my heart is Indian." Conanchet's final words to his wife, which are aimed only at preparing her for his death and her abandonment, urge her to give up the dream "dreamt among the trees," and to return to the settlements of her people. But Submission, presumable killer of his king and man without a last name, Conanchet leaves safe in the woods, perched in one of the trees that define the dream. He has declared already that their lives "are one," and he goes to his own death, leading a war-party of hostile Indians away from his "brother."

The passion which joins together the men of races forbidden to mingle in marriage is everywhere in Cooper, appearing finally in *The Chainbearer,* in which Mordaunt Littlepage falls in love at first sight with the old Indian known variously as Susquesus, Sureflint, and Trackless. The passage is quite remarkable. Sureflint advances with the customary declaration of loneliness, "No tribe—no squaw—no papoose"; and Littlepage comments, comparing the red-skin with the pale-face girl his family are urging him to marry, "Priscilla Bayard herself, however lovely, graceful, winning and feminine, had not created a feeling so strong and animated, as that which was awakened within me in behalf of old Sureflint." This quite extraordinary reaction is paralleled, as James Grossman points out, by Natty Bumppo's declaration to Jasper, his presumable rival for Mabel Dunham in *The Pathfinder:* "if I had to marry you, boy, I should give myself no consarn about my being well looked upon . . . ," though this time, for once, the beloved boy is white.

The final give-away comes, however, as Grossman is again acute enough to see, in *Jack Tier,* a sea story published toward the end of Cooper's writing career. In this novel, there is sketched an erotic relationship between two males—old buddies they seem at first glance, though one has forgotten or pretends to have forgotten the other—so complicated in its blend of love and hate, loyalty and rejection, that it is rivaled only by such Melvillean sinister homoerotic relationships as those of Redburn and Jackson, Billy Budd and Claggart. Cooper seems on the very verge of treating candidly the kind of feeling that, romanticized and idealized, had lent an attractive ambiguity to the companionship of Chingachgook and Natty Bumppo; but at the very last minute, he loses his nerve and "reveals" that the evil Captain Spike's strange friend, Jack Tier—is really a woman, Spike's wife, Molly Swash! By 1848, however, there was little Cooper could do to undercut his own creation; his version of a love between males, more enduring and purer than any heterosexual passion, had become an undying myth as had Natty and Chingachgook, perhaps the only two characters in American literature endowed with the kind of archetypal life otherwise lived by Don Juan, Don Quixote, Falstaff, and Robinson Crusoe.

PART TWO

ACHIEVEMENT AND FRUSTRATION

8

CLARISSA IN AMERICA:
TOWARD
MARJORIE MORNINGSTAR

NONE OF THE FORMS of the novel adapted from European prototypes has influenced American fiction more profoundly than the
sentimental tale of seduction. First of all, the seduction story
proper has never for long ceased to be written or read in the
United States; dismissed as old-fashioned, exhausted, intolerable,
it reappears not only as the best-seller but even as the advanced,
the New Novel. In the second place, the heroine of the seduction
struggle, the Protestant Virgin and redeemer first called Clarissa,
has continued to impose herself on American life and fiction alike,
outliving even the abandonment of the fable in which she confronted the Seducer. Third, and most important of all, the long
uncontested reign in America of sentimental archetypes and
clichés has made it almost impossible for our novelists to portray
adult sexual passion or a fully passionate woman.

On the most popular level, of course, the combat of the pure
woman and the seducer-rapist has never been abandoned, though
it seems for a while to have been exiled to the drama and from
there to have passed to the moving pictures. The earliest cinema
assimilated the fallen archetypes of seduction along with many
others; and in one sub-form of the lowbrow Western, the traditional sex combat is played out to the present moment, the white-
hatted hero intervening just before the black-hatted villain manages to violate the rancher's blond daughter. Even the old class
distinctions are dimly maintained, the seducer being given often
the status of dude, gambler, or banker, and wearing, until quite

217

recently, not only the black mufti of civilian life, but also an "Eastern," upper-class mustache. The horse-opera version of the seduction fable represents a male kidnaping of an originally female theme: the projection of an erotic daydream in which the Fair Maiden is first (almost) raped, then rescued to be legally possessed, but *cannot save herself.*

Both hero and villain of the latter-day sentimental story are, as we observed earlier, created by splitting the Lovelace figure into two components, whatever is truly masculine and cleanly attractive being identified with the "good," and whatever is grossly phallic or unduly polished being identified with the "bad." The nonrepentant Lovelace, who wants merely to enjoy Clarissa sexually, is made one man; and the repentant Lovelace, who wants to marry her, is made another. Sometimes, indeed, the white-hatted Lovelace is permitted a genital past, symbolized by a previous connection with some dark, preferably Mexican, prostitute, in which he has burned away all lust, purified himself for the blond Maiden. On the basis of such hints, or of none at all, the audience puts Humpty-Dumpty together again, joins in its own consciousness the halves of the fragmented hero-villain. The spectator tears the dress from the pale shoulder and breast of the struggling girl in the lonely cabin, and at the same time pounds toward the cabin on his lathered white horse to save her. His better and worse instincts simultaneously gratified, he cheers as the bunkhouse Clarissa, still safe though charmingly ruffled, learns that her virginity does not save but must be saved by the male deliverer, who will extort it from her (legally, legally!) as the price of her delivery.

Neither shifts in official morality, nor literary manifestos proclaiming sexual freedom, nor even actual changes in social behavior appear to have shaken the mystique of virginity on which our response to the threat of rape and seduction depends. It is our least rational attitudes toward sex to which the seduction story appeals; and on that level, the responses of men and women are sharply distinguished from each other. Women, at least, seem to find little archetypal satisfaction in the sub-variety of the Western which makes the heroine a contested pawn. Yet in the latter half of the nineteenth century, the female audience, pledgd to an almost intolerable gentility, no longer could relish without feelings of guilt the old fantasy in which the figures with which they identified were first ravished, then succeeded by their humility in castrating their ravishers. In its place, there appeared a mythic proto-literature in which women eternally suffer not from sexual assault but from the general failure of males—not, that is to say, from men's potency but from their weakness: their cowardice, lack of moral firmness, insufficient intelligence, proneness to get drunk or ill, or to die when most needed, The popular line of Richardsonianism ends in the seduction story without seduction!

Its history in the more serious novel is almost equally duplicitous. Cooper, like Scott, had accepted the decision of the genteel audience that ladies could no longer be seduced, at least in the pages of books; but like his Scotch predecessor, he felt free to permit lower-class characters to endure that ungenteel indignity, even to the point of becoming pregnant. Against Cora and Alice, he would not, as we have noticed, allow the threat of sexual violation to be raised, only that of a forced marriage and consignment to a wigwam; but Judith Hutter in *The Deerslayer* is far enough removed from the upper ranks of society to be portrayed as doubly involved in the seduction tangle. Cooper is desperately polite in his language, reticent to the point of obscurity; but it is clear that Judith is herself the offspring of a mother seduced or abandoned, and that her coquetry and her refusal to accept her station in life have, if not deprived her of her virginity, at least so compromised her honor that she is not a fit bride for Deerslayer. It is typical of Cooper—who reverses in this respect the meanings implicit in the seduction theme—that he makes of Judith's indiscreet involvement with the officers in the British garrison an occasion for a sermon not against the effrontery of upper-class seducers, but against the shamelessness of female social climbers, willing to barter their virtue for a rise in status.

Nonetheless, Cooper did not seem really at home with the seduction story, using it only this once and then quite peripherally; indeed, his major themes afforded him no scope for developing the deeper meanings of the Clarissa archetype. William Gilmore Simms, on the other hand, who is perhaps Cooper's most successful follower both in tales of Indian warfare and of the American Revolution, was attracted to the seduction fable in one of its most popular forms. In two novels, he succeeded in giving fictional form to the famous "Kentucky tragedy" which, occurring first as fact, passed almost immediately into literature, and has ever since continued to haunt the imagination of American writers. In *Charlemont*, which was published in 1856, and *Beauchampe*, actually a sequel to the first novel though it appeared in 1842, Simms tells a tale which had already served as the kernel of *Greyslear* (1840) by Charles Fenno Hoffman and an unfinished play by Edgar Allan Poe called *Politian* (1835-36). The account of how Anna Cooke persuaded a certain Jeroboam Beauchamp to kill for her sake a prominent Kentucky politician and attorney, Solomon P. Sharp, who had in her girlhood seduced her, and how the accomplices, after being sentenced to be hanged, committed suicide, makes a choice melodrama; the very embodiment of a Romantic era, which that era itself could not forbear turning into a myth. Not only Poe and Hoffman and Simms, but the playwrights Charlotte Barnes, John Savage, and T. H. Chivers took up the theme; and in *World Enough and Time* (1950), Robert Penn Warren returned to it once more, seeking in its mythic substance clues to the meanings of justice and honor in an age when Byronism had inflated those concepts with passionate rhetoric. The popular success of Warren's novel indicates how, under whatever aegis, the seduction story continues to stir the popular mind; and its uncomfortable rejection by many highbrow critics, who had until the appearance of this novel considered Warren one of their own, is a sign of how baffled the merely literary man may be by such archetypal material.

For Simms, some twenty years after the actual episode, the story offered the spectacular possibilities inherent in gossip about prominent personalities (he scarcely changed the real names of his protagonists), as well as the gothic appeal of dark violence and shrill melodrama. He was a writer with a truly operatic taste for posturing and high-flown language, so that when his heroine, called first Margaret Cooper, then Anna Cooke, cries out, "War always with my foe—war to the knife—war to the last!" we almost fancy we are hearing it sung. The terrific moments are all mercilessly exploited: the dying murderers in each other's arms; the stabbing of the cowardly Solomon Sharp by Beauchamp, who cannot provoke him to a duel; the desperate whispering of Sharp that he could not have been the father of Anna's child, since it was born black! Simms is, of course, a Southerner, who ended estranged from much of his audience over slavery and the Civil War, and the merest *hint* of miscegenation is about all he can manage, though in other matters he is so brutally explicit that Poe himself found him "revolting." " 'It was not mine!' " Simms has Sharp say of Anna's baby, " 'and to say whose it was is scarce so easy a matter, but—' and he drew nigh and whispered the rest of the sentence, some three syllables, into the ears of the husband."

Those three syllables the prurient, race-haunted imagination of the Southerner presumably had no difficulty in supplying.

Yet Simms was not interested only in the horror to be wrested from his material. Good Sentimentalist as well as belated gothicist, he extorts the tear as well as the shudder. Primarily, however, Simms thinks of himself as a historian, a sociologist; and he finds the roots of the double crime of passion and revenge in the social conditions of the border: that leading edge of the westward movement, that margin which symbolizes the yearning for innocence and its inevitable defeat. (It is an aspect of the story which particularly intrigues Warren later on.) "The population of a frontier country . . . scattered over a large territory," Simms writes in the "Advertisement" to *Charlemont,* "and meeting infrequently, feels the lack of social intercourse; and this tends to break down most of the barriers which a strict convention usually establishes for the protection . . . of sex and caste. . . . It follows, naturally, that they are frequently wronged and outraged, and just as naturally that their resentments are keen, eager and vindictive." It is an acute enough observation of the genesis of the "code of the West," a type of insight available to one who, born in Charleston, South Carolina, lived for some time as a young man under frontier conditions in Mississippi.

But Simms is not content to attribute the fall of Anna and her excessive lust for vengeance simply to "conditions." The very nature of the fable, in which the seduced girl does not immediately forgive and die, but lives long enough to strike back through a male avenger, who is merely the extension of her will; in which she does not convert and redeem by Christian example, but destroys by a border code of honor—contains an implicit condemnation of that girl for betraying her archetypal role. Simms's two-volume work is the first protest in our literature against woman's refusal in life to act out the humble, long-suffering part assigned her by the Richardsonian myth.

Simms is quite explicit on this score in the same "Advertisement." "Her character and career will illustrate most of the mistakes which are made by that ambitious class, among the gentle sex, who are now seeking so earnestly to pass out from that province of humiliation to which the sex has been circumscribed from the first moment of recorded history." And he goes out of his way to point out, as a warning to those not yet utterly lost, that the "proposed change in her condition threatens fatally some of her own and the best securities of humanity." Like a good Richardsonian Sentimentalist aware of living in an unfavorable age, he reminds the Anna Cookes of his time of what every Clarissa once knew, that her essential function is to typify the heart ("Her very influence over man lies in her sensibilities"), not to usurp the function of the head ("It will be a perilous fall . . . when . . . in the extreme development of the mere intellect, she shall forfeit a single one of those securities of her sex").

Simms is not, to be sure, a distinguished writer, as he himself well knew; he is only a symptomatic one. "Here lies one," he wrote in a modest epitaph composed for himself, "who, after a reasonably long life, distinguished by unceasing labors, has left all his better work undone." Yet once in his career he hit upon an archetypal theme and saw through to its meanings, which others had fumbled away. Unlike Poe or Mrs. Bragaldi, who transposed an essentially American and nineteenth-century fable to seventeenth-century Rome or fifteenth-century Milan, or C. F. Hoffman, who moved it back to Revolutionary days—watering the seduction down to a mere abduction—Simms kept his tale at that precise point in time when the American woman was sloughing off one role, known in all its possibilities, for another, dangerously unexplored. That he succeeded in adapting the seduction archetype to the inner needs of women and the inner fears of men in his own time is a tribute both to his own acuity and to the resiliency of the myth with which he worked.

I I

Hawthorne was engaged in a similar venture at just about the same time, portraying first in Hester in *The Scarlet Letter,* then in Zenobia in *The Blithedale Romance,* the spirit of impatience with their status that moved women in his world. There is something a little unconvincing in his projection of feminism back into the seventeenth century. He can attribute prophetic anticipations of female discontent to Hester, but there is nothing for her to *do* with them inside the scene Hawthorne has imagined for her, since they are portrayed by Hawthorne not as the causes of her seduction but as its consequence, irresponsible conceptions of a mind which has been condemned to live outside the law and society itself. Yet Hawthorne's description of Hester's theories makes them sound like the notions Simms attributes to Anna Cooke:

Indeed, the same dark question often rose into her mind, with reference to the whole race of womanhood. Was existence worth accepting, even to the happiest among them? . . . As a first step, the whole system of society is to be torn down and built up anew. Then, the very nature of the opposite sex, or its long hereditary habit, which has become like nature, is to be essentially modified, before woman can be allowed to assume what seems a fair and suitable position. Finally, all other difficulties being obviated, woman cannot take advantage of these preliminary reforms, until she herself shall have undergone a still mightier change; in which, perhaps, the ethereal essence, wherein she has her truest life, will be found to have evaporated.

Though he has earlier denied to females of Hester's era the "ethereal" quality of their later descendants, Hawthorne has at this point forgotten which world he is in. His quarrel is not with Hester but, through her, with the emancipated ladies of his own time.

It is for their sake that he has Hester finally disavow the temptation to become the deliverer of her sex, has her confess herself too "stained with sin, bowed down with shame" to perform a task which demands an "angel and apostle . . . lofty, pure and beautiful." By her submission, Hester saves herself from the fate of Zenobia, in whom feminism is real, contemporary, and unrepented (she is suspected of being a portrait of Margaret Fuller), and who is visited with a final fate more vindictively stage-managed than any other doom in Hawthorne. Described as "Woman, bruising herself against the narrow limitations of her sex," Zenobia is actually bruised against the ambivalent hostility of Miles Coverdale, the narrator of the novel in which she appears, and of Hawthorne, who speaks almost directly through the mask of Coverdale. It is hard to know which infuriates Hawthorne more, Zenobia's impassioned cry, "If I live another year, I will lift up my own voice in behalf of woman's wider liberty!" or her abject surrender to the brutally masculine reformer, Hollingsworth, who shouts down her plea for women's rights: ". . . if there were a chance of their attaining the end which these petticoated monstrosities have in view, I would call upon my own sex to use its physical force, that unmistakeable evidence of sovereignty, to scourge them back within their proper bounds!"

The impotent, failed poet Coverdale in some sense must mean his assurance that he would love to kneel before a woman ruler, bow in adoration to a Protestant Virgin; though he is convinced, too, that only a broken heart makes women reformers rather than passive lovers, that feminism is the result of ill-regulated or ill-bestowed passion. Perhaps, most of all, he distrusts Zenobia not for being an emancipated woman but for being a fully sexual one, for having forced him, at their first meeting, to imagine her naked ("in Eve's earliest garments," he delicately puts it), to respond to what in her is rich, warm, and dangerous. For having sinned in the flesh with men more masculine than he, and for having survived in all the opulence of that flesh to pollute his imagination, Zenobia must—in Coverdale's telling of the tale—die, the victim of her own despair. Hawthorne-Coverdale's portrait of the drowned Zenobia, fished up after her suicide, is a masterpiece of sadistic horror, pregnant with all the nuances proper not to her life but to the nauseating dream which betrays a shameful, unconfessed wish.

It is not only with the seduction of the corrupted woman, "high-spirited" or "headstrong," that Hawthorne deals, but also with that of the pale, the "ethereal'" Maiden; though he cannot find it in his heart—or more precisely, perhaps, within the limits of the decorum he shared with his age—to portray the actual ruin of any innocent. His "weakly maidens," eternally threatened, eternally escape; and even his full-blown passionate females are only *postulated* as sexually experienced. His reticence extends to describing the actual fall even of those indecorous females to whom the loss of chastity comes in part as a consequence of their own refusal to believe in its importance. It is notorious that *The Scarlet Letter* is a seduction story without a seduction, a parable of the Fall with the Fall offstage and before the action proper begins. Similarly, the hinted-at but never quite defined original sin of Zenobia or of Miriam in *The Marble Faun* must be taken on faith. Certain women move onto Hawthorne's fictional stage already deflowered; no woman is deflowered in his fictional present.

Hawthorne is the only American novelist of classic stature who deals centrally in his most important works with the seduction theme; yet there is no seduction scene (even the devirgination of Donatello, which is of a man by a woman, is accomplished in the outer darkness between chapters and could not be proved in court) in any of his works! Perhaps it is just as well that he never tried one, since the American conventions for describing such scenes were vulgar and false to a degree that defied redemption. How much more moving and even sexually exciting is Hawthorne's description of Hester's symbolic letting down of her hair before her lover in the forest clearing ("By another impulse, she took off the formal cap that confined her hair; and down it fell upon her shoulders, dark and rich, with at once a shadow and a light in its abundance . . .") than Simms's intendedly passionate evocation of Margaret-Anna's surrender in another forest (". . . and there they lingered! He, fond, artful, persuasive; she, trembling with the dangerous sweetness of wild, unbidden emotions. Ah! why did she not go? . . . The moon rose until she hung in the zenith . . . the rivulet ran along, still prattling through the groves . . . but they no longer heard the prattle of the rivulet . . . and it was only when they were about to depart, that poor Margaret discovered that the moon had all the while been looking down upon them . . .").

Yet from his very first novel on, Hawthorne had attempted to deal with the seduction theme, evoking in *Fanshawe* stereotypes right out of the stock of the genteel sentimental novel: the depraved Seducer, the virtuous Maiden, the brave young lover— Lovelace and Clarissa, plus the supernumerary male rescuer made necessary by the latter-day failure of nerve before the prospect of letting any real young lady get raped.

Any of the "d——d female scribblers," whom Hawthorne thought of as his rivals, could have done as well with the sentimental New-Comic plot: a virgin is tricked by a scoundrel with a forged letter, purportedly from her father, and led off into a lonely valley where she is on the point of being violated when she is rescued by her true lover. This absurdly conventional action is rendered in the style of the female epigones of Richardson, with no real inwardness, almost none of the sustained, almost painfully detailed psychological probing which is the forte of their master.

Sentiment seems, for all his choice of theme, to concern Hawthorne as little in *Fanshawe* as does psychology. He capitalizes scandalously little upon the sentimental possibilities of his story, milking for the proper quota of tears only the episode of a criminal at his mother's deathbed, and the scene in which the girl praying for her virtue dares call upon that criminal in the name of that abandoned mother. "I have thought of my mother . . . ," Hawthorne has him answer; "I remember the neglect, the wrong . . . that she received at my hands . . . by those words you have turned my heart to stone." Perhaps the lonely young man who had long lived in a widowed mother's house knew more about the feelings involved in the inevitable betrayals of mothers by sons than of the passion of a rapist. Beyond this hidden allusion to his own home life, Hawthorne is no more deeply involved in the pathos of abused innocence and the terror of hardened criminality than he is in the female satisfactions of a matrimonial happy ending. Neither emotional aspect of his ill-chosen fable accords with his need to project at the beginning of his writing career the self-distrust and self-pity which, under his irony and reserve, were to remain the hallmarks of his fiction. The dread of social, artistic, and sexual failure is imposed on the uncongenial theme, bends it toward the pathetic at least, if not the tragic. By a simple doubling of the heroic male protagonist, Hawthorne adopts the stereotypes of seduction to his own deepest personal exigencies.

His heroine, Ellen Langton, that is to say, has not the customary one, but two true lovers: Edward Walcott, who is handsome, vigorous, full of natural grace and forgivable "boyish" excesses; and Fanshawe, who is slight, pale, melancholy—afflicted by some mysterious "blight ere maturity." The latter is, in short, a Wertherlike portrait of the scholar-artist as a doomed young man, a type to whom Hawthorne elsewhere in his early work gives the name "Oberon" to indicate that he is not of this world. The Oberon character can by definition neither get the girl or live to full maturity, yet in *Fanshawe* he is permitted to beat his healthier competitor to the struggling maiden, actually to save her by his intervention. It is a concession to self-pity, the last kindness of the defeated artist to his own image; yet Hawthorne, even in so melting a mood, refuses to imagine Oberon-Fanshawe in actual physical combat with the forces of evil. His melancholy hero merely tosses a stone into the ravine where Ellen is pleading with her abductor, distracts that abductor from his purpose, and watches as the attacker, eager to destroy all witnesses to his crime, climbs the steep side of a cliff, slips and falls to his death.

After Ellen is thus saved, however, Fanshawe does not claim her hand; only in the moment of her swoon, when she seems more charming corpse than menacing live female, can he achieve a sort of consummation. "He lifted the motionless form of Ellen in his arms, and . . . gazed on her cheek of lily paleness with a joy, a triumph, that rose almost to madness. . . . He bent over her, and pressed a kiss—the first, and he knew it would be the last— on her pale lips. . . ." It is a way of *not* eating your cake and having it, too.

It is clear from the logic of Fanshawe's character as Hawthorne has conceived it that he cannot have the girl, any girl, that he is psychologically impotent; but Hawthorne prefers to have him disavow her, deliberately reject the salvation she offers, choosing instead an early grave, after which Ellen is free to marry Edward Walcott, whom her patience and faithfulness save from roistering and other "passions and pursuits that would have interfered with domestic felicity."

Fanshawe is finally an unsuccessful novel, but in it Hawthorne finds the pattern and invents the protagonists that inform almost all the rest of his work. In *The Blithedale Romance,* for instance, his next-to-the-last completed novel, the personae of *Fanshawe* reappear in a more richly worked out social context, and with a more complex kind of inwardness as well as a more consistent symbolic significance. Fanshawe has become Miles Coverdale, peeping Tom and unsuccessful artist, who is not permitted this time the luxury of saving anyone or even of dying, but only of confessing at the end that he has all along loved the girl he could not win for himself. Hollingsworth, who corresponds to Edward Walcott, aggressive, phallic, desired by women though in minor ways sadly astray, is once more allowed the marriage which is his salvation. This time, however, he is humbled even as he is saved, spiritually castrated, since in his case the "passions and pursuits that would have interfered with domestic felicity" are his ideas for social reform, the "philanthropy" which has been the vital core of his life. Poor, lucky Hollingsworth totters, almost crawls to the happy ending; it is Hawthorne-Oberon-Coverdale's secret revenge.

Between *Fanshawe* and *The Blithedale Romance,* the Oberon character, who embodies Hawthorne's earliest view of the function and fate of the artist, is variously transformed. In *The Scarlet Letter,* he becomes Dimmesdale, the artist as hypocrite, the man whose power over words and souls is based on an unconfessable guilt; and his secret sin is identified as seduction. Certainly, *The Scarlet Letter* is the only eminent American book before the

modern period to have made—or to have seemed to make—
passionate love its center, and it was this which moved the scan-
dalized critics to talk about the beginnings of "a French era" in
our chaste literature. Actually, Howthorne's short novel is not as
much against the American grain as it superficially appears to be.
Master of duplicity, he is especially duplicitous in this regard,
refusing, for instance, even to mention in his text the word
"adultery," though the "A" which symbolizes it glows at the
center of almost every scene. The little Puritan children of the
seventeenth century, franker than adults of the nineteenth, are
permitted "the utterance of the word that had no distinct purport
to their own minds, but was more than terrible to her [Hester]
. . ."; but the reader is not permitted to overhear it. As a matter
of fact, little children in more recent generations, taking the book
off the shelves in the children's library, where it has been permitted to stay by the most high-minded librarians, have doubtless
been puzzled over what the mysterious letter does stand for,
since no word for Hester's crime that is familiar to them begins
with that chaste letter.

Though sex is centrally present in *The Scarlet Letter* as it is
not in our other great novels, it is there rendered reticently, incomprehensibly enough to seem, though not innocent, perhaps, as
good as innocent. To understand just how shadowy and sterilized
its treatment of passion really is, it is only necessary to compare
Hawthorne's novella with a real example of the continental novel,
with Rousseau's *Nouvelle Héloïse,* for instance. We know he regarded that novel highly all his life, first reading it because it
was forbidden, and describing it as "admirable" in a list of books
which he prepared for himself at the age of sixteen. More importantly, he returned to it just when he was ready to produce *The
Scarlet Letter,* bogging down this time, but reviving in himself
a sense of that forbidden and secretly relished work. In the course
of a pilgrimage to the Rousseau country in 1859, he wrote:

> In Switzerland, I found myself more affected by Clarens, the
> scene of the love of St. Preux and Julia, than I have often been
> by the scenes of romance and poetry. I read Rousseau's ro-
> mance with great sympathy when I was hardly more than a boy;
> ten years ago or more I tried to read it again, without success;
> but from my feeling of yesterday I think it still retains its hold
> on my imagination.

It is possible to exaggerate the parallels between the book that moved Hawthorne in his youth and the one he wrote in his middle age, yet certain general similarities are really there. The three characters of Julie, Saint-Preux, and Wolmar correspond illuminatingly with Hester, Dimmesdale, and Chillingworth; and the basic pattern of the *Nouvelle Héloïse* is repeated in *The Scarlet Letter:* a second temptation after a first fall, ending in an unnatural triangle perpetuated under strange circumstances. The differences, however, are more striking and more significant, especially the expurgation in Hawthorne's book of all direct reference to the physical aspects of passion. From Hawthorne's imagination, fired in adolescence, Rousseau's fable must pass through his conscience, created in solitude and confirmed in his marriage to a good woman; and it emerges finally much transformed. The dangerous doctrines that passion justifies all and that adulterous love renounced on earth will be recognized in heaven survive in Hawthorne not as articles of faith, but as problematical convictions, temptations to Faustian pride. Moreover, passion is rendered in *The Scarlet Letter* not as lived, but as remembered or proposed. The reality of the flesh, which in Rousseau provides a counterbalance to his excessive sentimentality, tends to disappear in Hawthorne.

The anti-rhetoric of Hawthorne, which defends him against sentimentality, also prevents him from rendering sensuality, dissolves all ecstasies in ironies. Everywhere in his work a peculiar tension is created between the passionate analogues he evokes and the dispassionate quality of his actual text. Behind Dimmesdale and Hester, we are aware not only of Saint-Preux and Julie, but of the original Abelard and Héloïse, castrated priest and his beloved, and of David and Bathsheba, whose love is portrayed in the tapestries of Dimmesdale's house. Again and again in the text, references are made to the infamous Overbury case, Chillingworth being identified with the Dr. Forman who was its chief villain. But the filth involved in that case: the suggestions of homosexuality, the aphrodisiacs, the poison enemas, the wax mommets with a "thorn thrust through the privity"—all these are transmuted into abstract evocations of evil and concupiscence.

In the end, we are left with the sense that surely something more terrible than mere adultery is at stake behind all the reticences and taboos, that Hawthorne may be dealing, half-consciously at least, with the sin of incest, for which his mother's family, the Mannings, had once been publicly disgraced. So at least one commentator (Vernon Loggins in *The Hawthornes*) has suggested, and this Hawthorne's life-long preoccupation with the theme, as well as the moment at which he composed his greatest novel, would seem to confirm. *Felt's Annals,* referred to in the "Custom-House Introduction," records the unsavory case of the Mannings; and the pictures it evokes jibe with the key images of *The Scarlet Letter:* two girls in the market-place, each with an "I" in her cap; and their beloved brother fleeing through the lawless wilderness! Brother-sister incest: it is the kind of love, as we have seen, proper to the gothic tale, of which *The Scarlet Letter* is the supreme example in our fiction; but in that book, it has been translated down to a less terrible crime, which itself has been reduced to its own mere initial. Historically, a woman found guilty of adultery would have been condemned to wear the two letters "AD"; but this seems to Hawthorne not abstract enough, and he substitutes the single "A," that represents the beginning of all things, and that, in the primers of New England, stood for *Adam's Fall*—in which we (quite unspecifically) sinned all!

The carnal act upon which adultery depends is not merely unnamed in *The Scarlet Letter;* it is further deprived of reality by being displaced in time, postulated rather than described. So displaced, that act becomes in the psychologist's sense, prehistoric; affects us much as the spied-upon primal scene (mother and father intertwined in bed), blurred by the amnesia of guilt. It is an original sin, more an "emblem" or a "type," in Hawthorne's terms, than a deed. "Ye that wronged me are not sinful," Chillingworth says to his wife and her lover, "save in a kind of typical illusion." In one sense, the postulated original sin seems merely a convenient explanatory device. Certainly, it accounts naturalistically for the existence of Pearl, the illegitimate daughter of Hester. But Pearl seems less a real child than an allegorical representation of the fruits of sin; and we are offered, as if jestingly, the alternative explanation that she is a by-blow of the Devil. In addition, Hester must be from the very beginning a mother, though she appears among men who are, within the time of the story itself, rendered as impotent. The impotence of Dimmesdale, however, must be felt as a punishment, the typical self-castration of the seducer, celebrated in the American novel from the time of *Charlotte Temple;* and we are, therefore, asked to believe that at some point before the action begins he traduced Hester's innocence, thus unmanning himself. Actually, he is portrayed as one for whom sex is a remembered nightmare or a futilely longed-for hope; and he does not even kiss Hester at his moment of Satanic exhilaration in the forest.

If it is finally hard for us to believe *on a literal level* in the original adultery of Hester and Dimmesdale, this is because their whole prehistory remains shadowy and vague. Hawthorne's gestures at indicating the social backgrounds and historical contexts of his characters are half-hearted and unconvincing, a bow toward realism. And his book is finally dream-like rather than documentary, not at all the historical novel it has been often called— evoking the past as nightmare rather than fact. It is, therefore, easier to believe in the diabolical transportation of Chillingworth from Germany than in any more rational theory of his arrival on the scene; just as it is easier to imagine Pearl plucked from a rosebush than carried for nine months within her mother. All the characters come into existence when the book begins and do not survive. Hester is simply not there until the prison doors open; and at that moment Chillingworth drops from the air. So born they must die with the action's close—contrary to the traditions of the Victorian novel. For all his desire to end his book like his contemporaries, Hawthorne finds it difficult to say simply that Pearl left the country and married well. He is much more comfortable with the end of Chillingworth, who withered away, as is quite proper for a protagonist regarded by his author as a "shadowy figure," one of a "tribe of unrealities," who cease to exist when he stops thinking of them.

Actors in a dark hallucination, Hawthorne's protagonists are aptly moved by a guilt as hallucinatory as themselves: a crime as vaguely defined, though as inescapable in its consequences, as the unknowable transgression in Kafka's *The Trial.* It is enough for Hawthorne to suggest the Oedipus situation: an equivocal mother, an evil father—and between them, Dimmesdale, who is described as first as "child-like" and at last as "childish." The whole action moves toward the climactic moment, when, after years of cowardly silence and a momentary temptation to flee, that child-figure totters into the noonday public square to confess his fault before the whole community. At that point, Oedipus-Dimmesdale blends with the image of Doctor Johnson standing in the Uttoxeter market-place to make public amends for an offense against his father. It is a story which obsessed Hawthorne all his life, which he wrote out as an exemplary tale for children and told himself in his diary, a story obviously representing to him some buried guilt of his own.

That guilt the prehistoric fall of *The Scarlet Letter* explains, too, in encoded form. It is incarnate in Hester, most "gorgeous" of his Dark Ladies; for "gorgeous" is to Hawthorne a dirty word—a token of pollution. But why is gorgeousness a trap and love a crime, why beauty forbidden and joy banned to the nineteenth-century American? There was, *The Scarlet Letter* suggests, another fall in the Eden of the New World at precisely the moment at which the book unfolds, a communal fall to match Hester's private one. The very first page tells us that "whatever Utopia of human virtue and happiness" men may imagine in whatever land, they find it necessary "to allot a portion of the virgin soil as a cemetery, and another portion as the site of a prison." Before such a prison, Hawthorne's tale begins, and in such a cemetery, it comes to a close; and between, he attempts to explain how sin and death, for whose sake they exist, have come into the Puritan Commonwealth. Yet it is, finally, his own crisis of conscience that Hawthorne translates into a mythical history of America, his own experience of womanhood that he projects in Hester.

Sitting day after day beside the bed of his dying mother, confronted by his wife of whom she did not approve, and watching through the window his daughter Una playing the death scene to which she must eventually come—Hawthorne must have become aware with special poignancy of the web of femaleness in which we are involved from cradle to grave. But what this glimpse into the maternal mysteries did to him we do not know, except for the fact that he wept once when his mother died, again when he had finished the "hell-fired" book which is her memorial; and that somewhere between these two public betrayals of emotion, he suffered from what his family called "brain-fever."

The incest theme, however, even in its disguise of adultery, belongs primarily to the pre-plot of *The Scarlet Letter;* its plot is concerned with a second, quite different fall: a second temptation, in the face of which his characters, postulated as having been powerless before the "dark necessity" of their original fall, are portrayed as capable of free choice. Yet their freedom is ironic, for what they must learn freely to accept is the notion that freedom is the recognition of necessity. *The Scarlet Letter* is the most utopian of American books: not the Paradise Regained it seems at first, but only an Eden Revisited.

In the seeming Eden of the New World, a man and woman, who are still essentially the old Adam and Eve, deceive themselves for a moment into believing that they can escape the consequences of sin. The woman has served a prison term and bears on her breast the sign of her shame, and the man, who was the occasion of that shame, has lived secretly with his guilt and powerless remorse; yet in their deluded hope, they meet in the forest, plot a flight from the world of law and religion. For an instant, that hope seems to transfigure not only them, but the dark wood into which they have strayed. When Hester flings aside the scarlet letter and lets down her hair, the forest glows to life: "Such was the sympathy of . . . wild, heathen Nature . . . never subjugated by law, nor illumined by higher truth with the bliss of these two spirits. Love . . . must always create a sunshine that overflows upon the natural world."

Yet Hawthorne cannot grant these lovers even the mitigated bliss he earlier permitted the May King and Queen in "The Maypole of Merry Mount"; for between them lies the taboo of adultery, as real to him as to his ancestors. Hawthorne does not accept without qualification the judgment of his ancestors, though he condemns Hester's proposal of flight even as they would have, uses to describe it the Faustian metaphor. He is, after all, a modern, secular thinker, for whom nothing is self-evident, everything problematical; and he is being tempted as he writes to make a retreat from his own community very like Hester's. Yet, for all his quarrel with Puritanism and its persecuting zeal, he knows that no American can really leave behind the America which the Puritans have once and for all defined.

America represents for Hawthorne not only the marginal settlement, set between corrupt civilization and unredeemed nature, but also the rule of moral law in the place of self-justifying passion or cynical gallantry. In *The Scarlet Letter,* passion justifies nothing, while its denial redeems all. The fallen Eden of this world remains fallen; but the sinful priest purges himself by public confession, becomes worthy of his sole remaining way to salvation, death. Even Hester, though sin and suffering have made her an almost magical figure, a polluted but still terrible goddess, must finally accept loneliness and self-restraint instead of the love and freedom she dreamed. She cannot become the greater Ann Hutchinson she might have been had she remained unfallen, cannot redeem her sex from the indignities against which she once raged and plotted in secret. Passion has opened up for her no new possibilities, only closed off older ones.

The relationship of Hester and Dimmesdale is not, however, the only passionate connection in the novel. Through the five years covered by the book's action (the unwritten pre-plot takes up two more, from the marriage with Chillingworth to the birth of Pearl, thus adding up to the mystic seven), one relationship grows in intimacy, depth, and terror. In it, Dimmesdale plays a key role once more, though this time a passive, feminine one, his tremulous hand laid to his heart. Between him and Chillingworth, grows an intense, destructive emotion (a "dark passion," Hawthorne calls it), compounded of the intolerable intimacy of doctor and patient, analyst and analysand, husband and wife, father and son, cuckold and cuckolder. It is a bond like that which elsewhere in American literature joins together Simon Legree and Uncle Tom, Claggart and Billy Budd, Babo and Benito Cereno.

Both earlier and later in Hawthorne's own work, such connections exist between the sexes: father and daughter, as in "Rappaccini's Daughter"; husband and wife, as in "The Birthmark"; mesmerist and female subject, as in *The Blithedale Romance;* or lover and beloved, as in "Ethan Brand." In the last work, Hawthorne describes Esther as "the girl whom, with such cold and remorseless purpose, Ethan Brand had made the subject of a psychological experiment, and wasted, absorbed and perhaps annihilated her soul in the process." It is a pattern as old in our fiction as Brockden Brown's *Wieland;* and the prototype of the destructive lover is Carwin, in whom the seducer is merged (following Goethe's example) with the scientist, Don Juan with Faust. In Brown, however, as in Hawthorne everywhere else, the dark passion exists between a man and a woman. Chillingworth, however, is as much a devil as a man; while Dimmesdale is, of course, male: a one-time seducer reduced by unconfessed guilt to feminine passivity. And their relationship seems an odd combination of the tie between Faust and Gretchen, on the one hand, with that between Faust and Mephistopheles on the other.

The terms used to define the nature of their union are significant: "a kind of intimacy," a "paternal and reverential love," described by Dimmesdale's parishioners as the "best possible measure . . . unless he had selected some one of the many blooming damsels to become his devoted wife." Hester, who has been the wife of one and the mistress of the other, yet never as close to either as they are to each other, says reproachfully to Chillingworth: "no man is so near to him as you. . . . You are beside him, sleeping and waking. . . . You burrow and rankle in his heart. Your clutch is on his life." "Burrow" is the key word for Chillingworth's penetration of Dimmesdale's heart: "burrow into his intimacy . . . deep into the patient's bosom . . . delving . . . probing . . . in a dark cavern." The climax comes with the exposure of the secret of Dimmesdale's bosom, his own scarlet letter, embossed (perhaps!) in the very flesh. "He laid his hand on his bosom, and thrust aside the vestment," Hawthorne says at the moment of revelation, portraying Chillingworth in an ecstasy, leaping into the air. He knows at last the ultimate secret of his dearest enemy; and knowing it, has possessed him, accomplished a rape of the spirit beyond any penetration of the flesh. "He has violated," Hester comments, echoing Hawthorne's description of Ethan Brand, "the sanctity of the human heart."

Hawthorne is not content, however, to leave the last word with Hester, answering her in his own voice, his own typically hypothetical manner:

> It is a curious subject of observation and inquiry, whether hatred and love be not the same thing at bottom. Each, in its utmost development, supposes a high degree of intimacy and heart knowledge; each renders one individual dependent for the food . . . of his spiritual life upon another. . . . In the spiritual world, the old physician and the minister—may, unawares, have found their earthly stock of hatred and antipathy transmuted into golden love.

Out of the ambivalence of love and hatred, the constitutionally double-dealing Hawthorne has distilled an equivocation which undercuts, at the last moment, the whole suggested meaning of his book. He has not, to be sure, committed himself finally; but his last qualification for the passion of Chillingworth and Dimmesdale is favorable, while his last word on that of Hester and Dimmesdale is quite the opposite. Though earlier Hester has boasted, "What we did had a consecration of its own," the only proof of her assertion she could offer was, "We felt it so! We said so to each other!" Dimmesdale does not demur in the forest, where he is temporarily mad; but he answers Hester in the market-place, at his moment of greatest insight: "It may be that we forgot our God—when we violated our reverence for each other's soul. . . ."

As one bucket goes up, the other goes down; and we are left with the disturbing paradox (mitigated, to be sure, by Hawthorne's customary, pussyfooting subjunctives: "may have found," "may be that we forgot") that love may conceal a destructive impulse and work for ill, while hatred may be only a disguised form of love and eventuate in good. If on the one hand, *The Scarlet Letter* leads toward a Goethe-like justification of diabolism as an instrument of salvation, on the other hand, it insists, in a very American way, upon the dangers of passion. It is certainly true, in terms of the plot, that Chillingworth drives the minister toward confession and penance, while Hester would have lured him to evasion and flight. But this means, for all of Hawthorne's equivocations, that the eternal feminine does not draw us on toward grace, rather that the woman promises only madness and damnation. It is the eternal demonic—personified in the wronged husband—which leads Dimmesdale on; and saved by his personal Serpent, he can in turn save his Eve—his apparent weakness deliver her apparent strength.

There is, however, a turn of the screw even beyond this; for though Hester works, perhaps unwittingly, to destroy Dimmesdale, saps his courage and brings him to the verge of selling his soul, it is to her that he must turn for support. Morally, he is finally stronger than she, but physically he depends upon her as a child upon its mother. It is on her arm that he ascends the scaffold, on her breast that he rests his trembling head. "Is she angel or devil?" Hawthorne's wife had asked him of Beatrice Rappaccini, when he was in the process of creating that prototype of Hester; and his answer was that he did not know! With Hester herself, he is still equivocal; she is the female temptress of Puritan mythology, but also, though sullied, the secular madonna of sentimental Protestantism, a true descendant, via Julie, of Clarissa.

Similarly, Dimmesdale is a descendant of Lovelace via Saint-Preux; though he is further transformed, as we have noted, following the example of Mrs. Rowson's Montraville. There is, in Hawthorne, a certain irony in the treatment of the unmanned seducer who represents, if not himself, an important aspect of that self; yet not even Montraville staggers to his end as feebly as Dimmesdale. His final reduction makes explicit the relationship in which the man and woman, who in the book's pre-history played Lovelace and

Clarissa, now stand: "It was hardly a man with life in him that tottered on his path so nervelessly. . . . He still walked onward, if that movement could be so described, which rather resembled the wavering effort of an infant with its mother's arms in view. . . ." Such motherly arms do, indeed, wait to receive him, the arms of Hester, of whom earlier Hawthorne has written: "Had there been a Papist among the crowd of Puritans . . . he might have seen in this beautiful woman . . . the image of Divine Maternity. . . ." The guilty lovers' consummation plotted in the forest between the minister and the outcast does not take place; but that minister, become a child, embraces innocently that outcast, sanctified by motherhood. "They beheld the minister, leaning on Hester's shoulder and supported by his arm around him. . . . Hester partly raised him, and supported his head against her bosom. . . ." At the last moment of his life, Dimmesdale, the eternal son, has found his way back to the breast, no longer barred to him by law or taboo. The qualified happy ending comes this time not from *Paradise Lost* but *Paradise Regained:* "Home to his Mother's house private return'd." It is the most suitable of endings for a book produced out of the anguish of personal failure and the death of a mother.

The Scarlet Letter is, then, our only classic book which makes passion a central theme. Born into an age and a class pledged to gentility, Hawthorne was denied a vocabulary adequate to his subject, driven back on duplicity and cunning; and in the end, he seems to adorn that subject rather than present it, conceal it with fancy needlework, "so that the Capital A might have been thought to mean . . . anything other than Adulteress." Indeed, the phrase from "Endicott and the Red Cross," written some thirteen years before *The Scarlet Letter,* suggests that from the first the cryptic "A" may have represented to Hawthorne not only "Adultery" but "Art." Certainly, he regarded his own art as involving precisely that adornment of guilt by craft which he attributes to Hester's prototype: "sporting with her infamy, the lost and desperate creature had embroidered the fatal token with golden thread and the nicest art of needlework. . . ."

Unable to break through the limitations of his era or to repress the shame he felt at trifling with them, Hawthorne ended by writing in the form of a love story an elegiac treatise on the death of love. *The Scarlet Letter* is, in one of its major aspects, a portrayal of the attenuation of sex in America, the shrinking on our shores from

Brobdingnagian parents to Lilliputian children. In a note in his journal, Hawthorne reminds himself that Brobdingnag, where Gulliver once sat astride the nipples of gross, lusty girls, was located on the coast of North America, home of the mid-nineteenth-century fleshless bluestocking! *The Scarlet Letter* is concerned not only with passion but also with America (another possible signification of Hester's letter), that is to say, it attempts to find in the story of Hester and Dimmesdale a paradigm of the fall of love in the New World. The Puritans who move through Hawthorne's pages belong to a first-generation community, which, despite its revolt against the paternal figures of kings and bishops, has not itself lost "the quality of reverence" or contracted "the disease of sadness, which almost all children in these latter days inherit along with the scrofula. . . ." The inhabitants of Hawthorne's seventeenth-century world still live in the Elizabethan afterglow; "for they were the offspring of sires . . . who had known how to be merry. . . ." It is the generation which succeeds them that made gaiety a "forgotten art" by darkening American life with "the blackest shade of Puritanism."

Hawthorne recreates these first ancestors not merely as merry rebels, but as mythical progenitors. Twice over he describes them as they pass ceremonially, a "procession of majestic and venerable fathers," among them his own ultimate "dim and dusky grandsire . . . grave, bearded, sable-cloaked and steeple-crowned. . . ." And the mothers who inhabit Hawthorne's dream are scarcely less overwhelming. "The women . . . stood within less than half a century of the period when Elizabeth had been the not altogether unsuitable representative of her sex. . . . The bright morning sun, therefore, shone on broad shoulders and well-developed busts, and on round and ruddy cheeks, that . . . had hardly grown paler and thinner in the atmosphere of New England." Hawthorne is, to be sure, somewhat ambivalent about the abundant fleshliness of these mothers of his race, suggesting that their "moral diet was not a bit more refined" than the beef and ale with which they satisfied their bellies. Yet there is something nostalgic, even rueful about his acknowledgment that since those early days "every successive mother has transmitted to her child a fainter bloom, a more delicate and briefer beauty, and a slighter physical frame. . . ."

To the world of such lush and substantial women, Hester unquestionably belongs. She is not an "ethereal" latter-day invalid like Sophia Hawthorne, but "lady-like . . . after the manner . . . of those days; characterized by a certain state and dignity, rather than by the delicate, evanescent and indescribable grace, which is now recognized as its indication." Dimmesdale, however, is no father, no mythic progenitor at all; after his love affair, at least (in which surely he was more seduced than seducing), he has been shrunken to Lilliputian size—seems a modern, alienated, anguished artist, transported into a more heroic age. He is not a Puritan, but a child of the Puritans, their diminished offspring, inheritor of melancholy, and the prototype of Hawthorne's own fallen generation. His fall from potency and his return to the maternal embrace just before death constitute an "emblem" of the fate of the American male. And when he is reborn, he becomes first Clifford Pyncheon in *The House of the Seven Gables* and then the impotent, estranged Coverdale, whose very name re-echoes his own. Beyond this, there is, among Hawthorne's finished works, only *The Marble Faun,* in which Hawthorne insisted on marrying off his alienated artist (this time a sculptor called Kenyon) to a good woman—as pallidly Anglo-Saxon, as improbable in the marriage bed as himself.

Most ambiguous of all the avatars of Oberon-Fanshawe is Clifford Pyncheon, who is, indeed, oddly out of place in the cheery, middlebrow pages of *The House of the Seven Gables.* Symbol of the estranged artist, he seems in the book's philistine context a demi-idiot: half withered old man and half child, the passive victim of the world's brutality. He is finally more than this, however —a portrait of Oberon as the ghostly surviver of a world that has ceased to exist. The thirty years he has passed in the prison which the world prepares for such "sybarites" have left him broken, a quivering sensibility without will or passion. With no ethical commitment to temper it, the "necessity for the beautiful" has turned Clifford into a monster, who weeps because an organ-grinder's monkey is ugly, and turns from the face of his own loving but unlovely sister.

Against his decaying impotence is set the strength of the daguerreotypist and rebel, Holgrave, who is often confusingly referred to in the text as "the artist." He is not, however, in Clifford's way an "artist of the beautiful," but rather an artist of the practical: a man of the people, self-taught, a little vulgar. Half technician and half creator, he is what would be called in our time a producer of "mass culture"—and he is, appropriately enough, identified as a latter-day magician, a descendant of mesmerists.

Both he and Clifford long for the novel's ingenue, the good girl Phoebe, who is described at one point as "a religion in herself." But there is, of course, really no contest; Clifford wants finally only to ogle a little, and this favor Phoebe brings herself to grant him with no loss to her virginal *mana*.

The only question to be resolved by the action is whether Holgrave will ravish Phoebe or permit her to be his savior, whether he will play the part of *Fanshawe's* rapist or of its more virile halfhero. In the end, with a single gesture he disavows his youthful radicalism and his male aggressiveness, commits himself to marriage. "It will be far otherwise than you forebode," he reassures Phoebe, who is hesitating over his proposal. "The world owes all its onward impulse to men ill at ease. The happy man inevitably confines himself within limits. I have a presentiment that, hereafter, it will be my lot . . . to conform myself to laws, and the peaceful practice of society." For this avowal, he receives the reward promised in the genteel Love Religion to the male who rejects the Lovelace role. "The bliss which makes all things true, beautiful and holy shone around this youth and maiden. They were conscious of nothing sad or old. They transfigured the earth and made it Eden again, and themselves the first two dwellers in it." So man is restored to the Garden by the love of a good woman and not by utopian social schemes for remaking the world. No wonder that more sentimental critics never weary of insisting that the thematic resolution of *The House of the Seven Gables* "may well justify preference for it over *The Scarlet Letter.*" Such readers do not note, perhaps, the faint sigh of doubt with which Hawthorne qualifies the domesticated Edenic vision, "But how soon the heavy earth dream settled down again!" They remember only the Dickensian lightness of tone, the sunshine, the small boy buying sweets, the comic Old Venner—and are happy to recall that Hawthorne felt (or at least said he felt) *The House of the Seven Gables* a book "more proper and natural for me to write."

In *The Blithedale Romance,* the sunshine begins to dim, the pathos implicit in Hawthorne's four-sided triangle to reassert itself; and though in *The Marble Faun* Oberon-Kenyon manages to find a bride, the cheerfulness of *The House of the Seven Gables* is not recaptured. Toward the end of his life, Hawthorne finds himself once more confronting in all their original ambiguity and disorder the symbolic protagonists on whom briefly he had succeeded in imposing his sentimental will. One of the three unfinished novels with which he was wrestling before he died is *Septimius Felton;* and in the contradictory manuscript versions of that book which survive, Ellen and Fanshawe and Edward Walcott return to haunt him.

Septimius-Fanshawe, a pale, scholarly youth, competes for the hand of Rose Garfield, the ultimate Ellen, against the hearty Robert Hagburn, last embodiment of Edward Walcott. But even deeper imaginative elements arise and escape from the author's conscious control. A third lover, a British officer called Cyril Norton, enters the scene, attempts to kiss Rose and is killed in a duel by Septimius. He has brought with him, however, the incestuous ambiguities of Hawthorne's early story, "Alice Doane's Appeal," and the very names of the protagonists shift eerily as if trying to establish a meaning of which Hawthorne is not quite aware. At one point Rose Garfield is called Alice; and at another Robert Hagburn becomes Robert Garfield as if he were her brother, while Septimius is suddenly called Norton as if to indicate some blood relationship to the man he has killed. Finally, although Rose and Septimius have already become engaged, Hawthorne decides that these two at least *are* in fact half-brother and sister.

Meanwhile, symbolic figures of darkness move through the world of the more realistic protagonists: an *anima*-character called Sybil, identified with a bloody flower that grows from graves; a magician-Bad Father, whose companion and emblem is a gigantic spider. At the close of his career, Hawthorne loses himself in a *Walpurgisnacht* dream of father-hatred and incest, guilt and Faustian aspiration, quite like that from which he began in "Alice Doane's Appeal." The seduction theme has been restored to the gothic envelope in which his initial fear of sexuality had encysted it.

It is so encysted, of course, in Melville's sole attempt at a sentimental novel, *Pierre.* Like most of Melville's books—like *all* of them, Melville himself would have said—*Pierre* is finally a "botch" because it is the product of contradictory ambitions. Melville had been betrayed by the success of his earliest novels, pseudo-documentaries of escape from bourgeois life, into believing that it would be some day possible for him to earn his living as a writer; and in none of the works written at the peak of his powers is he innocent of some attempt to adapt them to the market. "Dollars damn me," he said quite frankly of his situation. Of all his novels, however, *Pierre* is the most deliberately aimed, in its opening pages at least, at the largest potential audience, which is to say, the female one.

Certainly, he declares his intentions concerning *Pierre* clearly enough in a letter to Mrs. Hawthorne: "But, My Dear Lady, I shall not again send you a bowl of salt water. The next chalice I shall commend, will be a rural bowl of milk." *Moby Dick* was written for Hawthorne, for the discriminating male reader; *Pierre,* for the wife of that reader, for a second-best audience. Its very style declares that it represents not only a shift of scene from ocean to countryside, but a change of tone appropriate to one who now addresses "My Dear Ladies": "There are some strange summer mornings in the country, when he who is but a sojourner from the city shall early walk forth . . . and be wonder-smitten with the trance-like aspect of the green and golden world." When into this Edenic world of green and gold, Melville introduces two fair, bright-eyed lovers ("Lucy!" "Pierre!"), and sets to preside over it no paternal Thunderer, but the Great Mother herself, the Queen of Heaven as aristocratic American lady—called Maria, of course —what more could a female reader ask? It is milk for milk that Melville offers: a return of nourishing warmth to the warm nourisher who had borne him.

The theme itself seems orthodox and womanly enough, too, the traditional subject of genteel literature since the beginnings of the novel in the United States: "the fatal Consequences of Seduction." For in a little while, the third avatar of the Great Goddess appears to stand beside Maria and Lucy—Pierre's half-sister Isabel, in whom Hecate joins Ceres and Kore; the trinity is complete: the mother, the promised bride, and the layer-out of the dead. Isabel is, however, no mere allegorical figure; for like Lucy in *Lucy Temple,* and Harriot in *The Power of Sympathy,* she is the standard bastard daughter of the father—revelation of his secret sin and bait in the trap of retributory incest. Working with such material, Melville must have felt justified in writing to his publisher, who had begun to grow uneasy over the lagging sales of *Moby Dick,* that his new effort, "a regular romance, with a mysterious plot to it & strong passions," was surely "very much more calculated for popularity than anything you have yet published of mine." Indeed, Melville thought that they might as well make a fresh start with so fresh a novel, and suggested, in order not to prejudice the possible new public, that they put on the flyleaf the name "Guy Winthrop" or simply *"By a Vermonter."*

Yet all along he knew that he had other ambitions for the book. "So now let us add Moby Dick to our blessing, and step from that," Melville wrote to Hawthorne. "Leviathan is not the biggest fish;—I have heard of Krakens." Surely, *Pierre* represents an attempt to haul some such ultimate monster of the deeps to the surface. Was Melville fooling only his publisher or himself, too— really convinced that he could conceal his Kraken in a bowl of milk? His critics and his audience were not deceived when the book appeared, raising charges of incoherence and indecency, even protesting against the time-honored incest theme, so remote had gentility grown from its own roots by the mid-nineteenth century. "Belongs to the German school," one reviewer, perspicacious as well as indignant, observed. "Yes! *'Pierre'* is a species of New York Werther, having all the absurdities and none of the beauties of Goethe's juvenile indiscretion."

III

Had he been willing to eschew all hopes of reaching the genteel female audience, or to give up the dream of pleasing the official arbiters of taste, Melville might have had the kind of quasi-respectable success attained by George Lippard, whose *The Quaker City; or, The Monks of Monk Hall,* first published in 1844, sold 60,000 copies the first year (compared with the 283 copies of *Pierre* sold ten months after publication) and which was still apparently being bought at the rate of 30,000 a year when Lippard died in 1854, not yet quite thirty-two years old. It is not necessary to believe the author's boast on the title page of *The Quaker City* that "No American novel has ever commanded so wide-spread an interest, as this work," or to credit completely the claim of the 1845 edition to represent a twenty-seventh printing; but one must take seriously the report of a Philadelphia newspaper at the time of Lippard's death that "He was the author of a number of novels, which have been read probably as extensively as those of any other writer in the country. . . ." It was not easy, certainly, to earn three or four thousand dollars a year by writing in Lippard's time; but this he managed to do, appealing to the lower middlebrow audience, which otherwise would have had to subsist on such imported fare as the novels of Eugene Sue, whose compound of gothicism and sentimental eroticism gave him the sweet-smelling savor of "dirtiness."

It is hard to know exactly what the nature of Lippard's audience was or precisely what satisfactions they sought in his books. He thought of himself as the inheritor of the tradition of Charles Brockden Brown, his fellow Philadelphian, about whom he wrote a touching magazine piece and to whom he dedicated *The Quaker City*. The combination of sex, horror, and advanced social thought that had once been the specialty of Brown Lippard provided, too —though on a slap-dash literary level considerably below that of his predecessor. He had, however, Brown's capacity for yielding up the imagination to a frenetic vision, out of which the author makes a book not so much by composing a fiction as by recording an uncensored nightmare. In such a novel as *The Quaker City,* the archetypal bugaboos of the popular mind—malicious hunchbacks, sinister Jews, hulking deaf-and-dumb Negroes, corrupt clergymen, and bloated bankers—murder, rape, carouse, and collapse finally into drunken stupors inside or beneath a gothic whorehouse, whose lowest level is a stagnant sewer. Unfaithful wives are poisoned, the skulls of old women bashed in, the virginity of sobbing young girls violated; but nothing is presented as gratuitous horror, the staple of the less pretentious dime novels; all is offered as a true revelation of *what really goes on inside*. In Lippard, pornography is justified as muckraking.

Gangster and banker, clergyman and bawd, lawyer and doctor —these are presumably the real rulers of society caught off guard; and the nightmarish evocations of the book a literal description of how the rich and their henchmen amuse themselves with the money they have sweated from the laboring man. This is the populist vision of upper-class life and the economic system which maintains it translated directly from private fantasy to fiction, without emendation or expurgation, but it is a religious fantasy as well as a political one, a poor man's apocalypse. In the small-town Protestant mind, the Big City is Sodom; and "Woe unto Sodom!" says the title-page illustration of Lippard's novel, evoking all the prurience associated with urban centers of iniquity by a thousand revival meetings.

Lippard himself was a pre-Marxian socialist, always armed under his Byronic cloak against the possibility of an attack by a hired assassin of the masters of society, and the founder of a secret order to fight back against them: the "Brotherhood of the Union," of which he was "Supreme Washington." His program was unequivocally revolutionary; "When Labor has tried all other means in vain—. . . . then we advise Labor to go to War . . . War with the Rifle, Sword and Knife!" He thought of his novels, stories, and pamphlets (he published twenty-three books in some twelve years) as weapons in the holy war of labor. Long before the Communist theory of art as a weapon had been developed, Lippard had anticipated it: "LITERATURE merely considered as an ART is a despicable thing. . . . A literature which does not work practically, for the advancement of social reform, or which is too dignified or too good to picture the great wrongs of the great mass of humanity, is just good for nothing at all."

It is not, however, literature in general that Lippard has to justify as a social weapon, but horror pornography in particular. Psychologically, of course, popular radicalism has always taken advantage of the tendency of relatively naive and uneducated people to project on the upper classes which they despise the erotic and sadist fantasies of which they are ashamed, thus providing themselves with the luxury of at once indulging and disavowing their own most shamefully masturbatory dreams. An ambitious, half-starved orphan boy just past twenty, knowing nothing of political reality except what his fancy suggests, makes an admirable spokesman for such a group. And just such a boy was George Lippard, near enough culturally to his readers to share their darkest fantasies, but far enough from them to articulate what they could only feel.

Understandably enough, it is seduction, the seduction of a poor girl by a pampered gentleman, which furnishes Lippard the key image for satisfying both the social and sexual demands of his audience; and in him, for the first time in America, perhaps, the Richardsonian theme takes on a fully conscious significance as a symbol of class war. "We'll be seduced no more!" the readers of *Pamela* had cried; and Lippard's readers echo more crudely, "You can't rape us!" The immediate occasion for *The Monks of Monk Hall* was an actual incident in which a Philadelphian who had killed the seducer of his sister, aboard the Camden ferry, was held in a New Jersey prison, tried in a New Jersey court, and then—to the relief and joy of his fellow citizens—acquitted by New Jersey justice. The sentimental popular acclaim that followed the release of the murderer led to the writing of the novel, which itself apparently helped swell an upsurge of public opinion that resulted in the passage of an anti-seduction law in the state of New York in 1849. It is a prime example of art as social action!

Lippard is eager to leave no doubt that seduction is the central theme of his crowded and complex "Romance of Philadelphia Life, Mystery and Crime." In his preface to one of the later editions, he writes, "I determined to write a book founded upon the following idea: *That the seduction of a poor and innocent girl, is a deed altogether as criminal as murder . . . the assassin of chastity and maidenhood is worthy of death by the hands of any man, and in any place.*" At the end of the main action of the book, editorial is translated into dithyramb, a song of triumph sung by a brother who has just avenged, with "the life current of the Libertine," the seduction of his sister: "Is that the murmur of a brook . . . is that the song of a bird? No, no, but still it is music—that gushing of the Wronger's Blood! . . . I would dance. Yes, Yes, I would dance over the Corse! . . . in sight of God and his angels, I would dance over the corse, while a wild song of joy fill the heavens. A song—huzza—a song! . . . This, this is the vengeance of a Brother!' "

It is by all odds the most false and forced passage in a novel not seldom false and forced, Lippard's amends for having lingered so lasciviously over the details of the rape, and for having encouraged the reader to relish those details with him. The fall of the seduction theme from gentility had freed it from the old restraints and reticences that had hedged it in; and Lippard profited to the full from this new freedom. At the level of Melville's *Pierre,* a charge of immorality meant the loss of sales and a blow to his quest for popularity; but at the level of *The Quaker City,* to be charged with having produced "the most immoral work of the age" meant to be even more widely read. Lippard cites the accusation against his morals proudly, taking it as a testimony to the truth and social efficacy of his novel; and he is not averse to exploiting it for sales. Like the very earliest American novelists, he boasts that he has torn the veils of delicacy aside in the interests of exposing the seducer; but unlike his predecessors, he lets us look our fill at the scandals behind the veil:

The left hand of Lorimer, gently stealing round her form, rested with a faint pressure upon the folds of her night-robe, over her bosom, which now came heaving tremulously into light. . . . Closer and more close, the hand of Lorimer pressed against the heaving bosom, with but the slight folds of the night-robe between. . . . Brighter grew the glow on her cheek, close pressed the hand on her bosom, warmer and higher arose that bosom in

the light. . . . In a moment, Mary raised her glowing countenance from his breast. . . . Her breath came thick and gaspingly.
Her cheeks were all a-glow, her blue eyes swam in a hazy dim-
ness. She felt as though she was about to fall swooning on the
floor . . . the languor came deeper and more mellow over her
limbs; her bosom rose no longer quick and gaspingly, but in
long pulsations, that urged the full Globes in all their virgin
beauty, softly and slowly into view . . . and her parted lips
deepened into a rich vermillion tint. 'She is mine!'

I V

Fifty years before *Sister Carrie,* Lippard had worked out a combination of sex and social protest in a style very like Dreiser's compound of conventional sentimental diction and colloquial speech.
Whether or not Dreiser himself read Lippard's brutal exposé of
Life in the Great City is hard to know; but certainly their books,
making due allowance for changes in taste, are strikingly similar—
parallel manifestations of a need in the nongenteel sub-audience
for a revival of the seduction archetype, a hunger that even the
endless reprintings of *Charlotte Temple* could not assuage. It was
in the '90's, after a half-century in which gentility had apparently
triumphed over passion, that the "fatal consequences of seduction"
began once more to assert themselves as a compelling theme of
serious literature. In 1893, a twenty-one-year-old writer called Stephen Crane published *Maggie—A Girl of the Streets;* in 1894,
Mark Twain's *Pudd'nhead Wilson* appeared; and in 1899, Theodore Dreiser, at the summer home of his closest friend Arthur
Henry ("If he had been a girl, I would have married him, of
course"), wrote down on a blank page the words "Sister Carrie"
—and wondered what they were intended to mean.

In plot, Crane's book is the most faithful of all to the stereotypes of the theme: an innocent girl is seduced, made pregnant,
cast out by her family, and ends committing suicide, while her
seducer is being victimized by the evil woman for whom he has
left her. It is not even a Lady whom Crane has portrayed, but—in
unconscious submission to bourgeois taboos—a girl of the people,
an operator in a sweatshop, who lives on the Bowery. Crane's intention, described in an inscription in a gift copy as making "room
in heaven for all sorts of souls, notably an occasional street girl,
who are not confidently expected to be there by many excellent

people," is surely not uncongenial to the great bleeding heart of sentimental America. Yet his book was a commercial failure; no respectable publisher could be persuaded to issue it, and the privately printed edition signed "Johnston Smith" remained unsold, despite Crane's attempt to promote it by having four men sit in front of the El all day reading it. The book provided no titillation at all—the physical seduction going undescribed—only a great, gray brutality of language (no "dirty" words, to be sure, though much profanity) and a constant play of irony, sometimes subtle, more often obvious. The violent, drunken mother acting out her expected indignation over the fall of her daughter, and the stupid, brutalized brother going through the standard motions of vengeance are travesties. Such parody of the "vengeance of a Brother" no ordinary reader could forgive, any more than he could forgive the literary pretensions of the novel: the tight form and the poetic language of the descriptive passages, which pull away from, when they do not condescend to, the characters described. *Maggie* is a good book neither in the critics' nor the great audience's sense; it is only the book of a good writer.

Twain's *Pudd'nhead Wilson* provides even fewer archetypal satisfactions. His fallen woman, Roxana, is a Negress, about whose seduction by a white man (accomplished before the action proper of the book begins) Twain himself refuses to be incensed; it is postulated in the book as a fact of life or an act of God, something that just happens to black wenches, useful for beginning a plot. A much lesser novelist, Albion W. Tourgée, had in his first novel *'Toinette* (1876) pictured the revolt of a slave girl, who after the Civil War demands marriage of the Southern gentleman who has been her lover and is the father of her child. Though she has only the slightest trace of Negro blood, her lover refuses in horror, and she leaves him. This issue Twain scarcely seems to know exists; what moral indignation he feels is directly against slavery as an institution and especially against sons who betray their mothers, rather than against Virginia gentlemen who betray slave girls. Neither in his respectable nor in his bootleg fiction is Twain really interested in the traditional meanings of the seduction theme.

It is only Dreiser who proves capable of reviving that theme for serious literature, for he takes it seriously: finding in the impregnation and abandonment of helpless women no mere occasions for melodrama (as in Twain) or for exercises in irony and contrasting style (as in Crane). Dreiser is qualified first of all by his essentially sentimental response to the plight of the oppressed, by what he himself calls—attributing the feeling to one of his characters—an "uncritical upswelling of grief for the weak and the helpless." There is in him none of the detachment and cynicism of Crane, none of the utter blackness and pessimism of Twain; he is as "positive" through his tears as any female scribbler. Even his famous determinism is essentially sentimental at root, amounting effectively to little more than the sob of exculpation: "Nobody's fault! Nobody's fault!" Much is made by his friendlier critics of the fact that just before the beginning of his writing career Dreiser discovered Balzac; much more should be made of the fact that long before that encounter, his imagination had already been formed by Ouida and Laura Jean Libby. If, on the one hand, the daughters of the non-Anglo-Saxon American poor find in him a voice, on the other, the stickier writers for women through him achieve literary respectability.

It is no accident that for several years he was able to edit successfully the Butterick magazines, purveyors of fashion, fiction, and useful articles ("What to Do When Diphtheria Comes") to lower-middlebrow women; nor was his writing for such an audience an unfortunate interruption in his career, a prostitution of his talent. Nobody, as many writers have learned to their grief through both success and failure, can deceive such an audience for very long; one hint of condescension gives the game away. If Dreiser managed to please such a group of readers, it was because *at the deepest level, he shared their values;* and the friends who worked so hard to save him from the deleterious effect of such "hack work," and finally persuaded him to abandon it—understood nothing. When Dreiser in " 'The Genius' " describes the youg artist, Eugene Witla (his barely disguised self-portrait), as beginning with a love of the the painting of that insufferable anti-artist Bouguereau, this is not just a revelation of the author's insufficient culture; it is also a revelation of his fundamental taste. For better or worse, Dreiser is bound in weakness and in strength to the values of the sentimental lower middle class.

When he wrote on rejection slips sent to contributors to *The Delineator,* "We like realism, but it must be tinged with sufficient idealism to make it all of a truly uplifting character. . . . The fine side of things—the idealistic—is the answer for us . . ." he was not merely playing with a straight face the part for which he had been hired. To his good friend H. L. Mencken, to whom surely he could speak frankly, he wrote in quite the same vein that he would like for another of his magazines (this one presumably freer from outside control), *The Bohemian*, no "tainted fiction," but stories that testified to their authors' "knowledge of life *as it is,* broad, simple, good-natured." If there is a fundamental flaw in Dreiser, it resides neither in his stylistic clumsiness, which for strength's sake is easily forgiven, nor in his tritely elegant literary vocabulary, the *kitsch* interior-decorating with which he cannot forbear touching up his scenes, but in the fact that his novels are in fact "uplifting" —which is to say, sentimental rather than tragic.

How, then, did Dreiser come to be, as one of his publishers was later to put it, "the one man to have first created an audience for daring books," the defendant in obscenity trials which came to seem to his contemporaries forums at which the cause of a new, frank literature could be advocated? It is hard now to see the sense in which Dreiser's books, whatever their other merits, are daring at all. Certainly, they do not describe the sexual act or its more passionate preliminaries with a frankness or pornographic intensity comparable to George Lippard's. Dreiser came of the kind of people who copulate in the dark and live out their lives without ever seeing their sexual partners nude; and he was brought up on the kind of book which made it impossible for him to write convincingly about the act of love; his subject was, like theirs, when erotic at all, the traditional "consequences of seduction."

His notion of a passionate interchange between lovers involves such "poetic" apostrophes as, "Oh, Flower Face! Oh, Silver Feet! Oh, Myrtle Bloom!" The erotic, that is to say, demanded for him a veneer of the poetic; and his concept of poetry is perhaps best indicated by the metrical chapter titles in *Sister Carrie:* "And This is Not Elf Land: What Gold Will Not Buy," "The Way of the Beaten: A Harp in the Wind." It is all a little like what his brother, Paul Dresser (also the champion of the fallen woman in "My Gal Sal"), was doing in the popular song. There is power in Dreiser, to be sure; no one gives better the sense of the dazzled entry of the small-town girl into the big city; no one renders better the seedy milieu of the status-hungry on their way up or down; but no American writer is more the victim of the sentimental wound, less capable of dealing with passion. When he resists the impulse to poeticize, Dreiser does love scenes like this: "Carrie rose up as if to step away, he holding her hand. Now he slipped his arm about her and she struggled, but in vain. He held her quite close. Instantly there flared up in his body the all-compelling desire. His affection took an ardent form. . . . She found him lifting her head and looking into her eyes. What magnetism there was she could never know. His many sins, however, were for the moment all forgotten." It is banality raised to the power of evasion, an implicit denial of the reality of passion.

He could never portray, for all his own later hectic career as a lover, any woman except the traditional seduced working girl of sentimental melodrama. Yet because the deceived woman, the seduced virgin are for Dreiser the images through which he understands America and himself, he stumbles into scandal. The man who makes good and the girl who goes bad, these stereotypes of the folk (occasionally reversed, for variety, to the girl who rises and the man who falls) are the sole symbols that move him to write, and it is with the fallen girl that he begins his career. He is in fact the avenging brother that earlier writers only imagine; and Sister Carrie, like Jennie Gerhardt after her, is a household image, one of those sisters of his own, who were always getting into trouble: running off with married men or embezzlers, coming home pregnant. The phrase which came unbidden into his mind was not a simple girl's name, as in the typical woman's book, but *"Sister Carrie,"* and in the novel itself he tries to justify the first word in various ways. Meeting her married sister in Chicago at the beginning of the book, Caroline Meeber is hailed by that full title, "half affectionately" bestowed on her, Dreiser tells us, by her family; and by the end of the story, when she is translated into a kind of unchurched nun, celibate, lonely, and dedicated to charity, it seems even more appropriate. Surely, the quasi-religious pun is intended; and yet, first of all, Carrie is not the sister of her fictional family or even a Little Sister of the Poor, but one of Dreiser's own sisters, redeemed from the shabby failures of her actual life. If not a brother's vengeance, *Sister Carrie* is his amends.

Why, then, did it irk and shock so many readers? How, to begin with, could so conventional an account of a small-town girl, seduced first by the flashy drummer, Drouet, then talked into a bigamous marriage with the repentant embezzler, Hurstwood, so horrify the wife of Dreiser's publisher? Legend at least tells us that she was so dismayed that she persuaded her husband not to promote the book which he had already contracted to print. There is no apparent moral ambiguity in Dreiser's presentation. Both Hurstwood's robbery and Carrie's love affairs are called evil, and

Hurstwood is quite satisfactorily punished, degraded to the level of a skid-row panhandler, left about to commit suicide in a flophouse. Before that, he has been harried from failure to failure, his pride and virility broken until he crawls in the slush, begs a few dollars from the woman he has wronged. Not even Montraville or Hollingsworth had been so degraded for their offenses! Even Carrie, though she has the kind of success denied her seducer, and achieves the material comforts of which she once scarcely knew how to dream, cannot find happiness in her career as an actress or in herself. To make the point clear, Dreiser lingers almost tearfully over Carrie's melancholy figure at the end, pauses to apostrophize her: "Oh, Carrie, Carrie! . . . know, then, that for you is neither surfeit or content. In your rocking chair, by your window dreaming, shall you long alone. In your rocking chair, by your window, shall you dream such a happiness as you may never feel." It is the lyrics of a popular song again—"Old Rocking Chair's Got Me," *obligato*. What more did Mr. and Mrs. Doubleday want? Blood? The death of the girl who had fallen? Crane had already provided that in a book which no one would print, which sold even fewer than the 650 copies of *Sister Carrie* that went out of the one thousand printed. Dreiser, with an instinct for self-dramatization, liked to speak of the "suppression" of his first book, but in fact it did as well as Melville's *Pierre*.

It is true that Dreiser lapsed at this point into ten years of silence, which is to say, a decade of editing, and writing articles and short stories, but no novels; yet this seems to have been less a lock-out on the part of the publishers (actually he was given an advance during this period on a book which he never finished) than some deep, psychological slow-down within him. Carrie had represented more than an expurgated version of his unfortunate sister (when he emended life it was always in favor of that "sufficient idealism" which he had urged on his contributors); she had been, in a way, a disguised portrait of himself: a Portrait of the Artist as a Girl Gone Wrong. "Thus in life there is ever . . . the mind that reasons, and the mind that feels," Dreiser had written in *Sister Carrie,* thinking of himself. "Of the one come the men of action . . . of the other, poets and dreamers—artists all. As harps in the wind, the latter respond to every breath of fancy, voicing in their moods all the ebb and flow of the ideal. Man has not yet comprehended the dreamer any more than he has the ideal. For him the laws and morals of the world are unduly severe. Ever hearkening to the sound of beauty, striving for the flash of its distant wings, he watches to follow. . . . So watched Carrie, so followed. . . ." In this respect, too, she is a sister to her author, also a "harp in the wind"; and it is perhaps precisely the bovaryism revealed in such a passage, the *Weltschmerz* and self-pity, the half-secret caviling at moral restraints which put off the popular reader.

In *Jennie Gerhardt*, Dreiser did not again make the mistake of portraying the anti-bourgeois sentimental artist in the girl who goes bad. This time he draws a portrait of his mother as reflected in the experience of his sisters, his poor suffering mother, whom he could never forget holding up to him as a child her shabby shoes and saying, "See poor mother's shoes? See the hole there?" He was the mama's boy par excellence, dreaming always of that figure "potent and alive," who had—despite the ogre papa—made their home seem "like Fairyland." In the novel, the mother-sister figure is identified not only with Jennie, but with all of "the distraught and helpless poor," while the figure of the father is fractured into the religious tyrant Mr. Gerhardt; Senator Brander, Jennie's first lover, who wants to marry her but dies too soon; and Lester Kane, son of a rich family, who deserts Jennie when he is threatened with disinheritance. None of the three, however, though each makes Jennie suffer in some way, can finally qualify as a villain, not even old Gerhardt. They are finally all melted down in the universal solvent of Dreiser's pity for victims—revealed as not the rejecting fathers they first seemed, but weak sons, pleading forgiveness from the eternally offended Jennie-Mother. It is only the abstract "system," which is the really Bad Father; and if the seduction novel in Dreiser's hands takes on social meanings once more, those meanings are not translatable into any conventional theory of the class struggle. In his books, humanity as a whole struggles against the inhuman nature of things as they are. Seducer and victim are equally betrayed, equally to be pitied: Lester Kane is condemned by his own weakness to die apart from his love, and Jennie for all her strength can only look through the iron grille of the cemetery at his coffin being lowered into the earth.

The fictional world of Dreiser is the *absolutely* sentimental world, in which morality itself has finally been dissolved in pity; and in such a world, Charlotte Temple is quite appropriately reborn. No theme but seduction can contain the meanings Dreiser is trying to express, no catastrophe but deflowering start his heroines on their way toward total alienation. But any allusion to deflowering had become in Dreiser's time taboo; and even the once-standard description of an unmarried mother's affection for her illegitimate child, a sympathetic rendering of her refusal to consider it unclean, had come to seem in bourgeois circles a flaunting of decency itself. To the anti-bourgeois camp in the literary world of the early twentieth century, Dreiser's orthodox sentimental plea for sympathy rather than scorn for the fallen woman seemed, therefore, a revolutionary manifesto, an emancipation proclamation! And in the context of the developing struggle, in the courts and in the magazines, he did, indeed, become the spokesman for the forces combating genteel censorship, winning in the end a freedom in the handling of sex which he himself was incapable of exploiting.

Meanwhile, his theme had become more and more explicitly the denial of personal moral responsibility, the assertion that the individual who was to be pitied could not be blamed. After a while, he was scarcely distinguishable from his friend Clarence Darrow, making a tearful, mechanistic courtroom plea for a criminal facing the sentence of death. It is appropriate, therefore, that the novel in which Dreiser gives full-dress treatment to the contention that nothing is anybody's fault should take place largely in the courtroom, quote extensive sections of an actual court record. In *An American Tragedy,* which was published in 1925, a poor boy on the make in society (his prototype in real life came from a fairly comfortable family) lets drown (his prototype deliberately plotted and executed the crime) a factory girl whom he has got pregnant, and who stands in the way of his marriage to a rich debutante. Even in the columns of the newspapers, Dreiser can only find new instances of what early reading and experience have made for him an obsessive theme. Whatever he thinks he is trying to prove, he must prove it by setting in motion the Seducer and the Seduced, the passionate or vain young man indulging his desire for power and the baffled girl, lonely and eager to be fed well, dressed well, inducted into the mysteries of beauty. What makes *An American Tragedy* particularly American is the fact that Clarissa falls prey not to Lovelace but to Horatio Alger!

For his services in reviving a myth as old as the bourgeois novel itself, Dreiser was identified as a "naturalist," a term of contempt to the genteel, and a rallying cry for those who were engaged in the struggle against gentility. And the battle which he fought inadvertently at first he engaged in quite consciously after a while; by those who hailed him as a great emancipator, he was persuaded that it had been his aim all along to release Americans in life and art for the pursuit of passion; and especially in *The Genius* he abandoned his more essential seduction theme to plead the cause of Don Juan. It is partly Dreiser's own fault, therefore, if he has come to seem part of the Lawrentian sexual revolution of the '20's, otherwise carried forward by that homegrown D. H. Lawrence, Sherwood Anderson; though perhaps most of the responsibility lies with such champions of his work as Dorothy Dudley. In her study of Dreiser's impact on America, Miss Dudley reports the following astonishing conversation between Dreiser and herself on the subject of his mother. " 'Was she really so alive, so "pagan" as you call her? Was your father enough for her then, or did she find others?' 'She did if she wanted to, I'm certain of that. She had a way of doing what she wanted to do without disturbing the rest of us. But I was too young, I don't know about that.' 'Well, maybe she did. Maybe your father was not your father. How do you know?' " This fondest fantasy of the erotic sentimentalism of the '20's— illegitimacy or putting one over on Father—Dreiser disavows. His mother's "paganism" he would apparently like to keep spiritual, abstract, and he shies at adultery, which is not, in any case, a main subject of his essentially American books. The new mystique of passion Dreiser never really embraced—not retroactively for his mother anyhow; but the older mystique of virginity he had left behind. And this defection perhaps cut him off from the kind of middlebrow popularity which, granted his gifts and limitations, he should have enjoyed.

That popularity Herman Wouk, profiting by the collapse of hyper-genteel taboos in the bourgeoisie itself, has managed to attain. The struggle of writers like Dreiser, ironically enough, made it possible to write in 1955 the pure bourgeois novel of seduction as originally created by the female Richardsonians. Only one fundamental revision has been made in the mythos of seduction between *Charlotte Temple* and *Marjorie Morningstar* (their very titles indicate their kinship): the newer genteel Sentimentalism will not let the fallen woman die. That Marjorie in losing her virginity has been permanently maimed, incapacitated for the full enjoyment of marriage, Mr. Wouk does not doubt; yet he insists on marrying her off into a bitter-sweet happy ending. The twentieth-century Clarissa no longer is condemned to end her life by suicide or a broken heart, when her honor is lost; she is granted the partial redemption of marriage to an athletic lawyer, ends not in the wretched hovel where Charlotte came to die, but in the split-level house beautiful of exurban New York. Perhaps this is why she can no longer save anyone but herself, though she is still capable of damning the man who devirginates her. Something of the old mythic power still clings to her, some last trace of the aura of Clarissa, that secular savior, whose piety and sexuality were felt, for all their absurdly conventional dress, as real and terrible. But Marjorie has followed the downward path of travesty already foreshadowed in Charlotte, seems finally only a silly girl who turns into a dull suburban lady, the ghost (dead she would have been more alive) of the Protestant virgin, oddly turned Jew.

Between Richardson and Wouk, falls the shadow of Flaubert, who has taught Wouk. Wouk, however, will not confess this truth, which even the facts of his own fable substantiate, but attempts to exorcise it by editorial comment and implicit moralizing, trying to lift our hearts high above such earthbound reflections. The voice which, despite his censorship, keeps whispering to him and his readers alike, "Clarissa is Bovary, Marjorie is Bovary, you are Bovary," he identifies with the voice of the Seducer, against whose wiles it is his function to warn the bourgeois American world.

Who is the Seducer in Wouk's novel, the modern counterpart of the irresistible Lovelace, whose struggle with the immovable Clarissa all Europe once followed through a million words? He is called Noel Airman, which is to say, *Luftmensch,* the impractical schemer who never touches the ground, though he was born Ehrman, which is to say, man of honor. Denying his Jewish birthright, Wouk apparently means to tell us, by denying his Jewish name, Noel also denies virtue; and we are not surprised to discover that he is not only an actor, pianist, and playwright, but also a valueless bohemian and, especially, Don Giovanni once more!

Airman, like Lovelace before him, is both seducer and freethinker, besides being possessed of a grace alongside of which bourgeois manners and morality seem grubbily and unpleasantly safe and sane. Lovelace, however, was an aristocrat, survivor of the class just then blending (as Richardson shows by the possibility of his wooing Clarissa) into the mercantile bourgeoisie; Airman is not sure where he belongs. He is intended to be a member of a self-appointed aristocracy of culture, a highbrow (miserable imitation of Noel Coward that he actually is): the equivalent to the middlebrow imagination of the Dandy and the *poète maudit.* And this finally is the true subject of Wouk's book, its underground theme. The bourgeoisie has won its fight against the old nobility, the last item on its agenda having been the Freedom from Seduction. But suddenly, from among its own sons, a new enemy appears to cry that there is no seduction, that all is permitted, that the values for which their fathers fought against the old nobility are lies.

There is some justification, after all, for recasting Lovelace as Airman, since, as we have seen, it was on the model of the former that Rousseau created his Saint-Preux, on whom in turn Goethe modeled Werther; and from Werther have stemmed all the portraits of the artist as a young seducer down to our own time. It is Wouk's unique contribution to American letters to have identified this bugaboo of middle-class ladies with the "Jewish intellectual," trading on a stereotype of such highbrows as cynical, bohemian, neurotic, negative, much given to idle talk about obscure books and Sigmund Freud. To the fear of the Jewish intellectual as seducer, which troubles the sleep of lower-middlebrow Anglo-Saxon maidens, he has finally given genteel literary expression. But beside his bad Jew, Wouk is careful to set good ones: soft-hearted, handball-playing professional men; kindly, old, ridiculous uncles; warm, expansive mamas—but especially Marjorie herself.

From the earliest moment, Jewish heroines have been viable in American novels; the rich widow, Mrs. Achsa Fielding, whom Arthur Mervyn marries in Brockden Brown's romance, is a Jewess, as is Hawthorne's Miriam in *The Marble Faun*. They soon become, however, forbidden exotics—dark, alien types whom the hero, after Brown, is not permitted to marry—for lurking behind and beside them is the Jewish villain, the Smiler with a Knife. Shylock and Jessica, Isaac and Rebecca: these are the prototypical pairs reflected in such American works as Melville's *Clarel* and *Mrs. Peixada* by "Sidney Luska," though it is Scott's model rather than Shakespeare's which our writers follow; since in their imaginations to marry the Jew's daughter does not cease to be a sin even if she is converted, whatever Shakespeare may once have believed. In *The Yoke of the Torah*, "Sidney Luska" de-mythicizes the Jew's daughter at last, portrays her as a dull, bourgeois girl whose marriage to the sensitive hero of the novel means his spiritual and moral death.

Marjorie is the end-product of this de-mythicizing process, by which Scott's Rebecca becomes Luska's Tillie (" 'Oh my daughter, she works like a horse. . . . And such a *good* girl. Only nineteen years old and earns more than a hundred dollars a month. . . . She's grand. She's an angel' "), but she is Tillie mythicized again, Tillie as Clarissa—out of the fire into the frying pan! However, there is a further, an essential difference. Marjorie is, first of all, detached from the melodrama of the encounter with the gentile, allowed to choose only between the Jewish intellectual and the Jewish bourgeois. The effect of putting her into so totally Jewish a context is to make her seem scarcely Jewish at all (though much is made of her difficulties with religion), hardly distinguishable from the Sweetheart of Sigma Chi. In another sense, Wouk's novel represents the entry of the newest shibboleth of sentimental liberalism into the sentimental novel of seduction, the assimilation of anti-anti-Semitism into the kind of book which had already assimilated abolitionism, Christian socialism, woman's rights, temperance, etc., etc.

Marjorie Morningstar is, in this respect, the first fictional celebration of the mid-twentieth-century *détente* between the Jews and middle-class America; and the movie which has followed, the *Time* story and the *Time* cover picture are, in effect, public acknowledgments of that fact. Among the enlightened minority audience of the arts, the transformation of the Jew from bugaboo to culture hero is as old as Kafka and James Joyce. In the high literature of Europe and, more slowly, in that of the United States, gentile and Jew have joined forces to portray the Jewish character as a figure representing man's fate in the modern, urbanized world. In general, the point of such portrayals is to suggest that we live in an age of rootlessness, alienation, and terror, in which the exiled condition so long thought peculiar to the Jew comes to seem the common human lot. This is neither a cheery nor a reassuring view; and it is therefore incumbent on the lower-middlebrow novelist, Wouk, to suggest a counter-view: the contention that the Jew was never (or is, at least, no longer) the rootless dissenter, the stranger which legend has made him, but rather the very paragon of the happy citizen at home, loyal, chaste, thrifty, pious, and moderately successful—in short, not Noel Airman but Marjorie Morningstar, which is to say, Charlotte Temple given a second chance.

9

GOOD GOOD GIRLS AND
GOOD BAD BOYS:
CLARISSA AS A JUVENILE

THERE WAS, HOWEVER, a period of thirty years or more (from the end of the '50's until the '90's had begun) when the seduction story was excluded from female middlebrow fiction—a period in which women, grown too genteel for sex, cast about for new fables to feed their fantasy. And in a certain kind of Western they found some satisfaction at least.

Owen Wister's *The Virginian* first made respectably popular the mythic romance of the cowboy and the schoolmarm and the ethical clash which nearly frustrates their love. The cowboy's commitment to honor, to the surviving code of the duel, and the schoolmarm's commitment to Christian forgiveness and nonviolence force an inevitable crisis, that nearly disrupts the marriage with which the novel has all along promised to end. On their wedding day, the Virginian and Mary Wood quarrel over whether he shall answer or evade the challenge of the villain, Trampas; and when he goes out, after all, to fight, Mary swears she will not marry him. His opponent killed, however, the Virginian returns, redolent with the sweet smell of gunpowder, virility, and success, to find his bride (her motivation scarcely examined) ready to embrace him. The Sermon on the Mount has yielded to the code of the West with only the most perfunctory of struggles. *The Virginian* is a fable, cloying and false, which projects at once the self-hatred of the genteel eastern sophisticate confronted with the primitive, and his dream of a world where "men are men," i.e., walk with smoking guns into the arms of women who cheerfully abdicate their roles as guardians of morality. The enduring appeal of this slight, slick novel (until recently required reading in many American high schools) is testified to by the unacknowledged plagiarism of its theme in the recent movie *High Noon,* in which Gary Cooper, in whom myth after myth has become flesh, incarnates the Virginian, too.*

Such a story did not, however, finally satisfy female readers, who even in the mid-nineteenth century yearned to see women portrayed as abused and suffering, and the male as crushed and submissive in the end. Though such readers joined the campaign to excise passion from the novel, they were not really happy either with the kind of literature that campaign produced in the later works of Harriet Beecher Stowe or in the whole body of fiction by William Dean Howells. The latter novelist is, indeed, the embodiment of the writer an age demanded and did not really want: the author of flawlessly polite, high-minded, well-written studies of untragic, essentially eventless life in New England—the antiseptic upper-middlebrow romance. Yet his forty books, in which there are no seductions and only rare moments of violence, are too restrictedly "realistic" to do justice to the reality of dream and nightmare, fantasy and fear. Only in *A Modern Instance,* written in 1882, does Howells deal for once with a radically unhappy marriage; and here he adapts the genteel-sentimental pattern which had substituted the bad husband (his Bartley Hubbard has "no more moral nature than a baseball") for the Seducer, the long-suffering wife for the Persecuted Maiden or fallen woman.

It is the theme Melville and Hawthorne had fumbled back and forth in the unwritten Agatha story, and which J. W. DeForest had written in *Miss Ravenel's Conversion.* In this study of the conflict of loyalties and love against a Civil War background (the book appeared in 1867), Lillie Ravenel turns down Edward Colbourne, obviously more worthy of her, for the "magnetic" Lieutenant-Colonel Carter. High-colored, with flashing black eyes and an ability to speak French—unlike the more plodding "good" protagonist—Carter would have been the Seducer in a franker time. But though he compares Carter to the "hideous apes with carnivorous appetites, whose desire it was to devour the approaching stranger," even the boldly realistic DeForest is victim enough of

* In an unforeseen reversal of the original plot, Arthur Miller has in *The Misfits* written a movie about the triumph of female values of love over the death-centered values of the code. To do this, however, he has had to transform the school teacher of the legend into the semblance of Marilyn Monroe.

the genteel mode to make his character no more than an embezzling, unfaithful spouse. Passionate and immoral, he still wants only, however unworthily, to marry Lillie.

Even in *St. Elmo* (1866), the pseudo-gothic villain-hero of Augusta Wilson's all-time best-seller who gives his name to the book is never permitted to threaten assault, ends by offering marriage to the persecuted orphan girl, Edna Earl. When it becomes too great a strain on credulity to believe in St. Elmo's self-control, he is shipped off on a long sea voyage, and the reader can turn with relief to the heroine in her now quite unexceptionable struggles. When he gets back into the fictional scene, St. Elmo has not only reformed but has become a clergyman, whose offer of marriage Edna cannot refuse. The unworthy wooer competes with the unworthy husband for the place of Lovelace in the sentimental fable; but even their unworthiness is sometimes tempered by the tenderness or squeamishness of the lady authors. The rejected suitor may be, as in Maria Cummins' *The Lamplighter* (on whose prose style Joyce's Gertie McDowell, thirty years later, still bases the rhetoric of her erotic daydreams), merely in appearance unworthy. He was not, it turns out, really flirting with the most notorious coquette in Saratoga Springs, only pleading with her to take better care of her sick mother!

Such perfunctory explanations or reconciliations seem often less important than the tear-extorting episodes of unmerited female suffering which precede them, and which lend to the wives and maidens of the sexless sentimental romances of the '60's an aura of martyrdom—equal almost to Clarissa's own. The double feat demanded of the respectable writer of the era is to create a Clarissa who is not raped (she turns out to be a debased Jane Eyre), and a Lovelace who is not a rapist (he is invariably a vulgarized Rochester). In this they must have succeeded, for they were read with fantastic avidity. *The Lamplighter* sold 40,000 copies in eight weeks, and one "limited" edition out of the scores in which *St. Elmo* was printed totaled 100,000 copies! Yet the successes of the purely commercial purveyors of domestic sentiment are unimportant except as they cast light on the contemporary failures of more serious writers.

Howells, who inhabits the quietest, upper-middlebrow levels of the genteel world, hangs on his wall the embroidered motto of Mrs. Hentz and Mrs. Wilson: "Keep it Clean!"—but he refuses to set up beneath it the ikon of the Suffering Woman, the idol of the secret religion of the sentimental lady writers. No more could he set up the image of any secular Aphrodite; in the niche of the White Goddess, a fully clothed, upper-class, middle-aged Anglo-Saxon lady sits holding a cup of tea and making conversation, moderate, gracious, and witty. This is why his books possess neither passionate nor "religious" overtones, but take up again the failed gambit of Brockden Brown's *Clara Howard* or Cooper's *Persuasion:* a tradition which William Gilmore Simms called "a very inferior school of writing, known as the social life novel." This literature of evasion, Howells, resolutely cheerful, progressive, and sane, considered both "scientific" and Anglo-Saxon. In his *Heroines of Fiction,* he insists that English and American readers are quite willing to permit the writer to handle "such relations of men and women as George Eliot treats in *Adam Bede"* (typically, he will not say the word "adultery"), if only the writer agrees to maintain "scientific decorum." And though he can adduce only one American book as an example, he argues that Anglo-Saxon literature has not really evaded the treatment of passion.

> It is quite false or quite mistaken to suppose our novels have left untouched these most important realities of life. They have only not made them their stock in trade; they have kept a true perspective in regard to them; they have relegated them in their pictures of life to the space and place they occupy in life itself, as we know it in England and America.

Yet whatever "space and place" sex may have occupied in Anglo-American life as observed by a self-made gentleman like Howells, it certainly once occupied most of the fictional "space and place" of the novel; and the diminution of its allotted area, according to the "true perspective" of gentility, left a vacuum into which new sentimental material immediately rushed. One source of such material is the spirit of social protest and the causes with which that movement occupied itself. Many critics have pointed out, detachedly or in anger, that the withdrawal of sexual passion from art leads to an increase of horror and sadism; it has not been similarly noted that such a withdrawal leads also to the disguised masochism of the "protest" novel.

To this very day, in such writers as John Hersey, Irwin Shaw, and James Michener, the sentimental novel of social protest survives, dedicating itself to such latter-day issues as anti-Semitism,

racial discrimination, the atom bomb, McCarthyism, etc., etc., eternally searching for new examples among the abused "little people"
to set in the position of the Persecuted Maiden. One result of the
eternal search of the reformer-sentimentalists for new causes is that
the old ones wear out, come to seem ridiculous. Nothing, for instance, seems to the enlightened of today more absurd than the
teetotal or the anti-tobacco campaigns (except possibly the drive
against sexual vulgarity); yet it was with such causes that the
socially conscious novel began. The campaign against liquor is, of
all reforming movements, the one most easily adapted to the demands of traditional Sentimentalism and the image of the Suffering
Woman. Even in such sophisticated works as *Miss Ravenel's Conversion* and *A Modern Instance,* drunkenness is used as a chief
symbol for the husband's betrayal of the wife; in the latter, indeed,
it is a substitute for the kind of sexual defection Howells is
squeamish about handling.

The saloon, of course, was for a long time felt as the anti-
type of the home, a refuge for escaping males nearly as archetypal as the wilderness and the sea. Ever since *Rip Van Winkle,*
the image of a bust with the boys has stood for the flight from the
shrew. Some deep sense of this surely is in all anti-saloon literature; and it is not surprising to learn that Timothy Arthur, author
of the comically stereotypical *Ten Nights in a Bar-Room* (1854),
was a man who devoted most of his career to fictional studies of
the break-up of marriage, by liquor, card-playing, and other causes
too complex to win for him the fame he achieved by exploiting the
simpler anti-domestic vices. The abused woman, beaten or neglected by the drunken bully, has become so standard a fixture in
the sentimental melodrama of life in America, that we can scarcely
believe it to have been invented at any given moment. Surely, the
child has bent under the swinging doors to cry "Is my father in
there?" from the beginning of time.

Walt Whitman was perhaps not the inventor of the form; but he
had in 1842 written in *Franklin Evans or The Inebriate* one of the
earliest temperance novels, a book he himself considered the first
in the field. It would be lovely to believe that the poet later called
"the dirtiest beast of the age" was also the creator of so philistine
a literary kind. *Franklin Evans* is, in any case, a deeply earnest
plea for total abstinence, though Whitman later tried to pass it off
as a mere potboiler, a joke on its readers. Periodically throughout
his life, Whitman was to swear off liquor, dedicate himself to health

and pure cold water; and whatever guilt prompted those vain pledges of abstinence is projected in *Franklin Evans,* through images sentimental (the hopeless drunk loses his job, watches his wife fade and die) and gothic (from a bout of drunken euphoria, the victim awakes to find himself married to an octoroon). The volume ends, after piling up example after example of the fatal consequences of drink, with an impassioned plea to the reader to join the ranks of the reformers, who are about to march on the "musical Saloons" in an effort to crush the "Red Fiend" and deliver the youth of America from those poisonous dens "where the mind and the body are both rendered effeminate together."

The greatest of all novels of sentimental protest is, however, dedicated not to the problem of drink but to that of slavery, though its author was a total abstainer, who would appear at literary luncheons only if promised that no wine would be served. The novel, of course, is Harriet Beecher Stowe's *Uncle Tom's Cabin,* which she read in installments to her children as she composed it in 1851 and 1852. They wept as they listened; and she wept, too, returned to each installment at such a pitch of frenzy that she began after a while to feel as if the volume were being dictated rather than invented. "The Lord himself wrote it!" she insisted later; and if He had, indeed, written and autographed it, it could not have sold better—some 300,000 copies in the very first year of publication, and millions in the following years, perhaps outstripping even *The Last of the Mohicans.* It is an astonishingly various and complex book, simplified in the folk mind, which has remembered in its place the dramatic version in which Mrs. Stowe had no hand and which she saw, secretly, only once.

In *Uncle Tom's Cabin,* there are two contrasting studies of marriage: one between an opportunistic, morally lax husband and an enduring Christian wife; another between a hypochondriacal, self-pitying shrew—an acute but cruel caricature of the Southern lady —and a gentle, enduring husband. The latter relationship between the St. Clares, who are mother and father to Little Eva, is from a purely novelistic point of view the most skillfully executed section of the book; but it is scarcely remembered by *Uncle Tom's* admirers. No more do the really erotic episodes stick in the collective memory of America: neither Legree's passionate relationship with the half-mad slave girl, Cassy, nor his breathless, ultimately frustrated attempt to violate the fifteen-year-old quadroon, Emmeline.

The story of the decline of Cassy from a protected Creole childhood, in which she is scarcely aware that she is a Negro, through
her lush bondage to a chivalrous white New Orleans lover, in
which she is scarcely aware she is a slave, to the point where she
is pawed publicly in the slave market and degraded to the level of
becoming Legree's unwilling mistress is fictional material of real
interest; merely sketched in by Mrs. Stowe, it has recently been
worked out in great detail by R. P. Warren in *Band of Angels.* Yet
it fades from the mind even just after we have read *Uncle Tom.*
It is not essential to the book which became part of our childhood.
Of the complex novel created by Mrs. Stowe (or God!), America
has chosen to preserve only the child's book.

Though we *know* Emmeline and Cassy are cowering in the attic
at the moment that Quimbo and Sambo under Legree's direction
are beating Uncle Tom to death, it is only the latter scene which
we *feel.* We respond to the suffering and the triumph and the dis-
tressingly tearful arrival, just too late, of Marse George, the boy
who has loved and remembered Tom and who is our surrogate in
the book. All the conventional loves and romances of the book slip
away, precisely because they are conventional, but also because
they are irrelevant: the boy-girl all-white love of Eva and her
cousin Henrique; and even, though it is a unifying thread joining
the first volume of the novel to the second, the separation, the
individual flights, and the joyous reunion in Canada of Eliza and
George. We remember Eliza and the bloodhound, Eliza on the
ice; we have to check the text to discover what happened to her
after she left the floes behind, to remember that with her husband
she emigrated to Liberia! Poor George—his existence is fictional
only, not mythic. Unlettered Negroes to this day will speak of a
pious compromiser of their own race, who urges Christian forbearance rather than militancy, as a "Tom" or "Uncle Tom"; it has
become a standard term of contempt. But no one speaks of the
advocate of force who challenges him as a "George," though Mrs.
Stowe's protagonist of that name was a very model for the righteous use of force against force.

Only Uncle Tom and Topsy and Little Eva have archetypal
stature; only the loves of the black man for the little white girl, of
the white girl for the black, of the white boy for the slave live the
lives of myths. Mrs. Stowe's laudable effort to establish a counter-
stereotype to the image of the black rapist that haunts the mind of
the South was a failure. We do not remember the turncoat puritan

Legree squeezing the virginal breast of Emmeline, eyeing her lust-fully; he is frozen forever, the last enduring myth of the book, in his role of slave-driver, at his purest moment of passion, himself the slave of his need to destroy the Christian slave Tom: "There was one hesitating pause, one irresolute relenting thrill, and the spirit of evil came back with sevenfold vehemence; and Legree, foaming with rage, smote his victim to the ground." It is at this moment that Legree seems the archetypal Seducer, ready for the final violation which the reader has all along feared and awaited with equal fervor.

For all the false rhetoric of Mrs. Stowe's description, that blow has an impact as wide in its significance as the assault of Lovelace, the attack of Cain; in it, the white man seals his guilt against the black, confesses his complicity in an act at once predestined and free. This is the moment that stays with us always, balanced against the counter-moment in which George grasps the hand of the dying Tom—*too late,* for Mrs. Stowe cannot help telling the truth—and weeps. The fact of brutality, the hope of forgiveness and mutual love: these are the twin images of guilt and reconciliation that represent for the popular mind of America the truth of slavery. How oddly they undercut the scenes of separated families, of baffled mother-love, at which Mrs. Stowe worked so hard—feeling perhaps that to her bourgeois readers slavery would stand condemned only if it were proved an offense against the sacred family and the suffering mother.

The chief pleasures of *Uncle Tom's Cabin* are, however, rooted not in the moral indignation of the reformer but in the more devious titillations of the sadist; not love but death is Mrs. Stowe's true Muse. For its potential readers, the death of Uncle Tom, the death of Little Eva, the almost-death of Eliza are the big scenes of *Uncle Tom's Cabin,* for they find in the fact and in the threat of death the thrill once provided by the fact or threat of sexual violation. Death is the supreme rapist who threatens when all other Seducers have been banished to the semi-pornographic pulps. And it is the sexless child who comes to seem his proper victim, after the nubile Maiden is considered too ambiguous and dangerous a subject for polite literature. The aroma of sexuality clings to this Maiden, in-nocent as she may be; and Eliza, for instance, caught by her pur-suers, might easily become the object not of bloodlust, which is considered safe, but of quite specific sexual desire. Mrs. Stowe was Puritan enough not to flinch from such problems, but most of her readers were not; and they selected from her gallery of abused females the sexless child to remember and revere.

Little Eva seemed the answer to a particularly vexing genteel dilemma. To save the female for polite readers who wanted women but not sex was not an easy matter. The only safe woman is a dead woman; but even she, if young and beautiful, is only half safe, as any American knows, recalling the necrophilia of Edgar Allan Poe. The only *safe,* safe female is a pre-adolescent girl dying or dead. But this, of course, is Little Eva, the pre-pubescent corpse as heroine, model for all the protagonists of a literature at once juvenile and genteelly gothic.

Though the essential theme of the novel is, as we have come to see, love, it has never been forbidden the spice of death; and in its beginnings, it presented both in one, though both in terms of a fully adult world. In the earliest bourgeois fiction, we remember, the reader was permitted to assist at the last moments of the betrayed woman, no more excluded from the deathbed than from the marriage bed or the couch of sexual betrayal. In the later, more genteel stages of the novel, however, when it was no longer considered permissible to witness female sexual immorality, the reader was banned from the bedrooms of mature women even at the moment of their deaths. He had to content himself with the spectacle of the immaculate child winning her father to God by her courage in the face of a premature end.

Little Eva is the classic case in America, melting the obdurate though kindly St. Clare from skepticism to faith. What an orgy of approved pathos such scenes provided in the hands of a master like Harriet Beecher Stowe, or the later Louisa May Alcott, who in *Little Women* reworked the prototype of Mrs. Stowe into a kind of fiction specifically directed at young girls! Here is the *locus classicus* from *Uncle Tom's Cabin.*

"Dear papa," said the child, with a last effort, throwing her arms about his neck. In a moment they dropped again; and, as St. Clare raised his head, he saw a spasm of mortal agony pass over the face—she struggled for breath, and threw up her little hands.

"O God, this is dreadful," he said, turning away in agony, and wringing Tom's hand. . . . "O, Tom, my boy, it is killing me!" . . .

The child lay panting on her pillows, as one exhausted—the

large clear eyes rolled up and fixed. Ah, what said those eyes, that spoke so much of heaven? Earth was past, and earthly pain; but so solemn, so mysterious, was the triumphant brightness of that face, that it checked even the sobs of sorrow. . . .

The bed was draped in white; and there, beneath the drooping angel-figure, lay a little sleeping form—sleeping never to waken!

If there seems something grotesque in such a rigging of the scene, so naked a relish of the stiffening white body between the whiter sheets; if we find an especially queasy voyeurism in this insistence on entering the boudoirs of immature girls, it is perhaps the fault of our post-Freudian imaginations, incapable of responding sentimentally rather than analytically to such images. The bed we know is the place of deflowering as well as dying, and in the bridal bed, a young girl, still virgin, dies to be replaced by the woman, mourning forever the white thing she once was. At least, so an age of innocence dreamed the event; they did not have to *understand* what they dreamed. With no sense of indecorum, they penetrated, behind Mrs. Stowe, the bedroom of the Pure Young Thing and participated in the kill. To be allowed (vicariously) to murder the deflowered Clarissa of the earlier novel is, perhaps, satisfactory enough, since the appeasement of guilt, the hatred of sin lies at its root; but to murder (just as vicariously) the pre-adolescent Virgin is to be granted the supreme privilege of assaulting innocence, appeasing the hatred of virtue, which must surely have stirred uneasily before such atrociously immaculate examples. And it is all done without recourse to "sex," as sex was then quite narrowly defined—*cleanly* sadistic to an age in which no one suspected that the shadow of the Marquis de Sade might fall upon the social reformer. All was permitted the writer capable of combining such erotic evocations of death with attacks on slavery or demands for the reorganization of debtors' prisons, boys' schools, and almshouses.

The notion that Mrs. Stowe (whose blend of morality and prurience led her to expose the love life of Byron and his sister, when she had run out of material closer to home) might be a pornographer was as unthinkable to the great audience of her age as the fact that Dickens, her teacher in this regard, drew all his life on his own odd taste for pre-nubile girls. That Dickens' Little Nell is the model for Little Eva seems probable enough; though, indeed, the atmosphere of the era makes the simultaneous emergence of such archetypal small girls far from unlikely. It is Dickens, however, who first provides in *The Old Curiosity Shop* (1842) the iconography of the Holy Family of the genteel Protestant bourgeoisie. Not the Divine Boy but the Good Good Girl is imagined, cuddled not in the arms of the mother but in those of the father, and not at the moment of birth but at that of death. When *The Old Curiosity Shop* first appeared, critics spoke of the affiliation of Little Nell to Cordelia; and indeed, the final scenes of *King Lear* must have suggested to Dickens the form of what has been called the Protestant *Pietà:* the white-clad daughter, dying or dead, in the arms of the old man, tearful papa or grandfather or (in America) the woolly-haired slave.

It is the unendurable happy ending, as the white slip of a thing too good for this world prepares to leave it for the next, while readers and parents, lovers all, sob into their handkerchiefs. The Good Good Girl, blond, asexual goddess of nursery or orphanage or old plantation house ("Always dressed in white," Mrs. Stowe writes of Eva, "she seemed to move like a shadow through all sorts of places, without contracting spot or stain; and there was not a corner or nook . . . where those fairy footsteps had not glided, and that visionary golden head, with its deep blue eyes, fleeted along"), must die not only so we may weep—and tears are, for the sentimentalist, the true baptism of the heart—but also because there is nothing else for her to do. There lies before the Little Evas of the world no course of action which would not sully them; allowed to grow up, Little Eva could only become—since she is forbidden the nunnery by the Protestant ethos and the role of the old maid is in our culture hopelessly comic—wife, mother, or widow, tinged no matter how slightly with the stain of sexuality, *suffered* perhaps rather than sought, but, in any case, *there!*

II

Only the girl-child seems, however, a sufficiently spotless savior to the imagination of America, which boggles at the notion of a pure boy. In Dickens, the pale dwarfish monsters of piety include not only Little Nells but boys, too: Tiny Tim and Paul Dombey and Oliver Twist, who though he does not ever quite die is constantly flirting with that final consummation. In the United States, however, such figures seem alien. Little Lord Fauntleroy is an import once much admired by Europeanizing females, but always scorned by nativists no matter how sentimental. He seems in our context the "little gentleman," miniature version of the polished, foreign seducer: an outsider who wears his Sunday clothes on weekdays and would rather walk shod than run barefoot. Sometimes he is called scornfully a "mamma's boy" but this term must be analyzed carefully, since *all* American boys belong to mother— even Tom Sawyer, traditional enemy of all "little gentlemen." Tom, indeed, has no father at all, his only parent that Aunt Polly whom he would die for rather than betray.

To betray the mother—to deny her like the young rogue in *The Prince and the Pauper*—this is the unforgivable sin. What then is the difference between the Good Good Boy and the Good Bad Boy, between Sid Sawyer, let us say, and Tom? The Good Good Boy does what his mother must pretend that she wants him to do: obey, conform; the Good Bad Boy does what she really wants him to do: deceive, break her heart a little, be forgiven. For a long time the Good Bad Boy was called the "bad boy" without qualification, since his goodness needed no adjective to declare itself to those who really knew him; and the very epithet was enough to insure a best-seller: *Confessions of a Bad Boy, Peck's Bad Boy,* etc. How much longer it took for a book to be called *Bad Girl* and how different the connotations of the title! "Oh, Tom, you bad boy!" Becky Thatcher cries to Tom and we take it as an endearment. It is the fate of the Good Good Girl (who must suffer, too, like the more mature savior-figures before her) to love such boys precisely because they play hooky, cuss, steal in a mild sort of a way, dream of violence. Where taboos forbid the expression of sexuality such delinquency is a declaration of maleness.

The Good Bad Boy is, of course, America's vision of itself, crude and unruly in his beginnings, but endowed by his creator with an instinctive sense of what is right. Sexually as pure as any milky maiden, he is a roughneck all the same, at once potent and submissive, made to be reformed by the right woman. No wonder our greatest book is about a boy and that boy "bad"! The book is, of course, *Huckleberry Finn* (with its extension back into *Tom Sawyer*), an astonishingly complicated novel, containing not one image of the boy but a series of interlocking ones. Tom Sawyer exists as the projection of all that Sid Sawyer, pious Good Good Boy, presumably yearns for and denies; but Huck Finn in turn stands for what Tom is not quite rebel enough to represent; and Nigger Jim (remade from boy to adult between the two books) embodies a world of instinct and primal terror beyond what even the outcast white boy projects.

In our national imagination, two freckle-faced boys, arm in arm, fishing poles over their shoulders, walk toward the river; or one alone floats peacefully on its waters, a runaway Negro by his side. They are on the lam, we know, from Aunt Polly and Aunt Sally and the widow Douglas and Miss Watson, from golden-haired Becky Thatcher, too—from all the reduplicated female symbols of "sivilization" It is these images of boyhood which the popular imagination further debases step by step via Penrod and Sam or O. Henry's "Red Chief" to Henry Aldrich on the radio or the insufferable Archie of the teen-age comic books. Such figures become constantly more false in their naïveté, in their hostility to culture in general and schoolteachers in particular; and it scarcely matters whether they are kept in the traditional costume of overalls or are permitted jeans and sweaters decorated with high-school letters.

Twain is surely not responsible for all the vulgar metamorphoses of his images of boyhood; but in one respect he is a conscious accomplice of the genteel kidnapers of Huck and Jim. Since not only in his avowed children's books, but almost everywhere in his work, Twain writes as a boy for a world accustomed to regarding the relations of the sexes in terms of the tie that binds mother to son. Not only does he disavow physical passion, refusing the Don Juan role traditional for European writers; but he downgrades even the Faustian role incumbent on American authors. In him, the diabolic outcast becomes the "little devil," not only comical but cute, a child who will outgrow his mischief, or an imperfect adult male, who needs the "dusting off" of marriage to a good woman. It was in the fading '60's that Twain's typical fictional devices were contrived, in the '70's that they were perfected—at a time, that is to say, when everywhere in the popular American novel the archetypes were being reduced to juveniles. As Clarissa becomes a small girl in *The Wide, Wide World,* so Werther becomes a child in Twain's total work, turns into the boy-author Mark Twain; and not only the American women who made Susan Warner's book a best-seller approve, but their husbands, too, who laughed at their wives' taste—just as Twain had at his wife's before being challenged to write *The*

Gilded Age. Even dirty, tired, adult Europe approves, finds no offense in *The Innocents Abroad* itself, since Twain was playing a role that European self-hatred and condescension to the United States demanded, acting the Good Bad Boy of Western culture. For everyone, male and female, European and American, he represents the id subverting tired ego-ideals, not in terror and anarchy, but in horseplay, pranks, and irreverent jests.

There is notoriously a price for assuming a mask, indeed, always a suspicion that what the mask hides is no face at all! And certainly one senses in Twain the need to act out for public laughter the aspects of himself which he feared might evoke private snickers. His buffoonery is obviously a camouflage for insecurity, the insecurity of a man with genteel ideas and bad manners, with pretensions to aristocratic origins and no formal education. Yet all along, he seems to have believed that somewhere beneath the high-jinks of Twain, there was a real and quite serious Sam Clemens: with serious ideas, too dangerous to utter; and serious ambitions, too lofty to risk in the market-place—even a serious vein of bawdry, too masculine and broad for the general reader. But his serious ideas eventuate in the sophomoric cynicism of "What is Man," his serious aesthetics in the sentimental banalities of *Joan of Arc,* his serious bawdry in the pseudo-archaic smutty jokes of *1601.*

Finally, Twain is betrayed not by his contempt for culture, which is involved, ironical, and sometimes wickedly witty, but by his pretensions to culture. He was a man fitfully intelligent when he did not know he was thinking, a spottily skillful stylist when he was not aware he was writing artistically; but he lacked critical judgment completely (his notion of criticism was a hunt for boners in the Leatherstocking Tales), and was tormented by an urge toward self-parody that verged on self-punishment. He is, therefore, an embarrassment to admiring critics, who tend either to swallow whole his dishearteningly uneven achievement; or to admire him only for the bitter wisdom presumably concealed from the vulgar beneath the hilarious surfaces of his work. There are corresponding traps for dissenting critics, who may find Twain the beneficiary of a cult of native humor finally more deadly than the cult of museums which he exposed; or cry out that his "philosophy" is the product of a childish mind, and his dissembling of it for popularity's sake shameful.

To make of Twain either a cult or a case, however, is finally to lose the sense of him as a poet, the possessor of deep and special mythopoeic powers, whose childhood was contemporaneous with a nation's; and who, remembering himself before the fall of puberty, remembered his country before the fall of the Civil War. The myth which Twain creates is a myth of childhood, rural, sexless, yet blessed in its natural Eden by the promise of innocent love, and troubled by the shadow of bloody death. The world in which his myth unfolds is one in which passion is less real than witchcraft, ghosts more common than adulterers; but it is also one in which a pure love between males, colored and white, triumphs over witches and ghosts and death itself. It is, of course, a world already dreamed in the fiction of Cooper and Poe, Dana and Melville, but never before labeled: "For Children Only!" And if we remember Twain's quite serious predecessors rather than his more sentimental followers (Stephen Crane, Booth Tarkington, etc.), we can understand how his novels define a boundary between myth and bathos, the highbrow Western and the boys' book.

It is hard to say whether the fear of sex, a strange blindness to the daily manifestations of sex, or the attenuation of sexuality itself drove the American novel back over the lintel of puberty in the declining years of the nineteenth century. Twain himself seems to have believed, not unlike Hawthorne before him, that it was the last; certainly, he had no sense of being *forbidden* to talk about a kind of passion which burgeoned everywhere in his society. In *1601*, at least, he seems to believe, though the conviction is offered in the guise of a joke, that genitality itself had withered to the vanishing point in America: "Then spake ye damned wyndmill, Sir Walter, of a people in ye uttermost parts of America that copulate not until they be five-and-thirty years of age, ye women being eight-and-twenty, and doe it then but once in seven yeares." In the mouth of "ye damned wyndmill," this is spoken contemptuously, but in his own voice, Twain (who did not in fact marry until he was past thirty) makes a similar assertion about the young people of his childhood community, this time with a certain amount of pride.

Chastity. There was the utmost liberty among young people— but no young girl was ever insulted, or seduced, or even scan-

dalously gossiped about. Such things were not even dreamed of
in a society, much less spoken of and referred to as possibilities.

The dream which Twain dreamed, at any rate, did not include
such possibilities; and *his* memories of the past, at least, were duly
expurgated, though just once in *Tom Sawyer* his censorship re-
laxes. For a single moment, we see Becky caught out peeking at the
dirty picture in the teacher's anatomy book, and for that moment
we are reminded of the living flesh beneath the pinafores and
roundabouts. But it does not finally matter; for Twain will not let
his protagonists, not Becky or Tom or Huck, over the borderline
of adolescence, playing such games with their ages that the reader
cannot tell from page to page whether they are barely out of kin-
dergarten (in *Tom Sawyer,* Tom is just losing his baby teeth) or
on the verge of manhood (in *Huckleberry Finn,* one summer later,
Huck, Tom's apparent co-eval, is fourteen). Yet Twain's dream of
boyhood begins with a dream of love in a sexless world; and, indeed, the "Boy's Manuscript," which he wrote in 1870, and which
is the seed of all the later books about Huck and Tom, is an account of a love affair between eight- or nine-year-olds—involving
flirtation, jealousy, and reconciliation, though not, of course,
passion.

Yet for all its sexual purity, Tom's childhood world is intimately acquainted with death. Violence is omnipresent, yet somehow is never considered to impugn innocence, so long as it does
not involve concupiscence. The plan of Injun Joe in *Tom Sawyer*
to take revenge on the Widow Douglas was apparently based on
an actual case involving the threat of rape, which Twain bowdlerized to a mere slitting of the nostrils and notching of the ears—
thus apparently making it suitable for child readers.

There is the sense everywhere in Twain that *violence doesn't
count,* the muting of sensitivity before aggression which is always
demanded by slapstick and the more brutal forms of farce; and it
is this which the one favorable review of *Huckleberry Finn* ap-
plauds as "a total absence of morbidness in the book," a proof that
"the *mal du siècle* has not yet reached Arkansas." Twain's treatment of the Grangerford-Shepherdson feud strikes the reviewer as
a prime example: "described only as it would appear to a semi-
civilized boy of fourteen, without the slightest condemnation or
surprise. . . ." But this is scarcely the whole story; for concurrent
with such a brutalized acceptance of terror in Twain, is a guilt-

ridden obsession with it, an inability to let it alone. Twain's attitude toward violence is finally as complicated, subtle, and deliberately ambiguous as his attitude toward sex is naive, sentimentalized, and hopelessly evasive. He is not only the creator of childhood idylls but a great poet of violence; and, indeed, even his humor depends upon a world in which there is neither a stable order nor civil peace.

His hope for order and peace he invested in the genteel Atlantic seaboard society into which he married, after years of drifting from job to job through West and East and South, looking for these qualities especially in his wife, whom he drafted as a super-ego, a living conscience. "I would . . . quit wearing socks if she thought them immoral," he said of his Livy, of whom he asked that she regularly "dust him off," make him worthy of the civilization she represented. He never chafed at Livy's demands, though he occasionally evaded them like the Good Bad Boy he never ceased to be, perhaps even regretted that she forbade too little; it would have made life more interesting if she *had* declared socks immoral! The society which had bred him, made him the untidy, disorderly boor he always felt before his wife, he recalled as a world of violence and horror. It seemed to him a chaotic middle ground between the South (with its no longer viable patriarchal ideals and its obsession with Sir Walter Scott), which his family had left behind just before his birth, and the true Western frontier (with its denial of all hierarchy and tradition), which had moved on ahead. Missouri he remembered as a slothful sub-frontier, in which the fathers no longer had any authority, and the mothers sought in vain to assert certain simple-minded standards of piety and decorum. Certainly, his own father had died in Twain's childhood, crying despairingly, "Let me die!"; while his mother had pleaded with him at the deathbed, "Only promise me to be a better boy. Promise not to break my heart."

Yet to Twain, Missouri was also a world of innocence and freedom and joy, a world in which *he,* at least, had been innocent and free and joyous, a naked boy, swimming and fishing and smoking on Jackson's Island. To the idyllic era of his childhood, Twain's mature mind reverted over and over, only to discover that the era had been lived out in a society marred by disorder and violence and slavery. It was the violence which he especially recalled: the dead man he had discovered after breaking into his father's office; the vagabond shot down in the street and gasping for breath beneath the heavy Bible laid on his chest; the hellish storm that had broken the night Injun Joe died, and had left him whimpering for the salvation of his soul; the tramp who had burned himself to death in the local jail, setting himself on fire (perhaps!) with matches the boy Twain had smuggled to him. Each terror brought with it the shadow of guilt: he should not have been sneaking into his father's office after dark; he should have been good enough to regard the crash of thunder with equanimity; he should have protested against laying so heavy and pious a burden on a dying man's chest; he should not have passed contraband through the bars.

Twain began to feel after a while that he carried with him the infection of death, out of the world he had left into the new world in which he sought peace. The death of his father, perhaps, and certainly that of his brother, Henry (whom he pilloried later as Sid all the same), he felt as somehow his responsibility; but these at least belonged to the life he had led before meeting Livy. When his son died, however, after an act of carelessness on his part, his favorite daughter, Susy, while he was absent in Europe ("died where she had spent all her life till my crimes made her a pauper and an exile"); when his daughter Jean developed epilepsy, and his wife ailed, he was more than ever ridden by a guilt which he could not allay, except by trying to persuade himself that death was a final good. "She has found," he said of Susy, "the richest gift the world can offer." Yet the books in which he tried, toward the end of his own life, to express his dark despair are flat and unconvincing or shrill and sophomoric. When Hannibal becomes Eseldorf, and Tom Sawyer is excluded from the final version of *The Mysterious Stranger,* all tension and ambiguity depart from Twain's work and with it his special charm.

His most profoundly sad books are the most mad and idyllic, his wisest those he wrote dreaming not thinking: dreaming the golden dream that threatens momentarily to turn into nightmare: and the wisest and saddest of them all, as it is also the craziest and most euphoric, is, of course, *Huckleberry Finn.* Indeed, to turn from *Huckleberry Finn* to the rest of Twain's work is disheartening; for there are only portions of other books which approach it; most of the first part of *Life on the Mississippi,* a good deal of *Pudd'nhead Wilson;* and to a lesser degree, *The Innocents Abroad, A Connecticut Yankee in King Arthur's Court, Tom Sawyer.* Beyond this, there is much that is merely occasional, even trivial; much that is without passion or point; much that is highfalutin or absurdly noble; much that is terrifyingly unfunny and empty. After a while, the reader who has made the mistake of reading too much Twain begins to feel that even the books he has liked cannot possibly be as good as he has thought them; that what Twain has left behind is not so much a real *oeuvre* as a bag of tricks: the accoutrements of a role, whose meaning has been lost to us with the death of its performer and a change in taste.

And then one reads *Huckleberry Finn* again, hears—intermittently at least—a voice which is neither Clemens' nor Twain's but genuinely Huck's, which is to say, not the voice of a genteel sentimentalist or a clown in full make-up, but of a boy-Ishmael: "the juvenile pariah of the village . . . idle, and lawless, and vulgar, and bad. . . ." The phrase is out of *Tom Sawyer,* of course, and it is with that earlier book that any discussion of *Huckleberry Finn* must begin; for it is Tom who discovers Huck, after his own book has begun, and discovering him, almost inadvertently, discovers also a great mythic theme. That theme succeeds in time in overwhelming the love story of Tom and Becky, which was the first inspiration of the book, and even thrusts aside the kind of genre picture ("Whitewashing the Fence"—the illustrator's dream!) which was its second. Of Tom Blankenship, the original of Huck, Twain writes in *The Autobiography:* "He was the only really independent person—boy or man—in the community . . ."; and in *Tom Sawyer,* adds that all the children, at least, "wished they dared be like him." The memory of "all the boy" Twain was or dreamed himself afterward is Tom; the memory of all he was not and only wished he dared aspire to be is Huck; and it is fitting that they be companions, the books named after each, sequels.

"Mark Twain's next book will bear the title of 'Huckleberry Finn, A Sequel to Tom Sawyer,' " a puff in *The Dial* for February, 1884, announced; and when the book actually appeared, it was called *Adventures of Huckleberry Finn (Tom Sawyer's Comrade),* but Twain was unwilling to depend on advertising and the title page alone to make his point. "You don't know about me," the first sentence of the new novel reads, "without you have read a book by the name of *The Adventures of Tom Sawyer. . . .*" And it is well, for once, to take Twain at his word, though there intervened between the publication of the first book (in 1876) and the second eight years, nearly seven of which Twain spent bogged down and unable to write a line, once his first impetus had taken him through the fifteenth chapter of the book as it presently stands. He did not know what to do when the raft had been taken out from under him and his characters! The point was, though it took Twain seven years to find it out, that his new book had ceased to be a continuation of the old, developing a much more complex relationship to it than that of a mere sequel.

Though *Huckleberry Finn* begins in the same long, idyllic summer of which *Tom Sawyer* had already consumed more than the normal number of weeks, and comes to a close in the following year, both boys have grown older by perhaps five or six years. And the author, too, has matured, is only *playing* now at producing an entertainment for children. If *Tom Sawyer* was always a boy's book, even when Twain thought he was writing for adults, *Huckleberry Finn* is from the start, on one of its levels at least, not merely an adult but a subversive novel, as the board of the Concord Public Library should have been congratulated for seeing. From time to time, Huck regresses to the age he was in the earlier book, chiefly when he comes face to face with a nubile, attractive girl, as in the Wilks episode—throughout which he is portrayed as feeling for the nineteen-year-old, red-haired Mary Ann the kind of nine-year-old passion little Billy Rogers had felt for a girl of the same age in the "Boy's Manuscript"; "I've seen the girl that is my doom. . . . Oh, she is *so* lovely! And she loves me. I know it. I could see it easy. She's nineteen years old Christmas. I never, never, never will part with *this* one! NEVER!" But such strategic retreats in time cannot conceal the basic change in Twain's conception of Huck, who has ceased to be merely a clownish foil to Tom, essentially *stupid* though good of heart. There is no mention in *Huckleberry Finn* of "Huck's slow mind," no condescending references to his efforts at thought as "a mental struggle."

It is, of course, Huck who tells the second tale with an apparent artlessness that touches true poetry, a kind of speech which characterizes him better than his author can. But the switch into first-person narrative does not in itself insure the new view of Huck. Twain attempts twice more to let Huck speak for himself, in *Tom Sawyer Abroad* and *Tom Sawyer Detective;* but in each case Huck lapses back into the role of obtuse oaf, his conversation sprinkled with burlesque boners: "diseased" for "deceased," "prostitution" for "prosecution," or "the solar sister" for "the solar system." Even in *Huckleberry Finn,* the first comic substitution has been smuggled (anything for a laugh!) into the Wilks episode, which is, in all respects, the falsest part of the book. And in *Huckleberry Finn,* too, Huck has been permitted occasionally to gush over the loneliness of life on the Mississippi in a schoolgirl style, which betrays his unsuspected affiliation to the female orphans of Susan Warner and Maria Cummins. Nothing in that book, however, descends to the level of *Tom Sawyer Abroad,* in which Huck hails a new bit of scenery as "the darlingest place there is" or improbably explains that "there was a dear little temple" between the paws of the Sphinx.

The language of Huck is a function of Twain's understanding of his character and role, and varies in authenticity with the author's sense of what both he and his character are doing. In all three Tom Sawyer stories, Huck is Tom's Noble Savage, a sentimentalized id-figure (and in this respect Jim is his double), representing the Good Bad Boy's dream of how bully life might be without parents, clothing or school; and in those books, Huck is even more condescended to than admired. In *Huckleberry Finn,* however, Huck does the condescending toward Tom, who represents in that book his misguided ego-ideal, the embodiment of a "literary" style which he cannot really afford. When he is truest to himself, Huck respects, in the teeth of all he has been taught, Nigger Jim, which is to say, an even more ultimate id-figure; in his weaker moments, he joins Tom in relegating the surrogate for the instinctive life to the world of make-believe, which is also a prison.

In general, the two boys represent to each other the writer's conception of "experience" and the nonreader's conception of "art." It would be pleasant to say that they fuse finally into a single figure: but even in the terms of Twain, they represent not so much two aspects of the same man as that man's sense of what he has become, opposed to what he has escaped becoming. In American life as a whole, the two are notoriously disjoined: the artist and the naïf, the man who has made it and the man who never knew it was there to be made. It is all very well to tell us that Huck's original ended as "a good citizen and greatly respected." This, we know, is not true of the fictional Huck, who is finally lost to Tom and respectability alike. Though in boyhood, Mark-Tom and Tom-Huck (surely, the inversion of the names is a deliberate joke!) were permitted to play hooky together; it is clear that once Mark-Tom decides to be good, to marry Livy, he will never again answer Tom-Huck's meow. Only in fantasy will he slide down the lightning rod again; but even his fantasy will end on a note of separation, not really belied by the desperate attempts, published and unpublished, to continue beyond *Huckleberry Finn* his childhood alliance with the village pariah.

If we think of the two books not as sequels but as alternative versions of the same themes (hopelessly concealed from the author himself in *Tom Sawyer,* more consciously developed in *Huckleberry Finn*), those themes will become clearer to us, reveal themselves in their mythic significance. Stripped of incidental ornaments, *Tom Sawyer* and *Huckleberry Finn* are seen as the same dream dreamed twice over, the second time as nightmare; though, to be sure, the terror of the second dream is already at work in the first, whose euphoria persists strangely into the second. In both books, there is a pretended, a quasi-ritual death to the community and its moral codes; though in *Tom Sawyer* that "death" is a lark, undertaken in childish pique, while in *Huckleberry Finn* it is a last desperate evasion, an act of self-defense. In both, there is a consequent spying on the community from cover to watch the effects of that death, the aftermath of regret: the childish dream of the suicide, who longs to be present at his own discovery, come true. In the one case, however, the spying is a prelude to a triumphant return, a revelation, in the other, to a further flight and concealment.

In both, there is an escape to an island, indeed, to the same island, on which the refugee lives, for a little while, with his good companions and in the bosom of nature, fishing, swimming, smoking the pipe forbidden by mothers. But in the one case, the natural Eden is purely a boys' paradise, from which one returns home as from a picnic; in the other, it is a temporary asylum not only from "sivilization" but from pursuit, enslavement, and death; and leaving it, the refugee plunges into further flight. The good companions, in the one case, are other boys, homesick almost from the start; in the other, the sole companion is a run-away slave, whose home is nowhere. In both, there is a night-journey across the river back into the abandoned world of obligations and restraints, a scouting foray into what has become enemy country; but in the one case, the scouting prepares for a return, in the other, a more desperate withdrawal.

In both, the escapee and presumed ghost watches from a place of concealment (how much in both books is peeked at, witnessed, overheard!) a sentimental *Pietà,* the sorrow of the "mother" over her mischievous and presumably lost boy. But how different is Huck's witnessing of Aunt Sally's tears, which are not even shed for him, from Tom's watching Aunt Polly cry. Though the descriptions are not unlike ("And twice I . . . see her setting there . . . with her eyes toward the road and tears in them. . . . And third time I waked up at dawn . . . and she was there yet . . . and her old grey head was resting on her hands, and she was asleep." "He had to keep still long after she went to bed, for she kept making broken-hearted ejaculations . . . and turning over. But at last she was still, only moaning a little in her sleep"), Tom is already prepared for his reconciliation with the offended mother while Huck is already incubating his great refusal. In Tom's pocket all the time is the message, *"We ain't dead—we are only off being pirates";* while Huck is preparing inwardly for the moment when he will declare: "But I reckon I got to light out for the territory ahead of the rest, because Aunt Sally she's going to adopt me and civilize me, and I can't stand it."

In both books, there is a terrorized flight from a threatening Satanic figure, who also stands outside of the comunity from which the boy-protagonist tries to escape in earnest or in play; and in each case, the outlaw figure represents a grotesque travesty of the boy himself, his innocence distorted into an image of guilt. Tom plays the robber, the pirate, which Injun Joe is in fact; Huck yearns in Widow Douglas' house for the life of ignorance and sloth, which his Pap actually lives. But in *Tom Sawyer,* the shadow of the protagonist is represented as utterly alien, a melodramatic half-breed out of a dime novel; in *Huckleberry Finn,* Huck's shadow is his own father: no creature of melodrama, but the town drunk—a vision of what he himself may well become! Pap Finn had, indeed, been cast for the role of Muff Potter in an early version of *Tom Sawyer,* but he was too real a terror for that theatrically gothic tale.

In both books, the shadow figure controls or threatens a treasure (the same "innocent" buried loot of dead murderers), which can be possessed in peace only after he has died; and in both, the plot involves a simultaneous revelation of that death and the protagonist's deliverance: his coming for the first time, or again, into a fortune. In both cases, the death of the demonic guardian of the hoard is rendered with special horror: Injun Joe at the cave's stony sill, a broken case-knife in his hand and the gnawed claws of bats beside him; Pap, naked and stabbed in the back, in the floating house of death, its walls scribbled with obscenities. But only in *Huckleberry Finn* is the full Oedipal significance of their deaths revealed, the terrible secret that the innocent treasure can be won only by the destruction of the Bad Father!

In both books, there is a good angel, too, a redemptive *anima* figure, contrasted with the threatening shadow. In *Tom Sawyer,* that figure appears in the form of Becky Thatcher, juvenile version of the snow maiden: "a lovely little blue-eyed creature with yellow hair plaited in two long tails, white summer frock." She is called, unequivocally enough, Tom's "new angel," and, for all her peeping at the forbidden picture in the teacher's book (what momentary demonic impulse prompted Twain to such a give-away?), will obviously grow up to be just such a good woman as Twain himself married and idolized. Meanwhile, she scarcely knows which she admires more in the Good Bad Boy Tom, his badness ("Oh, you bad thing!"), which it will give her pleasure to subdue, or his goodness ("Tom, how *could* you be so noble!"), which she calls forth and will sustain. It is of marriage with her that Tom dreams; for, as he explains to Huck, she is a "girl" not a "gal"! But marriage, to Huck, means only domestic strife and the abandonment of the world in which he is at home. Wistfully and a little jealously, he remarks, "Only if you get married I'll be more lonesomer than ever."

Yet Huck has his good angel, too, appropriately enough as black as Becky Thatcher is white: not a future good woman but a runaway slave, who represents his aspiration toward a deeper level of the primitive, even as Becky represents Tom's yearning for a "higher" level of civilization. Miss Watson's Jim is the Becky Thatcher of *Huckleberry Finn.* They cannot be present in the same book; Jim does not appear in *Tom Sawyer;* and when he enters the sequel Becky withdraws, making even her brief farewell bow under the name of Bessie Thatcher. With Jim, of course, Huck does not dream of any sexual relation, any more than Tom does with Becky; nor does he think of their union in terms of a marriage. Yet they pet and sustain each other in mutual love and trust: make on their raft an anti-family of two, with neither past nor future, only a transitory, perilous present of peace and joy.

Like Tom and Becky, Huck and Jim triumph over the petty pride that threatens to separate them in the midst of horror and pursuit, declare their affection without shame or fear of ridicule in the face of death; yet, like Tom and Becky, they seem to be already drifting apart after their moment of deliverance. For Huck and Jim, there is no possibility of a continuing love; Jim has a family, which will presumably claim him, and Huck must follow the centrifugal impulse which has made and will keep him the "only independent person . . . in the community." Moreover, he and Jim are separated not by the schoolyard code which forbids the fraternizing of boys and girls, but by the profound social gulf between black and white in ante-bellum Missouri. Huck himself knows that the talk of another lark involving Jim, the outing to the Indian territory will not really materialize, and that he will have to "light out . . . ahead of the rest." Twain could not ever quite manage to write anything publishable about the projected expedition, though he went to work on it almost immediately after finishing *Huckleberry Finn.* The prospect of "howling adventures amongst the Injuns" is merely another of Tom's artistic lies, a forecast as vain as his assurance in the earlier book that Huck will come and live with him after he and Becky are married.

Three's a crowd, whether the third be Becky or Jim, Tom's *anima* figure or Huck's; and after an unsuccessful try, in *Tom Sawyer Abroad,* to carry along both Huck and Jim on an adventure of Tom's (the two play scarcely distinguishable end-men to Tom's interlocutor), Twain settles in *Tom Sawyer Detective* for his original white pair. Jim presumably returns to his wife and children, whom Twain had temporarily forgotten; and, of course, Becky, in whom he never *quite* believed at all, makes no further appearance. Tom and Huck had, as a matter of fact, already stood alone at the close of both *Tom Sawyer* and *Huckleberry Finn;* for each book tries to end with a pact in which the Good Bad Boy and the juvenile pariah come to terms: the juvenile pariah agreeing to accept an adoptive mother, and the Good Bad Boy agreeing in return to accept the pariah into his world of make-believe—the robber gang or the expedition to the territory. Both the integration into the family and the playing of terror in the place of living it stand for a surrender of independence, since Tom, who thinks he wants to be like Huck, secretly wants Huck to be like him. In *Tom Sawyer,* the melancholy happy ending works; but *Huckleberry Finn,* which begins with the collapse of that first happy ending, closes with the hint it will not hold the second time either.

All of which means, finally, that *Huckleberry Finn* is a true book, *Tom Sawyer* only "mostly a true book" with "some stretchers," one of which is its ending. Huck can tell the truth about Tom, for though he lies by preference almost always, he *knows* when he is lying; but Tom is incapable of telling the truth about Huck, because he does not ever know when he is lying. At the point in *Huckleberry Finn* when Huck is about to disengage from the spell of Tom's long magical summer and plunge into his own, he sees quite clearly what Tom is like: "So then I judged that all that stuff was only just one of Tom Sawyer's lies. I reckoned he believed in the A-rabs and the elephants, but as for me I think different. It had all the marks of a Sunday-school." Toward the end of the book, however, when he has *become* Tom, Huck seems to lose this insight, and submits himself to the hoax of trying to steal Jim in fiction as he has already tried in fact; but at this point, the book has become Tom's, not his.

By and large, it is possible to say that *Tom Sawyer* is a fable of lost boyhood written by Tom, while *Huckleberry Finn* is that same fable transcribed by Huck. Somewhat misleadingly, Tom's version does not appear in first-person, though Twain considered telling it that way, and the "Boy's Manuscript," which is its germ, is actually written so. But its third-person narrative is finally even more right; for Tom is himself always an actor in a fiction of his own making, and, of course, he and Mark Twain are alternative sketches of the same character. Just as Tom speaks in a literary style compiled out of his favorite reading, so his book is a compound of genteel and gothic clichés, tempered with the condescension and humor which Twain considered proper in a book written for children. One of the chief functions of its style is to make the events it describes seem less real. The reality of the emotions it evokes is deliberately called into question by overwriting which verges on burlesque: "Life to him seemed hollow, and existence but a burden" or "He thought he loved her to distraction, he regarded his passion as adoration; and behold it was only a poor little innocent partiality." What we are asked to remember always is that the characters described so solemnly are eight- and nine-year-old kids!

Yet toward his own book as a whole, Twain adopts the same ironical tone, closing it with the words: "So endeth this chronicle. It being the history of a *boy,* it . . . could not go much further without becoming the history of a man." "So endeth this chronicle. . . ." It is at once a confession of falseness and an attempt to evade it, utterly different from the conclusion of *Huckleberry Finn:* "so there ain't nothing more to write about, and I am rotten glad of it. . . ." *Tom Sawyer* is the first of a long line of books intended to be read by a boy with his father looking over his shoulder, and thus to perpetuate for a new generation the legend of an older one. From it descends a tradition, which passes via Stephen Crane and Booth Tarkington to the creators of Henry Aldrich and the Good Bad Boys of contemporary comics: the ritual praise of good-badness as the true Americanism. "He warn't *bad,* so to say . . ." Aunt Polly insists, thinking Tom dead, "only misch*eev*ous. . . . *He* never meant any harm, and he was the best-hearted boy that ever was. . . ."

Huckleberry Finn, however, is not the progenitor of anything, because it is written neither by Tom nor Mark Twain, but by the evoked Huckleberry himself, who makes it quite clear at the end that he intends to write no more: "and if I'd 'a' knowed what trouble it was to make a book I wouldn't 'a' tackled it, and ain't a-going to no more." Nor could Twain himself make him change his mind, though he tried to call him up over and over for an encore. Only once did Huck really possess his presumable author, speak through him in his authentic voice. In the book called by his name, Huckleberry Finn exists, dictates his own style, his own moral judgments, his own meanings, which neither Twain nor the reader has to understand to experience. Tom Sawyer notoriously enters the book before it is finished, not letting Huck speak for himself again until the very last pages; but though he can counterfeit Huck's style, he cannot make him live, only move woodenly through the howling farce—which reveals the poverty of Tom's values and imagination, and exposes the falsity of his role. He is no more the "Tom" he claims to be than is Huck, but *really* Sid, the model boy whom he hates and whose name he assumes: Sid disguised as Robin Hood!

In one sense, *Huckleberry Finn* seems a circular book, ending as it began with a refused adoption and a projected flight; and certainly it has the effect of refusing the reader's imagination passage into the future. But there is a break-through in the last pages, especially in the terrible sentence which begins, "But I reckon I got to light out for the territory ahead of the rest. . . ." In these words, the end of childhood is clearly signaled; and we are forced to ask the question, which, duplicitously, the book refuses to answer: what will become of Huck if he persists in his refusal to return to the place where he has been before? It is easier to project Tom's future, and perhaps this is the best way to begin. Huck has been *forced,* in the course of the action, to become Tom; but Tom has eagerly taken on the role of Sid, and in doing so has given away the secret so well kept in *Tom Sawyer:* the Good Bad Boy and the Good Good Boy are not so different, after all—mother's boys, both of them. Tom will become a lawyer, a banker, a senator, at best—maintaining even into adulthood his permitted good-badness—a writer, which is to say, Mark Twain! Clemens did not deceive himself about the meaning of this, confessing to William Dean Howells: "If I went on now, and took him into manhood, he would just *lie,* like all the one-horse men in literature. . . ."

But what if Twain had taken "on into manhood" Huck Finn, who lies, to be sure, but never in any "one-horse" literary way? Having rejected the world of the mothers, Huck is condemned really to "go to Hell," to be lost in a sub-world of violence, a violence so universal that it is not judged but breathed like an atmosphere. It is a world in which one survives by his own wits and the stupidity of others: a world bounded on the one side by Pap, the corrupt victim; and on the other, by the Duke and the King, the feckless victimizers. When Huck catches his last glimpse of those two charming and vicious operators "astraddle of a rail," he expresses for them more pity than he finds to spare for anyone else in the book: "and I was sorry for them poor pitiful rascals, it seemed like I couldn't ever feel any hardness against them any more in the world."

One cannot help feeling that it is his own fate which Huck foresees in their plight, and that it is himself he weeps for. Even so he must end up, too, tarred and feathered, unless he dies like his father, stabbed in the back and set adrift on the river. When his father's fate is revealed to him by Jim at the novel's conclusion, Huck can find nothing to say. A happy ending is going on that Twain does not want to imperil; but had Huck been permitted to speak, one suspects that he might have paraphrased his own comment on the doomed crooks aboard the *Walter Scott:* "I felt a little bit heavy-hearted about Pap, but not much, for I reckoned if he could stand it I could." It is the only reaction really proper to the most lost of all American anti-heroes.

In his relationship to his lot, his final resolve to accept what is called these days his "terrible freedom," Huck seems the first Existentialist hero, the improbable ancestor of Camus's "stranger," or the protagonists of Jean-Paul Sartre, or the negative characters of the early Hemingway. But how contrived, literary, and abstract the others seem beside Huck! He is the product of no metaphysics, but of a terrible break-through of the undermind of America itself. In him, the obsessive American theme of loneliness reaches an ultimate level of expression, being accepted at last not as a blessing to be sought or a curse to be flaunted or fled, but quite simply as man's fate. There are mythic qualities in Ahab and even Dimmesdale; but Huck *is* a myth: not invented but discovered by one close enough to the popular mind to let it, this once at least, speak through him. Twain sometimes merely pandered to that popular mind, played the buffoon for it, but he was unalienated from it; and when he let it possess him, instead of pretending to condescend to it, he and the American people dreamed Huck—dreamed, that is to say, the anti-American American dream.

Yet this thoroughly horrifying book, whose morality is rejection and whose ambiance is terror, is a funny book, at last somehow a child's book after all; and the desperate story it tells is felt as joyous, an innocent experience. This ambiguity, this deep doubleness of *Huckleberry Finn* is its essential riddle. How can it be at once so terrible and so comfortable to read? It is, of course, a book which arises out of the part of the mind for which there are no problems, only experiences; and its terrors are those we know best how to live with, since our memories do not go back beyond the point where they had begun to haunt us. There is, moreover, the lyrical quality of much of the book, the colloquial poetry which celebrates the natural world and childhood as two aspects of a single thing. The historical moment to which Twain's child-centered imagination returned was the moment when America was passing out of a rural childhood into urban maturity; and the pattern of his own life seemed, therefore, the prototype of the national experience. As time has gone on, and for more and more Americans the world of nature has shrunk to the memory of faraway vacations and an occasional visit to the old folks; as even the river has been spanned and harnessed to industry, Twain's vanishing rural community has come to seem more and more mythic, strange, and beautiful. One of the troubling mysteries of our life is that we can only know as adults what we can only feel as children; and *Huckleberry Finn* manages to evoke the lost world of boyhood with all the horror and loveliness it once possessed for the child who lived it.

Besides, the book *is* funny; the Duke and the Dauphin as comical as they are unspeakable; the occasional quips riotous; the medley of burlesque and parody and understatement the performance of an old pro, a practiced and talented clown. Even the long ending, taken by itself, is a masterpiece of sustained farce hard to match in any literature. To deplore the ending has become one of the clichés of criticism; and it is true that it is worked out at so great length that it imperils the structure of the book; it is even apparently true that the gratuitous torturing of Jim is too brutal

and painful a joke to seem really funny to the sensitive or enlightened or genteel. Regarded closely enough, Tom's scheme for stealing away a Negro whom he knows to be free is not only sadistic
but thoroughly immoral, a confusion of literature and life, which
leads to the infliction of artistic tortures upon a real human being!
And why do Jim and Huck, too simple and marginal to be taken
in by Tom's affections, play along with his absurd plan? To them,
the need to escape is urgent and every delay a threat, for they do
not possess Tom's inside knowledge. In a way, of course, the horseplay is intended precisely to keep us from asking such questions,
to confuse our sense of what is illusory, what real. But we have a
right to demand answers all the same to questions which Twain has
himself, however ambiguously, posed; and the answers are not
hard to find. In the first place, the essential virtue of Huck and
Jim is to endure whatever befalls them; and to them, moreover,
there is nothing any more ridiculous about what Tom does than
there is about what society inflicts on them every day. After all,
what can a man, who all his life has known *he can be sold,* find
more absurd than that. To Huck as well as Jim, all heroism and
all suffering are equally "unreal," equally asinine; and the tom-
foolery of "Marse Tom" seems to them no stranger than the vagaries of Judge Thatcher. Similarly, the pretended royalty of the
two scoundrels strikes them as no more or less just and rational
than that of the legitimate rulers of Europe. The seediness of the
Duke and Dauphin undercuts the pretensions of all aristocrats,
even those who smell much sweeter, just as Tom's absurdities (for
which, after all, he is wounded!) show up the chivalry of the quite
serious Grangerfords and Colonel Sherburn, mock even Huck's
self-dramatization.

The burlesque tone of the finale manages to suggest such ideas,
but at the same time keeps them in the realm of slapstick, where
they do not appear either problematical or horrifying. The essential point of the ending is to reassert the duplicity of the book, to
play out its moral issues as *jokes;* for if we were once to stop
laughing, we would be betrayed out of the Neverland of childhood
back into an actual world of maturity. The book must end just
short of Huck's growing up, thus leaving us with the conviction
that his gesture of total rejection and the brief, harried honeymoon
which preceded it, are as endless as childhood's summers, really
eternal. Believing this, we can believe, too, that whatever Huck's
final decision may foreshadow or imply, his ending is, indeed,
happy—the book which describes it a book about happiness.

If *Huckleberry Finn* is, finally, the greatest of all books about childhood, this is because it renders with a child's tough-mindedness and a child's desperate hilarity a double truth fumbled by most other books on the subject: how truly wonderful it is to remember our childhood; and yet how we cannot recall it without revealing to ourselves the roots of the very terror, which in adulthood has driven us nostalgically to evoke that past.

It is easy to exaggerate the difference that a few generations and the "sexual revolution" have made in the Good Bad Boy in literature. Even though he is allowed now a certain amount of good clean sex * (not as the basis of an adult relationship but as an exhibition of prowess) and forbidden in exchange an equivalent amount of good clean violence, his standard repertory of permitted indiscretions remains pretty much the same. Like Tom Sawyer and Huck before him, the Good Bad Boy begins his revolt by playing hooky, though in these times of prosperity and extended adolescence, he runs away (at least in the books of J. D. Salinger or the "Beat" writers) not from grade school but from prep school or college. Similarly, he is allowed still to "hook" things, though in these lusher days the ante has gone up from the few candles or the side of bacon which made up the loot of Twain's books. Salinger and Jack Kerouac alike attempt to project images of their own lost youth in the guise of Huckleberry Finn, though like most Americans, they have him confused with Tom Sawyer. Rural no longer in their memories or nostalgia, they yearn still for boyhood, and speak in their books through the boy's mask in a language as far removed from literate adult speech as was Huck's. Their prepschool or hipsterish sub-languages fail, however, to become the kind of poetry which Twain succeeded in making, at their worst seem self-parodies: "And I said to myself, Wham, listen to that, man. That's the West, here I am in the West. . . . Whooee, I told my soul, and the cowboy came back and off we went to Grand Island."

Whether on the upper-middlebrow level of Salinger or the bohemian-*kitsch* level of Kerouac, such writers echo not the tragic *Huckleberry Finn* but the sentimental book with which it is intertwined. In *Catcher in the Rye,* Holden Caulfield comes to the dead

---

* On the model of Henry Miller, who like his master Walt Whitman, succeeded in becoming a Good Bad Bay only in middle age, but who continues even in old age to be the Tom Sawyer of the current generation, crying at all the windows, "Come on out and play."

end of ineffectual revolt in a breakdown, out of which he is impelled to fight his way by the Good Good Girl in the guise of the pure little sister, from whose hands he passes directly into those of the psychiatrist. In *On the Road,* whose characters heal themselves as they go by play-therapy, the inevitable adjustment to society is only promised not delivered. In the book itself all the stigma of Tom Sawyer are already present except for the return to Aunt Polly; Paul Goodman, in a recent review, without specifically recalling the stereotype, has identified them precisely:

> One is stunned by how conventional and law-fearing these lonely middle-class fellows are. They dutifully get legal marriages and divorces. The hint of a "gang-bang" makes them impotent. They never masturbate or perform homosexual acts. . . . To disobey a cop is 'all hell.' Their idea of crime is the petty shoplifting of ten-year-olds stealing cigarettes or of teen-agers joyriding in other people's cars. . . . Their behavior is a conformity *plus royaliste que le roi.*

The fact that one is tempted, even impelled to speak of such a writer as Kerouac at over thirty-five as a "boy," the fact that he writes as one of the boys is as symptomatic as the fact that middle-aged ladies in their bridge clubs call themselves "the girls." The flight from sexuality led to a literature about children written for the consumption of adults; but the reading of that literature has turned those adults in their own inmost images of themselves into children. Indeed, the Good Bad Boyhood has not merely impinged upon adult life, it has become, like everything else in America, a "career." The age of Kerouac's protagonists is just as ambiguous as that of Mark Twain's, though for opposite reasons. Twain blurred adolescence back into boyhood to avoid confronting the problem of sex; the newer writers, accepting the confusion of childhood and youth, blur both into manhood to avoid yielding up to maturity the fine clean rapture of childish "making out." The protagonists of the hipsters have crossed the borderline of genital maturity, but in all other respects they have not left Jackson's Island. *Plus ça change, plus c'est la même chose*—which in American means, "Boys will be boys."

10

THE REVENGE ON WOMAN:
FROM LUCY TO LOLITA

THE REIGN OF SENTIMENTALISM in the American novel not only made it exceedingly difficult for our writers to portray sexual passion, but prevented them as well from drawing convincing portraits of women. As late as 1901, we remember, William Dean Howells could find only *one* American fictionist before Henry James—Hawthorne—whose "heroines" seemed worthy of being ranked with those of Fannie Burney, Maria Edgeworth, Jane Austen, Miss Farrier, Mrs. Opie, and Mrs. Radcliffe! It should be remembered that Howells was not even looking for candor in the portrayal or vigor in the character; to him both Defoe and Richardson, for instance, seem outside the pale, living as they did in "the day before we began to dwell in decencies, before women began to read novels so much that the novel had to change the subject, or so limit its discussion that it came to the same thing."

For Howells, a proper literature ("There is nothing hurried or huddled in it, nothing confused or obscure, nothing excessive or inordinate"), in which proper women could flourish, begins with Goldsmith and is perfected by Jane Austen, both models of "the instinct of reticence . . . with its admirable limitations," and co-inventors of "the Heroine who was above all a Nice Girl . . ." Howells will in a pinch take the Nice Girl over the real girl (it is characteristic that he does not call her a "woman"), for he is himself a self-consciously cheerful adherent of Sentimentalism; yet he cannot find in our classic fiction heroines to satisfy even his bloodless taste. Our female entertainers are, by any standards, of small

291

account even beside Mrs. Opie; and our serious male novelists are trapped hopelessly between certain genteel prejudices which they share with the mass audience and a secret reluctance to abide by those prejudices. The *double* falsity of many American heroines— of Cooper's, for instance, and of Melville's—arises out of the compounding of the inadequacy of the sentimental prototypes by the writer's lack of faith in them.

There is something perfunctory and forced about Cooper's cataloguing of the standard attributes of "the most juvenile" of the "two females" in *The Last of the Mohicans*. He provides her almost automatically with a "dazzling complexion, fair golden hair and bright blue eyes," and we do not doubt that she is a type he would *like* to admire; but the metaphors with which he feels obliged to adorn her portrait lie lifeless on the page: "The flush which still lingered above the pines in the western sky was not more bright nor delicate than the bloom on her cheek; nor was the opening day more dewy than the animated smile which she bestowed on the youth. . . ." A writer like Poe, on the other hand, can scarcely bring himself to do more than list the stereotyped data which indicate the Fair Lady, attaching them to a name which one would like to take for a joke but does not quite dare: "the fair-haired and blue-eyed Lady Rowena Trevanion, of Tremaine." Hawthorne, of all Americans, tries hardest to redeem the figure of the Nice Girl, and has left behind a gallery of such types: from the lower-class Phoebe of *The House of the Seven Gables* ("a cheerful little body," "as graceful as a bird . . . as pleasant about the house as a gleam of sunshine falling on the floor through a shadow of tinkling leaves") to the New England virgin, Hilda in *The Marble Faun* ("A fair, young girl dressed in white," "how like a dove . . . the fair, pure creature," "without suspicion or shadow upon the snowy whiteness of her form . . ."). Surely, these are portrayals prompted by a secret hate!

Occasionally, beneath Hawthorne's life-long, patient apotheosis of the pale-face American girl, an undercurrent of dis-ease heaves queasily, betrays its presence. The very image of the snow maiden, which is his special metaphor for the Nice Girl, can with the slightest shift of emphasis become an explicit reproach. "Pretty fancies of snow and moonlight," he condescendingly calls Hilda's paintings in *The Marble Faun*, likening them to "so many feminine achievements in literature"; but his own books are, insofar as they glorify the Phoebe-Priscilla-Hilda type, not so very different from those "feminine achievements," and the epithet rebounds on him and his heroines at once. This, indeed, he knows at some level, though he is incapable of saying so directly; instead he entrusts the heretical criticism to one of his bad women. Just after the first appearance of Priscilla, the gorgeous and depraved Zenobia refers to the pallid outcast as "this shadowy snow-maiden, who, precisely at the stroke of midnight, shall melt away at my feet in a pool of ice-cold water and give me my death with a pair of wet slippers." But it is Coverdale, which is to say, Hawthorne himself, who almost immediately catches a cold of which he nearly dies; and shivering in his bed, he sighs, "How cold an Arcadia was this!"

The Lucy of Melville's *Pierre,* whose symbolic name identifies her immediately, is another sexless White Lady, her color appropriate to the book which its author thought of as a "rural bowl of milk." The first symbol of her presence, seen before we catch sight of her, is a "snow-white glossy pillow"; and when Melville begins to catalogue her charms, whiteness sets the tone: "Her cheeks were tinted with the most delicate white and red, the white predominating. Her eyes some god brought down from heaven; her hair was Danae's, spangled with Jove's shower; her teeth were dived for in the Persian sea." In short, she is white and gold and blue, the conventional color scheme, though Melville has a hard time simply saying so. It is only, Melville assures us, "the angelical part of Lucy" which interests him anyhow; but how can a man marry, go to bed with an angel—how can an author, even in fancy, deflower her? "One husbandly embrace," he has Pierre reflect, would cause her spirit to evaporate; and he cries out, "By heaven, but marriage is an impious thing!"

As late as the time of Henry Adams, the figure of a woman refined to the point where copulation with her seems blasphemous possesses the imagination of the most sophisticated American writers. Adams was convinced that no writer of his own day was capable of portraying women fairly. "Howells," he observed, "cannot deal with gentlemen or ladies; he always slips up. James knows almost nothing of women but the mere outside; he never had a wife." Practically alone among nineteenth-century writers, Adams is willing to abandon the physical image of the American young lady as a blond Goddess; his Esther, for instance, "has a bad figure, which she makes answer for a good one. She is too slight, too thin; she looks fragile. . . . Her features are imperfect. Except her ears, her voice, her eyes, which have a sort of brown depth like a trout brook, she has no very good points." Nonetheless, he cannot imagine a truly sexual heroine; and, indeed, the young ladies of both *Democracy* (1871) and *Esther* (1884) end by rejecting their suitors and the very notion of marriage as an "impious thing." Only in the image of the Virgin could Adams find an ideal of womanhood to which he subscribed; but "marked American type" that he was, he insisted on imposing that divine ideal on actual ladies whom he knew, though when he died, there was discovered in his wallet the following litany which he had composed:

> Simple as when I asked your aid before;
> Humble as when I prayed for grace in vain
> Seven hundred years ago; weak, weary, sore
> In heart and hope, I ask your help again.

Before the twentieth century, only Mark Twain among all our novelists, popular or serious, seems to have mocked outright the blue-eyed Protestant Virgin, who pre-empted in our fiction the position real women might have filled. But he was a privileged jester, set apart by the blessing-curse of never being taken at his word. In "Those Extraordinary Twins" (1894) he tells the reader quite candidly that he had planned at first to have "a silly young miss for heroine," who would fall in love with the "good" half of a pair of Siamese twins. The "bad" half, however, was to break up the match by drinking so much that his weaker brother would get scandalously drunk. But "Those Extraordinary Twins" began quite rapidly to turn into *Pudd'nhead Wilson,* which, among other things, meant that "the lightweight heroine" Rowena was pushed out of the center by the developing tragic character of Roxana.

The first name of the "lightweight heroine" recalls not only Poe's incredible "Lady Rowena Trevanion, of Tremaine," but more deliberately, perhaps, the fair Rowena, bland blonde of Scott's *Ivanhoe;* while her last name, which is Cooper, evokes the author of the Leatherstocking Tales, whom Twain so brutally ridiculed in the much-reprinted essay "Fenimore Cooper's Literary Offenses." Scott he detested with an even purer hatred, believing that he had utterly corrupted the Southern imagination by dreams of chivalry and romance, which made it quite impossible for any Southern writer to face reality or describe an actual woman! In *Life on the Mississippi* (1883), Twain quotes the following extract from a New Orleans newspaper: "On Saturday, early in the morning, the beauty of the place graced our cabin, and proud of her freight the gallant little boat glided up the bayou"; then launches into an impassioned attack on the prose style and the notions which underlie it: "the trouble with the Southern reporter is Women: Women, supplemented by Walter Scott and his knights and beauty and chivalry, and so on. . . . A curious exemplification of the power of a single book for good or harm is shown in the effects wrought by *Don Quixote* and those wrought by *Ivanhoe*. The first swept the world's admiration for the medieval chivalry silliness out of existence; and the other restored it."

Yet Twain himself is not immune to the Scott-disease which he diagnoses; Westerner and Southerner at once, his divided self carries on an endless civil war. It is the chivalrous Twain who gallops to the defense of Harriet Shelley, in a sentimental essay defending wife and home, unrivaled in our literature except by Mrs. Stowe's similar apology for the wife of Byron, just as it is the chivalrous Twain who invents Becky Thatcher in *Tom Sawyer* only to forget her in *Huckleberry Finn,* where he absent-mindedly refers to her as "Bessie." But there is one chivalric idol, one legendary embodiment of pure womanhood, he could never forget: Joan of Arc. In her, Twain was able to invest the baffled virgin-worship of the Protestant American male—remaking her, in her suffering and tragic triumph, into the image of Clarissa Harlowe, of whom, to be sure, he may never have heard.

In an early essay, Twain praises Joan's "patient endurance, her steadfastness, her granite fortitude," characteristics one and all of the standard suffering female of genteel literature. He protests against paintings which portray Joan as a peasant, "a strapping, middle-aged fish-wife," for he knows she must really have looked like the American Good Good Girl, like Charlotte Temple: "a lithe young slender figure . . . dear and bonny and lovable, the face beautiful and transfigured. . . ." In his fat, two-volumed pseudo-fiction devoted to her life, Twain makes Joan into a full-fledged female savior, "girlishly fair and sweet and saintly in her long white robe," and burned for our sins.

For a good American like Twain, all offenses are offenses against the woman; to be born is to rack the mother with pain; to be married is to blaspheme against purity; to have a child is to set a seal on such blasphemy, publish it to the world. Simply to be a man is to be impure, to betray; and there is nothing to do but to kneel at the feet of the offended female and cry for forgiveness. Twain's study is more an act of expiation than a book; and for this reason he worked at it as he worked at no other work. It is, however, precisely the piety of *Joan of Arc* which makes it unreadable to all but the most grossly sentimental. When it appeared in 1896, it was already absurdly old-fashioned, a piece of romantic medievalism that out-Scotted Scott. Yet *Maggie—A Girl of the Streets* had already been published, and *Sister Carrie* was only three years off; and while such books did not destroy Sentimentalism by any means, they replaced the Good Good Girl with the Good Bad one —the sanctified virgin with the hoyden or the whore with a heart of gold.

II

All through the history of our novel, there had appeared side by side with the Fair Maiden, the Dark Lady—sinister embodiment of the sexuality denied the snow maiden. The Indian, as we have seen, is divided into Mingo and Mohawk, Pawnee and Sioux— good Indian and bad; and similarly woman is bifurcated into Fair Virgin and Dark Lady, the glorious phantom at the mouth of the cave, and the hideous Moor who lurks within. In each case, the dark double represents the threat of both sex and death; the red Indian with his bloody scalping knife is also a rapist (however equivocal Cooper may pretend to be about it), just as the Dark Lady with her luxuriant flesh is a bearer of poison. In such a symbolic world, sex and death become one.

In the novel itself, however, the paired ladies, blonde and bru- nette, had come into existence for purely decorative purposes, be- fore they were adapted to symbolic ones. As early as *Clarissa,* the suffering heroine was provided with a foil, a gay Miss Howe to complement a somber Clary; and in Rousseau, the contrasted girls of *La Nouvelle Héloïse* are a simple study in mood and coloring. Charles Brockden Brown in *Arthur Mervyn* seems on the verge of exploiting to the full the encounter of fair and black when he sets Eliza Hadwin against Mrs. Achsa Fielding and requires his hero to choose between the poor young country girl or the rich Jewish widow, "unsightly as a *night-hag,* tawny as a Moor, the eye of a gypsy, low in stature, contemptibly diminutive. . . ." But Arthur chooses to wed the "night-hag," presumably to live happily ever after; and nothing is made of the promised contrast between simple health and worn-out sophistication.

Perhaps more to the point is Scott's use of the black-hired Jewess Rebecca as a foil to the blond Anglo-Saxon Rowena in *Ivanhoe,* which must have deeply impressed the mind of an American public that has not yet relinquished the story as an entertainment commodity. Scott, however, scarcely differentiates his girls— and when Ivanhoe abandons Rebecca for Rowena, it proves nothing except a revulsion on his author's part from mixed marriages. If there is any literary antecedent for the special American use of the split heroine, any motive for it beyond the split psyche of American writers, it is probably to be found in the sonnet sequence of Shakespeare.

The puritanical sense of conflict in the black and white melodrama of the *Sonnets* must surely have appealed to the Shakespeare-soaked Romantic writers of the nineteenth century; and, though they ignored—at a loss—his contrast of homoerotic and hetereosexual love, they must have welcomed his metaphor of the "fair" love and the love "colour'd ill." The primeval terror of darkness, the northern fear of the swarthy southerner, the ingrained European habit of identifying evil with blackness: all these contribute to make the vision of the Dark Lady of the sonnets seem archetypally appealing: "For I have sworn thee fair, and thought thee bright/Who art as black as hell, as dark as night." Shakespeare's lusted-for and hated black woman blends, at any rate, with the Romantics' concept of the *Belle dame sans merci* into the figure of the American Dark Lady; and both are reinforced by the resurgence out of the Christian past of the archetypes of Lilith and Eve who brought sin into the world.

It is Cooper who first permits the contrast its symbolic significance, as we have already noticed, in his opposition of the blooming, bold Cora and her pallid, swooning sister Alice, or the corrupt, lovely Judith and her unearthly, pure, mad sister, Hettie. That the girls be sisters, thus secretly confessing their kinship, is Cooper's invention, a device taken up by Hawthorne in *The Blithedale Romance,* where he saves it for a revelation, a surprise. It is not, however, until Hawthorne develops the theme, that it comes fully into its own; what was for Cooper an idea entertained by the way is for him an obsession. Married himself to an ethereal ice-lady, Hawthorne excelled in imagining all his life dark figures which have the irreality and queasy appeal of masturbatory fancies. How exotic they are, how *gorgeous* (it is Hawthorne's ambivalent adjective), and how poisonous: non-Anglo-Saxons, all of them, Mediterraneans, Orientals, Jews—or at least given to an oriental lushness in dress and in the flesh, not considered quite decent in New England society.

The prototype of them all is Beatrice Rappaccini, who grows up in her father's deadly garden among his strange, dangerous blooms, which are in "their gorgeousness . . . fierce, passionate, and even unnatural." They are the product, Hawthorne tells us in a revealing choice of words, of "adultery," an illegitimate crossing of species. Behind the hocus-pocus of the story, the gothic mystification, it is clear what the secret weapon of Beatrice is, the poison that would have made her superhuman, "as terrible . . . as beautiful." It is, of course, the full magic of sex with which she is endowed, that primal power bred out of ladies by civilized life, but deliberately bred back into Beatrice by her magician father. "Wouldst thou then, have preferred the condition of a weak woman, exposed to all evil and capable of none?" her baffled father asks her, when she seems to be rejecting his gift. And drinking the antidote that kills her, denying her genital potency for the sake of a less potent young man whom she loves, Beatrice answers—Good Bad Girl at the last—"Yes!"

It is an answer repeated by Hawthorne's other Dark Ladies, who seem always to share his own puritan conscience: Zenobia dies of love because her kind of love has no place in the genteel American world; Miriam in *The Marble Faun* endures captivity and suffering, subdues her gorgeous power to the capacity of the weaker man she desires. Even Hester finally submits, accepts a life which is a kind of Protestant nunship, though her beloved must die to convince her that not the unleashing of her passion but its denial means salvation.

In general, Hawthorne's Dark Ladies are superior to their pale sisters not only in their symbolic resonance but even in their evocation of the reality of the flesh; in their portraits, Hawthorne alternates between the absurdest allegorical devices and a vivid projection of their sexual allure. Even Howells could never forget the passage in which Coverdale tells us of Zenobia, "She was dressed as simply as possible, in an American print (I think the dry goods people call it so), but with a silken handkerchief, between which and her gown there was a glimpse of a white shoulder.

It struck me as a great piece of good fortune that there should be just that glimpse." Here is a genuine and genial sensuality, the rendering of the actual feel of a woman, so exceedingly rare in American fiction; and for a moment the style neither evades nor overstates. For the instant at least, Zenobia is no mere projection of the fear of and longing for the flesh. But it is only an instant; in a sentence or two, we are back to the improbable hot-house flower in her hair, "an exotic of rare beauty . . . so brilliant, so rare, so costly . . . ," and we have left the real world of American dry goods for the fake world of theatrical properties out of gothic stock. Such momentary transformations from theater to flesh *never* occur, however, in Hawthorne's handling of his Good Good women, which is, perhaps, why his one book without a Dark Lady, *The House of the Seven Gables,* is his most sentimental and philistine; while his single novel without a snow maiden, *The Scarlet Letter,* is the truest and most tragic.

In *Pierre,* Melville, just then in the full flush of his enthusiasm for Hawthorne's work, attempted to project onto the kind of scene congenial to Hawthorne images of a metaphysical "blackness ten times black." The unfortunate Pierre gives up the daylight graces of the White Maiden Lucy, which he cannot abide desecrating in marriage, for the "nameless beauty," "the long-suffering, hopeless anguish" of the Dark Isabel. Unlike Hawthorne's Dark Ladies, however, Isabel is not sexually aggressive; her darkness is the shadow of the incest taboo, cast by the sins of the father on the generation which follows. Yet in the end, Pierre, Lucy, and Isabel end up in an emblematic *ménage à trois,* based presumably upon mutual self-sacrifice, but actually redolent of unconfessable ambivalent desires. Pierre attempts to hold to him at once the White Maiden and the Dark, the longing for life and lust for death, the visible embodiments of the centripetal and centrifugal urges of his own divided soul; but it is a vain and fatal effort.

Isabel herself, who prefers the language of Shakespeare to that of flowers, calls herself the Bad Angel, Lucy the Good. The sentimental conventions of the novel, she takes for the eternal symbolism of God, reading into her own brunette coloring her meaning and fated role. "Is Lucy Tartan the name? . . . she came, with her blue eyes turned beseechingly on me; she seemed as if persuading me from thee . . . methought she was that good angel, which some say, hovers over every human soul; and methought—oh, methought that I was thy other—thy other angel, Pierre—. . . . Say,

Pierre, doth not a funerealness invest me? Was ever hearse so plumed?—Oh, God; that I had been born with blue eyes, and fair hair! Those make the livery of heaven! Heard ye ever yet of a good angel with dark eyes, Pierre?—no, no, no—all blue, blue, blue. . . ." And Pierre's penultimate words later echo her, "Away! —Good Angel and Bad Angel both!—for Pierre is neuter now!" Yet he is not quite "neuter" even at the last; for death is a denial of the white Lucy, an acceptance of the black Isabel, who (in the book's final words) "fell upon Pierre's heart, and her long hair ran over him, and arbored him in ebon vines."

Beside Melville's lucid self-consciousness, other writers seem almost inadvertent in their uses of Dark and Fair Ladies. Oliver Wendell Holmes comes close to a deliberate exploitation of the contrast in *Elsie Venner* (1861), where he sets up with some care the customary opposition of a "dependent, frail, sensitive" blue-eyed lady (she is a schoolmarm of brahmin stock) and the dark-eyed "ophidian" girl, Elsie, but he does not permit them to enter into the archetypal contest for the soul of the hero. Elsie possesses all the gothic stigmata of the Dark Lady ("black hair twisted in heavy braids . . . diamond eyes"), plus the eerie characteristics of a snake-woman (she hisses when she talks, and is preternaturally cold to the touch); but she is intended, Holmes tells us, to represent only the prenatal influence of snake bite!

Critics of Holmes's own day talked of Undine and Lamia, but he brushed them aside, disclaiming all mythic intent; and he would have been, perhaps—though he was a doctor and something of a psychologist himself—even more dismayed at modern suggestions about "phallic women" and the *vagina dentata*. Holmes turns to psychology in his "psychological romance," not to reveal hidden impulses in the lower depths of the mind, but to combat the old theology with the new science; to challenge "the dogma of inherited guilt and its consequences." That Elsie is not responsible for the promptings of a nature conditioned before she was born by the bite of a serpent, Dr. Holmes is sure all his readers will understand; and he asks us, therefore, to consider her not a sinner but a patient.

In other writers, the symbolic contrast recurs as a cliché or a scarcely noticed convention: the blond, scatter-brained Rowena and the tragic mulatto Roxana in *Pudd'nhead Wilson;* or the seduced and avenging Laura Van Brunt and the Quaker Nice Girl, Ruth Bolton, in Twain's one "serious" novel *The Gilded Age;* or the death-ridden Creole Margaret and Mrs. Conway with "her light

hair, blue eyes, and delicacy . . . of skin" who intrude so inappropriately upon Whitman's temperance novel, *Franklin Evans*. But
surely the ultimate *reductio* of the theme is found in *Uncle Tom's
Cabin* where the Pale Maiden as dying child, Little Eva, is paired
off with the Dark Lady as pesky brat, Topsy. Just as, in more adult
versions, the sexuality denied the pallid virgin is projected in the
gorgeous brunette, so here the mischief and normal juvenile cus-
sedness denied the little angel is projected in the figure of the little
(black) devil. Mrs. Stowe lingers over their dramatic confrontation, making what symbolic capital she can of it.

> There stood the two children, representative of the two extremes
> of society. The fair, high-bred child, with her golden hair, deep
> eyes, her spiritual, noble brow and prince-like movements; and
> her black, keen, subtle, cringing yet acute neighbour. They stood
> the representatives of their races. The Saxon, born of ages of
> cultivation, command, education, physical and moral eminence.
> The African, born of ages of oppression, submission, ignorance,
> toil, and vice!

The moral polarity has become an ethnic one!

True enough, from the beginning, the Dark Lady had represented the hunger of the Protestant, Anglo-Saxon male not only for
the rich sexuality, the dangerous warmth he had rejected as unworthy of his wife, but also for the religions which he had disowned
in fear, the racial groups he had excluded and despised. The black
woman is typically Catholic or Jew, Latin or Oriental or Negro.
Wherever the Dark Lady plays a serious role in our literature, she
is likely to represent either our relationship with the enslaved
Africa in our midst or with the Mediterranean Europe from which
our culture began; she is surrogate for all the Otherness against
which an Anglo-Saxon world attempts to define itself and a Protestant one to justify its existence. The figure of the Creole woman
especially possesses the imagination of the blond American, because she unites in one flesh the opposing European and African
poles.

In Mrs. Achsa Fielding, Brockden Brown almost invented the
first Dark Lady of our fiction—but he is not *afraid* enough either
of her experience in passion or her connection with things European to imbue her with a sufficiently sinister allure. His Arthur
Mervyn desires to become not innocent but mature; and the notion

of cosmopolitanism strikes him as a fulfillment rather than a threat. Only when innocence and Americanism come to seem a single thing, do the Catholic, the European, the Jew, the devirginated woman fuse into an archetypal image of terror. It is Hawthorne who first creates in *The Marble Faun* the international romance, in which the Fair Maiden and Dark Lady come clearly to stand for American innocence and European experience. He moves his scene to a mythic Italy—half the cultural mecca of Baedeker, half the demi-hell of Mrs. Radcliffe—an appropriate setting for his dark-haired Miriam, who evokes at once the tyranny of the Vatican, the bloody tale of the Cenci, and the mystery of the eternally alienated Jew.

Yet Miriam remains in *The Marble Faun* merely a spectacle for Hawthorne's visiting Americans, just another tourist attraction for the snow maiden, Hilda, and the genteel artist, Kenyon. Both willingly surrender her to Europe and embrace each other at the end, America discovering America, timidity a matching timidity even in the heart of malaria-infested Rome.

III

Even Hawthorne, however, only tentatively approaches the theme; it is not until Henry James that the Dark Lady-Fair Girl archetype and the myth of the American in Europe are fused into a rich and unified subject. Nowhere is James more deeply indebted to Hawthorne than in this area, and nowhere is he more deeply involved in the main American tradition; yet commentators seem scarcely to have noticed his use of the Hawthorne patterns of dark female and light. F. O. Matthiessen comes close with the guarded observation on *The Wings of the Dove:* "It may be an accidental residue of romanticism that, as was the usual practice of Hawthorne and Melville, the innocent heroine is fair, and the dangerous worldly girl dark." As a matter of fact, the conventional moral color-scheme is everywhere in James's best books, an integral part of his deepest symbolism. Though the Nice American Girl, who appears variously in *Portrait of a Lady, The Wings of the Dove,* and *The Golden Bowl,* is derived, on the one hand, from James's cousin, Minny Temple, who died of tuberculosis at the age of twenty-four, on the other hand, she is a descendant of Hilda in *The Marble Faun,* Hawthorne's prototypical sketch of the American Girl abroad.

Hilda is, in that book, portrayed as the Lady of the Doves, a dove herself, and that image is quite directly borrowed to characterize Milly Theale in *The Wings of the Dove,* as the title itself attests; they are downy, white birds both of them, ready to fly from guilt to America or death. Maggie Verver in *The Golden Bowl* is even more profoundly linked to Hilda, when James says of her that she is one who "wasn't born to know evil," "must never know it," thus joining her to the strange breed of human whom Hawthorne had first imagined as blond and snow-white enough to be exempt from original sin. Of Hilda he had said (and we are told that he was making a spiritual portrait of his own wife!): "Her womanhood is of the ethereal type, and incompatible with any shadow of darkness or evil. . . . She would die of her first wrongdoing,—supposing for a moment that she could be capable of doing wrong." Both James and Hawthorne, that is to say, confused the symbolic figure of innocence, projected by Sentimentalism as a blond Maiden, with certain fair girls whom they actually knew; and joined in the genteel conspiracy to persuade those girls themselves of their immunity to evil. It is a fantastic heresy against both orthodoxy and fact, as well as a terrible burden that women themselves were finally to cast off in the great sexual revolution of the early twentieth century.

James, at least, never questioned the sentimental heresy, only added to it the necrophiliac titillation (otherwise exploited by Poe and Mrs. Stowe) by identifying the immaculate virgin with the girl dying or dead. This identification is made as early in his work as *Daisy Miller* (1879), though it does not reach a climax until *The Wings of the Dove* (1902), the working title of which was *La Mourante.* It is from the dead that James's truest, richest inspiration comes, from a fascination with and a love for the dead, for death itself; and it is no accident that his Muse and his America are both figured forth by the image of a girl who died at twenty-four.

In a certain sense, all of his stories are ghost stories—evocations of a tenuous past; and his most distinguished minor work is quite baldly cast in this rather vulgar, popular form. "The 'ghost story,' " he wrote in one of his prefaces, "as we for convenience call it, has ever been for me the most possible form of the fairy tale." But at a deeper level than he consciously sought in doing his intended stories of terror (he called, we remember, even *The Turn of the Screw* "a potboiler"), James was forever closing in on the real subject that haunted him always: the necrophilia that has always so oddly been an essential part of American romance. In his notebooks, James kept writing to himself suggestions for a story about a girl whose long-awaited husband "comes in the form of death," or of the artist whose long-planned achievement comes in the same form. In "The Altar of the Dead" (1895), the protagonist burning candles for a dead girl and dead friends in a service not somehow quite religious, almost finds love in a fellow necrophile, but dies himself at the moment of surrender. In *The Sense of the Past* (1910), a young man retreats through an old portrait, i.e., traditional art, into a world of ghosts, where he himself seems a ghost; and no consummation to any relationship is possible. He had been driven into his retreat, symptomatically enough, by dismay at the modern American girl, whose love for the native and the contemporary, James remarks scornfully, makes her fittest mate the *cowboy!* But "Maud-Evelyn" is his oddest fiction of all; in this disturbing story, the protagonist, humoring parents unwilling to admit the death of their daughter, is overwhelmed by their mad faith: lives through an imaginary love affair with a dead girl, wooing, being engaged, wedding, and at last mourning the woman he had never had. It is, in a sense, a giveaway, yet also a final consummation of the American asexual affair with the Pure Maiden—a willful derangement of the senses that makes possible cohabitation with a ghost.

Not all of James's Pure Maidens are so frankly corpses, however; some lead complex lives of suffering and renunciation in the flesh. Occasionally he is content to portray his dove girl as standing alone, confronting the dark experience which complements her innocence in the form of a male wooer only. Such, at any rate, is the pattern of *Daisy Miller,* the best-loved by the popular audience of all his works. More often, however, he provides for them foils like Madame Merle in *Portrait of a Lady,* Kate Croy in *The Wings of the Dove,* or Charlotte Stant in *The Golden Bowl,* who are distinguished from their ethereal opposites by the traditional thick, dark hair and dark eyes. Such dark counter-virgins circle nervously about their more passive opposites, their destined prey—drawn by an ambivalent love, much like the passion that joined and divided Hawthorne's Zenobia and Priscilla. In *The Wings of the Dove,* James made quite explicit the interplay of his contrasted heroines' paleness and darkness, rest and restlessness: "the angular, pale princess . . . merely seated, merely still. The upright lady, with thick dark braids . . . makes the whole circuit and makes it again. . . ." It is scene-design, to be sure, interior decoration; but it is also a moral emblem.

Representing innocence and experience, the Pale Maiden and Dark Lady also stand in James's personal mythology for the American and the European, or more precisely, the American girl who has remained true to her essential Niceness and the American lady who has fallen to the level of European cynicism and moral improvisation. In James's recasting, the conventional figure of the blond virgin takes on new dimensions through the mere addition of wealth to her definition—by augmenting the charm of chastity with the magic of money. There is something dazzling, almost magnificent about the Jamesian *Principessa Americana,* though she remains traditionally modest all the same, an Heiress of All the Ages who is yet a Nice Girl. He seems to have taken a cue from Hawthorne, who in a summary note at the end of *The Scarlet Letter* projects the image of the heiress for the first time: "Pearl—the elf-child,—the demon offspring . . . became the richest heiress of her day, in the New World." Like Pearl before them, James's heroines aspire not only to be American aristocrats, ennobled by wealth, but *real* princesses, too. They seek, that is to say, Old World titles that will grace their newly won eminence with ancient sanctions, even as Little Pearl had done before them: "Letters came [to Hester], with armorial seals upon them, though of bearings unknown to English heraldry."

In return for her recognition by Europe, the Pale Maiden offers her recognition of it—an exchange of ambassadors, in effect. But her recognition is also a redemption; and if she seems superficially intent only on carrying Europe home as loot, souvenirs, museum pieces, this is merely her way of symbolizing the bringing of a lost continent to the light. For the cultural goods she bears off, including a certain kind of husband, she is willing to pay in dollars, but *in no other currency.* Certainly, she will surrender no jot of American morality or even punctilio; and, indeed, James's insistence on this point led less friendly critics to describe his earlier work as long-drawn out studies of why an American girl does *not* marry an earl. The Nice Girl in her Jamesian form seeks a European husband—Merton Densher, Prince Amerigo, Osmond—not because she desires to escape the moral limitations of her own life but because she is eager to proselytize in its behalf: to naturalize her bridegroom to the American ethos, as Clarissa or Pamela had sought once to naturalize their lovers to the world of bourgeois values. The not-quite-nice American girl, on the other hand, seeks to yield herself up to Europe and its ways, as do Kate Croy or Charlotte or Madame Merle. To Henry James the Fair Maiden, the Good Good Girl is quite simply America itself—her whiteness the outward manifestation of our mysterious national immunity to guilt, which he feels as at once lovely, comic, and quite terrible.

Of all the European husbands in James, only Prince Amerigo understands this mystery in all its implications, which is why he is called after the man, his presumable ancestor, who first discovered the New World. Amerigo has learned about the pure American woman, who is, in the European sense, not a woman at all (what lust he has for female flesh and spirit is satisfied by Charlotte Stant) by reading one of those typical American books without women, Edgar Poe's *The Narrative of A. Gordon Pym*. And he knows, therefore, that in moving into the polar world of American morality, he is leaving behind the moral "blackness of darkness" to which as an Italian he has grown up, to confront "a dazzling curtain of light, concealing as darkness conceals, yet of the color of milk or snow. . . ." The reflections of the Prince echo almost directly the words of the close of *Gordon Pym:* "The darkness had materially increased, relieved only by the glare of the water thrown back from the white curtain before us." But the "shrouded human figure" which emerges from the curtain at the end of the world, and the hue of whose skin is "the perfect whiteness of the snow," blends into the figures of the other castrating White Ladies of our literature: the snow maiden Priscilla and milky Lucy. Maggie Verver is at once the embodiment of a country which dreams such virgins of milk and snow, and another example of the type; but she is also the portrait of the artist who makes such a maiden his Muse—a self-portrait of Henry James. Poe in *The Narrative of A. Gordon Pym* had been content to portray the woman not as one of flesh, by which the classic American novelists have been haunted, but merely as a "white mist," a magnet and a devouring whirlpool; James recreates of the same aboriginal mist the figure of Maggie: more Christ than woman, more angel of death than Christ.

There are ambiguous undertones in all of James's renderings of the conflict of Dark Lady and White Maiden; for though he never doubts the moral superiority of the ethos projected by the Nice American Girl, he yearns for the grace and cultured ease of the European life-style. Yet in only one of his novels, does he permit

the representative of American values and Anglo-Saxon womanhood to show at a real disadvantage. In *The Ambassadors,* all the
delicacy and moral tact ordinarily represented by the Fair Maiden
are embodied in the male figure of Lambert Strether, surely the
most maidenly of all James's men. The American girl abroad is
caricatured as Mamie Pocock; and the Europeanized American
woman transfigured and redeemed as Maria Gostrey; but these
oddly transformed and transvalued renderings of the Fair Girl and
Dark Lady do not really stand at the center of the book or bear its
symbolic weight. In *The Ambassadors,* the sexual allure of Europe
is finally projected as a middle-aged French woman living in adultery; though, to be sure, she is an Aphrodite figure discreetly
draped to avoid shocking James's genteel readers. "A goddess still
partly engaged in a morning cloud," James himself calls his Madame de Vionnet, "a sea-nymph waist-high in a summer surge." If
we know by inference what lies below the waist of Madame de
Vionnet, we must thank our own experience, for James is reluctant
to make explicit the genital facts of the case.

Yet the real sense of the book demands that we understand
Strether as caught between the claim of America and the appeal of
Europe, a world desexed and morally engaged opposed to one
sexually potent and ethically lax. In *The Ambassadors,* however,
the world of American values is no longer imagined in the form of
the beautiful *mourante,* Minny Temple, fixed in an eternal youth
by the fact of death but rather in the shape of what Minny might
have become (what the American dream does indeed become) had
she lived on, hardened and matured. It is Mrs. Newsome who projects the American female, the Heiress of All the Ages come to
middle age, icy and imperious, the snow maiden turned into "some
particularly large iceberg in a cool blue northern sea." In a wonderful stroke, James excludes her from the actual sense of the
book; for she does not have to be present to be felt. The cold Atlantic winds that blow eastward from her immense frigidity represent her sufficiently. The sympathy of the aging, virginal hero (we
are told he has been married before, has a son, but we do not
believe it, scarcely remember it) goes this time quite unequivocally
toward the adulterous woman, the Dark European Lady. The blue
Iceberg has, however, in effect castrated him, and he cannot love
what he approves; and so ends urging others to enjoy what he is
incapable of possessing.

It is worth considering for a moment the fact that in the four novels of James now generally considered his best, the archetype of Dark Lady and Fair has arisen to possess him: to give his work not only technical authority and novelistic insight but a mythic dimension as well. Three of the four books, *Portrait of a Lady, The Wings of the Dove,* and *The Golden Bowl,* are successive attempts to work out the same pattern-story in which the deepest experiences of James's life cohere: his encounter with death in his cousin Minny's early end, his recognition of an authentic American art in the work of Hawthorne, the expansion of his moral horizon in his removal to Europe. It is worth noticing that in these works, too, he flirted with or actually faced the forbidden American theme, which he himself spoke of squeamishly as "the adulterine element in the subject." Yet no Nice American Girl could in James be guilty of adultery, which remained for him the European, the Mediterranean sin—quite understandable in citizens of a world where neither romance nor free choice entered into marriage, but utterly shocking in an American. One cannot imagine, for instance, James benignly desiring for the American Dark Lady Charlotte Stant the happiness he wishes, through Strether, for her French opposite number, Madame de Vionnet. There is a strange double standard for Europeans and Americans built into his particular version of the Fair-Dark polarity.

For James, certain women, who must be among other things Americans, are innocent by definition and forever; like Hawthorne he assumes a fundamental and ineradicable distinction between females born not to know evil and those born to endure the effects of sin. Melville in *Mardi* more dangerously suggests that the Fair Maiden once sexually possessed even in marriage, becomes—or is revealed as—the Dark Lady. *Mardi* is, however, a hectic and untidy book, in which Melville managed to find neither a satisfactory rhetoric nor a set of symbols; and his heretical suggestion is almost lost in a blur of contradictory intentions.

Mardi (1849) was apparently begun as a mock-documentary, an attempt to show up the critics who had caviled at the truth of *Typee* (1846) and *Omoo* (1847), books based in part on fact. Melville seems, however, to have rapidly abandoned his scheme "to see whether the fiction might not, possibly, be received for a verity; in some degree the reverse of my previous experience"; so that finally *Mardi* looks forward, toward his work to come, rather than backward to work already done. In one aspect a tentative approach to the style and themes of *Moby Dick,* in another it is the first version of the Fair Girl-Dark Lady archetype somewhat differently rendered in *Pierre.* In its earliest narrative pages, it bears a marked resemblance to *Gordon Pym,* which had appeared some ten years earlier, though Melville as far as we can tell never read Poe. Unlike Poe, however—and unlike his later self writing *Moby Dick* —Melville could not resist in *Mardi* the temptation to introduce a woman into his essential plot, an improbable Anglo-Saxon virgin who floats on a raft into his fable, disrupting utterly its probability and coherence.

The girl, who is kept prisoner by a Polynesian enchanter-priest and his three warrior sons, turns out to have blond hair, blue eyes, and milk-white skin, and must therefore be rescued from the emissaries of darkness by an onslaught which ends in the death of the old priest. Though ridden by guilt because of the murder which is her price, and unable to get from her any rational story of who she is, the protagonist settles down with the blond Maiden (she is called Yillah) on a convenient sub-tropical island. After a brief, rather unconvincing interlude in a South Seas bower of love, he wakes one morning to find his beloved gone. The purity represented by Yilliah is in Melville's treatment ambiguous from the start, for it makes its initial appearance in the hands of demonic agents, is won even temporarily only by the death of the old man, disappears upon possession, and is pursued at the risk of blasphemy, "the last, last crime." The desolate cry of Pierre, "By heaven, but marriage is an impious thing!" is already implicit in the theme.

As he trails Yillah through the archipelagos of the Pacific, Taji is "pursuer and pursued, over an endless sea," himself trailed by the three sons of the dead magician, the outraged "brothers" of the Fair Girl—even as he is lured on by three maidens, as dark as the three avengers, who bear him tokens from a swarthy enchantress called Hautia. Arrived at the womb-tomb sea-caverns of Hautia, Taji dives for the drowned image of his lost Yillah, which glimmers in their depths like a ghost side by side with the jewel of Hautia. He cannot manage, however, either to recover the ghost of innocence or to touch the bottom of experience, and is contemptuously dismissed, having learned only one thing: the dark-eyed handmaids of Hautia all somehow contain within them the vanished Yillahs of the world—and he can attain neither.

Mardi is, it must be remembered, a honeymoon book, the work into which Melville plunged almost immediately after his marriage; but in the single marriage ceremony described in the novel, the groom is pictured with a millstone attached to his neck, so disguised with flowers that he can scarcely recognize it. The fable itself, however, cuts deeper and more cruelly than any merely defensive male humor. Nothing less than the whole sentimental myth of redemption through marriage is challenged by Melville's suggestion that the milk-white bride is corrupted by the consummation of marriage. If the most husbandly embrace converts the Fair Maiden into her Dark opposite, reveals Clarissa as Circe— then man is doomed forever to choose between the blasphemous pursuit of an unattainable ideal and the self-destructive plunge into the gulf of sensuality. So at least *Mardi* seems to insist. Melville is reported to have read the installments of his work in progress regularly to his bride, and certainly, from time to time she helped him with the copying; but what she could have made of so disturbing a revelation of her husband's ambivalence toward women and sexual passion is hard to say. There is some evidence that mercifully she did not understand it at all; for in a letter to her mother she writes, "I suppose by this time you are deep in the 'fogs' of *Mardi*—if the mist ever does clear away, I should like to know what it reveals to *you*—" Indeed, it is doubtful that Melville himself knew quite what he was doing in a book which he tells us he wrote "Like a man walking in his sleep."

IV

In the nineteenth century at least, treasonable attacks on the cult of the Pure Woman are dreamed, not planned. Like James's unwitting revelation that the snow maiden is a corpse, Melville's exposure of her identity with the Dark Lady is invested in a kind of make-believe, an atmosphere of fantasy in which everything is permissible because nothing is proffered quite seriously. It is only when the stereotype of the Good Good Girl is challenged in "realistic" fiction, in novels which eschew the camouflage of gothicism and allegory, that the great audience is disturbed. The largest reading public, which is unaware of its vision of immaculate womanhood as a myth, does not rise to defend it as a myth; but cries out in horror when it is attacked on the level of fact—a simple truth about the wives, sisters, mothers, and daughters of America. This is why the same readers who were neither dismayed nor titillated by James's later conversion, via a "ghost story" or an offhand reference to the least-read work of Poe, of the Pale Maiden to a ghost, bought, eagerly read, and horrifiedly attacked James's portrait of the American Girl in *Daisy Miller*.

For better or worse, the popular James of his own times was the author of this little book; and it is chiefly in terms of their relationship to *Daisy Miller* that Howells describes the female readers of James: "to read him if for nothing but to condemn him is the high intellectual experience of the daughters of mothers whose indignant girlhood resented while it adored his portraits of American women." But what made such mothers indignant at and resentful of poor Daisy, with her unspeakable little brother, her shocked American admirer and her naïve resolve to consort with Italians just as she had with her "gentlemen friends" in Schenectady? That she be cut by her convention-bound compatriots in Rome seems probable enough; but that American editors should have rejected so American a book as somehow shocking is hard to believe.

As late as 1936, one historian of the American novel, though no longer prepared to describe Daisy as "an outrage on American girlhood," still found her a caricture and the product of a confusion. Any lady really endowed with "active innocence" and "personal daintiness," that critic argued, would not have acted like Daisy Miller because "she would not have cared to be conspicuous." It is a last, weak afterthrob of the spasm of fascinated revulsion with which the genteel female audience greeted *Daisy Miller* in 1879. The motives of that audience Howells, who managed to please it all his life, ticked off in his own impassioned apology for Daisy: "The American woman would none of Daisy Miller . . . because the American woman . . . was too jealous of her own perfection to allow that innocence might be reckless, and angels in their ignorance of evil might not behave as discreetly as worse people."

James is, however, careful to make it clear that Daisy is finally and unequivocally innocent. Though she went alone to the Colosseum with the Italian Giovanelli, and stood with him, unchaperoned and unobserved, in the moonlight until midnight, she remained quite intact. It is Giovanelli himself who says at her grave, " 'She was the most beautiful young lady I ever saw, and the most amiable,' and then he added, 'and she was the most innocent.' " Daisy is, in short, the prototype of all those young

American female tourists who continue to baffle their continental lovers with an innocence not at all impeached, though they have now taken to sleeping with their Giovanellis as well as standing with them in the moonlight. What the European male fails ever to understand is that the American Girl is innocent by definition, *mythically* innocent; and that her purity, therefore, depends upon nothing she does or says. But James's Daisy is also the Good Bad Girl, *only* the Good Bad Girl; and her creation impugns not at all the Clarissa-Charlotte Temple archetype.

She is an improbable sister to the hard-riding, hard-shooting sometimes cigar-smoking, heroines of the dime novel; for in serious literature and the popular paperback alike, the Good Bad Girl, with her heart of truest gold beneath the roughest of exteriors, survives to become a stock character of the movies, a living embodiment of the American faith that evil is appearance only. Model or waitress or dance-hall girl, the modern version of the falsely impugned Maiden is discovered staggering drunk in the roué's penthouse, watched climbing with overnight bag the gangplank to the philanderer's yacht, followed by the camera as she slips from table to table, embrace to embrace with a pert wiggle of her rear—only to be revealed at the dénouement as virginal though indiscreet. She represents an American, which is to say, an expurgated recasting of the continental image of the virtuous whore, a Grushenka with a maidenhead; and, indeed, in Dreiser the two images fade into one.

Yet Daisy is, in another sense a transitional figure, the hinge upon which the American adoration of pure womanhood swings over to reveal its underside of fear and contempt. The first notable anti-virgin of our fiction, the prototype of the blasphemous portraits of the Fair Goddess as bitch in which our twentieth-century fiction abounds, is quite deliberately called Daisy—after James's misunderstood American Girl. She is, of course, the Daisy Fay Buchanan of Scott Fitzgerald's *The Great Gatsby,* the girl who lures her lovers on, like America itself, with a "voice . . . full of money." More like James's Maggie Verver, perhaps, than Daisy Miller in the potency of her charm, she is yet another Heiress of All the Ages: great-great-granddaughter of that priceless Pearl, who got the best of the Old World and the New. She is an odd inversion of Clarissa-Charlotte Temple-Maggie Verver; no longer the abused woman, who only by her suffering and death castrates her betrayer, but the abusing woman, symbol of an imperialist rather than a colonial America. The phallic woman with a phallus of gold, she remains still somehow the magic princess James had imagined as the heroine of *The Golden Bowl:* "High in a white palace the king's daughter, the golden girl." To Fitzgerald, however, her fairy glamour is illusory, and once approached the White Maiden is revealed as a White Witch, the golden girl as a golden idol. On his palette, white and gold make a dirty color; for wealth is no longer innocent, America no longer innocent, the Girl who is the soul of both turned destructive and corrupt.

There is only one story that Fitzgerald knows how to tell, and no matter how he thrashes about, he must tell it over and over. The penniless knight, poor stupid Hans, caddy or bootlegger or medical student, goes out to seek his fortune and unluckily finds it. His reward is, just as in the fairy tales, the golden girl in the white palace; but quite differently from the fairy tales, that is not a happy ending at all. He finds in his bed not the white bride but the Dark Destroyer; indeed, there is no White Bride, since Dark Lady and Fair, witch and redeemer have fallen together. But it is more complicated even than this. Possessed of the power of wealth, Fitzgerald's women, like their wealthy male compeers, who seem their twins rather than their mates, are rapists and aggressors. Of both Daisy and her husband Tom, Fitzgerald tells us, "they smashed up things and creatures and then retreated back into their money." In a real sense, not Daisy but Jay Gatz, the Great Gatsby, is the true descendant of Daisy Miller: the naïf out of the West destined to shock the upholders of decorum and to die of a love for which there is no worthy object.

In Fitzgerald's world, the distinction between sexes is fluid and shifting, precisely because he has transposed the mythic roles and values of male and female, remaking Clarissa in Lovelace's image, Lovelace in Clarissa's. With no difficulty at all and only a minimum of rewriting, the boy Francis, who was to be a center of vision in *The World's Fair,* becomes the girl Rosemary as that proposed novel turned into *Tender Is the Night.* Thematically, archetypally even such chief male protagonists as Gatsby and Dick Diver are females; at least, they occupy in their stories the position of Henry James's Nice American Girls. It is they who embody innocence and the American dream, taking up the role the flapper had contemptuously abandoned for what was called in the '20's "freedom"; but they do not know this, projecting the dream which survives only in themselves upon the rich young ladies whom they desire. Early in *Tender Is the Night,* Dick Diver comes upon Nicole in Europe, and, dazzled by her "cream-colored dress . . . her very blonde hair . . . her face lighting up like an angel's," thinks of her as "a scarcely saved waif of disaster bringing him the essence of a continent. . . ." He reads into her, that is to say, the conventional meanings of the Good American Girl. But before his marriage with her has finally unmanned him, he comes to see her as an "evil-eyed" destroyer, and longs "to grind her grinning mask into jelly."

It is he, however, who is ground into jelly, crushed and driven from the imaginary sentimental paradise of married love to the lonely male refuge, the counter-paradise of mindless drunkenness. We see him last making the sign of the cross, a priest of Sentimental Love, who has arrived in the empty temple after the abdication of his goddess. Nicole, the goddess who failed, is postulated in the novel as a schizophrenic, in an attempt to explain her double role as Fair Lady and Dark, her two faces, angelic and diabolic, the melting and the grinning mask. But the schizophrenia is really in Diver, which is to say, in Fitzgerald, which is finally to say, in the American mind itself. There are not, in fact, two orders of women, good and bad, nor is there even one which seems for a little while bad, only to prove in the end utterly unravished and pure. There are only two sets of expectations and a single imperfect kind of woman caught between them: only actual incomplete females, looking in vain for a satisfactory definition of their role in a land of artists who insist on treating them as goddesses or bitches. The dream role and the nightmare role alike deny the humanity of women, who, baffled, switch from playing out one to acting out the other. Fitzgerald apparently never managed to accommodate to the fact that he lived at the moment of a great switch-over in roles, though he recorded that revolution in the body of his work. His outrage and self-pity constantly break through the pattern of his fiction, make even an ambitious attempt like *Tender Is the Night* finally too sentimental and whining to endure.

Only in *The Great Gatsby* does Fitzgerald manage to transmute his pattern into an objective form, evade the self-pity which corrodes the significance and the very shape of his other work—and this is perhaps because Gatsby is the most distant of all his protagonists from his real self. To Gatsby, Daisy appears in the customary semblance of the Fair Maiden, however; he finds her quite simply "the first 'nice' girl he had ever known." It is Howells' genteel epithet which occurs to him, though by Fitzgerald's time the capital letters are gone and the apologetic quotation marks have insidiously intruded. Daisy, rich and elegant and clean and sweet-smelling, represents to her status-hungry provincial lover, not the corruption and death she really embodies, but Success—which is to say, America itself. In Fitzgerald, the same fable that informs James is replayed, subtly transformed, for like James he has written an anti-Western, an "Eastern": a drama in which back-trailers reverse their westward drive to seek in the world which their ancestors abandoned the dream of riches and glory that has somehow evaded them. Fitzgerald's young men go east even as far as Europe; though unlike James's young women, they are in quest not of art and experience and the shudder of guilt, but of an even more ultimate innocence, an absolute America: a happy ending complete with new car, big house, money, and the girl.

In the symbolic geography of *The Great Gatsby,* the two halves of a nation are compressed into the two settlements on Long Island of West Egg and East Egg, from the first of which the not-quite arrived look yearningly across the water at those who are already *in,* Jay Gatsby at Daisy Buchanan. There is no need for a symbolic Europe to complete the scene; and, indeed, even in *Tender Is the Night,* Europe is only a place where the East Eggians go to play, a transatlantic extension of East Egg itself. In a concluding passage of great beauty and conviction, Fitzgerald manages to convey the whole world of aspiration which Daisy has represented to Gatsby, and transforms the book from a lament over the fall of the Fair Woman to an elegy for the lapsed American dream of innocent success:

And as the moon rose higher the inessential houses began to melt away until gradually I became aware of the old island here that flowered once for Dutch sailors' eyes—a fresh, green breast of the new world . . . the trees that had made way for Gatsby's house, had once pandered in whispers to the last and greatest of all human dreams; for a transitory enchanted moment man must have held his breath in the presence of this continent . . . face to face for the last time in history with something commensurate with his capacity for wonder.

And as I sat there brooding on the old, unknown world, I thought of Gatsby's wonder when he first picked out the green light at the end of Daisy's dock. He had come a long way to this blue lawn, and his dream must have seemed so close that he could hardly fail to grasp it. He did not know that it was already behind him, somewhere back in the vast obscurity beyond the city, where the dark fields of the republic rolled on under the night.

For Fitzgerald, "love" was essentially yearning and frustration; and there is consequently little consummated genital love in his novels, though he identified himself with that sexual revolution which the '20's thought of as their special subject. The adolescent's "kiss" is the only climax his imagination can really encompass; and despite his occasionally telling us that one or another of his charters has "taken" a woman, it is the only climax he ever realizes in a scene. In his insufferable early books, the American institution of *coitus interruptus,* from bundling to necking a favorite national pastime, finds at last a laureate; and even in his more mature works, his women move from the kiss to the kill with only the barest suggestion of copulation between. Hemingway, on the other hand, is much addicted to describing the sex act. It is the symbolic center of his work: a scene to which he recurs when nostalgically evoking his boyhood as "Up in Michigan"; illustrating the virtues of the sturdy poor as in *To Have and Have Not;* reflecting on civil strife and heroism as in *For Whom the Bell Tolls;* or projecting the fantasies of a man facing old age as in *Across the River and Into the Trees.* There are, however, no *women* in his books! In his earlier fictions, Hemingway's descriptions of the sexual encounter are intentionally brutal, in his later ones unintentionally comic; for in no case, can he quite succeed in making his females human, and coitus performed with an animal, a thing, or a wet dream is either horrible or ridiculous. If in *For Whom the Bell Tolls* Hemingway has written the most absurd love scene in the history of the American novel, this is not because he lost momentarily his skill and authority; it is a give-away—a moment which illuminates the whole erotic content of his fiction.

Hemingway is only really comfortable in dealing with "men without women." The relations of father to son, of battle-companions, friends on a fishing trip, fellow inmates in a hospital, a couple of waiters preparing to close up shop, a bullfighter and his manager, a boy and a gangster: these move him to simplicity and truth. Perhaps he is best of all with men who stand alone—in night-time scenes when the solitary individual sweats in his bed on the verge of nightmare, or arises to confront himself in the glass; though he is at home, too, with the Rip Van Winkle archetype, with men in flight from women. Certainly, he returns again and again to the fishing trip and the journey to the war—those two traditional evasions of domesticity and civil life. Yet he feels an obligation to introduce women into his more ambitious fictions, though he does not know what to do with them beyond taking them to bed. All his life, he has been haunted by a sense of how simple it all was once, when he could take his Indian girl into the clean-smelling woods, stretch out beside her on the pine-needles (her brother standing guard), and rise to no obligations at all. In a story called "Fathers and Sons," he writes a tribute to that prototypical, mindless, undemanding, scarcely human girl: "Could you say she did first what no one has ever done better and mention plump brown legs, flat belly, hard little breasts, well holding arms, quick searching tongue, the flat eyes, the good taste of mouth . . . and hemlock needles stuck against your belly. . . . Long time ago good. Now no good."

In Hemingway the rejection of the sentimental happy ending of marriage involves the acceptance of the sentimental happy beginning of innocent and inconsequential sex, and camouflages the rejection of maturity and of fatherhood itself. The only story in which he portrays a major protagonist as having a child is the one in which he remembers with nostalgia his little Trudy of the "well holding arms, quick searching tongue," and looks forward to the time when his son will have a gun and they can pop off to the forest like two boys together. More typically he aspires to be not Father but "Papa," the Old Man of the girl-child with whom he is temporarily sleeping; and surely there is no writer to whom childbirth more customarily presents itself as the essential catastrophe. At best he portrays it as a plaguey sort of accident which forces a man to leave his buddies behind at the moment of greatest pleasure as in "Cross Country Snow"; at worst, it becomes in his fiction that horror which drives the tender-hearted husband of "Indian Camp" to suicide, or which takes Catherine away from Lieutenant Henry in *A Farewell to Arms*.

Poor things, all they wanted was innocent orgasm after orgasm on an island of peace in a world at war, love-making without end in a scarcely real country to which neither owed life or allegiance.

But such a relationship can, of course, never last, as Hemingway-Nick Adams-Lieutenant Henry has always known: "They all ended the same. Long time ago good. Now no good." Only the dead woman becomes neither a bore nor a mother; and before Catherine can quite become either she must die, killed not by Hemingway, of course, but by childbirth! It is all quite sad and lovely at the end: the last kiss bestowed on what was a woman and is now a statue, the walk home through the rain. Poe himself could not have done better, though he was haunted not by the memory of a plump little Indian on the hemlock needles but a fantasy of a high-born maiden "loved with a love that was more than love" and carried away by death.

Had Catherine lived, she could only have turned into a bitch; for this is the fate in Hemingway's imagination of all Anglo-Saxon women. In him, the cliché of Dark Lady and Fair survives, but stood on its head, exactly reversed. The Dark Lady, who is neither wife nor mother, blends with the image of Fayaway, the exotic servant-consort reconstructed by Melville in *Typee* out of memories of an eight-year-old Polynesian girl-child. In Hemingway, such women are mindless, soft, subservient; painless devices for extracting seed without human engagement. The Fair Lady, on the other hand, who gets pregnant and wants a wedding, or uses her sexual allure to assert her power, is seen as a threat and a destroyer of men. But the seed-extractors are Indians or Latins, black-eyed and dusky in hue, while the castrators are at least Anglo-Saxon if not symbolically blond. Neither are permitted to be virgins; indeed, both are imagined as having been often possessed, though in the case of the Fair Woman promiscuity is used as a device for humiliating and unmanning the male foolish enough to have entered into a marriage with her. Through the Dark anti-virgin, on the other hand, a new lover enters into a blameless communion with the other uncommitted males who have possessed her and departed, as well as with those yet to come. It is a kind of homosexuality once-removed, the appeal of the whorehouse (Eden of the world of men without women) embodied in a single figure.

When Hemingway's bitches are Americans, they are hopeless and unmitigated bitches; symbols of Home and Mother as remembered by the boy who could never forgive Mama for having wantonly destroyed Papa's Indian collection! Mrs. Macomber, who, in "The Short Happy Life of Francis Macomber," kills her husband for having alienated the affections of the guide with whom she is having one of her spiteful little affairs, is a prime example of the type. And "the woman," in "The Snows of Kilimanjaro" another, who with her wealth has weaned her husband from all that sustained his virility, betrayed him to aimlessness and humiliation. Like Fitzgerald's betrayed men, he can choose only to die, swoon to the death he desires at the climax of a dream of escape.

The British bitch is for Hemingway only a demi-bitch, however, as the English are only, as it were, demi-Americans. Catherine is delivered from her doom by death; Brett Ashley in *The Sun Also Rises* (1926) is permitted, once at least, the gesture of herself rejecting her mythical role. But it is quite a feat at that, and Brett cannot leave off congratulating herself: "You know it makes one feel rather good deciding not to be a bitch." Yet Brett never becomes a woman really; she is mythicized rather than redeemed. And if she is the most satisfactory female character in all of Hemingway, this is because for once she is presented not as an animal or as a nightmare but quite audaciously as a goddess, the bitch-goddess with a boyish bob (Hemingway is rather fond of women who seem as much boy as girl), the Lilith of the '20's. No man embraces her without being in some sense castrated, except for Jake Barnes who is unmanned to begin with; no man approaches her without *wanting* to be castrated, except for Romero, who thinks naïvely that she is—or can easily become—a woman. Indeed, when Brett leaves that nineteen-year-old bullfighter, one suspects that, though she avows it is because she will not be "one of those bitches who ruins children," she is really running away because she thinks he might *make* her a woman. Certainly, Romero's insistence that she let her hair grow out has something to do with it: "He wanted me to grow my hair out. Me, with long hair. I'd look so like hell. . . . He said it would make me more womanly. I'd look a fright."

To yield up her cropped head would be to yield up her emancipation from female servitude, to become feminine rather than phallic; and this Brett cannot do. She thinks of herself as a flapper, though the word perhaps would not have occurred to her, as a member of the "Lost Generation"; but the Spaniards know her immediately as a terrible goddess, the avatar of an ancient archetype. She tries in vain to enter into the circle of Christian communion, but is always turned aside at the door; she changes her mind, she has forgotten her hat—the apparent reason never matters; she belongs to a world alien and prior to that of the Christian churches

in which Jake finds a kind of peace. In Pamplona, Brett is surrounded by a group of *riau-riau* dancers, who desert a religious
procession to follow her, set her up as a rival to Saint Fermin:
"Some dancers formed a circle around Brett and started to dance.
They wore big wreaths of white garlic around their necks. . . .
They were all chanting. Brett wanted to dance but they did not
want her to. They wanted her as an image to dance around." Incapable of love except as a moment in bed, Brett can bestow on
her worshipers nothing more than the brief joy of a drunken ecstasy—followed by suffering and deprivation and regret. In the
end, not only are her physical lovers unmanned and degraded, but
even Jake, who is her priest and is protected by his terrible wound,
is humiliated. For her service is a betrayal not only of his Catholic
faith but of his pure passion for bullfighting and trout-fishing; and
the priest of the bitch-goddess is, on the purely human level, a
pimp.

v

In the work of William Faulkner, the fear of the castrating woman
and the dis-ease with sexuality present in the novels of his contemporaries, Fitzgerald and Hemingway, attain their fullest and shrill-
est expression. Not content with merely projecting images of the
anti-virgin, he insists upon editorializing against the woman he
travesties in character and situation. No Jiggs and Maggie cliché of
popular anti-feminism is too banal for him to use; he reminds us
(again and again!) that men are helpless in the hands of their
mothers, wives, and sisters; that females do not think but proceed
from evidence to conclusions by paths too devious for males to
follow; that they possess neither morality nor honor; that they are
capable, therefore, of betrayal without qualm or quiver of guilt but
also of inexplicable loyalty; that they enjoy an occasional beating
at the hands of their men; that they are unforgiving and without
charity to other members of their own sex; that they lose keys and
other small useful articles with maddening regularity but are quite
capable of finding things invisible to men; that they use their sexuality with cold calculation to achieve their inscrutable ends, etc.,
etc.

Until his last books, Faulkner treated with respect only females,
white ladies or colored women, past the menopause. The elderly
maiden or widowed aunt is the sole female figure in his fiction

exempt from travesty and contempt. Up to the very verge of her climacteric, woman seems to Faulkner capable of the most shameless concupiscence, like Miss Burden in *Light in August,* cowering naked in the garden of the decaying house waiting to be captured and possessed in an obscene game of hide-and-seek. Faulkner sometimes gives the impression of the village misogynist swapping yarns with the boys at the bar in order to reveal a truth about women which shocks even himself. Like old Varner in *The Hamlet,* he keeps assuring his readers that he "cheerfully and robustly and undeviatingly" declines to accept "any such theory as female chastity other than as a myth to hoodwink young husbands. . . ." But there is little robust or cheerful about his attitudes, however undeviatingly he may assert them; he is less like Varner fundamentally than like Hightower, the scared and stinking refugee from life in *Light in August,* who cries out in despair that "the husband of a mother, whether he be the father or not is already a cuckold . . . what woman has ever suffered from any brute as men have suffered from good women?"

Pubescent or nubile women, for Faulkner, fall into two classes, roughly corresponding to those of Hemingway, though for the former both are terrifying: great, sluggish, mindless daughters of peasants, whose fertility and allure are scarcely distinguishable from those of a beast in heat; and the febrile, almost fleshless but sexually insatiable daughters of the aristocracy. Not the women he observes but those he dreams inhabit Faulkner's novels, myths of masculine protest: the peasant wench as earth goddess (Lena Grove in *Light in August,* Dewy Dell in *As I Lay Dying,* Eula Varner in *The Hamlet*), or the coed as nymphomaniac Venus (Cecily of *Soldiers' Pay,* Patricia in *Mosquitoes,* Temple Drake in *Sanctuary*). Their very names tend toward allegory, "Dewy Dell," for instance, suggesting both a natural setting and woman's sex, her sex as a fact of nature, while "Temple Drake" evokes both a ruined sanctuary and the sense of an unnatural usurpation: woman become a sexual aggressor—more drake than duck.

Unlike the natural women of Hemingway, Faulkner's dewiest dells turn out to be destroyers rather than redeemers, quicksands disguised as sacred groves. In his portrayal of Lena Grove, he relents for once into something like admiration; but his Eula Varner is more typical. Faulkner begins by describing Eula, the goddess who presides over the revels of *The Hamlet* and is married off in the end to its Devil, Flem Snopes, in terms of a pagan dithyramb to Aphrodite: "Her entire appearance suggested some symbology out of the old Dionysic Times, honey in sunlight and bursting grapes, the writhen bleeding of the crushed fecundated vine beneath the hard rapacious trampling goat-hoof." What begins as a pre-Christian eulogy to the inarticulate manifestation of sheer fertility imperceptibly slips over into a puritan cry of distress and distaste before unredeemed, burgeoning life.

When Faulkner abandons mythology for more direct physical description, his uneasiness before Eula's languor and inert lusciousness is even more clearly betrayed. "She simply did not move at all of her own volition, save to and from the table and to and from bed. She was late in learning to walk. . . . She remained in it [her perambulator] long after she had grown too large to straighten her legs out. . . . She did nothing. She might as well have been a foetus." If she is a foetus, however, Eula is an almost intolerably alluring one, a foetus-vampire, as it were; for hanging sluggishly in her mother's arms, she seems, Faulkner writes, even at the age of five or six, an "indisputably female burden like a bizarre and chaperoned Sabine rape." And after she begins to walk to school, men and boys gape, whistle, and howl in the unquenchable anguish and joy of pure desire. It is an absurd conceit, hysterical, a little mad—tolerable only because Faulkner so obviously believes in it, believes in the terror of mere inert female flesh not as a fact of life but as an article of faith!

Just as his Eula figures are all motionless, quivering, mammalian softness, Faulkner's Temple figures are sheer motion, a blur of dancing legs and wind-blown hair in a speeding car: "sexless yet somehow troubling." It is the assertion of femaleness which upsets him in Eula Varner; and it is its denial which disturbs him in Temple Drake. Temple is disconcertingly almost a man, almost phallic; and, indeed, at the moment of her rape by Popeye, it is difficult to tell which one is the phallus bearer, to whom the bloody corncob really belongs. "Then I thought about being a man," Temple says later, "and as soon as I thought it, it happened. . . . It made a kind of plopping sound, like blowing a little rubber tube wrong-side outward. . . . I could feel it, and I lay right still to keep from laughing about how surprised he was going to be . . ." In *Sanctuary,* Faulkner's revulsion from woman's betrayal of her traditionally submissive role reaches so shrill a pitch that, in simple self-defense, he has felt it necessary to disavow that novel as a pot-boiler; yet it is obviously written in earnest though at white heat, a nightmare directly transcribed. Fortunately, it is not quite convincing enough to be unbearable, though it possesses enough hallucinatory vividness to give it the baleful appeal of a Dickensian or Dostoevskian grotesque. *Sanctuary* is, on the one hand, the darkest of all Faulkner's books, a brutal protest to the quality of American life written in the pit of the Great Depression; but on the other hand, it is the dirtiest of all the dirty jokes exchanged among men only at the expense of the abdicating Anglo-Saxon Virgin.

Temple is not only a lady, but the very image of all those Fair Ladies whose fall or resistance had been the central subject of genteel literature ever since *Charlotte Temple* was published in the United States. That her name is an inversion of that of the prototypical American heroine is, perhaps, only an accident, one of the more satisfactory jokes of history; and certainly Faulkner did not know that the original of Maggie Verver was Henry James's cousin Minny Temple, whose frailness, white skin, and red hair also distinguish Temple Drake. The title of his book, however, makes it clear that Faulkner is fully aware that he is dealing not with a mere change in mores but with the desecration of a cult object. Out of the "high delicate head" of Faulkner's Temple, at any rate, look eyes which are "cool, predatory, and discreet," but their discretion is belied by the "bold painted mouth." She fools no one; the wife of a gangster into whose hideout she has stumbled sees immediately that though Temple, like her illustrious prototypes, is still the Girl on the Run, she no longer means to run quite fast enough to get away. And even Gowan Stevens, Temple's escort and male opposite number, is not too drunk to understand what she really wants, though drunk enough not to be able to take advantage of his knowledge. "Don't think I don't see your name where it's written on that lavatory wall!" he tells her in impotent spite. It is the final degradation; the holy name on the lavatory wall!

Before Faulkner is through, we have been compelled to watch the ex-snow maiden, the former golden girl, not only raped (which is nothing new, of course, since she was born being raped, was Clarissa before she was Maggie Verver), but begging to be had, whimpering for the consummation she had once fled in terror. Beside Temple, pleading with Red, brutal thug and stud, to satisfy her, even Daisy Buchanan seems in retrospect a quasi-lady, Brett not really a bitch at all. Western literature before the coming of Sentimentalism is rich in images of destructive women—Thaïs and

Cleopatra and Lilith herself; but Temple is more than a recrudescence of that rejected orthodox archetype. She represents a lust of
the nerves rather than of the flesh, a *programmatic* concupiscence
entered upon as a declaration of independence, is in short a queasy
male image of the flapper—the New Woman of the 1920's. Not
content to be violated, the woman becomes the violator and
Faulkner responds with nausea:

> He came toward her. She did not move. Her eyes began to grow
> darker and darker, lifting into her skull above a half-moon of
> white, without a focus, with the blank rigidity of a statue's eyes.
> She began to say Ah-ah-ah-ah in an expiring voice, her body
> arching slowly backward as though forced by an exquisite tor-
> ture. When he touched her she sprang like a bow, hurling her-
> self upon him, her mouth gaped and ugly like that of a dying
> fish as she writhed her loins against him. . . . With her hips
> grinding against him, her mouth gaping in straining protrusion,
> bloodless, she began to speak. "Let's hurry. Anywhere. . . .
> Come on. What're you waiting for?" She strained her mouth to-
> ward him, dragging his head down, making a whimpering moan.
> "Please. Please. Please. Please. You've got to. I'm on fire, I
> tell you."

Toward the end of his life, Faulkner seems to have repented of
his many blasphemies against woman and to have committed himself to redeeming one by one all his anti-virgins; but his attempts
at redemption somehow do not touch the level of acceptance
reached by his original travesties. In *Requiem for a Nun,* he portrays Temple as a mother, as married to Gowan Stevens, who once
read her name on the lavatory wall. Insanely burning once more
for a new Red, she is not permitted to abase herself again, but is
redeemed by the self-sacrifice of a Negro girl, and is left at the
play's end aching with a higher lust for religious belief, about to
follow her husband home. In *The Town,* Faulkner carries Eula's
refurbishing even further than he had Temple's, actually rewriting
Eula's past history as he pretends to recapitulate it, and turning
her into the very model of female courage and endurance. This
time the former avatar of female corruption herself performs the
act of self-sacrifice, dies to assure an honorable future for her
daughter—an innocent young girl, who is left at the novel's end
advancing, wide-eyed and pure, on Greenwich Village. The epi-

taph inscribed on Eula's grave by her impotent husband is, we are asked to believe, truer than that husband can guess or any decent citizen is prepared to grant:

EULA   VARNER   SNOPES
1889   1927
A Virtuous Wife is a Crown to her Husband
Her Children Rise and Call Her Blessed

And even this is not the end. In *The Long Hot Summer,* a film which lists Faulkner's name among the credits, Eula is de-mythicized as well as redeemed: made into the customary Hollywood image of the sexy but sincere young wife, who begins wriggling like a taken fish in the arms of her new husband, while the boys wolf-call and wail in the stifling dusk. In the end, however, she helps to win that husband from weakness to strength, returns to his arms and legitimate bliss, when he has proved himself a true son to his father and a good citizen! Eula and Temple alike fade into the stereotype of the Good Bad Girl, who in turn gives birth to the sweet young thing, and the Protestant Virgin is restored to her shrine; but it makes no difference. Faulkner's art fails him when he turns from nausea and despair to sentimentality and maudlin pity; and even the popular mind rejects his attempts at converting his archetypes into the stereotypes of market-place culture.

Not only in Hemingway and Faulkner and Fitzgerald, but in John Held, Jr. and in the Anita Loos of *Gentlemen Prefer Blondes,* the archetype of the snow maiden as gold-digger, the bad blonde takes over. The vampire, symbol of sexual aggression as cannibalism, first formulated as a male, had been turned by the Romantic imagination into the Dark Lady, the "vamp" as she was called when Zenobia had become Theda Bara. During the '20's, however, in a second revolutionary shift, Mary Pickford and Theda Bara became one, America's Sweetheart and the vampire amalgamated into the bleached blonde. The notion that fair hair is the product of the peroxide bottle rather than of race or culture, a disguise rather than an outward and visible sign of an inward and invisible grace, becomes an article of cynical un-faith. A whole disillusioned generation eyeing the peroxide blonde (after a while "platinum" rather than golden, as if the old symbol of wealth were not opulent enough) remarks nastily, "Yes, but what color is she below the waist?" Jean Harlow is the first avatar of that new and blasphemous dream, first of the series that includes Marilyn Monroe and Jayne Mansfield. The movies, out of respect for the Hays office, must pretend that they are Good Bad Girls one and all—Good Girls who only appear bad for a little while; but the mass audience knows better, knows they are really Bad Good Girls—Bad Girls who pass themselves off as good by wearing the hair and skin and eyes that were once the sacred investiture of the Protestant Virgin.

It is fitting that the most memorable and terrible woman in an American novel of the '30's is a portrait of the blond movie actress, a kind of *ersatz* Jean Harlowe. She is, of course, the Faye Greener of Nathanael West's *Day of the Locust,* and her very name is a fitting climax to the series we have been tracing through the history of our fiction: Charlotte Temple to Temple Drake, Daisy Miller to Daisy Fay to Faye Greener.*

In West's earliest fiction, there are traces of queasiness before woman's surrender of her traditional role, her usurpation of male privileges which so disturbed Faulkner. In *The Dream Life of Balso Snell* (1931), this is projected as a fantasy in which the female turns, at the moment of possession, into something disturbingly like a male. "Throwing his arms about her, Balso interrupted her recitation by sticking his tongue into her mouth. But when he closed his eyes to heighten the fun, he felt that he was embracing tweed. He opened them and saw that what he held in his arms was a middleaged woman dressed in a mannish suit and wearing horn-rimmed glasses." To such a betrayal, in which the erotic object becomes at once something mannish and schoolmarmish, there is only one answer: "By this time, Balso had gotten one of his hands free. He hit Miss McGeeney a terrific blow in the gut and hove her into the fountain."

The rest of West's fiction contains a series of precisely such blows in the female gut: travesties of the teasers and betrayers and lady rapists who assault and torment his male protagonists, baffle them in their search for a love which is more than desire. Even the most submissive of Good Girls only succeeds in enraging West, as the Betty of *Miss Lonelyhearts* enrages her lover. "She was like a kitten," he thinks, "whose soft helplessness makes one ache to hurt

---

* It seems odd that it did not occur to me earlier that her name suggests, too, how the grass is always greener on the other side—for West, the blond, gentile side.

it." And taking her nipple between his fingers, " 'Let me pluck this rose,' he said, giving a sharp tug. 'I want to wear it in my buttonhole.' " It is in *A Cool Million,* however, that the Good Good Girl, again called Betty, gets her full comeuppance, raped with appalling regularity from the time she is twelve, pursued by mad dogs, bullies and corrupt politicians, she fulfills her destiny as the final adornment of the Colonial American Room of Wu Fong's whorehouse, where she blends admirably into a background of "antimacassars, ships in bottles, carved whale bone, hooked rugs."

Betty is still the Good Good Girl, even as an unsuccessful prostitute, an American Justine, which is to say, a victim. But Faye Greener is the blond bitch in all her archetypal purity, a woman willing at last to take up the role that old Rappaccini had once vainly dreamed for his daughter: "to be endowed with marvellous gifts against which no power and strength could avail an enemy . . . to be as terrible as . . . beautiful." Like Temple Drake before her, Faye does her destroying on the run; pursued by everyone, possessed by anyone with the price, she is somehow unattainable still —certainly to the artist-narrator, Tod, who has seen her pawed by a seedy cowboy actor and a brutal Mexican hanger-on, but cannot quite bring himself to buy her. "If only he had the courage to throw himself on her. Nothing less violent than rape would do. The sensation he felt was like that he got when holding an egg in his hand. Not that she was fragile or even seemed fragile. It wasn't that. It was her completeness, her egg-like self-sufficiency, that made him want to touch her." But she cannot really be touched, for she is the dream dreamed by all of America, the dream of a love which is death; and in a strange sense she remains virginal as death is virginal: the immaculate, degraded *anima* of a nation, her realest existence on the screen.

It is because West's book is about Hollywood, and because he knows that Hollywood is where all America comes to die, that Faye is its proper center, dispensing what the bored hinterlanders do not quite know that they desire, as they press against the restraining ropes at a gala preview: a *Götterdämmerung,* an orgy of destruction. Precisely because she is a phantom bride, she is also a child, epitome of the quest for eternal youth which is the obverse of the lust for death: "Although she was seventeen, she was dressed like a child of twelve in a white cotton dress with a blue sailor collar. Her long legs were bare and she had blue sandals on her feet." The long legs are a further clue: those improbable legs which America has bred onto the naturally short-legged female form. "She was a tall girl," West tells us of Faye, "with wide, straight shoulders and long, sword-like legs." The rest is conventional enough: the long neck, the full face, the widely divided breasts, the platinum hair tied back with a blue ribbon, the sailor suit of a small girl; but it is the sword-legs which gave away the game.

"Her invitation wasn't to pleasure," West explains, "but to struggle, hard and sharp, closer to murder than to love. If you threw yourself on her, it would be like throwing yourself from the parapet of a skyscraper. You would do it with a scream. You wouldn't expect to rise again. Your teeth would be driven into your skull like nails into a pine board and your back would be broken. You wouldn't even have time to sweat or close your eyes." Only the fantasies of post-World War I Germany have reflected (in films like *The Blue Angel*) comparable excesses of male masochism; and Marlene Dietrich, who embodied the cruel woman of those fantasies, soon emigrated to the United States which appreciated even more than Germany the delicious threat of her million-dollar legs. But it is not male masochism alone which creates and acclaims images of the castrating bitch; there is a corresponding female sadism which greets such images and collaborates in their fabrication.

Though the long-suffering victim does not disappear from popular woman's literature, she is flanked in the mid-twentieth century by a new figure, the lady with the whip. Most often that newer figure is projected backward in time, cast as the heroine-villainess of a historical romance, as if to insist that the dangerous woman belongs to the there-and-then rather than to the here-and-now. The protagonists of such books are not possessed by their numerous lovers but possess them, use, exhaust, and abandon their men— leave them to defeat or death. "Avatars of the Bitch," Gershom Legman calls such villainous heroines in an indignant pamphlet called *Love and Death,* which is directed against the sadist travesties of women and the celebration of violence on all levels of our culture. *Gone With the Wind* draws his special wrath, though its bitch-lady, Scarlett O'Hara, seems mild enough beside the women of Faulkner or Nathanael West. As popular literature goes, Margaret Mitchell's novel is notably "clean," the sort of fat, traditional book on which high-school students make their "book reports" for the class, while they are busily reading *Peyton Place* outside.

Gone with the Wind's heroine, Scarlett O'Hara, is less the portrait of a woman than an embodiment of the Northern stereotypes
of the suffering South (the really orthodox Daughters of the Confederacy walked out on her!): corrupt, vain, though at last more
sinned against than sinning. The sentimentality of *Gone With the
Wind* is chiefly political; but its politics is embodied in an erotic
fable, whose heroine is permitted an act of violence beyond anything Brockden Brown allowed Constantia Dudley. She is allowed
not merely to kill a would-be attacker, but to *enjoy* the act with a
joy deeper, more organic than any she finds in love.

> Like lightning, she shoved her weapon over the banisters and
> into the startled bearded face. Before he could even fumble at
> his belt, she pulled the trigger. . . . The man crashed backwards
> to the floor. . . . Scarlett ran down the stairs and stood over him,
> gazing down into what was left of the face above the beard, a
> bloody pit where the nose had been, glazing eyes burned with
> powder. . . . Her eyes went to the stubby hairy hand on the
> floor so close to the sewing box and suddenly she was vitally
> alive again, vitally glad with a cool tigerish joy. She could have
> ground her heel into the gaping wound which had been his nose
> and taken sweet pleasure in the feel of his warm blood on her
> bare feet. She had struck a blow for Tara—and for Ellen.

For the old plantation and for the abused woman: these are the
causes in whose name the New Woman strikes; and avenging the
fallen Clarissas of the past, she becomes the bitch-killer.*

VI

Once the Good Good Girl has been exposed, no sentimental stereotype of womanhood is safe; first the mother and then the angel
child are revealed as bitches, too. Quite early in the game, Melville
had challenged the standard clichés of motherhood with the portrait of Mary Glendenning in *Pierre*. She is not, like Mrs. St. Clare
in *Uncle Tom's Cabin,* a traditional Bad Mother—descendant of

---

* But turning killer, she becomes fair game herself; and the way is
open for such male counter-fantasies as Norman Mailer's *An American
Dream,* in which the Dark Lady, turned wife, is murdered by the sympathetic protagonist, who also buggers the Bad Blonde, revealed as a Nazi,
while the Good Blonde is being snatched from him by the powers of
darkness. And in the end, all male murderers and desecrators go scot free.

the stepmothers in Grimm—who loves herself more than her child, but a *Good* Mother, whose very goodness is revealed as a threat, a loving mother, whose love serves only to unman her son. The sickly-sweet entanglement between Pierre and his mother, who flirt and flatter like a pair of lovers, ends in mutual misunderstanding and alienation. In pharisaic pride, the mother casts out her son, when he once dares to reject her rule and her notions of respectable behavior: "Then erected all her haughtiness again, and stood before Pierre in incurious, unappeasable grief and scorn for him. . . . 'Beneath my roof, and at my table, he who was once Pierre Glendenning no more puts himself.' "

So intense is Melville's involvement in the crisis of rejection which he attempts to transcribe, that he can find no language for it, falls into a rhetoric impossible to believe and even difficult to follow; and we remember that on his own marriage certificate, his mother's name is written in the place of his bride's! Like Mark Twain, who was also obsessed by the theme of the divorce between mother and son, Melville cannot abide thinking of that rupture as final. Twain's Good Bad Boy, Tom Sawyer or Tom Canty in *The Prince and the Pauper,* merely seem to deny the mother, only play at running away from home, but return at last to be forgiven and redeemed. Huck, to be sure, rejects a whole series of surrogate mothers from the Widow Douglas to Aunt Sally, but he is an orphan—postulated as a "motherless boy"; and, no more than his author, does he dare deny the value of what he is somehow unable to accept. Melville's reconciliations with the mother, however, are invariably projected as symbolic rather than real. Pierre can never recover on earth his first innocent relationship with Mary Glendenning (between them falls the shadow of the incest taboo); though the "orphan" Ishmael has been picked up at the close of *Moby Dick* by "the devious-cruising *Rachel . . .* in her retracing search after her children," rescued by the ship which represents eternally-suffering motherhood.

Only in the twentieth century is the charge of betrayal unequivocally leveled against the mothers themselves, the counterattack begun. The key work on the subject was imagined in the '20's, though never quite written, in the book which Fitzgerald called at one point *The Boy Who Killed His Mother,* but which he gradually transformed into *Tender Is the Night,* by changing its boy-hero into a girl, who gets along reasonably well with *her* mother! It is Fitzgerald's friend Hemingway, who, though he stops short of portraying matricide, launches the full-scale assault: turning Mother into a monster of piety, who despises the great clean outdoors of rod and gun, and rises from her copy of *Science and Sanity* to destroy Father's collection of Indian artifacts while he is off teaching junior to shoot. There is no question about junior's allegiance; through Nick, the boy Hemingway always in some sense remained, the choice is made once and for all in a short story called "The Doctor and the Doctor's Wife": " 'Your mother wants you to come and see her,' the doctor said. 'I want to go with you,' Nick said."

In the gallery of anti-mothers, perhaps the Addie Bundren of Faulkner's *As I Lay Dying* (1930) is the most icy and terrible. Marriage to her had meant chiefly an escape from teaching school, and from the children in whom she had found pleasure only when beating them: "I looked forward to the times when they faulted, so I could whip them." And when, after her marriage, she finds herself with child, a rage gathers in her against her husband that only cuckolding him can satisfy. "And when I knew that I had Cash," she thinks in her last reverie, "I knew that living was terrible and that this was the answer to it. . . . When he was born I knew that motherhood was invented by someone who had to have a word for it because the ones that had the children didn't care whether there was a word for it or not." The image of the mother of bastards, who hates the life which painfully grows in her, is passed on from Faulkner to his disciple, Robert Penn Warren. The mother of Jack Burden in *All the King's Men* is the special heiress of the Faulknerian rage. To her grown son, she seems "a woman without heart, who loved merely power over men and the momentary satisfaction to vanity or flesh which they could give her," in short, the conventional bitch of contemporary American fiction. And at the climax of the novel's action, she reveals to that son that he is, indeed, a bastard, his presumed father really betrayed; though it is from this moment of truth that a new relationship between them grows possible, one based neither on the traditional notions of maternal purity and faithfulness nor on a revulsion from them which debouches in hate.

On the more popular levels, that stage of reconciliation is never reached. Once more a sentimental cliché heaves over sickeningly in the ooze at the bottom of the mass mind, reveals its underside of delusion and horror; the hackneyed tribute "I owe it all to Mother!" turns into a self-pitying whine which converts the same words to a condemnation. The emasculated display everywhere their attenuated private parts; the Oedipal captives hold up their silver chains to the light; and a nation of mama's boys kick and scream that it is all mama's fault. The age demands that the Devil-Mom replace the saint-Mom; but no one asks that real women replace allegorical lay figures in the maternal role. The new stereotype is redeemed for literature, however, the anti-mother made flesh in a single distinguished novel, Wright Morris' *Man and Boy* (1951).

This is an oddly dispassionate little study of a bird-watching, maniacally tidy housewife, who pares her toe-nails with a knife stolen from her husband, and is called universally "Mother"— though her only son died before the action begins. She has, in effect, killed him; driven "the Boy" before her merciless, unremitting, and unsympathetic love, first into the household refuge of the bathroom, then to the more universal sanctuary of the war, in which he has died a hero's death. Early in the game, she had wrested from the Boy the gun, given to him by his defeated father as a token of manhood; and having no other way of making a big bang, "the Boy" ended by blowing himself up. Nowhere in our literature is the castrating mother-wife, shaving her legs, getting into her girdle, spreading newspapers on the newly washed floor, studied with less hysteria or self-pity. As Mother moves through her Big Day (she has been asked to christen a destroyer which is being named after the Boy) to its climax, everything crumbles before her assurance: her husband's feeble attempt at conspiratorial revolt with a chance accomplice, a dwarfed soldier called Seymour Lipido; the conventions and procedures of the United States Navy; the insolence of the children of the poor.

Oblivious, magnificent, and terrible, she advances on the docks, presumably under the escort of a naval officer, but really under the sole protection of an immense, stupid cleaning lady, who holds over her a green parasol and alone knows her divinity. The bottle broken and the ship duly dubbed, Mother insists upon making a speech, utterly irrelevant to the occasion, before a cowed crowd of listeners; and Seymour Lipido (who has already been converted enough to yell, "Viva Mrs. Ormsby—nuts to the Navy!") makes the response on which the book ends. " 'Here she comes,' he cried, 'Here comes Mother!' and rose from his seat in such a manner that Mr. Ormsby, like a man on a springboard, rose with him. As one man they rose together, some of them, like Mr. Ormby, a little stunned, but all of them able, with the help of their wives, to get to their feet. Coming toward them, soberly, was Mother, her flanks protected by the U.S. Navy, with Mrs. Myrtle Dinardo still in full charge of the sky."

The image of the golden girl child dies the hardest death of all in the American psyche; but this, too, yields before the general onslaught on the concept of pure womanhood. To this very day, the juvenile version of the Good Good Girl survives—not only in children's books and comic strips like "Little Annie Rooney," but even in the work of so serious a middlebrow writer as J. D. Salinger. His Esmé in "For Esmé—with Love and Squalor," like Holden's kid sister in *The Catcher in the Rye,* redeems from madness a mind at the point of surrender; and if in "A Perfect Day for Bananafish," the child Sybil cannot save the life of Seymour Glass, at least she illuminates for him the world of adult corruption. Salinger is as addicted as any contemporary to portraying full-grown women as bitches, but he clings to the pure child as a foil. He proffers Seymour Glass's erotic trifling with the golden-haired little Sybil (he plays with her fingers, kisses her feet) not as one more neurotic symptom, but as an attempt to escape from sexual bondage to the freedom of love; in his work, in short, the child becomes the rival of the wife.

Before the turn of the century, however, Stephen Crane had, in his *Whilomville Stories,* begun the debunking of the little angel, revealing the golden-curled, pink-and-white girl-child as a source of mischief and deceit, though the prevailing tone of these tales is so sentimental and cute that it is hard to take him seriously. The game of calling little angels little devils is an old and respectable one—quite unexceptionable to a popular audience, as long as it is clear that the author is really only kidding. The Good Bad Small Girl of this type is related to the "tomboy" figure, the rebel against femininity, who, as every genteel reader knows, will be transformed at the moment that she steps out of her overalls into her first party dress and is revealed as worthy of love! The lesbian implications of this image were not apparent to the great audience of the past, which would have found in any hint of female homosexuality the really unforgivable blasphemy against the conventions of womanhood. But Carson McCullers has taken full advantage of those implications, projecting in her neo-tomboys, ambiguous and epicene, the homosexual's sense of exclusion from the family and his uneasiness before heterosexual passion. Indeed, nothing is more suitable for such ends than the child's bafflement at weddings and honeymoons and the mystery of copulation, which these rituals at once declare and conceal. With the collaboration of Julie Harris, Mrs. McCullers has made the boy-girl of *Member of the Wedding* familiar to all of America; so that we have come to accept the Good Bad Tomboy, Huck Finn as F. Jasmine Adams, as a standard form of our nostalgia for pre-sexual bliss.

It is Faulkner, however, who first attempts to portray not merely the small Good Bad Girl, but the (expected) Good Girl as (actually) bad. In *Absalom, Absalom!*, the young girl Judith is discovered, leaning over the edge of a loft and screaming with the bloodlust her brother does not share (he trembles, nauseated), while her father wrestles, naked and bloody, with one of his Negro field hands. Judith is not merely the tomboy contrasted with the sissy brother; she is, though only in embryo, the child witch, travesty of the good woman as well as the pure child; and she belongs quite properly in the company of the ghouls and ghosts who make *Absalom, Absalom!* the most gothic of Faulkner's books. Yet Faulkner somehow cannot manage to keep Judith alive after her first scene; for the plot pushes her to the periphery, and she blends with a Negro servant woman and her old-maid aunt into a composite creature, a symbol of featureless femininity: "It was as though we were one being, interchangeable and indiscriminate . . . the three of us, three women. . . ."

In *The Hamlet,* he tries again with the young Eula Varner, who is formulated, in a book more comic than gothic, rather as the girl bitch than the child witch. The scene in which the schoolmaster Labove, helpless with the desire that an eleven-year-old girl has stirred up in him and will not satisfy, chases her mindless quivering flesh round and round the classroom comes closer than anything in American literature to the horrific vision of *Death in Venice:* a revelation that the pursuit of childhood is not harmless nostalgia but decadence and the will to self-destruction. In Faulkner, however, it is, in all its unmitigated horror, played for the laughs, culminates in a pratfall rather than a tragic death. Eula knocks her schoolmaster-lover down and " 'Stop pawing me,' she said. 'You old headless horseman Ichabod Crane.' "

Eula is the *femme fatale* as a small, fat girl; but she destroys only as the blind, fertile thrust of nature destroys, without malice or intent. Quite different is the female protagonist of William March's *The Bad Seed* (1954), who consciously desires evil but wears in the presence of adults a mask of innocence, which she has learned to simulate reading *Elsie Dinsmore*. The avowed themes of March's book: the question of whether criminal traits can be inherited and the decision of a mother to kill her own child—are of secondary importance; what thrilled the great audience and made this novel March's only best-selling work is his revelation of the sweet young thing as sadist and killer. It is this motif which filled the theaters and movie-houses with middlebrow, middle-class communicants eager to participate in the defilement of their own sacred images. That defilement is carried even further in Vladimir Nabokov's *Lolita* (1958), whose subject is the seduction of a middle-aged man by a twelve-year-old girl; and which has already achieved the two supreme successes possible to heretical works: an initial banning and a subsequent life as a best-seller, despite its endorsement by eminently respectable professors.

Nabokov's theme involves multiple ironies; for in his novel, it is the naïve child, the female, the American who corrupts the sophisticated adult, the male, the European. In a single work, Richardson, Mrs. Stowe, and Henry James are all controverted, all customary symbols for the encounter of innocence and experience stood on their heads. *Lolita, or the Confession of a White Widowed Male* is the international novel moved to America along with the émigré who is its male protagonist. As full as *The Marble Faun* or *The Ambassadors* of guidebook observations, it devotes them not to châteaux or museums or the Church of the Capuchins but to highways and motels and roadside cafés; its America comes out of the AAA Tourguide and Duncan Hines, as surely as the Europe of Hawthorne out of the Baedeker. Nowhere in our recent literature is there so detailed and acute a picture of our landscape, topographical and moral, as in *Lolita*. But more profoundly than the scenery and the setting, Lolita herself is America—just as Daisy or Hilda or Maggie were America before her; and representing America to the mind of a European, she is even more Annabel Lee than Maggie Verver. Indeed, the book begins with an evocation of Poe's "Kingdom by the Sea"; and before it is through, the names of his girl-love and Nabokov's fade into each other, blur to a single entangled formula: "Annabel Haze, alias Dolores Lee, alias Loleeta. . . ." Annabel Lee as nymphomaniac, demonic rapist of the soul—such is the lithe, brown Campfire Girl, who loves her mummy but was devirginated at the age of twelve (like Justine before her, Nabokov reminds us)!

Into Lolita and her mummy, the bitch-girl and the semi-preserved suburban predator, the pure American female has been split and degraded; but the European confronts her in both her latter-day avatars as helplessly as when she was still whole and dazzling in her purity. Like Prince Amerigo in *The Golden Bowl,* Nabokov's Humbert Humbert is still engaged in the discovery of America through Poe and the American woman; but unlike the Prince he is not redeemed, merely fascinated, raped, driven to murder, and left to die of a heart attack in jail. At every turn of its complications, the perverse theme of *Lolita* parodies some myth of the Sentimental Love Religion and the cult of the child. And it is surely for this reason that the book was banned and then blessed with a popular success; for it is the final blasphemy against the mythical innocence of the woman and the child, more than sufficient unto a day haunted by the fear that there may, after all, have been such an innocence—that somewhere underground it may still persist.

11

THE FAILURE
OF SENTIMENT AND
THE EVASION OF LOVE

THE FAILURE of the Sentimental Love Religion and the rejection of the Protestant Virgin are the two most critical and baffling facts of the history of the novel in America. But that failure and that rejection are inevitable, granted the profound division in the American awareness of women, arising from an impossible demand that they represent at once the ruined and redeeming virgin-bride dreamed by Sentimentalism, and the forgiving mother, necessary to sustain an imaginary American commonwealth of boy-children, camerados at work and play.

Perhaps the clue to an essential difficulty is here. If marriage dismays the American writer, though his earlier European prototypes assured him it was salvation itself; and if lawless passion unnerves him, though his later European colleagues assure him that it "justifies all"—this is because both marriage and passion impugn the image of woman as mother, mean the abandonment of childhood. The keynote of our special sentimentality had been set even before the mid-nineteenth-century American renaissance by Nathaniel Parker Willis. Writing of that soon-forgotten figure some fifty years after his debut, Oliver Wendell Holmes remembered that in 1830 "Willis was by far the most prominent young American author"! He recalled his epicene grace, "something between a remembrance of the Count D'Orsay and an anticipation of Oscar Wilde," and compared him to a portrait of Hippolytus: "the beautiful young man who had kindled a passion in the heart of his wicked step-mother."

337

There could be no apter image to preside over the birth of our literature: the evocation of a delicate homosexuality, fleeing from gross female assault and haunted by the incest taboo. And even more to the point are the verses which Holmes quotes from Willis, written when he had already won the fame he desired, but was appalled to realize that he had swapped time for success, was over the sill of manhood:

> I'm twenty-two, I'm twenty-two,—
> They idly give me joy,
> As if I should be glad to know
> That I was less a boy.

It is maturity above all things that the American writer fears, and marriage seems to him its essential sign. For marriage stands traditionally not only for a reconciliation with the divided self, a truce between head and heart, but also for a compromise with society, an acceptance of responsibility and drudgery and dullness. To this ultimate surrender, the Young Werther had preferred death; and Werther, as we have noticed earlier, was the moral guide of the first hero of American fiction.

It is more complicated even than this, however; for marriage also means an acceptance of the status of a father: an abandonment of the quest to deliver the captive mother and an assumption of the role of the ogre who holds her in captivity. There is no authentic American who would not rather be Jack than the Giant, which is to say, who would not choose to be "one of the boys" to the very end. The ideal American postulates himself as the fatherless man, the eternal son of the mother.

He does not, of course, see himself as the swaggering son of the continental imagination, the adulterer who in every cuckolded husband humiliates his father and revenges his mother. Romantic adultery is regarded with horror by the American bourgeois and the classic American novelist alike, for it is hopelessly involved with a European class society abandoned forever; by most of our writers it is not really regarded at all, only ignored at the prompting of a largely unconscious self-censorship. To our writers, for whom courtly love is something learned about in school, extramarital passion seems not only an offense against the mother, but also, like marriage itself, a disclaimer of childhood: a way of smuggling adult responsibility and guilt in through the back door.

Only a temporary alliance with a savage maiden whose language one cannot understand: a mindless, speechless, brief encounter in some tropical Happy Valley appears to our traditional writers a possible image for a love which does not compromise freedom. But in the end, even this seems to them not quite safe.

There is finally no heterosexual solution which the American psyche finds completely satisfactory, no imagined or real consummation between man and woman found worthy of standing in our fiction for the healing of the breach between consciousness and unconsciousness, reason and impulse, society and nature. Yet in no nation in the world are those cleavages more deeply felt, declared, indeed, in the very pattern of historical life, visibly represented by the frontier. And in no nation is the need to heal such divisions more passionately recognized. The quest which has distinguished our fiction from Brockden Brown and Cooper, through Poe and Melville and Twain, to Faulkner and Hemingway is the search for an innocent substitute for adulterous passion and marriage alike. Is there not, our writers ask over and over, a sentimental relationship at once erotic and immaculate, a union which commits its participants neither to society nor sin—and yet one which is able to symbolize the union of the ego with the id, the thinking self with its rejected impulses?

We have already noticed that the first legend to seize the American imagination is the story of Rip Van Winkle, which has outlived the general reputation of its author, and which for years continued, as a popular drama, to reach the kind of audience to whom books remain forever a mystery. It is all a joke, of course, the jocular tale of a man who wakes up to find, when he has slept off his superhuman drunk, that he has also slept away the life of the shrew who bullied him, as well as that of George III, who had oppressed his country. Even as such a jest, however, the Rip archetype possesses surprising vitality, surviving to this day in the comic strip "Bringing Up Father," whose very title refers ironically to American woman's image of herself as a culture bearer, the civilizer of her spouse.

Though the Catskills for which Jiggs lights out is Dinty Moore's saloon, the alcoholic aroma of his escape remains the same as Rip's; and though Maggie takes opera lessons and aspires to "high society," she is still Mrs. Rip, a status-striving shrew. There is something already a little old-fashioned about "Bringing Up

Father," both in its up-from-the-working-class background and in the frankness with which it reveals the power struggle between husband and wife. The true Rip type—whether embodied in Jiggs or Major Hoople or the Uncle Willie of "Moon Mullins"—seems faintly archaic, a hangover from a more brutal age, before one spouse had agreed to put down the rolling pin or the other to bend the elbow no longer. The successor of Rip-Jiggs is Dagwood Bumstead, who goes to work every day and welcomes the tyranny of Blondie as quite what his own inadequacy demands and merits. On the most popular level, the image of the wife as shrew seems to be dying, abandoned to middlebrow novelists like Philip Wylie or quite serious calumniators of the female like Faulkner or Hemingway or Wright Morris. The disreputable figure of Rip himself dies harder, appearing with all his old scapegrace charm in, for instance, Faulkner's "Uncle Willy," where he is portrayed as the small boys' ally in their war against the mothers. "He wasn't anybody's uncle, but all of us, and grown people, too, called him . . . Uncle Willy." It is a hopeless war these days, the war against good women; and Uncle Willy, who cannot sleep away the lifetime of his opponents, is driven out of town.

Sometimes, in more serious books, Rip doffs his comic role and appears in new guises, less the clown but still essentially the man on the run from his wife. In the unwritten story of "Agatha," he teased the imaginations of Hawthorne and Melville in the form of the sailor, Robertson: that anti-Enoch Arden who returns from a long absence to find his former wife, not married again but still waiting—and flees again westward to a new escape. In *The Wonder Book,* Hawthorne through his alter ego Eustace Bright had already gone on record as refusing to re-tell the tale of Rip in its original version, though begged to by eager children. "Among those misty hills, he said, was a spot where some old Dutchmen were playing an everlasting game of nine-pins and where an idle fellow whose name was Rip Van Winkle had fallen asleep and slept away twenty years at a stretch." It is interesting to note how gun, dog and wife disappear from this discreet summary, to which Eustace Bright will add no more. "But the student replied that the story had been told once already, and better than it ever could be told again, and that nobody would have a right to alter a word of it until it should have grown as old as 'The Gorgon's Head.' . . ." "The Gorgon's Head"—it is an odd association, which evokes the missing wife at a symbolic remove, as the female face which turns the beholder to stone!

Despite his disclaimer, however, Hawthorne actually did rewrite Irving's tale, or at least embodied certain of its elements in the shadowy sketch which he called "Wakefield." It is not quite a story, this ironic little portrait of a man endowed with "a quiet selfishness . . . a peculiar sort of vanity . . . a disposition to craft," who one day steps out of his door and, for the legendary twenty years, remains away, merely as "a little joke . . . at his wife's expense," "a long whimwham." But the joke is finally at Wakefield's expense, since outside the purlieus of his own home, he becomes for Hawthorne a hopelessly alienated man: "the Outcast of the Universe." Hawthorne's story is racked, that is to say, by a guilt entirely absent in Irving's tale, in which there is no note of equivocation about the joyousness of Rip's deliverance: "there was one species of despotism under which he had long groaned and that was petticoat government. Happily that was at an end; he had got his neck out of the yoke of matrimony, and could go in and out whenever he pleased. . . ."

What is posed originally as an innocent lark soon becomes problematic; for the myth of Rip is more than just another example among the jollier fables of masculine protest; it is the definition, made once and for all—as Eustace Bright justly observes—of a fundamental American archetype. In some ways, it seems astonishingly prophetic: a forecast of today's fishing trip with the boys, tomorrow's escape to the ball park or the poker game. Henpecked and misunderstood at home, the natural man whistles for his dog, Wolf, picks up his gun and leaves the village for Nature—seeking in a day's outing what a long life at home has failed to provide him. It is hard to tell whether he is taking a vacation or making a revolution, whether his gesture is one of evasion or of subversion; but in any case, he seeks some ultimate Good symbolized by the keg of excellent Hollands and the male companions, who do not even talk (that is the province of his wife), merely indicate the liquor and continue with their game—their eternal playtime in the hills.

It is scarcely surprising that such a legend would have a special appeal for Melville, whose whole writing career represents, as it were, an escape to an inner Catskills, a Happy Valley of natural ease and male camaraderie, into which his imagination had translated the experience of his early manhood. To no one did marriage seem so utterly Paradise lost (as we have observed in looking at *Mardi*); to no one did bachelorhood appear so enviable a state. In "Benito Cereno," the innocent ship which Captain Delano leaves to plunge into a web of horror and intrigue is called *The Bachelor's Delight;* in *Moby Dick,* the last glimpse of joy and peace enjoyed by the crew of the *Pequod* comes in their encounter with another whaler named the *Bachelor;* while one of Melville's most intriguing short stories contrasts "The Tartarus of Maids" with "The Paradise of Bachelors." No wonder, then, that Melville turns at the end of his life to the most traditional of all American fables of anti-marriage. His idyllic tale, a composite of verse and prose, was intended as part of a volume he was preparing in his last years to dedicate to his wife. Like that other ambiguous tribute, *Mardi,* "Rip Van Winkle's Lilac" demands some knowledge of the language of flowers for a full understanding; but even to a cursory reader its essential meaning is clear. Melville's tale is an apology for the original Rip, put in the mouth of a bohemian painter, who prefers the shadow of the lilac tree reputed to have been planted by Rip's own hand to the shelter of the whitewashed church. The implication is that art is nurtured not by institutionalized religion but by the impulse which leads man to overthrow petticoat tyranny and head for the hills.

But why has Melville symbolized Rip's heritage by a lilac? For what precisely does it stand, this casual gift of the lazy reprobate to the American artist? We are told two things about it: first, that its blossoms have replaced Dame Van Winkle's pot of pinks and hollyhocks; and second, that its trunk stands in the place of a willow which endured as long as the house lasted and could not be cut down by Dame Van Winkle's ax. But pinks represent both boldness and woman's love, while hollyhocks stand for ambition and fecundity. Opposed to these symbols of aggressive, fertile femaleness, the lilac bloom betokens humility and the joy of youth —appropriate to the modest companionship of boys. The willow, of course, figures forth mourning, the blight that cannot be removed as long as hearth and home continue; while the lilac bush means joy, the rapture which arises when both have become dust. The gift book for Mrs. Melville, who in its code is called "Winnifred" (which means, appropriately enough "White Phantom"!), is entitled *Weeds and Wildings, with a Rose or Two.* What tender meanings roses had for Melville, we know from his portrait of that rosy and beloved boy Billy Budd; but Mrs. Melville, it is interesting to note, suffered from rose fever!

I I

Though the myth of Rip Van Winkle embodies the sketch of an alternative to married life, in Irving's version, the mountain spree is tucked away in a few lines, Rip plunged unceremoniously into his Big Sleep—as if to suggest that the escape from the shrew can only be dreamed, not lived. Even on a more serious level, some American writers follow his lead, making not the search for an erotic substitute but the simple failure of married love their essential theme. Hawthorne, for instance, peoples his tales, as we have already seen, with a succession of Wakefieldian "outcasts," capable only of beholding love but not of sharing it. Disconcertingly, he offers such impotent Peeping Toms as prototypes of the American artist.

The metaphor of the trapped spectator is a kindlier one than that of the Peeping Tom, but it describes the same kind of peripheral observer, who is reborn in the form of James's Lambert Strether in *The Ambassadors*. Though the remote original of his character was William Dean Howells, James refused in the end to make him an artist, even a *poète manqué* like Coverdale. "I can't make him a novelist—too like W.D.H.," he wrote to himself. ". . . But I want him 'intellectual' . . . fine, clever, literary almost: it deepens the irony, the tragedy. The Editor of a Magazine—that would come nearest. . . ." A good deal of Howells remains, nonetheless, and even a judgment on Howells; for the "happy ending" of *The Ambassadors* is one of the saddest in all our literature, leaving us with the heartbreaking image of Strether as the man who *sees* everything but can do nothing, understands everything but can possess nothing.

James is not quite candid, however, insisting that Strether's choice of impotence is a willed, a moral act, and that his very voyeurism is insight and "vision." Miss Gostrey, however, is not deceived. When she asks Strether quite directly whether he will not remain in Europe, not take his reward, not, in effect, take her— Strether answers that to be right he must "not, not out of the whole affair . . . have got anything" for himself except "wonderful impressions," which is to say, thrilling peeps into reality. "It's you

who would make me wrong," he tells Maria Gostrey; but she protests, "It isn't so much your *being* 'right'—it's your horrible sharp
eye for what makes you so." But Strether is really nothing but that
"horrible sharp eye," which is his sole organ of morality; and, in
this sense at least, he is his own author: less Howells than Henry
James who began with "pedestrian gaping" along Broadway, and
remained always the big-eyed child, imagining "the probable taste
of the bright compound wistfully watched in the confectioner's
window, unattainable, impossible. . . ." It is this James who invents the technique of the "center of consciousness," i.e., a device
for making the peeper the focus of a work of art, and who insists
that "art deals with what we see." It is only in the work of art
that James, like Coverdale before him, can possess symbolically
what in reality he cannot touch; and of his very limitations he
makes the form and substance of his fiction, which is not, as he
liked to boast, "felt life" so much as *"seen* life."

For all his subtlety and tact, James is basically, hopelessly innocent, an innocent voyeur, which is to say, a child! And he is, indeed, the first novelist to do in full consciousness what Twain in
Huckleberry Finn did just once unawares: present the complexities
of adult experience as perceived by a pre-adolescent mind. The
child character, made compulsory in our books by the restrictions
of gentility and the fear of sex, is first used in *What Maisie Knew*
to confront rather than evade experience. James's novel, like the
later books which follow its pattern, is a kind of initiation story,
though it deals not with a full-scale initiation from innocence to
maturity but with a quasi initiation that ends in a withdrawal. In
the Jamesian version of the Fall of Man, at any rate, there are four
actors, not three: the man, the woman, the serpent, and the child,
presumably watching from behind the tree.

The Peeping Child is only a junior version of the Peeping Tom
as pallid poet or aging editor of a magazine; but it has had a special appeal to the American imagination. In *What Maisie Knew,*
James not only invents the fable, but sets the technique for presenting it; and, indeed, the vicarious ocular initiation presupposes the
convention of controlled point of view. Once James has shown
how to do it, novelist after novelist sets himself to portraying the
corrupt world as reflected in the innocent eye. Eye to the crack in
the door, ear attuned from the bed where he presumably sleeps—
curious or at idle play, the innocent observer stumbles upon the

murderer bent over the corpse, the guilty lovers in each other's arms, the idolized jockey in a whorehouse, a slattern on his knee, and, like the boy in Sherwood Anderson's story, is left, crying, "What did he do it for? I want to know why."

The end of innocence via the ocular initiation is bafflement and nausea; beyond the cry of the kid at the window, it is hard to imagine a real acceptance of adult life and sexuality, hard to conceive of anything but continuing flight or self-destruction. This many American writers besides Anderson see quite clearly; Faulkner, for instance, presents a similar insight, though with a brutality and terror beside which Anderson's sentimentality is revealed in all its inadequacy. Quentin Compson, who has watched as a child an adult drama of passion and death in "That Evening Sun Go Down," relives it as an adolescent witness and peripheral actor in *The Sound and the Fury* and *Absalom, Absalom!;* then dies by his own hand on the verge of manhood, refusing to step over the mystic barrier of twenty-one. Joe Christmas, in *Light in August,* on the other hand, manages to reach the age of Christ at the crucifixion, even after his induction into nausea at the age of five. But at fourteen, he cruelly kicks the naked black girl upon whom he might have lost his virginity; and at thirty-three, decapitates the aging woman who has made him her lover, thus assuring his own eventual lynching. Impotence and sadist aggression, suicide direct or indirect; it is not only to Faulkner that these seem the choices for an American whose imagination is fixed forever on one of the two major crises of pre-adolescent emotional life. Yet it is around these crises that our literature compulsively circles: the stumbling on the primal scene, mother and father caught in the sexual act (or less dramatically, the inference of that scene from creaking springs and ambiguous cries); or the discovery of heterosexual "treachery" on the part of some crush, idolized in innocent homosexual adoration.

In our time, the subterfuges which have traditionally concealed from author and audience alike the true nature of the castrated peeper are no longer necessary. By 1926, it was possible for Hemingway in *The Sun Also Rises* (and thirty years later, even a movie version could make the point unequivocally—though not without some show of daring) to portray an emasculated Jake Barnes, all of whose desperate clutching of Brett creates between them a friction which only erodes, never sparks to life. To be sure, Hemingway tells us that it is "the War" which has afflicted

Jake with the absurd wound which he examines in the mirror of his lonely room; but "the War" is merely a convenient tag for the failure of values and faith which converted a generation of young American writers to self-hatred, bravado, and expatriation. The same forces, at any rate, which have "emancipated" Brett have unmanned Jake; forced him into the role not only of witness to Brett's love affairs, but of pimp as well—setter-up of scenes which, beheld or imagined, can only drive him to queasy despair. From the time of Hemingway, impotence has been a central symbol in our fiction, a felt clue to the quality of American life, erotic and spiritual.

Faulkner, who is Hemingway's contemporary and admirer, has exploited the same theme, conceiving as eunuchs both Flem Snopes, symbol of the new bourgeoisie, the sterile lover of money, and Popeye, the spawn of urban alleys, Prohibition, and the hysteria of the Great Depression. The self-pity, which in Hawthorne, James, and even Hemingway has softened the horror of the portrait of the American as impotent voyeur, the insistence that, for better or worse, he is an intellectual, "one of us"— disappears in *Sanctuary*. The dreadfully intelligent eye of Strether has become the absurd and moronic stare which the name Popeye implies; and it looks not out of the face of a gentleman, but from the rat's face (when he watches her in the barn, Popeye seems to Temple one of the smaller rodents) of a killer. He is the ultimate, as he is the most revolting, avatar of the desexed seducer, but he is also a terrible caricature of the child witness, not like Peter Pan one who chooses not to grow up, but one who cannot. "And he will never be a man properly speaking," a doctor says of Popeye when he is five, ". . . he will never be any older than he is now."

When Popeye leans over the bed in Madame Reba's whorehouse, watching Temple Drake perform the act of darkness of which he is incapable ("the two of them would be nekkid as two snakes, and Popeye hanging over the foot of the bed without even his hat off, making a kind of whinnying sound"), he is projecting a brutal travesty of the American artist, helpless and fascinated before the fact of genital love. Similarly, in that other central "love" scene, in which Popeye rapes Temple with the corncob, Faulkner is parodying his own blasphemy of the Pale Protestant Virgin—portraying the hysterical masculine protest of his time in the image of the maimed male, revenging himself on

woman who has maimed him with the first instrument that comes
to hand, a weapon in place of the phallus.

But he is revealing, too, the secret of the descendants of
Natty Bumppo in popular literature: those cowboys, for instance,
who ride off into the sunset leaving the girls they have rescued
behind; and they have been postulated as virile without sexuality,
their only weapons (like Popeye's) in their hands, for only thus
can they be imagined as representing the innocence of the West.
The taboo that separates them from the women they preserve is
so unself-consciously accepted, so widely known, that a television
comedian can set the nation to laughing with a quip about the
unconventional cowboy who insisted on kissing the girl in the
last scene and was trampled to death by his jealous horse.

But just as Natty became with the westward expansion a cow-
puncher, with the retreat from the frontier, he was urbanized into
the image of the private detective, called—in the language of that
literature itself—the "private eye," the peeper institutionalized at
last. Through the corrupt city, the innocent tough guy who finally
sees all, though he is slugged, doped, sapped, shot at, and bribed
on the way to his vision, moves on an immaculate journey. The
undraped daughters of the rich, tight-breasted virgins and nymphomaniac night-club entertainers, tempt him with their proffered
bodies; but he is faithful only to his buddies, and like Lambert
Strether, to "what is right."

In a typical gesture, the shamus of *The Maltese Falcon* (1930)
sends the sexually attractive woman who loves him off to jail; but
even this rejection is finally not decisive enough. From Dashiell
Hammett, the private eye is passed on to Raymond Chandler and
from him to Mickey Spillane, who recreates him at last for the
ultimate audience—the readers of pocket-books, who put down
their quarters in millions in search of myths more appropriate
to their lives than those of high literature. In Spillane's Mike
Hammer, Faulkner's Popeye is reborn as a culture hero, a
chevalier of the city streets, blasting down the female he never
manages quite to possess, and who, dead in one book, rises up
in the next, phallic and aggressive, deadly whether clothed or
nude. "She was a beautiful evil goddess with a gun in her hand,"
he writes in *The Big Kill* of Marsha, who lies dead a moment
later, shot by the kid she has spurned and wounded: "the tongue
of flame that blasted from the muzzle seemed to lick out across
the room with a horrible vengeance that ripped all evil from her

face, turning it into a ghastly wet red mask that was really no face at all." The climax of *Vengeance Is Mine,* however, is really more satisfactory, since it is Mike Hammer himself who does the shooting, and he blasts not the face of the goddess but the naked body of a luscious blonde, making the only penetration possible to the cripple of love with the slug of a .45.

III

When the Hawthorne-James-Faulkner gambit is refused and the American writer does not make impotence itself his subject, he is left to choose between the two archetypes of innocent homosexuality and unconsummated incest: the love of comrades and that of brother and sister. From his trip to Europe, undertaken just after he had finished *Moby Dick,* Melville brought back with him not only the oleograph reproduction of Guido Reni's "Beatrice Cenci" mentioned earlier but also a life-long memory of the relief sculpture of Antinoüs, favorite boy of the Emperor Hadrian, a work of art ("head like moss-rose with curls and buds —rest all simplicity") then on display in the Villa Albani. He returned, that is to say, from his cultural pilgrimage with an icon of incest justified and of homosexuality glorified, in memory of which it is perhaps fair to call the themes we have been describing the Antinoüs archetype and the Cenci archetype.

Both themes are juvenile and regressive, that is, narcissistic; for where woman is felt to be a feared and forbidden other, the only legitimate beloved is the self. Pure narcissism cannot, however, provide the dream and tension proper to a novel; the mirror-image of the self is translated in the American novel either into the flesh of one's flesh, the sister as *anima;* or into the comrade of one's own sex, the buddy as *anima.* Certainly, Melville's greatest work is essentially an account, as he himself hints, of "Narcissus, who because he could not grasp the tormenting, mild image he saw in the fountain, plunged into it and was drowned": but the alter ego of Narcissus-Ishmael is projected as the Polynesian cannibal, Queequeg, in whom the seeker in quest of his own "tormenting, mild image" finds a genuine other. Marriage to a woman would have seemed to Melville's hero intolerable; only through a pure wedding of male to male could he project an engagement with life which did not betray the self.

This is an alternative deeply appealing to the American mind and essentially congenial to the American experience. If one considers the series of distinguished fictions which begins with Cooper's Leatherstocking Tales and passes through Poe's *Narrative of A. Gordon Pym* (as well as his abortive *Journal of Julius Rodman*), Dana's *Two Years Before the Mast,* Melville's whole body of work culminating in *Moby Dick,* Twain's *Huckleberry Finn* and Henry James's "The Great Good Place," and is refurbished in our own time in such works as Faulkner's "The Bear" as well as Hemingway's *The Sun Also Rises* and *The Old Man and the Sea,* it is evident that there is an archetype at work, a model story, appearing and reappearing in a score of guises, haunting almost all our major writers of fiction.

What is hard to understand at first is why middle-class readers were not appalled at the implications of the homoerotic* fable, opposed as it is to almost everything in which middle-class society pretends to believe. Only by assuming an unconscious marginal rejection of the values of that society on the part of all or most of its members can we come to terms with its glorification of a long line of heroes in flight from woman and home. Cooper's Natty flees the settlements and the prospect of marriage with squaw or pale-face maiden; Melville's Ishmael rejects his cruel stepmother and the whole world of security she represents; Poe's Gordon Pym deceives and defies his family to go to sea; Twain's Huck evades all the women who try, with rigor or gentleness, to redeem his orphaned state; James's Dane flees from his social commitments to ladies and ladies' luncheons. None of these protagonists, moreover, manages to disown all female ties without seeming to reject life itself. "Whenever it is a damp, drizzly November in my soul," Ishmael remarks, "then, I account it high time to get to sea as soon as I can. This is my substitute for pistol and ball. With a philosophical flourish Cato throws himself upon his sword; I quietly take to ship."

Yet for a man to love death is not nearly so suspect in bourgeois America as for him to love another man; and in all the classic American books we have been examining, there are hints of such

---

* "Homoerotic" is a word of which I was never very fond, and which I like even less now. But I wanted it to be quite clear that I was not attributing sodomy to certain literary characters or their authors, and so I avoided when I could the more disturbing word "homosexual." All my care has done little good, however, since what I have to say on this score has been at once the best remembered and most grossly misunderstood section of my book. *Ubi morbus, ibi digitus.*

a love: in some, buried deep beneath the ken of the authors themselves, in others moving just beneath a transparent surface. How could Antinoüs come to preside over the literature of the nineteenth-century United States, which is to say, at a time and in a place where homosexuality was regarded with a horror perhaps unmatched elsewhere and ever? Certainly, in the popular literature of the period, the "sissy," the effeminate boy, nearest thing to a fairy mentionable in polite books, was a target upon which the fury of a self-conscious masculinity vented itself with especial venom. In the long run, however, so violent a disavowal of male inversion fostered an ignorance of its true nature; the "sin" or "crime" of homosexuality was conceived only in the grossest physical terms, so that a love as abstract and unconsummated as Dante's for Beatrice (or Shakespeare's for his aristocratic boy!) seemed unexceptionable to the most genteel. Mothers, indeed, rejoiced at "harmless" romantic attachments between their sons, conceiving of them as protections against the lure of the flesh, which might lead to venereal diseases or the impregnation of quite undesirable lower-class girls. Even in the minds of women, that is to say, "evil love" could only be conceived of in connection with "evil women," and the relations of males seemed therefore healthy by definition. Indeed, to this very day, anyone who suggests that such relations are occasionally at least ambiguous is regarded as a disturber of the peace, a public enemy.

In our native mythology, the tie between male and male is not only considered innocent, it is taken for the very symbol of innocence itself; * for it is imagined as the only institutional bond in a paradisal world in which there are no (heterosexual) marriages or giving in marriage. Paradisal, however, means for hardheaded Americans not quite real; and there is, in fact, a certain sense of make-believe in almost all portrayals of the holy mar-

---

* Things have changed radically in this regard, however. When the traditional sentimental relationship of white man and colored is evoked these days, it is likely to be quite the opposite of innocent, as the following passage from James Purdy's *Cabot Wright Begins* spectacularly indicates: "Taking Winters Hart's left hand in his, Bernie held his friend's dark finger on which he wore a wedding-ring, and pressed the finger and the hand. Far from being annoyed at this liberty, Winters Hart was, to tell the truth, relieved and pleased. Isolation in a racial democracy, as he was to tell Bernie later that night, as they lay in Bernie's bed together, isolation, no thank you."

riage of males, set as they typically are in the past, the wilderness, or at sea—that is to say, in worlds familiar to most readers in dreams. After Mark Twain, one of the partners to such a union is typically conceived of as a child, thus inviting the reader to identify the Great Good Place where the union is consummated with his own childhood, a region more remote and less real to the grown man than the dimmest reaches of pre-history. It is Stephen Crane who finds the proper name for that Neverland, calling it "Whilomville," which is to say a town which never had an "is" but only a half-recalled, half-invented "was." Everywhere in our classic fiction—in Cooper's use of the historical past, in Melville's evocation of his own receding youth, in Twain's or Faulkner's reversion to a rural boyhood, there is implicit a suggestion that the Edenic affair is lived out in a Garden in the process of being destroyed. The sound of axes is heard; the trees fall; the ground is broken for factories and stores; and the reader feels that he is being asked to recreate in fantasy a place to which neither he nor the author can ever return—the "home" to which the American writer complains he cannot go back again.

In our classic fiction, the heroes of such attempts at evasion are shown, at their stories' close, remanded to the world of reality. Ishmael, "alone escaped alive," comes back to tell his tale, Gordon Pym to write down his authentic account of adventure, Huck Finn to take another whirl at being civilized. Though he is already speaking of his next escape, even the motherless boy is last presented at the moment of his restitution to the society of women. Henry James, too sophisticated to equivocate about the reality of the Great Good Place, portrays his hero as awaking from a simple dream, from a twelve-hour sleep. Natty alone is never portrayed outside the universe of fantasy; pursuing the elusive West to the very end, he makes of his death the ultimate escape, for which his later avatars yearn but which they can never seem quite to attain. Those others act out not a permanent removal from the society which irks them, but an outing, a long excursion. Tom Sawyer's career as a pirate parodies the dream to which his author subscribed, gives the whole game away: the vows of eternal alienation and the message to Aunt Polly concealed in a pocket all the time: "We ain't dead—we are only off being pirates."

Perhaps it is this sense of make-believe which redeems so

subversive a theme for the most genteel and diffident reader. It represents a projection, entertained *without final faith,* of a way of life hostile to the accepted standards of the American community: a counter-family that can only flourish in a world without women or churches or decency or hard work, living what one is tempted to call "life with father," or, more precisely, "life with foster-father." Such terms seem to hold up well enough, superficially at least, in describing the erotic tie at the heart of *Huckleberry Finn,* for instance, or those in fictions like Faulkner's "The Bear" and *Intruder in the Dust,* as well as in certain stories by Stephen Crane and Sherwood Anderson. In these fictions, a small boy is represented as turning to a colored foster-father in revulsion from a real father, felt as brutal or ineffectual or effete; or he is portrayed as seeking out the dark-skinned, outcast male in an attempt to escape the mothers of his world, who are wholly committed to respectable codes of piety and success.

Such a reading, however, only seems satisfactory if we set a book like Mark Twain's in the context of a popular tradition which falsifies him even as it derives from him: the vulgarized juvenile, which descends by way of Stephen Crane's *Whilomville Stories* to the heavy-handed cuteness of Booth Tarkington's *Penrod.* In that middlebrow line of descent, the filial relationship of Negro and child is transformed into the stereotype which William Lyon Phelps describes condescendingly in a foreword to Crane's tales of childhood: "Little children and big Africans make ideal companions, for the latter have the patience, inner sympathy, forbearance, and unfailing good humor necessary to such an association. Both Stephen Crane and Booth Tarkington have given us permanent drawings in black and white." Twain's treatment of Jim in *Huckleberry Finn* is, however, complex enough to preserve him from becoming a merely stereotypical darkie; and that very complexity makes it impossible to describe him as just a substitute father. Sometimes he seems more servant than father, sometimes more lover than servant, sometimes more mother than either! His relationship with Huck must be seen not against the later sentimental tradition of "little children and big Africans," but against an earlier tradition of more nearly coeval loving pairs like Natty and Chingachgook, Gordon Pym and Dirk Peters, Ishmael and Queequeg. In Jim, Huck finds the pure affection offered by Mary Jane without the threat of marriage; the escape from social obligations offered

by Pap without the threat of beatings; the protection and pet-
ting offered by his volunteer foster-mothers without the threat
of pious conformity; the male companionship offered by the
Grangerfords without the threat of the combat of honor; the
friendship offered by Tom without the everlasting rhetoric and
make-believe. Jim is all things to him: father and mother and
playmate and beloved, appearing naked and begowned and be-
whiskered and painted blue, and calling Huck by the names
appropriate to their multiform relationship: "Huck" or "honey"
or "chile" or "boss," and just once "white genlman."

It is an impossible society which they constitute, the outcast
boy and the Negro, who, even for Huck, does not really exist
as a person: a society in which, momentarily, the irreparable
breach between black and white seems healed by love. Huck,
who offends no one else, begins by playing in Tom's company
a stupid joke on the sleeping Jim; then almost kills him as the
result of another heartless stunt; teases him to the point of tears
about the reality of their perils on the river; and finally joins
with Tom once more to inflict on Jim a hundred pointless torments, even putting his life in unnecessary danger. And through
it all, Jim plays the role of Uncle Tom, enduring everything,
suffering everything, forgiving everything—finally risking a lynching to save "Marse Tom's" life. It is the Southerner's dream,
the American dream of guilt remitted by the abused Negro, who,
like the abused mother, opens his arms crying, "Lawsy, I's
mighty glad to git you back agin, honey."

Only on the unstable surface of the river and in the dark of
night, can such a relationship exist, and its proper home is the
raft, which floats on the surge of flood-time into the story, a gift
from the non-Christian powers of Nature. "There warn't no home
like a raft, after all . . . ," Huck reflects. "You feel mighty free
and easy and comfortable on a raft." But the very essence of life
on a raft is unreality. "The motion of the raft is gentle, and
gliding, and smooth, and noiseless . . . ," Twain writes in *A Tramp
Abroad;* "under its restful influence . . . existence becomes a
dream . . . a deep and tranquil ecstasy." Yet the dream of life
on the river always threatens to turn for Twain into a nightmare.
In 1906, he comments on a recurring dream in which he was once
more piloting a boat down the Mississippi:

It is never a pleasant dream, either. I love to think about those
days, but there's always something sickening about the thought

. . . and usually in my dream I am just about to start into a
black shadow without being able to tell whether it is Selma
Bluff, or Hat Island, or just a black wall of night.

The idyll of Huck and Jim is a dream at whose heart lurks a
nightmare. All about them on the lawless river, crime is plotted
and violence done, while the river itself is ever ready to mislead
and destroy with fog or storm or snag. Thieves and murderers
seek the same avenue of escape which Huck and Jim follow in
domestic peace. And at last, in the persons of the Duke and
Dauphin, the evil of river life invades the raft itself. The floating
island paradise becomes an occupied country, a place where
absurd and sodden scoundrels hatch deceit and seek to avoid
retribution. There is no way to escape evil forever, no absolute
raft; and once the home of Huck and Jim has been invaded, they
cannot manage to establish their little Eden again. For a moment
after the fiasco at the Wilks', it seems as if Huck and Jim are
about to recapture their first freedom: "it *did* seem so good to be
free again and all by ourselves on the big river, and nobody to
bother us." But the King and Duke appear at the last minute, and
Huck collapses into despair: "it was all I could do to keep from
crying."

If one moves from a literal to a symbolic level, the difficulties
involved in reading Jim and Huck as father and son become even
greater. It is hard to think of a figure, union with whom signifies
a coming to terms with the natural and impulsive, as finally
paternal; much more suitable is the metaphor of the spouse. Only
marriage is a relationship complicated enough to stand for so
complicated and ambiguous a cluster of meanings; the search for
a parent, a master, a slave, an equal, a companion, a soul—a
union with one's deepest self which is simultaneously a rejection
of the community to which one was born. This Melville, at least,
most canny and conscious of all exploiters of this common theme,
realized with great clarity, working out the metaphor of the holy
marriage in great detail in the pages of *Moby Dick,* to which we
must turn for clues to what elsewhere remains confusing and
confused.

Three elements are necessary for the *hierogamos:* the longed-
for spouse, the questing lover, and the sacred setting. The setting,
though it is, of course, only another projection of the world of

instinct represented by the desired spouse, is of great symbolic importance. It is an Eden, to be sure, which is to say, a place out of time and history, as well as beyond the bounds of society; but it is a natural Eden, nature as Eden. Only in the mind of Henry James is that Great Good Place portrayed as an ordered and cultivated garden, though even for him it provides a vantage point from which one can look out "over a long valley to a far horizon," like some "old Italian picture." More typically, it is portrayed as a camp-site in the wilderness, a raft floating down the river, an isolated valley on a South Sea island, a lonely wood sought as a refuge from combat, a ship on the open sea. What it cannot be is city or village, hearth or home; for isolation is the key, the non-presence of the customary—in the words of Henry James, "the absence of what he didn't want." And what "he" especially does not want is *women!*

In America, the earthly paradise for men only is associated, for obvious historical reasons, with the "West"; and it is possible to regard the classic works which he have been discussing, in this sense, as "Westerns." Despite certain superficial differences, they are, indeed, all closely related to the pulp stories, the comic-books, movies, and TV shows, in which the cowhand and his side-kick ride in silent communion through a wilderness of sagebrush, rocks, and tumbleweed. The Western, understood in this way, does not even require an American setting, being reborn, for instance, in Hemingway's *The Sun Also Rises* in the improbable environs of Paris and Burguete. One must not be confused by the exotica of expatriation: bullfights, French whores, and *thés dansants*. Like the American East, Paris in Hemingway's book stands for the world of women and work, for "civilization" with all its moral complexity, and it is presided over quite properly by the bitch-goddess Brett Ashley. The mountains of Spain, on the other hand, represent the West: a world of male companions and sport, an anti-civilization, simple and joyous, whose presiding genius is that scarcely articulate arch-buddy, "good, old Bill."

For Hemingway there are many Wests, from Switzerland to Africa; but the mountains of Spain are inextricably associated in his mind with the authentic American West, with Montana whose very name is the Spanish word for the mountains that make of both isolated fastnesses holy places. It is in the Hotel Montana that Lady Ashley ends up after her abortive romance with the bullfighter Romero; and it is from the University of Montana that

Robert Jordan, hero of *For Whom the Bell Tolls,* takes off to the Spanish Civil War. But it is not only a pun that binds together for Hemingway his two paradisal retreats; it is also the sacred sport of fishing. Though the monastery of Roncesvalles stands on a peak high above Jake's place of refuge, it serves only to remind Hemingway's characters of a religion now lapsed for them. "It's a remarkable place," one of them says of the monastery; but Bill, the good companion, observes mournfully, "It isn't the same as fishing, is it?"

It is in the trout stream of Burguete that Jake and Bill immerse themselves and are made whole again and clean; for that stream links back to the rivers of Hemingway's youth, the rivers of upper Michigan, whose mythical source is the Mississippi of Tom Sawyer and Huck Finn. "We stayed five days at Burguete and had good fishing. The nights were cold and the days were hot. . . . It was hot enough so that it felt good to wade in the cold stream, and the sun dried you when you came out. . . ." They are boys again, back on Jackson's Island, which is to say, safe in the Neverland of men without women. Jake is, in his quest for the Great Good Place, at one with almost all the other heroes of Hemingway; though somehow it is he who has managed to find again the magical stream of which the wounded, half-mad *tenente* in "Now I Lay Me" can only dream: "I would think of a trout stream I had fished along when I was a boy and fish its whole length carefully in my mind. . . . But some nights I could not fish, and on those nights I was cold-awake and said my prayers over and over. . . ."

In the double-barreled story, "Big Two-Hearted River," it is impossible to tell whether the hero (called Nick this time) is moving through reality or fantasy. We can know only that he has returned, or dreams he has returned, once more to the River that is always different and always the same; and that this time he fishes it inch by inch to the edge of the tragic swamp which he will not enter. This time there is no question of choosing between fishing and praying; fishing has become clearly a prayer, or at least a ritual, in the midst of which a disguised prayer is uttered in the guise of a childish epithet. "Chrise," Nick says at one point, when he knows he is at last really *there,* "Geezus Chrise," and Hemingway tells us he says it "happily." In the dreams of the River both in "Now I Lay Me" and "Big Two-Hearted River," however, the Hemingway hero imagines himself alone; in *The Sun Also Rises,* a second self is with him, a companion to share the inarticulate sentimentality that becomes finally too embarrassing to bear, bursting with pure masculine love. " 'Old Bill' I said. 'You bum!' " And when the time for parting comes, when the bluff, immaculate honeymoon is over, when the telegram arrives to announce that the outsiders are coming, Brett and Cohen, woman and Jew, it is a third fisherman, an Englishman called Harris, who blurts out in his drunkenness what neither Jake nor Bill can quite confess: "I've not had so much fun since the war. . . . We *have* had a good time."

What Hemingway's emphasis on the ritual murder of fish conceals is that it is not so much the sport as the occasion for immersion which is essential to the holy marriage of males. Water is the symbol of the barrier between the Great Good Place and the busy world of women; and everywhere in our fiction, the masculine paradise is laved by great rivers or the vast ocean, washed by the ripples of Lake Glimmerglass or the spume of Glens Falls, even— in Poe—drowned, swallowed up in a liquid white avalanche: "and now we rushed into the embraces of the cataract, where a chasm threw itself open to receive us." Not only in chronicles of shipwreck like *Gordon Pym* or *Moby Dick,* but even in so mild an account of masculine evasion as James's "The Great Good Place," the metaphor of a descent into the waters prevails; though to be sure, in the case of James we are reminded of the bathtub or hydrotherapy rather than a plunge into the maelstrom: "He didn't want, for a time, anything but just to *be* there, to steep in the bath. He was in the bath yet, the broad deep bath of stillness. They sat in it together now with the water up to their chins. . . . He had been sunk that way before, sunk . . . in another flood. . . . *This* was a curtain so slow and tepid that one floated practically without motion and without chill."

To descend into the charmed waters where one can float "practically without motion" is, in effect, to die; and the flight to the watery world is a kind of suicide, a quietus self-imposed. Melville, in whom much that is elsewhere implicit is made explicit, makes it clear that the land is the realm of the super-ego, the water that of the id; and he at least does not hesitate long between them. Like Bulkington, the supernumerary hero of *Moby Dick,* he turns his own back on the "leeward land": "The port would fain give succor; the port is pitiful; in the port is safety, comfort, hearthstone, supper, warm blankets, friends, all that's kind to our mortalities. . . . But in landlessness alone resides the highest truth, shoreless, indefinite as God—so better is it to perish in that howling infinite, than to be ingloriously dashed upon the lee, even if it were safety."

Better death than castration, articulate Melville cries; but he does not foresee death as inevitable for the man who plunges into the "all-subduing" element, the shoreless wastes of his own unconsciousness. What seems a suicide may be in the end a baptism and a transfiguration, an immersion and a resurrection. "Take heart, take heart, O Bulkington . . . ," Melville writes at the close of the "six-inch chapter" which he calls Bulkington's "stoneless grave"; "Up from the spray of thy ocean-perishing—straight up, leaps thy apotheosis!" So (in gentle parody) Tom Sawyer is resurrected after "drowning," while Huck, presumably slaughtered like a pig, takes the plunge and lives again; so Ishmael, drawn into the ocean whirlpool, or Gordon Pym, sucked into the chasm beneath the cataract, emerge unscathed to write gospel accounts of their survival. The picnic, the day's outing from which the male fugitive returns, is also a watery grave; and though, like the Ancient Mariner, the survivor lives on chiefly to tell his tale, he returns purged and guiltless.

In fact, only he is guiltless in our world; for—our classical novelists believe with Shakespeare—no man born of woman is innocent enough to combat evil without being converted into its image. Each must be born again, the second time not of the murky flood of blood, amniotic fluid, and milk which characterizes female gestation, but out of the immaculate flux of waters which characterizes a birth into the world of men without women. A new birth implies a new family, a wifeless and motherless one, in which the good companion is the spouse and nurse, the redeemed male the lover and child, each his own progenitor and offspring. The disgust of the American male at our original birth is most clearly and passionately expressed in Melville's sketch called "The Tartarus of Maids." In this extraordinary piece, Melville describes the processes of natural gestation (to him a mechanical and brutal function) from inside, as it were—in terms of a guided tour through a paper mill. Proceeding from a "large bespattered place, with two great round vats in it, full of a wet, weedy-looking stuff, not unlike the albuminous part of an egg" into a "room, stifling with a strange, blood-like, abdominal heat," he beholds at last the end product of a process which takes "nine minutes to the second": "suddenly, I saw a sort of paper-fall, not wholly unlike a water-fall; a scissory sound smote my ears, as of some cord being snapped; and down dropped an unfolded sheet of perfect foolscap, with my 'Cupid' half faded out of it, and still moist and warm . . . here was the end of the machine." To convert into "royal sheets" the "imperfect foolscap" produced by a female machine, which is powered by the fall of "Blood River" through what Melville calls the "Black Notch," is no easy task. They must either be reimmersed, as we have seen, in the waters of life which seem those of death, or else be dipped into an altogether alien bloodstream.

The alternative to immersion and rebirth is the baptism in the blood of a beast. Quite often, indeed, the holy marriage is sanctified by the ritual killing of a totem, the ram offered in the place of Isaac; though in the American version of the fable of sacrifice it is Isaac who kills the beast, becomes his own father at the moment of killing him, while the colored mother-midwife-beloved stands by as witness. From Natty Bumppo's first deer to the buck whose shooting by young Ike McCaslin is described in Faulkner's "Delta Autumn," such doomed animals play a leading role in American fiction. When Ike is smeared with the blood of his victim by Sam Fathers, half-Indian, half-Negro ("and Sam dipped his hands into the hot blood and marked his face forever while he stood trying not to tremble"), even the scarcely literate can understand the ritual that is being performed. Indeed, with the expulsion of sex from polite novels and the consequent demotion of the hero to childhood, such outdoor stories became a staple of middlebrow literature. In the forest rather than brothel or bedroom, through murder rather than sex, the child enters manhood, trembles with nausea over the broken bird or lifeless rabbit rather than the spread-eagled whore.

In our more serious fictions, from *Moby Dick* to Faulkner's "The Bear" or Hemingway's *The Old Man and the Sea,* such tales are redeemed from sentimentality by making of the animals involved not mere occasions for the loss of virginity but monstrous embodiments of the natural world in all its ambiguous and indestructible essence. Either, like Moby Dick, such totemic beasts are ubiquitous and immortal; or, like Big Ben, the bear of Faulkner's story, they cannot be destroyed until "the last day"; or, like the giant swordfish of *The Old Man and the Sea,* they cannot be brought back as trophies. They are sacred embodiments of power, taboo objects whose death is a blasphemy if it it not a rite. Behind all such tales echoes the reproach of God to Job: "Canst thou catch Leviathan with a hook!" and their guilt-ridden protagonists regret the violence they enact even as they enact it. It is the boast of the young Isaac McCaslin and his hunting companions that they go to the woods once a year "not to hunt bear and deer but to keep yearly rendezvous with the bear which they did not even intend to kill." Yet *finally* the bear dies as lesser bears have died before him, the whale is harpooned and stripped, the swordfish mounted above the fireplace, and (as was foretold) the innocent world ends; for Ishmael and Ike McCaslin live, after all, in America, where the way is opened for the rape of nature by the pioneers who come to it in love and in search of communion. At any moment, the pure huntsman may find himself transformed into his anti-image, the Faustian man—Captain Ahab, who thrusts at the unfallen world not in reverence but in rage.

But worse is yet to come—for after the tragic betrayal, the comic anti-climax follows fast. Natty Bumppo gives way to the bounty-hunter, to Buffalo Bill; and Buffalo Bill is followed by the dude with pack animal and guide and whisky bottle, playing Indian and fleeing his wife! The real end of the flight to the forest never changes, only the equipment and the ideological justification. Like the dude who emulates him, the hero did not go out alone to encounter the spirit of the wilderness—but traveled always with a companion and guide; and like the hero, the dude still hunts some excuse to justify the ideal community of buddies isolated from the world, pursues the "primitive area," in which alone such a community can survive.

IV

But who are these good companions in their archetypal reality, as dreamed by our greatest writers rather than travestied by our poor selves?

The questing lover is, in general, a surrogate for the artist, the articulate man (Natty, grandfather of them all, is garrulous to a fault), whose tale is presented typically in the form of a first-person narrative, journal, diary, or running reminiscence: "And I only am escaped alone to tell thee." He is the artist projected as a pariah, an Ishmael—not *le grand écrivain américain,* which was, on occasion at least, as we have noticed, Cooper's conscious self-image. In Poe, for instance, Julius Rodman, the hero of his incomplete Western, is obviously intended to suggest the author; dwarfed, hypochondriac, oddly Semitic in appearance ("He was . . . not more than five feet three or four inches high . . . with legs somewhat bowed. . . . His physiognomy was of a Jewish cast . . ."), Rodman anticipates the westward trek of Lewis and Clark "urged solely by a desire to seek in the bosom of the wilderness, that peace which his peculiar disposition would not suffer him to enjoy among men."

It is Melville, however, who most consciously works out the figure of the fugitive-lover artist and gives him his generic name. In his series of portraits of the artist as outcast, he blends the Old Testament archetype of Hagar's unwanted son (Redburn is already called a "sort of Ishmael") with the figure of the taboo wanderer, about whom he had learned something during his sojourn in the islands of the South Pacific. Sometimes the rejected son is a merely comic character in Melville, a *schlemiel* with an absurd name, a ridiculous jacket, an outlandish vocabulary, and pretensions to gentility; but he is always threatening to take on tragic overtones. And often, indeed, he is mythicized into an almost divine presence, at once accursed and a source of blessing, Prometheus himself. The "I" of *Typee* is incapable of taking seriously his own godhead, but he has been renamed Tommo and started on the long road toward apotheosis; while the very title of Melville's next book, *Omoo,* is a Polynesian word for the untouchable Wanderer. In *Mardi,* the protagonist is not merely called Taji, another name for the taboo man, but is transformed into that semi-mythical figure. *Redburn* and *White Jacket,* intended potboilers, return to the comic version of the theme, qualifying its serious implications with a playful irony; but in *Moby Dick,* Ishmael takes on once again the full stature of the alienated man, though he enters the novel as a rather absurd greenhorn, apparently fitter for gags and pratfalls than the tragic illumination toward which he really moves.

Everywhere the figure of the Stranger moves through Melville's work: as the rich boy turned writer in *Pierre,* as the early avatars of the Confidence Man, as the exiled Israel Potter, as the ultimately alienated protagonist of "Bartleby the Scrivener," condemned to prison and madness and death. Snob, greenhorn, madman, *schlemiel,* god and exile: the Outsider has a score of forms in Melville's fiction, but he remains, in his various masquerades, always the artist, society's rejected son with his "splintered heart

and maddened hand . . . turned against the wolfish world." Though
Outsider, he is not alien; invariably a native white American in
Melville, he remains so as Twain's Huck and Faulkner's Ike
McCaslin and Hemingway's Nick Adams or Jake Barnes: lonelier
and lonelier in a country overrun by other stocks; "Chinese and
African and Aryan and Jew, all breed and spawn together until
no man has time to say which one is which nor cares. . . ."

Typically white and Anglo-Saxon (even Poe's Rodman turns
out really to have been "a native of England where his relatives
were of excellent standing"), the artist surrogate in the homoerotic Western is a disaffected child of the reigning race and class.
He is no late arrival, no member of a dusky or non-Aryan race
(when Saul Bellow re-imagined Huck Finn as a young Chicago
Jew in *The Adventures of Augie March,* scarcely any of his readers recognized the affiliation), but a renegade from respectability
and belongingness. He has cut himself out of the community that
bred him in a desire to embrace some alien shadow-figure symbolizing the instinctive life despised by his white, Anglo-Saxon
parents and his fated white, Anglo-Saxon wife.

But who is the alien helpmeet for him? There are various versions of the shadow-spouse in our literature, fumblings in various
directions toward the definition of a type symbolically appropriate;
but they finally cohere in a single image.

In the remote prototype of Irving, there is no single good companion but an indefinite group of European ghosts out of which
a single voice speaks the only word Rip Van Winkle hears—his
own name! In Melville, there are several attempts at portraying
the appropriate mate, from Toby, who is the narrator's companion
in the valley of the Typees, to the various avatars of Jack Chase,
the Handsome Sailor who appears in person in *White Jacket* and
who haunted Melville until the end of his life. The Sailor is represented by Bulkington in *Moby Dick* ("full six feet in height,
with noble shoulders, and a chest like a cofferdam . . ."), and
finally by Billy himself in *Billy Budd,* whose dedication recalls
in Melville's last days his first love: "To Jack Chase . . . Wherever
that great heart may now be . . ." But Billy is Jack Chase recast
in the image of Antinoüs ("head like moss-rose with curls and
buds"), so "welkin-eyed," angelic and beautiful that he threatens
to quite give away the homosexual secret he embodies. The first
Jack Chase is the idol of White Jacket, but more usually the love
which the Handsome Sailor stirs is more ambiguous, verges on

hatred and destruction. It is as if something in Melville himself, aware of what is from the conventional point of view dangerous in his yearning for his six-foot, Anglo-Saxon beauties, drove him to portray that yearning chiefly in dark parody; the relationship of Billy Budd and Claggart, who could have loved Billy "but for fate and ban."

Even outside his treatment of the Handsome Sailor theme, Melville turned on occasion to descriptions of such murderous and passionate relations between males. Steeling himself to kill his cousin and boyhood friend, thus insuring his own eventual death, Pierre cries out, "Oh Glen! Oh Fred! most fraternally do I leap to your rib-crushing hugs! Oh, how I love ye two, that yet can make me lively hate. . . ." And even the utterly hostile cohabitation of Benito Cereno and the slave Babo is an obscene parody of the intimate bond of lovers.

Melville is, of course, not alone among American writers in portraying such sinister relationships; and one of the most notable examples is to be found in the work of Hawthorne, whose own relation to Melville turned from an initial deep affection to coldness and distrust. Surely no loving tie is closer than the one established between Chillingworth and Dimmesdale in *The Scarlet Letter,* as the cuckold penetrates in icy intimacy his cuckolder's psyche. Hester, Chillingworth, and Dimmesdale stand to each other in that odd relationship which European critics call the unnatural triangle, in which two men are bound to each other through the woman they jointly possess, as they cannot "for fate and ban" possess each other.

In our own time, the unnatural triangle recurs in Saul Bellow's *The Victim* (1947), where it assumes a peculiarly American mutilated form, being, in effect, a triangle without an apex or with only a hypothetical one, which is to say, a triangle without a woman! Indeed, the whole of Bellow's work is singularly lacking in real or vivid female characters; where women are introduced, they appear as nympholeptic fantasies, peculiarly unconvincing. His true world is a world of men in boarding houses, men whose wives are ill, or have left them, or have gone off on vacation; and the deepest emotions he evokes are those which simultaneously join together and separate father and son, brother and sister, con-man and victim. This holds true throughout the body of his work, from *Dangling Man* to *Seize the Day,* and is even seen, in a bizarre context, in *Henderson the Rain King,* in which Bellow actually

returns (three times over) to the convention of the dark companion.* But in no book does the involvement of mates quivering
between poles of attraction and repulsion take on a more crucial
importance than it has in *The Victim*. Asa Leventhal, the hero
of that novel, finds his lover-enemy Kirby Allbee in his very bed,
but finds him there not with his wife but a casual whore. What
binds the two men together is not the ambivalent tie of the
cuckold and the cuckolder but of the Jew and anti-Semite. Bourgeois and bohemian, secure citizen and self-torturing bum, Semite
and Anglo-Saxon, recent immigrant and old American—they are
bound together by their manifold contrasts. Nothing renders them
more "dependent for the food of spiritual life" upon each other
than Allbee's indecent need for Jews to define his existence by
defining a difference, or Leventhal's secret hunger for a hatred
that can mark off the boundaries of his identity.

It is this realization on Bellow's part which differentiates his
book from the host of righteous, liberal tract-novels about the
problem of anti-Semitism, makes it a complex study of the deeper
levels of life, on which the erotic and political fuse into a single
passion, baffling but human. That passion is founded in a terrible
physical intimacy which Bellow renders in terms of sheer nausea.
"Leventhal . . . was so conscious of Allbee, so certain he was
being scrutinized, that he was able to see himself as if through
a strange pair of eyes: the side of his face, the palpitation of his
throat, the seams of his skin. . . . Changed in this way into his
own observer, he was able to see Allbee, too . . . the weave of
his coat, his raggedly overgrown neck . . . the color of the blood
on his ear; he could even evoke the odor of his hair and skin.
The acuteness and intimacy of it astounded him, oppressed and
intoxicated him." And when Allbee begs to touch Leventhal's
hair—that alien, wiry, Jewish hair—actually reaches out and
takes it in hand, the gesture is like a sexual assault; "He fingered

---

* With the publication of *Herzog,* Bellow has simultaneously entered
the lists of best-sellers and embraced the subject matter of popular ladies'
fiction (my best friend betrayed me with my wife); but Madeleine, the
wife, seems a nightmare projection bred by baffled malice rather than a
realized woman; and Herzog's passionate involvement with her remains,
therefore, unconvincing. The most moving and credible relationship in the
book is that between Herzog and his faithless friend, Valentine Gershbach,
who turns out to be the most vital and believable human being created in
the book. Bellow remains the laureate of such disturbing and ambiguous
encounters.

Leventhal's hair, and Leventhal found himself under his touch and felt incapable of doing anything. But then he pushed his hand away, crying 'Lay off!' " After this, there is no climax possible except the "rib-crushing hug." Leventhal, the physical spell broken, drives the shoddy parasite out of his apartment by brute force. "Allbee fell back a few steps and, seizing a heavy glass ashtray, he aimed it menacingly. . . . Leventhal made a rush at him. . . . Pinning his arms, he wheeled him around and ran him into the vestibule. . . . The door, as Leventhal jerked it open, hit Allbee in the face. He did not resist. . . ." It is the consummation: an orgasm of violence, entailing a separation.

It is a long way from *Billy Budd* to *The Victim;* and by Bellow's time the Anglo-Saxon beauty, seedy and corrupt, has become the tormentor, while his swarthy opponent has taken on the sympathetic role. Melville is not yet ready to dissolve in irony the contrast of good blonde and evil brunette; as a matter of fact, his Billy is simply the Fair Maiden translated in sex—too much the Anglo-Saxon Virgin still to represent the dangerous and forbidden Eros which the good companion must embody. A *white* anti-bride will not in the long run really do: not the Good Bad Boys who accompany Tom Sawyer to Jackson's Island or their grown-up equivalent, the "old Bill" of *The Sun Also Rises,* not certainly the "Brother" of Henry James's "The Great Good Place," "a man of his own age, tired distinguished modest kind. . . ." In *Gordon Pym,* one can watch Poe learning as he goes that the Anglo-Saxon alter ego is no fit partner in the holy marriage of males, see how he abandons Pym's white shipmate, Augustus Bernard, to clear the way for the half-breed Dirk Peters. But the prototype had already been established by Cooper in the dusky figures of the Last Mohicans, father and son.

In dreams of white men, psychologists tell us, the forbidden erotic object tends to be represented by a colored man, such a figure as the "black pagod of a fellow," the "grand sculptured bull," "so intensely black that he must needs have been . . . of the unadulterable blood of Ham" whom Melville evokes for a moment at the beginning of *Billy Budd.* So in the communal American dream of love (beneath which lurks, for all the idyllic surface, a sense of trifling with taboos), the spouse of the pariah is properly of another race, a race suppressed and denied, even as the promptings of the libido are suppressed and denied. In the

Leatherstocking Tales, the anti-wife is the dispossessed Indian; in *Gordon Pym,* the half-mad breed; in *Huckleberry Finn,* the Negro slave; in *Moby Dick,* the uprooted Polynesian (even as in *Two Years Before the Mast,* which may have given Melville his cue); in Faulkner's "The Bear," the old man, half Chickasaw and half Negro. In Sam Fathers, "son of a Negro slave and a Chickasaw chief," one meaning of the dark skin is made clear; for his coloredness is taken as an ensign of kinship with the wilderness and the beasts who inhabit it. "Because there was," Faulkner writes, "something running in Sam Fathers' veins which ran in the veins of the buck too. . . ." Edenic nature, the totem, and the dark spouse: these are three symbols for the same thing—for the primitive world which lies beyond the margins of cities and beneath the lintel of consciousness.

v

Whatever the symbolic necessities which demand that the male *hierogamos* be inter-racial as well as homoerotic, that marriage takes on, by virtue of crossing conventional color lines, a sociological significance as well as a psychological and metaphysical one.* The elopement of the good companions comes, therefore, to stand for the healing of the social conflicts which most irk us, and before which we feel most powerless and baffled. Such a sociological extension of meaning by no means cancels out but rather enriches other, more profound significances and gives to them their peculiarly American form.

There is, of course, in the European novel—and even the drama, epic, and romance which precede the emergence of that genre—a tradition of the pseudo-marriage of males, stretching from, say, Don Quixote and Sancho Panza through Leporello and Don Juan, Robinson Crusoe and Friday to Pickwick and Sam Weller. *Robinson Crusoe,* in particular, seems to embody an

---

* Recently, we have grown more and more aware of how in the Civil Rights Movement the aspirations of Negroes for full freedom and the struggle of homosexuals to be accepted are oddly intermingled. And it is no use protesting (as Ralph Ellison has done, for instance) that they should be kept separate and pure. For better or for worse, they are mythically one in our deepest imaginations, as, indeed, James Baldwin has tried to make manifest—however shrilly and ineptly—in *Another Country.*

archetype much like that which haunts our classic fiction; and this is proper enough for a novel so bourgeois and Protestant that one is tempted to think of it as an American novel before the fact. The protagonists are not only black and white, but they exist on the archetypal island, cut off from the home community by the estranging sea. Cannibal and castaway, man-eater and journal-keeper, they learn to adjust to each other and to domesticity, on what is surely the most meager and puritanic Eden in all literature.

In *Robinson Crusoe,* however, the male relationship, even after shipwreck and abandonment, is kept rigidly within the European class-patterns of master and man. Within this convention (the Shakespearean convention, one wants to call it, for it is part of the basic symbolic structure of Shakespeare's work) the advocacy of the "natural" way of life is entrusted to the servant, and by virtue of that fact, clearly identified as inferior. The servant is, by definition, a comic character, who can never be taken quite seriously, never really understood as an ideological rival to his master. He can be cowardly, greedy, and carnal without stirring anything in us but smug condescension (cf. the role of the lazy, fearful tom-catting darkie in the popular arts up to the very present); he can eat flesh on Friday or loose his bowels over his horse in a moment of terror like Sancho Panza, for *nothing is at stake.* The servant may represent the protest of the unconscious against the ego ideals for which his master stands, but there is no equivocation about their relative rank or importance. To side with Leporello against Don Juan, Caliban against Prospero is unthinkable; and even Robinson Crusoe, good bourgeois that he is, teaches Friday "master" as his first word!

In America, however, we are a nation of Calibans and Leporellos and Sancho Panzas—of "fugitive slaves." Europe is the master from which we have all fled. It is hard therefore for even the most class-conscious writer to keep his characters in their traditional places; Cooper himself, Tory-democrat that he is, proves incapable of defining Natty and Chingachgook in terms of a strict hierarchical relationship either to each other or to the "ladies and gentlemen," those supernumeraries in the plot who are presumably their betters. Melville, Twain, Faulkner, even a homemade dandy like Poe, quite frankly abandon the attempt. Who is the better man, Gordon Pym or Dirk Peters, Isaac Mc-Caslin or Sam Fathers, Huck or Nigger Jim, Ishmael or Queequeg? Though Jim is presumably a slave and calls even Huck a "young gentleman," the whole point of the work is that Jim is "free as any cretur." The rapid mobility of American social life, as well as its establishment by masterless men, makes it only too easy to conceive the relationship of instinct and ego, white and black, not as a tie between servant and master but as a marriage of equals.

Yet there are forces in our life, almost as profound and aboriginal, which work against such a concept. The Northern European white, blue-eyed stock which originally settled the United States, shabby as it was in its origins, soon set itself up as a ruling class eager to protect its hegemony and its purity, a purity especially identified with its pale, genteel women busy in schools and churches. The drama of an equal meeting and mating of Caucasian and colored men was remanded quite early to a mythical *state of nature,* or at least to the nearest equivalent of that state, the frontier, where trapper and Indian guide bedded down together. In the settlements, such equality could scarcely survive beside the facts of social organization: the Negro confined to his ghettos, the Indian harried and driven continually westward, the Polynesian sailor restricted to the waterfront city of cheap saloons and brothels.

There is an almost hysterical note to our insistence that the love of male and male does not compete with heterosexual passion but complements it; that it is not homosexuality in any crude meaning of the word, but a passionless passion, simple, utterly satisfying, yet immune to lust—physical only as a handshake is physical, this side of copulation. And yet we can never shake off the nagging awareness that there is at the sentimental center of our novels, where we are accustomed to find in their European counterparts "platonic" love or adultery, seduction, rape, or long-drawn-out flirtation, nothing but the love of males! What awaits us are the fugitive slave and the no-account boy side by side on a raft borne by the endless river toward an impossible escape; or the pariah sailor waking in the tattooed arms of the brown harpooner on the verge of some impossible quest. To emphasize the purity of such unions, the fact that they join soul to soul rather than body to body, they are typically contrasted with mere heterosexual passion, the dubious desire which threatens always to end in miscegenation. Yet, though such confrontations seem only to contrast the homoerotic and heterosexual ways of joining white and black, they suggest disconcertingly a general superiority of the love of man for man over the ignoble lust of man for woman.

It is for this reason, perhaps, that the colored rival of the wife is presented typically with the stigmata of something dangerous and disgusting as well as forbidden. Chingachgook wears a death's-head on his chest and a scalp at his belt, while Queequeg is horridly tattooed and bears with him a phallic god and shrunken head; even Jim, who possesses no particularly repulsive characteristics, makes his first appearance with his head muffled in a blanket—scaring Huck half to death—and is dyed, before the voyage is over, a sickening blue. The most monstrous of all the dark companions is Poe's hybrid Dirk Peters, who assumes in the course of Poe's description of him not only a bestial aspect but something of the appearance of a gnome or kobold, which is to say, the surviving image in the mind of *homo sapiens* of the stunted proto-men that they destroyed, the first dispossessed people, whose memory survives to haunt our fairy tales and nightmares. But the Neanderthal gnome is also the model for popular notions of "devils" or "demons," quite properly assimilated to the primordial figure that symbolizes our broken link with the animal world. For better or worse, the love-affair with the "Black Man" carries with it diabolic implications, hints of a union with infernal forces, as well as salvational overtones, promises of psychic redemption. And in *Moby Dick* Melville attempts to embody both in the two dark-skinned characters, supernumeraries in the action, who represent the polar aspects of the id, beneficent and destructive. The first is the Polynesian harpooner, Queequeg, whose relationship to Ishmael threatens to take over the entire book in its first portion; and the second is the Parsee, Fedallah, who is yoked to Ahab by a link as passionate, though quite different from that which joins the first two. The Parsee and the Polynesian are associated with two other representatives of the primitive, also harpooners, the Indian, Tashtego, and the African, Dagoo. Yellow, brown, red, and black, they seem, considered together, rather emblems than characters, signifying the four quarters of the globe and the four elements as well, for Dagoo is carefully identified with the earth, Tashtego with the air, the Parsee with fire, and Queequeg with water. Only Queequeg and Fedallah *thematically* matter, however, since they alone are used to represent the basic conflict which lies at the heart of the book, the struggle between love and death. Queequeg stands for the redemptive baptism of water (or sperm), and around him the "Western" or sentimental story which is one half of *Moby Dick* develops; while Fedallah stands for the destructive baptism of fire (or blood), and around him the gothic or Faustian romance which is its other half unfolds. But it is Queequeg who wins, though the two never meet face to face, Eros which triumphs over Thanatos.

Moby Dick can be read then not only as an account of a whale-hunt, but also as a love story, perhaps the greatest love story in our fiction, cast in the peculiar American form of innocent homosexuality. During 1851, the year in which he completed *Moby Dick,* Melville scored and underscored two passages, which he had come on in his current reading, and which must have seemed to him confirmations of his own deepest feelings. The first is from the *Maid's Tragedie* and runs:

> For aught I know, all husbands are like me;
> And every one I talk with of his wife,
> Is but a well dissembler of his woes
> As I am; would I knew it, for the rareness afflicts me now . . .

The second is picked out of the tale of David and Jonathan in Samuel II: "Thy love to me was wonderful, passing the love of women." Taken together, they define clearly enough what sort of love Melville would choose, what avoid to represent the force which conquers death; but the first indicates as well his uneasiness over his convictions, his fear that he may stand alone in preferring to the comforts of marriage the sentimental companionship of males.

In *Moby Dick,* the redemptive love of man and man is represented by the tie which binds Ishmael to Queequeg, while the commitment to death is portrayed in the link which joins Ahab to Fedallah; but the two relationships are disturbingly alike: both between males, one white and one colored. Indeed, the very darkness of Queequeg betrays a doubt about the angelic companion, oddly confuses him with the Satanic one. Melville is more conscious than he seems at first glance of the ambiguous nature of the love which he celebrates in *Moby Dick,* and which, beginning with the encounter of Ishmael and Queequeg, grows ever more general and inclusive, but never less suspect, as the story unfolds.

In Chapter XCIV, which is called "A Squeeze of the Hand," Ishmael is granted a final vision of the nature of love while he is busy with his shipmates squeezing the sperm of Stubb's whale. Though Melville is deliberately playing from the start with the double meaning of the word "sperm" (he comments on how "in old times sperm was such a favorite cosmetic," knowing well enough that it was semen not blubber which the medieval cosmeticians prized), the passage seems for a while an idyllic prose poem: "As I bathed my hands among the soft, gentle globules of infiltrated tissue . . . as they richly broke to my fingers . . . as I snuffed up that uncontaminated aroma . . . I forgot all about our horrible oath; in that inexpressible sperm, I washed my hands and heart of it. . . . I felt divinely free from all ill will or petulance or malice of any sort whatever. . . ." In sperm, that is to say, Ishmael has washed himself clean of the pledge to destroy and pursue, his implication in the blasphemous quest of Ahab; it is a counter-baptism to that of fire.

But the passage moves on to even more explicit and embarrassing erotic images, until at last (surely, not without a certain sly humor) Ishmael calls upon the whole world to perform a similar service of love: "nay, let us all squeeze ourselves into each other; let us squeeze ourselves universally into the very milk and sperm of kindness." Beyond this there is only the comic vision of the "angels in paradise, each with his hands in a jar of spermaceti," and an encyclopedic interlude, which prepares us for the following frankly phallic chapter, "The Cassock." The Cassock itself turns out to be the foreskin of the whale, and represents only the first of a series of allusions and puns, which, running through the brief chapter, play off against each other Christianity and male sexuality, the religion Melville rejected and the improbable place to which he turned in search of another.

The "unaccountable cone,—longer than a Kentuckian is tall," which is all that remains of the whale's phallus is associated in what seems a casual phrase ("and jet-black as Yojo, the ebony idol of Queequeg") with the love of Ishmael and the Polynesian harpooner. And we remember that before that image, Ishmael had salaamed twice or thrice, even kissed its nose, in the course of celebrating his holy marriage with Queequeg. The convocation of the two idolatries is deliberate, and both are identified with an even more abominable original by Ishmael's reference to what is "darkly

set forth in the fifteenth chapter of the first book of Kings." The
Biblical text to which Ishmael sends the reader deals with the rites
practiced by the wicked Queen Maachah before just such a phallic
idol, and makes a specific connection between those rites and sodomy: "And he took away the sodomites out of the land, and removed all the idols that his fathers had made." There is a certain
playful contempt in this allusion, an assumption that the reader
will not search out the reference or finding it not understand—any
more than he will understand the crude anti-ecclesiastical pun with
which the chapter ends. Ishmael has described how a section of
the whale's foreskin is made into a garment for the "mincer," who
cuts up the horse-pieces of blubber for the pots; and he stands back
admiringly to look at him: "Arrayed in decent black; occupying a
conspicuous pulpit; intent on bible leaves; what a candidate for an
archbishoprick . . . !" There is something a little childish finally
about the camouflaged anti-clerical bravado.

It will not do to sentimentalize or Christianize Melville's pagan
concept of love. It is not *caritas* which he celebrates; and his symbol for the redeeming passion is Priapus rather than the cross.
Perhaps it is least misleading to think of the love which redeems
Ishmael as Platonic, in the authentic historical sense of the word.
Rising from the particular object to the universal, it remains suspect nonetheless; for like the ideal Eros of *The Symposium,* it is
grounded in a relationship unequivally rejected by the Judaeo-
Christian tradition. Genteel or orthodox advocates of love should
look hard at Melville's text before deciding to applaud the conquest of death he celebrates in *Moby Dick.* Yet it is love in the
fullest sense which that book makes its center; not a brutal or
casual relationship, but one which develops on the pattern of a
marriage: achieving in the course of a single voyage the shape of a
whole lifetime shared, and symbolizing a spiritual education.

Ishmael, who begins as a comic character, somewhat green,
more than a little pedantic, everybody's butt, plays in the account
of his meeting with Queequeg the role of the sacred virgin. He
seems quite improbably, to have no notions during his last days
ashore of picking up a woman, visiting a brothel, even getting
drunk. Indeed, he is something of a prohibitionist, prissy as well as
timid; and it takes all of his energy and spirit simply to find a bed
for the night. Ishmael reacts just as his joking landlord had foreseen at his first glimpse of the barbaric fellow with whom he must
share his bed. Everything about Queequeg appalls him: his tattoo-

ing, the shrunken head he carries about for sale, the ugly, black idol—and especially his great, glowing tomahawk pipe, half symbol of peace, half weapon of assault: "this wild cannibal, tomahawk between his teeth, sprang into bed beside me. I sang out . . . and giving a grunt of astonishment he began feeling me . . ." It is an inauspicious enough beginning, and the maidenly Ishmael is terrified: "I rolled away from him against the wall and . . . conjured him . . . to keep quiet and let me up."

"Coffin, Angels! save me!" Ishmael cries, appealing to the landlord and to the powers above. He does not yet know (though Melville perhaps does) that Queequeg is his dark angel, and that on Queequeg's coffin he will escape death at the book's close. He sees only that his tattooed and savage bedmate, like an enlightened spouse, immediately ceases his attack, rolls over and away from him as much as to say—"I won't touch a leg of ye . . ."; and what began in fright ends in security: "I never slept better in my life." During Ishmael's peaceful sleep, matters have developed, however; and he awakens in the harpooner's embrace: "I found Queequeg's arm thrown over me in the most loving and affectionate manner. You had almost thought I had been his wife. . . ." It is worth noting that Ishmael tends to think of himself in the passive, the feminine role; but even more critical is his immediate sense of their relationship as a *marriage,* which is to say, a permanent commitment: the sort of indissoluble union, which he, as a detached wanderer, has presumably been fleeing. To be sure, it all seems quite comic and unreal, this bedroom scene with a Polynesian sailor— only a gross parody of marriage; and Ishmael reflects ironically on "the unbecomingness of hugging a male in that matrimonial style. . . ."

Yet he begins to grow a little disturbed, too, at the thought of being somewhat trapped. "For though I tried to . . . unlock his bridegroom clasp . . . he still hugged me tightly, as though naught but death should part us twain." The final words echo the marriage service, but in evoking the shadow of death, they also betray an access of panic, arising from an old association between sexual satisfaction and punishment. This suggestion is fortified by the recollection of a childhood nightmare, itself symbolic of rejection, paralysis, castration, and death. Somehow the pseudo-matrimonial aspects of his waking bring to Ishmael's mind memories of his stepmother: another unsuitable bedfellow, perhaps, who may once have "expostulated" with him on "the unbecomingness of hugging . . .

in that matrimonial style," when he crawled in beside her for night-time or morning comfort. The actual context in which he recalls her, however, has nothing to do with hugging; she is remembered as a legendary stepmother, a Bad Mother "who was all the time whipping me or sending me to bed supperless."

Oddly enough, this juvenile domestic tragedy of being misunder-stood and rejected by mama is almost the only specific piece of information offered, in what is surely the vaguest of Melville's books, about Ishmael's past. We learn nothing of the adult indig-nities which have presumably set his "splintered heart and mad-dened hand against the wolfish world"; indeed, it is as if there were nothing but a runaway boy behind the outwardly mature form of the narrator of *Moby Dick*. It is tempting to read into Ishmael's little anecdote of crime and punishment a sense of guilt and power-lessness associated with the boy's special sin of masturbation. Cer-tainly, it is the "hand" which plays a key role in the waking night-mare: "a phantom hand," "not daring to drag away my hand"; and in the larger pattern of Ishmael's experience, too, that word recurs in sensitive places. Not only does he describe his estrange-ment in terms of "his maddened hand" set against the "wolfish world"; but his reconciliation comes, as we have seen, in a chapter called "A Squeeze of the Hand," when he tells us that he has at last "washed my hands and heart," and cries out his appeal: "Come, let us squeeze hands all around. . . ."

In the childhood episode recalled in Queequeg's arms, the boy Ishmael was not as usual slippered, though he begged for that cus-tomary punishment. He was forced, instead, to remain in bed all through the longest day of the year: "sixteen entire hours must elapse before I could hope for a resurrection." He was, in effect, condemned to impotence and death; and to this condemnation his own unconscious subscribed, calling up the phantom hand that held him powerless, awake but involved still in nightmare terror. In his own fantasy, the sentence of a single, endless day had been extended through all eternity: never, never (in either sense) to rise again! And for what crime had he presumably been punished—"some caper or other," about which he claims not to be sure, but which he thinks may have involved an attempt to climb up his mother's chimney. It is a fantasy more than a fact; and its inter-pretation suggests itself immediately, casts light on the meaning of chimneys for Melville in such a later story as "I and My Chimney."

Finding himself in a matrimonial deadlock with Queequeg, Ishmael feels again the old threat of impotence and death. But though he is in bed, in that forbidden hugging-place, he is not this time trying to crawl up his mother's chimney. He embraces no woman, no obvious surrogate for the banned mother, only another male, a figure patriarchal enough, in fact, to remind him of George Washington! Surely, the matrimonial hug of such a companion is innocent, only a joke, an accidental result of trying to find a room in an overcrowded town. And though the memory of the nightmare terror of childhood recurs, it recurs purged; for Ishmael has forgiven himself and is free at last to rise: "take away that awful fear, and my sensations . . . were very similar." Actually, he is free for a reconciliation with the tabooed mother; but this he will not know until the book's end, when, an orphan, he is picked up by "the devious cruising *Rachel.*" His long sentimental re-education has now just begun.

Its first stage is represented by the disappearance of Ishmael's fear of Queequeg's tomahawk. That "wild pipe of his" becomes now only a peace pipe, "regularly passing between us . . ."; and their alliance can be regularly solemnized: "he pressed his forehead against mine, clasped me around the waist, and said that henceforth we were married." Ishmael hastens to add, of course, "meaning, in his country's phrase, that we were bosom friends"; for the innocence of their connection must be asserted continually. This is Platonism without sodomy, which is to say, marriage without copulation: the vain dream of genteel ladies fulfilled in a sailor's rooming-house by two men. Queequeg promises that "he would gladly die for me, if need should be"; and die he does, for there *is* need. Indeed, only by his self-sacrifice is Ishmael's sentence of death finally commuted; only in his symbolic body is Ishmael snatched from death.

But all this is not to be for a little while; more immediately, they divide between them Ishmael's worldly goods (Melville, who cannot resist overdetermining everything, makes it thirty pieces of silver) and discuss the counter-claims of their rival religions. It is a scene half broadly comic, half subtly satiric: as Melville, on the one hand, gently parodies the problem of church allegiance in mixed marriages, and on the other, reflects in the style of *Typee* and *Omoo* on the insularity and rigidity of Protestant Christianity. Its real climax comes, however, with the kissing of the grotesque phallic idol, a bowing down before the less savory aspects of the natural and impulsive world which, for all its horror, seems to Melville the only source of love. And the chapter ends in bed, on a simple note of peace, never attained again in the rest of the book: "There, then, in our hearts' honeymoon, lay I and Queequeg—a cosy, loving pair."

Though this is, in a sense, a happy ending, Melville does not abandon his lovers here. There follows an account of their waking, Queequeg's Ramadan, the signing together on the *Pequod* for a whaling voyage, a series of minor incidents, including a sightseeing tour. In the course of those incidents, we learn a good deal about Queequeg's early life and see a display of heroism on his part, begin to feel that Melville is preparing for some shipboard climax —which never comes. Queequeg is not abandoned once the voyage starts, as is Bulkington; but he passes from the center to the periphery of the action. What matters to the reader is his relationship to Ishmael, but their occasions for meeting once they are aboard are few. Queequeg becomes Starbuck's harpooner, but his association with the first mate remains purely formal, devoid of typical significance and passion alike; and for the sake of the book's symbolic coherence, Melville smuggles in an encounter or two between the sundered lovers. Together, for instance, they work at making a sword-mat, with Ishmael acting "the attendant or page of Queequeg," and they find themselves in the same boat whenever there is a launching; but the most crucial of the scenes involving them as a pair comes in the chapter called "The Monkey-Rope," which presents, in effect, a picture of married life after the honeymoon.

It is in this chapter, that Melville, apparently the only time in the whole book, makes a deliberate change in the facts of whaling procedure, describing how Ishmael and Queequeg are tied together during the process of cutting in, in which one man balances on the whale's back, while the other, leaning over the side, helps him keep his slippery balance. "It was a humorously perilous business for both of us . . . ," Ishmael observes, "for better or worse, we two, for the time, were wedded . . . my own individuality was now merged in a stock company of two . . . another's mistake or misfortune might plunge innocent me into unmerited disaster and death." "Nor," he comments further, "could I possibly forget that, do what I would, I only had the management of one end of it." As if even this were not enough to make his point, Melville adds a footnote which explains that "only in the *Pequod* . . . the monkey and his holder were ever tied together. This improvement . . . was introduced . . . in order to afford the imperiled harpooner the strongest possible guarantee for the faithfulness and vigilance of his monkey-rope holder." For an instant, Melville seems to be thinking of the relations of husbands and wives in general rather than of the ideal marriage of Ishmael and Queequeg; and he reverts to the wry derisive tone of his comment on matrimony in *Mardi*.

When Ahab enters the book, however, the theme of love and marriage is pushed into the background, from which it emerges (in the unforeseen posthumous consummation of the relationship between Ishmael and Queequeg) only after Ahab has destroyed himself and the whole shipboard world he has subverted. Ishmael himself has been bent temporarily to Ahab's will, totally committed to the fulfillment of his monomaniac quest until the moment of his sperm-squeezing conversion; but he can do nothing even at that point, remains still the spectator he has become from the moment of Ahab's ascendancy over him. But as a spectator and Ahab's man, he has no longer any use for Queequeg, who is also converted into an accomplice to the blasphemous hunt. Ishmael begins Chapter XXIV with the words, "As Queequeg and I are now fairly embarked on this business of whaling . . . ," but before the chapter is over, Queequeg has been relegated to a supernumerary role in the gothic drama that stars Captain Ahab; the sentimental romance is temporarily over.

Corresponding to the gothic mood of *Moby Dick* after the voyage has begun is another relationship between a white man and a colored one, a quite different projection of the commitment of the ego to a life of impulse and instinct. In Ishmael, the heart of Western white civilization reaches out to the uncorrupted sources of natural life; in Ahab, the head of Western man turns to the same sources in search of power and fear. Queequeg's counterpart is Fedallah, the Parsee, who becomes Ahab's harpooner. He and his crew, however, are not signed on to the *Pequod,* but smuggled aboard, bootlegged on a commercial voyage by a madman; and once the ship is at sea, they rise out of the hold like nightmares. The first hint of their existence has come from Elijah, who has asked Ishmael, "Did ye see anything looking like men going toward the ship a while ago?" This Ishmael takes as a "plain matter-of-fact question," though he is baffled when he tries to pursue it; and we do not hear again of the dusky figures he is not sure whether he has seen or not, until in the moonlight watch two sailors hear the muffled noises of "somebody down in the after-hold that has not yet been seen on deck."

It is not, however, until the first lowering that Fedallah and his tiger-yellow cohorts make a daylight appearance. "With a start all glared at dark Ahab, who was surrounded by five dusky phantoms that seemed fresh formed of air." The coyly noncommittal "seemed" reminds us of Hawthorne; but once the figure of Fedallah "tall and swart . . . with one white tooth evilly protruding from its steel-like lips" has hissed "Ready" to Ahab, he and his crew are handled in terms of peculiarly Melvillean melodrama:

> But what was it that inscrutable Ahab said to that tiger-yellow crew of his—these were words best omitted here; for you live under the blessed light of the evangelical land. Only the infidel sharks in the audacious sea may give ear to such words, when, with tornado brow, and eyes of red murder, and foam-glued lips, Ahab leaped after his prey.

The style, overstated, hysterical, a little ridiculous, dismays the modern reader, as do the stock descriptions of Ahab as the gothic hero-villain. Indeed, the whole relationship of Ahab to Fedallah is rendered in precisely so artificial and unconvincing a mode, from their first lowering to Ahab's last sight of the Parsee tangled in the harpoons on Moby Dick's back.

The most recent moving-picture version of the book quite simply cut him out, apparently because the director was convinced that not even a medium invented to make falsity credible could redeem such material from absurdity. Yet the Parsee stands at the center of the whole machinery of signs and portents and prophecies, which lend the book its characteristically Satanic tone. In him is made manifest the spirit of Ahab's quest, all that impels "the rushing *Pequod,* freighted with savages, and laden with fire, and burning a corpse, and plunging into that blackness of darkness," and makes her "the material counterpart of her monomanic commander's soul." It is the Parsee who prays blasphemously at the forging of Ahab's magical harpoon, that is tempered in the pagan blood of the barbaric harpooners: " 'Ego non baptizo te in nomine patris, sed in nomine diaboli,' deliriously howled Ahab, as the malignant iron scorchingly devoured the baptismal blood." But this moment, over which the Parsee presides, and at which is spoken the "secret motto" of *Moby Dick,* is the thematic center of the book—at least insofar as it is Ahab's.

Without the Parsee to make explicit his damnation, Ahab is merely crazy, *Moby Dick* meaningless. But Melville does not really know how to handle him; for he is not a "character" at all, in the sense that Ishmael is a character—or even Queequeg. He possesses not literal reality but representative truth, and should be understood as a conventional device for portraying inwardness, a projected nightmare. Even Ahab, with his Machiavellian posturing, his rhetoric half out of Byron, half out of the Elizabethans, is almost equally absurd when understood literally. Though in the purely novelistic scenes with Starbuck, he must be taken as a genuine protagonist, with a mind and a past, in his relationship with Fedallah, he has no more mind than Moby Dick; for, like the whale, he is a projection: an emblem of the head itself, cut off from the heart and driven toward its own destruction in its sultanic loneliness. But he is also Faust, as the Parsee is also the Devil, both of them archetypes as well as projections. Certainly, Ahab lives a Faustian life: a "godlike ungodly old man" pressing on beyond all limits to penetrate the ultimate mysteries in despite of God himself; and certainly, he dies a Faustian death, howling defiance to the end: "Oh, lonely death on lonely life! Oh, now I feel my topmost greatness lies in my topmost grief. . . . Towards thee I roll, thou all-destroying but unconquering whale, to the last I grapple with thee; from hell's heart I stab at thee; for hate's sake I spit my last breath at thee. . . ."

Such a life and such a death Melville can render, however rhetorically, at least without embarrassment; but the compact with the Devil upon which they both depend for their meanings, and for whose sake, indeed, he has invented Fedallah, he cannot bring himself to portray. Only obliquely through the comic comments of Stubb and Flask, do we come to suspect that the bargain which makes Ahab a Faust has already been struck: "Flask, I take that Fedallah to be the devil in disguise . . . the reason why you don't see his tail is because he tucks it up out of sight, carries it coiled away in his pocket, I guess . . ."; "the devil there is trying to come round him and get him to swap away his silver watch or his soul, or something of that sort, and he'll surrender Moby Dick. . . ." If the point of such evasions is not a simple failure of nerve, but a desire to undercut ironically the whole Faustian myth, why is Fedallah in the action to begin with, and why do his Macbethian predictions so precisely and tantalizingly come true? What sort of double game is Melville playing with the very myth which lies at the center of his work? The second American Faust, like the first, was written by a man who did not know whether he believed in the Devil, and was embarrassed by the machinery of gothicism, which he was unable to abandon. Yet finally *Moby Dick* triumphs over the shoddiness of its gothic devices, as it triumphs over the naïveté and parochialism of its "Western" love story by deeply mythicizing both its components, and thus liberating them from novelistic restrictions and the implicit judgment of realism: by becoming, in short, the most improbable of all epic poems.

In the latter part of *Moby Dick,* even Queequeg is gradually transformed from a character into a myth, though he never quite loses his status as a fully realized protagonist—never seems, like Fedallah, *merely* what he stands for. His erotic function we have already noticed, but his role as a tutelary spirit of midwifery remains still to be examined. Not only does he act as a cicerone in the Grand Armada episode, pointing out, in the midst of woe and death, the newborn whale still umbilically attached to his dam; but earlier he has played the actual obstetrician, himself bringing Tashtego out of the womb-tomb of the whale's head. The Indian, who, while "cutting in," had been trapped in that suddenly sinking head ("coffined, hearsed, and tombed in the secret inner chamber and santum sanctorum of the whale"), first presents a leg at the opening which Queequeg has cleaved to rescue him. But Queequeg refuses the unorthodox presentation, turning him about until "he came forth in the good old way—head first. . . . Thus through the courage and skill in obstetrics of Queequeg, the deliverance or rather the delivery of Tashtego, was successfully accomplished. . . ." It is not Queequeg's first underwater rescue (he had earlier fished out of the waters of New Bedford the bumpkin who had mocked him), but this time the rescue is presented clearly as a symbolic act of resurrection.

Controller of life and death, Queequeg's own existence is in his power; and indeed, he is shown at one point as simply refusing to

die, though a fever has brought him almost to his "endless end."
Recalling, Ishmael tells us, some uncompleted obligations, the
harpooner returns to life, after everyone has given him up, but not
before he has made his own coffin from "some heathenish . . .
lumber . . . cut from the original groves of the Lackaday Islands."
On this coffin, after his recovery, Queequeg spends long hours
copying the signs from his body, which not only stand for his identity, but constitute as well "a mystical treatise on the art of attaining truth." For a little while, this wondrously engraved coffin serves
as his sea-bag; then, at Queequeg's own hint, it is converted into
a lifebuoy to replace one that has been lost. Upon its strange metamorphoses, Ahab himself comments in a Hamlet-like soliloquy
which follows an exchange with the carpenter who refurbishes it.
He teases himself for a moment with the question, which he considers himself too far gone on the "dark side of earth" to fully
credit: "Can it be that in some spiritual sense the coffin is, after
all, but an immortality preserver?"

Of all the ship's accoutrements, only the coffin-lifebuoy survives
("owing to its great buoyancy, rising with great force") after Moby
Dick has rammed the *Pequod;* and graven with the symbols of
Queequeg's identity, standing in Queequeg's stead, it rises to the
hand of Ishmael, who alone among the crew has risen to the surface of the sea. "Buoyed up by that coffin, for almost one whole
day and night, I floated on a soft and dirge-like main." It is as if
the prayer which Ishmael did not understand when he uttered it,
has been answered. "Coffin, Angels! save me!" The coffin-lifebuoy
is not, however, the only symbolic analogue for Queequeg the
savior in the complex pattern of the book. Wherever the choice is
made, of a seeming death which is really life, a suicidal plunge
which eventuates in a resurrection, the holy marriage with Queequeg is being analogically repeated. Queequeg, who represents
Oceania, the watery area of the world, is equated with the sea and
with the whale who inhabits its depths. This is, of course, to say,
with *Ishmael's* sea and *Ishmael's* whale; for Ahab's version of
both are quite different, and are associated with the Satanic Fedallah. The descent into either (as opposed to the assault upon
either), like the love-union with the dark savage (as opposed to
the pact with him), signifies a life-giving immersion in nature or
the id, a death and rebirth. That is why such erotic terminology is
used to describe both the innards of the whale and the depths of

the sea: the vestibule of the whale called "the bridal chamber of his mouth"; the bottom of the sea referred to as "the very pelvis of the world."

In his mythical descent, Ishmael ceases to be the latest avatar of Natty Bumppo, one more instance of a peculiarly American proto-type, and fades into an archetype much more ancient by far. The whole movement of the book is from land to sea, from time to timelessness; and Melville succeeds in converting all that is provin-cial in his subject into the universal by removing it from the land-bound world of history back toward the oceanic, which is to say, an archaic, an "antemosaic" world of portents and monsters, un-changed since the days of creation. The romance of Ishmael (even as the tragedy of Ahab) is finally seen against a dream landscape, where time has not yet come into existence; and where the acts of men are motivated not by psychology but by mythic patterns, set thousands of years before America was discovered.

It is with Jonah that Melville identifies Ishmael, the archetypal runaway; but his name further complicates the identification, mak-ing him an Ishmael who is a Jonah: an outcast son who is cast into the depths and brought forth again by the God whom he is fleeing. What Ishmael saw in his plunge into the depths we are not directly told; but we assume that his experience must have been like that of Jonah, to whom wisdom came in the belly of the whale.

We do learn, however, what Ishmael saw looking down into the sea in the midst of the Grand Armada, following the pointing finger of Queequeg. At the heart of the pod of frightened and frightening whales, at the very center of "consternation and af-frights," he discovers "dalliance and delight"—which is to say, birth and copulation but *no* death. And this he reads as a sign that there is within the human self a place in which the "eternal mild-ness of joy" prevails deep below "the ponderous planets of unwan-ing woe." Ishmael interprets his glimpse into the world of natural immortality, where life is endlessly renewed by physical generation, as a guarantee that there is a renewal of the spirit, too, in human "dalliance and delight," which is all the immortality man can ever achieve. For this natural renewal of the soul, the Holy Marriage of Males, immune to the spiritual death implicit in fleshly marriage with women, is an alternative symbol.

Against this accidental glimpse into the heart of living mysteries, which constitutes Ishmael's real descent into the whale, Melville counterposes an account of a royally-sponsored, priest-guided tour through a whale's skeleton in the Bower of the Arsacides. From the spout-hole of the King's dead and grounded whale, a perpetual stream of vapor ascends, a presumable token that there is no death; but it is a fake, an "artificial smoke" manufactured by the priests to compel belief. Deep within the whitening skeleton, to which Ishmael penetrates like a man threading a maze, there is simply nothing: "no living thing; naught was there but bones." For Melville, this sterile showplace of prepared illusions represents all organized religion, especially the Presbyterianism to which he himself was raised; and he has Ishmael cry out in revulsion, "Only in the heart of the quickest perils . . . only in the profound unbounded sea, can the fully invested whale be truly and livingly found out."

To find out "the fully invested whale" is the end of Ishmael's quest, from which he was temporarily diverted by Ahab's magnetic charm; and wherever he dives deep he is faithful to that goal: in his acceptance of Queequeg's embrace; in his penetration of the Grand Armada; in his final descent toward the "button-like black bubble," the "vital center" of the vortex left by the sinking *Pequod*. All of these symbolize the life-giving immersion represented elsewhere in the book by Father Mapple, who first invokes the myth of Jonah, and who himself seems "kneeling and praying at the bottom of the sea"; by Bulkington, who is buried and resurrected in a single chapter: "Up from the spray of thy ocean perishing— straight up leaps thy apotheosis!"; by Pip, abandoned and rescued by those who never understand what he has seen; by Tashtego, whose thrashing arm above the sea seems an "arm thrust forth from the grass over the grave." Understood as a series of linked analogies, organized not as in a novel but as in a poem, *Moby Dick* displays an unsuspected unity. Even the cetological passages, those apparent digressions with their endless and apparently impertinent documentation, are revealed as a final Ishmael-Queequeg analogue: one more descent into the whale, this time a scholarly exploration, inch by inch, from skin to sex. "Have a care how you seize the privilege of Jonah," Ishmael warns himself, as he girds up his loins for the plunge into Leviathan.

Infinitely rich in significance, the descent into the depths is a theme in the oldest epic literature of our civilization; but it represents only one half of the archetypal adventures of the epic hero, who must not only disappear into the sea and rise again, but must also slay the dragon of the deep. Ishmael is, then, but one part of the split epic hero (and surely his splitting is a sign in itself of the divided state of the psyche in modern life), whose other part is Ahab. In the case of the latter, too, there is a tension established between the primary suggestion of the name Ahab, a wicked king whose blood was licked by dogs, and the secondary mythical association with Perseus and St. George: deliverers both and slayers of monsters. Ahab, however, saves no one, not even himself. He is the hero who is lost, even as Ishmael is the coward who is saved; for in Melville's scheme, the warrior who attacks the ravening beast goes down to death, while the prophet who runs away is preserved alive. Though like Ishmael Ahab seeks the whale "in the heart of quickest perils," he seeks him not to plunge into his jaws and be swallowed up but to attack and destroy him.

The one is a would-be murderer, the other a symbolic suicide. Ishmael goes to sea "as a substitute for pistol and ball"; Ahab embarks to "strike through the mask." But it is Ahab who must die, precisely because he has sought the death of the Other rather than of himself; for *Moby Dick* is based on the fundamental paradoxes which outlive in the Western mind the religion that once sustained them. Not only does the chant of the cheating witches of *Macbeth* ring through the book: "Fair is Foul and Foul is Fair!" but also the older assertion, more promise than threat, that Death is Life and Life Death. In Father Mapple's sermon, which appears quite early in the book, the fundamental proposition is asserted: "But what then? Methinks we have hugely mistaken this matter of Life and Death. Methinks that what we call my shadow here on earth is my true substance. . . ." Such paradoxes are worked out in great detail: Queequeg's coffin is, as we have noticed, a lifebuoy, while the great ship, which images forth the living world, is revealed as a hearse; Ahab, who only half-jestingly calls himself immortal ("I am immortal then on land or sea"), dies forever; but Ishmael, who considers himself already dead ("a quiet ghost with a clean conscience"), is reborn.

But why is Ahab doomed, the once heroic act of Perseus become in him an analogue of the Faustian bargain with the Devil? What does it mean to kill the monster anyway? As rich in significance as the baptismal descent, the battle with the dragon can be interpreted as the victory of light over storm and darkness; an attack of the son against the father; a destruction of whatever is dark, repressive, and authoritarian in the psyche itself; a combat with the Devil or with God or with an inscrutable being who may be either; an assault on the irrational in nature and an attempt to resolve the world's mysteries by liquidating them. For Melville, such an onslaught is suspect in several ways. Not only does he sense a kind of Oedipal guilt in Ahab's frenzy against the "fiery father," in whose despite he seeks to hunt down the whale, but perceives that in him the struggle against the monstrous becomes the struggle against a Calvinist God, whom Ahab confuses with the traditional figure of the Devil!

Is not Moby Dick, after all, identified with Leviathan himself; and is not Leviathan the immortal symbol of the inscrutability of the created world, a mystery not to be resolved until the end of days? Is not that lower inscrutability, moreover, a type of the higher, of the ultimate mystery of the divine? Melville, for whom in *Moby Dick* the precepts of the New Testament are irrelevant, and who put in Christ's place a Polynesian harpooner, could not close his ears to the Old Testament challenge: "Canst thou catch Leviathan with a hook?" And does not the man who tries, does not Ahab become, in his alienation, his sultanism, his pride, blasphemy, and diabolism, finally more monstrous than the beast he hunts? When, on the last day, they confront each other, which is the Monster, Moby Dick in his "gentle joyousness," his "mighty mildness of repose," or Ahab screaming his mad defiance?

In complete contempt of the three-thousand-year-old pattern of myth, Melville permits the dragon-slayer to be slain, the dragon to escape alive; but it is hard to tell whether he really stands the legend on its head, allows evil to survive and heroism to perish. Only Ahab believes that the whale represents evil, and Ahab is both crazy and damned. Yet no child can abide the ending as it stands—in the book which parents and librarians alike expect them to enjoy; and in the comic-book version, revised for their special benefit, Moby Dick goes down with Ahab, whose death becomes merely the heroic price he pays for victory. For simple minds, the salvation of Ishmael is not enough; they cannot project their dreams of glory upon so passive a sufferer: the fugitive from life cast upon after a three-day chase, which both represents and parodies the immersion of Jonah as a type of Christ's burial and resurrection.

Ahab lost and Ishmael saved, the destroyer destroyed and the lover preserved by the symbolic body of his beloved: it is not finally quite so obvious and pat. Though Ahab and Ishmael are opposites, they are also one—two halves of a single epic hero; and only in their essential unity is the final unity of the book to be found. What Melville disjoined, in a typically American stratagem of duplicity, the reader must re-unite. In *Moby Dick,* the king-god-culture hero, who kills and is redeemed, is split into an active older brother and a passive younger, different sons of the same terrible father, who move, as it were, through separate works of art: the first through a belated horror tragedy, the latter through a nineteenth-century *Bildungsroman.* Yet though the agent in the first is projected as a finally rejected "he," and the witness in the second as a beloved "I," even structurally their two actions become one. The tragic play is encysted, enclosed in a comic narrative frame, on a model suggested, perhaps, by the Book of Job; though in Job, the chief protagonist is the same in the drama and frame-story. In *Moby Dick,* the protagonist of the frame-story is Ishmael, who becomes the trapped spectator of the drama of Ahab's fall, experiencing the catharsis of which Ahab is incapable. The heart, that is to say, witnessing the mad self-destruction of the head is itself purged and redeemed.

Heart and head, however, Ishmael and Ahab begin by confronting the same problem; for they are both described as rejected sons. The stepmother motif, first suggested by Ishmael's nightmare reminiscence in Queequeg's arms, is taken up again, toward the close of the book, in a chapter called "The Symphony." It opens on a moment just before the final three-day chase of Moby Dick and the catastrophe, which at this point seems inevitable; yet in that moment, all the world except for Ahab seems to relent. The two great principles, maternal and paternal, which divide the world and the minds of men, which make Ahab Ahab and Ishmael Ishmael, "the gentle . . . feminine air" and the "strong, troubled, murderous . . . masculine sea"—seem for once at peace with each other. "Those two seemed one; it was only the sex, as it were, that distinguished them." And at this point, even the stepmother, who had symbolically condemned Ishmael to death, symbolically returns to promise Ahab life:

That glad, happy air, that winsome sky, did at last stroke and caress him; the step-mother world, so long cruel—forbidding—

now threw affectionate arms around his stubborn neck; and did seem to joyously sob over him, as if over one, that however wilful and erring, she could yet find it in her heart to save and to bless.

Earlier, Ahab has appealed to the demonic Father God, in his blustering and bullying way, for just such a revelation: "My sweet mother, I know not. Oh, cruel! what hast thou done with her?" But when he has his answer, learns that the "sweet mother" resides still in the beauty of the natural world (it is precisely what was revealed to Ishmael in the midst of the Grand Armada), he will not listen. In the end, he proves not really interested in the reconciliation with the Mother, wanting nothing less than to grapple with the "fiery Father" himself, to be joined to him in an assault which is also an embrace: "I leap with thee; I burn with thee; would fain be welded with thee. . . ." He seeks madly to identify himself with the castrating power shadowed forth in the whale: the power that has scarred and maimed him and made his wife a widow, though they are scarcely wed. But the desire to be one with the forbidding fire is merely another version of the Faustian temptation, to be as a god; and all this is figured forth in Ahab's relationship with the Parsee, fire-worshiper and Devil, presiding genius of the infernal baptism.

Yet Ishmael, too, we remember, has temporarily at least lost faith in water and subscribed to fire, lent his voice to the pledge of the maddened crew to pursue the abominable quest. He, too, has dreamed of catching Leviathan with a hook, thus confirming his unity with Ahab in a common mythical identification. Though the one is Jonah, the one Perseus, both are Job: Job as Jonah, Job as Perseus. "Give not thyself up, then, to fire," Ishmael warns the reader in "The Tryworks," "lest it invert thee, deaden thee, as for a time it did me. There is a wisdom that is woe; but there is a woe that is madness." Multiple ambiguities undercut the simple polarity which the book superficially suggests. Even Queequeg, good angel and representative of the baptism to life, gives his blood along with Tashtego's and Dagoo's for the Satanic tempering of Ahab's harpoon; while the very sperm in which Ishmael washes himself clean of hate comes from a whale struck by the infuriated hunters, the very whale whose death meant the casting away of his alter ego, Pip.

Yet there is an irony beyond all of these. If Queequeg dies for

Ishmael, so does Ahab; though, to be sure, the one dies in deliberate self-sacrifice, the other in blind hybris. It is, however, Ahab's destruction which ransoms Ishmael's life, the playing out of Ahab's fury which instructs Ishmael in love. If, as Ishmael asserts at one point, a whaling ship was his Harvard and Yale College, Ahab was his major professor. The head, driven by woe past woe to sacrilege and murder, burns itself out in a terror by which the heart is purified: left alone in the sea of the unlimited, clinging to the symbolic body of the dark beloved, who seemed death and was really life. Only thus is the Father of Fury appeased. The sea rolls again in primeval calm, "as it rolled five thousand years ago," which is to say, before man had committed the primal offense. The instruments of rage are put away: the beaks of the hawks, which snatched violently at Ahab's hat, "sheathed"; the sharks' mouths, which gnawed hungrily at Ahab's oars, "padlocked."

The outcast son is buoyed up on the charmed sea, preserved until discovered by the cruising *Rachel,* that is, the Mother, whom he thought of as rejecting him, but who all along has wept for her children, refusing to be comforted. But the return to the Mother is a return also to God, to the numinous felt as maternal, to what Melville knew enough of Hebrew mysticism, even at the time of writing *Mardi,* to call the *Shekhinah:* "an awful glory. Sphere in sphere it burned:—the one Shekinah! The air was flaked with fire; deep in which, fell . . . tears . . ." The *Shekhinah* is the presence of God in the natural world, his spirit which he has sent into exile with all his outcasts, and which there weeps for them. "I have written a wicked book," Melville wrote to Hawthorne, "and feel spotless as the lamb." It is the final expression of the profound duplicity and unity of *Moby Dick:* I have written a wicked book (boasts Ahab-Melville), and feel spotless as the lamb(Ishmael-Melville rejoins).

Such a happy ending, however qualified, is more and more desperately insisted upon these days in the face of the contradictions between the relationships we dream and the relationships we live. In the motion picture *The Defiant Ones,* the old story is told again: Huck and Jim run from their pursuers through field and swamp once more—though this time they are escapees from a chain gang; and to emphasize their terrible bond they are chained together (the link that binds them is referred to wryly at one point as a wedding ring!). Though they are captured at the end, they have learned to love each other with a love pure enough to transcend their mutual prejudices and bitterness. The white man, wounded by an evil woman who would have separated the two good companions and feels no love, only a lust that does not even demand to know the name of the phallus-bearer who satisfies it, ends up lying in the arms of the colored man, who sings to him like a mother to a child; and still together, more than ever together, they are borne off to jail. As the old myth sinks deeper and deeper into the national mind, intertwined with nostalgic memories of books that we have read as children, like our fathers before us and theirs before them, it comes to seem truer than the reality of headlines. At the psychic levels, from which works of art proceed and to which they seek to return, not Little Rock but Hannibal is the place where black and white confront each other; not Eniwetok but the *Pequod* is the meeting-ground of the Kanaka and the American sailor.

Since the locus of our deepest response to the conflict of races is legend, we find it easy to believe that our dark-skinned beloved will rescue us from the confusion and limitations of a society which excludes him. Certainly, our classic writers assure us that when we have been cut off or have cut ourselves off from the instinctive sources of life, he will receive us without rancor or the insult of forgiveness. He will fold us in his arms saying "honey" or "Aikane"; he will comfort us, as if he knew our offense against him were only symbolic—an offense against that in ourselves which he represents—never truly *real*. And yet our novelists can never quite let us forget our guilt; the fictions which embody the myth of the *hierogamos* dramatize compulsively not only the role of the colored man as bugaboo but also as victim. The Polynesian sailor Hope in Dana's *Two Years Before the Mast* is shown dying of the white man's syphilis; Queequeg is wracked by a fever caught crawling in the hold on the white man's business; Crane's Negro is disfigured by the slow drip of acid in a burning house where he blindly attempts to rescue a white man's son; Cooper's Indian smolders in a drunken old age, victim of the white man's whisky; Jim is portrayed burdened with chains and weakened by a score of foolish torments imagined by Tom in the name of a white man's notion of "bulliness"; Lucas Beauchamp is hunted and chivvied, almost lynched in the name of the white man's justice.

The immense barrier of guilt between white man and dark man is no more mitigated in our classic fiction than is the gulf of color and culture itself; both, indeed, are emphasized to the point of melodrama, so that the final reconciliation may seem more tender and miraculous. The archeteype makes no attempt to deny the facts of outrage or guilt; it is nurtured by them. It merely portrays them as meaningless in the face of a passion immune to what Melville calls "that climax which is so fatal to ordinary love." "It's too good for true, honey," Jim says to Huck. "It's too good for true."

12

THE BLACKNESS
OF DARKNESS:
EDGAR ALLAN POE
AND THE DEVELOPMENT
OF THE GOTHIC

IN HIS HARRIED CAREER as a journalist, book-reviewer, short-story writer, poet, and critic, Edgar Allan Poe tried twice to write a full-length novel, reworking each time chronicles of American exploration on sea and land. Both *The Narrative of A. Gordon Pym* (1837-38) and *The Journal of Julius Rodman* (1840) strike us as improbable books for Poe to have attempted, concerned as they are with the American scene and the great outdoors. The former is based upon accounts of pioneering expeditions to the South Seas, and especially a South Polar expedition projected by an acquaintance of Poe called J. N. Reynolds; while the second borrows heavily from the journals of Lewis and Clark, purporting to describe a trip across the Rockies which had preceded theirs.

There is little doubt that Poe was trying to cash in on contemporary interest in the remote and the unexplored, exploited, on the one hand, by such popular histories as Washington Irving's *Astoria* or *Adventures of Captain Bonneville,* and, on the other, by the Indian novels of James Fenimore Cooper. In the course of a review of the latter's *Wyandotté,* written in 1843, Poe reflects on the Leatherstocking Tales and remarks a little ruefully:

> . . . we mean to suggest that this theme—life in the Wilderness —is one of intrinsic and universal interest, appealing to the heart of man in all phases; a theme, like that of life upon the ocean, so unfailingly omniprevalent in its power of arresting and absorbing attention, that while success or popularity is, with

such a subject, expected as a matter of course, a failure might be properly regarded as conclusive evidence of imbecility on the part of the author. . . .

He goes on to add, however, that "the two theses in question," that is, the wilderness and life upon the ocean, are subjects to be avoided by the "man of genius . . . more interested in fame than popularity," for they belong to the lesser of the "two great classes of fiction," the "popular division" at whose head Cooper stands. Of this category, Poe remarks that "the author is lost or forgotten; or remembered, if at all, with something very nearly akin to contempt." He considers his own fiction in general part of the other great class, which includes the work of "Mr. Brockden Brown, Mr. John Neal, Mr. Simms, Mr. Hawthorne," of whom it can be said that "even when the works perish, the man survives."

Yet in *Gordon Pym* and *Julius Rodman,* Poe tried his hand at the two popular themes, attempting, for the first time perhaps, to treat the sort of legendary material which had appeared in Leatherstocking Tales with the scrupulous documentation of Irving's nonfictional accounts. The kind of book at which Poe aimed Melville was to produce with eminent success, beginning less than a decade later with the best-selling *Typee* (1846) and *Omoo* (1847), and raising the genre to unexpected power in *Moby Dick*. Poe is considerably less successful, failing completely in the case of the unfinished *Julius Rodman* to lend fictional life to borrowed documents; and achieving in *Gordon Pym* a work so hopelessly unpopular (in America at least), that only within the last very few years has a major attempt to redeem it been undertaken. Poe himself, some time after its appearance, was willing to write off *Gordon Pym* as a "silly book"; and certainly from the first he had considered it, or pretended to consider it, a shameless bid for popular success.

The whole apparatus which surrounds the anonymous final form of *Gordon Pym* is apologetic: an involved attempt on Poe's part to convince himself that his primary purpose in publishing the tale was to perpetrate a hoax on the reader. But this is an almost compulsive aspect of Poe's art in general, arising from a dark necessity, which dogged not only him among American writers, of remaining in ignorance about his own deepest aims and drives. Just so Cooper was obligated to believe that he was mocking his wife's literary taste before he could become an author, while Melville eternally persuaded himself that he was on the verge of producing a best-seller, and Twain pretended he was a writer of books for boys.

The apologetic and playful preface to *Pym* has for us now chiefly biographical interest, illuminating the author but not the work. Whatever Poe's ostensible or concealed motives, he created in his only complete longer fiction not a trivial hoax but the archetypal American story, which would be recast in *Moby Dick* and *Huckleberry Finn*. Why, then, did Poe's book not achieve either the immediate acclaim accorded the latter or the slowly growing reputation won by the former? All the attributes of the highbrow Western are present in his novel: the rejection of the family and of the world of women, the secret evasion from home and the turning to the open sea. Only a bevy of black squaws and a few female corpses ("scattered about . . . in the last and most loathesome state of putrefaction") intrude into the world of pure male companionship which Poe imagines; and they provide no competition to the alliance of Pym either with his boyhood friend and Anglo-Saxon compeer, Augustus Barnard, or with his dusky demon, the "hybrid line-manager," Dirk Peters.

Rioting and shipwreck and rescue at sea do not break the rhythm of the flight that bears Pym farther and farther from civilization toward a primitive isolation, symbolized by the uncharted island and the lost valley, the derelict ship, and the small boat adrift at sea. Even Rip Van Winkle's initiatory draught, the alcoholic pledge to escape and forgetfulness, is represented in *Pym*. Buried in a coffin-like refuge in the black hull of a riot-torn ship, Gordon Pym finds at hand a bottle to console him; and later he and his companions fish up out of the flooded hold a flask of Madeira!

There are totemic beasts to spare in the pages of Poe's Western: a great white bear dramatically slaughtered, as well as legendary and exotic animals, compounded surrealistically out of incongruous familiar forms, and even stranger tabooed birds, who float lifelessly on a tepid and milky sea. And through it all, the outcast wanderer—equally in love with death and distance—seeks some absolute Elsewhere, though more in woe than wonder. Poe's realm of refuge and escape seems finally a place of death rather than one of love: the idyllic American dream turned nightmare as it is dreamed in its author's uneasy sleep. If the West means archetypically some ultimate innocence, there is no West in Poe's book at all—only an illusory hope that draws men toward inevitable disenchantment and betrayal. It is not merely that a gothic horror balances the quest for innocence in *Gordon Pym;* such a balance is the standard pattern of all highbrow Westerns. Only in Poe's novel, however, is the dark counterpoint permitted to drown out the *cantus firmus* of hopeful joy or to mar a final harmonic resolution.

Huckleberry Finn closes on a note of high euphoria, sustained by rescue and redemption and promises of new beginnings, which quite conceal from the ordinary reader the tragic implications of the conclusion; while *Moby Dick* ends with the promise of adoption, the symbolic salvation of the orphaned Ishmael by the crushing, motherly *Rachel.* Only at the close of *Gordon Pym* is the Great Mother identified with total destruction, a death without resurrection, a sterile, white womb from which there is no exit. "And now we rushed into the embraces of the cataract, where a chasm threw itself open to receive us. But there arose in our pathway a shrouded human figure, very far larger in its proportions than any dweller among men. And the hue of the skin of the figure was of the perfect whiteness of snow."

The book is finally an anti-Western disguised as the form it travesties; and this fact the great public, which will not in such matters be fooled, perceived—and perceiving, rejected the work. From the beginning, a perceptive reader of *Gordon Pym* is aware that every current sentimental platitude, every cliché of the fable of the holy marriage of males is being ironically exposed. Man's best friend, the dog, turns into a slavering monster ready to tear his master's throat to appease his hunger and thirst; a presumably loyal crew, led by the kind of standard black cook who plays the grinning and subservient comedian even in *Moby Dick,* mutinies; a bird flies through the pure blue air to drop "with a sullen splash" at the feet of a half-famished group of sailors "a portion of clotted and liverlike substance," a chunk of decayed human flesh; an approaching ship, hailed as a source of rescue, turns out to be a vessel loaded only with human carrion, from which issues "a smell, a stench, such as the whole world has no name for." Even the friendly bottle, traditional symbol of innocent male companionship, induces not joy but the D.T.'s, "an indescribable state of weakness and horror . . . a violent ague."

Most disconcerting of the parodies in *Pym* is that of the theme of resurrection itself, which later carries so much symbolic weight in both *Moby Dick* and *Huckleberry Finn.* Like Ishmael or Huck,

Gordon Pym is presumably slain only to rise again, immersed and entombed only to be reborn—in his case, not once but over and over. Out of the coffin in the hold and out of a swoon that seems death itself, he is brought to life, but only to face mutiny and a new threat of destruction; and he emerges in the disguise of a ghost, his face coated with white chalk and blotched with blood, his clothes stuffed to resemble the bloated stomach of a swollen corpse. The threat of murder once again avoided, he is the victim of ship-wreck; and almost dead once more (his life meagerly sustained by drinking the blood of a murdered shipmate), he is rescued by a passing ship, only to fall victim to a last catastrophe which leaves him buried alive just as in the beginning. A "living inhumation," Poe calls the state of life-in-death, to which his long circle brings him back; and he lingers almost sensuously over the details: "The blackness of darkness . . . the terrific oppression of the lungs, the stifling fumes from the damp earth . . . the allotted portion of *the dead.*" But even from this plight, Pym is rescued, this time by his blood-stained, demonic mate, Dirk Peters; and the two together approach the ultimate plunge into a white polar chasm, from which there is no reason to believe either can emerge. Indeed, it is precisely such an end which the pariah poet-sailor has prayed for, has loved in anticipation: "death or captivity among barbarian hordes . . . a lifetime dragged out in sorrow and tears, upon some grey and desolate rock."

Since Pym lusts for Gehenna rather than Eden, the companions he chooses on his quest embody not fertility or patient endurance but impotence and terror. Augustus Barnard, his first specter bride-groom, dies horribly, rots away visibly on a parody before-the-fact of Huck's raft: "His arm was completely black from the wrist to the shoulder, and his feet were like ice. . . . He was frightfully emaciated; so much so that . . . *he now did not weigh more than forty or fifty* [pounds] *at the farthest.* His eyes were . . . scarcely perceptible, and the skin of his cheeks hung so loosely as to prevent his masticating any food . . . without great difficulty." His painful death is not even sacrificial, merely another device to produce a shudder, especially at the point where his entire leg comes off in the hand of the man who is attempting to heave his rotten corpse into the sea!

Augustus' impromptu grave-digger is his successor; for it is Dirk Peters who tosses the first good companion over the side to the sharks who gather with gnashing teeth. But Peters is, as we have already noticed, a very ogre: such a monster, one of Poe's critics describes him, as children draw to scare themselves, a nightmare out of our racial beginnings. He is, in fact, as Marie Bonaparte suggests, the accursed hero who has destroyed the Father, taking on himself the guilt of the artist who only writes or dreams such horror. He protects the artist-surrogate of the plot with almost maternal tenderness, fights his battles like a big brother; and like a lover, holds him safe and warm when the defeated wanderer seeks his bloody embrace, impotent and whimpering. Yet the sought-for embrace is a rape and a betrayal, a prelude to certain death.

The climax of the relationship of Pym and Peters comes at the moment when the two are trapped on the Island of Tsalal, where all their companions have been killed by an artificial landslide contrived by the bloodthirsty black aborigines. The two survivors are trying to find their way out of a cleft in the earth that has providentially sheltered them; and Pym is suspended in fright on a sheer cliff wall.

> For one moment my fingers clutched compulsively upon their hold, while, with the movement, the faintest possible idea of escape wandered, like a shadow, through my mind—in the next my whole soul was pervaded with a *longing to fall;* a desire, a yearning, a passion utterly uncontrollable. I let go at once my grasp upon the peg, and, turning half round from the precipice, remained tottering for an instant against its naked face. But now there came a spinning of the brain; a shrill-sounding and phantom voice screamed within my ears; a dusky, fiendish and filmy figure stood immediately beneath me; and, sighing, I sank down with a bursting heart, and plunged within its arms.

The "dusky, fiendish . . . figure" is, of course Peters, the halfbreed; and the studied ambiguity of the passage, in which the language of horror becomes that of eroticism, the dying plunge becomes a climactic embrace, makes it clear that the *longing to fall* and the desire for the dark spouse are one, a single perverseness. Peters is not made an angelic representative of instinct and nature even at this critical instant; he remains still a fiend, even in the act of becoming a savior.

Poe espouses the view of instinctual life which is the common property of those writers whom he regards as "men of genius," the view of Brockden Brown and Hawthorne; and he quite consciously rejects the sentimentalizing of the savage which he finds in popularizers like Cooper. Indeed, Poe's aristocratic pretensions make it impossible for him to adopt such an attitude without the equivocations and soul-searching demanded of such liberal gothicists as the young Brockden Brown. His fictional world needs no good Indians because he believes in none; and try as he will, he cannot keep quite distinct the mutinous black cook, whom he calls a "perfect demon," from the "dusky, fiendish" figure of Dirk Peters. *Theoretically*, the tale of *Gordon Pym* projects through its Negroes the fear of black rebellion and of the white man's perverse lust for the Negro, while symbolizing in the red man an innocent and admirable yearning for the manly violence of the frontier; but in the working out of the plot, the two are confused.

It is true that the half-breed line-manager offers protection against the shipboard mutineers and the vicious natives of Tsalal; but his sheltering embrace is identified with the mortal hug of the grizzly bear, whose skin he wears to cover his bald pate. The figure of the black man blends ambiguously with that of the slave, while that of the red man blurs into that of the wild beast! The West, at any rate, was always for Poe only half real, a literary experience rather than a part of his life; but the South moved him at the deepest personal level. Insofar as *Gordon Pym* is finally a social document as well as a fantasy, its subject is slavery; and its scene, however disguised, is the section of America which was to destroy itself defending that institution. It is, indeed, to be expected that our first eminent Southern author discover that the proper subject for American gothic is the black man, from whose shadow we have not yet emerged.

Though the movement of *Gordon Pym* seems to bear us away from America, once Nantucket and New Bedford have been left behind, and to carry us through remoter and remoter seas toward the exotic Antarctic, it ends in a region quite unlike the actual polar regions. Heading toward an expected world of ice and snow, Pym finds instead a place of tepid waters and luxuriant growth; seeking a white world, he discovers, beside and within it, a black one. What has gone wrong? It is necessary for Poe to believe, in that blessed ignorance which frees forbidden fancies, that Pym's fictional voyage is bearing him toward the polar region, just as it was necessary for him to believe the whole story a delicious hoax;

but we, as latter-day readers, need not be the victims of either delusion. For all the carefully worked-up details about penguins, *biche de mer,* galapagos tortoises (bait for the audience which was later to subscribe to the *National Geographic*), Poe follows the footsteps not of Captain Cook but of his own first voyage in the arms of his mother, undertaken before his memory began, from New England to the South. In his deepest imagination, any flight from the North bears the voyager not toward but away from the snow—not to the South Pole, but to the American South.

Certainly, it grows not colder, but warmer and warmer, as Pym aboard the last ship to rescue him, the *Jane Gay,* pushes closer and closer to the Pole. "We had now advanced to the southward more than eight degrees farther than any previous navigators. We found . . . that the temperature of the air, and latterly of the water, became milder." Whatever pseudo-scientific explanations Poe may have believed would sustain this improbable notion of a luke-warm Antarctica, certain *symbolic* necessities were of more importance; he is being, in fact, carried back to Ole Virginny—as the color of the natives he meets on the Island of Tsalal (latitude 83° 20′, longitude 43° 5′ W.) clearly indicates. They are brawny, muscular, and jet black, with "thick and woolen hair," "thick and clumsy lips," these "wretches," whom Pym describes, after they have destroyed all the white men but him and Peters, as "the most wicked, hypocritical, vindictive, bloodthirsty, and altogether fiend-ish race of men upon the face of the globe." And he sets them in a world distinguished not only by blackness and warmth, but by a certain disturbing sexuality quite proper to Southern stereotypes of Negro life.* That sexuality can only be expressed obliquely by Poe, who was so squeamish about matters of this kind that the much franker Baudelaire was driven to remark, *"Dans l'oeuvre d'Edgar Poe, il n'y a jamais d'amour."* The phallicism of the island he, therefore, suggests not in human terms but by a reference to the islanders' chief crop, the *biche de mer*—a kind of sea-cucumber of which, Poe informs us, the authorities say that it "renews the exhausted system of the immoderate voluptuary."

The inhabitants of Tsalal are not, of course, the burlesque

---

* *Pym* represents the first serious attempt at introducing Negroes into our literature; and perhaps for that reason it is ignored (along with Melville's "Benito Cereno") by D. H. Lawrence in his *Studies in Classic American Literature.* Lawrence, at any rate, prefers his savages, Noble and Ignoble alike, Red rather than Black, and has written a history of our fiction with No Negroes Allowed.

Negroes, those black "rascals" or "scamps," named pompously "Jupiter" or "Pompey," who lend a minstrel-show note to Poe's lighter tales. Woolly-pated and bow-legged, these characters play the role of mischievous, cowardly, stupid and faithful dependents, good always for a laugh when they say "soldiers" for "shoulders" or "clause" for "cause." The dark hordes of Too-Wit project the image of what the Southerner privately fears the Negro may be; just as the comic body-servant of Poe's other fiction projects the image of what the anti-abolitionist publicly claims he is. It is the darker image, however, which is true to Poe's memories of his boyhood and youth in the Allen household; while the lighter belongs only to certain patriarchal legends, to which he learned to subscribe during his days on *The Southern Literary Messenger.* In the single reference to the Negro in his correspondence, Poe complains to his step-father (the date is 1827): "You suffer me to be subjected to the whim & caprice, not only of your white family, but to the complete authority of the blacks."

At the climax of *Gordon Pym,* Poe dreams himself once more, though a grown man, subject to that nightmare authority; and the book projects his personal resentment and fear, as well as the guilty terror of a whole society in the face of those whom they can never quite believe they have the right to enslave. In Tsalal, blackness is no longer the livery of subjection but a sign of menace; so utterly black, that even the teeth concealed by their pendulous lips are black, the Antarctic savages inhabit a black land in which the vegetation and the animals, water itself are all subdued to the same dismal color. The voyage of Pym has transported him into the black belt, a black belt transformed from the level of sociology to that of myth, in whose midst the reigning Caucasian is overwhelmed by a sense of isolation and peril. Not even the glimmer of white teeth bared in a heartening smile cuts the gloom of this exclusive and excluding dark world, whose ultimate darkness is revealed in that final chasm in which Pym and Peters are trapped after the treacherous destruction of their white shipmates. "We alone had escaped from the tempest of that overwhelming destruction. We were the sole living white men upon the island." At this point, the darkness of "Nigger-town" merges at last into the darkness of the womb which is also a tomb, an intestinal chamber from which there is apparently no way of being born again into a realm of light.

How has Pym arrived here, in this place where whiteness itself is taboo, where even the flicker of a handkerchief, the flash of sunlight on taut sails, a little flour in the bottom of a pan stir terror, and doom the white man who feels at home in a world full of such pale symbols? Pym has sought a polar whiteness and has discovered instead a realm of the domination of black. It was (as Marie Bonaparte and other analytical critics have made clear) his mother whom Poe was pursuing in his disguise as Pym: that lost, pale mother, white with the whiteness of milk and the pallor of disease; and the imaginary voyage is a long regression to childhood. But hostilely guarding the last access to the White Goddess, stands the black killer, Too-Wit. In the ultimate reaches of his boyhood, where he had confidently looked for some image of maternal comfort and security, Poe-Pym finds *both* the white chasm and cascade and the black womb sealed off by black warriors.

II

Down through the history of the minstrel show, a black-faced Sambo (smeared with burnt cork, whether Negro or white, into the grotesque semblance of the archetypal nigger) tries to exorcise with high-jinks and ritual jokes the threat of the black rebellion and the sense of guilt which secretly demands it as penance and purge. But our more serious writers return again and again to the theme: Melville, for instance, in "Benito Cereno" treating quite explicitly the tragic encounter between certain sentimental and comic stereotypes of the Negro and a historic instance of a slave mutiny. In that story, Captain Amasa Delano fails to recognize the rebellion on a Spanish slave-ship which he encounters, precisely because he is a good American. He is endowed, that is to say, with an "undistrustful good nature" and will not credit "the imputation of malign evil in man." This means in fact that he is quite willing to believe almost any evil of a European aristocrat, like the Don Benito who gives the tale its title; and is prepared to accept the most incredible behavior as the kind of "sullen inefficiency" to be expected of a Latin crew. On the other hand, he is incapable of believing a Negro, particularly a body servant, anything but a "faithful fellow."

It is just this phrase which occurs to Captain Delano as he watches Babo, a black slave who is actually holding his master prisoner, threatening death with the razor he presumably wields to shave him. " 'Faithful fellow!' cried Captain Delano, 'Don Benito, I envy you such a friend, slave I cannot call him.' " But Melville will not let it go, adding on his own behalf—in a tone less ironical than one would expect:

> Most negroes are natural valets and hairdressers. . . . There is . . . a smooth tact about them in this employment. . . . And above all is the great gift of good-humour . . . a certain easy cheerfulness . . . as though God had set the whole negro to some pleasant tune . . . to this is added the docility arising from the unaspiring contentment of a limited mind, and that susceptibility of bland attachment sometimes inhering in indisputable inferiors. . . . Like most men of a good, blithe heart, Captain Delano took to negroes . . . just as other men to Newfoundland dogs.

But Babo is, in fact, the leader of a black uprising that has already murdered his master's closest friend and bound his corpse to the prow; and Captain Delano in his unwillingness to imperil his fondness for Negroes, almost kills Don Benito when he makes a last, desperate attempt to escape. Still convinced that the true source of moral infection is to be found only in the decaying institutions of Europe, Captain Delano cannot understand why, even after the exposure of Babo, Benito Cereno continues to pine away and seems to long only for death.

Though the fact of slavery, out of which all the violence and deceit aboard the Spanish ship has been bred, remains a part of his own democratic world as well as Don Benito's aristocratic one, Amasa Delano is undismayed. Though only an incident has been dealt with and its deep causes left untouched, he finds in this no cause for despair, but demands that the Spaniard join with him in recognizing a happy ending. "You are saved . . . ," he cries to Don Benito; "You are saved: what has cast such a shadow upon you?" And he will not understand when the Spanish captain answers, "The negro." Indeed, Melville seems to share the bafflement of his American protagonist; a Northerner like Captain Delano, Melville finds the problem of slavery and the Negro a little exotic, a gothic horror in an almost theatrical sense of the word. Before his story is done, at any rate, he lets it lapse back into the language of the written record when he had to look for it in the first instance—quite unlike Poe who found this particular theme at the very center of his own experience.

In this regard, Mark Twain is much more like Poe than Melville. Whatever his conflicting allegiances, he was a Southerner in his roots and origin, who all his life long carried on a family quarrel with the part of the country in which he had long ceased to live. He had enlisted briefly on the side of the Confederacy, though he became finally a convert to the abolitionist cause and wrote in his finest book an attack on slavery; and he could never really disavow the Southern notion of "honor," though he mocked all his life Sir Walter Scott and the mad chivalric codes which the South had derived from Scott's books. The town in which Twain was born and to which his imagination compulsively returned existed on a boundary between South and West; and, indeed, his two youthful careers led him to turn first in one direction then in the other. As a riverboat pilot before the Civil War, he followed the Mississippi down to New Orleans, as a journalist and fortune-hunter after Abolition, he headed across that same river toward Nevada and California. Both worlds lured him, turn and turn about; and in his two most profound books, he faces first one way then the other, but reverses the actual order of his life.

Huckleberry Finn ends with Huck pointed west, ready to light out for the territory in search of a freedom he had deludedly and vainly sought with Jim by going down the Mississippi. Why, critics have asked ever since the book appeared, did Huck not cross the river to the Illinois side, go east to where freedom really existed as a political fact? But the East, though it claimed Twain at last, had no symbolic meaning for him; the motion toward childhood is for him a motion toward the South, down the river. It was, therefore, down to Arkansas that Twain moved the Missouri farm of his mother's sister and her husband, the Great Good Place of his earliest years, which is celebrated in the most moving and lyrical section of the *Autobiography,* and which had appeared earlier as a mythical refuge in *Huckleberry Finn* (1885) and *Tom Sawyer Detective* (1896). Like Poe, Twain thought of the trip home as a voyage south; but like the earlier writer, too, he felt that trip a descent into hell. Though Twain was always consciously more attracted than repelled by the ambivalent Eden of his boyhood, and in his memoirs tends to idealize its terror almost out of existence, his fiction tells quite another story. Huck Finn is able to reject Aunt Sally's utopia out of hand—for all the redolence of its good home cooking; and in *Tom Sawyer Detective,* it takes all of Tom's ingenuity to exorcise murder and the threat of madness from the earthly paradise. In neither of these works, however, does Twain make it quite clear what has cast a shadow upon his idyllic world, what *particular* terror haunts his most nostalgic memories.

Only in *Pudd'nhead Wilson,* his most gothic book and an almost diagrammatic study in black and white, does he reveal that his specter is identical with Poe's and Don Benito's: "The negro." *Puddn'head Wilson* begins and ends in the village where *Huckleberry Finn* began and *Tom Sawyer* was played out, on the banks of the same symbolic river and in the same mythical pre-Civil War years. But between the "St. Petersburg" of the earlier books and the "Dawson's Landing" of the later one, there is a terrible difference. Pudd'nhead is represented as a mature and cynical stranger coming into the place at which Twain had never managed before to look from the outside. To his two boy heroes, it is so totally and entirely their world that they know it no more than their own faces. Only the outsider, the estranged adult Twain had become, rather than the unalienated child he remembered himself, offers an opportunity for perspective; and the opening of the novel pans slowly down on the village: its rose-clad houses, its cats, its sleepiness, and its fragrance—all preparing for the off-hand giveaway of the sentence beginning, "Dawson's Landing was a slave-holding town. . . ."

Striving to return as a grownup to the limit of a boy's memory, Twain arrives at the fact of slavery, once as imperceptible to him as the town itself. The Civil War is the watershed, in Twain's life, between childhood and manhood, innocence and experience, joy and despair; and this very fact insures that in his time of experience and despair he come to know that his innocence and joy, as well as the life that sustained them, were based on the labor and indignities of slaves. Yet the lost happiness, however based, was real; and Twain, whose dogmatic anti-Christianity can conceive no other paradise, cannot leave off returning to it in reminiscence and in art. All the same, he cannot deny the shamefulness of his plight, the pity of being forced to dream a boy's dream of freedom acted out in the world of slavery.

In *Tom Sawyer,* the paradox at the heart of Twain's essential myth is hushed up for nostalgia's sake and in the interests of writing a child's book; in *Huckleberry Finn,* it is present as a constant tension, though camouflaged by the poetry and high spirits of the text; in *Pudd'nhead Wilson,* it falls apart into horror

and horseplay. In that novel, Hannibal is rendered from the very
start not as a Western but as a Southern town. The river is no
longer presented as a just-passed frontier, a defining limit between
the realms of civilization and nature, a boundary which America
touches and crosses on its way west; it is felt as a passageway into
the deep South. "Down the river" is the phrase that gives a kind
of musical unity to the work: a guilt-ridden, terrible motif repeated with variations, from the jesting taunts of its heroine, the
Negress Roxana, to a fellow slave, "If you b'longed to me I'd sell
you down the river 'fo' you git too fur gone . . ." to the bleak irony
of the novel's final sentence, "The Governor . . . pardoned Tom at
once, and the creditors sold him down the river."

The contrast with *Huckleberry Finn* inevitably suggests itself;
for here the direction of the river Twain loved is regarded as pointing *only* into the ultimate Southern horror, the unmitigated terror
of conscienceless and brutal slavery. The movement of the plot, the
very shape of *Pudd'nhead Wilson* is determined by this symbolic
motion toward the Gulf of Mexico—the movement of the Father of
Waters toward a confluence with the great maternal sea; though
here that symbolic motion represents no longer a dream of the
flight to freedom, but only a nightmare of the passage into captivity. And at the center of the motion and the plot, stands the figure
of the slave-girl Roxana, who has held at her breast both her own
child and her master's, black and white milk-brothers. Roxana,
however, defies all clichés; she is no gross, comfortable, placid
source of warmth, all bosom and grin, but a passionate, complex,
and beautiful mulatto, a truly living woman distinguished from the
wooden images of virtue and bitchery that pass for females in most
American novels. She is "black" only by definition, by social convention, though her actual appearance as described by Twain,
"majestic . . . rosy . . . comely," so baffled the platitude-ridden
illustrator of the official edition that he drew in her place a plump
and comic Aunt Jemima!

Her own child, called Valet de Chambre, or Chambers, has been
sired by Cecil Burleigh Essex, a white Virginia gentleman, and
hence is even less the woolly-haired, swart, blubber-lipped caricature than she. Indeed he is scarcely distinguishable with his "blue
eyes and flaxen curls" from his milk-brother, Thomas à Becket
Driscoll, so that Roxana has no trouble switching the two in their
cradles when Valet de Chambre is threatened with being sold down

the river. Twain makes clear that there is in the South no absolute distinction of black and white, merely an imaginary line—crossed and recrossed by the white man's lust—that makes one of two physically identical babies "by a fiction of law and custom a negro." Once the "negro" Valet de Chambre has been dressed in a soft muslin robe and the "white" Thomas à Becket Driscoll in a tow-linen shirt, their roles are reversed and each plays the traditional role of his imagined race. The real Tom persists in protecting his "young master" despite the beatings he receives at his hands, and even saves him from drowning. But when, after his rescue, the white fellows of the false Tom tease him by calling his rescuer his "nigger pappy," the false Tom attempts to kill that rescuer. He cannot abide the suggestion that "he had a second birth into life, and that Chambers was the author of his new being," cannot assent to the American archetype embodied in Jim and Huck in *Huckleberry Finn*—and so drives a knife into his savior. No more can he abide being the son of a Negress, and ends by selling his mother down the river.

But it is not only the literally "false" Toms who betray their black mothers and play Cain to their Negro brothers; Twain's protagonists merely make melodramatically evident the fact that every mistreatment of a Negro, the simple continuance of slavery as an institution, is both a betrayal of the breast at which the Southerner who calls himself white has sucked, and of the brother he calls black, who has sucked at the breast beside him. In the mythical dénouement of Twain's book, it is suggested that all sons of the South, whether counted in the census as black or white, are symbolically the offspring of black mothers and white fathers, products of a spiritual miscegenation at the very least, which compounds the evil of slavery with an additional evil. The whitest aristocrat has nestled up to a black teat; the dullest slave may have been sired by some pure-blooded F. F. V. blade, discharging his blind lust upon a field wench or a house servant.

The family pattern of *Pudd'nhead Wilson* is opposite to that of *Huckleberry Finn;* for while the former is the portrait of a Southern, which is to say, a patriarchal society, the latter portrays a Western or matriarchal one. In the earlier book, the "sivilization" which Huck finally rejects is a world of mothers, that is, of what Christianity has become among the females who maintain it just behind the advancing frontier. It is a relatively simple-minded world, whose goal is virtue, which is defined as not cursing, stealing, smoking, or lying, but rather keeping clean, wearing shoes, and praying for spiritual gifts. In this world, the male principle is represented, if at all (Tom Sawyer has no father), by outcasts and scoundrels like Huck's unredeemable Pap—or some representative of nature and instinct like the runaway slave, Nigger Jim. In *Pudd'nhead Wilson,* on the other hand, it is the fathers who represent society, who are the defenders of a chivalric code which Twain elsewhere affects to despise, and the descendants of cavaliers. York Leicester Driscoll, Percy Northumberland Driscoll, Pembroke Howard, and Colonel Cecil Burleigh Essex: the names make the point perhaps too obviously. This is a world continuous with that of Renaissance England, a world in which "honor" is the sole code.

The patriarchal world of "honor" is also one of gallantry, of a kind of lustiness associated in Twain's mind with the court of Elizabeth, which for him represented a lost sexual Eden, contrasted (in his privately circulated *1601*) with a debilitated America, where men "copulate not until they be five-and-thirty years of age . . . and doe it then but once in seven yeeres." Though the men of Dawson's Landing, being Virginians, are potent still, their white women, who languish and retreat and die, are latter-day Americans, almost asexually genteel, so that only the Negress can match the vigor of the fathers with a corresponding fertility and power. Roxy is just such a Negress, and her union with Cecil Burleigh Essex represents not only a sociological but a symbolic truth. If the fathers of the South are Virginia gentlemen, the mothers are Negro girls, casually or callously taken in the parody of love, which is all that is possible when one partner to a sexual union is not even given the status of a person.

Twain's own judgment of sexual relations between black and white, slave and free is not explicitly stated; but there seems no doubt that he regarded the union between Roxy and Essex with a certain degree of horror, regarded it as a kind of fall—even in itself and a source of doom to all involved. There are two possible relations, two kinds of love between colored and white projected in our fiction, one of which is innocent, one guilty; one of which saves, one damns. The first provides a sentimental relation for the highbrow Western, the second a terrible one for the Southern gothic romance. The innocent relationship can exist only between men, or a man and a boy; the other suspect and impure, tries to join the disjoined in heterosexual passion, and its end is a catastrophe: a catastrophe symbolized by the "blackness" of the Negro, outward sign of an inward exclusion from grace.

At one level, Twain seems willing to accept the tragic position of the Negro as an inexplicable curse, crying out through the mouth of the pseudo-Tom in his moment of bafflement and despair, "What crime did the uncreated first nigger commit that the curse of birth was decreed for him. . . ." And certainly Roxy seems to share her master's assumption that blackness of the skin, the invisible taint of the blood carries with it an inevitable moral weakness. Her son's malice and cowardice, she is disconcertingly willing to attribute to the quantum of Negro blood which she has bequeathed him. "It's de nigger in you, dat's what it is," she screams at her son when he has refused to fight a duel; "Thirty-one parts o' you is white en on'y one part nigger, en dat po' little one part is yo' soul." Conversely, she has assured him at an earlier moment, after revealing to him the secret of his birth ("You's a *nigger—bawn* a nigger en a *slave!*"), that his white father at least had been a great man, who had been honored with "de bigges' funeral dis town ever seed." "Dey ain't another nigger in dis town dat's as high-bawn as you is . . . jus you hold yo' head up as high as you want to—you has de right. . . ."

This is, of course, a conventional kind of humor, and Twain is after the laughs which are easy enough to get by portraying one Negro calling another "nigger" in the proper dialect. But certain ironies proliferate disturbingly beneath the burlesque; and we are left baffled before the spectacle of slaves and outcasts accepting, as they insult each other, not only the offensive epithet "nigger," but all the assumptions implicit in that epithet. Insofar as Twain asks us to accept certain vaudeville gags as social history, we find his book and its meanings distasteful, an uncomfortable reminder of his own human failings; but we cannot help suspecting that behind the horseplay and grotesque melodrama of his plot, he may be attempting to translate an account of local prejudice into a fable revealing man's more universal implication in guilt and doom. If the false Tom is meant to represent not merely a Negro vainly pretending to be white, but the fruit of the betrayal and terror and profaned love which join all men, white and black, in our society —he must be made to embody the seeds of self-destruction which that relationship contains within it. He must therefore lie, steal, kill, and boast of his crimes, until, out of hybris, he reveals himself as a secret slave.

Though it is Pudd'nhead Wilson, local character, fingerprint expert and amateur detective, who presumably unmasks the impostor and wins the town's applause, it is really the false Tom himself who brings on his own downfall. Twain cannot resist a courtroom dénouement, a revelation and reversal sprung by some self-appointed sleuth at the darkest moment of a plot. Tom Sawyer, indeed, exists precisely to make such exposures not only in the books called by his name, but even in the one written in Huckleberry Finn's. Most readers will remember (and the reader of *Pudd'nhead Wilson* must to fully savor that book) how at the climax of *Huckleberry Finn,* Tom Sawyer, "his eyes hot, and his nostrils opening and shutting like gills," cries out of Jim: "They hain't no *right* to shut him up. . . . Turn him loose! He ain't no slave; he's as free as any cretur that walks this earth!" "As free as any cretur," the boy hero declares, blithely convinced that freedom is real, realer than the illusion of slavery; and, putting down that sanguine book, we believe him.

But a wry joke is already implicit in the phrase, which Twain no more sees than does Tom; and we as readers are not permitted to see it, as long as we remain within the spell of the happy ending. In *Pudd'nhead Wilson,* however, the protagonist, who is obviously Tom himself permitted at long last to grow up, rises to answer his own earlier courtroom cry, in just such a situation as he has always loved: " 'Valet de Chambre, Negro and slave . . . make upon the window the fingerprints that will hang you!" The double truth is in that instant complete: the seeming slave is free, but the free man is really a slave. It is an odd dénouement to a detective story enlivened by touches of farce: this revelation which condemns a hitherto free man to a life of servitude down the river, and leaves his mother sobbing on her knees, "De Lord have mercy on me, po' miserable sinner dat I is!" There is a happy ending this time for no one really except David Wilson (no longer called contemptuously "Pudd'nhead"), if one considers his acceptance by the philistine community really a blessing. To be sure, the same fingerprints which prove the presumed Tom a slave, establish the presumed Chambers as free; but his "curious fate" is equivocal if not actually tragic. Neither black nor white in his self-consciousness, he is excluded by long conditioning from the world of upper-class society, and barred from the "solacing refuge" of the slave kitchens by the fact of his legal whiteness. Had he turned on his foster-brother at the moment of revelation, he could only have yelled what he earlier cried out to his presumed mother, "Yah-yah-yah! . . . Bofe of us is imitation *white*—dat's what we is. . . ." And what would he have made of Twain's afterthought, one of the final jottings in his journal, "the skin of every human being contains a slave"?

Certainly, Pudd'nhead Wilson, in his exhibitionist courtroom speech, when he rises to announce once more the old scandal that the son has killed his father (Twain somewhat timidly makes them only step-father and step-son), does not succeed in restoring to the community a sense of its own innocence by establishing the guilt of a single culprit. Yet this, as W. H. Auden convincingly argues, is the archetypal function of the detective story, to which genre *Pudd'nhead Wilson* seems to belong. It is, in fact, an *anti*-detective story, more like *The Brothers Karamazov* than *The Innocence of Father Brown,* its function to expose communal guilt: our moral bankruptcy, horror and shame, the stupidity of our definition of a Negro, and the hopeless trap of our relations with him. Wilson's disclosure of Roxy's hoax coalesces with Mark Twain's exposure to America of its own secret self. Each of Twain's chapters is headed by a quotation from "Pudd'nhead Wilson's Calendar," a collection of small-town dangerous thoughts; and at the head of the final chapter, under the rubric "Conclusion," he inscribes the following text: *"October 21, The Discovery.* It was wonderful to find America, but it would have been more wonderful to miss it." It is the most improbable of endings for a detective story, which depends precisely upon its readers' faith in discovery; but it is one appropriate enough for the anti-Western novel at the moment that it becomes anti-American in its revulsion from all clichés of innocent, new frontiers.

The assault upon the Western and its image of America did not, of course, die with Twain. In our time, it is most notably carried forward by Robert Penn Warren, a poet, critic, and pedagogue as well as a novelist, who has attempted the risky game of presenting to our largest audience the anti-Western in the guise of the Western, the anti-historical romance in the guise of that form itself. In this enterprise, he has followed the example of Twain himself, who pretended to be writing in *Pudd'nhead Wilson* a popular detective story even as he mocked the form; and who in "A Double-Barrelled Detective Story" carried the process even further, specifically parodying the methods of Conan Doyle. It is with historical fiction that Warren prefers to deal, seeing himself perhaps as the researcher (his first book dealt with the life of John Brown) just as Twain sees himself as the sleuth. In *World Enough and Time* (1952), at any rate, Warren attacks directly the myth of the West, using for his purposes the famous Beauchamp case, which had been treated earlier by Simms and Edgar Allan Poe. Warren, however, is not primarily interested in the fable of seduction and revenge, on which we have commented earlier; by shifting the point of interest from the Persecuted Maiden to her avenging lover, whom he calls Jeremiah Beaumont, he converts the tale from a study of the encounter of innocence and lust to a study of the encounter of romanticism and reality. Through all his attempts to substitute for life, or impose on life itself a sentimental dream of life, Beaumont has assumed the existence of a paradisal West, an unfallen Eden to which he can flee when all else fails him. In the end, Warren permits him to escape hanging (changing the facts of the original story for this purpose) and to seek out the wilderness of which he has so long dreamed. But that wilderness he finds to be no more than a festering swamp, in which he is ultimately murdered and his beloved, withered and haggard, commits suicide; and presiding over the travesty of the Great Good Place, no noble and immaculate Natty Bumppo, but a hump-backed monster dying in sensuality and filth: *la grande Bosse,* river pirate and nightmare made flesh, the visible shape of original sin which Beaumont's sentimental version of the West had denied.

In *Brother to Dragons* (1953), a long verse narrative, Warren continues his assault on the theory of original innocence, drafting Thomas Jefferson as a ghostly witness to a particularly brutal and meaningless crime committed by two of his nephews, who slaughter in a meat-house, for trivial reasons, a Negro—acting out ritually the guilt of the white man toward those he has enslaved.*

* The ghost of Merriwether Lewis haunts Warren's poem and has recently begun to haunt me, too—so blithe in his beginnings, so tragic in his end. He represents and his journals record an attempt to penetrate the American West erotically, joyously—to assimilate it in heterosexual love. But his death at thirty-five (murdered? a suicide?) marks the failure of that attempt as well as Lewis's personal defeat.

It is not until *Band of Angels* (1955), however, that Warren, a Southerner himself and once involved in the Agrarian movement, turns to a full-scale treatment of the subject Twain had broached in *Pudd'nhead Wilson,* the plight of the white Negro. By turning the false Tom into a girl, however, Warren transforms the novel of miscegenation from the masculine murder mystery to the feminine bosom book, the erotic historical romance, creating a hybrid form whose strange pedigree would read: out of Margaret Mitchell by Mark Twain! Its fable deals with Amantha Starr, a young woman who discovers on her father's death that she is legally a slave and a Negro—and of her difficulty in deciding what, beneath "the fiction of law and custom," she really is.

The problem of identity is not for her as simple as it was for the exposed Valet de Chambre; what his mother confides in him and Pudd'nhead declares in open court, he himself believes. But Amantha does not know what to believe, for she has been sent as a child to an enlightened and pious college, where she has acquired a set of abolitionist clichés as useless to her in understanding the realities of slavery and being a Negro as are the opposite clichés of the Southern slaveholders. Nonetheless, an aura of miscegenation hangs over the series of love affairs which make up the history of Amantha, threatening to dissolve each embrace into a spasm of nausea or to convert it into a rape; yet she will not, she cannot bring herself to say, "I am a Negro!" No more capable of declaring herself white, she chooses to be nothing: an abstract victim without a particular identity. Like the hero of Ralph Ellison's *Invisible Man,* she fades from sight because she becomes nothing except her role; but in her case, the invisibility is willed. Her decision justifies her lovers in approaching her with disgust or condescension or pity—anything, that is to say, but love; and it is for that reason, that they are destroyed. Only when her white husband comes to realize that he, too, is a victim, she, too, a human ("The skin of every human being contains a slave" and its obverse), is he able to live with her not as a master or a benefactor, but as one weak and suffering being with another; and Amantha is at last free. It is a finally sentimental resolution, a retreat from the tragic blackness toward which Mark Twain had, however falteringly, moved.

To find a writer capable of accepting the darker implications of Twain's gothicism and pressing on to even more terrible resolutions, we must turn back to Warren's immediate master, William Faulkner. Faulkner instinctively begins with the realization, which we have discovered in Twain, that not murder only but miscegenation, too, must preside over the relations of black and white to produce the full gothic shiver. More shocking to the imagination of the South than the fantasy of a white man overwhelmed by a hostile black world is the fear that finally all distinctions will be blurred and black and white no longer exist. On what can the assurance of a God-given right to enslave Negroes or deprive them of rights be based, when no man can say with security who is the real Thomas à Becket Driscoll, who some black pretender? Precisely this prevision of total assimilation and chaos is entrusted to the young Canadian Shreve at the end of Faulkner's *Absalom, Absalom!* (1935):

> I think that in time the Jim Bonds are going to conquer the western hemisphere. Of course it won't be quite in our time and of course as they spread toward the poles they will bleach out again like the rabbits and birds do, so they won't show up so sharp against the snow. But it will still be Jim Bond; and so in a few thousand years, I who regard you will also have sprung from the loins of African kings.

But Jim Bond in the novel is an idiot, elusive as a ghost, a specter haunting the ravaged white family whose blood he shares.

In Faulkner's work, the threat of miscegenation is posed not only in terms of future racial contamination, but also in those of a present sexual threat. Out of the semi-obscene sub-literature of Southern racists, he captures and redeems the hysterical vision of the black rapist, the Negro who, by stealth or force (in Faulkner it is typically by stealth, which is to say, under the cover of a pseudo-white skin), possesses a white woman. The archetype answers precisely the abolitionist myth of the helpless Negro servant girl assaulted by her master. Against Roxana, pitifully proud of her relationship with the gentleman who leaves her pregnant with a flaxen-haired slave, is set the mother of Joe Christmas in *Light in August* (1932), trying to convince the doctor who attends her that the man who had fathered her bastard "was a Mexican. When old Doc Hines could see in his face the black curse of God Almighty." And against Simon Legree in *Uncle Tom's Cabin,* pursuing the terrified and virginal Emmeline, is balanced (in *Absalom, Absalom!*) the figure of Charles Bon, who has persuaded a white woman to marry him. A charming and handsome Negro, who has "passed" without difficulty, he turns to the somewhat younger white man, who has adulated him and to whose sister he is engaged, deliberately evoking the vulgar taunt of the crudest Negro-baiters, "I'm the nigger that's going to sleep with your sister. Unless you stop me, Henry." And Henry, as he must, though only after long delay, shoots him.

Yet just before Bon speaks the words that doom him, Henry has cried to him, "You are my brother." Such brotherhood is more than a metaphor in *Absalom, Absalom!,* more even than the bond of having shared a single breast that links Twain's Tom to Chambers. In Faulkner's plot, the white man and the Negro who love and destroy each other are quite literally the sons of the same father, of Thomas Sutpen, the passionate, damned hero of the action. The younger, white son was born of a timid, genteel, rustic, puritanical creature, married for the sake of the status and respectability she could bestow; the older, black one was the offspring of a Haitian breed, foisted on an ignorant and ambitious young man by her unscrupulous parents. White and black, they find themselves locked finally in a terrible triangle, the two brothers more in love with each other than either with the sister (perhaps Bon loves no one, only wants to provoke his proud father into admitting the relationship from which he has fled), and the threat of incest over them all.

This is the final turn of the screw, the ultimate gothic horror which serves both to produce one more shock and to add one more level of symbolic relevance to the action: the man who screams in panic that some black buck is about to rape his sister is speaking of one who is, indeed, his brother, and whom secretly he loves. But the event of such love is only guilt and death and a retreat into a dark house, already sacked and gutted in a war fought to maintain the order which had bred the relationship itself. Sutpen and his Negro bride had already mated, already produced a child neither white nor black; and the frustration of a second incestuous match saves nothing. It serves only to prevent the grafting onto the narrow, Protestant provincialism of the rural South of a Catholic and urban grace, nurtured in Creole New Orleans. The adulterated Sutpen line eventuates not in the sensuous, elegant hybrid that might have been produced out of a mating of Charles Bon and Sutpen's white daughter, but in Jim Bond, mindless child of the offspring of

Bon's self-punishing marriage to an ignorant, ugly Negress: ". . . there was nothing left now, nothing out there now but that idiot boy to lurk around those ashes and those four gutted chimneys and howl until someone came and drove him away. They couldn't catch him and nobody ever seemed to make him go very far away, he just stopped howling for a little while."

Jim Bond (the name which meant "good" corrupted to one which means "slave") is not so much living flesh and blood as the terrible ghost that haunts the mind of such Southerners as Quentin Compson, who has been driven to uncover step by step the mystery of the Sutpens, and who represents the conscience of Faulkner himself. No wonder he grows frantic under his roommate's questioning: " 'Now I want you to tell me just one thing more. Why do you hate the South?' 'I dont hate it,' Quentin said, quickly, at once, immediately; 'I dont hate it,' he said. *I dont hate it* he thought, panting in the cold air, the iron New England dark; *I dont. I dont! I dont hate it! I dont hate it!"* These are the final words of the book; but they are followed by a genealogy, in which we read of Quentin Compson that he died in the very year in which he uncovered the secret of the death of Charles Bon, not yet twenty years old: a suicide, we learn in another place. It is the only possible ending to a novel in which the "Southern" as a genre reaches its final form. At the same time that *Absalom, Absalom!* solves the detective-story problem of who killed Charles Bon, it is answering another, profounder question, satisfying the Southerner's need to "know at last why God let us lose the war." The query is as desperate as that posed by Captain Delano: "What has cast such a shadow upon you?" And the answer is the same: "The Negro."

Yet the theme we have been examining does not exhaust the meanings of Faulkner's book. It represents only a single strand in an intricately constructed and immensely complex work, a showpiece of sustained rhetoric, whose total effect makes it at first bewildering, but which, in the long run, seems the most deeply moving of all American gothic fictions. In the history of that genre, *Absalom, Absalom!* is remarkable for having first joined to the theme of slavery and black revenge, which is the essential sociological theme of the American tale of terror, that of incest, which is its essential erotic theme.

In Poe the incest theme belongs to the private world of his own tortured psyche rather than the broader arena of social life in the South. Over and over, the writer, who married his scarcely nubile cousin and called her Sis, returns to the theme, particularly in that series of tales involving dark and terrible ladies, which is his most authentic and convincing achievement. The first of these stories is "Berenice" ("Berenice and I were cousins, and we grew up together in my paternal halls . . ."); and the line continues on through "Eleanora" ("She whom I loved in youth . . . was the sole daughter of the only sister of my mother long departed") to reach a climax in "The Fall of the House of Usher," in which the doomed beloved is at last identified as the protagonist's sister. Sometimes, as in "Morella" and "Ligeia," the dying succubus-bri le is portrayed as not even being kin to her husband; but always she is clearly a dark projection of his psyche, as intimately related to him as his own image in the mirror. And always, too, she bears the stigmata of a tabooed figure: the dark eyes and hair, which mark her as the carrier of madness and death. She tends to become, indeed, the symbol of mortality, the figure of death itself—combining the characteristics of shadow and *anima,* as if intended to signify that the soul of a man and his death are one thing.

The uses of incest in sentimental and gothic fiction are, as we have already noticed, many; but in Poe, who deals customarily with problems of impotence rather than of power, the death-wish is always uppermost; and the desire to embrace the sister-bride means for him first of all a yearning to *fall*—a perverse longing to plunge into the destructive embrace of his own image in a dark tarn. The ending of "The Fall of the House of Usher" expresses directly the lust for a union with death which is Poe's ruling passion. Madeline, the sister of Usher, whom he has buried alive, returns from the grave to claim her brother just as he has, almost equally, feared and desired:

> Without those doors there DID stand the lofty and enshrouded figure of the Lady Madeline of Usher. There was blood upon her white robes, and the evidence of some bitter struggle upon every portion of her emaciated frame. For a moment she remained trembling and reeling to and fro upon the threshold,

then, with a low moaning cry, fell heavily inward upon the person of her brother, and in her violent and now final death agonies, bore him to the floor as a corpse. . . .

It is the most horrific of *Liebestods,* the ultimate expression of Poe's obsessive dream of being possessed by the dead, raped by a cadaverous sister-beloved, elsewhere projected in the story of Ligeia, who returns from death to take over the body of a second bride. But there is in Poe a complementary desire to possess the dead, to return embrace for embrace, violation for violation. At its mildest and most conventional, this longing is satisfied in fantasies of lovers joined as fellow ghosts beyond the grave or chatting cozily after the cataclysmic destruction of the world. In such tales, the erotic commerce of the specters is confined to speech, as in "The Colloquy of Monos and Una" or "The Conversations of Eiros and Charmion." Occasionally, however, Poe's necrophiliac heroes descend living into the tomb, like the protagonist of "Berenice," who returns with the bloody teeth of his beloved, or the narrator of "Ulalume," who scarcely knows why he has drifted back to the "dank tarn of Auber." Most frank of all Poe's celebrations of the union with a corpse is confided to the disarmingly sweet verses of "Annabel Lee":

> And so, all the night-tide, I lie down by the side
> Of my darling—my darling—my life and my bride,
> In the sepulchre there by the sea—
> In her tomb by the sounding sea.

The odd syndrome of child-love, necrophilia, and incest in Poe is too personal and pathological to shed much light on the general meaning of the latter theme in American literature and life. It is not without interest, however, to reflect that the tales of Poe have come to be thought of as a children's classic; and his fantasies—in which adults never copulate in the flesh, only rape each other's minds, at least as long as they are alive—are considered proper selections for classroom anthologies. In any case, he has had little direct influence on later serious American writers, until, perhaps, the time of Vladimir Nabokov, in whose *Lolita* the example of Poe is combined so oddly with that of Gogol. When gothic incest became a major theme in the mid-nineteenth century, it was embodied not in the figure of Madeline Usher but that of Beatrice Cenci.

The most gothic books of both Hawthorne and Melville are presided over by the mythic face of this lady as painted by Guido Reni and adulated by two generations of American tourists. Over *The Marble Faun* of the one and the *Pierre* of the other, Beatrice Cenci casts a shadow of parricide and incest, suggests an added dimension of horror that Hawthorne at least was too cautious to specify in his own plot. It is important to remember that it was not really the original seventeenth-century painting of her in the Palazzo Barberini to which both Hawthorne and Melville made the obligatory pilgrimage; for both alike were possessed by a literary tradition which had grown up around the portrait, finally making it impossible to see past the myth of "a fallen angel," as Hilda calls her in *The Marble Faun,* "fallen, and yet sinless."

In response to the *myth* of the portrait, both American writers vibrated in accord; but about what it looked like they totally disagree. "With blue eyes and fair complexion, the Cenci's hair is golden," Melville writes; while Hawthorne informs us that from beneath Beatrice's turban "strayed a lock or two . . . of auburn hair. The eyes were large and brown. . . ." Since each had approached the picture as literature, each re-envisioned it in his own style. For Melville, the incest-stained innocent *must* be blond in order to make his symbolic point (elsewhere worked out in *Typee* and *Mardi*) that in some women the Fair Maiden and the Dark Lady are disturbingly confused:

> . . . physically . . . all is in strict, natural keeping: which, nevertheless, still the more intensifies the suggested anomaly of so *blonde* a being, being double-hooded, as it were by the black crape of the two more horrible crimes . . . possible to civilized humanity—incest and parricide.

It is, indeed, the blond Lucy of his own *Pierre* who, in that novel, stands before the portrait, which reflects the incest and terror that she has not recognized, not allowed herself to recognize in her closest companions, Isabel and Pierre.

Hawthorne goes even further by suggesting an actual resemblance between his Anglo-Saxon snow maiden and the mysterious portrait, that to him symbolizes not so much the ambiguity of light and dark as the mystery of alienation: "It was the saddest picture ever painted or conceived; it involved an unfathomable depth of sorrow . . . a sorrow that removed this beautiful girl out of the sphere of humanity, and set her in a far-off region, the remoteness of which . . . makes us shiver as at a spectre." In Hawthorne, the copy of Guido's Beatrice that plays a part in his own tale, is not the product—as in Melville—of an unknown hand, but has been lovingly painted by the Fair Girl herself, by his dove-like Hilda. Looking into her mirror, she fancies a similarity between her own expression and that of the Beatrice before whom she has sat so long. Hawthorne, however, hastens to make it clear that not her own sin but that of another had frightened Beatrice Cenci "into a remote and inaccessible region, where no sympathy would come," and that it is a similar fate which is shadowed on Hilda's face. Just as the earlier innocent had been crushed by a sense of her father's guilt, Hilda risks being crushed by an awareness of the crime of her friend, the Dark Lady, Miriam.

It is Miriam who is involved in a mysterious scandal which binds her to the sinister palace of the Cenci itself, Miariam to whom Hawthorne's mouthpiece, Kenyon, says, "I shudder at the fatality that seems to haunt your footsteps, and throws a shadow of crime about your path, you being guiltless." But what precise crime has cast a shadow upon her, Hawthorne cannot bring himself to tell. It is connected, we know, with the hairy Model who dogs her footsteps, and who is bound to her, it is suggested, by blood as well as complicity, a man "so evil, so vile, and yet so strangely subtle, as could only be accounted for by the insanity which often develops itself in old, closekept races of men when long unmixed with newer blood." This suggestion of immemorial inbreeding, joined with the repeated allusions to Miriam's implication in "one of the most dreadful and mysterious events that have occurred within the present century," implies surely the sin of incest; but Hawthorne is at once too genteel and too fond of playful mystification to speak out that dread word.

Hawthorne had dealt openly with the subject of incest only in his early story "Alice Doane's Appeal," whose basic fable oddly resembles Faulkner's *Absalom, Absalom!* It opens with a murder whose solution involves the exposure of the feelings that bind together in an unnatural triangle a young man, his sister, and a stranger whom he suspects of being her lover, but who proves in the end brother to both. "He was my very counterpart," says Leonard Doane of Walter Broame; and this uncanny resemblance seems to him reason enough for his sister Alice to "inevitably love him . . . with all the strength of sisterly affection, added to that impure passion which alone engrosses all the heart." Driven half-mad by imaginings which project onto the stranger his own unconfessed desire for his sister, and infuriated further by that stranger's boasts of having conquered her, Leonard kills him. At the moment of death, however, he sees in the face of the man he has murdered "a likeness of my father."

As in Faulkner's novel, the brothers are as culturally unlike as they are physically the same; for just as in the twentieth-century fiction, one has been educated "in the cities of the old world" and one "in this rude wilderness." Cosmopolitan sybarite and rustic stalwart, they represent in their conflict not the struggle of Creole black and Puritan white brother, but the encounter of Old World and New World sons of the same fatherland, loyalist and colonial in a struggle for possession of the body of America. In the end, Hawthorne's fragmentary story threatens to become a parable of the American Revolution—a gothic treatment of the international theme, set back into the period when our national consciousness was in the process of being forged.

In the final years of his life, Hawthorne tried once more to create a substantial fiction dealing, beneath its spectacular machinery of bloody footsteps, ancestral curses, and lost wills, with the bloody confrontation of England and America. He achieved only a handful of fragmentary manuscripts in which the theme of incest struggles to assert itself, as it must in any fable treating a guilt-ridden fraternal relationship which begins in love and ends in murder.

In light of Hawthorne's life-long obsession with the subject, one is tempted to believe the contention of certain critics (finally unproven) that the incestuous Pierre of Melville's gothic romance is intended to be a portrait of Hawthorne; that the book was Melville's attempt to confess for his alienated friend the secret sin which presumably haunted him through all his years. Melville seems to have believed, at any rate, that he had penetrated the heart of Hawthorne's mystery; for when Hawthorne's son visited him in 1883, Melville told him—so Julian Hawthorne wrote later —"that there was some secret in my father's life which had never been revealed, and which accounted for the gloomy passages in his books." Julian was not much impressed, however, observing dryly, "It was characteristic of him to imagine so; there were many secrets untold in his own career." Whether, indeed, the "secret" revealed in *Pierre* is Melville's or Hawthorne's or neither's matters little; what is important is that it is the major underground concern of American gothicists in general, the erotic relationship proper to that form: brother-sister incest. *Pierre* represents the major attempt in the history of our fiction at making of that theme great art, at redeeming it from the stereotypes into which it had fallen, and wresting from it whatever symbolic meaning it had all along contained.

Even in the first chapters of *Pierre,* suggestions of a sickly incestuousness hover over the euphoric rustic scene. The young Pierre not merely flutters about his mother with the excessive gallantries of a courtly lover, tying her ribbon, her shoe-lace, but he addresses her as "Sister Mary"; and she, speaking of the blond Lucy who is to be Pierre's wife, refers to her as a "little sister." There is more than a trace of pride registered in the adjective, for Pierre's mother is securely aware of her sexual superiority to "little" Lucy, reflecting later that beside her son's fiancée she herself seems a quart decanter of port next to a pint decanter of pale sherry! But Pierre is not content just to *play* at incest with his mother, and marry—as an assurance of his fidelity to her—a girl who is clearly no sexual rival. Instead, he turns to a dark, alien figure, the complete denial of everything in his mother's milky, blue, pink, and gold idyllic world, but a reminder of what his wild father might have been before his marriage.

To complicate matters further, Isabel, the swart *anima*-figure who may be his sister, is half-mad and an outcast; so that to espouse her cause can be made to seem moral dedication and an attack on conformity. When Pierre decides finally to run off with Isabel, to pretend to the world that they are man and wife—so that he can at once protect her and not expose his father as a breeder of bastards—he is able to feel himself Christ-like, and his act a more than human self-sacrifice. Melville, however, refuses either him or the reader the privilege of living long with this illusion, pointing out that in attempting to transcend the codes of conventional society, Pierre has risked becoming a scandalous sinner rather than a moral hero. In the end, he is not the Christ or Titan he dreams himself, not even a Memnon or Hamlet, but a latter-day Widow of Ephesus. Like the woman of that legend, who, in dedicating herself to an impossible ideal of fidelity, ended by desecrating the grave of her husband in lust and hanging his body on a public gallows, Pierre invents for himself crimes beyond the ken of ordinary men, a dénouement almost as comic as it is terrible.

Even at the moment when he first confides to Isabel his decision to run off with her and accept the world's blame, conscious of his blamelessness, Pierre really knows what he is after. The secret motive of his ostensible sacrifice enters his awareness.

He held her tremblingly; she bent toward him; his mouth wet her ear; he whispered it. . . . Over the face of Pierre there shot a terrible self-revelation; he imprinted repeated burning kisses upon her; pressed her hand; would not let go her sweet and awful passiveness.

Then they changed; they coiled together, and entangledly stood mute.

The image of the serpent signals the presence of the serpentine horror of incest, already implicit in the pressure of a damp mouth at the ear; but there is a further fall to come. After Pierre has fled to the city, and has found there only failure and the torments of guilt, he comes to his dark sister to be consoled, to be held in her arms in "the peace of the twilight." But folded into that "sweet and awful passiveness" again, he leaps up in anguish, crying, "If to follow Virtue to her uttermost vista . . . if by that I take hold on hell, and if the uttermost virtue, after all, prove but a betraying pander to the monstrousest vice,—then close in and crush me, ye stony walls, and into one gulf let all things tumble together!"

It is pseudo-Shakespearean rant, the rhetoric of the cheapest gothic melodrama, a theatrical debasement of the pure Faustian cry of terror; but beneath its superficial falseness, there is at work an insidious attack on the platitudes of Romanticism, which had made of fraternal affection the symbol of an impossible purity. The gothic mode is essentially a form of parody, a way of assailing clichés by exaggerating them to the limit of grotesqueness; and in *Pierre,* Melville is mocking the banal tender plea, "Let me be a sister to you!", just as in *Absalom, Absalom!,* Faulkner was to mock the banal harsh taunt, "Would you want a nigger to sleep with your sister!" Yet there is rage in Melville, too, anguish at the thought that there cannot be an immaculate love of brother and sister; that this, too, is one of "The Ambiguities" referred to by the subtitle of his novel.

At this point, Pierre begins to rethink the evidence which has convinced him that Isabel was, indeed, his father's illegitimate daughter: her perhaps imagined resemblance to a portrait of his father as a young man, her disordered memories, an initialed hand-kerchief. "Call me brother no more!" he cries in despair; and the next moment he tries to argue away the concepts of virtue and vice, even as he has argued away their blood relationship. Only the denial of one or the other can save him from confessing his utter damnation, and he scarcely knows which to disavow first. He brushes aside "these two shadows cast from one nothing" and goes on to insist that "these, seems to me are Virtue and Vice. . . . It is all a dream that we dreamed we dream. . . . From nothing proceeds nothing, Isabel! How can one sin in a dream." But when Isabel, content with his dismissal of sin, unconcerned in her passivity, says simply, "Let us sit down again, my brother," Pierre is driven to repeat his first denial, "I am Pierre." Isabel still unruffled amends her request, "Let us sit down again, Pierre . . ." and together in the growing dark with no lamp lit, they fade into each other in their fatal embrace.

Just as he sins (or perhaps does not) in the dream which is his life, Pierre also dreams within that dream; and his dream within a dream contains Melville's own reading of his book, a guide to future critics. The most analytic of novelists, Melville insisted always on being the explicator of his own symbols and themes; and incest was for him not a bedrock fact but a symbol, beyond which the reader must go in search of total comprehension, a riddle to be solved. Pierre sees in his dream a mountain shaped like a Promethean man, an outcropping of rock near his ancestral home, which fades into the figure of Enceladus, the mutilated but "deathless son of Terra"; and in turn this "American Enceladus," half-buried and castrated ("Nature . . . performed an amputation, and left the impotent Titan without one serviceable ball-and-socket above the thigh"), fades into the image of Pierre: "but on the Titan's armless trunk, his own duplicate face and features gleamed upon him with prophetic discomfiture and woe."

When he awakes from "that ideal horror to all his actual grief," Pierre calls upon all his knowledge of myth and legend, hammers away at the riddle like Moses at the rock, until he has made clear to his own and Melville's satisfaction the meaning of his vision:

> Old Titan's self was the son of incestuous Coelus and Terra, the son of incestuous Heaven and Earth. And Titan married his mother Terra, another and accumulatively incestuous match. So

Enceladus was both the son and grandson of an incest; and even thus, there had been born from the organic blended heavenliness and earthliness of Pierre, another mixed, uncertain, heaven-aspiring, but still not wholly earth-emancipated mood; which again, by its terrestrial taint held down to its terrestrial mother, generated there the present doubly incestuous Enceladus within him; so that the present mood of Pierre—that reckless sky-assaulting mood of his, was nevertheless on one side the grand-son of the sky. For it is according to eternal fitness, that the pre-cipitated Titan should still seek to regain his paternal birthright even by fierce escalade.

It seems almost more an evasion than an explanation; and certainly Melville permits himself to get trapped in the intricacies of his image, becoming as much its victim as its exploiter. What he seems to be saying on the simplest level is that in each individual there is a fundamental conflict of two principles, called variously earth and heaven, nature and spirit, id and super-ego; and that every human action is bred of a marriage of these principles, or of a union be-tween one of them and some previous action bred of an earlier marriage. In Western civilization, these principles are typically identified with the mother and father, and any attempt to allegorize them produces, on the literal level, a story of incest. To become somehow one with the father—even at the risk of seeming to be-tray the mother or of threatening the sovereignty of the paternal principle itself—this is for Melville the meaning of Enceladus' escalade and of Pierre's elopement.

Whether or not this seems finally satisfactory as an explanation of the fable of Melville's book, it is, perhaps, the only example in our literature of a writer's conscious attempt to know what he is unconsciously meaning when he takes up the subject of incest. At the opposite pole from this is Poe, who was content simply to be possessed by his subjects (when pressed he could always pretend they were parodies or hoaxes, or disown them as "silly"), and whose works, therefore, seem in large part symptoms rather than achievements.

IV

Yet Poe produced, after all, one completely achieved work of art in his writing career, a character who belongs specifically to none of his stories though he is, in part, the creation of all of them—a composite of Julius Rodman, Gordon Pym, William Wilson, Roderick Usher, and all the other pale, tormented failures at aggression, exploration, and love, who are haunted, buried alive, or clasped in the arms of corpses. That character, who is, of course, Edgar Allan Poe (even the middle name is an invention, part of the legend), Poe not only wrote but *lived*—taking cues from Brockden Brown and Byron and Bulwer Lytton; and adding, where necessary, the appropriate lies. He told incompatible stories about his birth, falsified his age, claimed to have gone off to Greece to help in the fight for freedom; and when he died, bequeathed his life-long task of composing a Poe-image to a particularly hostile executor, Rufus Griswold. It was perhaps Poe's last hoax, a perverse joke on himself and his public; for Griswold, as Poe must have foreseen, proceeded to blacken Poe's reputation with all the aplomb of a self-consciously righteous man exposing a scoundrel. To make Poe seem an utterly irresponsible villain, Griswold was not above forging letters or lifting appropriate passages out of popular novels and fitting them into his account. Like Poe himself, that is to say, Griswold approached his subject's life as if it were a work of art.

So also did Baudelaire, that second and unforeseen collaborator in the posthumous rewriting of Poe, who was moved by a passion equal and opposite to Griswold's. In need of a hero, an alter ego, a model for his own version of the *poète maudit,* Baudelaire took up the still plastic image of Poe and made of it that French *symboliste* once-removed, the *Edgairpo* of the Europeans, which to this day baffles visitors from our side of the Atlantic. Baudelaire saw Poe simultaneously as the victim of America and as a second Christ whose cross was alcohol. Speaking from the first view, he says: "Some of the documents which I have seen persuade me that Poe found in the United States a large prison from which all his life he was making desperate efforts to escape"; and from the second, "I say without shame, because I feel that it springs from a profound sense of pity and affection, that I prefer Edgar Poe, drunk, poor, persecuted and a pariah, to a calm and virtuous Goethe or Walter

Scott. I should willingly say of him and of a special class of men what the catechism says of our Lord: 'He has suffered much for us!' "

It is easy enough to discount both statements of Baudelaire as examples of a new sentimentality, the sentimentality of the anti-bourgeois European poet, who tries to put art in the vacant place of God and America and mass society in that of the Devil. Poe was by no means the first or only writer in the United States to find himself at odds with his country. It is, indeed, the typical relationship between Americans and serious native writers of all kinds, even James Fenimore Cooper (who represented to Poe the antithesis of that to which he aspired) having found himself estranged from his fellow citizens, hostile to their way of life. But whatever quarrels Cooper may have had with the American public, he was never alienated from the deepest levels of the American mind. If, at his death, he was being read less and less, still his passing was felt as an occasion for national mourning, and Daniel Webster, the official spokesman of the era, called upon to pronounce his funeral oration. Poe, on the other hand, lay without a tombstone for twenty-six years, and when one was erected, the only notable American present was Walt Whitman. Yet it was not Cooper but Poe who became for the American imagination the eternal prototype of the American Writer. Cooper, who could make a nation's myths, could not himself become such a myth; while Poe, who created no archetypal figure to rival Natty Bumppo, himself became a legend. This is perhaps not quite what Poe meant when he referred in reviewing Cooper to two kinds of literature, in one of which "the books sometimes live, while the authors usually die"; while in the other, "even when the works perish the man survives"; but it is close enough to it to indicate that dimly he felt the nature of his own mythical role as well as that of the highbrow writer in general.

Poe represents, of course, the artist as outcast or outsider, surrogate for all in himself that the common reader secretly regrets having to reject in the name of morality or success; and as such, he is our own local instance of an almost universal archetype. Just before Poe's day, Byron (to whom Baudelaire compared Poe, calling the latter *"le Byron égaré dans le mauvais monde"*) had played that mythic role for all of Europe and America, composing his public figure by combining the image of Don Juan with that of the gothic hero-villain, whose ancestry we have traced back to Richardson and Prévost. The most ancient avatar of the alienated artist, however, is Euripides—that is to say, the legendary creature fabricated by Greek commentators and called by that tragedian's name. The pattern is typical in all respects: born of poor and disreputable parents, himself sullen and disagreeable, Euripides is portrayed as returning contempt for contempt, withdrawing to a seaside grotto to be alone with the books he prefers to men; and at the last, it is told, he is torn to pieces by dogs or, preferably, by enraged women!

The final apocryphal anecdote is, of course, drawn from the legend of Orpheus, a mythical being with whom the actual historical figure of the poet was hopelessly confused. But what does the Orpheus archetype, of which Poe was the improbable New World avatar, signify? It is intended, apparently, to express the dismay of the popular mind before the kind of poet who is no longer content to represent bardically the traditions of a closed society, but speaks in his own person—invents, as it were, personal consciousness. In such a poet, the community foresees its own imminent fall from the unity and peace of pre-conscious communal life, and they condemn him to death. But the spokesman for the ego is destroyed by representatives of the id—Maenads, the devotees of Dionysus, wild beasts—and in his moment of destruction is made divine, becomes one with Dionysus himself. Even at its most primitive level, the myth of the outcast poet does not end with his exclusion and death. He has had to suffer and be despised; yet he is loved, even apotheosized precisely for that suffering and despite.

In the nineteenth century, the alienated artist still functions as a scape-hero, though by this time he knows his own role in advance, collaborates in his life and work with the community who seek to impose the traditional role on him. Perhaps, he is a little too self-conscious of what he is doing, a little too much in love with his own pain and exclusion to ring quite true; but society needs him still, demanding of the poet that he enact in his life the rejected values of heedlessness, disorder, and madness—and also that he permit himself to be abused and rejected for enacting them; that he take upon himself both sin and punishment, and so free the community from the burden of its repressed longings and its secret guilt.

This poor Poe was, for his own good masochistic reasons, only too willing to do; and where he did not quite conform to the necessary pattern, Griswold amended the facts of his life, converting the dandy, the lonely aristocrat of the spirit, the lost Byron of the Western world into a willful drunkard, a dope addict, a feckless bohemian. Failing to understand the archetypal necessities of the

case, certain respectable scholars of our own time have attempted
to redeem Poe from his legend—perhaps because their own peace
of mind depends on their proving that all the great writers of our
past were as sane and orderly as any member of the Kiwanis Club,
to which they themselves are likely to belong. One such critic
writes, for instance, "One would like, for all time, to destroy fictions that Poe was a drunkard . . . ; he was not a dope fiend . . . :
and he was not a rake. His life was, in fact, one of the dullest any
figure of literary importance has lived in the past two hundred
years." But Poe did, after all, marry a thirteen-year-old child and
watch her die painfully over five years; did at least believe himself
the victim of D.T.'s, and yet fling himself into frantic bouts of
drinking when faced by sexual problems he could not solve; was
at last picked up in the streets of Baltimore senseless, and turned
over to a doctor, who wrote: "There is a gentleman, rather the
worse for wear, at Ryan's 4th ward polls, who goes under the
cognomen of Edgar A. Poe, and who appears in great distress . . .";
did die, four days later, of alcoholic poisoning. It is not quite as
lively a death scene as that attributed by legend to Euripides, but
it is surely not the dullest in the past two hundred years. And it
haunts us still in the pages of Hart Crane's *The Bridge,* in which
the poet fixes once and for all the truth no scholar can really
desecrate:

> And when they dragged your retching flesh,
> Your trembling hands that night through Baltimore—
> That last night on the ballot rounds, did you
> Shaking, did you deny the ticket, Poe?

The image of Poe which for over a century has possessed the
American mind is that image of failure and impotence so necessary
to us in a world of success and power: an image of one who is the
victim of society and of himself. But it is more specifically, perhaps
essentially, the image of the *poet as drunkard,* the weak-stomached,
will-less addict, forever swearing off and forever succumbing again.
"For more than ten days I was totally deranged . . . ," Poe writes
in a letter. "All was hallucination arising from an attack which I
had never before experienced—an attack of mania-a-potu. May
heaven grant that it prove a warning to me for the rest of my
days. . . ." Mania-a-potu: it is the same somewhat unusual word
Poe has used in *Gordon Pym* for *delirium tremens.* But D.T.'s are

a part of American folklore, like drinking itself the source of an endless stream of uneasy jokes: "Close the windows; they're coming through the door!" The morning-after, the malfunctioning liver, the "shakes"—no jest will finally charm away the shadow which they throw over the idyllic dream of an innocent night at the bar with the boys.

In Poe's life, the fiction of "social drinking" is given the lie; for to him, even the first drink was a plunge toward dissolution, a kind of symbolic suicide. He plays in the American mind the role of an anti-Rip Van Winkle, projecting the fear that after the bust, one does not awake to a new and wifeless world, but continues to sleep the tormented sleep of the damned. If the figure of Poe in Baltimore refuses to be exorcised from the national imagination, it is because Poe's terrible death befell him in a moment of typically American evasion; not only did he fall drunken beside a balloting place (and to be drunk on Election Day is surely the most American of acts!), but his drunkenness was prompted by a flight from women and marriage. No wonder the folk mind never wearies of crying, "Let him die for the act we dream! Let him die the death we secretly desire!" It is in this sense, not Baudelaire's, that America was guilty of Poe's death—as it was guilty afterward of Scott Fitzgerald's and Hart Crane's and Dylan Thomas': those latter-day scape-heroes, who found not only sacrificial ends similar to Poe's but even Griswolds of their own to celebrate them.

The figures Poe created in his work were never as satisfactory, unfortunately, as the figure he composed with his life. Certainly Gordon Pym—though he moves into the first major scene "not a little intoxicated" and early confesses himself a member of the "numerous race of the melancholy"—does not ever come alive as a significant character, much less assume the tragic dimensions attained by Poe himself. Poe lacks as a writer a *sense of sin,* and therefore cannot raise his characters to the Faustian level which alone dignifies gothic fiction. When he tries to treat in his tales (in the "Duc de l'Omelette," for instance) the Satanic pact, he is embarrassed and seeks refuge in the heavy-handed horseplay he took for humor. The relations of Pym with Peters suggest from time to time the terrible bargain between Faust and Mephisto; but Poe will not permit Peters to become a real Devil, and Pym has obviously no soul to sell. Poe liked to boast that he had transformed the gothic from a "horror of Germany" to a "horror of the soul"; but by "soul" he seems to have meant only what we should call "sensibility." Certainly Pym, who in this respect resembles all of Poe's protagonists, responds even to torment aesthetically rather than morally; and for all his concern with evil, Poe provides only what Wallace Stevens would call an *Esthétique du mal*. If his own life seems to offer a more genuinely metaphysical shudder, this is thanks not to him but to the Puritan conscience of Griswold, which made of him a kind of vulgar Faust for the American market, just as Baudelaire made of him a *poète maudit* for the French one. If there seem to be even now two Poes, it is because he left a half-finished self that has been completed in one way for the American middlebrow audience, and in quite another for the highbrow French public.

13

THE POWER OF
BLACKNESS:
FAUSTIAN MAN AND
THE CULT OF VIOLENCE

IF EDGAR ALLAN POE fails finally to transform the gothic into the tragic, this is because he lacks that ultimate "power of blackness," which, as Melville observed, "derives its force from its appeal to that Calvinistic sense of Innate Depravity and Original Sin, from whose visitations, in some shape or other, no deeply thinking mind is always and wholly free." Scarcely any other of our classic writers, however, shares Poe's immunity to Calvinism; and it is, indeed, in their efforts to come to terms with a Puritan heritage, to render its insights in secular terms, that our chief nineteenth-century novelists reach the level of tragedy. By the nineteenth century, to be sure, American Puritanism had lost its original unity as well as its controlling position in American life, and had developed in two quite opposite directions toward two quite irreconcilable positions.

One wing had passed via eighteenth-century "enthusiasm" and Methodism toward a hysterical evangelism, which produced revivals like the Great Awakening of 1742, and which survives to this day in the meetings which fill for a moment otherwise empty movie houses up and down the land. This movement derives from the extreme Calvinist emphasis on Grace and on the personal nature of salvation; and ends by despising everything but Grace—rejecting learning and scholarship and intelligence itself. A hatred of all hallowed forms and a love for plainness in the church architecture and ritual is joined to an utter rejection of all "secondary goods." Inherent in their position is a fear of art that cuts as deep as the fear of sex; and there is, therefore, no possibility of literature developing out of their lowbrow, plebeian Puritanism, though of course a satirical literature attacking it has come regularly from the pens of rebels against it.

Middlebrow, middle-class Puritanism, on the other hand, preserves the respect for learning which made the original American Calvinists the founders of great universities. Its impetus carries it, by way of rationalism and religious liberalism, to Unitarianism and beyond to a series of post-Christian, syncretistic beliefs in which the notion of ecclesiastical "purification" is extended to a point where all ritual and dogma disappear, bearing away with them first the notions of the divinity of Christ and of original sin, and then of the necessity for an organized church. Religion is finally defined as a vague call to social service and "duty," and as anti-materialism, which is to say, a refusal to accept the body and its limitations (including death itself!) as real. Such a commitment to "spiritual" values leads, on the one hand, to a bland cosmic optimism, which denies "innate depravity" and considers evil an illusion or a mistake; and on the other hand, to a bloodless sort of asceticism, often combined with advanced social ideas.

The mid-nineteenth-century culmination of that faith is, of course, Transcendentalism: a creed constructed out of scraps of Carlyle, Swedenborg, German Idealist philosophy, and Hindu religion. More movement than system, Transcendentalism rests upon a series of assumptions sustained not by reason but by feeling and a homemade mythology. Some of the key assumptions are: that the real world is a world of ideas not apparent to the senses; that nature is beneficent and rational, and that man is, therefore, *at home* * in the universe; that, in fact, both man and Nature participate in God, who is not finally separate from either; that consequently the fittest church is unadorned Nature itself and the truest Bible the heart of the lonely thinker; that a man alone with himself is closest to perfection and that mass society tends to corrupt him; that there is no evil illusion and distrust of the self. Such beliefs urge upon man as his essential duty the act of saying "Yea!" to everything, of crying out "I accept the Universe!"

---

* Once more, Henry Miller comes to mind—though perhaps Benjamin Franklin, who easily and somewhat smugly believed the universe to be his home, is a better analogue than Emerson, who seems to have had always to strain a little in order to convince himself that he was really at ease in the cosmos.

The influence of Transcendentalism on the American essay and on American poetry through Emerson, Thoreau, Whitman, and their lesser disciples is marked, though not always fortunate; but in our classic fiction, the Transcendentalist appears chiefly as a comic character "cracked right across the brow," mocked by Hawthorne, for instance, in *The Blithedale Romance* and by Melville in both *Pierre* and *The Confidence Man.* Yet in their own time, Hawthorne and Melville alike were called "Transcendentalists" by book-reviewers (including Edgar Allan Poe), who handled that term with all the irresponsibility with which the word "existentialist" is now bandied about. These two writers represent, in fact, a third line of development from Puritanism, the only strain in which the rich paradoxes and tensions of Calvinism are not simplified in the interests of simple-minded orthodoxy or sentimental liberalism; and they engage in a common attempt to redeem the complex values of Puritanism from religion to art. It is hard to find a name for their view of the world; but perhaps the term "tragic Humanism" will do as well as any.

Among the assumptions of Melville and Hawthorne are the following: that the world of appearance is at once real and a mask through which we can dimly perceive more ultimate forces at work; that Nature is inscrutable, perhaps basically hostile to man, but certainly in some sense alien; that in man and Nature alike, there is a "diabolical" element, a "mystery of iniquity"; that it is impossible to know fully either God or ourselves, and that our only protection from destructive self-deceit is the pressure and presence of others; that to be alone is, therefore, to be lost; that evil is real, and that the thinking man breaks his heart trying to solve its compatibility with the existence of a good God or his own glimmering perceptions of goodness. From this it follows that the writer's duty is to say, "Nay!", to deny the easy affirmations by which most men live, and to expose the blackness of life most men try deliberately to ignore. For tragic Humanists, it is the function of art not to console or sustain, much less to entertain, but to *disturb* by telling a truth which is always unwelcome; and they consequently find it easy to view themselves in Faustian terms, to think of their dangerous vocations as a bargain with the Devil. It is for these reasons that they speak of their books not, like Poe, as hoaxes or burlesques, but as "hell-fired" and "wicked." Melville is not merely playing at Satanism when he confides to Hawthorne that the secret motto of *Moby Dick* is: *"Ego baptizo non in nomine patris, filii et spiritus sancti sed in nomine diaboli."* In 1850, the sole name for what we would call the unconscious was "hell"; and forays into that region were therefore regarded as courting damnation.

It is because they come to terms so frankly with the Faustian implications of their own enterprise that writers like Melville and Hawthorne (later Twain and Faulkner, too) are able to create Faustian characters, and to satisfy the dimly perceived need of many Americans to have their national existence projected in terms of a compact with the Devil. In Hawthorne, the scientist and the social reformer; in Melville, the ruthless exploiter of nature and the magnetic leader of men; in Twain, the refugee from culture, the young man who goes West; in Faulkner, the self-made man fighting for status and security—in each, some standard and respected American type is identified with the black magician who bartered away his soul. There is scarcely a heroic ideal of our native life which is not, in one or another of these writers' gothic books, illuminated by a weird and lurid light. Such ideals are not, it should be clear, merely travestied and debunked; they are rather revealed as equivocal, problematic—redeemed from easy sentimental acceptance and raised to a tragic power. It is Hawthorne who first opens up in our literature, as Melville himself explained, the tragic way; and the greatest of his gothic fictions, the first American tragedy is *The Scarlet Letter*. A "Puritan *Faust*," it has been called, as if there could be in the United States any other sort of *Faust;* but it is important all the same to be aware that it was Hawthorne who set the diabolical pact in a Puritan context and cast upon the beginnings of life in America a gothic gloom that not even Longfellow's middlebrow idylls could relieve.

The Scarlet Letter is finally not essentially a love story at all; and though it is possible to gain some insights into its theme and tone by considering it an American, which is to say, a denatured and defleshed, *Nouvelle Héloïse,* it is more valuable to approach it as an American, which is to say, a less violent and hopeless, version of *The Monk.* Like Lewis' horror novel, Hawthorne's book deals with a man of God led by the desire for a woman to betray his religious commitment, and finally almost (Hawthorne repents at the last moment, as Lewis does not) to sell his soul to the Devil. Certainly, it makes more sense to compare the figure of Hester

with that of the active Matilda, and Dimmesdale with the passive
Ambrosio, who is seduced by her, than to try to find analogues for
the American pair in Goethe's Gretchen and Faust. If Hawthorne's
novella is, indeed, as has often been suggested, an American *Faust,*
it is a *Faust* without a traduced maiden. Much less sentimental and
Richardsonian than Goethe, Hawthorne is not concerned with the
fall of innocence at the seducer's hand or with that seducer's salvation by the prayers of his victim.

The Faustianism of Hawthorne is the melodramatic Faustianism of the gothic romances: of Lewis, whom he read avidly, and
of Maturin, from whose *Melmoth the Wanderer* he borrowed the
name of a minor character in *Fanshawe.* Not only Lewis and
Maturin, but Mrs. Radcliffe and Brockden Brown were favorite
authors of the young Hawthorne; and from them he learned how to
cast on events the lurid lights, the air of equivocal terror which
gives *The Scarlet Letter* its "hell-fired" atmosphere. The very color
scheme of the book, the black-and-whiteness of its world illuminated only by the baleful glow of the scarlet letter, come from the
traditional gothic palette; but in Hawthorne's imagination, those
colors are endowed with a moral significance. Black and white are
not only the natural colors of the wintry forest settlement in which
the events unfold, but stand, too, for that settlement's rigidly distinguished versions of virtue and vice; while red is the color of sexuality itself, the fear of which haunts the Puritan world like a
bloody specter. The book opens with a description of "the black
flower of civilized society, a prison" and closes on a gravestone, a
"simple slab of slate," whose escutcheon is "sombre . . . and relieved only by one everglowing point of light gloomier than a
shadow:—ON A FIELD SABLE, THE LETTER A, GULES."

It is the scarlet letter itself which is finally the chief gothic property of Hawthorne's tale, more significant than the portents and
signs, the meteors in the midnight sky, or even "the noise of
witches; whose voices, at that period, were often heard . . . as they
rode with Satan through the air. . . ." Into that letter are compressed the meanings of all the demonic fires, scarlet blossoms, and
red jewels which symbolize passion and danger in his earlier tales.
It glows with a heat genital and Satanic at once—burning his fingers even centuries later, Hawthorne tells us in his introduction,
like "red-hot iron"; and its "lurid gleam," the text declares, is derived "from the flames of the infernal pit." Its "bale-fire," at any
rate, lights up the book with a flickering glare representing at once

Hester's awareness of guilt and Hawthorne's: his doubts over his plunge into the unconscious, and hers over her fall through passion into the lawless world of Nature.

What Hester inwardly perceives the book makes explicit: that the scarlet letter belongs not to her alone but to the whole community which has sought to exclude her. It is repeated everywhere: in the child she bears, who is the scarlet letter made flesh; in the heavens of secret midnight; on the tombstone which takes up her monitory role after she is dead; and especially in the secret sign on the breast of the minister, whom the community considers its special saint. In his dumb flesh is confessed what his articulate mouth cannot avow, not his transgression alone but that of all men who have cast the first stone. At the heart of the American past, in the parchment scroll which is our history, Hawthorne has discovered not an original innocence but a primal guilt—and he seeks to evoke that past not in nostalgia but terror.

It is on the frontier, the margin where law meets lawlessness, the community nature, that Hawthorne imagines his exemplary drama played out; but his primitive world is much more like Brockden Brown's than Cooper's. To him, the "dark inscrutable forest" seems rather the allegorical *selva oscura* of Dante than Natty Bumppo's living bride: the symbol of that moral wilderness into which man wanders along the byways of sin, and in which he loses himself forever. In its darkness, Hawthorne says of Hester at one point, "the wildness of her nature might assimilate itself with a people alien to the law. . . ." He projects no idyllic dream of finding in the forest the Noble Savage, only a nightmare of confronting the barbaric warrior and the Devil whom he serves; and the occasional Indian who emerges from his wilderness takes up a place not beside the pariah-artist but the black magician.

The virgin sea seems to him as unredeemed as the land, a second realm of gloomy lawlessness. For him sailors are ignoble savages, too: "the swarthy-cheeked wild men of the ocean, as the Indians were of the land. . . ." Neither Hawthorne's Indians nor seamen, however, play a critical part in the development of the action; they merely stand symbolically by, in their appropriate garb, speaking no word but watching "with countenance of inflexible gravity, beyond what even the Puritan aspect could attain." In the two important scenes at the foot of the scaffold, which so symmetrically open and close the book, there are red men in attendance, on the second occasion flanked by their even wilder confreres, the mariners "rough-looking desperadoes, with sun-blackened faces, and an immensity of beard." Yet neither the black desperadoes of the deep nor the swarthy and stolid Indians play the role in *The Scarlet Letter* entrusted to Cooper's Mingoes or the gothic savages of Brockden Brown.

The Magua of Hawthorne's novella is Chillingworth, the white doctor and man of science, so oddly at home in the alien world of the primitive. "By the Indian's side, and evidently sustaining a companionship with him, stood a white man, clad in a strange disarray of civilized and savage costume"; "old Roger Chillingworth, the physician, was seen to enter the market-place, in close and familiar talk with the commander of the questionable vessel." From his Indian captors and friends, Chillingworth has learned a darker "medicine" to complement his European science; but he has not ceased to be still "the misshapen scholar . . . eyes dim and bleared by lamplight," whose "scientific achievements were esteemed hardly less than supernatural." If on the one hand, Chillingworth is portrayed as the heir to the lore of the "savage priests," on the other, he is presented as a student of the black magic of "Doctor Forman, the famous old conjurer." To represent the horror of Europe, however, Chillingworth must be white, while to stand for that of America he must be colored; he is, in fact, a white man who grows black. Even the other protagonists notice his gradual metamorphosis ("his dark complexion seemed to have grown duskier . . .") into the very image of the Black Man, which is to say, Satan himself: "a striking evidence of man's faculty of transforming himself into a devil . . . if he only will . . . undertake a devil's office."

In general, one of the major problems involved in reading *The Scarlet Letter* is determining the ontological status of the characters, the sense in which we are being asked to believe in them. Caught between the analytic mode of the sentimental novel and the projective mode of the gothic, Hawthorne ends by rendering two of his five main characters (Hester and Dimmesdale) analytically, two ambiguously (Chillingworth and Pearl), and one projectively (Mistress Hibbins). Hester and Dimmesdale are exploited from time to time as "emblems" of psychological or moral states; but they remain rooted always in the world of reality. Chillingworth, on the other hand, makes so magical an entrance and exit that we find it hard to believe in him as merely an aging scholar, who has nearly destroyed himself by attempting to hold together a loveless marriage with a younger woman; while Pearl, though she is presented as the fruit of her mother's sin, seems hardly flesh and

blood at all, and Mistress Hibbins is quite inexplicable in naturalistic terms, despite Hawthorne's perfunctory suggestion that she is
simply insane.

The latter three are, perhaps, best understood as the "daemons"
or "shadows" of the more actual protagonists. Chillingworth is
clearly enough the shadow of Dimmesdale, a paternal image, the
Bad Father who speaks with the voice of Dimmesdale's Calvinist
heritage. He is a tormenting alter ego, capable of slipping past the
barriers of cowardice and self-pity to touch the hidden truth. When
Dimmesdale, hounded to penitence by his shadow, mounts the
scaffold to expose his own long-hidden scarlet letter, Hawthorne
offers us what seem alternative explanations of its genesis. It may
be, he suggests, the result of some hideous self-inflicted torture, the
psychosomatic effect of remorse, or the work, scientific or magical,
of Chillingworth; but these we can see are only apparent alternatives, which properly translated reduce to a single statement:
Dimmesdale and Chillingworth are one, as body and soul are one.

Certainly, Chillingworth cannot survive the minister's death,
after which "he positively withered up, shrivelled away, almost
vanished from sight." And when the process is complete, the old
physician gone, leaving to the bastard child of his wife enough
money to make her "the richest heiress of her day"—both that
child and her mother disappear, too. From their refuge in the Old
World, Hester returns alone to her place of shame and assumes
again the burden of her guilt; for there is no longer any function
for the "demon child" who was her shadow. From the first, Pearl
has been projected as "a forcible type . . . of the moral agony
which Hester Prynne had borne." Redeemed, however, by her
father's last penance, and endowed with the wealth of his shadow,
she vanishes, too, not out of the world but *into* it: "A spell was
broken . . . and as her tears fell upon her father's cheek, they were
the pledge that she would grow up amid human joy and sorrow,
nor forever do battle with the world, but be a woman in it. Towards her mother, too, Pearl's errand . . . was all fulfilled."

Taken as a character constructed in psychological depth, Pearl
is intolerable. Though she is the first child in American fiction
whose characterization is based on painstaking observation of a
real little girl (an astonishing number of details in her portrayal
come from the notes Hawthorne took on his little daughter, Una),
she is so distorted in the interests of her symbolic role that she
seems by turns incredible and absurd. It is partly a question of the
tone in which her actions are described, a tone sometimes senti-

mental and condescending (Hawthorne's son, Julian, interpreted the book as essentially a defense of bastards!), sometimes mystifying and heavily gothic. Daemonic Pearl certainly is, in her immunity to man-made law, her babbling in strange tongues, her uncanny insight into her mother's heart. But she is disconcertingly benign—as often compared to a blossom from a rosebush as to a witch! Her name is the clue to her essential nature, as surely as is Chillingworth's icy appellation; for she is "the gem of her mother's bosom," the Pearl of great price: not only Hester's torment, but also her salvation. "Thus early had this child saved her from Satan's snare. . . ."

Unaware of exactly what he is doing with his shadow characters: incapable of committing himself unreservedly to the gothic modes, but unable either to translate them into terms of psychological inwardness—Hawthorne tempers the daemonic in Chillingworth's case with melodrama, in Pearl's with sentimentality, and in Mistress Hibbins' with a kind of skeptical irony. The wizard Hawthorne can regard with horror, the elf-child with condescension; but to the full-blown witch, he responds with uneasy evasions, unwilling perhaps to grant reality to the nightmare which had aroused the persecuting zeal of his ancestors. Mistress Hibbins is, nonetheless, the third daemon of the book, the shadow of a sixth protagonist that we have not yet named: the Puritan community itself, which Hawthorne portrays as haunted by "the noise of witches; whose voices at that period, were often heard to pass over the settlements or lonely cottages, as they rode with Satan through the air."

The name of Mistress Hibbins is mentioned in Hawthorne's text before that of any of the other major characters of the book; and at four critical moments she appears on the scene. On her first appearance, she pleads with Hester to come with her to the forest and sign her name in the Black Man's book; on her second, she peers from her window into the darkness where the minister stands alone on the scaffold and cries out in anguish; on her third, she hails the minister as a fellow-communicant of Satan after he has met Hester in the forest and agreed to run off. The fourth scene is the longest, involving an interchange with Hester in which Mistress Hibbins claims fellowship not only with her and her lover, but impugns the whole community, for whose undermind of filth and fear she speaks: "Many a church-member saw I, walking behind the music, that has danced in the same measure with me when Somebody was fiddler, and, it might be, an Indian powwow or a

Lapland wizard changing hands with us!" Yet despite her critical role in the book, the dour-faced witch lady is rendered more as hallucination than fact. Her first entrance is hedged about with such phrases as: "it is averred" and "if we suppose this interview . . . to be authentic and not a parable . . ."; her second ends: "the old lady . . . vanished. Possibly, she went up among the clouds"; the third introduces the disturbing phrase, "and his encounter, if it were a real incident . . ." Only the fourth does not qualify its assertion of what happened with doubt, merely attributes Mistress Hibbins' diatribe to her "insanity, as we would term it."

Yet hedged about with doubts and characterized as mad, Magistrate Bellingham's sister is the mouthpiece through which the Faustian theme is introduced into the book. The Faustian theme, however, constitutes the very center of *The Scarlet Letter:* a profound crisis of the soul, for which Hawthorne was able to find no other image than one appropriate to the crazy dreams of a self-styled witch, or the blood-curdling story told to a child. Chapters XVI to XX, which make up the center of Hawthorne's tale, describe the encounter of Dimmesdale and Hester, the evocation of their old love, their momentary illusion of freedom, and the minister's moral collapse; but what begins as romance ends in gothic horror. It is Pearl who gives us the clue, asking her mother to tell the very story that she and her love have been acting out: "a story about the Black Man. . . . How he haunts this forest, and carries a book with him,—a big, heavy book, with iron clasps, and how this ugly Black Man offers his book and an iron pen to everybody that meets him here among the trees; and they are to write their names with their own blood. And then he sets his mark on their bosoms!" This is, indeed, the tale which Hawthorne tells in *The Scarlet Letter,* though for his characters the problem is not, as in the older versions of the story, whether they *shall* make such a pact, but whether they *have made* it; for in this new Faustian legend, one may enter into such an agreement unawares.

Over and over the essential question is asked. Pearl herself puts it to her mother just after her request for a gothic story, "Didst thou ever meet the Black Man, mother?" and Hester answers, "Once in my life I met the Black Man! . . . This scarlet letter is his mark!" Even earlier, Hester has inquired of Chillingworth, "Art thou like the Black Man that haunts the forest round about us? Hast thou enticed me into a bond that will prove the ruin of my soul?" But Chillingworth, smiling, has only evaded her query, "Not thy soul. . . . No, not thine!" It is Dimmesdale whom he implies he has lured into the infernal pact; and it is Dimmesdale who questions himself finally, though impelled by Hester's temptation rather than Chillingworth's torment, "Am I mad? or am I given over utterly to the fiend? Did I make a contract with him in the forest, and sign it with my blood?" This time it is Hawthorne himself who answers: "The wretched minister! He had made a bargain very like it! Tempted by a dream of happiness he had yielded himself with deliberate choice, as he had never done before, to what he knew was deadly sin."

For Hawthorne, the Faustian man is one who, unable to deny the definitions of right and wrong by which his community lives, chooses nonetheless to defy them. He is the individual, who, in pursuit of "knowledge" or "experience" or just "happiness" places himself outside the sanctions and protection of society. His loneliness and alienation are at once his crime and his punishment; for he commits a kind of suicide when he steps outside of society by deciding to live in unrepented sin; and he can only return to haunt the world of ordinary men like a ghost. Every major protagonist of *The Scarlet Letter* is such a specter. Of Hester, we are told that "she was as much alone as if she inhabited another sphere," and that "It was only the darkened house which could contain her. When sunshine came, she was not there." Dimmesdale asks of himself, "Then what was he?—a substance?—or the dimmest of shadows?"; and Hawthorne tells us of Chillingworth that "he chose . . . to vanish out of life as completely as if he indeed lay at the bottom of the ocean." Pearl, born of the original sin which has obliterated the substance of her elders, begins as "a born outcast of the infantile world. . . . Mother and daughter stood in the same circle of seclusion from human society."

Neither hate nor love can penetrate the spheres of unreality to which Hester, Dimmesdale, and Chillingworth have consigned themselves. The old physician proves incapable of believing himself a fiend or the two lovers sinners except in a "typical illusion"; and meeting after seven years, the minister and Hester "questioned one another's actual and bodily existence, and even doubted of their own. . . . Each a ghost, and awe-stricken at the other ghost!" Indeed, Hawthorne has the same trouble believing his characters real that they have themselves. "But to all these shadowy beings, so long our acquaintances," he says by way of valedictory, "we would fain be merciful." And we realize the sense in which he himself was, like Dimmesdale or Hester, alienated, removed to a sphere from which like some ghostly Paul Pry he peered down on the ghosts of his imagining. We have spoken of Hester and Dimmesdale as more actual than their shadows; but their actuality is a thin and tenuous thing, though the best at the command of a writer whom Poe advised, in critical impatience, to get a bottle of visible ink!

Not only alienation, however, defines Hawthorne's Faustian protagonists. They dream also of being *free*—uncommitted and unbound by history or moral responsibility. "Let us not look back," says Hester, playing the tempter to Dimmesdale, "the past is gone. . . . With this symbol, I undo it all. . . ." It is an American creed which she espouses, and like a good American, she looks to the world of nature for its consummation: "Doth the universe lie within the compass of yonder town. . . . Whither leads yonder forest track? Deeper it goes, and deeper, into the wilderness. There thou art free!" It is the dream already old by the time of Hawthorne of "lighting out for the territory," pursuing the endlessly retreating horizon of innocence into an inexhaustible West: the seed of a million Saturday matinees. "Begin all anew. . . . There is happiness to be enjoyed. There is good to be done. . . ." Really to believe this, however, is to leave behind the world of moral responsibility inhabited by Puritan saint and sinner alike, and to become a make-believe cowboy.

Here is the critical point at which the sons of Natty Bumppo part company with the descendants of Faust. The former cry out with their mythic progenitor in *The Deerslayer:* "When the colony's laws, or even the King's laws, seem agin the laws of God, they get to be onlawful and ought not to be obeyed." But who is qualified to say what God's laws are: a half-educated trapper without a cross in his blood, an unrepentant adulteress, an orphan boy on a raft with a stolen slave? *Vox dei, vox populi,* says the sentimental populist, and dissents in happy innocence; but the gothic rebel revolts against the will of God itself, saying a little naïvely with Huck, "All right, then, I'll *go* to Hell!" or shouting melodramatically with Ahab, "From hell's heart I strike at thee"; or, at least, insisting desperately with Dimmesdale, "But now,—since I am irrevocably doomed,—wherefore should I not snatch the solace allowed to the condemned culprit before his execution?"

Yet Dimmesdale is finally incapable of maintaining the Faustian stance. If *The Scarlet Letter* is, indeed, an American *Faust,* Dimmesdale is not really Faust himself but Gretchen, a secondary sinner lured on to destruction by a stronger one whom he loves, a tremulous victim led astray by daring arguments. It is true that in the end his weakness proves stronger than Hester's strength, leading him to repentance and public confession, while she dreams still of flight; but his is a Christian triumph, which cheats both the Devil who would damn him and the Faustian woman who considers that damnation bliss! Chillingworth is no more Faust than he, only a self-made Mephistopheles, the nearest thing to a real Devil Hawthorne could permit himself in his cautiously gothic tale; but he is a timid Devil at that. He and Dimmesdale are, at any rate, portrayed in one scene, ranging wide in terrible intimacy over the whole field of faith, and approaching the brink of apostasy: "It was as if a window were thrown open, admitting a freer atmosphere into the close and stifled study. . . . But the air was too fresh and chill. . . . So the minister, and the physician with him, withdrew within the limits of what their church defined as orthodoxy." Neither the Devil-doctor in his hate nor the guilty pastor in his ambivalent vanity dares throw himself into the uncertain depths of Faustian speculation or quarrel with the Calvinist God.

Hester, however, has no such scruples, but during her seven years of outward chastity and inward turmoil of the soul, leaves all limits behind: "she cast away the fragments of a broken chain. The world's law was no law for her mind." Ideas "as perilous as demons" became her familiars, persuading her to question the basic tenets of her faith, the place of woman, the very sanctity of life itself. "At times a fearful doubt strove to possess her soul, whether it were not better to send Pearl at once to heaven, and go herself to such futurity as Eternal Justice should provide." Met in the "vast and dismal forest" by the minister whom she has not confronted for seven years, except in his official role as defender of the religion against which they both have sinned, Hester greets him in the name of a rival, a pagan faith. He is at a loss in the "untamed forest," but she secure; for "her intellect and her heart had their home, as it were, in desert places, where she had roamed as freely as the Indian in his woods." How naturally the metaphor occurs to Hawthorne for whom the woods are haunted and the redskin a Satanic figure.

"She had wandered, without rule or guidance, in a moral wilderness," and consequently regarded "whatever priests or legislators had established . . . with hardly more reverence than the Indian would feel. . . ." It is a final satisfactory touch that a woman be not only the first Faust of classic American literature, but also the wildest Indian of them all!

There are finally no heroes in Hawthorne, for whom the illusion of heroism, the dream of transcending one's humanity, is the last diabolic temptation; neither man nor woman can break back into Eden, though man and woman together can momentarily restore Paradise on earth. That is to say, there are in his work no redeemed individuals, only redeemed *couples,* husband and wife, like the pair who, in "The Maypole of Merry Mount," accept expulsion from the Garden of irresponsible indulgence; or the one which goes out in "The Canterbury Pilgrims" from the Garden of icy abstinence; or the one which abandons at the end of "The Great Carbuncle" the Garden of unshareable bliss. Similarly, Holgrave and Phoebe in *The House of the Seven Gables,* Hollingsworth and Priscilla in *The Blithedale Romance,* both Kenyon and Hilda, Donatello and Miriam in *The Marble Faun,* by choosing marriage over passion and loneliness submit "to earth's doom of care and sorrow, and troubled joy. . . ." Hawthorne's muted, resigned conclusions reflect the final lines of Milton's *Paradise Lost* —the mitigated catastrophe of the seventeenth-century Puritan poet becoming unexpectedly the mitigated happy ending of the nineteenth-century Puritan fictionist:

> Some natural tears they drop't, but wip'd them soon;
> The World was all before them, where to choose
> Thir place of rest, and Providence thir guide:
> They hand in hand with wandring steps and slow,
> Through *Eden* took thir solitarie way.

In Hawthorne, this becomes more abstract and more sentimental. "As the moral gloom of the world overpowers all systematic gayety, even so was their home of wild mirth made desolate amid the sad forest. They returned to it no more. . . . They went heavenward, supporting each other along the difficult path which it was their lot to tread, and never wasted one regretful thought on the vanities of Merry Mount." Between Milton and Hawthorne lie nearly two hundred years of Sentimentalism, which sought to make of marriage another, better Eden, and of woman an innocent savior capable of restoring man to it. Hawthorne's fallen pairs, therefore, walk forth from their several false Gardens to a truer bliss; and his Gretchen-Eves sustain their trembling Adams, aware that, unlike their primal mother, they at least have not brought sin into the world.

"O felix culpa!" is the secret motto of all the novels of Hawthorne after *The Scarlet Letter,* novels in which he tries to relieve the gloom of the tragic vision of his greatest work. But unlike Augustine, Hawthorne comes to feel the fall of man a fortunate calamity not because it leads to the coming of Christ, but because it prepares the ground for marriage and the bourgeois family. It is a bathetic turn: a rejection of that "blackness ten times black" which Melville had discovered in *Mosses from an Old Manse,* in favor of the positive view of life, into which American writers are so often tempted after their first success—and which condemns them to subsequent failure. When Holgrave in *The House of the Seven Gables* chooses to become a husband rather than a magician, and will not play the mesmeric game of his Maule forebears, though another Pyncheon is within his power, he has made symbolically the great refusal which saps Hawthorne's later work of the tragic power that he fully tapped only once. After Holgrave finishes telling Phoebe the story of the strange control so dreadfully exerted by his ancestor over hers, he sees that her head is beginning to droop, her eyes to close:

> A veil was beginning to be muffled about her, in which she could only behold him and live in his thoughts and emotions. . . . It was evident that, with but one wave of his hand and a corresponding effort of his will, he could complete his mastery over Phoebe's free and virgin spirit. . . . To a disposition like Holgrave's, at once speculative and active, there is no temptation so great as the opportunity of acquiring empire over the human spirit. Let us, therefore . . . allow him integrity . . . since he forbade himself to twine that one link more which might have rendered his spell over Phoebe indissoluble.

Having refused the double temptation of Don Juan and Faust, the power to deflower a "virgin spirit" and to control another life, Holgrave is required also to surrender his reformer's dream that "the moss-grown and rotten Past is to be torn down, and lifeless institutions to be thrust out of the way, and their dead corpses, buried, and everything begin anew." In *The Blithedale Romance,* Hawthorne splits the single figure of Holgrave into two characters, the seducer-mesmerist Westervelt and the philanthropic reformer Hollingsworth, permitting the former to leave the scene unrepentant, while the latter capitulates to woman and marriage. In *The Marble Faun,* the scientific experimenter with souls is replaced by the alienated artist, who has bartered his place in humanity for a power over cold stone; but he, too, is finally led to the altar, while his alter ego (this time a jesuitical plotter and loathesome criminal) plunges to a bloody death. Only at the end of his life, Hawthorne seems to have tried again to find the tragic note that would redeem his gothic effects from triviality and theatricality; but he could not recover his pristine purity, so long compromised for the sake of Dickensian effects and concessions to genteel sentimentalism.

It is not for his saved protagonists but for his lost ones that modern readers remember Hawthorne, for his unreconstructed utopians and damned magicians—but especially for his lonely outcasts who prefigure the plight of modern, alienated man. In "Wakefield," he treats with irony the utopia of bachelorhood, which from the time of Washington Irving has had so special an appeal for American readers. In "The Man of Adamant," he deals with the utopia of absolute dissent, portraying a kind of *reductio ad absurdum* of Protestantism itself, which brings a man at last into so rigid and lonely an orthodoxy that he becomes the prisoner of himself, but chiefly he is concerned with the solitude of the artist in the utopia of his art, and his half-willful condemnation of himself to impotence and death.

In Hawthorne's imagination, the figure of the artist, whom he calls Oberon,* is always fading into that of the scientist, whose traditional name we know; for to him both seem men who, in the impassioned pursuit of a craft and the knowledge it yields, come to reject "brotherhood with man and reverence for God." To know, to create, to control, they are willing to step beyond all established bounds, suspend all customary moral standards and make them-

---

* A singularly suggestive choice of names, it occurs to me now; for in *A Midsumer Night's Dream,* Oberon is not only the master of illusion but also of his wife, whose essential passion he reveals as lust for a dumb beast, even as he wins from her the favors of the Ganymede-like boy for whose possession they contend.

selves alone the judges of the rightness of what they do. In Rappaccini and Aylmer and Ethan Brand, Hawthorne projects before the fact the dilemma of the atomic scientists in our time and predicts their essentially immoral stand. Aylmer in "The Birthmark" is the most utterly utopian of the crew; unable to abide the imperfections of mortality, the tiny scarlet hand of passion betrayed on the marble skin of his wife, he produces a perfection which is death —destroys what he loves. Ethan Brand is the coldest, the most detached researcher: a social scientist, really, who, seeking by mass interviews to discover the nature of the unpardonable sin, learns that it is "pure research." "He was now a cold observer, looking on mankind as the subject of his experiments, and, at length, converting man and woman to be his puppets, and pulling the wires that moved them to such degrees of crime as were demanded for his study." "Ethan Brand," however, has survived more as a fragment than a real tale. "A Chapter from an Abortive Romance" Hawthorne called it, yet—with the possible exception of "Young Goodman Brown"—it is his most explicit short treatment of the Satanic pact, and it ends on the proper melodramatic note of damnation. "O Mother earth," Ethan Brand cries just before casting himself into a lime-burner's furnace, "who art no more my Mother . . . O mankind, whose brotherhood I have cast off . . . O stars of heaven, that shone on me of old . . . farewell all, and forever. Come, deadly element of Fire,—henceforth my familiar friend! Embrace me, as I do thee!"

The intent is tragic, but the tone is false, and what began in terror ends in mere rant. "Young Goodman Brown," however, resists the impulse to inflated rhetoric and is finally the most successful, as it is the most subdued, of the Faustian tales. Committed to finding out beyond the limits to which human curiosity is permitted to penetrate, the real virtue of his neighbors, his ancestors, his wife, Brown commits himself to the Devil and is granted a vision of universal depravity and damnation. The whole community is revealed to him as hypocritical and evil: his grandfather proves indistinguishable from Satan himself; and even his wife, for all her freshness and fluttering pink ribbons, is discovered disporting herself at a witches' sabbath. But Brown's lonely vision in the heathen forest brings him no more security than peace; it cuts him off forever from his fellow men, fixes him in a terrible solitude, but it leaves him with no assurance that what he has seen is true. "Had Goodman Brown fallen asleep in the forest and only dreamed the dream of a witch-meeting?" Though he can never know the answer, never be sure whether the horror he experienced exists in the community or in the depths of his own foul heart, he can find no bliss in domesticity, no salvation in marriage. Confronted by his wife, who is called, of course, Faith, and who has slipped out eagerly to meet him on his return, he "looked sternly and sadly into her face, and passed on without a greeting. . . . And when he had lived long, and was borne to his grave a hoary corpse . . . they carved no hopeful verse upon his tombstone, for his dying hour was gloom." It is surely the most perfect in form and tone, as it is in import the most tragic of Hawthorne's tales, a piece of symbolic gothicism whose promise is fulfilled only in *The Scarlet Letter.*

Yet even in *The Scarlet Letter,* Hawthorne has begun to play the typically American game with damnation, to suggest that, after all, it is more menace than fact: an eternally unfulfilled threat, cheated of fulfillment at the last minute by divine mercy. Though all three of his major characters make the Faustian commitment, they are providentially tricked into Grace. Hester at first hampered by the holy burden of her child and later spared the last folly of flight by Dimmesdale's confession and death, remains in the place of her sin, attaching once more and forever to her breast the glorious badge of her shame. So earlier, Dimmesdale has, by penitence and self-immolation, transformed himself from a tormented victim of sin to "spirit sinking into deep repose," while Chillingworth—at that point more Devil than man—could only scream in rage, "Thou hast escaped me."

Of Chillingworth alone is Hawthorne willing to declare that "it only remained for the unhumanized mortal to betake himself whither his Master would find him tasks enough, and pay him his wages duly." But Chillingworth has ceased to be the ambiguous hero-villain who is Faust, becoming rather a simple embodiment of evil with which neither reader nor author is tempted to identify. Satan that he makes himself in the end, however, Chillingworth began at least as the wronged husband; and his final fate is mitigated as the doom of Hawthorne's succeeding melodramatic villains is not. Judge Pyncheon, latter-day Puritan turned businessman and pharisee, who has persecuted and robbed the innocents who share his blood, is dispatched from the pages of *The House of the Seven Gables* with all the stigmata of damnation upon him. In a chapter pat and moralistic enough to have become a classroom set-piece, Hawthorne consigns him to eternal darkness: "There is no face! An infinite, inscrutable blackness has annihilated sight! where is our universe? All crumbled away from us; and we, adrift in chaos, may hearken to the gusts of homeless wind, that go sighing and murmuring about, in quest of what was once a world!"

With the mesmerist Westervelt, the corresponding villain in *The Blithedale Romance,* Hawthorne manages to do little, dismissing him with a hasty parting curse put into the mouth of Miles Coverdale: "Heaven deal with Westervelt according to his nature and deserts!—that is to say, annihilate him." But Westervelt seems only a scapegoat, a conventional villain, whose unequivocal damnation serves chiefly to distract our attention from Hawthorne's unwillingness to face up to the problem of Zenobia's eternal fate. It is typical of Hawthorne that he can best imagine the Faustian role, in all its essential moral ambiguity, in terms of a woman: one of those Dark Ladies, whom Hester prefigures, and whom he has carefully excluded from his single sunny romance, *The House of the Seven Gables.* Whether Zenobia did, indeed, die unrepentant and presumably lost, he cannot persuade himself to decide. When her body is dragged up from the lake into which she has thrown herself in despair, she is found frozen into a position that projects the author's bewilderment before her fate. "She knelt as if in prayer . . ." he begins hopefully, then adds in quick qualification, "But her arms! They were bent before her, as if she struggled against Providence in never ending hostility." Yet this qualification in turn seems too unequivocal to leave without amendment, and he pushes it aside. "Away with the hideous thought. The flitting moment after Zenobia sank into the dark pool . . . was so long, in its capacity of God's infinite forgiveness, as the lifetime of the world."

His last female Faust is the somber, oriental Miriam of *The Marble Faun,* who, like her prototypes Hester and Zenobia, not only defies sexual taboos but thinks deep and dangerous thoughts, chafing at the limitations imposed on her sex by law and convention. With one terrible look, Miriam has caused the death of her persecutor and put in peril the soul of her beloved, who has followed the signal of her glance; but blood is not demanded for blood. Only that persecutor comes, in the course of the book, to a violent end; while both Miriam and Donatello, her lover, seem more nearly redeemed than lost in their consequent penance and sorrow. Miriam is disclosed finally, it is true, as a veiled and tragic penitent; but her own defense is left ringing in the reader's ears as she has passionately spoken it to the sculptor Kenyon: "Was the crime . . . was it a blessing in that disguise? Was it a means of education, bringing a simple nature to the point . . . which it could have reached under no other discipline? . . . The story of the fall of man! Is it not repeated in our romance of Monte Beni? . . . Was that very sin—into which Adam precipitated himself and all his race . . . the destined means by which, over a long pathway of toil and sorrow, we are to attain a higher, brighter and profounder happiness . . . ?"

It is a more complex and heretical version of the fortunate Fall than any of the sentimental reworkings, in the earlier tales, of the conclusion of Milton's *Paradise Lost*. But is it intended finally to mitigate the tragic nemesis of the Faustian legend, deprive us of the finale in which the hero-villain is dragged shrieking through a trap door to hell? Or is it supposed to represent only one more, the last and most treacherous of the Faustian temptations? And who is being tempted, Hawthorne or Miriam? The ambiguity of Hawthorne deliberately suspends such questions out of the reach of certainty; more bewilderingly than is his bewildering wont, he teases the reader first toward one conclusion, then another. Though the sculptor, who speaks for the author in the novel, has protested on first hearing Miriam's theory, "It is too dangerous, Miriam! I cannot follow you!", he ends by repeating her arguments to Hilda. "Is sin, then,—which we deem such a dreadful blackness in the universe, —is it, like sorrow, merely an element of human education. . . . Did Adam fall, that we might ultimately rise to a far loftier paradise than his?"

Put in Kenyon's blunt terms, the Faustian theory of the meaning of Faustian action only shocks the snow maiden Hilda, who cries, "Oh, hush! . . . This is terrible; and I could weep for you, if you indeed believe it." At her perhaps unexpectedly violent response, Kenyon hedges with quite Hawthorne-like adaptability, "Forgive me, Hilda! I never did believe it!" It is only loneliness, he explains —the artist's curse of solitude—which has led him to play with such perilous speculations, from which marriage to her, association with the "white wisdom" which she embodies, would save him once and for all. "O Hilda," he pleads abjectly, "guide me home!" But this is not the final word either; for Hawthorne is at last unwilling to rest on either an orthodox horror before heterodoxy or the intellectual's retreat toward domesticity and accommodation. Good Christian that she is, Hilda is more sentimental than strict, more genteel optimist than gloomy Calvinist; and when the question is asked, "What was Miriam's life to be?" the author can only defer, like Kenyon in the novel, to her "white wisdom." "But Hilda had a hopeful soul and saw sunlight on the mountain-tops."

Melville was truer, finally, to the vision of blackness, which he pretended to have discovered in Hawthorne, than was Hawthorne himself. The reality of damnation he never denied; but the *meaning* of it, for one committed to a skeptical and secular view, he questioned. Especially in his later works, he presented the "mystery of iniquity" in such complexly ironical contexts that the wariest of readers is occasionally baffled. Nevertheless, he kept faith throughout his fiction not only with the gothic vision in general, but with the Faustian theme; creating, along two main lines of descent, a notable series of gothic hero-villains, in each of whom a genuine Faust struggles to be born. The first line of descent begins with *Mardi,* whose hero, Taji or the Wanderer, none of the customary satisfactions of men can hold: not a union with the image of female purity (Yillah) or absolute passion (Hautia), or even with the *Shekhinah,* the personified presence of God, whom his companion, Mohi, perceives in a vision.

He presses on past the countries of the civilized world, allegorically represented by imaginary South Sea islands; and leaves behind even the utopian kingdom of Serenia, a kind of Unitarian Great Good Place, whose messengers bear the flower symbols of victory, immortality, and love, and whose citizens believe that Alma (Christ) and Right Reason are one. Even Taji's most faithful companions turn from him, when they realize he has left Serenia behind not temporarily but forever. "Nay, madman!" they cry by way of warning, "Serenia is our haven. Through yonder strait for thee perdition lies. And from the deep beyond, no voyager ever puts back." But this, of course, is precisely what Taji desires. "Let *me,* then, be the unreturning wanderer," he answers them; and ignoring their final plea, "Nay, Taji! commit not the last, last crime!" shouts his Satanic defiance: "Now, I am my soul's emperor; and my first act is abdication!" Maddened, he races seaward, still seeking the ungraspable spirit which has slipped from his honeymoon clasp, and still sought by three sons of the Old Man he killed to attain her: "Pursuers and pursued, over an endless sea."

It is an authentic, an unmitigated Faustian conclusion to a book which confronts directly the problem of the limits imposed by caution and convention on man's quest for knowledge and experience; but in *Mardi,* both the conclusion and the confrontation are hopelessly imbedded in matter which Melville's first readers found indigestible, "not only tedious but unreadable." Melville himself seems finally to have felt the impulse out of which he had produced *Mardi* as perilous if not downright diabolic; at any rate he determined to suppress the "unmanageable" element, which he held responsible for the book's failure, and to turn out next "a plain, straight forward, amusing narrative," "no metaphysics . . . nothing but cakes and ale." Those cakes-and-ale narratives are *Redburn* and *White Jacket,* the former of which he especially despised in retrospect, calling it "the beggarly *Redburn,*" and remarking that he had only written it to buy tobacco. Yet in both there are themes present, only half-consciously developed, out of which he was to create later some of his profoundest and most terrible effects. One such theme, which we have already examined from another point of view, is the love-conflict between the shipboard bully and the Handsome Sailor—a subject already stereotypical in popular fiction but handled by Melville in an extraordinary way.

Perhaps the most unforeseen consequence of his special handling of the theme is his transformation of the bully into a second version of the Faustian hero-villain—a version to which he was perhaps driven by the popular rejection of his sailor-*poète maudit,* but one to which he returned throughout his writing career. As late as *Billy Budd,* which he left unpublished, Melville was trying still to work out to his own satisfaction the meaning of the attraction-repulsion which drove the evil seaman and the innocent sailor to their mutual destruction. He had made in *Redburn* a first attempt, creating in Jackson an image of "natural depravity" capable of charming even those who saw through to his evil center. In his copy of *King Lear,* Melville, pondering the problem still, was to write some years later, "The infernal nature has a valor often denied to innocence"; and this valor, along with an extraordinary power over his shipmates, he bestows on Jackson. Though that utterly corrupt sailor "was as yellow as gamboge" and hairless to boot, though "his nose had brown down in the middle, and he squinted with one eye," nevertheless "one glance of his squinting eye was as good as a knockdown, for it was the most deep, subtle, infernal . . . eye . . . ever lodged in a human head."

Under its gaze, Jackson's fellows cringe, crawl to him, laugh at his sadistic jokes, do the work which he evades; while Redburn, whom Jackson inexplicably hates, becomes an Ishmael on the ship. It is quite simply the power of evil in Jackson, the sense of his damnation implicit in every gesture, which cows the crew like a superhuman mystery; the most unsubtle of seamen knows that "in truth, he carried about with him the traces of these things, and the mark of a fearful end nigh at hand. . . ." But what subdues everyone else, only exacerbates the rage of Jackson himself; his awareness that he "must die like a dog, in consequence of his sins" stirs in him a hatred for all mankind. He is presented as the victim not merely of the manifold diseases that rack his body, but of divine vengeance itself, "seamed and blasted by lightning." And he assumes as his end nears a kind of dark nobility, inextricably intertwined with the Faustian role he visibly plays: "The prospect of the speedy and unshunnable death now before him, seemed to exasperate his misanthropic soul into madness; and if he had indeed sold his soul to Satan, he seemed determined to die with a curse between his teeth."

The Satanic bargain is spoken of only hypothetically, but Jackson does, indeed, die with a blasphemy on his lips and a torrent of blood from his lungs spattering the sail, on which he is working as death strikes him down into the sea. It is of Tiberius, "the diabolical Tiberius at Caprae," that Melville, speaking through Redburn, is reminded; and he makes the proud vaunt: "I account this Yankee Jackson fully as dignified a personage as he. . . . Though he was a nameless vagabond without an epitaph, and none, but I, narrate what he was." It is the first stirring of an odd notion in Melville that in the classless world of democracy, aristocratic distinction is bestowed by entering into the diabolic compact; but he was not to be able to work it out explicitly until *Moby Dick*.

In *White Jacket,* he does not know what to do at all with the figure that demands to become Faust; unable to reject him utterly, he presents him as Bland, the master-at-arms, but cannot invent a fiction worthy of him. Melville does find his shipboard villain a new face this time, providing him with a mouth "somewhat small, Moorish-arched, and wickedly delicate" besides the customary "snaky black eye"; and before this "charming blackleg," White Jacket himself, the Ishmael of the later book, stands entranced: "I could not but abominate him when I thought of his conduct; but I pitied the continual gnawing, which under all his deftly donned disguises, I saw lying at the bottom of his soul. I admired his heroism. . . ." Yet Melville can find no real devil's work for him to do, only portray him as a petty smuggler broken in rank for a time, then restored to office.

There is in *White Jacket* a true Handsome Sailor, Jack Chase, who is Bland's ideal opponent in every sense, separated out from the *schlemiel*-hero with whom he is fused in *Redburn;* but he is never allowed to meet Bland head on. Melville may perhaps have felt, on one level of consciousness or another, that their relationship could not have been developed without suggesting the theme of overt homosexuality, which comes closer to the surface in this novel than in any other of his works, but is consigned to silence in a summary paragraph:

> The sins for which the cities of the plain were overthrown still linger in some of these wooden-walled Gomorrahs of the deep. . . . The landsman who has never read Walpole's *Mysterious Mother,* nor Sophocles' *Oedipus Tyrannus,* nor the Roman story of *Count Cenci,* dramatized by Shelley, let that landsman guardedly remain in his ignorance of even worse horrors than these, and forever abstain from seeking to draw aside this veil.

Like Jackson, a Yankee emperor, unsung except by Melville, Ahab is like him, too, "seamed and blasted" by lightning; like Bland, he is the victim of an inward "continual gnawing," and like both, is gifted with a "snaky eye" capable of cowing all opposition, enlisting the indifferent on an infernal quest. In Ahab's relationship with Fedallah, however, the Faustian bargain becomes explicit for the first time, pushing into the background the love-combat with the Handsome Sailor. There is such a sailor in *Moby Dick,* the beloved Bulkington, so carefully introduced and so abruptly, though apologetically, shuffled off the scene in Chapter XXIII. Surely, at some point in his writing of the novel, Melville must have imagined between Ahab and Bulkington the encounter that finally was yielded up to make place for Ahab's confrontation of the whale itself and of the power he attempted to strike at through the whale. The end, however, is the same; like Jackson, Ahab ends with blasphemy on his lips and damnation in his soul; though, much less equivocally, there is attributed to him the imperial dignity, proffered and then withdrawn from his prototype.

For all the magnificence of Ahab, Melville cannot even after *Moby Dick* surrender the Jackson prototype, or the theme with which he is associated from the start; but in the posthumous *Billy*

Budd, he tries once more. We recognize Claggart when he enters, though by this time there has been imposed on the face of evil the actual stone image of Tiberius, which Melville had finally seen in Rome in 1857, noting in his journal: "a look of sickly evil,— intellect without manliness and sadness without goodness." The uncanny, beardless yellow of Jackson's aspect has become almost marmoreal, "a pallor tinged with a faint shade of amber akin to the hue of time-tinted marbles of old"; but the same compelling eye still subdues all beholders with its dark glance, still stirs in Melville the old questions about the attractiveness of evil, and, even more disturbingly, about the mystery of its existence. "What was the matter with the master-at-arms?" he asks; and his answer (a Radcliffean answer, he tells us) is: "Natural Depravity: a depravity according to nature." To this natural depravity there corresponds a natural innocence, represented by Billy Budd, who is Jack Chase recast in the image of Antinoüs, even as Claggart is Bland recast in that of Tiberius.

In the Christian world, however, where the beauty of innocence cannot be made the minion to the lust of imperial evil, the encounter of the two is played out as passionate *hatred,* eventuates in melodrama. Claggart, who hates Billy with a helpless and ambivalent fury, accuses him to the captain of the ship on which they both serve, meanwhile fixing him with a "mesmeric glance"—"like the hungry lurch of a torpedo fish." Billy, falsely accused and unprepared for treachery, cannot speak but swings in exasperation at Claggart, killing him with a single blow; and over his sinewless body (more like "a dead snake" than a man), the captain can only exclaim, "Struck dead by an angel of God. Yet the angel must die." Not God himself this time but the instrument of God acted to destroy the blasphemer, and that instrument must bear—according to the laws of men—blood guilt and legal blame. The focus has shifted, with the shifting of Melville's concern and the burning out of his own diabolism, from the Faustian villain-hero to the innocent avenger; and with that shift, Melville's art has moved from the realm of the gothic to that of the sentimental. The abhorrence and pity for the "godlike, ungodly man," crucified on his own evil, kept in so desperate a balance in *Moby Dick,* has reverted again to the imbalance of *Redburn.* In *Billy Budd,* however, Claggart is not even permitted the Faustian death-speech of defiance and contempt; the only last words allowed are the submissive ones of Billy,

"God bless Captain Vere." That Devil, in whose name *Moby Dick* received its bloody baptism, has been disowned!

Between *Moby Dick* and *Billy Budd* come many works and many changes of heart, but, first of all, the astonishing, though finally unsuccessful experiment of *Pierre*. In this book, the Taji of *Mardi* is reborn, though he is removed from the sea which was the very symbol of his commitment to the unlimited. Pierre is the lonely spoiled child, the intellectual adventurer, the alienated artist in search of a devil to whom to sell his soul. Unlike Claggart or Jackson or Bland he is not evil by birth and definition, but by choice and vocation; he becomes the Devil's agent by rejecting the morality of the community in which he has lived at peace, ends by calling the concepts of vice and virtue which he cannot really deny the substance of a dream. He is the only hero of Melville who attempts to earn his living as a writer, a highbrow writer, who has determined (at the moment of his acutest financial need) to abandon the kind of literature that has made him a youthful success and write a work dedicated to nothing but truth. That this work turns out to be the very book in which he is a character is an illusionistic device by which Melville makes it clear that he and Pierre are symbolically one, and that the Faustian commitment of Pierre is indistinguishable from the creation of the work in which he exists.

Yet about Pierre's ultimate damnation, Melville does not equivocate. Pierre himself foresees his doom, as he must to make it fully terrible; and true to his Faustian role, he dies crying out that knowledge defiantly: "Now, 'tis merely hell in both worlds. Well, be it hell. I will mold a trumpet of the flames, and, with my breath of flame, breathe back my defiance." It is an acceptance, however, only of the fact of damnation but not of its justice—a little like Huck's cry from the heart, "All right, I'll *go* to Hell!" Melville does not cheat in the end like Twain, revealing that the "girl in Saddle Meadows" was not Pierre's sister after all (as Jim is revealed not to have been a slave), and Pierre therefore as innocent of incest as Huck of "nigger-stealing"; but there is an implicit protest all the same in Pierre's self-condemnation—a protest not against mistaken interpretation of God's law but against that law itself. Ahab himself had not questioned the price he was asked to pay, the just settlement of a bargain deliberately entered upon; but Pierre has acted in terms of charity not blasphemy, and that his end be damnation, too, that the end of love be hell seems to Melville to call in question the very meanings of "damnation" and "hell." "It is ambiguous still!" Pierre exclaims; and in this final word he is at one with his author.

The ambiguities of *Pierre* are further compounded in *The Confidence Man,* which is not a gothic romance at all, but an oddly wry and dry satire that never quite manages to explode into the release of laughter. Critics argue still about whether the multiformed hero of that book—who begins as the absolute Stranger, an "impostor from the East," and learns to be all things to all men—is Christ or Satan. Certainly, he begins in the guise of Christ (his first avatar is a deaf-and-dumb, submissive butt of the arrogant mob, dressed in white garments, which are the outer sign of his essential humility) and he preaches the orthodox gospel of Faith—or Confidence, Hope, and Charity. The question of whether the practice of those virtues leads mankind to loss or gain is, however, left tantalizingly open; and, in the end, we come to realize that we are being asked to consider not whether the Confidence Man is Saviour or Adversary, but *whether Christ is the Devil!* If this is, indeed, the case, then only Faustian doubt can deliver us from the ultimate con game, the trap of religious belief.

Melville's ironies are finally not unlike those at work in Mark Twain's equally skeptical but more avowedly Satanic story, *The Mysterious Stranger,* though in *The Confidence Man* neither those who have faith nor those who have doubt are rewarded. In Twain's book, on the other hand, the characters who enter into a pact with his amiable young Devil are favored above the pious Christians, granted insanity or early death, which—for Twain—are man's sole protections against suffering and vain regret. *The Mysterious Stranger* appears, to be sure, a little crude and sophomoric beside the subtleties of Melville's quietly mad novel; for, unlike Melville, Twain remained always a profoundly ignorant man, doomed to sound like the village atheist when he aspired to speak like Faust. There is a certain superficial resemblance between Pierre's Faustian assertion that "these two shadows cast from one nothing; these, seems to me, are Virtue and Vice. . . . I am a nothing. It is all a dream that we dreamed we dream . . ." and the statement of Twain's boy-demon that "there is no God, no universe, no human race, no earthly life, no hell. It is all a dream—a grotesque and foolish dream." The former avowal is, however, presented dramatically as the rationalization of a self-declared moral hero on the verge of incest; while the other is put forward as a final word of truth, a summary conclusion.

If Twain's status as a gothic writer depended only upon *The Mysterious Stranger,* he would not rank very high; for it is finally an obvious book, composed by one convinced that whatever shocked his genteel wife would make the foundations of organized Christianity tremble! Typically enough, the Faustian role in *The Mysterious Stranger* is shared by three youngsters (familiar pre-Civil War Hannibal types, disguised as late-sixteenth-century Austrians), who live in a town called Eseldorf, described as "a paradise for boys." It is the only kind of Paradise Twain could ever imagine; and the serpent who enters it is appropriately a juvenile demon, a kind of superhuman Huck Finn, who teaches his companions to amuse themselves by making *golems* and performing minor witchcraft in place of the less spectacular highjinks of the earlier novels. Before young Satan has inducted them into such higher make-believe, the Eseldorf boys have contented themselves with listening to ghost stories and learning to smoke from a servant in the village castle, called Felix Brandt though he is obviously Nigger Jim in whiteface.

It is perhaps because there are no Negro slaves in Eseldof, that Twain cannot evoke in its environs the full gothic horror which he attains in *Pudd'nhead Wilson.* Unable to play on the theme which evoked for him the essential shudder: "the skin of every man contains a slave," he is driven back on Pudd'nhead's second-best observation, his thought for April 1: "This is the day upon which we are reminded of what we are on the other three hundred and sixty-four." This amounts to an essentially banal observation about men, the stuff of comedy rather than of Faustian tragedy; and *The Mysterious Stranger* can never, therefore, seem quite serious to the adult mind. The boy Faust who is its narrator subscribes at the close to the Devil's doctrine ("He vanished and left me appalled, for I knew, and realized, that all he had said was true"); but it is harder to be moved at his words than at Huck's presumably comic decision to go to hell.

Huckleberry Finn is essentially a book about a marginal American type, who only wants to stay alive; but who does not find this very easy to do, being assailed on the one side by forces of violence, which begrudge him the little he asks, and on the other, by forces of benevolence, which insist that he ask for more. Against

the modesty and singleness of his purpose, everything else is meas-
ured and weighed: religion, the social order, other men. Huck
exists on a sub-moral level; for he cannot afford, in his minimal
economy, the luxury of living by the moral codes of the Widow
Douglases of his small-town world. Such codes assume a standard
of security, if not actual prosperity, to which he does not even
aspire: "She told me what she meant—I must help other people,
and do everything I could for other people and look out for them
all the time, and never think about myself. . . . I went out in the
woods and turned it over in my mind a long time, but I couldn't
see no advantage in it—except for the other people; so that at last
I reckoned I wouldn't worry about it any more, but just let it go."
Huck has not yet fallen, manages to live still without that "moral
sense," which his last avatar, the young devil in *The Mysterious
Stranger*, describes as the blight of mankind.

Yet Huck is not, of course, a devil or even a savage, only a
semi-barbarian; and having grown up on the edge of civilization,
he has always known, even before his brief indoctrination by Miss
Watson, the ethical precepts of her world. No more free-thinker
than savage, he not only knows, but, in an abstract way, believes
in these codes, by which he could not survive for an instant in the
lawless sub-society which he inhabits. There is, therefore, a constant disjunction in his mind (very like irony—and exploited by
Twain for irony's sake) between what he considers he *ought* to do,
and what he is aware that he *must* do; and it is this disjunction
which underlies the moral crisis of the book. Huck begins with
such minor crimes as lying and cussing, smoking and petty theft;
and, indeed, the first is so habitual a reflex that he scarcely knows
what to do at a point where apparently only telling the truth can
help him.

> I reckon a body that ups and tells the truth when he is in a tight
> place is taking considerable many resks, though I ain't had no
> experience, and can't say for certain . . . and yet here's a case
> where I'm blest if it don't look like the truth is better and actuly
> safer than a lie. . . . I never seen nothing like it.

These lines are spoken by Huck in the Wilks episode, when
Twain's own reality-principle is being sold out to sentimentality;
but they reflect still the basic set which distinguishes the juvenile
pariah from the Good Bad Boy.

There is occasionally a certain bravado about Huck in his relationship to the world of morality, which he can neither abide nor disavow. When, for instance, Miss Watson (to whom "scrunching up" or yawning during lessons is a sin punishable in hell) tells Huck about the "bad place," he says he wishes he were there; and is considerably cheered to learn that Tom is likely to end up there, too. A moment later, however, he is in a state of depression and terror, imagining that he hears the voice of a ghost that "can't rest easy in its grave," seeing evil omens everywhere and performing his own rites of exorcism. "I got up and turned around in my tracks three times and crossed my heart every time." One must assume that he is beset by similar feelings of guilt and despair after his later nonchalant declaration: "Well, then, says I, what's the use you learning to do right when it's troublesome to do right and ain't no trouble to do wrong, and the wages is just the same? . . . So I reckoned I wouldn't bother no more about it, but after this always do whichever comes handiest at the time."

Huck had just made the first decisive move toward stealing Jim out of slavery, and feels that he has graduated at last from petty crimes to major ones. It never enters his head for a moment that protecting Jim against recapture is anything but *wrong;* for he has no abolitionist ideas and questions the justice of slavery no more than did Aristotle. He considers, however, that as an outcast he has little to lose; and is only overcome with horror when the Good Bad Boy Tom seems about to become his accomplice. His whole world of values is momentarily threatened, and only re-establishes itself when he learns that Jim has been all along free and Tom has known it: ". . . I couldn't ever understand before . . . how he could help a body set a nigger free with his bringing up." Huck believes in the equality of the races as little as he does in abolition; and when, after his long association with Jim, he is asked by Aunt Sally whether anyone was hurt in a steamboat accident, he answers blandly, "No'm, killed a nigger." There is no intended irony either in Huck's comment about Tom or in his response to Aunt Sally; Twain may *use* them ironically, but this must not mislead us. If Huck lies, runs, and hides for Jim's sake, even as he has lied, run, and hid for his own, this is not because he thinks he is acting in behalf of some higher moral code, but because he has extended his area of self-interest to a family of two. He loves Jim quite literally as himself, and is willing to go to hell for him, even as he was willing to go there for the sake of "scrunching" a little or cussing or smoking.

There is no irony, either, in the self-reproach, the acceptance
of his own damnation which Huck finally speaks; whatever games
Twain may be playing with his declaration, Huck quite simply
believes it:

> . . . something inside of me kept saying, There was the Sunday-
> school, you could 'a' gone to it; and if you'd 'a' done it they'd 'a'
> learnt you there that people that acts as I'd been acting about
> that nigger goes to the everlasting fire.
> It made me shiver. And I about made up my mind to pray,
> and see if I couldn't try to quit being the kind of boy I was and
> be better . . . but deep down in me I knowed it was a lie, and
> He knowed it. You can't pray a lie—I found that out.

His attempted prayer a failure, Huck tries to write a letter to Miss
Watson, telling her where Jim is, and thus putting things right with
his conscience; but though doing it makes him feel "washed clean
of sin for the first time," his love for Jim returns. He remembers
not some abolitionist slogan or moral tag about the equal rights of
all mankind, only how Jim "would always call me honey, and pet
me, and do everything he could think of for me . . ." and he
decides not to send the letter.

> . . . I studied a minute, sort of holding my breath, and then
> says to myself: "All right, then I'll *go* to Hell"—and tore it up.
> It was awful thoughts and awful words, but they was said.
> And I let them stay said; and never thought no more about re-
> forming. I shoved the whole thing out of my head, and said I
> would take up wickedness again, which was in my line, being
> brung up to it, and the other warn't.

At this point, the Faustian theme is improbably reborn in the
midst of comedy and nostalgia. Lionel Trilling compares Huck at
the moment of his decision to a courtly lover submitting to eternal
torment for the sake of his beloved; but he seems more Faust than
Lancelot: one with Ahab and Pierre and Hester and Ethan Brand.
To be sure, Twain is toying with the theme, evading final responsibility; for he knows that the most genteel post-Civil-War reader,
secure in a world without slavery, will see Huck, not as a Satanic
and hybristic rebel, setting the promptings of his own ignorant heart
over the law of the land and the teaching of his church—but as a

moral hero. Yet in Huck, for an instant at least, the marginal
loafer, the uncommitted idler is revealed as the American Faust;
the dark side turned up of what *Huckleberry Finn's* first reviewer
called "the ruffianism that is one result of the independence of
Americans." Yet the revelation is made in so witty and charming
and ambiguous a way, that the same reviewer has described Huck's
terrible decision as "most instructive and amusing."

Twain has a further duplicitous device, which is quite simply to
make his shiftless Faustian drifter a boy, a child with, he keeps
assuring us, a truly virtuous heart. Not only does Twain shrug off
the issues, social and moral, involved in a life based on lying and
stealing with the implicit comment that "Boys will be boys!"; but
he further confounds confusion by identifying his juvenile pariah
with the sentimental stereotypes of the child as Noble Savage and
the child as victim of society. Huck is, whatever his other faults,
the most nonviolent of American fictional children, more like
Oliver Twist than Tom Sawyer, who is his companion. Unlike
Tom, he never fights with his fists; and though he takes up a rifle
once against his delirious father, who has threatened him with a
knife, he does not fire it. He never quite shoots even in self-
defense; and during the Grangerford feud, for instance, finds a
perch in a tree and merely watches, trembling, the foolish bravery
of others. He runs, hides, equivocates, dodges, and, when he can
do nothing else, suffers. Though admiring critics speak of him
sometimes as "manly" or "courageous," he is actually timid almost
to the point of burlesque—the anti-type of the foolhardy Tom. To
be sure, aboard the *Walter Scott,* he whips up courage enough to
eavesdrop on the quarreling crooks by reminding himself of what
Tom Sawyer would have done ("and I says to myself, Tom Sawyer
wouldn't back out now, and I won't either"); but more customarily, discretion is the whole of his valor. He is quite frank about
his fears, telling us over and over: "I warn't feeling very brash,
there warn't much sand in my craw"; "I was too scared"; "Well,
I catched my breath and most fainted"; "It made me so sick I most
fell out of the tree." And when the lynch mob, after which he has
tagged along, breaks and runs before the defiance of Colonel Sherburn, Huck observes in self-mockery, "I could 'a' stayed if I wanted
to, but I didn't want to."

He has, indeed, the right to be afraid, for he has no effective
protectors. A "motherless boy," his father is his worst enemy; and

he is, by the time he enters the scene, incapable of paying the price of membership in a respectable household, immune to "civilization." Moreover, his civilizers prove strangely unable to defend him; for when his own origins rise against him (he is, after all, the child of ignorance and drunkenness and violence), the polite community, disabled by sentimentality and a commitment to legal process, stands helplessly by. Not only do the half-world, which bred him, and the genteel community, which tried to adopt him, betray him; but Nature herself, to which he flees as a final refuge, proves a treacherous parent, offering, along with moments of joy and calm, times of terror in storm and fog. No wonder Huck is a strangely melancholy child—not only possessed of a sense of alienation ("lonesome" is almost his favorite adjective), but obsessed by, more than half in love with death.

From the first, the reader is made aware of Huck's dark preoccupations: "I felt so lonesome I most wished I was dead. . . . I heard an owl . . . who-whooing about somebody that was dead, and a whippoorwill and a dog crying about somebody who was going to die." And, indeed, he plays dead in order to survive, rigs a scene of murder to persuade his Pap (who has taken him for the angel of death!) and the world that he is beyond their reach: "They won't ever hunt the river for anything but my dead carcass. They'll soon get tired of that, and won't bother no more about me." Afterwards, he seems a ghost to everyone who knew him; and even at the moment just before what he calls his rebirth ("it was like being born again") at the Phelps farm, his original melancholia returns:

> there was them kind of faint dronings of bugs and flies in the air that makes it seem so lonesome and like everybody's dead and gone . . . it makes a body wish *he* was dead, too, and done with it all. . . . When I got a little ways I heard the dim hum of a spinning-wheel wailing along up and sinking along down again; and then I knowed for certain I wished I was dead—for that *is* the lonesomest sound in the whole world.

"Lonesome" and "dead": the two words are inextricably linked; and they rise in Huck's mind at the moment just before he leaves and just as he is about to re-enter the matriarchal world—which is all the civilization he knows.

"Hannibal" is Mark Twain's name for the world of belongingness and security, of school and home and church, presided over by the mothers. There are men on the upper levels of this respectable world (Judge Thatcher, for instance, self-important and pompous), but they are not, in *Huckleberry Finn,* presented as its rulers or its conscience. Tom, of course, has no father at all, is responsible only to Aunt Polly; while Huck is found at the book's start in the all-female household of the widow Douglas and the old maid, Miss Watson. "I never seen anybody but lied one time or another," Huck remarks at the outset, "without it was Aunt Polly, or the widow, or maybe Mary." These are the super-ego figures of the book, these husbandless mothers or fatherless daughters who cannot lie, only love. But the kindly widow is given a dour double in Miss Watson, as if to reveal the threat always lurking beneath matriarchal tenderness: the rigid piety, the petty discipline, the belief in soap—the love of money! Miss Watson, we remember, tempted by a slave-trader's generous offer, plans to sell her nigger, Jim, down the river and away from his family! The world of mothers, after all, believes not only in Providence and cleanliness and affection, but in slavery, too. Yet it is the best of all conceivable worlds to Mark Twain.

Into it all girls are inducted, apparently, simply by being born; for there are, in Mark Twain's Hannibal, no bad girls, only good ones, marriage with whom means an initiation into piety and conformity, the end of freedom. But as long as childhood lasts, Twain's boys are granted a special immunity from the codes of the mothers. Those mothers do not, of course, openly announce this privilege, only secretly hope that, against their avowed wishes, their sons will rebel, be properly "misch*ee*vous." The boy who conforms too soon, the Good Good Boy represented by Sid Sawyer, is despised a little by the mothers themselves, who prefer the Good Bad Boy, Tom—and long to convert into his image the juvenile pariah with the heart of gold, Huck Finn. There are no Bad Bad Boys in Twain's legendary town, no vicious delinquents beyond all hope of reform; such a thing is as impossible as a vicious woman! Even outside of his fiction, in personal reminiscence, Twain could not bring himself to grant that Huck's sisters had been prostitutes.

Evil he can imagine only in terms of a fully adult male, a Bad Father—like Injun Joe in *Tom Sawyer* or Pap in *Huckleberry Finn:*

His hair was long and tangled and greasy, and hung down, and you could see his eyes shining through like he was behind vines.

. . . There warn't no color in his face, where his face showed; it was white; not like another man's white, but a white to make a body sick, a white to make a body's flesh crawl—a tree-toad white, a fish-belly white.

But sharing the same sub-world which Pap inhabits, the world of those who will not accept or are not permitted to assume social responsibility, is Nigger Jim, whose good blackness is ironically contrasted with Pap's evil whiteness. Once Jim has run away, he no longer really belongs to Hannibal at all, but to the river: symbol of flight and the moral indifference of Nature. It is to the river that Pap comes at the moment of his sordid death; on the river that the crooks trapped aboard the *Walter Scott* die, too; the river that the Duke and Dauphin seek in their eternal flight from the vengeance of the towns. And beyond the river is Indian territory, the ultimate reach of alienation and anti-civilization.

This is the moral geography of the world in which Huck stands poised just before the moment of adolescence, and his choices are limited by the narrow possibilities of that world. Either he can accommodate like Tom or Sid, become the mothers' boy, after all; or he can turn back into his father's sub-world, the tanyard, the hogshead, the wharves—accept a perpetual outsideness. He cannot, of course, stay where he is in the no-man's land of boyhood, where the two adult worlds meet, because the simple passage of time will drive him out. For all his illusion of choice, he is not really free, but imprisoned in his "independence"; for he is incapable of remaining inside the respectable community. There is, on the one hand, too much of his father in him; and he is actually happy when Pap carries him off: "It was pretty good times up in the woods there, take it all around." On the other hand, there is too much Miss Watson in all mothers: "a poor chap would stand considerable show with the widow's Providence, but if Miss Watson's got him there warn't no help for him any more."

Huck's problem is, therefore, not to find his fate but to accept it; and *Huckleberry Finn* is the history of his vain attempts to escape that fate. He believes at first that he is running not from himself but from his father and Miss Watson, from both limits of the only society he knows. But he does not know to *what* he is escaping, except into nothing: a mere anti-society, in which he is a cipher, a ghost without a real name. "All I wanted was to go somewheres," he tells Miss Watson, "all I wanted was a change, I warn't particular." Huck is heading for no utopia, since he has heard of none; and so he ends up making flight itself his goal. He flees from the impermanence of boyhood to that of continual change; and, of course, it is a vain evasion except as it leads him to understand that *no* society can fulfill his destiny.

It is to the river that he turns, since the river is the only avenue of escape he knows; but the river betrays him, even as it betrays Jim in his complementary search for freedom. Bearing Huck toward the South, the river carries him from a matriarchal world to a patriarchal one, from one which believes in Providence to one which believes in honor ("Colonel Grangerford was a gentleman, you see. He was a gentleman all over . . ."); but for Huck, honor is a concept as unviable as good works or prayer. The chivalric world of the Grangerfords offers to take him in, to make him a little gentleman just as the Widow had wanted to make him a small Christian. There is even a patriarchal version of Tom Sawyer, young Buck, to be his companion and link to that world; but the end of chivalry is violence, for which Huck has even less taste than he has for telling the truth. And he stands at last, after the feud with the Shepherdsons has erupted into furious and wholesale slaughter, looking down at the dead bodies of two boys, who, unlike him, had been brought up to fight rather than run. "I covered up their faces, and got away as quick as I could. I cried a little when I was covering up Buck's face."

In the end, Huck has got out of the whole experience only a vague sense of guilt (he did carry the message which touched off the final combat), and another nightmare to add to his already full store. "I wished I hadn't ever come ashore that night to see such things, I ain't ever going to get shut of them—lots of times I dream about them." The episode of Colonel Sherburn does little to change his picture of life in the South, only adding a brutal murder (the shooting down for honor's sake of an unarmed, drunken lout, not very different from Huck's Pap) and a failed lynching, from which Huck turns away to go to a circus. The final condemnation of the South is spoken by Colonel Sherburn himself, who is the victim of its mad code of honor, but not of its hypocrisy: "If any real lynching's going to be done, it will be done in the dark, Southern fashion; and when they come they'll bring their masks. . . ."

The Wilks episode is transitional, still set in the patriarchal

world of the South, but centered, for Huck, around the figure of
Mary Jane, "most awful beautiful . . . her eyes . . . all lit up like
glory," on whom he develops a hopeless small-boy crush, seeming
suddenly five years younger. The whole section is unforgivably sentimental and melodramatic—a compound of sticky nobility and
stage gothicism, in the midst of which Huck's pure love is contrasted with the slobbering lustfulness of the Dauphin. At no point
in *Huckleberry Finn* is its protagonist so untrue to himself, or
Twain so near to yielding up the truth of his book to sentiment. Yet
finally Huck moves on past the temptation of puppy love, as he
has already passed through those of chivalry and courage. There is
no mock marriage, or even a dream of a future one, as in *Tom
Sawyer,* only a somewhat unconvincing touch of pathos, when the
only girl is left behind:

> I hain't ever seen her since that time that I see her go out of that
> door, no, I hain't ever seen her since, but I reckon I've thought
> of her many and many a million times, and her saying she would
> pray for me and if ever I'd 'a' thought it would do any good for
> me to pray for *her,* blamed if I wouldn't 'a' done it or bust.

Beyond this, there is Aunt Sally's farm, which looks at first
glance very like the Grangerfords'. There is the same double log
cabin, the same howling dogs to greet Huck; but his reception committee is quite different from the "three big men with guns pointed
at me," who welcomed "George Jackson" into the world of feuding
gentlemen. At the Phelpses', it is a Negro woman with a rolling pin
in her hand, then Aunt Sally herself, "her spinning stick in her
hand." We have moved from the world of gun-bearing fathers into
that of mothers, armed only with the symbols of domesticity. The
man of the house is the doddering, ineffective Hiram, scarcely real
beside his vivid wife. We are, in effect, back in Hannibal (Twain
in *The Autobiography* tells us that the original of the Phelps place
was in Missouri, but "I moved it down to Arkansas. It was all of
six hundred miles but it was no trouble"), and Huck is not
George Jackson, Sarah Williams, George Peters, or Adolphus; he
is, disconcertingly, Tom Sawyer! For a little while, he even thinks
like Tom, forgets the prescience of death that came over him with
the first sound of Aunt Sally's spinning wheel, and accepts her
house as if it were his Great Good Place, too. "It was a heavenly

place for a boy," Twain writes years later; but precisely for this reason it was no place for a boy who had chosen hell in its despite. In Twain, indeed, only children are permitted to reject society and success; adults grow up into compromise and adjustment. Pudd'nhead Wilson represents, in a sense, Twain's version of Pierre, the alienated intellectual cast adrift in a community of philistines; and as Pierre confides his doubts about the world's morality to his unpopular novel, so Pudd'nhead sets his down in his "Calendar." Yet Pudd'nhead, unlike Pierre, has no consuming desire to publish his dangerous work; but shows it only to a single reader, resents it as a betrayal when that reader exposes it to the unappreciative public. Twain's own attitude toward the "Calendar" is more than a little disconcerting; reporting on the community's reaction to Puddn'head's satirical notes, Twain observes that "they read those playful trifles in the solidest earnest." But "playful trifle" seems hardly an adequate characterization of such a comment as: "Whoever has lived long enough to find out what life is, knows how deep a debt of gratitude we owe to Adam, the first great benefactor of the human race. He brought death into the world."

It is, perhaps, only a final twist of Twain's irony to pretend to dismiss such bitterness as trifling, but it is a protective irony, too, a defense of himself as well as Pudd'nhead. Indeed, though he distributed much of the "Calendar" through the novel in the form of chapter headings, he saved out a few that he considered too shocking, kept him in manuscript until his death. Wilson is, like his author, a man unsure of just when he is kidding himself, when the public; and his assumption of the role of humorist protects him against the day when he will be ready to change overnight from clownish Faust to eccentric detective, receive the full benefits of the happy ending which Twain has all along had in store for him. After his courtroom triumph, cheering crowds of citizens gather to acclaim Pudd'nhead, and match their praise of him with reproach of themselves. "His long fight against hard luck and prejudice was ended," Twain reports blandly; "he was a made man for good." If there is an undertone of irony in this, it is impossible to prove; and, indeed, there is scarcely room for it to exist in the minimal distance Twain has left between author and character. Like Pudd'nhead, Mark Twain, too, wants to have it both ways at once: to insult the society he lives in in the guise of tossing off "playful trifles," and to be hailed as a hero for discovering what no one really wants to know! If Pudd'nhead has seemed to play the role of Faust or Pierre, this is only because "hard luck and prejudice" have conspired to miscast him. His overwhelming desire for success (not alienation!) and the price he was willing to pay for it he has declared frankly enough in the epigraph to Chapter I: "Tell the truth or trump—but get the trick!"

I I

From the time of Twain to that of Faulkner, it is hard to find a true Faustian character in American fiction. On the middlebrow level, that mythic figure is officially excluded by an orthodoxy of cheerfulness and acceptance. On the highbrow level, he is confused with the closely related archetype of the *poète maudit,* which descends ultimately from Werther and is influenced by French reworkings of Edgar Allan Poe. There is in such characters the Faustian potential, but most often their tragic possibilities are dissipated in posturing and self-pity. Their secret motto comes improbably from Emerson—not "to be great is to be damned," but "to be great is to be misunderstood." From the heroes of Henry Harland to those of Scott Fitzgerald, such not-quite tragic sufferers (they dream of expatriation rather than alienation, of going to Paris rather than hell!) continue to testify and perish, either on behalf of art alone or—more and more as the influence of Freud and Lawrence is felt—on behalf of sexual freedom, too. It is in the name of experience that they challenge the world, and it is against law that they chiefly chafe. But whether they are more innocent than their conforming fellow citizens or more guilty they cannot decide; and their authors write, therefore, books which are neither gothic nor Western, the kind of morally incoherent, sentimental works produced by Sherwood Anderson or Thomas Wolfe or Ross Lockridge.

World War I spurred the proliferation of such books; for in the minds of certain authors (the John Dos Passos of *Three Soldiers* is a key example), mass warfare came to seem essentially a conspiracy against the artistic sensibility, even more brutal than peacetime bourgeois life. The typical anti-war novel of the '20's is, therefore, more sentimental than political, rather like the "social" novels of Dickens, which judge society on the basis of how it treats the child —except that for writers like Dos Passos, not the child but the artist is the touchstone.* After World War II, the novelists, who succeeded in finding no new forms, revived once more the prototypes of twenty years before; and the American version of the *poète maudit* stalks again through the pages of Irwin Shaw's *The Young Lions,* a copy of Joyce's *Ulysses* under his bunk to make his affiliation clear. This time, however, he is permitted to fight back, to succeed rather than fail in the face of "hard luck and prejudice," to play Pudd'nhead Wilson—and thus to move even farther from the role of Faustian rebel. Successes or failures, however, such figures can never blaspheme, only shally endlessly between withdrawal and accommodation, self-pity and self-congratulation; for they live in a world which has no name for sin.

Of all the avatars of self-pity who have possessed our literature for five decades, perhaps the only one to approach legendary dimensions is Eugene Gant, who first appears in *Look Homeward Angel* and strives desperately to change and die in Wolfe's other thick, repetitious novels. Distinguished from our other innocent *poètes maudits* by his size, which has to match that of his author, Gant finally becomes neither heroic nor Gargantuan, but remains a great panting, blubbering hulk of an adolescent, who can age but not grow up. In a certain sense, he is more the successor to Huck Finn than to Stephen Dedalus, who was his immediate model. Joyce's Dedalus, both in *Portrait of the Artist as a Young Man* and *Ulysses,* broke out of the trap of self-pity and narcissism, pledging allegiance (while his detached and ironic author smiled) to the Satanic slogan: *Non serviam,* "I will not obey!" And he is harried into maturity, driven from home by the ghost of his mother, beside whose deathbed he had refused to kneel in prayer: "Silence, exile, and cunning," are the weapons he takes up in self-defense, weapons proper to the lonely Faustian man, who rejects in full awareness the pieties of family, church, and state. Gant's protective devices are nostalgia, *Weltschmerz,* and *Schwärmerei* (the German terms are inevitable in speaking of the single modern American author whom the Nazis found irresistible), the devices proper to the lonely child, who wants really only to recapture his lost, unknowable Mother. "Naked and alone we came into exile. In her

---

* So also the anti-Hollywood novel (written and rewritten as late as Mailer's *The Deer Park*) and the anti-University novel (represented in the first part of Philip Roth's *Letting Go* and the whole of Bernard Malamud's *A New Life*) continue to charge those two institutions with the ultimate literary crime: betraying the writer, and thus proving themselves no better than the War to End War itself.

dark womb we did not know our mother's face. . . . Which of us is not forever a stranger and alone? . . . O lost, and by the wind grieved, ghost, come back again." *Look Homeward Angel, You Can't Go Home Again:* the titles tell the story of the search and the frustration; and beyond them, the books reveal the love of that frustration and the seeking self: the little boy lost, for whom no world is real and satisfactory once mama's breast has been withdrawn, papa has died, and big brother has become a ghost endlessly mourned. There is no room for the Faustian passion where one is an outcast not because he has fallen but because he was born. And Wolfe's work finds its place, therefore, not even in the children's library, in which all terrible myths except those of passionate love can survive, but in the high school department, on the shelf of masturbatory dreams.

It is, perhaps, because in Faulkner's fiction alone, in the first half of the twentieth century, the Faustian figure persists as a living obsession, that Faulkner has come to seem our greatest contemporary novelist. What would strike us otherwise as mere hectic rhetoric and conventional gothic décor is transformed by this central concern into a tragic cry and an evocation of terror. In three of his major novels, Faulkner deliberately chooses the gothic mode, attempts to create the full-scale tale of terror, though everywhere he uses the devices of the form to invest with horror his vision of a chaotic and lost world. The first of these novels is *Sanctuary,* whose atrocities are presided over by Popeye, a two-dimensional, soulless machine of pure rapacity. The second is *Light in August,* whose Satanic segment unfolds under the aegis of Joe Christmas, the almost will-less offspring of a mating of black and white, possessed by the demons of rape and castration, murder and miscegenation. The third is *Absalom, Absalom!,* through which Thomas Sutpen, more ogre than man, stalks furiously toward his own destruction. It is only in the latter, however, that the authentic Faustian protagonist is created. *Sanctuary* is, on its more conscious levels at least, the least mythic of all Faulkner's works, and *Light in August* is, for all its bitterness and hysteria, a book about two saviors: Lena Grove, whom nothing can stop in her almost mindless quest of a father for her child, an inarticulate, unvirginal Mary in search of a Joseph; and Joe Christmas, in his inevitable crucifixion both Christ and anti-Christ. Born on Christmas Day without an acknowledged father, named at a venture "Christmas, the son of Joe," he dies, at the traditional age of thirty-three, nailed to the cross of his blood. And at the moment of his castration, which preludes his death even as the thrust of the lance into the side of Jesus, he seems to ascend to heaven on the spout of blood which the shocked reader realizes at that point has been shed for many:

> the pent black blood . . . seemed to rush out of his pale body like the rush of sparks from a rising rocket; upon that black blast the man seemed to rise soaring into their memories forever and ever. They are not to lose it, in whatever peaceful valleys, beside whatever placid and reassuring streams of old age, in the mirroring faces of whatever children they will contemplate old disasters and newer hopes. . . .

Only in Sutpen does Faulkner attempt the creation of the Faustian figure in whom the gothic achieves its thematic fulfillment. It is worth noting that he does not find his Faust among the humble peasants, black and white, who merely "endure"; nor does he discover him in the world of the aristocracy, of the Sartorises and their friends, in whom the old codes of honor of the South are remembered if not lived. Sutpen is a man without either honor or humility, only with a "grand design"; he is a poor white on the rise, the self-made man, whom Faulkner has elsewhere mocked and scorned, fighting his way toward acceptance and respectability. "He wasn't a gentleman," one of the narrators of *Absalom, Absalom!* insists, "he wasn't *even* a gentleman." A ragged and dirty boy, he is driven from a white man's house (whose owner rocks in a barrel-stave hammock, his leisure ensured by black sweat) by a Negro servant, though he has come in innocence to speak a helpful word; and he vows to make a secure place for himself in the world so that he need never again submit to such an indignity! For that secure place, he is willing to enter into whatever agreement hell may demand of him: "this Faustus, this demon, this Beelzebub fled hiding from some momentary flashing glare of his Creditor's outraged face . . . hiding, scuttling into respectability like a jackal into a rockpile. . . ." Yet though he is accused by Shreve (the Canadian roommate of Quentin Compson who speaks these words) of having made a compact with the Devil, Sutpen is not really credited with having a soul to sell. Commenting on Sutpen's coolness, the bravado which especially characterizes him, Shreve tries to write it off as "a part of the price he had got for whatever it was he had sold the Creditor, since according to the old dame he had never had a soul." In Shreve's irreverent account, the Satanic nature of Sutpen is treated with undergraduate levity. Not only does Shreve insist on referring to Sutpen's diabolic Master as "the Creditor" (apt enough metaphor in terms of the world of Sutpen who has ended by running a store), but he jokes about Sutpen's hiding his tail and horns "beneath human raiment and a beaver hat." It is not a new device for the American author embarrassed by the Faustian myth; indeed, it echoes quite directly the device by which Melville in *Moby Dick* lets jesting Stubb and Flask do most of the talking about Ahab's bargain with Fedallah.

Yet Shreve is surely not *only* making a dull joke over and over when he compulsively refers to Sutpen as "the demon." His epithet blends with those of the novel's other spokesmen: "fiend black-guard and devil," "ogre in an ogre-bourne with two phantom chil-dren," to create a common image more terrible and pathetic than comic or grotesque. Not only does Sutpen make his entrance into the story as the typical gothic hero-villain, emaciated and taciturn, his eyes "visionary and alert," guardedly watching out of a face baked black by some mysterious "oven's fever," but he grows in tragic stature as he struggles to achieve that grand design which brings only loneliness and madness and destruction to his children and himself. From the moment we see him first, naked and plas-tered with black mud, toiling in the virgin swamp beside his wild Negroes, to the point at which he falls beneath a scythe wielded by the father of a girl whom he has studded as if she were a beast, he becomes ever more monstrous and more admirable. In him, the very innocence that mitigates the Faustian guilt of other American heroes serves only to exacerbate that guilt; his invulnerable moral virginity merely increases the poignancy of the struggle, in which his "solitary despair" closes "in titan conflict with the lonely and foredoomed and indomitable iron spirit." Only the great mythic name is adequate to describe him; an old man selling calico to country girls in a tiny shack of a store, he is still somehow an "ancient and varicose and despairing Faustus . . . with the Credi-tor's hand already on his shoulder."

But Faulkner cannot sustain, from his ambivalent vantage-point, so tragic a view of the storekeeper, the status-hungry American on the make, the petty-bourgeois inheritor of a South that had be-longed to his ancestors. Sutpen killed by Wash is revived as a Snopes, first as Ab, then as his son Flem. His past history is bestowed in some detail upon his successors; like Sutpen, the Snopeses also approach the grand house of a white man, still rocking in the same barrel-stave hammock, and are driven like him from the front door by a black servant. To be sure, Ab Snopes has approached not in innocent benevolence but with malice already in his heart, not inadvertently tracking mud onto the white porch, but deliberately walking through manure in order to sully the immaculate floors of the kind of man he despairingly and impotently hates.

The Snopeses, however, represent in Faulkner's mythology not only meanness of spirit and active malice; they are, by definition, clowns, who introduce into *Sanctuary* itself a note of sheer burlesque, when two of the tribe register in a whorehouse which they take for a hotel. When Flem Snopes makes his appearance in *The Hamlet* (1940), he is wearing a celluloid collar and a patent-leather bow tie, carrying a straw satchel; he is, in short, a comic character. It is as if Faulkner had in mind Marx's maxim about history repeating itself, the first time as tragedy, the second as comedy. For Flem is a second-generation figure, a post-Civil War representative of the demonic drive which earlier had propelled Sutpen toward his doom. This time, however, the Satanic social climber is distinguished not by the titanic despair and loneliness which compel pity and terror, but by a single-minded meanness of spirit against which laughter is the only defense.

Comic as he is, however, the Flem Snopes of *The Hamlet* is still a comic Faust. Though he moves through a world of the broadest farce, of back-country yarns, which swell and burgeon in the unreal atmosphere of tale-swapping in the gathering twilight of a summer's day, Flem becomes at last so genuinely sinister a figure that around him laughter dies to a chilled silence or rises to the pitch of hysteria. Only hell seems adequate to define his icy cunning, the cold aplomb with which he takes possession piece by piece of the whole crumbling world of the South. The voice of reason in the novel belongs to the sewing-machine salesman, Ratliffe, who speaks for Faulkner more directly than any other character in *The Hamlet;* but it is Ratliffe who dreams, or perhaps, more properly, has a vision of Flem's Descent into Hell. There is consternation among the minor devils at the point when he is ready to be "redeemed into eternal torment," for they cannot find his soul. Like Sutpen before him, he has none at all—only "a little kind of dried-up smear under one edge" of the asbestos box, where his most precious part has presumably been kept against the day of the running out of his contract. Worse, however, is to come; before the comedy is played out, it becomes clear that Flem has come to "the Creditor" not to submit to punishment but to take over hell itself. At the end, the Infernal Prince, scarcely knowing what has happened, discovers himself on his knees, looking up at Flem who sits calmly on his erstwhile throne. And he cries wildly, "Take Paradise!" while "the wind roars up and the dark roars down and the Prince scrabbling across the floor, clawing and scrabbling at the locked door, screaming. . . ." It is a simple-minded gag, really—not Faust but Satan begging for mercy at the last; but it is hard to laugh away.

That the South has remained through the last three decades our preferred literary arena of terror is, in great part, the achievement of Faulkner, a product of his mythopoeic genius; but it is also a product of the spirit of the times. As the dark-skinned peoples of the world stir uneasily, begin to make their bid for power, readers white and black turn to the imaginative record of the first large-scale encounter of the two races at close quarters, the struggle of Negro and white in the United States. Long before Little Rock, the attitudes of European intellectuals toward the American South and the American Negro were set by Faulkner's fiction; and, indeed, not only the white man's consciousness of the colored man but the colored man's own self-consciousness have been determined in large part by literary images, from Mrs. Stowe's Uncle Tom to Faulkner's Dilsey and Lucas Beauchamp. The European has unfortunately tended to read Faulkner's gothic and symbolic distortion of life in Mississippi as literal sociological reporting; and Jean-Paul Sartre's *The Respectful Prostitute* provides a classic (and ridiculous) example of what happens when complex art is taken as simple fact. Only the American tradition of symbolic gothicism, which from Poe and Melville to Twain and Faulkner has never ceased to confront the problem of the Negro, has proved in an age of realism adequate to the complexities of life in the American South; and it is to Faulkner that young writers, Negro and white, continue to turn for clues to the "power of blackness" in our contemporary life.

Especially in Faulkner's early gothicism, succeeding novelists have discovered an example which has sustained them in their search for their own authentic themes and styles. One such line of development, which we have already noticed, is seen in the novels of Robert Penn Warren, the single long fiction of John Peale Bishop, *Act of Darkness,* and such novels of Erskine Caldwell as *Tobacco Road* and *God's Little Acre.* Caldwell, originally a short-story writer of considerable power, though always with a tendency toward melodrama, has deliberately vulgarized his themes, exaggerating the grotesquerie of Faulkner in the direction of the merely shocking, and creating a special brand of horror-pornography (grandpa eaten by the hogs, while brother is seducing sister in the splashing swill) that has made him one of the all-time best-sellers among the paperbacks. In him, the Faulknerian legend of the South reaches the wide audience capable only of the grossest responses and searching always for a violence capable of shaking their own torpor. Tough, tortured, and, at their best, determinedly intellectual, the masculine Faulknerians deal with the matter of the South not, like Caldwell, for its exoticism and suggestions of horror, nor even merely for the sake of atmosphere and tone, but because they are concerned with the complex moral and social problems at its heart, particularly those arising from the conflict and confluence of white and black.

Much more influential and varied, however, is a second Faulknerian line of descent in which women have rather consistently, though quite improbably, taken a leading part. Among the first generation of distaff Faulknerians are included such talented female fictionists as Katherine Anne Porter, Eudora Welty, and Carson McCullers; while in the succeeding generation Elizabeth Spencer and Flannery O'Connor have already achieved reputations. In the work of the earlier group, the obsessive concerns of Faulkner, and especially his vision of the South as a world of gothic terror disguised as historical fact, ceases to be the property of a single, eccentric author and becomes a living tradition; thanks to their transitional work, Mississippi has taken on for the imagination of the world the symbolic values attributed in the earliest years of the gothic to Italy. Against a background of miasmic swamps and sweating black skins, the Faulknerian syndrome of disease, death, defeat, mutilation, idiocy, and lust continues to evoke in the stories of these writers a shudder once compelled only by the supernatural. What tends to be dissipated in their fiction is the grossness, the sheer dirtiness, the farce and howling burlesque, all that keeps Faulkner from ever seeming precious, or, in any meaningful sense of the word, decadent. In Katherine Anne Porter, the grotesque tensions and masculine vigor of Faulkner still largely survive; in Eudora Welty, they tend to disappear among the more delicate nuances of sensibility; in Carson McCullers, especially after her first book, they have been quite subdued; and in Truman Capote, who is the heir of the feminizing Faulknerians, tone and style have been accommodated to notions of chic nurtured by such fashion magazines as *Harper's Bazaar.* In recent years, these journals have been remade in accordance with a new ideal of sensibility, defined by a taste for *haute couture,* classical ballet, baroque opera, certain more elegant rituals of the Church—and, above all, for the last, delicate distillation of Faulknerianism, a literature at once sensitive and Satanic.

Although (or perhaps because) this sensibility is quite frankly homosexual, it appeals to certain wealthy American women with cultural aspirations, and is, therefore, sponsored in their salons and published, with elegant taste, in magazines that cater to their other needs. The development of new markets for young writers who find themselves at home in those salons and magazines has gone hand in hand with the extension to America of the high bohemia which now includes New York as well as Venice or Ischia: a community hospitable to those who are internationalist and anti-bourgeois, so long as they are not sordid or sullen or bluntly political. The American writers who flourish best in this international society tend to be from the South; and, indeed, such a climate of expectation has been created in this regard, that aspirants to the chic audience are likely to pretend to Southern origins when they do not legitimately possess them.

In Faulkner, such writers find a ready-made *paysage moralisé,* through which to move their epicene protagonists, the landscape of the South already endowed with the proper symbolic values of decay and brooding evil. And in Faulkner, they find, too, a fear and distrust of women which they respond to according to their own lights. But it was not until the female intermediaries had begun the grafting of Jamesian sensibility onto the Southern gothic stem, that the true Magnolia Blossom or Southern homosexual style could be produced: pseudo-magical, pseudo-religious, pseudo-gothic.

Such fiction is often merely fashionable, for all its ostensible dedication to style and subtlety. Even Truman Capote, who from the beginning possessed considerable skill as a writer (it is impossible to imagine him writing anything as inept as Faulkner's *Mosquitoes*), has come more and more to play a part in print and out: to act for the benefit of his own limited world the elegant, sad androgyne—half reigning beauty and half freak. His promise has frittered away into journalism, as various magazines hasten to exploit him, send him on commissions to Russia, to Hollywood, etc. But even his novel, *Other Voices, Other Rooms,* already represents a falling away from the slight, authentic music of such an early story as "Children on their Birthdays." At the present moment, the queen has been replaced even in the superslicks by the beatnik; * but for perhaps ten years after World War II, the work of such fictionists as Capote and Carson McCullers profited by a *détente* in the middleclass, middlebrow war against homosexuality, just as the work of certain Jewish writers benefited by a similar relaxation on the anti-Semitic front. The new enlightenment according to psychoanalysis and intergroup tolerance has made it impossible for the right-minded to reject either fairy or Jew as subjects for our fiction, without self-reproach; and they have taken up the burden of *understanding* such deviants, often as their only remaining claim to liberalism.

In the lee of that understanding, certain writers, who only a generation or two ago would have had to produce semi-pornographic or encrypted books, have been able to make their ostensible subject what has so long been disguised or evaded in our classic fiction. Overt homosexuality carries with it, however, still the sense of taboo, and is almost always rendered, therefore, in gothic terms; though, as a covert theme, it informed the open-air Western mode. On the middlebrow and popular levels the new homosexuality is only now coming fully into its own. Capote (as artist rather than journalist) and Gore Vidal (as novelist rather than TV entertainer) have come to seem a little old hat, and even Paul Bowles begins to look like an enthusiasm of yesterday, while a serious new writer like Robert Phelps produces in *Heroes and Orators* (1958) a complex and troubling study of homosexual love that goes unnoticed; but Tennessee Williams and William Inge, moving from the stage to the screen, mold the imagination of our

---

* Both giving way in 1966 to that blend of beatnik and queer, the pop artist, whose camp style is at once a travesty and an emulation of the slicks themselves.

largest audience, and even in paperback detective stories, lesbian and queer become common properties.* Quite astonishingly, the gum-chewing popcorn-consuming hordes of the remotest hinterlands have accepted a new archetype of love (projected ideally by Anna Magnani and Marlon Brando) in which an aging, slovenly, aggressive woman—in a black slip—vainly assaults the innocence of a clean, incorruptible, beautiful young man—without a shirt. In ten thousand movie houses, the moment in which that infinitely desirable youth strips to the waist has come to represent the expected climax of the more arty film. His invert's strip tease takes place, of course, in a decaying clapboard house, outside of which the Spanish moss hangs ghostlike in the Southern night.

The child and the freak haunt such landscapes, too, images created out of the homosexual's conviction of the impossibility of love; and they move, not yet fallen into a world of acceptance and differentiated sex, through a society in which passion leads only to thralldom and suffering. Carson McCullers, in one book at least, manages to break through the parochialism and self-pity implicit in such a view of life, creating in *The Heart is a Lonely Hunter* an utterly convincing and terrible fiction. Written when she was only twenty-two, the book appeared in 1940, and is, in one sense, the last of the "proletarian novels," a true Depression book. Indeed, its success may be rooted precisely in the tension between public hysteria, proper to an age of social protest, and private anguish, proper to the sensibility of its author.

The Heart is a Lonely Hunter is a latter-day Southern love story, which is to say, a study of the failure of love, in this case the passion which unequally binds together two male deaf-mutes, one of them an almost bestial moron. That passion is rendered through the consciousness of one of those boy-girl adolescents shortly to become stereotypes; but in Mrs. McCullers' first novel, nothing is yet stereotypical. The melancholy Southern town, the deaf-and-dumb protagonists are completely satisfactory as fact and as symbol, fused into a single authentic vision suspended in the eye of a child, herself suspended at the verge of maturity. Mrs. McCullers' themes are common to the whole group to which she belongs: the impossibility of reciprocal love, the sadness of a

---

* The rise of Terry Sothern represents a later, analogous development—the passing of a kind of humor originally relished by audiences largely homosexual into the larger omni-sexual arena of popular culture—and its strange marriage with liberal anti-war protest in the best-selling movie, *Dr. Strangelove.*

world in which growing up means only learning that isolation is the lot of everyone. Mick (her very name makes the same point as her chopped-off hair) is the first of this writer's ambiguously boyish girls who stand outside of everything, even their own sex, feeling themselves freaks and seeking a society of freaks. But Mick is no Faust, even in the sense in which Huck was a Faust, and she becomes, in the course of her author's development, the Frankie of *Member of the Wedding,* a sentimental parody of herself, who exists to stir the easy tear at the pity of it all: a child victim, to be wept over condescendingly even as she weeps over a younger child victim, her cousin, or to be responded to with vague warmth as she cuddles in the arms of her black mammy—comes, oddly, back to the raft!

III

Not only the South, however, and the encounter of Negro and white have seemed to recent writers themes which literary modes based on reason and superficial observation must inevitably falsify. Modern war and the twentieth-century city have struck our novelists as phenomena more irrational and terrifying than the ghosts and haunted castles to which the gothic first addressed itself. Modes that once conveyed the shudder of man before the terror of the past as it persists into the present, come now to portray our horror before the evidences in contemporary society of a frightful future. The tale of terror seems more and more the most prophetic of all fictional genres: invented in the first surge of reaction to the Age of Reason, driven underground in a succeeding period of progress and civil peace, but again come into its own in an era of universal war, alienation from nature, failed revolutions, genocide, and ideological self-deception.

The modern war novel with its portrayal of incomprehensible violence, incoherent anguish, and ennui aspires toward the gothic form, but has been almost everywhere betrayed to sentimentality. Only in *The Enormous Room* of E. E. Cummings has a poet, already committed to hallucination and disjunction, proved capable of dealing with World War I in terms appropriate to its horror. Cummings' novel evokes a world in which reality slips fluidly in and out of focus in the rhythm of its protagonist's hysteria and despair, a world in which the real is haunted by itself. Other more "realistic" treatments of similar material, more popular at the moment of publication, have become now unreadable—seeming less adequate to the contemporary sense of what mass warfare is than Stephen Crane's impressionist *Red Badge of Courage,* which preceded them and was written by a man who had never seen combat.

Even Faulkner's *Soldiers' Pay,* not published until 1930, reflects still the standard disenchantment and self-pity of the middlebrow novel of anti-war protest; and *A Fable,* which he worked on up to 1954, represents his second try at making of the same materials, or profounder ones, something worthy of the experience of the A.E.F. It is a strangely moving effort to turn time back, to create after an uneasy period of peace and a second universal conflict, the book he and his contemporaries had failed to write the first time around. But *A Fable* is a dull, sentimental parable, tricked out with Faulkner's latter-day rhetoric, and projecting an intolerable backwoods Negro savior, who provides a second Christ-figure to balance the allegorical French corporal, who apparently bored Faulkner himself. Only in its occasional reversions to pure horror, its evocation, for instance, of the fetid atmosphere of a mass burial vault, does the book come to life. Not even the talent of Faulkner plus a commitment that brought him back again to the difficult subject has been able to break through the barrier that stands between the imagination of America and its experience in mass war. Travesties we have in great plenty, witting and unwitting entertainments, earnest tracts, anguished memoirs: all in the end defenses against that experience rather than illuminations of it.

If the novels written after World War I seem to become clichés even as they are committed to print, the novels of World War II are echoes of those clichés, products of minds so conditioned by the stereotypes of the earlier works that they seem never to have lived through the events of 1939-1945 at all. Only two recent books have risen above the dull slickness or sincerity of *The Young Lions* and *The Naked and the Dead.** Saul Bellow's *Dangling Man,* which deals with the pathetically comic nightmare of induction and stops just short of combat; and John Hawkes's incomprehensibly neglected *The Cannibal,* which deals with the comically pathetic nightmare of postwar occupation. Compounded

* Joseph Heller's *Catch-22* is a more recent exception—rendering with the techniques of the Black Vaudevillian a vision of war as ultimate burlesque, an event too farcical for tears.

of farce, fantasy, and macabre invention, his vision of the Europe left by two wars seems more appropriate to what we know than the inevitably rationalist falsifications of history. The rise and destruction of Nazism we have recorded in old newspapers and new textbooks as documented truth, actuality; but we have lived its course in our viscera and our nerves as a bad dream, in which, though we die for it, we cannot really believe.

Though the peculiar, wholesale horror of the great wars has eluded our greatest fictionists, and will exist for future ages only as a handful of clichés, the terror of the great Depression has fared better. The '30's thought of itself as a political period, and we have continued to think of it in a similar way, without being sufficiently aware that what it called politics was essentially apocalyptics: a commitment to revolution which is essentially a dedication to horror. Yet the typical fiction writer of the '30's would have been shocked to think himself a gothicist; if he were ideological enough not to mind being labeled, he would have called himself a "proletarian novelist."

The proletarian novel (sponsored in the first five years of the decade by the Communist critics, who had the sense of being the spokesmen for writers as different from themselves and each other as Dos Passos, Erskine Caldwell, and Hemingway) is not necessarily a book about proletarians. It is alternatively about poor farmers, members of the lower middle class, and, often enough, about intellectuals—specifically, about the intellectual's attempt to identify himself with the oppressed elements in society and with the movement which claimed to represent them. The proletarian novel was, theoretically, an attempt to glorify the Soviet Union and the Communist Party, and to prove that that Party was the consciousness of the working class in America. Yet the most characteristic aspect of such novels completely escapes all theories and definitions, for it is a product of the age as it worked on writers beneath the level of consciousness. This is the *tone* of the proletarian novel: the note of sustained and self-satisfied hysteria bred, on the one hand, of Depression years' despair and, on the other, of the sense of being selected as brands to be snatched from the fire.

From Marxism itself, the line of social thought which feeds into the proletarian novel had inherited a quasi-religious messianism. Two quite different sorts of feeling are involved, often confused with each other though logically separable: on the one hand, the desire that the good, clean, healthy workers of the future take over and destroy the whole heritage of the past, including the writer himself and his tradition; and on the other, the impulse of the writer to identify himself with the future, to feel himself strong and brutal enough to crush a world which has frustrated him. In the novel of the '30's, everything from sex to politics is assimilated into terror. It is, perhaps, the first fully self-conscious *secular* tale of terror, its object being to destroy not the phantoms of the past, but the institutions of the present, which are converted in its lurid light into ogres, as Wall Street is transformed into its haunted castle. All ghosts have been laid except "the specter" which, in 1848, Marx had announced was "haunting Europe," the specter of Communism. This means, in effect, a specter haunting a world of specters, horror confronting horror. And the proletarian novelists did, indeed, project violence in their fictions not only as that from which society was to be delivered, but also as the method of deliverance. In the shabby, gray days during which they wrote, the dream of violence possessed the American imagination like a promise of salvation. Politics was violent and a-politics equally so; whatever else a man publicly accepted or denied, he did not deny terror.

Obviously, the '30's did not invent terror and violence as fictional themes. They could find them not only in the picket-lines around them and in the Bonus Marchers, but in our classic novels as well. As far back as American books go, there are images of horror: the torn corpse stuffed up the chimney; the skull split by a tomahawk; the whale spouting blood. There are, however, two final transformations in the function and treatment of violence in fiction, which go even beyond the simple fact of its "neutralization"—its demotion from the world of the supernatural to that of everyday life. The first is the *urbanization of violence;* that is to say, violence is transferred from nature to society, from the given world that man must endure to the artificial world he has made, presumably to protect himself from the ravages of the first. There is, of course, a special horror in considering the law of fang and claw walled in but unmitigated in the brick and glass of the city-planners.

The city had been treated as a place of terror quite early in the nineteenth century by Dickens and by Baudelaire, who had variously transformed London and Paris into phantasmagoria of poverty and crime, lust and ennui; and behind both, there is the classic example of Dante, who at the very dawn of the modern city had already used his native Florence as a model for hell. In earlier American fiction, however, there are few instances of the gothic city, since most of our writers were pursuing memories of the frontier town, the colonial settlement in the clearing, when they were not simply escaping into the forest or out to sea. Brockden Brown, to be sure, had evoked the city under plague, a Philadelphia converted to a nightmare by disease and death; but Poe, who was, in a sense, his chief successor, abandoned, along with Brown's resolve to create horror without falling back on the supernatural, Brown's concern with American places. Poe surrenders the actual urban scene for unreal courts, the vaults beneath imaginary European towns, and especially lonely estates located on no maps. George Lippard, to be sure, returned to Philadelphia, which was his own native place as well as Brockden Brown's, and recreated it in his fantasy into a hellish sink.

The more sober and respectable writers of Lippard's own day, when they did not project their vision of the diabolical city back into the past, were likely to imagine it in the old world, like the Liverpool of Melville's *Redburn or* the Rome of Hawthorne's *The Marble Faun.* Even Twain, in his raucous populist way, and James, in more urbane fashion, played on the American ambivalence which regarded the European tour as at once a journey toward the culture of museums and guidebooks and a descent into hell. In *Pierre,* it is true, Melville tried his hand at creating a gothic version of New York: in the symbolic setting of that book, the city is the inferno into which the hero falls once he has excluded himself from the bucolic earthly paradise of Saddle Meadows. Over dark and merciless roads that leave the traveler bewildered and bruised, Pierre and Isabel come at night to the gloomy streets of Manhattan, where they find themselves at the mercy of the coachmen, "Charon ferry-men to corruption and death."

Yet it is, finally, not so much hell as Babylon into which Pierre brings his strange ménage, the "city of orgies" dreamed in the provinces by pious boys, whose visions of sin are derived from the Book of Proverbs and the Revelations of St. John; and the essential gothic tone is disrupted by sentimentality and melodrama.

"I say, my pretty one! Dear! Dear young man!! Oh, love, you are in a vast hurry, aren't you? Can't you stop a bit, now, my dear. . . ."

Pierre turned; and in the flashy, sinister, evil cross-lights of a druggist's window, his eye caught the person of a wonderfully beautifully-featured girl; scarlet-cheeked, glaringly arrayed, and of a figure all natural grace but unnatural vivacity. . . .

"My God!" shuddered Pierre, hurrying forward, "the town's first welcome to the youth!"

Precisely this provincial image, sentimental and lubricious, presides over the main line of American city novels from Whitman's *Franklin Evans,* through Crane's *Maggie,* up to the fiction of Dreiser and the "muckrakers"; and in its evocation, popular entertainer and serious "realist" are one, so long as both alike are young men from the midwest, making their tremulous way into the wicked Big Town, upon which they have projected all that their mothers and preachers have warned them of, and for which they ferociously long. Only in the '30's does the American city come at long last to seem, in the books of men born in those cities, not a latter-day reflection of Nineveh, but a horror in its own right—not less terrible but more so, since for such writers the city is quite simply all there is. The '30's mark the climax, too, of a second and even more critical change in the literary uses of violence: the *ennobling of violence* as "the midwife of history." Under the name of "the revolution," violence becomes not something to be fled, not the failing of otherwise admirable men, not a punishment for collective guilt— but the climax of social action. The process which had begun just after 1789 with the Terror, and had been hailed in the United States by the theoretically bloody-minded Jefferson, received in an age of mechanized warfare and mass production its final form. The lust for pain of Nietzsche and the hypostasizing of History by Hegel culminated in the twin horrors of Nazi and Soviet brutality; but a worse indignity had already been worked on the minds of the intellectuals, conditioned in advance to become apologists for one or the other system.

In light of this, it is easy to understand that questions of ideology are secondary, that it is the naked love-fear of violence which distinguished the novel of the '30's: a kind of passion not unlike that which moved the Germans before their final defeat, a desire for some utter cataclysm to end the dull dragging out of impotent suffering. Not only Communist-oriented writers produced urban horror literature in those days, but Southerners like Faulkner (in *Sanctuary*), John Peale Bishop (in *Act of Darkness*), or Robert

Penn Warren (in *At Heaven's Gate*). Where such writers had been
already established or were to continue long careers, they produced
books which seem in their total work eccentric, products of the
age rather than of the men. Hemingway himself made an obeisance
to the hectic mode in his oddly inept *To Have and Have Not;* and
a mild, upper-middlebrow traditionalist like James Gould Cozzens
produced, in *Castaway,* a novella uncharacteristically mad and, by
that token, convincing beyond all his other books. It is a pity that
his shrill parody of Robinson Crusoe, in which a castaway in a
gothic department store can only discover his own footprint, has
remained relatively unknown, while pointless critical disputes have
raged over his fat failure, *By Love Possessed.*

The most admired novelists of the period itself, whose popularity
has waned with the subsidence of the mood and sentiment which
they helped define, are remembered now for their evocations of
terror and despair—rather than for messages of hope or reform
that they sometimes rather perfunctorily supplied in lieu of the
more bourgeois happy endings. Not Steinbeck's advocacy of agri-
cultural resettlement or the brotherhood of man but his rendering
of the ambiguous terror of picket-line conflict in *In Dubious Battle;*
not Dos Passos' dream of a redeemed U.S.A. but his bloody evocation of the lynched and castrated labor leader, Wesley Everest,
hanging from a railroad bridge; not the May Day Parade in *Studs
Lonigan,* but Farrell's picture of Studs lying in the gutter in his
own vomit, contracting the pneumonia that is to kill him: these
remain in the reader's mind—an exhibition of social horrors. In
retrospect, the period of the '30's—at least during its first six or
seven years, before Americans lost the awareness of living at the
tail-end of a postwar period and began to feel themselves in a pre-
war era—seems now a time in which new gothic forms were being
created by writers who were determined not to know what they
were doing.

If Nathanael West appears to us from our present vantage point
the chief neglected talent of the age, this is largely because he was
immune to the self-deceit which afflicted his contemporaries; he
knew what he was doing. Despite his own left-wing political sympathies and the pressures of friends more committed than he, he
refused to subscribe to the program for proletarian fiction laid down
by the official theoreticians and critics of the Communist movement. And he turned unashamedly to the business of rendering the

naked anguish he felt, rather than projecting the commitment to action and faith it was assumed he should feel. Even more importantly he rejected the concept of realism-naturalism, refused to play the game (variously connived at by Dos Passos and Steinbeck and Farrell) of pretending to create documents rather than poetry. He returned, despite the immediate example of three decades of falsely "scientific" writing, which sought to replace imagination with sociology, the symbol with the case report, to the instinctive realization of the classic American fictionists that literary truth is not synonymous with fact. West's novels are a deliberate assault on the common man's notion of reality; for violence is not only his subject matter, but also his technique.

His apprenticeship was served in Europe, in the world of the Left Bank, where from the Surrealists he learned (his finger-exercises are to be found in his first book, *The Dream Life of Balso Snell*) a kind of humor expressed almost entirely in terms of the grotesque, that is to say, on a perilous border-line between jest and horror. Yet his Surrealist-inspired techniques—the violent conjunctions; the discords at the sensitive places where squeamishness demands harmony; the atrocious belly-laughs that shade off into hysteria—are not very different, after all, from the devices of *Pudd'nhead Wilson* or *Gordon Pym*. West is, in a sense, then, only reclaiming our own; yet, in another, he is introducing into the main line of American fiction a kind of sophistication, a view of the nature of art, of which our literature was badly in need.

It is possible for an American, of course, to find in his native sources, his native scene and his American self cues for the special kind of horror-comedy which characterizes West's novels. The uneducated Twain once did precisely that, and the half-educated Faulkner has pretended at least to follow his example. Yet in Twain everywhere, and in Faulkner more and more as the years go by, there is evident a presumptuous, home-made quality, which mars their work whenever they pass from the realm of myth to that of ideas. Nothing is more bald and thin than the back-porch atheism of Twain's *The Mysterious Stranger,* except perhaps the red-neck Protestantism of Faulkner's *A Fable*.

The religious dimension which they failed to achieve, West attains in part because he is aware of a European tradition in thought and art, out of which Kafka, so like him in certain ways, had earlier emerged. It is not accidental that both these anguish-ridden comedians, as uncompromisingly secular as they are profoundly religious, should be Jews; for Jews seem not only peculiarly apt at projecting images of numinous power for the unchurched, but are skillful, too, at creating myths of urban alienation and terror. The '30's, not only in America (where Daniel Fuchs and Henry Roth— the latter in a single astonishing book, *Call It Sleep*—are outstanding figures) but everywhere, is a period especially favorable for the Jewish writer bent on universalizing his own experience into a symbol of life in the Western world. More and more it has seemed to such writers that what they in their exile and urbanization have long been, Western man in general is becoming. This is, presumably, the claim implicit in West's name (he was originally called Nathan Wallenstein Weinstein), his boast that he is an American Everyman; though surely to none does the epigram of C. M. Doughty apply more tellingly than to West, who quotes it in *Balso Snell:* "The Semites are like to a man sitting in a cloaca to the eyes, and whose brows touch heaven."

Yet West is a peculiarly American case, too. In one of his few published critical notes he declares: "In America violence is idiomatic, in America violence is daily." And it is possible to see him as just another of our professional tough guys, one of the "boys in the backroom" (the phrase is applied by Edmund Wilson, in a little study of our fiction, to West along with John O'Hara). This is not to deny, though West himself tried to, that West is, in some meaningful sense, a Jew. He is enough the child of a long tradition of nonviolence to be racked by guilt in the face of violence, shocked and tormented every day in a world where violence is, of course, daily and most men are not at all disturbed. In *Miss Lonelyhearts,* he creates the portrait of a character, all nerves and no skin, the fool of pity, whom the quite ordinary horror of ordinary life lacerates to the point of madness. His protagonist is given the job of answering "letters to the lovelorn" on a daily newspaper; and he finds in this job, a joke to others (he must pretend in his column to be a woman, for only women presumably suffer and sympathize), a revelation of human misery too acute for him to bear. It is the final modern turn of the gothic screw: the realization that not the supernatural, the extraordinary, but the ordinary, the everyday are the terrors that constrict the heart.

Dear Miss Lonelyhearts—
   . . . I would like to have boy friends like other girls and go out on Saturday nites, but no boy will take me because I was

born without a nose—although I am a good dancer and have a nice shape and my father buys me pretty clothes.

I sit and look at myself all day and cry. I have a big hole in the middle of my face that scares people even myself so I can't blame the boys for not wanting to take me out. . . .

What did I do to deserve such a terrible bad fate? I asked Papa and he says he doesnt know, but that maybe I did something in the other world before I was born or that maybe I was being punished for his sins. I dont believe that because he is a very nice man. Ought I commit suicide?

Sincerely yours,
Desperate

Miss Lonelyhearts is, finally, the comic butt who takes upon himself the sins of the world: the *schlemiel* as Everyman, the skeptical and unbelieved-in Christ of a faithless age. But such a role of absurd Christ is West's analogue for the function of the writer, whom he considers obliged unremittingly to regard a suffering he is too sensitive to abide; and in no writer is there so absolute a sense of the misery of being human, though he also believes that such misery is a more proper occasion for laughter than tears. He is child enough of his time to envision an apocalypse; but his apocalypse is a defeat for everyone. The protagonist of *Miss Lonelyhearts* is shot reaching out in love toward a man he has unwillingly offended; while the hero-*schlemiel* of the more deliberately farcical *A Cool Million: or The Dismantling of Lemuel Pitkin* (in theme and style a parody of Horatio Alger), staggers from one ridiculous, anti-heroic disaster to another, becoming after his death the idol of an American fascist movement. But the true horror-climax of his life and the book comes when, utterly maimed, he stands on the stage between two corny comedians, who wallop him with rolled-up newspapers in time to their jokes, until his wig comes off (he has been at one point scalped), his glass eye pops out, and his wooden leg falls away; after which, they provide him with new artificial aids and begin again.

It is not until *The Day of the Locust,* however, which is West's last book, and the only novel on Hollywood not somehow made trivial by its subject, that one gets the final version of the Apocalypse according to Nathanael West. At the end of the book, a painter, caught in a rioting mob of fans at a Hollywood première, dreams, as he is being crushed by the rioters, the phantasmagoric masterpiece he has never finished painting, "The Burning of Los Angeles." West does not seem finally a really achieved writer; certainly, no one of his books is thoroughly satisfactory, though there are astonishing local successes in all of them. His greatness lies like a promise just beyond his last novel, and is frustrated by his early death; but he is the inventor of a peculiar kind of book, in which the most fruitful strain of American fiction is joined to the European tradition of avant-garde, anti-bourgeois art, native symbolism to imported *symbolisme*. The Westian or neo-gothic novel has opened up possibilities, unavailable to both the naturalistic semi-documentary and the over-refined novel of sensibility, possibilities of capturing the quality of experience in a mass society—rather than retreating to the meaningless retailing of fact or the pointless elaboration of private responses to irrelevant sensations. Putting down a book by West, a reader is not sure whether he has been presented with a nightmare endowed with the conviction of actuality or with actuality distorted into the semblance of a nightmare; but in either case, he has the sense that he has been presented with a view of a world in which, incredibly, he lives.

Yet the importance of West's work was scarcely realized in his own day; and it would be misleading even now to speak of his general influence. Though his novels continued to move younger writers, and though the last few years have witnessed not only a growing critical acclaim, but attempts to extend his audience by stage adaptations and moving-picture versions, West is still more admired than directly emulated.* S. J. Perelman, who is West's brother-in-law and was a contributor to the little magazine *Contact,* which West helped edit, has been conducting a strange experiment, whose end is the transformation of Surrealist gallows humor into commercial entertainment. It is all part of an extraordinary process, which begins for literature in the columns of *The New Yorker,* and for art in the cartoons of the same magazine, as well as in certain shop-windows decorated by Salvador Dali—but whose end is not yet in sight. The avant-garde images of twenty-five years ago and

* Not so in 1966, when West's attitudes and devices have been assimilated into what already seems a new convention: that much-touted Black Humor, with which many of our latest writers seem perforce to begin, and the somewhat older practitioners of which (Bruce Jay Friedman, for example) have come to seem in a very few years established models and guides.

the grotesquerie which distinguished the short-lived *Contact* have become now the common property of gifte shoppes and greeting-card racks, fall as stereotypes from the lips of hip twelve-year-olds. "Hate cards" and ashtrays adorned with "Nebbishes" (the surreal, Jewish sad sack of West reduced to the level of *kitsch*) spread now the self-contempt, the anti-bourgeois virulence, the contempt for home, mother, birthdays, and Christmas, once the exclusive stock-in-trade of bohemians; and the "sick" joke popularizes the nause-ated giggle before violence, which not so long ago belonged only to books like *Miss Lonelyhearts.* "Can Johnny come out to play, Mrs. Jones?" "You know Johnny has no arms and legs!" "We don't want players. We need bases." *

It is not only a matter, however, of neo-gothicism becoming a prevailing mode on the level of popular culture; on more serious levels, too, the mode of West, if not his example, is evident. The alienated *schlemiel*-heroes of Saul Bellow surely owe something to West's protagonists, whose anguish never quite overbalances their absurdity; and everywhere in the Jewish American novelists of the last two decades, West's influence is felt, if only as a temptation toward sheer terror rejected in favor of sentimentality or some ab-stract espousal of love. Though lonely in his own time, West was not really alone in his attempt to redeem French horror for the American soul, as Poe had once redeemed that of Germany; Djuna Barnes (whom he probably did not even know) had made a simi-lar, even less popular assay in *Nightwood* (1937). The dislocated lyricism, hallucinated vision, and oddly skewed language of Miss Barnes's black little book were introduced to the United States by T. S. Eliot, with a rather unconvincing assurance of their ultimately religious import. In his preface, Eliot argues, at any rate, that the homosexual ambience of *Nightwood,* its ecstatic evocations of disease and death reflect a genuine concern with the problem of evil and not just an obsession with the properties of decadent gothi-cism. Linguistically, *Nightwood* is too complex, and thematically, it is too little concerned with the experience of America to achieve even the belated and limited success of West's work; it lives now chiefly in the minds of a limited number of admirers and in quota-

---

* The last and most winningly atrocious representative of sick jokery (the Jewish-heterosexual wing, of course, rather than the Southern-homo-sexual) is Lenny Bruce, in whom the distance between literature and enter-tainment, high art and low comedy threatens to disappear.

tions included in anthologies of modern verse, though it inspired in part the considerable achievement of Malcolm Lowry, whose cult threatens to overwhelm that of his predecessor.

Nonetheless, such a book as John Hawkes's *The Cannibal,* begun though it was before the author had ever read *Nightwood,* recalls its passionate commitment to extorting from terror a poetry that will not mitigate or deny that terror. Though it is in part the product of World War II, as we have observed earlier, Hawkes's novel is also the fruit of the impact of Surrealim on the American mind. Written when the author was only twenty-three, it manages to evoke the nightmare Germany of 1945 (super-imposed upon a persistent, ghost-like image of the same country during World War I), through which a lonely American soldier on a motor-bike rides frantically toward his inevitable death. Hawkes's Germany is a world in which the past haunts the present, the present the past; and both conspire to insure that the future (a nationalist German revolt is being plotted throughout the action, with the narrator as its chief, and succeeds as the book closes) will know itself also a ghost-ridden ghost as soon as it is born. In no official document or journalist's report is the "German problem" rendered so faithfully in terms of the monstrous unreality which is its essence. Certain scenes, minor incidents remain in the mind with a vividness hard to explain; and a glimpse, for instance, dreamed rather than observed, of a man dead two wars ago seems somehow an essential clue to a mystery at which historians nibble away in vain:

> There the Merchant, without thoughts of trade, dressed only in grey, still fat, had died on his first day at the front and was wedged, standing upright, between two beams, his face knocked backwards, angry, disturbed. In his open mouth there rested a large cocoon, protruding and white, which moved sometimes as if it were alive. The trousers, dropped about his ankles, were filled with rust and tufts of hair.

Not only Left Bank Surrealism, but the example of Kafka, too, has reinforced latter-day American gothicism, as Tieck and Hoffmann provided examples for Poe and Hawthorne a hundred years before. Translated by an Englishman and relished first of all by Americans, Kafka's books have in their posthumous career moved especially our writers and our critics, as seems only fair for an author who called one of his longer works *Amerika*. It is the most comic of his books, a tale which looks westward not only in its title but in its fable, the account of a flight to our shores; and it parodies throughout, by way of tribute, *Huckleberry Finn*. Kakfa is, moreover, though a Czech by birth and a German in language, an urban Jew in his deepest self-consciousness; and his most direct influence in the United States has been on certain second-generation American Jews, brought up in New York and Chicago, to whom his prophetic visions of a universal bureaucracy have seemed blueprints of the world into which they were born. Nathanael West, so much like Kafka in spirit, had never read him; but the Jewish writers of the '40's and after draw on him directly. Isaac Rosenfeld and Paul Goodman have recreated in their short stories a symbolism as shifty and evasive as Kafka's own, as well as a technique, half-essayistic, half-poetical, based on his example. They have, in addition, specified and expanded his Freudian insights, and made explicit the revolutionary implications of his vision, without losing the mad humor which is his essence. Though their stories have remained relatively unpopular, an unwitting travesty of their American adaptation of Kafka, "The Lottery" by Shirley Jackson, has become a standard middlebrow anthology piece, perhaps because it lacks the intelligence and wit of their best work.

Neither Rosenfeld (prematurely dead) nor Goodman has succeeded in creating a full-scale novel in the Kafkaesque mode,* which may be essentially too fragmentary and lyrical (Kafka himself finished none of his longer books) for the larger form. Their work is, moreover, too bound to their model to seem either quite authentic or really free—and too ideological to allow room for rich invention. Freer in his uses of Kafka and the whole Surrealist tradition is Bernard Malamud, whose first novel, *The Natural* (1952), was largely ignored, perhaps because the lively play of fancy, the trifling with illusion which characterize it disconcerted those who had picked it up expecting a "good baseball yarn." Actually it *is* a baseball story, disconcertingly out of Ring Lardner by T. S. Eliot: an account of the tragic career of a ball-player called Roy Hobbs, last hero of a culture which is not sure whether it needs more to

---

* Goodman has made a big try since, gathering together and augmenting some of his earlier short fictions. But *Empire City* is finally a disappointing work, and since its appearance Goodman seems to have turned entirely to the essay, hashing and rehashing his left-wing critique of American education.

cherish or to destroy its heroes. Out of the hectic atmosphere of the ball park (not specially set in Brooklyn, but reminiscent of that mythical place), the legends of the sports page, *The Natural* creates a magical universe—in which white witch and black witch struggle for the soul of a secular savior, who will restore the Waste Land to fertility, by winning the pennant for the home team. Naturally it is a pennant that cannot be won; and in the final scene, the hero is more Casey at the Bat than Grail Knight; but the humor only accents without destroying the tragic impact of the close. The special tone of *The Natural,* its lovely, absurd madness, tends to disappear from Malamud's later work, except in the title story of his short-story collection *The Magic Barrel;* and with that tone goes the poetic language that sustained it. In *The Assistant,* he turns back to the muted, drab world of the Depression as remembered two decades later, and the quality of his prose is adapted to the denial of the marvelous to which he has committed himself.

The gothic provides a way into not only the magical world inhabited by the baseball fan, and the child dreaming of King Arthur who still lives within that fan, but also into certain areas of our social life where nightmare violence and guilt actually exist. To discuss, for instance, in the light of pure reason the Negro problem in the United States is to falsify its essential mystery and unreality; it is a gothic horror of our daily lives. If Ralph Ellison's *Invisible Man* seems, as a novel written by a Negro about the Negro's plight, superior to any of the passionate, incoherent books of Richard Wright, this is because Ellison has bypassed all formulas of protest and self-pity and cast off the restrictions of mere realism. Only James Baldwin's *Go Tell It on the Mountain* has a comparable freshness and directness, but it lacks finally the madness which gives to *Invisible Man* a special kind of conviction. The whole middle of Ellison's book takes on a special quality of grotesqueness, because he begins and ends it with a Surrealist nightmare. The invisible man (invisible, of course, because he is black—and being black cannot be seen through a wall of clichés) crouches in a cellar retreat lighted by "exactly 1,369 lights." His electric power he steals from the Monopolated Light and Power, using it not only for illumination but also to keep his record-player going. On that player spins endlessly Louis Armstrong's "What Did I Do to Be So Black and Blue," to which the invisible man listens as he eats his favorite dessert of vanilla ice-cream and sloe gin.

Invisible Man is, like most neo-gothic fiction, a technical achievement as well as a statement of an important theme; indeed, its technique is keyed to the world of absurdity and violence which it projects, and its author rejects the last falsification of irrelevant or inert form. It is the special distinction of this kind of fiction that it neither fakes a concern with technique (like the *U.S.A.* of Dos Passos, all of whose *ersatz* experimentalism seems contrived to conceal a shallowness of characterization and a lack of over-all unity) or abandons all such concerns as beside the point (like much documentary fiction from Farrell to James Jones). The gothicist understands that it is the angle of perception which determines a novelist's meaning, reveals a world haunted and infernal, or subscribes to the illusion of one rational and dull. The gothic novel has been from the first experimental, not merely because it is pledged to the slogan, "Make it new!", but, much more importantly, because it sets itself the task of persuading skeptical readers to believe in ghosts or invisible men, to believe in themselves as ghosts or invisible men! This is, of course, ridiculous; and the gothicist must learn to be, as all American exponents of the mode since Poe have known, self-consciously funny, if he does not choose to be inadvertently silly. Beside the solemn experimentalist, there has existed in the United States the comic one, from the West of *Balso Snell* to the John Barth of *The Floating Opera;* and it is the latter who has seemed most often to suggest the deepest truth about our existence —which is always, in one way or another, absurd.

Perhaps the most distinguished of our recent, serious comic novelists is Wright Morris, who from *My Uncle Dudley* to *The Field of Vision* has been trying to convince his readers that Nebraska is the absurd hell we all inhabit. His commercial unsuccess, in spite of critical acclaim that for ten years has been greeting the amazing patience, ingenuity, wit, and tact of his work, is one of the puzzling cultural phenomena of our time. Perhaps his subject matter is a little too American for those who can appreciate the subtlety of his form;* the subtlety of his form a little baffling to those with a real taste for his provincial subject matter; his macabre humor at once too honest and too violent for anyone. He expresses a kind of

---

* John Barth, on the eve of his fourth novel, faces a similar problem, for what Nebraska is to Morris, Maryland has been to him. But *The Sotweed Factor* has won him wide critical acclaim; and perhaps his next work may yet win through to the big urban audience.

hopelessly American anti-Americanism unparalleled since Mark Twain; as is attested by the fact that his favorite enemy is Norman Rockwell. Other writers simply ignore Rockwell, though some of them recreate in *The New Yorker, Harper's,* or *The Hudson Review* the images which he more profitably and naïvely projects on the covers of *The Saturday Evening Post;* Morris insists on meeting him head-on on his own home ground. He contests with Rockwell, that is to say, the American inheritance, raises the critical question: to whom does the ball signed by Babe Ruth, Ty Cobb's glove really belong? To the easy affirmer or the man who says no? To Pudd'n-head Wilson or Huckleberry Finn?

There is no doubt about which side Morris is on. Like Ellison's invisible man, he declares over and over in all his books, "So I became ill of affirmation, of saying 'yes' against the nay-saying of my stomach—not to mention my brain"; but he does not consider this a surrender of his birthright, a prelude to expatriation or internal exile. On the contrary, he thinks of this (as he has attempted to demonstrate in his recent critical book, *The Territory Ahead*) as making him one with the great nay-sayers of our classical novel, with those who have, in revulsion from the life around them, penetrated even deeper into the only real America, "the territory ahead." Morris is not, however, in any sense a provincial in technique or form; he tells, with devices that depend on but do not imitate the experiments of European modernists, his native horror-story—and he tells it, like the Dadaists and Twain who anticipated them, for the laughs! Indeed, it is the balance of horror and comedy in his work which keeps it from turning, on the one hand, into mere farce and on the other into horror-pornography.

I V

From the time of Poe, two possibilities have been open to the gothic: the pursuit of genuine terror, "the hideous Moor" who lurks at the back of the cave; or the evocation of sham terror, the calling-up of ghosts in which no one believes. The one is a confrontation of the violence which is essential to our lives, the other an indulgence in it, a flirtation with horror for the sake of a shameful thrill. The popular audience has always demanded the pseudo-fiction of terror, which in all of its major forms Poe perfected for the American market-place: the ghost story, the detective story, and science fiction. The archetypal nature of such forms is indicated by the fact that their readers do not think of themselves as reading particular books or even the works of certain authors, but rather as seeking out and consuming the latest examples of the forms themselves. Though the three forms overlap somewhat in time, they really illustrate a sequence in the development of popular taste. The classic ghost story seems now an obsolescent subgenre, though as late as Henry James's *Turn of the Screw* or "The Jolly Corner," it could be used by a quite serious artist to project the frightfulness of secret concupiscence, or the encounter between what the ego has made of itself and the monstrous thing it might have become had certain repressed impulses been actuated. Since the full impact of Freudianism, however, ghosts have tended to seem metaphors rather than facts of experience—except in certain naïve works, in which they are evoked to thrill the kind of mind which otherwise finds satisfaction in shabby séances and table-tapping. An occasional ghost moves through the murky ambience of Truman Capote's stories, shouldering aside frail children and psychoanalysts; but, by and large, the form has fallen into the hands of middlebrow craftsmen like Lovecraft and Gerald Heard, who cater to the dated addictions of a rapidly shrinking audience.

After science has progressed to the point of explaining, or claiming at least to have explained, the under-soul, ghosts can be granted only the half-mocking credence accorded the Hallowe'en midnight show, at which the clichés of the oldest gothic tales: creaking doors, clutching hands, screams out of the dark (all explained in the last reel)—are taken once more out of stock. To be sure, certain favorite monsters return decade after decade: Dracula and the creature of Frankenstein; but they are classified these days as "fantasy," which tends to blur into science fiction. Science fiction denies, however, in its basic assumptions the belief upon which the ghost story properly depends: "There are more things in heaven and earth, etc." In its world, all haunting terrors are explicable; and there is nothing not dreamed of in the physics laboratory, or the classrooms where Dr. Rhine lectures on extra-sensory perception. But though science fiction had already begun with Poe's *Gordon Pym* (imitated by both Jules Verne and Conan Doyle) and his post-cataclysmic dialogues like *Eros* and *Charmion,* and though an essential protagonist of the form was created when Hawthorne imagined Aylmer, the conscienceless experimenter, science fiction as an official genre with a commonly accepted name had to wait for World War II and the explosion of the atomic bomb.

In the interim period, the detective story, or more properly the murder mystery (the first label pretends that the form is a kind of cool, clean puzzle-game, the second admits its obsession with death), has performed for the middlebrow reader the function of evoking and purging terror. Half artist, half scientist, Poe's C. Auguste Dupin imposes upon a world of irrational horror the semblance of order, proves over and over that the most grotesque nightmare (the mutilated bodies stuffed up a chimney in a room no one seems to have entered) can be understood, given acumen and a talent for analysis. The detective story in this form is based on an extension of the gothic device of the explained supernatural; but it is set in a frame, apparently invented by Poe himself, in which a narrator, more confused and terrified than the reader, watches the performance of a detective, more perspicuous and cool than that reader. The narrator is a somewhat duller than average man-in-the-street and the detective his version of the *poète maudit:* a lonely recluse who deigns to aid the society from which he has withdrawn. Such tales of detection, in the hands of serious writers, are used to project a pathetic image of the author himself as *socially useful,* however spurned and misunderstood.

Indeed, Poe himself was driven to dissolve completely the barriers between art and life, C. Auguste Dupin and Edgar Allan Poe, providing in *The Mystery of Marie Roget* a solution to an actual unsolved case of his own time, and in *Eureka* (where the mask of Dupin is dropped at last) the answer to the most baffling whodunit of them all, the solution to the case of Creation! But the detective story, in American literature at least, has always represented symbolically the *capitulation* of the recalcitrant artist to the bourgeois community—and is, moreover, itself such an act of capitulation. All of Poe's fictions represent a complex adjustment between his desire to mock his audience and to be accepted by it; but there is a wide range of difference in the degree of accommodation to popular taste, from the difficulty of *Gordon Pym* to the accessibility of the detective stories. The latter have been among the most widely admired of all his tales, even Abraham Lincoln, who, according to the best records, read no other fiction, having made an exception in their case. In the hands of mere hacks—and the form attracts the hack irresistibly—the detective story has continued to be the favorite off-hours reading of tired Presidents, as well as harried businessmen, novelists, professors, and other public figures in search of a minor vice with no unpleasant consequences.

Mark Twain, who mocked Sherlock Holmes in "A Double-Barrelled Detective Story," himself turned to the form over and over: in *Tom Sawyer Detective, Simon Wheeler, Detective* (attempted twice unsuccessfully, as a play and a novel), and *Pudd'nhead Wilson*. In the latter, he uses typically enough the moment of reversal and recognition, when Wilson, the amateur sleuth, reveals innocence and guilt in a single gesture, to mark the moment of his accommodation to the philistine community. Similarly, Faulkner's Gavin Stevens, another lawyer and amateur detective, who first appeared in a series of *Saturday Evening Post* stories (later collected as *Knight's Gambit*), represents Faulkner's own attempt to make peace with the South, America, and the world. Windbag and baffled lover, Stevens seems a mating of Senator Claghorn and J. Alfred Prufrock, an impotent revealer of the truth, pitifully proud of his own rhetoric and his Phi Beta Kappa key. The successive spokesmen for Faulkner in his books represent his successive images of himself, from Quentin Compson to Gavin Stevens, images of despair giving way to images of accommodation. The self-torturing and doomed Quentin, we remember, was a kind of detective, too, in *Absalom, Absalom!* moving doggedly toward the truth about the South that would destroy him. Stevens, on the other hand, though he also pursues ultimate questions of guilt and responsibility in *Intruder in the Dust* and *Requiem for a Nun*, heads not toward suicide but a middle-aged romance and the happy ending of marriage! It is Stevens who presides over Faulkner's retreat from horror toward sentimentality and easy affirmation; and it is fitting that he be Pudd'nhead Wilson reborn.

On the middlebrow level, the pseudo-scientific novel of detection is nearly dead in the United States; and, indeed, though invented in America, it has flourished chiefly in the form of British importations from Conan Doyle and Chesterton to Agatha Christie and Dorothy Sayers. After Dupin, we have produced no deductive amateur sleuths worthy of being set beside Holmes or Father Brown, Hercule Poirot or Lord Peter Wimsey, with the possible exception of S. S. Van Dine's Philo Vance; and Holmes himself pretended to despise even Dupin. Our essential contribution to the form in the twentieth century is a strange offshoot of the '30's novel of urban violence: a "realistic" exposé of corruption in the big city, presided over by the private eye. But the private eye is not the dandy turned sleuth; he is the cowboy adapted to life on the city streets, the embodiment of innocence moving untouched through universal guilt. As created by Dashiell Hammett, the blameless shamus is also the honest proletarian, illuminating by contrast the decadent society of the rich; and he speaks not with the pedantic condescension of Poe's Dupin but in the language of the people. The style of the urban mystery story, that is to say, descends from Hemingway via Dashiell Hammett and Raymond Chandler to Mickey Spillane, one of the great artificial styles of our time, the sophisticated counterfeit of simplicity turned cliché.

As it has descended the long way from Sam Spade to Mike Hammer, the proletarian thriller has come to treat the riddle of guilt and innocence more and more perfunctorily, as its occasion rather than its end. Though it has never abandoned violence and death, it has radically altered their impact by associating them ever more intimately with sex—that subject so pointedly ignored in the prototypical tales of Poe. Murder laced with lust, mayhem spiced with nymphomania: this is the formula for the chief surviving form of the murder mystery in America, though, indeed, that form has not surrendered its native birthright of anti-feminism.* It insists, however, on undressing its bitches, surveying them with a surly and concupiscent eye before punching, shooting, or consigning them to the gas-chamber. Not only in the cruder and more successful books of Mickey Spillane, but in the more pretentious ones of Raymond Chandler, the detective story has reverted to the kind of populist semi-pornography that once made George Lippard's *The Monks of Monk Hall* a black-market best-seller. Now, even as a hundred years ago, lower-middlebrow Americans find it possible to countenance bared breasts and bellies in their literature only when violence is threatening, or when somewhere in the outer darkness a gangster plots his kill. And now, even as a hundred years ago, such

---

* The recent triumphs of James Bond represent a new development of the thriller, in which, like Mailer's heroes, the Secret Agent triumphs over women not with the "equalizer" (which is to say, the deadly weapon) but the "avenger" (which is to say, the lively one). Ian Fleming is, to be sure, British, but he has learned from American prototypes; and it is the American mass audience which finds special satisfaction in his hero's sexual conquest of a Lesbian called Pussy Galore whose troop of fellow Lesbians from Harlem have been bleached white and turned approximately heterosexual in the movie version.

readers relish thinking that the sadist fantasies in which they find masturbatory pleasure are revelations of social disorder, first steps toward making a better world. "The realist in murder," Hammett writes of his own school, "writes of a world in which gangsters can rule nations and almost rule cities, in which hotels and apartment houses and celebrated restaurants are owned by men who made their money out of brothels, and in which a screen star can be the fingerman for a mob. . . ." And through this world, he continues, walks the private eye, the man of honor who is also the poor man, the common man. "If there were enough like him," Chandler concludes, "the world would be a safe place to live in. . . ."

The appeal of Chandler and Hammett has faded with the decline of Popular Front liberalism and their latest imitators provide more and more vulgar sensationalism without even the pretense of virtuous politics, quite losing the righteous middlebrow audience. That audience, particularly in its male segment, has turned to science fiction, which is to say, the gothicism of the future. The first wave of popular gothicism drew on the fear of the past, which haunted a revolutionary epoch on guard against counter-revolution and the restoration of old authority; and the last trace of this fear survives in the ghost story, which looks for terror only in the graveyard, from what is presumably dead and buried. The second wave of popular gothicism reflected a fear of the present, a need to be reassured that the recrudescence of violence and guilt in the vicarage, the country house, or on the old plantation could be controlled by the use of reason, the "scientific" discovery of the truth. This is the source of the classic detective story, and more remotely helps determine even the thrillers of Hammett and Chandler; though in their books not reason but only counter-violence can defeat decadence and corruption—counter-violence and dumb luck, which is to say, grace.

The third wave of popular gothicism appeals to the fear of the future, and is based on a fundamental ambivalence toward science, which is shaping that future. Yet it can appeal only to science itself to regulate its own dangerous course; and the fact that it calls its chief genre "science fiction" indicates the depth of its commitment to technology and the more "scientific" approaches to social problems. Its politics is reasonably liberal, which is to say, it generally favors strong social controls though only for the most unselfish ends; and its world-view is moderately secular, which is to say, it believes God is dead, but sees no reason for getting hysterical about it. For all their vaguely anti-capitalist commitment to planning, most of its writers are if not anti-utopian, at least suspicious of utopias; and in their deepest imagination, the physicist tends to turn in their imaginations into the magician, black or white. In their thoroughly rational universe, all the traditional feats of magic for which respectable scientific terms can be found are accepted as a matter of course: the passage of objects through unbroken barriers (teleportation), the calling-up of the dead (time-travel), the creation of *homunculi* (perfection of multipurpose robots with positronic brains), demonic possession (control of thought-centers by disembodied interplanetary wanderers).

Chiefly, however, it is the dissolution of the earth in fire, which so haunted Poe, a vision of the apocalypse, which obsesses the writers of science fiction, though in their language such ultimate events are referred to as the Third World War, the explosion of the cobalt bomb, etc. The ghost story deals with a terror that threatens to destroy the individual soul; the detective story with a hidden guilt that threatens to destroy the self-contained community, or, more contemporaneously, the social fabric of a city; science fiction evokes a cataclysmic horror that threatens the entire earth, the solar system, galaxy—or even the total universe. Science fiction, on its upper-middlebrow levels, at least, does not admit that it is essentially terror fiction; but with not untypical Anglo-Saxon self-righteousness (it is primarily an Anglo-Saxon form) insists that its ends are insight and morality. Its writers propagate, for instance, non-Aristotelian logic, engram psychology, interracial (even, in advance, interplanetary) tolerance, and, of course, the general cause of science. Yet simultaneously they pander to fantasies of flight, dreams of omnipotence—and, not least of all, the shameful pleasure of imagining the stench of burning bodies, the acrid dust of crumbling cities, the desolation of the man lost in space, the anguish of the oppressed in totalitarian utopias as yet unborn.

In the lowest-brow manifestations of the genre, in comic-books or movies made for adolescents, the theme of the bug-eyed monster predominates: the nightmare of the invasion from space, in which an audience of teen-agers (who otherwise daydream the invasion *of* space) watch on the screen their contemporaries being ingested by a shapeless and inexorable blob of hungry matter. But this is only the most vulgar projection of a more universal theme, implicit on all levels of science fiction: a loss of faith in the potentialities of humanity itself and a prevision of its destruction, a masochistic delight in imagining a future in which mutants, robots, extraterrestrials, dogs, or simply *nothing* takes over. It is the hallucinatory form of the fantasy of an American defeat in the next war, a victory for the Others—called simply Russia in the daily newspaper, but transformed into beings more alien and terrible in the depths of the unconscious. But it is also a reflection of the guilt of the scientists themselves, some of whom actually write sciencefiction novels and all of whom presumably read solemn discussions of them in *The Bulletin of the Atomic Scientists*. The bomb, which is haunting not only those immediately concerned in its making, but all those committed to a faith in the scientific world-view somehow compromised in its production, plays in science fiction the role of the haunted castle in the earliest gothic romances. Yet on its surfaces, in its intruded editorials, science fiction is often cheerful, looks forward to the space age and a new inexhaustible West among the stars. The hope on the surface and the terror beneath: it is a customary enough American pattern, not untrue fundamentally to the life we live; yet it has turned much science fiction into hypocritical horror-pornography, and stands in the way of its ever being converted into literature of real worth. Certainly, it is the only neo-gothic form which has never been used by a writer of the first rank to tell the kind of truth no middlebrow can confront.*

Yet not only science fiction, but gothic literature on all levels runs the risk of becoming horror-pornography: the extortion of a shudder for its own sake, the submission to reveries of violence for the sake of their voluptuous appeal. Even a writer of intendedly highbrow fictions like Paul Bowles, who served his apprenticeship writing for *transition* and has never abandoned the postures of the avant-garde, can end by providing for readers of the little magazines the same furtive, sadist satisfactions that ten-year-olds find in *Horror Comics*:

---

* William Golding's *Lord of the Flies* is no real exception to this, for though its modes are those of science fiction, its values are middlebrow. But Anthony Burgess's *Clockwork Orange* is, as are the novels of the French pataphysician, Boris Vian; and William Burroughs ever since *The Naked Lunch* has drawn more and more on the conventions of the Gothic of the Future, for ends that challenge the middle-class liberal. The early pages of *The Soft Machine* are, in fact, a masterpiece of the genre.

The man moved and surveyed the young body lying on the stones. He ran his finger along the razor's blade; a pleasant excitement took possession of him. He stepped over, looked down and saw the sex that sprouted from the base of the belly. Not entirely conscious of what he was doing, he took it in one hand and brought his other arm down with the motion of a reaper wielding a sickle. It was swiftly severed. A round, dark hole was left, flush with the skin; he stared a moment, blankly. Driss was screaming. The muscles all over his body stood out, moved.

It is only the beginning of a monstrous sequence, in which the author is palpably an accomplice, invites us to become accomplices, too; and at the end, a little ashamed, we cannot convince ourselves that the point has been to demonstrate "that violence arising out of the clash of the Westerner with the alien world of the East." Only a touch of humor, a conversion at the last moment of *volupté* to farce could have redeemed the scene from pornography to true gothicism; but it is all played straight-faced and breathless.

Still, this kind of travesty is a risk the gothicist *must* run, a danger to which most serious writers sooner or later expose themselves in America, where, for reasons we have indicated, the novelist tends to be defeated in his attempts to deal with love, sentimentally or analytically. In gothicism, the American novelist not only finds opportunities to render inward experience symbolically, to present the world which typically strikes him as a riddle in riddling terms: but in it, too, he discovers ways of mythicizing the brutality and terror endemic to our life. There is, moreover, incumbent on the American author an obligation to negativism, which the sentimental genres cannot fulfill and which realism converts to mere pamphleteering. All fictionists are committed, surely, whatever their other concerns, to revealing the inevitable discrepancy between what life at any moment is imagined and what it is, between what man dreams and what he achieves, between what he would like to believe and what he fears is true. But the "what he fears is true" is the subject par excellence of the gothic, when it is more than mere trifling and titillation.

Nowhere in the world does the writer feel more deeply than in the United States the secret appeal of the community at large that he deny their publicly asserted orthodoxies, expose their dearly preserved deceits. Nowhere is his nay-saying, his "treachery" more desperately needed. There is little temptation really for any American author to play too blatantly affirmative a role; he knows, from the moment he learns to read, that no one wants him to be the Good Good Boy, not even his mother who says so. The danger is not that he will become Sid Sawyer, but that he will learn to play the part of Tom, the Good Bad Boy, the pseudo-rebel with the note in his pocket assuring Aunt Polly of his undying love. To be Huck Finn he must be willing not to "light out for the territory" (Tom was prepared to take that Western outing, too!), but to "go to Hell," which becomes in modern terms, to be "unadjusted," "nihilistic," or "sterile." The words change, but the chorus of sympathetic and dismayed voices crying out in favor of "salvation" or "adjustment" or "commitment" or "love" never ceases: "Nay, Taji: commit not the last, last crime!" Against their allure, the writer has to fortify him chiefly his own sense of the failure of passion and skill in his fellow artists at precisely the point when they abandon blasphemy and turn back toward one or another Serenia. He knows, though high-minded critics occasionally try to obscure the fact, the fatal falling-off between *The Scarlet Letter* and *The House of the Seven Gables,* between *Absalom, Absalom!* and *A Fable, Moby Dick* and the first part of *Pierre* (Melville alone among American writers could plot but never carry through the betrayal of himself), *Huckleberry Finn* and *Joan of Arc.* And he recognizes that, in each case, the author has abandoned with the gothic mode and its negative message his truest self.

Our classic books are not, however, nakedly and openly nihilistic; despite their obsession with terror they provide endings moral and happy enough for any middlebrow reader. Indeed, their gothicism itself is part of their profound duplicity, for the gothic has always been a popular mode, since in a world where fewer and fewer men believe in the Devil, the diabolic stance can be passed off as an amusing sham. Not only the professional funny man, Mark Twain, but Hawthorne and Melville, even Faulkner disguise the diabolical bargains which are the centers of their great books with horseplay and self-conscious farce. Yet read properly that horseplay itself as well as the specious happy endings are revealed as final macabre ironies, blasphemous jokes at the expense of the unwary reader. "I have written a wicked book, and feel spotless as the lamb," Melville writes, giving away the secret; but he does not speak it aloud, only confides it in the ear of his fellow conspirator

Hawthorne, from whom he believed he had learned "the grand truth":

> There is the grand truth about Nathaniel Hawthorne. He says No! in thunder; but the Devil himself cannot make him say *yes.* For all men who say *yes,* lie; and all men who say *no,*—why, they are in the happy condition of judicious, unencumbered travellers in Europe; they cross the frontiers into Eternity with nothing but a carpet bag,—that is to say, the Ego.

INDEX

506

But Toole's greatest achievement is Ignatius Reilly himself, intellectual, ideologue, deadbeat, goof-off, glutton, who should repel the reader with his gargantuan bloats, his thunderous contempt and one-man war against everybody—Freud, homosexuals, heterosexuals, Protestants, and the assorted excesses of modern times. Imagine an Aquinas gone to pot, transported to New Orleans from whence he makes a wild foray through the swamps to LSU at Baton Rouge, where his lumber jacket is stolen in the faculty men's room where he is seated, overcome by mammoth gastro-intestinal problems. His pyloric valve periodically closes in response to the lack of a "proper geometry and theology" in the modern world.

I hesitate to use the word *comedy*—though comedy it is—because that implies simply a funny book, and this novel is a great deal more than that. A great rumbling farce of Falstaffian dimensions would better describe it; *commedia* would be closer to it.

It is also sad. One never quite knows where the sadness comes from—from the tragedy at the heart of Ignatius's great gaseous rages and lunatic adventures or the tragedy attending the book itself.

The tragedy of the book is the tragedy of the author—his suicide in 1969 at the age of thirty-two. Another tragedy is the body of work we have been denied.

It is a great pity that John Kennedy Toole is not alive and well and writing. But he is not, and there is nothing we can do about it but make sure that this gargantuan tumultuous human tragicomedy is at least made available to a world of readers.

WALKER PERCY

There is a New Orleans city accent . . . associated with downtown New Orleans, particularly with the German and Irish Third Ward, that is hard to distinguish from the accent of Hoboken, Jersey City, and Astoria, Long Island, where the Al Smith inflection, extinct in Manhattan, has taken refuge. The reason, as you might expect, is that the same stocks that brought the accent to Manhattan imposed it on New Orleans.

....

"You're right on that. We're Mediterranean. I've never been to Greece or Italy, but I'm sure I'd be at home there as soon as I landed."

He would, too, I thought. New Orleans resembles Genoa or Marseilles, or Beirut or the Egyptian Alexandria more than it does New York, although all seaports resemble one another more than they can resemble any place in the interior. Like Havana and Port-au-Prince, New Orleans is within the orbit of a Hellenistic world that never touched the North Atlantic. The Mediterranean, Caribbean and Gulf of Mexico form a homogeneous, though interrupted, sea.

A. J. Liebling,
THE EARL OF LOUISIANA

A
Confederacy
of DUNCES

one

A GREEN HUNTING CAP squeezed the top of the fleshy balloon of a head. The green earflaps, full of large ears and uncut hair and the fine bristles that grew in the ears themselves, stuck out on either side like turn signals indicating two directions at once. Full, pursed lips protruded beneath the bushy black moustache and, at their corners, sank into little folds filled with disapproval and potato chip crumbs. In the shadow under the green visor of the cap Ignatius J. Reilly's supercilious blue and yellow eyes looked down upon the other people waiting under the clock at the D. H. Holmes department store, studying the crowd of people for signs of bad taste in dress. Several of the outfits, Ignatius noticed, were new enough and expensive enough to be properly considered offenses against taste and decency. Possession of anything new or expensive only reflected a person's lack of theology and geometry; it could even cast doubts upon one's soul.

Ignatius himself was dressed comfortably and sensibly. The hunting cap prevented head colds. The voluminous tweed trousers were durable and permitted unusually free locomotion. Their pleats and nooks contained pockets of warm, stale air that soothed Ignatius. The plaid flannel shirt made a jacket unnecessary while the muffler guarded exposed Reilly skin between earflap and collar. The outfit was acceptable by any theological and geometrical standards, however abstruse, and suggested a rich inner life.

Shifting from one hip to the other in his lumbering, elephantine fashion, Ignatius sent waves of flesh rippling beneath the tweed and flannel, waves that broke upon buttons and seams. Thus rearranged, he contemplated the long while that he had been waiting for his mother. Principally he considered the discomfort he was beginning to feel. It seemed as if his whole being was ready to burst from his swollen suede desert boots, and, as if to verify this, Ignatius turned his singular eyes toward his feet. The feet did indeed look swollen. He was prepared to offer the sight of those bulging boots to his mother as evidence of her thoughtlessness. Looking up, he saw the sun beginning to descend over the Mississippi at the foot of Canal Street. The Holmes clock said almost five. Already he was polishing a few carefully worded accusations designed to reduce his mother to repentance or, at least, confusion. He often had to keep her in her place.

She had driven him downtown in the old Plymouth, and while she was at the doctor's seeing about her arthritis, Ignatius had bought some sheet music at Werlein's for his trumpet and a new string for his lute. Then he had wandered into the Penny Arcade on Royal Street to see whether any new games had been installed. He had been disappointed to find the miniature mechanical baseball game gone. Perhaps it was only being repaired. The last time that he had played it the batter would not work and, after some argument, the management had returned his nickel, even though the Penny Arcade people had been base enough to suggest

2

that Ignatius had himself broken the baseball machine by kicking it.

Concentrating upon the fate of the miniature baseball machine, Ignatius detached his being from the physical reality of Canal Street and the people around him and therefore did not notice the two eyes that were hungrily watching him from behind one of D. H. Holmes' pillars, two sad eyes shining with hope and desire.

Was it possible to repair the machine in New Orleans? Probably so. However, it might have to be sent to some place like Milwaukee or Chicago or some other city whose name Ignatius associated with efficient repair shops and permanently smoking factories. Ignatius hoped that the baseball game was being carefully handled in shipment, that none of its little players was being chipped or maimed by brutal railroad employees determined to ruin the railroad forever with damage claims from shippers, railroad employees who would subsequently go on strike and destroy the Illinois Central.

As Ignatius was considering the delight which the little baseball game afforded humanity, the two sad and covetous eyes moved toward him through the crowd like torpedoes zeroing in on a great woolly tanker. The policeman plucked at Ignatius' bag of sheet music.

"You got any identification, mister?" the policeman asked in a voice that hoped that Ignatius was officially unidentified.

"What?" Ignatius looked down upon the badge on the blue cap. "Who are you?"

"Let me see your driver's license."

"I don't drive. Will you kindly go away? I am waiting for my mother."

3
..

"What's this hanging out your bag?"

"What do you think it is, stupid? It's a string for my lute."

"What's that?" The policeman drew back a little. "Are you local?"

"Is it the part of the police department to harass me when this city is a flagrant vice capital of the civilized world?" Ignatius bellowed over the crowd in front of the store. "This city is famous for its gamblers, prostitutes, exhibitionists, anti-Christs, alcoholics, sodomites, drug addicts, fetishists, onanists, pornographers, frauds, jades, litterbugs, and lesbians, all of whom are only too well protected by graft. If you have a moment, I shall endeavor to discuss the crime problem with you, but don't make the mistake of bothering *me*."

The policeman grabbed Ignatius by the arm and was struck on his cap with the sheet music. The dangling lute string whipped him on the ear.

"Hey," the policeman said.

"Take that!" Ignatius cried, noticing that a circle of interested shoppers was beginning to form.

Inside D. H. Holmes, Mrs. Reilly was in the bakery department pressing her maternal breast against a glass case of macaroons. With one of her fingers, chafed from many years of scrubbing her son's mammoth, yellowed drawers, she tapped on the glass case to attract the saleslady.

"Oh, Miss Inez," Mrs. Reilly called in that accent that occurs south of New Jersey only in New Orleans, that Hoboken near the Gulf of Mexico. "Over here, babe."

"Hey, how you making?" Miss Inez asked. "How you feeling, darling?"

"Not so hot," Mrs. Reilly answered truthfully.

"Ain't that a shame." Miss Inez leaned over the glass case and forgot about her cakes. "I don't feel so hot myself. It's my feet."

"Lord, I wisht I was that lucky. I got arthuritis in my elbow."

"Aw, no!" Miss Inez said with genuine sympathy. "My poor old poppa's got that. We make him go set himself in a hot tub fulla berling water."

"My boy's floating around in our tub all day long. I can't hardly get in my own bathroom no more."

"I thought he was married, precious."

"Ignatius? Eh, la la," Mrs. Reilly said sadly. "Sweetheart, you wanna gimme two dozen of them fancy mix?"

"But I thought you told me he was married," Miss Inez said while she was putting the cakes in a box.

"He ain't even got him a prospect. The little girl friend he had flew the coop."

"Well, he's got time."

"I guess so," Mrs. Reilly said disinterestedly. "Look, you wanna gimme half a dozen wine cakes, too? Ignatius gets nasty if we run outta cake."

"Your boy likes his cake, huh?"

"Oh, Lord, my elbow's killing me," Mrs. Reilly answered.

In the center of the crowd that had formed before the department store the hunting cap, the green radius of the circle of people, was bobbing about violently.

"I shall contact the mayor," Ignatius was shouting.

"Let the boy alone," a voice said from the crowd.

"Go get the strippers on Bourbon Street," an old man added. "He's a good boy. He's waiting for his momma."

5

"Thank you," Ignatius said haughtily. "I hope that all of you will bear witness to this outrage."

"You come with me," the policeman said to Ignatius with waning self-confidence. The crowd was turning into something of a mob, and there was no traffic patrolman in sight. "We're going to the precinct."

"A good boy can't even wait for his momma by D. H. Holmes." It was the old man again. "I'm telling you, the city was never like this. It's the communiss."

"Are you calling me a communiss?" the policeman asked the old man while he tried to avoid the lashing of the lute string. "I'll take you in, too. You better watch out who you calling a communiss."

"You can't arress me," the old man cried. "I'm a member of the Golden Age Club sponsored by the New Orleans Recreation Department."

"Let that old man alone, you dirty cop," a woman screamed. "He's prolly somebody's grampaw."

"I am," the old man said. "I got six granchirren all studying with the sisters. Smart, too."

Over the heads of the people Ignatius saw his mother walking slowly out of the lobby of the department store carrying the bakery products as if they were boxes of cement.

"Mother!" he called. "Not a moment too soon. I've been seized."

Pushing through the people, Mrs. Reilly said, "Ignatius! What's going on here? What you done now? Hey, take your hands off my boy."

"I'm not touching him, lady," the policeman said. "Is this here your son?"

Mrs. Reilly snatched the whizzing lute string from Ignatius.

"Of course I'm her child," Ignatius said. "Can't you see her affection for me?"

"She loves her boy," the old man said.

"What you trying to do my poor child?" Mrs. Reilly asked the policeman. Ignatius patted his mother's hennaed hair with one of his huge paws. "You got plenty business picking on poor chirren with all the kind of people they got running in this town. Waiting for his momma and they try to arrest him."

"This is clearly a case for the Civil Liberties Union," Ignatius observed, squeezing his mother's drooping shoulder with the paw. "We must contact Myrna Minkoff, my lost love. She knows about those things."

"It's the communiss," the old man interrupted.

"How old is he?" the policeman asked Mrs. Reilly.

"I am thirty," Ignatius said condescendingly.

"You got a job?"

"Ignatius hasta help me at home," Mrs. Reilly said. Her initial courage was failing a little, and she began to twist the lute string with the cord on the cake boxes. "I got terrible arthuritis."

"I dust a bit," Ignatius told the policeman. "In addition, I am at the moment writing a lengthy indictment against our century. When my brain begins to reel from my literary labors, I make an occasional cheese dip."

"Ignatius makes delicious cheese dips," Mrs. Reilly said.

"That's very nice of him," the old man said. "Most boys are out running around all the time."

"Why don't you shut up?" the policeman said to the old man.

"Ignatius," Mrs. Reilly asked in a trembling voice, "what you done, boy?"

"Actually, Mother, I believe that it was he who started everything." Ignatius pointed to the old man with his bag of sheet music. "I was simply standing about, waiting for you, praying that the news from the doctor would be encouraging."

"Get that old man outta here," Mrs. Reilly said to the policeman. "He's making trouble. It's a shame they got people like him walking the streets."

"The police are all communiss," the old man said.

"Didn't I say for you to shut up?" the policeman said angrily.

"I fall on my knees every night to thank my God we got protection," Mrs. Reilly told the crowd. "We'd all be dead without the police. We'd all be laying in our beds with our throats cut open from ear to ear."

"That's the truth, girl," some woman answered from the crowd.

"Say a rosary for the police force." Mrs. Reilly was now addressing her remarks to the crowd. Ignatius caressed her shoulder wildly, whispering encouragement. "Would you say a rosary for a communiss?"

"No!" several voices answered fervently. Someone pushed the old man.

"It's true, lady," the old man cried. "He tried to arrest your boy. Just like in Russia. They're all communiss."

"Come on," the policeman said to the old man. He grabbed him roughly by the back of the coat.

"Oh, my God!" Ignatius said, watching the wan little policeman try to control the old man. "Now my nerves are totally frayed."

8
..

"Help!" the old man appealed to the crowd. "It's a takeover. It's a violation of the Constitution!"

"He's crazy, Ignatius," Mrs. Reilly said. "We better get outta here, baby." She turned to the crowd. "Run, folks. He might kill us all. Personally, I think maybe *he's* the communiss."

"You don't have to overdo it, Mother," Ignatius said as they pushed through the dispersing crowd and started walking rapidly down Canal Street. He looked back and saw the old man and the bantam policeman grappling beneath the department store clock. "Will you please slow down a bit? I think I'm having a heart murmur."

"Oh, shut up. How you think I feel? I shouldn't haveta be running like this at my age."

"The heart is important at any age, I'm afraid."

"They's nothing wrong with your heart."

"There will be if we don't go a little slower." The tweed trousers billowed around Ignatius' gargantuan rump as he rolled forward. "Do you have my lute string?"

Mrs. Reilly pulled him around the corner onto Bourbon Street, and they started walking down into the French Quarter.

"How come that policeman was after you, boy?"

"I shall never know. But he will probably be coming after us in a few moments, as soon as he has subdued that aged fascist."

"You think so?" Mrs. Reilly asked nervously.

"I would imagine so. He seemed determined to arrest me. He must have some sort of quota or something. I seriously doubt that he will permit me to elude him so easily."

"Wouldn't that be awful! You'd be all over the

9

papers, Ignatius. The disgrace! You musta done something while you was waiting for me, Ignatius. I know
you, boy."

"If anyone was ever minding his business, it was I,"
Ignatius breathed. "Please. We must stop. I think I'm
going to have a hemorrhage."

"Okay." Mrs. Reilly looked at her son's reddening
face and realized that he would very happily collapse at
her feet just to prove his point. He had done it before.
The last time that she had forced him to accompany her
to mass on Sunday he had collapsed twice on the way to
the church and had collapsed once again during the
sermon about sloth, reeling out of the pew and creating
an embarrassing disturbance. "Let's go in here and sit
down."

She pushed him through the door of the Night of
Joy bar with one of the cake boxes. In the darkness that
smelled of bourbon and cigarette butts they climbed
onto two stools. While Mrs. Reilly arranged her cake
boxes on the bar, Ignatius spread his expansive nostrils
and said, "My God, Mother, it smells awful. My stomach is beginning to churn."

"You wanna go back on the street? You want that
policeman to take you in?"

Ignatius did not answer; he was sniffing loudly and
making faces. A bartender, who had been observing the
two, asked quizzically from the shadows, "Yes?"

"I shall have a coffee," Ignatius said grandly.
"Chicory coffee with boiled milk."

"Only instant," the bartender said.

"I can't possibly drink that," Ignatius told his
mother. "It's an abomination."

"Well, get a beer, Ignatius. It won't kill you."

"I may bloat."

"I'll take a Dixie 45," Mrs. Reilly said to the bartender.

"And the gentleman?" the bartender asked in a rich, assumed voice. "What is his pleasure?"

"Give him a Dixie, too."

"I may not drink it," Ignatius said as the bartender went off to open the beers.

"We can't sit in here for free, Ignatius."

"I don't see why not. We're the only customers. They should be glad to have us."

"They got strippers in here at night, huh?" Mrs. Reilly nudged her son.

"I would imagine so," Ignatius said coldly. He looked quite pained. "We might have stopped somewhere else. I suspect that the police will raid this place momentarily anyway." He snorted loudly and cleared his throat. "Thank God my moustache filters out some of the stench. My olfactories are already beginning to send out distress signals."

After what seemed a long time during which there was much tinkling of glass and closing of coolers somewhere in the shadows, the bartender appeared again and set the beers before them, pretending to knock Ignatius' beer into his lap. The Reillys were getting the Night of Joy's worst service, the treatment given unwanted customers.

"You don't by any chance have a cold Dr. Nut, do you?" Ignatius asked.

"No."

"My son loves Dr. Nut," Mrs. Reilly explained. "I gotta buy it by the case. Sometimes he sits himself down and drinks two, three Dr. Nuts at one time."

"I am sure that this man is not particularly interested," Ignatius said.

"Like to take that cap off?" the bartender asked.

"No, I wouldn't!" Ignatius thundered. "There's a chill in here."

"Suit yourself," the bartender said and drifted off into the shadows at the other end of the bar.

"Really!"

"Calm down," his mother said.

Ignatius raised the earflap on the side next to his mother.

"Well, I will lift this so that you won't have to strain your voice. What did the doctor tell you about your elbow or whatever it is?"

"It's gotta be massaged."

"I hope you don't want me to do that. You know how I feel about touching other people."

"He told me to stay out the cold as much as possible."

"If I could drive, I would be able to help you more, I imagine."

"Aw, that's okay, honey."

"Actually, even riding in a car affects me enough. Of course, the worst thing is riding on top in one of those Greyhound Scenicruisers. So high up. Do you remember the time that I went to Baton Rouge in one of those? I vomited several times. The driver had to stop the bus somewhere in the swamps to let me get off and walk around for a while. The other passengers were rather angry. They must have had stomachs of iron to ride in that awful machine. Leaving New Orleans also frightened me considerably. Outside of the city limits the heart of darkness, the true wasteland begins."

"I remember that, Ignatius," Mrs. Reilly said absently, drinking her beer in gulps. "You was really sick when you got back home."

"I felt better *then*. The worst moment was my arrival in Baton Rouge. I realized that I had a round-trip ticket and would have to return on the bus."

"You told me that, babe."

"The taxi back to New Orleans cost me forty dollars, but at least I wasn't violently ill during the taxi ride, although I felt myself beginning to gag several times. I made the driver go very slowly, which was unfortunate for him. The state police stopped him twice for being below the minimum highway speed limit. On the third time that they stopped him they took away his chauffeur's license. You see, they had been watching us on the radar all along."

Mrs. Reilly's attention wavered between her son and the beer. She had been listening to the story for three years.

"Of course," Ignatius continued, mistaking his mother's rapt look for interest, "that was the only time that I had ever been out of New Orleans in my life. I think that perhaps it was the lack of a center of orientation that might have upset me. Speeding along in that bus was like hurtling into the abyss. By the time we had left the swamps and reached those rolling hills near Baton Rouge, I was getting afraid that some rural rednecks might toss bombs at the bus. They love to attack vehicles, which are a symbol of progress, I guess."

"Well, I'm glad you didn't take the job," Mrs. Reilly said automatically, taking *guess* as her cue.

"I couldn't possibly take the job. When I saw the chairman of the Medieval Culture Department, my hands began breaking out in small white bumps. He was a totally soulless man. Then he made a comment about my not wearing a tie and made some smirky remark about the lumber jacket. I was appalled that so

13

meaningless a person would dare such effrontery. That lumber jacket was one of the few creature comforts to which I've ever been really attached, and if I ever find the lunatic who stole it, I shall report him to the proper authorities."

Mrs. Reilly saw again the horrible, coffee-stained lumber jacket that she had always secretly wanted to give to the Volunteers of America along with several other pieces of Ignatius' favorite clothing.

"You see, I was so overwhelmed by the complete grossness of that spurious 'chairman' that I ran from his office in the middle of one of his cretinous ramblings and rushed to the nearest bathroom, which turned out to be the one for 'Faculty Men.' At any rate, I was seated in one of the booths, having rested the lumber jacket on top of the door of the booth. Suddenly I saw the jacket being whisked over the door. I heard footsteps. Then the door of the restroom closed. At the moment, I was unable to pursue the shameless thief, so I began to scream. Someone entered the bathroom and knocked at the door of the booth. It turned out to be a member of the campus security force, or so he said. Through the door I explained what had just happened. He promised to find the jacket and went away. Actually, as I have mentioned to you before, I have always suspected that he and the 'chairman' were the same person. Their voices sounded somewhat similar."

"You sure can't trust nobody nowadays, honey."

"As soon as I could, I fled from the bathroom, eager only to get away from that horrible place. Of course, I was almost frozen standing on that desolate campus trying to hail a taxi. I finally got one that agreed to take me to New Orleans for forty dollars, and the driver was selfless enough to lend me his jacket. By the time we arrived here, however, he was quite depressed about losing his license and had grown rather surly. He also appeared to be developing a bad cold, judging by the frequency of his sneezes. After all, we were on the highway for almost two hours."

"I think I could drink me another beer, Ignatius."

"Mother! In this forsaken place?"

"Just one, baby. Come on, I want another."

"We're probably catching something from these glasses. However, if you're quite determined about the thing, get me a brandy, will you?"

Mrs. Reilly signaled to the bartender, who came out of the shadows and asked, "Now what happened to you on that bus, bud? I didn't get the end of the story."

"Will you kindly tend the bar properly?" Ignatius asked furiously. "It is your duty to silently serve when we call upon you. If we had wished to include you in our conversation, we would have indicated it by now. As a matter of fact, we are discussing rather urgent personal matters."

"The man's just trying to be nice, Ignatius. Shame on you."

"That in itself is a contradiction in terms. No one could possibly be nice in a den like this."

"We want two more beers."

"One beer and one brandy," Ignatius corrected.

"No more clean glasses," the bartender said.

"Ain't that a shame," Mrs. Reilly said. "Well, we can use the ones we got."

The bartender shrugged and went off into the shadows.

15

II

In the precinct the old man sat on a bench with the others, mostly shoplifters, who composed the late afternoon haul. He had neatly arranged along his thigh his Social Security card, his membership card in the St. Odo of Cluny Holy Name Society, a Golden Age Club badge, and a slip of paper identifying him as a member of the American Legion. A young black man, eyeless behind spaceage sunglasses, studied the little dossier on the thigh next to his.

"Whoa!" he said, grinning. "Say, you mus belong to everthin."

The old man rearranged his cards meticulously and said nothing.

"How come they draggin in somebody like you?" The sunglasses blew smoke all over the old man's cards. "Them po-lice mus be gettin desperate."

"I'm here in violation of my constitutional rights," the old man said with sudden anger.

"Well, they not gonna believe that. You better think up somethin else." A dark hand reached for one of the cards. "Hey, wha this mean, 'Colder Age'?"

The old man snatched the card and put it back on his thigh.

"Them little card not gonna do you no good. They throw you in jail anyway. They throw everbody in jail."

"You think so?" the old man asked the cloud of smoke.

"Sure." A new cloud floated up. "How come you here, man?"

"I don't know."

"You don know? Whoa! That crazy. You gotta be here for somethin. Plenty time they pickin up color peoples for nothin, but, mister, you gotta be here for somethin."

"I really don't know," the old man said glumly. "I was just standing in a crowd in front of D. H. Holmes."

"And you lif somebody wallet."

"No, I called a policeman a name."

"Like wha you callin him?"

" 'Communiss.' "

"Cawmniss! Ooo-woo. If I call a po-lice a cawmniss, my ass be in Angola right now for sure. I like to call one of them mother a cawmniss, though. Like this afternoon I standin aroun in Woolsworth and some cat steal a bag of cashew nuts out the 'Nut House' star screamin like she been stab. Hey! The nex thing, a flo'walk grabbin me, and then a police mother draggin me off. A man ain got a chance. Whoa!" His lips sucked at the cigarette. "Nobody findin them cashews on me, but that po-lice still draggin me off. I think that flo'walk a cawmniss. Mean motherfucker."

The old man cleared his throat and played with his cards.

"They probly let you go," the sunglasses said. "Me, they probly gimma a little talk think it scare me, even though they know I ain got them cashews. They probly try to prove I got them nuts. They probly buy a bag, slip it in my pocket. Woolsworth probly try to send me up for life."

The Negro seemed quite resigned and blew out a new cloud of blue smoke that enveloped him and the old man and the little cards. Then he said to himself, "I wonder who lif them nuts. Probly that flo'walk hisself."

A policeman summoned the old man up to the desk in the center of the room where a sergeant was seated.

17

The patrolman who had arrested him was standing there.

"What's your name?" the sergeant asked the old man.

"Claude Robichaux," he answered and put his little cards on the desk before the sergeant.

The sergeant looked over the cards and said, "Patrolman Mancuso here says you resisted arrest and called him a communiss."

"I didn't mean it," the old man said sadly, noticing how fiercely the sergeant was handling the little cards.

"Mancuso says you says all policemen are communiss."

"Oo-wee," the Negro said across the room.

"Will you shut up, Jones?" the sergeant called out.

"Okay," Jones answered.

"I'll get to you next."

"Say, I didn call nobody no cawmniss," Jones said. "I been frame by that flo'walk in Woolsworth. I don even like cashews."

"Shut your mouth up."

"Okay," Jones said brightly and blew a great thundercloud of smoke.

"I didn't mean anything I said," Mr. Robichaux told the sergeant. "I just got nervous. I got carried away. This policeman was trying to arress a poor boy waiting for his momma by Holmes."

"What?" the sergeant turned to the wan little policeman. "What were you trying to do?"

"He wasn't a boy," Mancuso said. "He was a big fat man dressed funny. He looked like a suspicious character. I was just trying to make a routine check and he started to resist. To tell you the truth, he looked like a big prevert."

18
....

"A pervert, huh?" the sergeant asked greedily.

"Yes," Mancuso said with new confidence. "A great big prevert."

"How big?"

"The biggest I ever saw in my whole life," Mancuso said, stretching his arms as if he were describing a fishing catch. The sergeant's eyes shone. "The first thing I spotted was this green hunting cap he was wearing."

Jones listened in attentive detachment somewhere within his cloud.

"Well, what happened, Mancuso? How come he's not standing here before me?"

"He got away. This woman came out the store and got everything mixed up, and she and him run around the corner into the Quarter."

"Oh, two Quarter characters," the sergeant said, suddenly enlightened.

"No, sir," the old man interrupted. "She was really his momma. A nice, pretty lady. I seen them downtown before. This policeman frightened her."

"Oh, listen, Mancuso," the sergeant screamed. "You're the only guy on the force who'd try to arrest somebody away from his mother. And why did you bring in grampaw here? Ring up his family and tell them to come get him."

"Please," Mr. Robichaux pleaded. "Don't do that. My daughter's busy with her kids. I never been arrested in my whole life. She can't come get me. What are my granchirren gonna think? They're all studying with the sisters."

"Get his daughter's number, Mancuso. That'll teach him to call us communiss!"

19

"Please!" Mr. Robichaux was in tears. "My granchirren respect me."

"Jesus Christ!" the sergeant said. "Trying to arrest a kid with his momma, bringing in somebody's grampaw. Get the hell outta here, Mancuso, and take grampaw with you. You wanna arrest suspicious characters? We'll fix you up."

"Yes, sir," Mancuso said weakly, leading the weeping old man away.

"Ooo-wee!" Jones said from the secrecy of his cloud.

III

Twilight was settling around the Night of Joy bar. Outside, Bourbon Street was beginning to light up. Neon signs flashed off and on, reflecting in the streets dampened by the light mist that had been falling steadily for some time. The taxis bringing the evening's first customers, midwestern tourists and conventioneers, made slight splashing sounds in the cold dusk.

A few other customers were in the Night of Joy, a man who ran his finger along a racing form, a depressed blonde who seemed connected with the bar in some capacity, and an elegantly dressed young man who chainsmoked Salems and drank frozen daiquiris in gulps.

"Ignatius, we better go," Mrs. Reilly said and belched.

"What?" Ignatius bellowed. "We must stay to watch the corruption. It's already beginning to set in."

The elegant young man spilled his daiquiri on his bottle-green velvet jacket.

20

"Hey, bartender," Mrs. Reilly called. "Get a rag. One of the customers just spilled they drink."

"That's *quite* all right, darling," the young man said angrily. He arched an eyebrow at Ignatius and his mother. "I think I'm in the wrong bar anyway."

"Don't get upset, honey," Mrs. Reilly counseled. "What's that you drinking? It looks like a pineapple snowball."

"Even if I described it to you, I doubt whether you'd understand what it is."

"How dare you talk to my dear, beloved mother like that!"

"Oh, hush, you big thing," the young man snapped. "Just look at my jacket."

"It's totally grotesque."

"Okay, now. Let's be friends," Mrs. Reilly said through foamy lips. "We got enough bombs and things already."

"And your son seems to delight in dropping them, I must say."

"Okay, you two. This is the kinda place where everybody oughta have themselves some fun." Mrs. Reilly smiled at the young man. "Let me buy you another drink, babe, for the one you spilled. And I think I'll take me another Dixie."

"I really must run," the young man sighed. "Thanks anyway."

"On a night like this?" Mrs. Reilly asked. "Aw, don't pay no mind to what Ignatius says. Why don't you stay and see the show?"

21

The young man rolled his eyes heavenward.

"Yeah." The blonde broke her silence. "See some ass and tits."

"Mother," Ignatius said coldly. "I do believe that you are encouraging these preposterous people."

"Well, you're the one wanted to stay, Ignatius."

"Yes, I did want to stay as an observer. I am not especially anxious to mingle."

"Honey, to tell you the truth, I can't listen to that story about that bus no more tonight. You already told it four times since we got here."

Ignatius looked hurt.

"I hardly suspected that I was boring you. After all, that bus ride was one of the more formative experiences of my life. As a mother, you should be interested in the traumas that have created my worldview."

"What's with the bus?" the blonde asked, moving to the stool next to Ignatius. "My name's Darlene. I like good stories. You got a spicy one?"

The bartender slammed the beer and the daiquiri down just as the bus was starting off on its journey in the vortex.

"Here, have a clean glass," the bartender snarled at Mrs. Reilly.

"Ain't that nice. Hey, Ignatius, I just got a clean glass."

But her son was too preoccupied with his arrival in Baton Rouge to hear her.

"You know, sweetheart," Mrs. Reilly said to the young man, "me and my boy was in trouble today. The police tried to arress him."

"Oh, my dear. Policemen are always so adamant, aren't they?"

"Yeah, and Ignatius got him a master's degree and all."

"What in the world was he doing?"

"Nothing. Just standing waiting for his poor, dear momma."

"His outfit is a little bizarre. I thought he was a performer of some sort when I first came in, although I tried not to imagine the nature of his act."

"I keep on telling him about his clothes, but he won't listen." Mrs. Reilly looked at the back of her son's flannel shirt and at the hair curling down the back of his neck. "That's sure pretty, that jacket you got."

"Oh, this?" the young man asked, feeling the velvet on the sleeve. "I don't mind telling you it cost a fortune. I found it in a dear little shop in the Village."

"You don't look like you from the country."

"Oh, my," the young man sighed and lit a Salem with a great click of his lighter. "I meant Greenwich Village in New York, sweetie. By the way, where did you ever get that hat? It's truly fantastic."

"Aw, Lord, I had this since Ignatius made his First Communion."

"Would you consider selling it?"

"How come?"

"I'm a dealer in used clothing. I'll give you ten dollars for it."

"Aw, come on. For this?"

"Fifteen?"

"Really?" Mrs. Reilly removed the hat. "Sure, honey."

The young man opened his wallet and gave Mrs. Reilly three five dollar bills. Draining his daiquiri glass, he stood up and said, "Now I really must run."

"So soon?"

"It's been perfectly delightful meeting you."

"Take care out in the cold and wet."

23

The young man smiled, placed the hat carefully beneath his trench coat, and left the bar.

"The radar patrol," Ignatius was telling Darlene, "is obviously rather foolproof. It seems that the cab driver and I were making small dots on their screen all the way from Baton Rouge."

"You was on radar," Darlene yawned. "Just think of that."

"Ignatius, we gotta go now," Mrs. Reilly said. "I'm hungry."

She turned toward him and knocked her beer bottle to the floor where it broke into a spray of brown, jagged glass.

"Mother, are you making a scene?" Ignatius asked irritably. "Can't you see that Miss Darlene and I are speaking? You have some cakes with you. Eat those. You're always complaining that you never go anywhere. I would have imagined that you would be enjoying your night on the town."

Ignatius was back on radar, so Mrs. Reilly reached in her boxes and ate a brownie.

"Like one?" she asked the bartender. "They nice. I got some nice wine cakes, too."

The bartender pretended to be looking for something on his shelves.

"I smell wine cakes," Darlene cried, looking past Ignatius.

"Have one, honey," Mrs. Reilly said.

"I think that I shall have one, too," Ignatius said. "I imagine that they taste rather good with brandy."

Mrs. Reilly spread the box out on the bar. Even the man with the racing form agreed to take a macaroon.

"Where you bought these nice wine cakes, lady?" Darlene asked Mrs. Reilly. "They're nice and juicy."

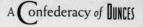

"Over by Holmes, sugar. They got a good selection. Plenty variety."

"They are rather tasty," Ignatius conceded, sending out his flabby pink tongue over his moustache to hunt for crumbs. "I think that I shall have a macaroon or two. I have always found coconut to be good roughage."

He picked around in the box purposefully.

"Me, I always like some good cake after I finish eating," Mrs. Reilly told the bartender, who turned his back on her.

"I bet you cook good, huh?" Darlene asked.

"Mother doesn't cook," Ignatius said dogmatically. "She burns."

"I use to cook too when I was married," Darlene told them. "I sort of used a lot of that canned stuff, though. I like that Spanish rice they got and that spaghetti with the tomato gravy."

"Canned food is a perversion," Ignatius said. "I suspect that it is ultimately very damaging to the soul."

"Lord, my elbow's starting up again," Mrs. Reilly sighed.

"Please. I am speaking," her son told her. "I never eat canned food. I did once, and I could feel my intestines starting to atrophy."

"You got a good education," Darlene said.

"Ignatius graduated from college. Then he stuck around there for four more years to get him a master's degree. Ignatius graduated smart."

" 'Graduated smart,' " Ignatius repeated with some pique. "Please define your terms. Exactly what do you mean by 'graduated smart.' "

"Don't talk to your momma like that," Darlene said.

"Oh, he treats me bad sometimes," Mrs. Reilly said loudly and began to cry. "You just don't know. When I think of all I done for that boy . . ."

"Mother, what are you saying?"

"You don't appreciate me."

"Stop that right now. I'm afraid that you've had too much beer."

"You treat me like garbage. I been good," Mrs. Reilly sobbed. She turned to Darlene. "I spent all his poor Grammaw Reilly's insurance money to keep him in college for eight years, and since then all he's done is lay around the house watching television."

"You oughta be ashamed," Darlene said to Ignatius. "A big man like you. Look at your poor momma."

Mrs. Reilly had collapsed, sobbing, on the bar, one hand clenched around her beer glass.

"This is ridiculous. Mother, stop that."

"If I knew you was so crool, mister, I wouldna listened to your crazy story about that Greyhound bus."

"Get up, Mother."

"You look like a big crazyman anyway," Darlene said. "I shoulda known. Just look how that poor woman's crying."

Darlene tried to push Ignatius from his stool but sent him crashing into his mother, who suddenly stopped crying and gasped, "My elbow!"

"What's going on here?" a woman asked from the padded chartreuse leatherette door of the bar. She was a statuesque woman nearing middle age, her fine body covered with a black leather overcoat that glistened with mist. "I leave this place for a few hours to go shopping and look what happens. I gotta be here every

26

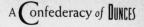

minute, I guess, to watch out you people don't ruin my investment."

"Just two drunks," the bartender said. "I've been giving them the cold shoulder since they come in, but they've been sticking like flies."

"But you, Darlene," the woman said. "You're big friends with them, huh? Playing games on the stools with these two characters?"

"This guy's been mistreating his momma," Darlene explained.

"Mothers? We got mothers in here now? Business already stinks."

"I beg your pardon," Ignatius said.

The woman ignored him and looked at the broken and empty cake box on the bar, saying, "Somebody's been having a picnic in here. Goddamit. I already told you people about ants and rats."

"I beg your pardon," Ignatius said again. "My mother is present."

"It's just my luck to have this crap broken all over here just when I'm looking for a janitor." The woman looked at the bartender. "Get these two out."

"Yes, Miss Lee."

"Don't you worry," Mrs. Reilly said. "We're leaving."

"We certainly are," Ignatius added, lumbering toward the door, leaving his mother behind to climb off her stool. "Hurry along, Mother. This woman looks like a Nazi commandant. She may strike us."

"Wait!" Miss Lee screamed, grabbing Ignatius' sleeve. "How much these characters owe?"

27
····

"Eight dollars," the bartender said.

"This is highway robbery!" Ignatius thundered. "You will hear from our attorneys."

Mrs. Reilly paid with two of the bills the young man had given her and, as she swayed past Miss Lee, she said, "We know when we not wanted. We can take our trade elsewheres."

"Good," Miss Lee answered. "Beat it. Trade from people like you is the kiss of death."

After the padded door had closed behind the Reillys, Miss Lee said, "I never liked mothers. Not even my own."

"My mother was a whore," the man with the racing form said, not looking up from his paper.

"Mothers are full of shit," Miss Lee observed and took off her leather coat. "Now let's you and me have a little talk, Darlene."

Outside, Mrs. Reilly took her son's arm for support, but, as much as they tried, they moved forward very slowly, although they seemed to move sideward more easily. Their walking had developed a pattern: three quick steps to the left, pause, three quick steps to the right, pause.

"That was a terrible woman," Mrs. Reilly said.

"A negation of all human qualities," Ignatius added. "By the way, how far is the car? I'm very tired."

"On St. Ann, honey. Just a few blocks."

"You left your hat in the bar."

"Oh, I sold it to that young man."

"You sold it? Why? Did you ask me whether I wanted it to be sold? I was very attached to that hat."

"I'm sorry, Ignatius. I didn't know you liked it so much. You never said nothing about it."

"I had an unspoken attachment to it. It was a contact with my childhood, a link with the past."

"But he gave me fifteen dollars, Ignatius."

"Please. Don't talk about it anymore. The whole

business is sacrilegious. Goodness knows what degenerate uses he will find for that hat. Do you have the fifteen dollars on you?"

"I still got seven left."

"Then why don't we stop and eat something?" Ignatius pointed to the cart at the corner. It was shaped like a hot dog on wheels. "I believe that they vend footlong hot dogs."

"Hot dogs? Honey, in all this rain and cold we gonna stand outside and eat weenies?"

"It's a thought."

"No," Mrs. Reilly said with somewhat beery courage. "Let's get home. I wouldn't eat nothing outta one of them dirty wagons anyway. They all operated by a bunch of bums."

"If you insist," Ignatius said, pouting. "Although I am rather hungry, and you have, after all, just sold a memento of my childhood for thirty pieces of silver, so to speak."

They continued their little pattern of steps along the wet flagstones of Bourbon Street. On St. Ann they found the old Plymouth easily. Its high roof stood above all the other cars, its best feature. The Plymouth was always easy to find in supermarket parking lots. Mrs. Reilly climbed the curb twice trying to force the car out of the parking place and left the impression of a 1946 Plymouth bumper in the hood of the Volkswagon in the rear.

"My nerves!" Ignatius said. He was slumped down in the seat so that just the top of his green hunting cap appeared in the window, looking like the tip of a promising watermelon. From the rear, where he always sat, having read somewhere that the seat next to the driver was the most dangerous, he watched his mother's wild and inexpert shifting with disapproval. "I suspect that you have effectively demolished the small car that someone innocently parked behind this bus. You had better succeed in getting out of this spot before its owner happens along."

"Shut up, Ignatius. You making me nervous," Mrs. Reilly said, looking at the hunting cap in the rear view mirror.

Ignatius got up on the seat and looked out of the rear window.

"That car is a total wreck. Your driver's license, if you do indeed have one, will doubtlessly be revoked. I certainly wouldn't blame them."

"Lay down there and take a nap," his mother said as the car jerked back again.

"Do you think that I could sleep now? I'm afraid for my life. Are you sure that you're turning the wheel the right way?"

Suddenly the car leaped out of the parking spot and skidded across the wet street into a post supporting a wrought-iron balcony. The post fell away to one side, and the Plymouth crunched against the building.

"Oh, my God!" Ignatius screamed from the rear. "What have you done now?"

"Call a priest!"

"I don't think that we're injured, Mother. However, you have just ruined my stomach for the next few days." Ignatius rolled down one of the rear windows and studied the fender that was pressed against the wall. "We shall need a new headlight on this side, I imagine."

"What we gonna do?"

"If I were driving, I would put the auto in reverse and back gracefully away from the scene. Someone will certainly press charges. The people who own this wreck of a building have been waiting for an opportunity like this for years. They probably spread grease on the street after nightfall hoping that motorists like you will spin toward their hovel." He belched. "My digestion has been destroyed. I think that I am beginning to bloat!"

Mrs. Reilly shifted the worn gears and inched slowly backward. As the car moved, the splintering of wood sounded over their heads, a splintering that changed into splitting of boards and scraping of metal. Then the balcony was falling in large sections, thundering on the roof of the car with the dull, heavy thud of grenades. The car, like a stoned human, stopped moving, and a piece of wrought-iron decoration shattered a rear window.

"Honey, are you okay?" Mrs. Reilly asked wildly after what seemed to be the final bombardment.

Ignatius made a gagging sound. The blue and yellow eyes were watering.

"Say something, Ignatius," his mother pleaded, turning around just in time to see Ignatius stick his head out of a window and vomit down the side of the dented car.

Patrolman Mancuso was walking slowly down Chartres Street dressed in ballet tights and a yellow sweater, a costume which the sergeant said would enable him to bring in genuine, bona fide suspicious characters instead of grandfathers and boys waiting for their mothers. The costume was the sergeant's punishment. He had told Mancuso that from now on he would be strictly responsible for bringing in suspicious characters, that police headquarters had a costume wardrobe

31

that would permit Mancuso to be a new character every day. Forlornly, Patrolman Mancuso had put on the tights before the sergeant, who had pushed him out of the precinct and told him to shape up or get off the force.

In the two hours that he had been cruising the French Quarter, he had captured no one. Twice things had looked hopeful. He had stopped a man wearing a beret and asked for a cigarette, but the man had threatened to have him arrested. Then he accosted a young man in a trench coat who was wearing a lady's hat, but the young man had slapped him across the face and dashed away.

As Patrolman Mancuso walked down Chartres rubbing his cheek, which still smarted from the slap, he heard what seemed to be an explosion. Hoping that a suspicious character had just thrown a bomb or shot himself, he ran around the corner onto St. Ann and saw the green hunting cap emitting vomit among the ruins.

t w o

"WITH THE BREAKDOWN of the Medieval system, the gods of Chaos, Lunacy, and Bad Taste gained ascendancy." Ignatius was writing in one of his Big Chief tablets.

After a period in which the western world had enjoyed order, tranquility, unity, and oneness with its True God and Trinity, there appeared winds of change which spelled evil days ahead. An ill wind blows no one good. The luminous years of Abélard, Thomas à Beckett, and Everyman dimmed into dross; Fortuna's wheel had turned on humanity, crushing its collarbone, smashing its skull, twisting its torso, puncturing its pelvis, sorrowing its soul. Having once been so high, humanity fell so low. What had once been dedicated to the soul was now dedicated to the sale.

"That is rather fine," Ignatius said to himself and continued his hurried writing.

Merchants and charlatans gained control of Europe, calling their insidious gospel "The Enlightenment." The day of the locust was at hand, but from the ashes of humanity there arose no Phoenix. The humble and pious peasant, Piers Plowman, went to town to sell his children to the lords of the New Order for purposes that we may call questionable at best. (See Reilly, Ignatius J., *Blood on Their Hands: The Crime of It All, A study of some selected abuses in sixteenth century Europe*, a Monograph, 2 pages, 1950, Rare Book Room, Left Corridor, Third

33
....

Floor, Howard-Tilton Memorial Library, Tulane University, New Orleans 18, Louisiana. Note: I mailed this singular monograph to the library as a gift; however, I am not really certain that it was ever accepted. It may well have been thrown out because it was only written in pencil on tablet paper.) The gyro had widened; The Great Chain of Being had snapped like so many paper clips strung together by some drooling idiot; death, destruction, anarchy, progress, ambition, and self-improvement were to be Piers' new fate. And a vicious fate it was to be: now he was faced with the perversion of having to GO TO WORK.

His vision of history temporarily fading, Ignatius sketched a noose at the bottom of the page. Then he drew a revolver and a little box on which he neatly printed GAS CHAMBER. He scratched the side of the pencil back and forth across the paper and labeled this APOCALYPSE. When he had finished decorating the page, he threw the tablet to the floor among many others that were scattered about. This had been a very productive morning, he thought. He had not accomplished so much in weeks. Looking at the dozens of Big Chief tablets that made a rug of Indian headdresses around the bed, Ignatius thought smugly that on their yellowed pages and wide-ruled lines were the seeds of a magnificent study in comparative history. Very disordered, of course. But one day he would assume the task of editing these fragments of his mentality into a jigsaw puzzle of a very grand design; the completed puzzle would show literate men the disaster course that history had been taking for the past four centuries. In the five years that he had dedicated to this work, he had produced an average of only six paragraphs monthly. He could not even remember what he had written in some of the tablets, and he realized that several were filled principally with doodling. However, Ignatius thought calmly, Rome was not built in a day.

Ignatius pulled his flannel nightshirt up and looked at his bloated stomach. He often bloated while lying in bed in the morning contemplating the unfortunate turn that events had taken since the Reformation. Doris Day and Greyhound Scenicruisers, whenever they came to mind, created an even more rapid expansion of his central region. But since the attempted arrest and the accident, he had been bloating for almost no reason at all, his pyloric valve snapping shut indiscriminately and filling his stomach with trapped gas, gas which had character and being and resented its confinement. He wondered whether his pyloric valve might be trying, Cassandralike, to tell him something. As a medievalist Ignatius believed in the *rota Fortunae*, or wheel of fortune, a central concept in *De Consolatione Philosophiae*, the philosophical work which had laid the foundation for medieval thought. Boethius, the late Roman who had written the *Consolatione* while unjustly imprisoned by the emperor, had said that a blind goddess spins us on a wheel, that our luck comes in cycles. Was the ludicrous attempt to arrest him the beginning of a bad cycle? Was his wheel rapidly spinning downward? The accident was also a bad sign. Ignatius was worried. For all his philosophy, Boethius had still been tortured and killed. Then Ignatius' valve closed again, and he rolled over on his left side to press the valve open.

"Oh, Fortuna, blind, heedless goddess, I am strapped to your wheel," Ignatius belched. "Do not crush me beneath your spokes. Raise me on high, divinity."

35

"What you mumbling about in there, boy?" his mother asked through the closed door.

"I am praying," Ignatius answered angrily.

"Patrolman Mancuso's coming today to see me about the accident. You better say a little Hail Mary for me, honey."

"Oh, my God," Ignatius muttered.

"I think it's wonderful you praying, babe. I been wondering what you do locked up in there all the time."

"Please go away!" Ignatius screamed. "You're shattering my religious ecstasy."

Bouncing up and down on his side vigorously, Ignatius sensed a belch rising in his throat, but when he expectantly opened his mouth he emitted only a small burp. Still, the bouncing had some physiological effect. Ignatius touched the small erection that was pointing downward into the sheet, held it, and lay still trying to decide what to do. In this position, with the red flannel nightshirt around his chest and his massive stomach sagging into the mattress, he thought somewhat sadly that after eighteen years with his hobby it had become merely a mechanical physical act stripped of the flights of fancy and invention that he had once been able to bring to it. At one time he had almost developed it into an art form, practicing the hobby with the skill and fervor of an artist and philosopher, a scholar and gentleman. There were still hidden in his room several accessories which he had once used, a rubber glove, a piece of fabric from a silk umbrella, a jar of Noxema. Putting them away again after it was all over had eventually grown too depressing.

Ignatius manipulated and concentrated. At last a vision appeared, the familiar figure of the large and devoted collie that had been his pet when he was in high school. "Woof!" Ignatius almost heard Rex say once again. "Woof! Woof! Arf!" Rex looked so lifelike. One ear dropped. He panted. The apparition jumped over a fence and chased a stick that somehow landed in the middle of Ignatius' quilt. As the tan and white fur grew closer, Ignatius' eyes dilated, crossed, and closed, and he lay wanly back among his four pillows, hoping that he had some Kleenex in his room.

II

"I come about that porter job you got advertise in the paper."

"Yeah?" Lana Lee looked at the sunglasses. "You got any references?"

"A po-lice gimme a reference. He tell me I better get my ass gainfully employ," Jones said and shot a jet of smoke out into the empty bar.

"Sorry. No police characters. Not in a business like this. I got an investment to watch."

"I ain exactly a character yet, but I can tell they gonna star that vagran no visible mean of support stuff on me. They told me." Jones withdrew into a forming cloud. "I thought maybe the Night of Joy like to help somebody become a member of the community, help keep a poor color boy outta jail. I keep the picket off, give the Night of Joy a good civil right ratin."

"Cut out the crap."

"Hey! Whoa!"

"You got any experience as a porter?"

"Wha? Sweepin and moppin and all that nigger shit?"

"Watch your mouth, boy. I got a clean business."

"Hell, anybody do that, especially color peoples."

"I've been looking," Lana Lee said, becoming a grave personnel manager, "for the right boy for this job for several days." She put her hands in the pockets of her leather overcoat and looked into the sunglasses. This was really a deal, like a present left on her doorstep. A colored guy who would get arrested for vagrancy if he didn't work. She would have a captive porter whom she could work for almost nothing. It was beautiful. Lana felt good for the first time since she had come upon those two characters messing up her bar. "The pay is twenty dollars a week."

"Hey! No wonder the right man ain show up. Ooo-wee. Say, whatever happen to the minimal wage?"

"You need a job, right? I need a porter. Business stinks. Take it from there!"

"The las person workin in here musta starve to death."

"You work six days a week from ten to three. If you come in regular, who knows? You might get a little raise."

"Don worry. I come in regular, anything keep my ass away from a po-lice for a few hour," Jones said, blowing some smoke on Lana Lee. "Where you keep them motherfuckin broom?"

"One thing we gotta understand is keeping our mouth clean around here."

"Yes, *ma'm*. I sure don wanna make a bad impressia in a fine place like the Night of Joy. Whoa!"

38

The door opened and Darlene came in wearing a satin cocktail dress and a flowered hat, flouncing her skirt gracefully as she walked.

"How come you're so late?" Lana screamed at her. "I told you to be here at one today."

"My cockatoo come down with a cold last night, Lana. It was awful. The whole night he was up coughing right in my ear."

"Where do you think up excuses like that?"

"Well, it's true," Darlene answered in an injured voice. She put her huge hat on the bar and climbed on a stool up into a cloud that Jones had blown. "I hadda take him to the vet's this morning to get a vitamin shot. I don't want that poor bird coughing all over my furniture."

"What got into your head that made you encourage those two characters last night? Every day, every day, Darlene, I try to explain to you the kind of clientele we want in here. Then I walk in and find you eating crap off my bar with some old lady and a fat turd. You trying to close down my business? People look in the door, see a combination like that, they walk off to another bar. What I have to do to make you *understand*, Darlene? How does a human being get through to a mind like yours?"

"I already told you I felt sorry for that poor woman, Lana. You oughta seen how her son treated her. You oughta heard the story he told me about a Greyhound bus. And all the time that sweet old lady sitting there paying for his drinks. I *had* to take one of her cakes to make her feel good."

"Well, the next time I find you encouraging people like that and ruining my investment, I'm gonna kick you out on your behind. Is that clear?"

"Yes, ma'm."

"You sure you got what I said?"

"Yes, ma'm."

"Okay. Now show this boy where we keep our brooms and crap and get that bottle that old lady broke cleaned up. You're in charge of getting this whole god-dam place as clean as a pin for what you did me last night. I'm going shopping." Lana got to the door and turned around. "I don't want nobody fooling with that cabinet under the bar."

"I swear," Darlene said to Jones after Lana had swung through the door, "this place is worse than the army. She just hire you today?"

"Yeah," Jones answered. "She ain exactly *hire* me. She kinda buyin me off a auction block."

"At least you gonna get a salary. I only work on commission for how much I get people to drink. You think that's easy? Try to get some guy to buy more than one of the kinda drinks they serve in here. All water. They gotta spend ten, fifteen dollars to get any effect at all. I swear, it's a tough job. Lana even pumps water in the champagne. You oughta taste that. Then she's all the time complaining about how business stinks. She oughta buy a drink at this bar and find out. Even when she's got only about five people drinking in here she's making a fortune. Water don't cost nothing."

"Wha she go shoppin for? A whip?"

"Don't ask me. Lana never tells me nothing. That Lana's a funny one." Darlene blew her nose daintily. "What I really wanna be is an exotic. I been practicing in my apartment on a routine. If I can get Lana to let me dance in here at night, I can get me a regular salary and quit hustling water on commission. Now that I think of it, I oughta get me some commission for what them people drank up in here last night. That old lady sure drank up a lotta beer. I don't see what Lana's got to complain about. Business is business. That fat man and his momma wasn't much worse than plenty we get in here. I think the thing got Lana was that funny green cap he had stuck up on his head. When he was talking, he'd pull the earflap down, and when he was listening, he'd stick it up again. By the time Lana got here, everybody was hollering at him, so he had both flaps stuck out like wings. You know, it looked sorta funny."

"And you say this fat cat travlin around with his momma?" Jones asked, making a mental association.

"Uh huh." Darlene folded her handkerchief and slipped it into her bosom. "I sure hope they don't ever decide to hang around here again. I'll really be in trouble. Jesus." Darlene sounded worried. "Look, we better do something about this place before Lana comes back. But listen. Don't knock yourself out cleaning up this dump. I never seen it really clean since I been here. And it's so dark in here all the time, nobody can tell the difference. To hear Lana talk, you'd think this hole was the Ritz."

Jones shot out a fresh cloud. Through his glasses he could hardly see anything at all.

III

Patrolman Mancuso enjoyed riding the motorcycle up St. Charles Avenue. At the precinct he had borrowed a large and loud one that was all chromium and baby blue, and at the touch of a switch it could become a pinball machine of flashing, winking, blinking red and white lights. The siren, a cacophany of twelve crazed bobcats, was enough to make suspicious characters within a half-mile radius defecate in panic and rush for cover. Patrolman Mancuso's love for the motorcycle was platonically intense.

The forces of evil generated by the hideous—and apparently impossible to uncover—underground of suspicious characters seemed remote to him this afternoon, though. The ancient oaks of St. Charles Avenue arched over the avenue like a canopy shielding him from the mild winter sun that splashed and sparkled on the chrome of the motorcycle. Although the days had lately been cold and damp, the afternoon had that sudden, surprising warmth that makes New Orleans winters gentle. Patrolman Mancuso appreciated the mildness, for he was wearing only a T-shirt and Bermuda shorts, the sergeant's costume selection for the day. The long red beard that hooked over his ears by means of wires did manage to warm his chest a little; he had snatched the beard from the locker while the sergeant wasn't looking.

Patrolman Mancuso inhaled the moldy scent of the oaks and thought, in a romantic aside, that St. Charles Avenue must be the loveliest place in the world. From time to time he passed the slowly rocking streetcars that seemed to be leisurely moving toward no special destination, following their route through the old mansions on either side of the avenue. Everything looked so calm, so prosperous, so unsuspicious. On his own time he was going up to see that poor Widow Reilly. She had looked so pitiful crying in the middle of that wreck. The least he could do was try to help her.

At Constantinople Street he turned toward the river, sputtering and growling through a declining neighborhood until he reached a block of houses built in the 1880s and 90s, wooden Gothic and Gilded Age relics that dripped carving and scrollwork, Boss Tweed suburban stereotypes separated by alleys so narrow that a yardstick could almost bridge them and fenced in by iron pikes and low walls of crumbling brick. The larger houses had become impromptu apartment buildings, their porches converted into additional rooms. In some of the frontyards there were aluminum carports, and bright aluminum awnings had been installed on one or two of the buildings. It was a neighborhood that had degenerated from Victorian to nothing in particular, a block that had moved into the twentieth century carelessly and uncaringly—and with very limited funds.

The address that Patrolman Mancuso was looking for was the tiniest structure on the block, aside from the carports, a Lilliput of the eighties. A frozen banana tree, brown and stricken, languished against the front of the porch, the tree preparing to collapse as the iron fence had done long ago. Near the dead tree there was a slight mound of earth and a leaning Celtic cross cut from plywood. The 1946 Plymouth was parked in the frontyard, its bumper pressed against the porch, its taillights blocking the brick sidewalk. But, except for the Plymouth and the weathered cross and the mummified banana tree, the tiny yard was completely bare. There were no shrubs. There was no grass. And no birds sang.

Patrolman Mancuso looked at the Plymouth and saw the deep crease in its roof and the fender, filled with concave circles, that was separated from the body by three or four inches of space. VAN CAMP'S PORK AND BEANS was printed on the piece of cardboard taped across the hole that had been the rear window. Stopping by the grave, he read REX in faded letters on the cross. Then he climbed the worn brick steps and heard through the closed shutters a booming chant.

43

Big girls don't cry.
Big girls don't cry.
Big girls, they don't cry-yi-yi.

> They don't cry.
> Big girls, they don't cry . . . yi.

While he was waiting for someone to answer the bell, he read the faded sticker on the crystal of the door, "A slip of the lip can sink a ship." Below a WAVE held her finger to lips that had turned tan.

Along the block some people were out on their porches looking at him and the motorcycle. The shutters across the street that slowly flipped up and down to get the proper focus indicated that he also had a considerable unseen audience, for a police motorcycle in the block was an event, especially if its driver wore shorts and a red beard. The block was poor, certainly, but honest. Suddenly self-conscious, Patrolman Mancuso rang the bell again and assumed what he considered his erect, official posture. He gave his audience his Mediterranean profile, but the audience saw only a small and sallow figure whose shorts hung clumsily in the crotch, whose spindly legs looked too naked in comparison to the formal garters and nylon socks that hung near the ankles. The audience remained curious, but unimpressed; a few were not even especially curious, the few who had expected some such vision to visit that miniature house eventually.

> Big girls don't cry
> Big girls don't cry.

44

Patrolman Mancuso knocked savagely at the shutters.

> Big girls don't cry.
> Big girls don't cry.

"They home," a woman screamed through the shutters of the house next door, an architect's vision of Jay Gould domestic. "Miss Reilly's prolly in the kitchen. Go around the back. What are you, mister? A cop?"

"Patrolman Mancuso. Undercover," he answered sternly.

"Yeah?" There was a moment of silence. "Which one you want, the boy or the mother?"

"The mother."

"Well, that's good. You'd never get a hold of him. He's watching the TV. You hear that? It's driving me nuts. My nerves is shot."

Patrolman Mancuso thanked the woman's voice and walked into the dank alley. In the back yard he found Mrs. Reilly hanging a spotted and yellowed sheet on a line that ran through the bare fig trees.

"Oh, it's you," Mrs. Reilly said after a moment. She had almost started to scream when she saw the man with the red beard appear in her yard. "How you doing, Mr. Mancuso? What them people said?" She stepped cautiously over the broken brick paving in her brown felt moccasins. "Come on in the house and we'll have us a nice cup of coffee."

The kitchen was a large, high-ceilinged room, the largest in the house, and it smelled of coffee and old newspapers. Like every room in the house, it was dark; the greasy wallpaper and brown wooden moldings would have transformed any light into gloom, and from the alley very little light filtered in anyway. Although the interiors of homes did not interest Patrolman Mancuso, still he did notice, as anyone would have, the antique stove with the high oven and the refrigerator with the cylindrical motor on top. Thinking of the electric fryers, gas driers, mechanical mixers and beaters, waffle plates, and motorized rotisseries that seemed to be always whirring, grinding, beating, cooling, hissing, and broiling in the lunar kitchen of his wife, Rita, he wondered what Mrs. Reilly did in this sparse room. Whenever a new appliance was advertised on television, Mrs. Mancuso bought it no matter how obscure its uses were.

"Now tell me what the man said." Mrs. Reilly began boiling a pot of milk on her Edwardian gas stove. "How much I gotta pay? You told him I was a poor widow with a child to support, huh?"

"Yeah, I told him that," Patrolman Mancuso said, sitting erectly in his chair and looking hopefully at the kitchen table covered with oilcloth. "Do you mind if I put my beard on the table? It's kinda hot in here and it's sticking my face."

"Sure, go ahead, babe. Here. Have a nice jelly doughnut. I just bought them fresh this morning over by Magazine Street. Ignatius says to me this morning, 'Momma, I sure feel like a jelly doughnut.' You know? So I went over by the German and bought him two dozen. Look, they got a few left."

She offered Patrolman Mancuso a torn and oily cake box that looked as if it had been subjected to unusual abuse during someone's attempt to take all of the doughnuts at once. At the bottom of the box Patrolman Mancuso found two withered pieces of doughnut out of which, judging by their moist edges, the jelly had been sucked.

"Thank you anyway, Miss Reilly. I had me a big lunch."

"Aw, ain't that a shame." She filled two cups half full with thick cold coffee and poured the boiling milk in up to the rim. "Ignatius loves his doughnuts. He says to me, 'Momma, I love my doughnuts.' " Mrs. Reilly slurped a bit at the rim of her cup. "He's out in the parlor right now looking at TV. Every afternoon, as right as rain, he looks at that show where them kids dance." In the kitchen the music was somewhat fainter than it had been on the porch. Patrolman Mancuso pictured the green hunting cap bathed in the blue-white glow of the television screen. "He don't like the show at all, but he won't miss it. You oughta hear what he says about them poor kids."

"I spoke with the man this morning," Patrolman Mancuso said, hoping that Mrs. Reilly had exhausted the subject of her son.

"Yeah?" She put three spoons of sugar in her coffee and, holding the spoon in the cup with her thumb so that the handle threatened to puncture her eyeball, she slurped a bit more. "What he said, honey?"

"I told him I investigated the accident and that you just skidded on a wet street."

"That sounds good. So what he said then, babe?"

"He said he don't want to go to court. He wants a settlement now."

"Oh, my God!" Ignatius bellowed from the front of the house. "What an egregious insult to good taste."

"Don't pay him no mind," Mrs. Reilly advised the startled policeman. "He does that all the time he looks at the TV. A 'settlement.' That means he wants some money, huh?"

"He even got a contractor to appraise the damage. Here, this is the estimate."

Mrs. Reilly took the sheet of paper and read the typed column of itemized figures beneath the contractor's letterhead.

47
....

"Lord! A thousand and twenty dollars. This is terrible. How I'm gonna pay that?" She dropped the estimate on the oilcloth. "You sure that is right?"

"Yes, ma'm. He's got a lawyer working on it, too. It's all on the up and up."

"Where I'm gonna get a thousand dollars, though? All me and Ignatius got is my poor husband's Social Security and a little two-bit pension, and that don't come to much."

"Do I believe the total perversion that I am witnessing?" Ignatius screamed from the parlor. The music had a frantic, tribal rhythm; a chorus of falsettos sang insinuatingly about loving all night long.

"I'm sorry," Patrolman Mancuso said, almost heartbroken over Mrs. Reilly's financial quandary.

"Aw, it's not your fault, darling," she said glumly. "Maybe I can get a mortgage on the house. We can't do nothing about it, huh?"

"No, ma'm," Patrolman Mancuso answered, listening to some sort of approaching stampede.

"The children on that program should all be gassed," Ignatius said as he strode into the kitchen in his nightshirt. Then he noticed the guest and said coldly, "Oh."

"Ignatius, you know Mr. Mancuso. Say 'Hello.' "

"I do believe that I've seen him about," Ignatius said and looked out the back door.

Patrolman Mancuso was too startled by the monstrous flannel nightshirt to reply to Ignatius' pleasantry.

"Ignatius, honey, the man wants over a thousand dollars for what I did to his building."

"A thousand dollars? He will not get a cent. We shall have him prosecuted immediately. Contact our attorneys, Mother."

48
....

"Our attorneys? He's got a estimate from a contractor. Mr. Mancuso here says they's nothing I can do."

"Oh. Well, you shall have to pay him then."

"I could take it to court if you think it's best."

"Drunken driving," Ignatius said calmly. "You haven't a chance."

Mrs. Reilly looked depressed.

"But Ignatius, a thousand twenty dollars."

"I am certain that you can procure some funds," he told her. "Is there any more coffee, or have you given the last to this carnival masker?"

"We can mortgage the house."

"Mortgage the house? Of course we won't."

"What else we gonna do, Ignatius?"

"There are means," Ignatius said absently. "I wish that you wouldn't bother me with this. That program always increases my anxiety anyway." He smelled the milk before putting it into the pot. "I would suggest that you telephone that dairy immediately. This milk is quite aged."

"I can get a thousand dollars over by the Homestead," Mrs. Reilly told the silent patrolman quietly. "The house is good security. I had me a real estate agent offered me seven thousand last year."

"The ironic thing about that program," Ignatius was saying over the stove, keeping one eye peeled so that he could seize the pot as soon as the milk began to boil, "is that it is supposed to be an *exemplum* to the youth of our nation. I would like very much to know what the Founding Fathers would say if they could see these children being debauched to further the cause of Clearasil. However, I always suspected that democracy would come to this." He painstakingly poured the milk

49
....

into his Shirley Temple mug. "A firm rule must be imposed upon our nation before it destroys itself. The United States needs some theology and geometry, some taste and decency. I suspect that we are teetering on the edge of the abyss."

"Ignatius, I'm gonna have to go by the Homestead tomorrow."

"We shall not deal with those usurers, Mother." Ignatius was feeling around in the cookie jar. "Something will turn up."

"Ignatius, honey, they can put me in jail."

"Ho hum. If you are going to stage one of your hysterical scenes, I shall have to return to the living room. As a matter of fact, I think I will."

He billowed out again in the direction of the music, the shower shoes flapping loudly against the soles of his huge feet.

"What I'm gonna do with a boy like that?" Mrs. Reilly sadly asked Patrolman Mancuso. "He don't care about his poor dear mother. Sometimes I think Ignatius wouldn't mind if they did throw me in jail. He's got a heart of ice, that boy."

"You spoiled him," Patrolman Mancuso said. "A woman's gotta watch she don't spoil her kids."

"How many chirren you got, Mr. Mancuso?"

"Three. Rosalie, Antoinette, and Angelo, Jr."

"Aw, ain't that nice. I bet they sweet, huh? Not like Ignatius." Mrs. Reilly shook her head. "Ignatius was such a precious child. I don't know what made him change. He used to say to me, 'Momma, I love you.' He don't say that no more."

"Aw, don't cry," Patrolman Mancuso said, deeply moved. "I'll make you some more coffee."

"He don't care if they lock me up," Mrs. Reilly

sniffed. She opened the oven and took out a bottle of muscatel. "You want some nice wine, Mr. Mancuso?"

"No thanks. Being on the force, I gotta make a impression. I gotta always be on the lookout for people, too."

"You don't mind?" Mrs. Reilly asked rhetorically and took a long drink from the bottle. Patrolman Mancuso began boiling the milk, hovering over the stove in a very domestic manner. "Sometimes I sure get the blues. Life's hard. I worked hard, too. I been good."

"You oughta look on the bright side," Patrolman Mancuso said.

"I guess so," Mrs. Reilly said. "Some people got it harder than me, I guess. Like my poor cousin, wonderful woman. Went to mass every day of her life. She got knocked down by a streetcar over on Magazine Street early one morning while she was on her way to Fisherman's Mass. It was still dark out."

"Personally, I never let myself get low," Patrolman Mancuso lied. "You gotta look up. You know what I mean? I got a dangerous line of work."

"You could get yourself killed."

"Sometimes I don't apprehend nobody all day. Sometimes I apprehend the wrong person."

"Like that old man in front of D. H. Holmes. That's my fault, Mr. Mancuso. I shoulda guessed Ignatius was wrong all along. It's just like him. All the time I'm telling him, 'Ignatius, here, put on this nice shirt. Put on this nice sweater I bought you.' But he don't listen. Not that boy. He's got a head like a rock."

"Then sometimes I get problems at home. With three kids, my wife's very nervous."

"Nerves is a terrible thing. Poor Miss Annie, the

51

next-door lady, she's got nerves. Always screaming about Ignatius making noise."

"That's my wife. Sometimes I gotta get outta the house. If I was another kind of man, sometimes I could really go get myself good and drunk. Just between us."

"I gotta have my little drink. It relieves the pressure. You know?"

"What I do is go bowl."

Mrs. Reilly tried to imagine little Patrolman Mancuso with a big bowling ball and said, "You like that, huh?"

"Bowling's wonderful, Miss Reilly. It takes your mind off things."

"Oh, my heavens!" a voice shouted from the parlor. "These girls are doubtless prostitutes already. How can they present horrors like this to the public?"

"I wish I had me a hobby like that."

"You oughta try bowling."

"Ay-yi-yi. I already got arthuritis in my elbow. I'm too old to play around with them balls. I'd wrench my back."

"I got a aunt, sixty-five, a grammaw, and she goes bowling all the time. She's even on a team."

"Some women are like that. Me, I never was much for sports."

"Bowling's more than a sport," Patrolman Mancuso said defensively. "You meet plenty people over by the alley. Nice people. You could make you some friends."

"Yeah, but it's just my luck to drop one of them balls on my toe. I got bum feet already."

"Next time I go by the alley, I'll let you know. I'll bring my aunt. You and me and my aunt, we'll go down by the alley. Okay?"

"Mother, when was this coffee dripped?" Ignatius demanded, flapping into the kitchen again.

"Just about a hour ago. Why?"

"It certainly tastes brackish."

"I thought it was very good," Patrolman Mancuso said. "Just as good as they serve at the French Market. I'm making some more now. You want a cup?"

"Pardon me," Ignatius said. "Mother, are you going to entertain this gentleman all afternoon? I would like to remind you that I am going to the movies tonight and that I am due at the theater promptly at seven so that I can see the cartoon. I would suggest that you begin preparing something to eat."

"I better go," Patrolman Mancuso said.

"Ignatius, you oughta be ashamed," Mrs. Reilly said in an angry voice. "Me and Mr. Mancuso here just having some coffee. You been nasty all afternoon. You don't care where I raise that money. You don't care if they lock me up. You don't care about nothing."

"Am I going to be attacked in my own home before a stranger with a false beard?"

"My heart's broke."

"Oh, really." Ignatius turned on Patrolman Mancuso. "Will you kindly leave? You are inciting my mother."

"Mr. Mancuso's not doing nothing but being nice."

"I better go," Patrolman Mancuso said apologetically.

"I'll get that money," Mrs. Reilly screamed. "I'll sell this house. I'll sell it out from under you, boy. I'll go stay by a old folks' home."

She grabbed an end of the oilcloth and wiped her eyes.

53

"If you do not leave," Ignatius said to Patrolman Mancuso, who was hooking on his beard, "I shall call the police."

"He *is* the police, stupid."

"This is totally absurd," Ignatius said and flapped away. "I am going to my room."

He slammed his door and snatched a Big Chief tablet from the floor. Throwing himself back among the pillows on the bed, he began doodling on a yellowed page. After almost thirty minutes of pulling at his hair and chewing on the pencil, he began to compose a paragraph.

Were Hroswitha with us today, we would all look to her for counsel and guidance. From the austerity and tranquility of her medieval world, the penetrating gaze of this legendary Sybil of a holy nun would exorcise the horrors which materialize before our eyes in the name of television. If we could only juxtapose one eyeball of this sanctified woman and a television tube, both being roughly of the same shape and design, what a phantasmagoria of exploding electrodes would occur. The images of those lasciviously gyrating children would disintegrate into so many ions and molecules, thereby effecting the catharsis which the tragedy of the debauching of the innocent necessarily demands.

Mrs. Reilly stood in the hall looking at the DO NOT DISTURB sign printed on a sheet of Big Chief paper and stuck to the door by an old flesh-colored Band-aid.

"Ignatius, let me in there, boy," she screamed.

"Let you in here?" Ignatius said through the door. "Of course I won't. I am occupied at the moment with an especially succinct passage."

"You let me in."

"You know that you are never allowed in here."

Mrs. Reilly pounded at the door.

54

"I don't know what is happening to you, Mother, but I suspect that you are momentarily deranged. Now that I think of it, I am too frightened to open the door. You may have a knife or a broken wine bottle."

"Open up this door, Ignatius."

"Oh, my valve! It's closing!" Ignatius groaned loudly. "Are you satisfied now that you have ruined me for the rest of the evening?"

Mrs. Reilly threw herself against the unpainted wood.

"Well, don't break the door," he said finally and, after a few moments, the bolt slid open.

"Ignatius, what's all this trash on the floor?"

"That is my worldview that you see. It still must be incorporated into a whole, so be careful where you step."

"And all the shutters closed. Ignatius! It's still light outside."

"My being is not without its Proustian elements," Ignatius said from the bed, to which he had quickly returned. "Oh, my stomach."

"It smells terrible in here."

"Well, what do you expect? The human body, when confined, produces certain odors which we tend to forget in this age of deodorants and other perversions. Actually, I find the atmosphere of this room rather comforting. Schiller needed the scent of apples rotting in his desk in order to write. I, too, have my needs. You may remember that Mark Twain preferred to lie supinely in bed while composing those rather dated and boring efforts which contemporary scholars try to prove meaningful. Veneration of Mark Twain is one of the roots of our current intellectual stalemate."

55

"If I know it was like this, I'd been in here long ago."

"I do not know why you are in here *now*, as a matter of fact, or why you have this sudden compulsion to invade my sanctuary. I doubt whether it will ever be the same after the trauma of this intrusion by an alien spirit."

"I came to talk to you, boy. Get your face out them pillows."

"This must be the influence of that ludicrous representative of the law. He seems to have turned you against your own child. By the way, he has left, hasn't he?"

"Yes, and I apologized to him over the way you acted."

"Mother, you are standing on my tablets. Will you please move a little? Isn't it enough that you have destroyed my digestion without destroying the fruits of my brain also?"

"Well, where I'm gonna stand, Ignatius? You want me to get in bed with you?" Mrs. Reilly asked angrily.

"Watch out where you're stepping, please!" Ignatius thundered. "My God, never has anyone been so totally and so literally stormed and besieged. What is it anyway that has driven you in here in this state of complete mania? Could it be the stench of cheap muscatel that is assaulting my nostrils?"

"I made up my mind. You gonna go out and get you a job."

Oh, what low joke was Fortuna playing on him now? Arrest, accident, job. Where would this dreadful cycle ever end?

"I see," Ignatius said calmly. "Knowing that you are congenitally incapable of arriving at a decision of this importance, I imagine that that mongoloid law officer put this idea into your head."

"Me and Mr. Mancuso talked like I used to talk to your poppa. You poppa used to tell me what to do. I wish he was alive today."

"Mancuso and my father are alike only in that they both give the impression of being rather inconsequential humans. However, your current mentor is apparently the type of person who thinks that everything will be all right if everyone works continually."

"Mr. Mancuso works hard. He's got a hard road at the precinct."

"I am certain that he supports several unwanted children who all hope to grow up to be policemen, the girls included."

"He's got three sweet chirren."

"I can imagine." Ignatius began to bounce slowly. "Oh!"

"What are you doing? Are you fooling with that valve again? Nobody else got him a valve but you. *I* ain't got no valve."

"*Everyone* has a valve!" Ignatius screamed. "Mine is simply more developed. I am trying to open a passage which you have succeeded in blocking. It may be permanently closed now for all I know."

"Mr. Mancuso says if you work you can help me pay off the man. He says he thinks the man might take the money in installments."

"Your friend the patrolman says a great deal. You certainly bring people out, as they say. I never suspected that he could be so loquacious or that he was capable of such perceptive comment. Do you realize that he is trying to destroy our home? It began the moment that he attempted that brutal arrest in front of

57

D. H. Holmes. Although you are too limited to comprehend it all, Mother, this man is our nemesis. He's spun our wheel downward."

"Wheel? Mr. Mancuso is a good man. You oughta be glad he didn't take you in!"

"In my private apocalypse he will be impaled upon his own nightstick. Anyway, it is inconceivable that I should get a job. I am very busy with my work at the moment, and I feel that I am entering a very fecund stage. Perhaps the accident jarred and loosened my thought. At any rate, I accomplished a great deal today."

"We gotta pay that man, Ignatius. You wanna see me in jail? Wouldn't you be ashamed with your poor momma behind bars?"

"Will you please stop talking about imprisonment? You seem to be preoccupied with the thought. Actually, you seem to enjoy thinking about it. Martyrdom is meaningless in our age." He belched quietly. "I would suggest certain economies around the house. Somehow you will soon see that you have the required amount."

"I spend all the money on you for food and whatnots."

"I have found several empty wine bottles about lately, the contents of which I certainly did not consume."

"Ignatius!"

"I made the mistake of heating the oven the other day before inspecting it properly. When I opened it to put in my frozen pizza, I was almost blinded by a bottle of broiled wine that was preparing to explode. I suggest that you divert some of the monies that you are pouring into the liquor industry."

58
....

"For shame, Ignatius. A few bottles of Gallo muscatel, and you with all them trinkets."

"Will you please define the meaning of *trinkets?*" Ignatius snapped.

"All them books. That gramaphone. That trumpet I bought you last month."

"I consider the trumpet a good investment, although our neighbor, Miss Annie, does not. If she beats on my shutters again, I'll pour water on her."

"Tomorrow we looking at the want ads in the paper. You gonna dress up and go find you a job."

"I am afraid to ask what your idea of 'dressing up' is. I will probably be turned into an utter mockery."

"I'm gonna iron you a nice white shirt and you gonna put on one of your poppa's nice ties."

"Do I believe what I am hearing?" Ignatius asked his pillow.

"It's either that, Ignatius, or I gotta take out a mortgage. You wanna lose the roof over your head?"

"No! You will not mortgage this house." He pounded a great paw into the mattress. "The whole sense of security which I have been trying to develop would crumble. I will not have any disinterested party controlling my domicile. I couldn't stand it. Just the thought of it makes my hands break out."

He extended a paw so that his mother could examine the rash.

"That is out of the question," he continued. "It would bring all of my latent anxieties to a head, and the result, I fear, would be very ugly indeed. I would not want you to have to spend the remainder of your life caring for a lunatic locked away somewhere in the attic. We shall not mortgage the house. You must have some funds somewhere."

"I got a hundred fifty in the Hibernia Bank."

"My God, is that all? I hardly thought that we were existing so precariously. However, it is fortunate that you have kept this from me. Had I known how close we were to total penury, my nerves would have given out long ago." Ignatius scratched his paws. "I must admit, though, that the alternative for me is rather grim. I doubt very seriously whether anyone will hire me."

"What do you mean, babe? You a fine boy with a good education."

"Employers sense in me a denial of their values." He rolled over onto his back. "They fear me. I suspect that they can see that I am forced to function in a century which I loathe. That was true even when I worked for the New Orleans Public Library."

"But, Ignatius, that was the only time you worked since you got out of college, and you was only there for two weeks."

"That is exactly what I mean," Ignatius replied, aiming a paper ball at the bowl of the milk glass chandelier.

"All you did was paste them little slips in the books."

"Yes, but I had my own esthetic about pasting those slips. On some days I could only paste in three or four slips and at the same time feel satisfied with the quality of my work. The library authorities resented my integrity about the whole thing. They only wanted another animal who could slop glue on their best sellers."

"You think maybe you could get a job there again?"

"I seriously doubt it. At the time I said some rather cutting things to the woman in charge of the processing department. They even revoked my borrower's card. You must realize the fear and hatred which my *weltanschauung* instills in people." Ignatius belched. "I won't mention that misguided trip to Baton Rouge. That incident, I believe, caused me to form a mental block against working."

"They was nice to you at college, Ignatius. Now tell the truth. They let you hang around there a long time. They even let you teach a class."

"Oh, it was basically the same. Some poor white from Mississippi told the dean that I was a propagandist for the Pope, which was patently untrue. I do not support the current Pope. He does not at all fit my concept of a good, authoritarian Pope. Actually, I am opposed to the relativism of modern Catholicism quite violently. However, the boldness of this ignorant lily-white redneck fundamentalist led my other students to form a committee to demand that I grade and return their accumulated essays and examinations. There was even a small demonstration outside the window of my office. It was rather dramatic. For being such simple, ignorant children, they managed it quite well. At the height of the demonstration I dumped all of the old papers— ungraded, of course—out of the window and right onto the students' heads. The college was too small to accept this act of defiance against the abyss of contemporary academia."

"Ignatius! You never told me that."

"I did not want to excite you at the time. I also told the students that, for the sake of humanity's future, I hoped that they were all sterile." Ignatius arranged the pillows about his head. "I could never have possibly read over the illiteracies and misconceptions burbling from the dark minds of these students. It will be the same wherever I work."

61

"You can get you a good job. Wait till they see a boy with a master's degree."

Ignatius sighed heavily and said, "I see no alternative." He twisted his face into a mask of suffering. There was no use fighting Fortuna until the cycle was over. "You realize, of course, that this is all your fault. The progress of my work will be greatly delayed. I suggest that you go to your confessor and make some penance, Mother. Promise him that you will avoid the path of sin and drinking in the future. Tell him what the consequence of your moral failure has been. Let him know that you have delayed the completion of a monumental indictment against our society. Perhaps he will comprehend the magnitude of your failing. If he is my type of priest, the penance will no doubt be rather strict. However, I have learned to expect little from today's clergyman."

"I'm gonna be good, Ignatius. You'll see."

"There, there, I shall find some employment, although it will not necessarily be what you would call a *good* job. I may have some valuable insights which may benefit my employer. Perhaps the experience can give my writing a new dimension. Being actively engaged in the system which I criticize will be an interesting irony in itself." Ignatius belched loudly. "If only Myrna Minkoff could see how low I've fallen."

"What that girl's doing now?" Mrs. Reilly asked suspiciously. "I put out good money for you to go to college, and you have to pick up with somebody like that."

"Myrna is still in New York, her native habitat. No doubt she is trying to taunt the police into arresting her in some demonstration at this very moment."

"She sure used to get me nervous playing on that

guitar of hers all over this house. If she's got money like you said, maybe you shoulda married her. You two might of settled down and had a nice baby or something."

"Do I believe that such obscenity and filth is coming from the lips of my own mother?" Ignatius bellowed. "Now run along and fix me some dinner. I must be at the theater on time. It's a circus musical, a heralded excess which I have been waiting to see for some time. We study the want ads tomorrow."

"I'm so proud you gonna work at last," Mrs. Reilly said emotionally and kissed her son somewhere in his damp moustache.

IV

"Look at that old gal," Jones mused to his psyche as the bus bounced and threw him against the woman sitting beside him. "She think cause I color I gonna rape her. She about to throw her grammaw ass out the window. Whoa! I ain gonna rape nobody."

He moved discreetly away from her, crossing his legs and wishing that he could smoke on the bus. He wondered who the fat cat in the green cap was who was suddenly all over town. Where would that fat mother show up next? There was something ghostly about that green-cap freak.

"Well, I gonna tell that po-lice I gainfully employ, keep him off my back, tell him I met up with a humanitaria payin me twenty dollar a week. He say, 'That fine, boy. I'm glad to see you straighten out.' And I say, 'Hey!' And he say, 'Now maybe you be becomin a member of the community.' And I say, 'Yeah, I got me a nigger job and nigger pay. Now I really a member of the community. Now I a real nigger. No vagran. Just nigger.' Whoa! What kinda change you got?"

The old woman pulled the bell cord and got out of the seat, trying self-consciously to avoid any contact with the anatomy of Jones, who watched her writhing through the detachment of his green lenses.

"Look at that. She think I got siphlus and TB and a hard on and I gonna cut her up with a razor and lif her purse. Ooo-wee."

The sunglasses watched the woman climb off the bus into a crowd standing at the bus stop. Somewhere in the rear of the crowd an altercation was going on. A man with a rolled up newspaper in his hand was striking another man who had a long red beard and was wearing bermuda shorts. The man in the beard looked familiar. Jones felt uneasy. First there was the green-cap phantom and now this person he couldn't identify.

Jones turned from the window when the man in the red beard ran off and opened the *Life* magazine that Darlene had given him. At least Darlene had been pleasant to him at the Night of Joy. Darlene subscribed to *Life* for purposes of self-improvement and, in giving it to Jones, had suggested that he might find it helpful, too. Jones tried to plow through an editorial about American involvement in the Far East but stopped midway, wondering how something like that could help Darlene to become an exotic, the goal that she had referred to again and again. He turned back to the advertisements, for they were the things that interested him in magazines. The selection in this magazine was excellent. He liked the Aetna Life Insurance ad with the picture of the lovely home that a couple had just bought. The Yardley Shaving Lotion men looked cool and rich. That's how the magazine could help him. He wanted to look just like those men.

V

When Fortuna spins you downward, go out to a movie and get more out of life. Ignatius was about to say this to himself; then he remembered that he went to the movies almost every night, no matter which way Fortuna was spinning.

He sat at attention in the darkness of the Prytania only a few rows from the screen, his body filling the seat and protruding into the two adjoining ones. On the seat to his right he had stationed his overcoat, three Milky Ways, and two auxiliary bags of popcorn, the bags neatly rolled at the top to keep the popcorn warm and crisp. Ignatius ate his current popcorn and stared raptly at the previews of coming attractions. One of the films looked bad enough, he thought, to bring him back to the Prytania in a few days. Then the screen glowed in bright, wide technicolor, the lion roared, and the title of the excess flashed on the screen before his miraculous blue and yellow eyes. His face froze and his popcorn bag began to shake. Upon entering the theater, he had carefully buttoned the two earflaps to the top of his cap, and now the strident score of the musical assaulted his naked ears from a variety of speakers. He listened to the music, detecting two popular songs which he particularly disliked, and scrutinized the credits closely to find any names of performers who normally nauseated him.

When the credits had ended and Ignatius had noted that several of the actors, the composer, the director, the hair designer, and the assistant producer were all people whose efforts had offended him at various times in the past, there appeared in the technicolor a scene of many extras milling about a circus tent. He greedily studied the crowd and found the heroine standing near a sideshow.

"Oh, my God!" he screamed. "There she is."

The children in the rows in front of him turned and stared, but Ignatius did not notice them. The blue and yellow eyes were following the heroine, who was gaily carrying a pail of water to what turned out to be her elephant.

"This is going to be even worse than I thought," Ignatius said when he saw the elephant.

He put the empty popcorn bag to his full lips, inflated it, and waited, his eyes gleaming with reflected technicolor. A tympany beat and the soundtrack filled with violins. The heroine and Ignatius opened their mouths simultaneously, hers in song, his in a groan. In the darkness two trembling hands met violently. The popcorn bag exploded with a bang. The children shrieked.

"What's all that noise?" the woman at the candy counter asked the manager.

"He's here tonight," the manager told her, pointing across the theater to the hulking silhouette at the bottom of the screen. The manager walked down the aisle to the front rows, where the shrieking was growing wilder. Their fear having dissipated itself, the children were holding a competition of shrieking. Ignatius listened to the bloodcurdling little trebles and giggles and gloated in his dark lair. With a few mild threats, the manager quieted the front rows and then glanced down the row in which the isolated figure of Ignatius rose like some great monster among the little heads. But he was treated only to a puffy profile. The eyes that shone under the green visor were following the heroine and her elephant across the wide screen and into the circus tent.

For a while Ignatius was relatively still, reacting to the unfolding plot with only an occasional subdued snort. Then what seemed to be the film's entire cast was up on the wires. In the foreground, on a trapeze, was the heroine. She swung back and forth to a waltz. She smiled in a huge close-up. Ignatius inspected her teeth for cavities and fillings. She extended one leg. Ignatius rapidly surveyed its contours for structural defects. She began to sing about trying over and over again until you succeeded. Ignatius quivered as the philosophy of the lyrics became clear. He studied her grip on the trapeze in the hope that the camera would record her fatal plunge to the sawdust far below.

On the second chorus the entire ensemble joined in the song, smiling and singing lustily about ultimate success while they swung, dangled, flipped, and soared.

"Oh, good heavens!" Ignatius shouted, unable to contain himself any longer. Popcorn spilled down his shirt and gathered in the folds of his trousers. "What degenerate produced this abortion?"

"Shut up," someone said behind him.

"Just look at those smiling morons! If only all of those wires would snap!" Ignatius rattled the few kernels of popcorn in his last bag. "Thank God that scene is over."

When a love scene appeared to be developing, he bounded up out of his seat and stomped up the aisle to the candy counter for more popcorn, but as he returned to his seat, the two big pink figures were just preparing to kiss.

"They probably have halitosis," Ignatius announced over the heads of the children. "I hate to think of the obscene places that those mouths have doubtlessly been before!"

"You'll have to do something," the candy woman told the manager laconically. "He's worse than ever tonight."

The manager sighed and started down the aisle to where Ignatius was mumbling, "Oh, my God, their tongues are probably all over each other's capped and rotting teeth."

three

IGNATIUS STAGGERED UP the brick path to the house, climbed the steps painfully, and rang the bell. One stalk of the dead banana tree had expired and collapsed stiffly onto the hood of the Plymouth.

"Ignatius, baby," Mrs. Reilly cried when she opened the door. "What's wrong? you look like you dying."

"My valve closed on the streetcar."

"Lord, come in quick out the cold."

Ignatius shuffled miserably back to the kitchen and fell into a chair.

"The personnel manager at that insurance company treated me very insultingly."

"You didn't get the job?"

"Of course I didn't get the job."

"What happened?"

"I would rather not discuss it."

"Did you go to the other places?"

"Obviously not. Do I appear to be in a condition that would attract prospective employers? I had the good judgment to come home as soon as possible."

"Don't feel blue, precious."

" 'Blue'? I am afraid that I never feel 'blue.' "

"Now don't be nasty. You'll get a nice job. You only been on the streets a few days," his mother said and looked at him. "Ignatius, was you wearing that cap when you spoke to the insurance man?"

"Of course I was. That office was improperly heated. I don't know how the employees of that company manage to stay alive exposing themselves to that chill day after day. And then there are those florescent tubes baking their brains out and blinding them. I did not like the office at all. I tried to explain the inadequacies of the place to the personnel manager, but he seemed rather uninterested. He was ultimately very hostile." Ignatius let out a monstrous belch. "However, I told you that it would be like this. I am an anachronism. People realize this and resent it."

"Lord, babe, you gotta look up."

"Look up?" Ignatius repeated savagely. "Who has been sowing that unnatural garbage into your mind?"

"Mr. Mancuso."

"Oh, my God! I should have known. Is he an example of 'looking up'?"

"You oughta hear the whole story of that poor man's life. You oughta hear what this sergeant at the precinct's trying . . ."

"Stop!" Ignatius covered one ear and beat a fist on the table. "I will not listen to another word about that man. Throughout the centuries it has been the Mancusos of the world who have caused wars and spread diseases. Suddenly the spirit of that evil man is haunting this house. He has become your Svengali!"

"Ignatius, get a holt of yourself."

70

"I refuse to 'look up.' Optimism nauseates me. It is perverse. Since man's fall, his proper position in the universe has been one of misery."

"I ain't miserable."

"You *are*."

"No, I ain't."

"Yes, you are."

"Ignatius, I *ain't* miserable. If I was, I'd tell you."

"If I had demolished private property while intoxicated and had thereby thrown my child to the wolves, I would be beating my breast and wailing. I would kneel in penance until my knees bled. By the way, what penance has the priest given you for your sin?"

"Three Hail Mary's and a Our Father."

"Is that all?" Ignatius screamed. "Did you tell him what you did, that you halted a critical work of great brilliance?"

"I went to confession, Ignatius. I told Father everything. He says, 'It don't sound like your fault, honey. It sounds to me like you just took a little skid on a wet street.' So I told him about you. I says 'My boy says I'm the one stopping him from writing in his copybooks. He's been writing on this story for almost five years.' And Father says, 'Yeah? Well, don't sound too important to me. You tell him to get out the house and go to work.'"

"No wonder I cannot support the Church," Ignatius bellowed. "You should have been lashed right there in the confessional."

"Now tomorrow, Ignatius, you go try some other place. They got plenty jobs in the city. I was talking to Miss Marie-Louise, the old lady works in the German's. She's got a crippled brother with a car phone. He's kinda deaf, you know? He got himself a good job over by the Goodwill Industries."

"Perhaps I should try there."

"Ignatius! They only hire blind people and dummies to make brooms and things."

71

"I am certain that those people are pleasant co-workers."

"Let's us look in the afternoon's paper. Maybe they got a nice job in there!"

"If I must go out tomorrow, I am not leaving the house so early. I felt very disoriented all the while I was downtown."

"You didn't leave here until after lunch."

"Still, I was not functioning properly. I suffered several bad dreams last night. I awoke bruised and muttering."

"Here, listen to this. I been seeing this ad in the paper every day," Mrs. Reilly said, holding the newspaper very close to her eyes. " 'Clean, hard-worker man. . . .' "

"That's 'hard-work*ing*.' "

" 'Clean, hard-working man, dependable, quite type. . . .' "

" '*Quiet* type.' Give that to me," Ignatius said, snatching the paper from his mother. "It's unfortunate that you couldn't complete your education."

"Poppa was very poor."

"Please! I couldn't bear to hear that grim story again at the moment. 'Clean, hard-working, dependable, quiet type.' Good God! What kind of monster is this that they want. I am afraid that I could never work for a concern with a worldview like that."

"Read the rest, babe."

" 'Clerical work. 25–35 years old. Apply Levy Pants, Industrial Canal and River, between 8 and 9 daily.' Well, that's out. I could never get all the way down there before nine o'clock."

"Honey, if you gonna work, you gotta get up early."

72

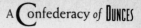

"No, Mother." Ignatius threw the paper on top of the oven. "I have been setting my sights too high. I cannot survive this type of work. I suspect that something like a newspaper route would be rather agreeable."

"Ignatius, a big man like you can't pedal around on no bike delivering newspapers."

"Perhaps you could drive me about in the car and I could toss the papers from the rear window."

"Listen, boy," Mrs. Reilly said angrily. "You gonna go try somewheres tomorrow. I mean it. The first thing you gonna do is answer this ad. You playing around, Ignatius. I know you."

"Ho hum," Ignatius yawned, exhibiting the flabby pink of his tongue. "Levy Pants sounds just as bad if not worse than the titles of the other organizations I have contacted. I can see that I am obviously beginning to scrape the bottom of the job market already."

"Just you wait, babe. You'll make good."

"Oh, my God!"

II

Patrolman Mancuso had a good idea that had been given to him by, of all people, Ignatius Reilly. He had telephoned the Reilly's house to ask Mrs. Reilly when she could go bowling with him and his aunt. But Ignatius had answered the telephone and screamed, "Stop molesting us, you mongoloid. If you had any sense, you would be investigating dens like that Night of Joy in which my beloved mother and I were mistreated and robbed. I, unfortunately, was the prey of a vicious, depraved B-girl. In addition, the proprietress is a Nazi.

We barely escaped with our lives. Go investigate that gang and let us alone, you home-wrecker."

Then Mrs. Reilly had wrestled the phone away from her son.

The sergeant would be glad to know about the place. He might even compliment Patrolman Mancuso for getting the tip. Clearing his throat, Patrolman Mancuso stood before the sergeant and said, "I got a lead on a place where they got B-girls."

"You got a lead?" the sergeant asked. "Who gave you the lead?"

Patrolman Mancuso decided against dragging Ignatius into the matter for several reasons. He settled on Mrs. Reilly.

"A lady I know," he answered.

"How come this lady knows about the place?" the sergeant asked. "Who took her to this place?"

Patrolman Mancuso couldn't say "her son." It might reopen some wounds. Why couldn't conversations with the sergeant ever go smoothly?

"She was there alone," Patrolman Mancuso said finally, trying to save the interview from becoming a shambles.

"A lady was in a place like that alone?" the sergeant screamed. "What kinda lady was this? She's probly a B-girl herself. Get outta here, Mancuso, and bring me in a suspicious character. You ain't brought in one person yet. Don't gimme no tips from B-girls. Go look in your locker. You're a soldier today. Beat it."

Patrolman Mancuso drifted sadly off to the lockers, wondering why he could never do anything right for the sergeant. When he was gone, the sergeant turned to a detective and said, "Send a couple men over to that Night of Joy some night. Someone there might've been just dumb enough to talk to Mancuso. But don't tell him. I don't want that goon taking any credit. He stays in costume until he brings me in a character."

"You know, we got another complaint on Mancuso today from somebody who says a small man wearing a sombrero pressed up against her in a bus last night," the detective said.

"No kidding," the sergeant said thoughtfully. "Well, any more complaints like that, and we *arrest* Mancuso."

III

Mr. Gonzalez turned the lights on in the small office and lit the gas heater beside his desk. In the twenty years that he had been working for Levy Pants, he had always been the first person to arrive each morning.

"It was still dark when I got here this morning," Mr. Gonzalez would say to Mr. Levy on those rare occasions when Mr. Levy was forced to visit Levy Pants.

"You must be leaving home too early," Mr. Levy would say.

"I was standing out on the steps of the office this morning talking to the milkman."

"Oh, shut up, Gonzalez. Did you get my plane ticket to Chicago for the Bears' game with the Packers?"

"I had the office all warm by the time everybody else came in for work."

"You're burning up my gas. Sit in the cold. It's good for you."

"I did two pages in the ledger this morning when I was in here all by myself. Look, I caught a rat near the water cooler. He didn't think anybody was around yet, and I hit him with a paper weight."

"Get that damned rat away from me. This place depresses me enough. Get on the phone and make my hotel reservations for the Derby."

But the criteria at Levy Pants were very low. Promptness was sufficient excuse for promotion. Mr. Gonzalez became the office manager and took control of the few dispirited clerks under him. He could never really remember the names of his clerks and typists. They seemed, at times, to come and go almost daily, with the exception of Miss Trixie, the octogenarian assistant accountant, who had been copying figures inaccurately into the Levy ledgers for almost half a century. She even wore her green celluloid visor on her way to and from work, a gesture that Mr. Gonzalez interpreted as a symbol of loyalty to Levy Pants. On Sundays she sometimes wore the visor to church, mistaking it for a hat. She had even worn it to her brother's funeral, where it was ripped from her head by her more alert and slightly younger sister-in-law. Mrs. Levy, though, had issued orders that Miss Trixie was to be retained, no matter what.

Mr. Gonzalez rubbed a rag over his desk and thought, as he did every morning at this time when the office was still chilly and deserted and the wharf rats played frenetic games among themselves within the walls, about the happiness that his association with Levy Pants had brought him. On the river the freighters gliding through the lifting mist bellowed at one another, the sound of their deep foghorns echoing among the rusting file cabinets in the office. Beside him the little heater popped and cracked as its parts grew warmer and expanded. He listened unconsciously to all the sounds that had begun his day for twenty years and lit the first of the ten cigarettes that he smoked every day. When he had smoked the cigarette down to its filter, he put it out and emptied the ashtray into the wastebasket. He always liked to impress Mr. Levy with the cleanliness of his desk.

Next to his desk was Miss Trixie's rolltop desk. Old newspapers filled every half-opened drawer. Among the little spherical formations of lint under the desk a piece of cardboard had been wedged under one corner to make the desk level. In place of Miss Trixie, a brown paper bag filled with old pieces of material, and a ball of twine occupied the chair. Cigarette butts spilled out of the ashtray on the desk. This was a mystery which Mr. Gonzalez had never been able to solve, for Miss Trixie did not smoke. He had questioned her about this several times, but had never received a coherent answer. There was something magnetic about Miss Trixie's area. It attracted whatever refuse there was in the office, and whenever pens, eyeglasses, purses, or cigarette lighters were missing they could usually be found somewhere in her desk. Miss Trixie also hoarded all of the telephone books, which were stored in some cluttered drawer in her desk.

Mr. Gonzalez was about to search Miss Trixie's area for his missing stamp pad when the door of the office opened and she shuffled in, scuffing her sneakers across the wooden floor. She had with her another paper bag that seemed to contain the same assortment of material and twine, aside from the stamp pad which was sticking out of the top of the bag. For two or three years Miss Trixie had been carrying these bags with her, sometimes accumulating three or four by the side of her desk, never disclosing their purpose or destination to anyone.

"Good morning, Miss Trixie," Mr. Gonzalez called in his effervescent tenor. "And how are we this morning?"

"Who? Oh, hello, Gomez," Miss Trixie said feebly and drifted off toward the ladies' room as if she were tacking into a gale. Miss Trixie was never perfectly vertical; she and the floor always met at an angle of less than ninety degrees.

Mr. Gonzalez took the opportunity of her disappearance to retrieve his stamp pad from the bag and discovered that it was covered with what felt and smelled like bacon grease. While he was wiping his stamp pad, he wondered how many of the other workers would appear. One day a year ago only he and Miss Trixie had shown up for work, but that was before the company had granted a five-dollar monthly increase. Still, the office help at Levy Pants often quit without even telephoning Mr. Gonzalez. This was a constant worry, and always after Miss Trixie's arrival he watched the door hopefully, especially now that the factory was supposed to begin shipment of its spring and summer line. The truth of the matter was that he needed office help desperately.

Mr. Gonzalez saw a green visor outside the door. Had Miss Trixie gone out through the factory and decided to reenter through the front door? It was like her. She had once gone to the ladies' room in the morning and been found by Mr. Gonzalez late that afternoon asleep on a pile of piece goods in the factory loft. Then the door opened, and one of the largest men that Mr. Gonzalez had ever seen entered the office. He removed the green cap and revealed thick black hair plastered to his skull with Vaseline in the style of the 1920s. When the overcoat came off, Mr. Gonzalez saw rings of fat squeezed into a tight white shirt that was vertically divided by a wide flowered tie. It appeared that Vaseline had also been applied to the moustache for it gleamed very brightly. And then there were the unbelievable blue and yellow eyes laced with the finest tracing of pinkish veins. Mr. Gonzalez prayed almost audibly that this behemoth was an applicant for a job. He was impressed and overwhelmed.

Ignatius found himself in perhaps the most disreputable office that he had ever entered. The naked light bulbs that hung irregularly from the stained ceiling cast a weak yellow light upon the warped floorboards. Old filing cabinets divided the room into several small cubicles, in each of which was a desk painted with a peculiar orange varnish. Through the dusty windows of the office there was a gray view of the Poland Avenue wharf, the Army Terminal, the Mississippi, and, far in the distance, the drydocks and the roofs of Algiers across the river. A very old woman hobbled into the room and bumped into a row of filing cabinets. The atmosphere of the place reminded Ignatius of his own room, and his valve agreed by opening joyfully. Ignatius prayed almost audibly that he would be accepted for the job. He was impressed and overwhelmed.

"Yes?" the dapper man at the clean desk asked brightly.

"Oh. I thought that the lady was in charge," Ignatius said in his most stentorian voice, finding the man the only blight in the office. "I have come in response to your advertisement."

"Oh, wonderful. Which one?" the man cried

79

enthusiastically. "We're running two in the paper, one for a woman and one for a man."

"Which one do you think I'm answering?" Ignatius hollered.

"Oh," Mr. Gonzalez said in great confusion. "I'm very sorry. I wasn't thinking. I mean, the sex doesn't matter. You could handle either job. I mean, I'm not concerned with sex."

"Please forget it," Ignatius said. He noticed with interest that the old woman was beginning to nod at her desk. Working conditions looked wonderful.

"Come sit down, please. Miss Trixie will take your coat and hat and put them in the employees' locker. We want you to feel at home at Levy Pants."

"But I haven't even spoken with you yet."

"That's all right. I'm sure that we'll see eye to eye. Miss Trixie. Miss Trixie."

"Who?" Miss Trixie cried, knocking her loaded ashtray to the floor.

"Here, I'll take your things." Mr. Gonzalez was slapped on the hand when he reached for the cap, but he was permitted to have the coat. "Isn't that a fine tie. You see very few like that anymore."

"It belonged to my departed father."

"I'm sorry to hear that," Mr. Gonzalez said and put the coat into an old metal locker in which Ignatius saw a bag like the two beside the old woman's desk. "By the way, this is Miss Trixie, one of our oldest employees. You'll enjoy knowing her."

80

Miss Trixie had fallen asleep, her white head among the old newspapers on her desk.

"Yes," Miss Trixie finally sighed. "Oh, it's you, Gomez. Is it quitting time already?"

"Miss Trixie, this is one of our new workers."

"Fine big boy," Miss Trixie said, turning her rheumy eyes up toward Ignatius. "Well fed."

"Miss Trixie has been with us for over fifty years. That will give you some idea of the satisfaction that our workers get from their association with Levy Pants. Miss Trixie worked for Mr. Levy's late father, a fine old gentleman."

"Yes, a fine old gentleman," Miss Trixie said, unable to remember the elder Mr. Levy at all anymore. "He treated me well. Always had a kind word, that man."

"Thank you, Miss Trixie," Mr. Gonzalez said quickly, like a master of ceremonies trying to end a variety act that had failed horribly.

"The company says it's going to give me a nice boiled ham for Easter," Miss Trixie told Ignatius. "I certainly hope so. They forgot all about my Thanksgiving turkey."

"Miss Trixie has stood by Levy Pants through the years," the office manager explained while the ancient assistant accountant babbled something else about the turkey.

"I've been waiting for years to retire, but every year they say I have one more to go. They work you till you drop," Miss Trixie wheezed. Then losing interest in retirement, she added, "I could have used that turkey."

She began sorting through one of her bags.

"Can you begin work today?" Mr. Gonzalez asked Ignatius.

"I don't believe that we have discussed anything concerning salary and so forth. Isn't that the normal procedure at this time?" Ignatius asked condescendingly.

"Well, the filing job, which is the one you'll have because we really need someone on the files, pays sixty dollars a week. Any days that you are absent due to sickness, et cetera, are deducted from your weekly wage."

"That is certainly far below the wage that I had expected." Ignatius sounded abnormally important. "I have a valve which is subject to vicissitudes which may force me to lie abed on certain days. Several more attractive organizations are currently vying for my services. I must consider them first."

"But listen," the office manager said confidentially. "Miss Trixie here earns only forty dollars a week, and she does have some seniority."

"She does look rather worn," Ignatius said, watching Miss Trixie spread the contents of her bag on her desk and sort through the scraps. "Isn't she past retirement?"

"Sshh," Mr. Gonzalez hissed. "Mrs. Levy won't let us retire her. She thinks it's better for Miss Trixie to keep active. Mrs. Levy is a brilliant, educated woman. She's taken a correspondence course in psychology." Mr. Gonzalez let this sink in. "Now, to return to your prospects, you are very fortunate to start with the salary I quoted. This is all part of the Levy Pants Plan to attract new blood into the company. Miss Trixie, unfortunately, was hired before the plan went into effect. It was not retroactive, and therefore doesn't cover her."

82

"I hate to disappoint you, sir, but I am afraid that the salary is not adequate. An oil magnate is currently dangling thousands before me trying to tempt me to be his personal secretary. At the moment, I am trying to decide whether I can accept the man's materialistic

A onfederacy *of* DUNCES

worldview. I suspect that I am going to finally tell him, 'Yes.' "

"We'll include twenty cents a day for carfare," Mr. Gonzalez pleaded.

"Well. That does change things," Ignatius conceded. "I shall take the job temporarily. I must admit that the 'Levy Pants Plan' rather attracts me."

"Oh, that's wonderful," Mr. Gonzalez blurted. "He'll love it here, won't he, Miss Trixie?"

Miss Trixie was too preoccupied with her scraps to reply.

"I find it strange that you have not even asked for my name," Ignatius snorted.

"Oh, my goodness. I completely forgot about that. Who are you?"

That day one other office worker, the stenographer, appeared. One woman telephoned to say that she had decided to quit and go on relief instead. The others did not contact Levy Pants at all.

IV

"Take those glasses off. How the hell can you see all that crap on the floor?"

"Who wanna look at all that crap?"

"I told you to take the glasses off, Jones."

"The glasses stayin *on*." Jones bumped the push broom into a bar stool. "For twenty dollar a week, you ain running a plantation in here."

Lana Lee started snapping a rubber band around the pile of bills and making little piles of nickels that she was taking out of the cash register.

"Stop knocking that broom against the bar," she

83

screamed. "Goddamit to hell, you making me nervous."

"You want quiet sweeping, you get you a old lady. I sweep *yawng.*"

The broom bumped against the bar several more times. Then the cloud of smoke and the broom moved off across the floor.

"You oughta tell your customer use they ashtray, tell them peoples you workin a man in here below the minimal wage. Maybe they be a little considerate."

"You better be glad I'm giving you a chance, boy," Lana Lee said. "There's plenty colored boys looking for work these days."

"Yeah, and they's plenty color boy turnin vagran, too, when they see what kinda wage peoples offerin. Sometime I think if you color, it better to be a vagran."

"You better be glad you're working."

"Ever night I'm fallin on my knee."

The broom bumped against a table.

"Let me know when you finish with that sweeping," Lana Lee said. "I got a little errand I want you to run for me."

"Erran? Hey! I thought this a sweepin and moppin job." Jones blew out a cumulus formation. "What this erran shit?"

"Listen here, Jones," Lana Lee dumped a pile of nickels into the cash register and wrote down a figure on a sheet of paper. "All I gotta do is phone the police and report you're out of work. You understand me?"

"And I tell the po-lice the Night of Joy a glorify cathouse. I fall in a trap when I come to work in this place. Whoa! Now I jus waitin to get some kinda evidence. When I do, I really gonna flap my mouth at the precinct."

"Watch your tongue."

"Times changin," Jones said, adjusting his sunglasses. "You cain scare color peoples no more. I got me some peoples form a human chain in front your door, drive away your business, get you on the TV news. Color peoples took enough horseshit already, and for twenty dollar a week you ain piling no more on. I getting pretty tire of bein vagran or workin below the minimal wage. Get somebody else run your erran."

"Aw, knock it off and finish my floor. I'll get Darlene to go."

"That po gal." Jones explored a booth with the broom. "Hustlin water, runnin erran. Whoa!"

"Ring up the precinct about her. She's a B-drinker."

"I waitin till I can ring up the precinct about *you*. Darlene don *wanna* be a B-drinker. She *force* to be a B-drinker. She say she wanna go in show biz."

"Yeah? Well, with the brains that girl's got she's lucky they haven't shipped her off to the funny farm."

"She be better off there."

"She'd be better off if she just put that mind of hers to selling my liquor and quit with the dancing crap. I can just imagine what somebody like her would do on my stage. Darlene's the kinda person ruin your investment if you don't watch her."

The padded door banged open and a young boy clicked into the bar, scraping the metal taps on his flamenco boots across the floor.

"Well, it's about time," Lana said to him.

85

"You got a new jig, huh?" The boy looked out at Jones through his swirls of oiled hair. "What happened to the last one? He die or something?"

"Honey," said Lana blandly.

The boy opened a flashy hand-tooled wallet and gave Lana a number of bills.

"Everything went okay, George?" she asked him. "The orphans liked them?"

"They liked the one on the desk with the glasses on. They thought it was some kinda teacher or something. I want only that one this time."

"You think they want another like that?" Lana asked with interest.

"Yeah. Why not? Maybe one with a blackboard and a book. You know. Doing something with a piece of chalk."

The boy and Lana smiled at each other.

"I get the picture," Lana said and winked.

"Hey, you a junkie?" the boy called to Jones. "You look like a junkie to me."

"You be lookin pretty junky with a Night of Joy broom stickin out your ass," Jones said very slowly. "Night of Joy broom old, they good and splintery."

"Okay, okay," Lana screamed. "I don't want a race riot in here. I got an investment to protect."

"You better tell your little ofay kid friend move along." Jones blew some smoke on the two. "I ain takin no insult with this kinda job."

"Come on, George," Lana said. She opened the cabinet under the bar and gave George a package wrapped in brown paper. "This is the one you want. Now go on. Beat it."

George winked at her and banged out the door.

"That suppose to be a messenger for the orphans?"

Jones asked. "I like to see the orphans he operatin for. I bet the United Fun don know about them orphans."

"What the hell are you talking about?" Lana asked angrily. She studied Jones's face, but the glasses prevented her reading anything there. "There's nothing wrong with a little charity. Now get back on my floor."

Lana started to make sounds, like the imprecations of a priestess, over the bills that the boy had given her. Whispered numerals and words floated upward from her coral lips, and, closing her eyes, she copied some figures onto a pad of paper. Her fine body, itself a profitable investment through the years, bent reverently over the formica top altar. Smoke, like incense, rose from the cigarette in the ashtray at her elbow, curling upward with her prayers, up above the host which she was elevating in order to study the date of its minting, the single silver dollar that lay among the offerings. Her bracelet tinkled, calling communicants to the altar, but the only one in the temple had been excommunicated from the Faith because of his parentage and continued mopping. An offering fell to the floor, the host, and Lana knelt to venerate and retrieve it.

"Hey, watch out," Jones called, violating the sanctity of the rite. "You droppin your profit from the orphans, butterfinger."

"Did you see where it went to, Jones?" she asked. "See if you can find it."

Jones rested his mop against the bar and scouted for the coin, squinting through his sunglasses and smoke.

"Ain this the shit," he mumbled to himself while the two searched the floor. "Ooo-wee!"

87

"I found it," Lana said emotionally. "I got it."

"Whoa! I'm sure glad you did. Hey! You better not be droppin silver dollars on the floor like that, Night of Joy be going bankrup. You be havin trouble meetin that big payroll."

"And why don't you try keeping your mouth shut, boy?"

"Say, who you callin 'boy'?" Jones took the handle of the broom and pushed vigorously toward the altar. "You ain Scarla O'Horror."

V

Ignatius eased himself into the taxi and gave the driver the Constantinople Street address. From the pocket of his overcoat he took a sheet of Levy Pants stationery, and borrowing the driver's clipboard for a desk, he began to write as the taxi joined the dense traffic on St. Claude Avenue.

I am really quite fatigued as my first working day draws to a close. I do not wish to suggest, however, that I am disheartened or depressed or defeated. For the first time in my life I have met the system face to face, fully determined to function within its context as an observer and critic in disguise, so to speak. Were there more firms like Levy Pants, I do believe that America's working forces would be better adjusted to their tasks. The obviously reliable worker is completely unmolested. Mr. Gonzalez, my "boss," is rather a cretin, but is nonetheless quite pleasant. He seems eternally apprehensive, certainly too apprehensive to criticize any worker's performance of duty. Actually, he will accept anything, almost, and is therefore appealingly democratic in his retarded way. As an example of this, Miss Trixie, our Earth Mother of the world of commerce, inadvertently set flame to some important orders in the process of lighting a heater. Mr.

Gonzalez was quite tolerant of this *gaffe* when one considers that the company of late has been receiving fewer and fewer orders and that the orders were a demand from Kansas City for some five hundred dollars ($500!) worth of our product. We must remember, though, that Mr. Gonzalez is under orders from that mysterious tycooness, the reputedly brilliant and learned Mrs. Levy, to treat Miss Trixie well and to make her feel active and wanted. But he has also been most courteous to me, permitting me to have my will among the files.

I intend to draw Miss Trixie out rather shortly; I suspect that this Medusa of capitalism has many valuable insights and more than one pithy observation to offer.

The only sour note—and here I degenerate into slang to more properly set the mood for the creature whom I am about to discuss—was Gloria, the stenographer, a young and brazen tart. Her mind was reeling with misconceptions and abysmal value judgments. After she had made one or two bold and unsolicited comments about my person and bearing, I drew Mr. Gonzalez aside to tell him that Gloria was planning to quit without notice at the end of the day. Mr. Gonzalez, thereupon, grew quite manic and fired Gloria immediately, affording himself an opportunity at authority which, I could see, he rarely enjoyed. Actually, it was the awful sound of Gloria's stake-like heels that led me to do what I did. Another day of that clatter would have sealed my valve for good. Then, too, there was all of that mascara and lipstick and other vulgarities which I would rather not catalogue.

I have many plans for my filing department and have taken—from among the many empty ones—a desk near a window. There I sat with my little gas heater at full force throughout the afternoon, watching the ships from many an exotic port steaming through the cold, dark waters of the harbor. Miss Trixie's light snore and the furious typing of Mr. Gonzalez provided a pleasant counterpoint to my reflections.

Mr. Levy did not appear today; I am given to understand that he visits the business rarely, that he is actually, as Mr. Gonzalez puts it, "trying to sell out as soon as possible." Perhaps the three of us (for I shall endeavor to make Mr. Gonzalez dismiss the other workers if they arrive tomorrow; too many people in that office will probably prove distracting)

89
····

in the office can revitalize the business and restore the faith of Mr. Levy The Younger. I have several excellent ideas already, and I know that I, for one, will eventually make Mr. Levy decide to put his heart and soul in the firm.

I have, incidentally, made a very shrewd bargain with Mr. Gonzalez: I convinced him that because I had helped him save the expense of Gloria's salary, he could respond by transporting me to and fro by taxi. The haggling that ensued was a blot upon an otherwise pleasant day, but I finally won my point by explaining to the man the dangers of my valve and of my health in general.

So we see that even when Fortuna spins us downward, the wheel sometimes halts for a moment and we find ourselves in a good, small cycle within the larger bad cycle. The universe, of course, is based upon the principle of the circle within the circle. At the moment, I am in an inner circle. Of course, smaller circles within this circle are also possible.

Ignatius gave the driver the clipboard and a variety of instructions upon speed, direction, and shifting. By the time they had reached Constantinople Street there was a hostile silence in the taxi, which was only broken by the driver's request for the fare.

As Ignatius pulled himself angrily up and out of the taxi, he saw his mother coming down the street. She was wearing her short pink topper and the small red hat that tilted over one eye so that she looked like a refugee starlet from the *Golddiggers* film series. Ignatius noticed hopelessly that she had added a dash of color by pinning a wilted poinsettia to the lapel of her topper. Her brown wedgies squeaked with discount price defiance, as she walked redly and pinkly along the broken brick sidewalk. Even though he had been seeing her outfits for years, the sight of his mother in full regalia always slightly appalled his valve.

"Oh, honey," Mrs. Reilly said breathlessly when

they met by the rear bumper of the Plymouth, which blocked all sidewalk traffic. "A terrible thing's happened."

"Oh, my God. What is it now?"

Ignatius imagined it was something in his mother's family, a group of people who tended to suffer violence and pain. There was the old aunt who had been robbed of fifty cents by some hoodlums, the cousin who had been struck by the Magazine streetcar, the uncle who had eaten a bad cream puff, the godfather who had touched a live wire knocked loose in a hurricane.

"It's poor Miss Annie next door. This morning she took a little fainting spell in the alley. Nerves, babe. She says you woke her up this morning playing on your banjo."

"That is a lute, not a banjo," Ignatius thundered. "Does she think that I'm one of these perverse Mark Twain characters?"

"I just come from seeing her. She's staying over by her son's house on St. Mary Street."

"Oh, that offensive boy." Ignatius climbed the steps ahead of his mother. "Well, thank God Miss Annie has left for a while. Now perhaps I can play my lute without her rasping denunciations assailing me from across the alley."

"I stopped off at Lenny's and bought her a nice little pair of beads filled with Lourdes water."

"Good grief. Lenny's. Never in my life have I seen a shop filled with so much religious hexerei. I suspect that that jewelry shop is going to be the scene of a miracle before long. Lenny himself may ascend."

"Miss Annie loved them beads, boy. Right away she started saying a rosary."

"No doubt that was better than conversing with you."

"Have a chair, babe, and I'll fix you something to eat."

"In the confusion of Miss Annie's collapse, you seem to have forgotten that you shipped me off to Levy Pants this morning."

"Oh, Ignatius, what happened?" Mrs. Reilly asked, putting a match to a burner that she had turned on several seconds before. There was a localized explosion on the top of the stove. "Lord, I almost got myself burnt."

"I am now an employee of Levy Pants."

"Ignatius!" his mother cried, circling his oily head in a clumsy pink woolen embrace that crushed his nose. Tears welled in her eyes. "I'm so proud of my boy."

"I'm quite exhausted. The atmosphere in that office is hypertense."

"I knew you'd make good."

"Thank you for your confidence."

"How much Levy Pants is gonna pay you, darling?"

"Sixty American dollars a week."

"Aw, that's all? Maybe you should of looked around some more."

"There are wonderful opportunities for advancement, wonderful plans for the alert young man. The salary may soon change."

"You think so? Well, I'm still proud, babe. Take off your overcoat." Mrs. Reilly opened a can of Libby's stew and tossed it in the pot. "They got any cute girls working there?"

Ignatius thought of Miss Trixie and said, "Yes, there is one."

"Single?"

"She appears to be."

Mrs. Reilly winked at Ignatius and threw his overcoat on top of the cupboard.

"Look, honey, I put a fire under this stew. Open you a can of peas, and they's bread in the icebox. I got a cake from the German's, too, but I can't remember right off where I put it. Take a look around the kitchen. I gotta go."

"Where are you going now?"

"Mr. Mancuso and his aunt, they gonna pick me up in a few minutes. We going down by Fazzio's to bowl."

"What?" Ignatius screamed. "Is that true?"

"I'll be in early. I told Mr. Mancuso I can't stay out late. And his aunt's a grammaw, so I guess she needs her sleep."

"This is certainly a fine reception that I am given after my first day of work," Ignatius said furiously. "You can't bowl. You have arthritis or something. This is ridiculous. Where are you going to eat?"

"I can get me some chili down by the bowling alley." Mrs. Reilly was already going to her room to change clothes. "Oh, honey, a letter come for you today from New York. I put it behind the coffee can. It looks like it came from that Myrna girl because the envelope's all dirty and smudged up. How come that Myrna's gotta send out mail looking like that? I thought you said her poppa's got money."

"You can't go bowling," Ignatius bellowed. "This is the most absurd thing that you have ever done."

Mrs. Reilly's door slammed. Ignatius found the envelope and tore it to shreds in opening it. He pulled out some art theater's year-old schedule for a summer film festival. On the reverse side of the rumpled schedule

93

there was a letter written in the uneven and angular hand that constituted Minkoffian penmanship. Myrna's habit of writing to editors rather than friends was always reflected in her salutation:

Sirs:
What is this strange, frightening letter that you have written me, Ignatius? How can I contact the Civil Liberties Union with the little evidence that you have given me? I can't imagine why a policeman would try to arrest you. You stay in your room all the time. I might have believed the arrest if you hadn't written about that "automobile accident." If both of your wrists were broken, how could you write me a letter?

Let us be honest with each other, Ignatius. I do not believe a word of what I read. But I am frightened—for you. The fantasy about the arrest has all the classic paranoid qualities. You are aware, of course, that Freud linked paranoia with homosexual tendencies.

"Filth!" Ignatius shouted.

However, we won't go into that aspect of the fantasy because I know how dedicated you are in your opposition to sex of any sort. Still your emotional problem is very apparent. Since you flunked that interview for the teaching job in Baton Rouge (meanwhile blaming it on the bus and things—a transferral of guilt), you have probably suffered feelings of failure. This "automobile accident" is a new crutch to help you make excuses for your meaningless, impotent existence. Ignatius, you must *identify* with something. As I've told you time and again, you must commit yourself to the crucial problems of the times.

"Ho hum," Ignatius yawned.

Subconsciously you feel that you must attempt to explain away your failure, as an intellectual and soldier of ideas, to actively participate in critical social movements. Also, a satisfying sexual encounter would purify your mind and body. You need the therapy of sex desperately. I'm afraid—from what I know about clinical cases like yours—that you may end up a psychosomatic invalid like Elizabeth B. Browning.

"How unspeakably offensive," Ignatius spluttered.

I don't feel much sympathy for you. You have closed your mind to both love and society. At the moment my every waking hour is spent in helping some dedicated friends raise money for a bold and shattering movie that they are planning to film about an interracial marriage. Although it will be a low-budget number, the script itself is chock full of disturbing truths and has the most fascinating tonalities and ironies. It was written by Shmuel, a boy I've known since Taft High days. Shmuel will also play the husband in the movie. We have found a girl from the streets of Harlem to play the wife. She is such a real, vital person that I have made her my very closest friend. I discuss her racial problems with her constantly, drawing her out even when she doesn't feel like discussing them—and I can tell how fervently she appreciates these dialogues with me.

There is a sick, reactionary villain in the script, an Irish landlord who refuses to rent to the couple, who by this time have been married in this subdued Ethical Culture ceremony. The landlord lives in this little womb-room whose walls are covered with pictures of the Pope and stuff like that. In other words, the audience will have no trouble reading him as soon as they get one glimpse at that room. We have not cast the landlord yet. You, of course, would be fantastic for the part. You see, Ignatius, if you would just decide to cut the umbilical cord that binds you to that stagnant city, that mother of yours, and that bed, you could be up here having opportunities like this. Are you interested in the part? We can't pay much, but you can stay with me.

I may play a little mood music or protest music on my guitar for the soundtrack. I hope that we can finally get this magnificent project on film soon because Leola, the unbelievable girl from Harlem, is beginning to bug us about salary.

95
....

Already I've bled about $1,000 from my father, who is suspicious (as usual) of the whole enterprise.

Ignatius, I've humored you long enough in our correspondence. Don't write to me again until you've taken part. I hate cowards.

M. Minkoff

P.S. Also write if you'd like to play the landlord.

"I'll show this offensive trollop," Ignatius mumbled, throwing the art theater schedule into the fire beneath the stew.

f o u r

LEVY PANTS WAS TWO structures fused into one macabre unit. The front of the plant was a brick commercial building of the nineteenth century with a mansard roof that bulged out into several rococo dormer windows, the panes of which were mostly cracked. Within this section the office occupied the third floor, a storage area the second, and refuse the first. Attached to this building, which Mr. Gonzalez referred to as "the brain center," was the factory, a barnlike prototype of an airplane hangar. The two smokestacks that rose from the factory's tin roof leaned apart at an angle that formed an outsized rabbit-eared television antenna, an antenna that received no hopeful electronic signal from the outside world but instead discharged occasional smoke of a very sickly shade. Alongside the neat gray wharf sheds that lined the river and canal across the railroad tracks, Levy Pants huddled, a silent and smoky plea for urban renewal.

Within the brain center there was more than the usual amount of activity. Ignatius was tacking to a post near his files a wide cardboard sign that said in bold blue Gothic lettering:

DEPARTMENT OF RESEARCH AND REFERENCE
I. J. REILLY, CUSTODIAN

He had neglected the morning filing to make the sign, spreading himself upon the floor with the cardboard and blue poster paint and painting meticulously for more than an hour. Miss Trixie had stepped on the sign during one of her occasional pointless tours of the office, but the damage was limited to only a small sneaker print on one corner of the cardboard. Still, Ignatius found the tiny imprint offensive, and over it he painted a dramatic and stylized version of a fleur-de-lis.

"Isn't that nice," Mr. Gonzalez said when Ignatius had stopped hammering. "It gives the office a certain tone."

"What does it mean?" Miss Trixie demanded, standing directly beneath the sign and examining it frantically.

"It is simply a guidepost," Ignatius said proudly.

"I don't understand all this," Miss Trixie said. "What's going on around here?" She turned to Ignatius. "Gomez, who is this person?"

"Miss Trixie, you know Mr. Reilly. He's been working with us for a week now."

"Reilly? I thought it was Gloria."

"Go back and work on your figures," Mr. Gonzalez told her. "We have to send that statement to the bank before noon."

"Oh, yes, we must send that statement," Miss Trixie agreed and shuffled off to the ladies' room.

"Mr. Reilly, I don't want to pressure you," Mr. Gonzalez said cautiously, "but I do notice that you have quite a pile of material on your desk that hasn't been filed yet."

"Oh, that. Yes. Well, when I opened the first drawer this morning, I was greeted by a rather large rat which seemed to be devouring the Abelman's Dry

Goods folder. I thought it politic to wait until he was sated. I would hate to contract the bubonic plague and lay the blame upon Levy Pants."

"Quite right," Mr. Gonzalez said anxiously, his dapper person quivering at the prospect of an on-the-job accident.

"In addition, my valve has been misbehaving and has prevented me from bending over to reach the lower drawers."

"I have just the thing for that," Mr. Gonzalez said and went into the little office storeroom to get, Ignatius imagined, some type of medicine. But he returned with one of the smallest metal stools that Ignatius had ever seen. "Here. The person who used to work on the files used to wheel back and forth on this along the lower drawers. Try it."

"I don't believe that my particular body structure is easily adaptable to that type of device," Ignatius observed, a gimlet eye fixed upon the rusting stool. Ignatius had always had a poor sense of balance, and ever since his obese childhood, he had suffered a tendency to fall, trip, and stumble. Until he was five years old and had finally managed to walk in an almost normal manner, he had been a mass of bruises and hickeys. "However, for the sake of Levy Pants, I shall try."

Ignatius squatted lower and lower until his great buttocks touched the stool, his knees reaching almost to his shoulders. When he was at last nestled upon his perch, he looked like an eggplant balanced atop a thumb tack.

"This will never do. I feel quite uncomfortable."

"Give it a try," Mr. Gonzalez said brightly.

Propelling himself with his feet, Ignatius traveled anxiously along the side of the files until one of the miniature wheels lodged in a crack. The stool tipped slightly and then turned over, dumping Ignatius heavily to the floor.

"Oh, my God!" he bellowed. "I think I've broken my back."

"Here," Mr. Gonzalez cried in his terrorized tenor. "I'll help you up."

"No! You must never move a person with a broken back unless you have a stretcher. I won't be paralyzed through your incompetence."

"Please try to get up, Mr. Reilly." Mr. Gonzalez looked at the mound at his feet. His heart sank. "I'll help you. I don't think you're badly injured."

"Let me alone," Ignatius screamed. "You fool. I refuse to spend the remainder of my life in a wheel chair."

Mr. Gonzalez felt his feet turn cold and numb.

The thud of Ignatius' fall had attracted Miss Trixie from the ladies' room; she came around the files and tripped on the mountain of supine flesh.

"Oh, dear," she said feebly. "Is Gloria dying, Gomez?"

"No," Mr. Gonzalez said sharply.

"Well, I'm certainly glad of that," Miss Trixie said, stepping onto one of Ignatius' outstretched hands.

"Good grief!" Ignatius thundered and sprang into a sitting position. "The bones in my hand are crushed. I'll never be able to use it again."

"Miss Trixie is very light," the office manager told Ignatius. "I don't think she could have hurt you much."

"Has she ever stepped on you, you idiot? How would you know?"

Ignatius sat at the feet of his co-workers and studied his hand.

"I suspect that I won't be able to use this hand again today. I had better go home immediately and bathe it."

"But the filing has to be done. Look how behind you are already."

"Are you talking about filing at a time like this? I am prepared to contact my attorneys and have them sue you for making me get on that obscene stool."

"We'll help you up, Gloria." Miss Trixie assumed what was apparently a hoisting position. She spread her sneakers far apart, toes pointing outward, and squatted like a Balinese dancer.

"Get up," Mr. Gonzalez snapped at her. "You're going to fall over."

"No," she answered through tight, withered lips. "I'm going to help Gloria. Get down on that side, Gomez. We'll just grab Gloria by the elbows."

Ignatius watched passively while Mr. Gonzalez squatted on his other side.

"You are distributing your weight incorrectly," he told them didactically. "If you are going to attempt to raise me, that position offers you no leverage. I suspect that the three of us will be injured. I suggest that you try a standing position. In that way you can easily bend over and hoist me."

"Don't be nervous, Gloria," Miss Trixie said, rocking back and forth on her haunches. Then she fell forward onto Ignatius, throwing him on his back once again. The edge of her celluloid visor hit him in the throat.

"Oof," gurgled from somewhere in the depths of Ignatius' throat. "Braah."

"Gloria!" Miss Trixie wheezed. She looked into the full face directly beneath hers. "Gomez, call a doctor."

"Miss Trixie, get off Mr. Reilly," the office manager hissed from where he squatted beside his two underlings.

"Braah."

"What are you people doing down there on the floor?" a man asked from the door. Mr. Gonzalez' chipper face hardened into a mask of horror, and he squeaked, "Good morning, Mr. Levy. We're so glad to see you."

"I just came in to see if I have any personal mail. I'm driving back to the coast right away. What's this big sign over here for? Somebody's going to get his eye knocked out on that thing."

"Is that Mr. Levy?" Ignatius called from the floor. He could not see the man over the row of filing cabinets. "Braah. I have been wanting to meet him."

Shedding Miss Trixie, who slumped to the floor, Ignatius struggled to his feet and saw a sportily dressed middle-aged man holding the handle of the office door so that he could flee as rapidly as he had entered.

"Hello there," Mr. Levy said casually. "New worker, Gonzalez?"

"Oh, yes sir. Mr. Levy, this is Mr. Reilly. He's very efficient. A whiz. As a matter of fact, he's made it possible for us to do away with several other workers."

"Braah."

"Oh, yeah, the name on this sign." Mr. Levy gave Ignatius a strange look.

102

"I have taken an unusual interest in your firm," Ignatius said to Mr. Levy. "The sign which you noticed upon entering is only the first of several innovations which I plan. Braah. I will change your mind about this firm, sir. Mark my word."

"You don't say?" Mr. Levy studied Ignatius with certain curiosity. "What about the mail, Gonzalez?"

"There's not much. You received your new credit cards. Transglobal Airlines sent you a certificate making you an honorary pilot for flying one hundred hours with them." Mr. Gonzalez opened his desk and gave Mr. Levy the mail. "There's also a brochure from a hotel in Miami."

"You'd better start making my spring practice reservations. I gave you my itinerary of practice camps, didn't I?"

"Yes, sir. By the way, I have some letters for you to sign. I had to write a letter to Abelman's Dry Goods. We always have trouble with them."

"I know. What do those crooks want now?"

"Abelman claims that the last lot of trousers we shipped him were only two feet long in the leg. I'm trying to straighten out the matter."

"Yeah? Well, stranger things have happened around this place," Mr. Levy said quickly. The office was already beginning to depress him. He had to get out. "Better check with that foreman in the factory. What's his name? Look, suppose you sign those letters like always. I have to go." Mr. Levy pulled the door open. "Don't work these kids too hard, Gonzalez. So long, Miss Trixie. My wife asked about you."

Miss Trixie was sitting on the floor relacing one of her sneakers.

"Miss Trixie," Mr. Gonzalez screamed. "Mr. Levy is talking to you."

"Who?" Miss Trixie snarled. "I thought you said he was dead."

"I hope that you will see some vast changes the

next time that you drop in on us," Ignatius said. "We are going to revitalize, as it were, your business."

"Okay. Take it easy," Mr. Levy said and slammed the door.

"He's a wonderful man," Mr. Gonzalez told Ignatius fervently. From a window the two watched Mr. Levy get into his sports car. The motor roared, and Mr. Levy sped away within a few seconds, leaving a settling cloud of blue exhaust.

"Perhaps I shall get to the filing," Ignatius said when he found himself staring out the window at only an empty street. "Will you please sign that correspondence so that I can file the carbon copies. It should now be safe to approach what that rodent has left of the Abelman folder."

Ignatius spied while Mr. Gonzalez, painstaking, forged *Gus Levy* to the letters.

"Mr. Reilly," Mr. Gonzalez said, carefully screwing the top onto his two-dollar pen, "I am going into the factory to speak with the foreman. Please keep an eye on things."

By *things*, Ignatius imagined that Mr. Gonzalez meant Miss Trixie, who was snoring loudly on the floor in front of the file cabinet.

"*Seguro*," Ignatius said and smiled. "A little Spanish in honor of your noble heritage."

As soon as the office manager went through the door, Ignatius rolled a sheet of Levy stationery into Mr. Gonzalez' high black typewriter. If Levy Pants was to succeed, the first step would be imposing a heavy hand upon its detractors. Levy Pants must become more militant and authoritarian in order to survive in the jungle of modern commercialism. Ignatius began to type the first step:

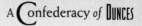

Abelman's Dry Goods
Kansas City, Missouri
U. S. A.

Mr. I. Abelman, Mongoloid, Esq.:

We have received via post your absurd comments about our trousers, the comments revealing, as they did, your total lack of contact with reality. Were you more aware, you would know or realize by now that the offending trousers were dispatched to you with our full knowledge that they were inadequate so far as length was concerned.

"Why? Why?" you are in your incomprehensible babble, unable to assimilate stimulating concepts of commerce into your retarded and blighted worldview.

The trousers were sent to you (1) as a means of testing your initiative (A clever, wide-awake business concern should be able to make three-quarter length trousers a by-word of masculine fashion. Your advertising and merchandising programs are obviously faulty.) and (2) as a means of testing your ability to meet the standards requisite in a distributor of our quality product. (Our loyal and dependable outlets can vend any trouser bearing the Levy label no matter how abominable their design and construction. You are apparently a faithless people.)

We do not wish to be bothered in the future by such tedious complaints. Please confine your correspondence to orders only. We are a busy and dynamic organization whose mission needless effrontery and harassment can only hinder. If you molest us again, sir, you may feel the sting of the lash across your pitiful shoulders.

Yours in anger,
Gus Levy, Pres.

Happily pondering the thought that the world understood only strength and force, Ignatius copied the Levy signature onto the letter with the office manager's pen, tore up Mr. Gonzalez' letter to Abelman, and slipped his own into the correspondence Outgoing box. Then he tiptoed carefully around the little inert figure of Miss Trixie, returned to the filing department, picked up the stack of still unfiled material, and threw it into the wastebasket.

II

"Hey, Miss Lee, that fat mother got him the green cap, he comin in here anymore?"

"No, thank God. It's characters like that ruin your investment."

"When your little orphan frien comin here again? Whoa! I like to fin out what goin on with them orphan. I bet they be the firs orphan the po-lice be interes in ever."

"I told you I send the orphans things. A little charity never hurt nobody. It makes you feel good."

"That really soun like Night of Joy chariddy when them orphan payin in a lotta money for whatever they gettin."

"Stop worrying about the orphans and start worrying about my floor. I got enough problems already. Darlene wants to dance. You want a raise. And I got worse problems on top of that." Lana thought of the plainclothesmen who had suddenly started to appear in the club late at night. "Business stinks."

"Yeah. I can tell that. I starvin to death in this cathouse."

"Say, Jones, you been over to the precinct lately?" Lana asked cautiously, wondering whether there was an outside chance that Jones might be leading the cops to the place. This Jones was turning out to be a headache, in spite of the low salary.

"No, I ain been visitin all my po-lice frien. I waitin till I get some good evidence." Jones shot out a nimbus formation. "I waitin for a break in the orphan case. Ooo-wee!"

Lana twisted up her coral lips and tried to imagine who had tipped off the police.

III

Mrs. Reilly could not believe that it had really happened to her. There was no television. There were no complaints. The bathroom was empty. Even the roaches seemed to have pulled up stakes. She sat at the kitchen table sipping a little muscatel and blew away the one baby roach that was starting to cross the table. The tiny body flew off the table and disappeared, and Mrs. Reilly said, "So long, darling." She poured another inch of wine, realizing for the first time that the house smelled different, too. It smelled as close as it ever did, but her son's curious personal odor, which always reminded her of the scent of old tea bags, seemed to have lifted. She lifted her glass and wondered whether Levy Pants was beginning to reek a little of used pekoe.

Suddenly Mrs. Reilly remembered the horrible night that she and Mr. Reilly had gone to the Prytania to see Clark Gable and Jean Harlow in *Red Dust*. In the heat and confusion that had followed their return home, nice Mr. Reilly had tried one of his indirect approaches, and Ignatius was conceived. Poor Mr. Reilly. He had never gone to another movie as long as he lived.

107

Mrs. Reilly sighed and looked at the floor to see whether the baby roach was still around and functioning. She was in too pleasant a mood to harm anything. While she was studying the linoleum, the telephone rang in the narrow hall. Mrs. Reilly corked her bottle and put it in the cold oven.

"Hello," she said into the telephone.

"Hey, Irene?" a woman's hoarse voice asked. "What you doing, babe? It's Santa Battaglia."

"How you making, honey?"

"I'm beat. I just finished opening four dozen ersters out in the backyard," Santa said in her rocky baritone. "That's hard work, believe me, banging that erster knife on them bricks."

"I wouldn't try nothing like that," Mrs. Reilly said honestly.

"I don't mind. When I was a little girl I use to open ersters up for my momma. She had her a little seafood stand outside the Lautenschlaeger Market. Poor momma. Right off the boat. Couldn't speak a word of English hardly. There I was just a little thing breaking them ersters open. I didn't go to no school. Not me, babe. I was right there with them ersters banging away on the banquette. Every now and then momma start banging away on me for something. We always had a lotta commotion around our stand, us."

"Your momma was very excitable, huh?"

"Poor girl. Standing there in the rain and cold with her old sunbonnet on not knowing what nobody was saying half the time. It was hard in them days, Irene. Things was tough, kid."

"You can say that again," Mrs. Reilly agreed. "We sure had us some hard times down on Dauphine Street. Poppa was very poor. He had him a job by a wagon works, but then the automobiles come in, and he gets his hand caught in a fanbelt. Many's the week we lived on red beans and rice."

"Red beans gives me gas."

"Me, too. Listen, Santa, why you called, sugar?"

"Oh, yeah, I almost forgot. You remember when we was out bowling the other night?"

"Tuesday?"

"No, it was Wednesday, I think. Anyway, it was the night Angelo got arrested and couldn't come."

"Wasn't that awful. The police arresting one of they very own."

"Yeah. Poor Angelo. He's so sweet. He sure got trouble at that precinct." Santa coughed hoarsely into the telephone. "Anyway, it was the night you come for me in that car of yours and we went to the alley alone. This morning I was over by the fish market buying them ersters, and this old man comes up to me and says, 'Wasn't you by the bowling alley the other night?' So I says, 'Yeah, mister, I go there a lot.' And he says, 'Well, I was there with my daughter and her husband and I seen you with a lady got sorta red hair.' I says, 'You mean the lady got the henna hair? That's my friend Miss Reilly. I'm learning her how to bowl.' That's all, Irene. He just tips his hat and walks out the market."

"I wonder who that could be," Mrs. Reilly said with great interest. "That's sure funny. What he looks like, babe?"

"Nice man, kinda old. I seen him around the neighborhood before taking some little kids to Mass. I think they his granchirren."

"Ain't that strange? Who'd be asking about me?"

"I don't know, kid, but you better watch out. Somebody's got they eye on you."

"Aw, Santa! I'm too old, girl."

"Listen to you. You still cute, Irene. I seen plenty men giving you the eye in the bowling alley."

"Aw, go on."

"That's the truth, kid. I ain't lying. You been stuck away with that son of yours too long."

"Ignatius says he's making good at Levy Pants," Mrs. Reilly said defensively. "I don't wanna get mixed up with no old man."

"He ain't *that* old," Santa said, sounding a little hurt. "Listen, Irene, me and Angelo coming by for you about seven tonight."

"I don't know, darling. Ignatius been telling me I oughta stay home more."

"Why you gotta stay home, girl? Angelo says he's a big man."

"Ignatius says he's afraid when I leave him alone here at night. He says he's scared of burgulars."

"Bring him along, and Angelo can learn him how to bowl, too."

"Whoo! Ignatius ain't what you'd call the sporting type," Mrs. Reilly said quickly.

"You come along anyways, huh?"

"Okay," Mrs. Reilly said finally. "I think the exercise is helping my elbow out. I'll tell Ignatius he can lock himself up in his room."

"Sure," Santa said. "Nobody's gonna hurt him."

"We ain't got nothing worth stealing anyways. I don't know where Ignatius gets them ideas of his."

"Me and Angelo be by at seven."

"Fine, and listen, precious, try and ask by the fish market who that old man is."

IV

The Levy home stood among the pines on a small rise overlooking the gray waters of Bay St. Louis. The exterior was an example of elegant rusticity; the interior was

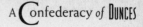

a successful attempt at keeping the rustic out entirely, a permanently seventy-five-degree womb connected to the year-round air-conditioning unit by an umbilicus of vents and pipes that silently filled the rooms with filtered and reconstituted Gulf of Mexico breezes and exhaled the Levys' carbon dioxide and cigarette smoke and ennui. The central machinery of the great life-giving unit throbbed somewhere in the acoustically tiled bowels of the home, like a Red Cross instructor giving cadence in an artificial respiration class, "*In* comes the good air, *out* goes the bad air, *in* comes the good air."

The home was as sensually comfortable as the human womb supposedly is. Every chair sank several inches at the lightest touch, foam and down surrendering abjectly to any pressure. The tufts of the acrylic nylon carpets tickled the ankles of anyone kind enough to walk on them. Beside the bar what looked like a radio dial would, upon being turned, make the lighting throughout the house as mellow or as bright as the mood demanded. Located throughout the house within easy walking distance of one another were contour chairs, a massage table, and a motorized exercising board whose many sections prodded the body with a motion that was at once gentle yet suggestive. Levy's Lodge—that was what the sign at the coast road said—was a Xanadu of the senses; within its insulated walls there was something that could gratify anything.

Mr. and Mrs. Levy, who considered each other the only ungratifying objects in the home, sat before their television set watching the colors merge together on the screen.

"Perry Como's face is all green," Mrs. Levy said

111

with great hostility. "He looks like a corpse. You'd better take this set back to the shop."

"I just brought it back from New Orleans this week," Mr. Levy said, blowing on the black hairs of his chest that he could see through the V of his terry cloth robe. He had just taken a steam bath and wanted to dry himself completely. Even with year-round air conditioning and central heating one could never be sure.

"Well, take it back again. I'm not going to go blind looking at a broken TV."

"Oh, shut up. He looks all right."

"He does not look all right. Look how green his lips are."

"It's the makeup those people use."

"You mean to tell me they put green makeup on Como's lips?"

"I don't know what they do."

"Of course you don't," Mrs. Levy said, turning her aqua marine-lidded eyes toward her husband, who was submerged somewhere among the pillows of a yellow nylon couch. She saw some terry cloth and a rubber shower clog at the end of a hairy leg.

"Don't bother me," he said. "Go play with your exercising board."

"I can't get on that thing tonight. My hair was done today."

She touched the high plasticized curls of her platinum hair.

"The hairdresser told me that I should get a wig, too," she said.

"What do you want with a wig? Look at all the hair you've got already."

"I want a brunette wig. That way I can change my personality."

"Look, you're already a brunette anyway, right? So why don't you let your hair grow out naturally and buy a blonde wig?"

"I hadn't thought of that."

"Well, think about it for a while and keep quiet. I'm tired. When I went into town today I stopped at the company. That always makes me depressed."

"What's happening there?"

"Nothing. Absolutely nothing."

"That's what I thought," Mrs. Levy sighed. "You've thrown your father's business down the drain. That's the tragedy of your life."

"Christ, who wants that old factory? Nobody's buying the kind of pants they make anymore. That's all my father's fault. When pleats came in in the thirties, he wouldn't change over from plain-front trousers. He was the Henry Ford of the garment industry. Then when the plain front came back in the fifties, he started making trousers with pleats. Now you should see what Gonzalez calls 'the new summer line.' They look like those balloon pants the clowns wear in circuses. And the fabric. I wouldn't use it for a dishrag myself."

"When we were married, I idolized you, Gus. I thought you had drive. You could have made Levy Pants really big. Maybe even an office in New York. It was handed all to you and you threw it away."

"Oh, stop all that crap. You're comfortable."

"Your father had character. I respected him."

"My father was a very mean and cheap man, a little tyrant. I had some interest in that company when I was young. I had plenty interest. Well, he destroyed all that with his tyranny. So far as I'm concerned, Levy Pants is *his* company. Let it go down the drain. He blocked every good idea I had for that firm just to prove that he

113

was the father and I was the son. If I said, 'Pleats,' he said, 'No pleats! Never!' If I said, 'Let's try some of the new synthetics,' he said, 'Synthetics over my dead body.'"

"He started peddling pants in a wagon. Look what he built that into. With your start you could have made Levy Pants nationwide."

"The nation is lucky, believe me. I spent my childhood in those pants. Anyway, I'm tired of listening to you talk. Period."

"Good. Let's keep quiet. Look, Como's lips are turning pink."

"You've never been a father figure to Susan and Sandra."

"The last time Sandra was home, she opened her purse to get cigarettes and a pack of rubbers falls on the floor right at my feet."

"That's what I'm trying to say to you. You never gave your daughters an image. No wonder they're so mixed up. *I* tried with them."

"Listen, let's not discuss Susan and Sandra. They're away at college. We're lucky we don't know what's going on. When they get tired, they'll marry some poor guy and everything will be all right."

"Then what kind of a grandfather are you going to be?"

"I don't know. Let me alone. Go get on your exercising board, get in the whirlpool bath. I'm enjoying this show."

"How can you enjoy it when the faces are all discolored."

"Let's not start that again."

"Are we going to Miami next month?"

"Maybe. Maybe we could settle there."

"And give up everything we have?"

"Give up what? They can fit your exercising board in a moving van."

"But the company."

"The company has made all the money it's ever going to make. Now is the time to sell."

"It's a good thing your father's dead. He should have lived to see this." Mrs. Levy gave the shower shoe a tragic glance. "Now I guess you'll spend all your time at the World Series or the Derby or Daytona. It's a real tragedy, Gus. A real tragedy."

"Don't try to make a big Arthur Miller play out of Levy Pants."

"Thank goodness I'm around to watch over you. Thank goodness *I* have an interest in that company. How's Miss Trixie? I hope she's still relating and functioning pretty well."

"She's still alive, and that's saying a lot for her."

"At least I have an interest in her. You would have thrown her out in the snow long ago."

"The woman should have been retired long ago."

"I told you retirement will kill her. She must be made to feel wanted and loved. That woman's a real prospect for psychic rejuvenation. I want you to bring her out here someday. I'd like to really get to work on her."

"Bring that old bag here? Are you nuts? I don't want a reminder of Levy Pants snoring in my den. She'll wet all over your couch. You can play with her by long distance."

"How typical," Mrs. Levy sighed. "How I've stood this heartlessness through the years I'll never know."

"I've already let you keep Trixie at the office, where I know she must drive that Gonzalez nuts all day long.

When I went there this morning everybody was on the floor. Don't ask me what they were doing. It could have been anything." Mr. Levy whistled through his teeth. "Gonzalez is on the moon, as usual, but you should see this other character working in there. I don't know where they got him from. You wouldn't believe your eyes, believe me. I'm afraid to guess what those three clowns do in that office all day long. It's a wonder nothing's happened already."

V

Ignatius had decided against going to the Prytania. The movie being shown was a widely praised Swedish drama about a man who was losing his soul, and Ignatius was not particularly interested in seeing it. He would have to speak with the manager of the theater about booking such dull fare.

He checked the bolt on his door and wondered when his mother would be coming home. Suddenly she was going out almost every night. But Ignatius had other considerations at the moment. Opening his desk, he looked at a pile of articles he had once written with an eye on the magazine market. For the journals of opinion there were "Boethius Observed" and "In Defense of Hroswitha: To Those Who Say She Did Not Exist." For the family magazines he had written "The Death of Rex" and "Children, the Hope of the World." In an attempt to crack the Sunday supplement market he had done "The Challenge of Water Safety," "The Danger of Eight-Cylinder Automobiles," "Abstinence, the Safest Method of Birth Control," and "New Orleans, City of Romance and Culture." As he looked through the old manuscripts, he wondered why he had failed to send any of them off, for each was excellent in its own way.

There was a new, extremely commercial project at hand, though. Ignatius quickly cleared the desk by brushing the magazine articles and Big Chief tablets smartly to the floor with one sweep of his paws. He placed a new looseleaf folder before him and printed slowly on its rough cover with a red crayon THE JOURNAL OF A WORKING BOY, OR, UP FROM SLOTH. When he had finished that, he tore the Blue Horse bands from the stacks of new lined paper and placed them in the folder. With a pencil he punched holes in the sheets of Levy stationery which already held some notes and inserted them in the front section of the folder. Taking up his Levy Pants ballpoint pen, he began writing on the first sheet of new Blue Horse paper:

Dear Reader,
Books are immortal sons defying their sires.

—Plato

I find, dear reader, that I have grown accustomed to the hectic pace of office life, an adjustment which I doubted I could make. Of course, it is true that in my brief career at Levy Pants, Limited, I have succeeded in initiating several work-saving methods. Those of you who are fellow office workers and find yourselves reading this incisive journal during a coffee break or such might take note of one or two of my innovations. I direct these observations to officers and tycoons, also.

I have taken to arriving at the office one hour later than I am expected. Therefore, I am far more rested and refreshed when I do arrive, and I avoid that bleak first hour of the working day during which my still sluggish senses and body make every chore a penance. I find that in arriving later, the work which I do perform is of a much higher quality.

My innovation in connection with the filing system must remain secret for the moment, for it is rather revolutionary, and I shall have to see how it works out. In theory the innovation is magnificent. However, I will say that the brittle and yellowing papers in the files constitute a fire hazard. A more special aspect that may not apply in all cases is that my files apparently are a tenement for assorted vermin. The bubonic plague is a valid Medieval fate; I do believe, though, that contracting the plague in this dreadful century would be only ludicrous.

Today our office was at last graced by the presence of our lord and master, Mr. G. Levy. To be quite honest, I found him rather casual and unconcerned. I brought to his attention the sign (Yes, reader, it has finally been painted and posted; a rather imperial fleur-de-lis now gives it added significance.), but that, too, elicited little interest on his part. His stay was brief and not at all businesslike, but who are we to question the motives of these giants of commerce whose whims rule the course of our nation. In time he will learn of my devotion to his firm, of my dedication. My example, in turn, may lead him to once again believe in Levy Pants.

La Trixie still keeps her own counsel, thereby proving herself even wiser than I had thought. I suspect that this woman knows a great deal, that her apathy is a façade for her seeming resentment against Levy Pants. She grows more coherent when she speaks of retirement. I have noticed that she needs a new pair of white socks, her current pair having grown rather gray. Perhaps I shall gift her with a pair of absorbent white athletic socks in the near future; this gesture may affect her and lead her to conversation. She seems to have grown fond of my cap, for she has taken to wearing it rather than her celluloid visor on occasion.

As I have told you in earlier installments, I was emulating the poet Milton by spending my youth in seclusion, meditation, and study in order to perfect my craft of writing as he did; my mother's cataclysmic intemperance has thrust me into the world in the most cavalier manner; my system is still in a state of flux. Therefore, I am still in the process of adapting myself to the tension of the working world. As soon as my system becomes used to the office, I shall take the giant step of visiting the factory, the bustling heart of Levy Pants. I have heard more than a little hissing and roaring through the factory door, but my presently somewhat enervated condition precludes a descent into that particular inferno at the moment. Now and then some factory worker straggles into the office to illiterately plead some cause (usually the drunkenness of the foreman, a chronic tosspa). When I am once again whole, I shall visit those factory people; I have deep and abiding convictions concerning social action. I am certain that I can perhaps do something to aid these factory folk. I cannot abide those who would act cowardly in the face of a social injustice. I believe in bold and shattering commitment to the problems of our times.

Social note: I have sought escape in the Prytania on more than one occasion, pulled by the attractions of some technicolored horrors, filmed abortions that were offenses against any criteria of taste and decency, reels and reels of perversion and blasphemy that stunned my disbelieving eyes, that shocked my virginal mind, and sealed my valve.

My mother is currently associating with some undesirables who are attempting to transform her into an athlete of sorts, depraved specimens of mankind who regularly bowl their way to oblivion. At times I find carrying on my blossoming business career rather painful, suffering as I do from these distractions at home.

Health note: My valve did close quite violently this afternoon when Mr. Gonzalez asked me to add a column of figures for him. When he saw the state into which I was thrown by the request, he thoughtfully added the figures himself. I tried not to make a scene, but my valve got the better of me. That office manager could, incidentally, develop into something of a nuisance.

> Until later,
> Darryl, Your Working Boy

Ignatius read what he had just written with pleasure. The *Journal* had all sorts of possibilities. It could be a contemporary, vital, real document of a young man's problems. At last he closed the looseleaf folder and contemplated a reply to Myrna, a slashing, vicious attack upon her being and worldview. It would be better to wait until he had visited the factory and seen what possibilities for social action there were there. Such boldness had to be handled properly; he might be able to do something with the factory workers which would make Myrna look like a reactionary in the field of social action. He had to prove his superiority to the offensive minx.

Picking up his lute, he decided to relax in song for a moment. His massive tongue rolled up over his moustache in preparation and, strumming, he began to sing, "Tarye no longer; toward thyn heritage/ Hast on thy weye, and be of ryght good chere."

"Shut up!" Miss Annie hollered through her closed shutters.

"How dare you!" Ignatius replied, ripping open his own shutters and looking out into the dark, cold alley. "Open up there. How dare you hide behind those shutters."

He ran furiously to the kitchen, filled a pot with water, and rushed back to his room. Just as he was about to throw the water on Miss Annie's still unopened shutters, he heard a car door slam out on the street. Some people were coming down the alley. Ignatius closed his shutters and turned off the light, listening to his mother speaking to someone. Patrolman Mancuso said something as they passed under his window, and a woman's hoarse voice said, "It looks safe to me, Irene. There ain't no lights on. He must of gone to the show."

Ignatius slipped his overcoat on and ran down the hall to the front door as they were opening the kitchen door. He went down the front steps and saw Patrolman Mancuso's white Rambler parked before the house. Bending over with great effort, Ignatius stuck a finger into the valve of one of the tires until the hissing stopped and the tire's bottom pancaked across the brick gutter. Then he walked down the alley, which was just wide enough for his bulk, to the rear of the house.

Bright lights were burning in the kitchen, and he could hear his mother's cheap radio through the closed window. Ignatius climbed the back steps silently and looked in through the greasy glass of the back door. His mother and Patrolman Mancuso were sitting at the table around an almost full fifth of Early Times. Patrolman Mancuso looked more downtrodden than ever, but Mrs. Reilly was tapping one foot on the linoleum and laughing shyly at what she was watching in the center of the room. A stocky woman with kinky gray hair was dancing alone on the linoleum, shaking her pendulous breasts, which were slung in a white bowling blouse. Her bowling shoes pounded the floor purposefully, carrying the swinging breasts and rotating hips back and forth between the table and the stove.

So this was Patrolman Mancuso's aunt. Only Patrolman Mancuso could have something like that for an aunt, Ignatius snorted to himself.

"Whoo!" Mrs. Reilly screamed gaily. "Santa!"

"Watch this, kids," the gray-haired woman screamed back like a prize fight referee and began shaking lower and lower until she was almost on the floor.

"Oh, my God!" Ignatius said to the wind.

"You gonna bust a gut, girl," Mrs. Reilly laughed. "You gonna go through my good floor."

"Maybe you better stop, Aunt Santa," Patrolman Mancuso said morosely.

"Hell, I ain't stopping now. I just got here," the woman answered, rising rhythmically. "Who says a grammaw can't dance no more?"

Holding her arms outward, the woman bumped across the linoleum runway.

"Lord!" Mrs. Reilly said and guffawed, tipping the whiskey bottle to her glass. "What if Ignatius comes home and sees this?"

"Fuck Ignatius!"

"Santa!" Mrs. Reilly gasped, shocked but, Ignatius noticed, slightly pleased.

"You people cut it out," Miss Annie screamed through her shutters.

"Who's that?" Santa asked Mrs. Reilly.

"Cut it out before I ring up the cops," Miss Annie's muffled voice cried.

"*Please* stop," Patrolman Mancuso pleaded nervously.

f i v e

DARLENE WAS POURING WATER into the half-filled liquor bottles behind the bar.

"Hey, Darlene, listen to this shit," Lana Lee commanded, folding the newspaper and weighting it down with her ashtray. " 'Frieda Club, Betty Bumper, and Liz Steele, all of 796 St. Peter St., were arrested from El Caballo Lounge, 570 Burgundy St., last night and booked with disturbing the peace and creating a public nuisance. According to arresting officers, the incident started when an unidentified man made a proposal to one of the women. The woman's two companions struck the man, who fled from the lounge. The Steele woman threw a stool at the bartender, and the other two women menaced customers in the lounge with stools and broken beer bottles. Customers in the lounge said that the man who fled was wearing bowling shoes.' How's about that? People like that are ruining the Quarter. Some honest Joe tries to make off with one of those dykes and they try to beat him up. Once upon a time it was nice and straight around here. Now it's all dykes and fairies. No wonder business stinks. I can't stand dykes. I can't!"

"The only people we get in here at night anymore is plainclothesmen," Darlene said. "How come they don't get a plainclothesman after women like that?"

"This place is turning into a goddam precinct. All I'm putting on is a benefit show for the Policeman's Benevolent Association," Lana said disgustedly. "A lotta empty space and few cops throwing signals at each other. Half the time I gotta watch you, brain, to see you don't try to sell them a drink."

"Well, Lana," Darlene said. "How I'm supposed to know who's a cop? Everybody looks the same to me." She blew her nose. "I try to make a living."

"You tell a cop by his eyes, Darlene. They're very self-assured. I been in the business too long. I know every dirty cop angle. The marked bills, the phony clothes. If you can't tell by the eyes, then take a look at the money. It's full of pencil marks and crap."

"How I'm supposed to see the money? It's so dark in here I can hardly see the eyes even."

"Well, we're gonna have to do something about you. I don't want you sittin out here on my stools. You're gonna try to sell a double martini to the chief of police one of these nights."

"Then let me get on the stage and dance. I got a socko routine."

"Oh, shut up," Lana hollered. If Jones knew about the police in the place at night, then goodbye, discount porter. "Now look here, Darlene, don't tell that Jones we suddenly got the whole force in here at night. You know how colored people feel about cops. He might get scared and quit. I mean, I'm trying to help the boy out and keep him off the streets."

"Okay," Darlene said. "But I ain't making no money I'm so afraid the guy on the next stool is the police. You know what we need in here to make money?"

"What?" Lana asked angrily.

"What we need in here is a animal."

"A what? Jesus Christ."

"I ain cleanin up after no animal," Jones said, bumping his mop noisily against the legs of the barstools.

"Come on over and check under these stools," Lana called to him.

"Oh! Whoa! Where I miss a spot? Hey!"

"Look in the paper, Lana," Darlene said. "Almost every other club on the street's got them an animal."

Lana turned to the entertainment pages and through Jones's fog studied the nightclub ads.

"Well, little Darlene's on the ball. I guess you'd like to become the manager of this club, huh?"

"No, ma'm."

"Well, remember that," Lana said and ran a finger along the ads. "Look at this. They got a snake at Jerry's, got them some doves at the 104, a baby tiger, a chimp . . ."

"And that's where the people are going," Darlene said. "You gotta keep up with things in this business."

"Thanks a lot. Since it's your idea, you got any suggestions?"

"I suggest we vote unanimous agains changing over to a zoo."

"Keep on the floor," Lana said.

"We could use my cockatoo," Darlene said. "I been practicing a smash dance with it. The bird's very smart. You oughta hear that thing talk."

"In color bars peoples all the time tryina keep birds *out*."

"Give the bird a chance," Darlene pleaded.

"Whoa!" Jones said. "Watch out. Your orphan frien just pullin in. It's humanitaria time."

125

George was slouching through the door in a bulky red sweater, white denims, and beige flamenco boots with slim-pointed toes. On both his hands there were tatoos of daggers drawn with ball-point pencil.

"Sorry, George, nothing for the orphans today," Lana said quickly.

"See that? Well them orphan they better star applyin to the United Fun," Jones said and blew some smoke on the daggers. "We having trouble with salary as it is. Chariddy begin at home."

"Huh?" George asked.

"They sure keeping a buncha hoods in the orphanages these days," Darlene observed. "I wouldn't give him nothing, Lana. He's operating some kinda shakedown racket, if you ast me. If this kid's a orphan, I'm the queen of England."

"Come here," Lana said to George and led him out onto the street.

"Whatsa matter?" George asked.

"I can't talk in front of those two jerks," Lana said. "Look, this new porter's not like the old one. This smartass has been asking me about this orphan crap since he first saw you. I don't trust him. I got cop trouble already."

"Then get yourself a new jig. There's plenty around."

"I couldn't get a blind Eskimo for the salary I'm paying him. I got him on something of a deal, like discount price. And he thinks if he tries to quit, I can get him arrested for vagrancy. The whole thing's a deal, George. I mean, in my line of business, you gotta keep your eye peeled for a bargain. Understand?"

"But what about me?"

"This Jones goes out to lunch from twelve to

twelve-thirty. So you come around about twelve-forty-five."

"What am I supposed to do with them packages all afternoon? I can't do nothing till after three. I don't want to be carrying that stuff around."

"Go check it in the bus station. I don't care. Just be sure they're safe. I'll see you tomorrow."

Lana went back into the bar.

"I sure hope you told that kid off," Darlene said. "Somebody oughta report him to the Better Business Bureau."

"Whoa!"

"Come on, Lana. Give me and the bird a chance. We're boffo."

"It used to be the old Kiwanis types liked to come in and watch a cute girl shake it a little. Now it's gotta be with some kinda animal. You know what's wrong with people today? They're sick. It's hard for a person to earn an honest buck." Lana lit a cigarette and matched Jones cloud for cloud. "Okay. We audition the bird. It's probably safer for you to be on my stage with a bird than on my stools with a cop. Bring in the goddam bird."

II

Mr. Gonzalez sat next to his little heater listening to the sounds of the river, his peaceful soul suspended in a Nirvana somewhere far above the two antennae of Levy Pants. His senses subconsciously savored the clatter of rats and the smell of old paper and wood and the possessed feeling that his pair of baggy Levy Pants gave him. He exhaled a thin stream of filtered smoke and aimed the cigarette's ashes like a marksman directly at the center of his ashtray. The impossible had happened: life at Levy Pants had become even better. The reason was Mr. Reilly. What fairy godmother had dropped Mr. Ignatius J. Reilly on the worn and rotting steps of Levy Pants?

He was four workers in one. In Mr. Reilly's competent hands, the filing seemed to disappear. He was also quite kind to Miss Trixie; there was hardly any friction in the office. Mr. Gonzalez was touched by what he had seen the previous afternoon—Mr. Reilly on his knees changing Miss Trixie's socks. Mr. Reilly was all heart. Of course, he was part valve, too. But the constant conversation about the valve could be accepted. It was the only drawback.

Looking happily about, Mr. Gonzalez noticed the results of Mr. Reilly's handiwork in the office. Tacked to Miss Trixie's desk was a large sign that said MISS TRIXIE with an old-fashioned nosegay drawn in crayon in one corner. Tacked to his desk was another sign that said SR. GONZALEZ and was decorated with the crest of King Alfonso. A multisectioned cross was nailed to a post in the office, the LIBBY'S TOMATO JUICE and KRAFT JELLY on two sections awaiting what Mr. Reilly had said would be brown paint with some black streaks to suggest the grain of the wood. In several empty ice cream cartons on top of the filing cabinets beans were already sprouting little vines. The purple monkscloth drapes that hung from the window next to Mr. Reilly's desk created a meditative area in the office. There the sun cast a claret-colored glow over the three-foot plaster statue of St. Anthony that stood near the wastebasket.

There had never been a worker like Mr. Reilly. He was so dedicated, so interested in the business. He was even planning to visit the factory when his valve was better to see how he could improve conditions there. The other workers had always been so unconcerned, so slipshod.

The door opened slowly as Miss Trixie made her day's entrance, a large bag preceding her.

"Miss Trixie!" Mr. Gonzalez said in what was, for him, a very sharp tone.

"Who?" Miss Trixie cried frantically.

She looked down at her tattered nightgown and flannel robe.

"Oh, my goodness," she wheezed. "I thought I felt a little chilly outside."

"Go home right now."

"It's cold outside, Gomez."

"You can't stay at Levy Pants like that. I'm sorry."

"Am I retired?" Miss Trixie asked hopefully.

"No!" Mr. Gonzalez squeaked. "I just want you to go home and change. You only live around the block. Hurry up."

Miss Trixie shuffled through the door, banging it closed. Then she came in again to get the bag, which she had left on the floor, and banged out again.

By the time Ignatius arrived an hour later, Miss Trixie had not returned. Mr. Gonzalez listened to Mr. Reilly's heavy, slow tread on the stairs. The door was thrust open, and the marvelous Ignatius J. Reilly appeared, a plaid scarf as large as a shawl wound around his neck, one end of it stuffed down into his coat.

"Good morning, sir," he said majestically.

"Good morning," Mr. Gonzalez said with delight. "Did you have a nice ride here?"

"Only fair. I suspect that the driver was a latent speed racer. I had to caution him continually. Actually, we parted company with a degree of hostility on both sides. Where is our little distaff member this morning?"

"I had to send her home. She came to work this morning in her nightgown."

Ignatius frowned and said, "I do not understand why she was sent away. After all, we are quite informal here. We are one big family. I only hope that you have not damaged her morale." He filled a glass at the water cooler to water his beans. "You may not be surprised to see me appear one morning in my nightshirt. I find it rather comfortable."

"I certainly don't mean to dictate what you people should wear," Mr. Gonzalez said anxiously.

"I should hope not. Miss Trixie and I can only take so much."

Mr. Gonzalez pretended to look for something in his desk to avoid the terrible eyes that Ignatius had turned on him.

"I shall finish the cross," Ignatius said finally, removing two quarts of paint from the pouchlike pockets of his overcoat.

"That's wonderful."

"The cross is top priority at the moment. Filing, alphabetizing—all of that must wait until I have completed this project. Then, when I finish the cross, I am going to have to visit the factory. I suspect that those people are screaming for a compassionate ear, a dedicated guide. I may be able to aid them."

130

"Of course. Don't let me tell you what to do."

"I won't." Ignatius stared at the office manager. "At last my valve seems to permit a visit to the factory. I must not pass up this opportunity. If I wait, it may seal up for several weeks."

"Then you must go to the factory today," the office manager agreed enthusiastically.

Mr. Gonzalez looked at Ignatius hopefully, but he received no reply. Ignatius filed his overcoat, scarf, and cap in one of the file drawers and began working on the cross. By eleven o'clock he was giving the cross its first coat, meticulously applying the paint with a small watercolor brush. Miss Trixie was still AWOL.

At noon Mr. Gonzalez looked over the stack of papers on which he was working and said, "I wonder where Miss Trixie can be."

"You have probably broken her spirit," Ignatius replied coldly. He was dabbing at the rough edges of the cardboard with the brush. "However, she may appear for lunch. I told her yesterday that I was bringing her a luncheon meat sandwich. I have discovered that Miss Trixie considers luncheon meat a rather toothsome delicacy. I would offer you a sandwich, but I am afraid that there are only enough for Miss Trixie and me."

"That's quite all right." Mr. Gonzalez produced a wan smile and watched Ignatius open his greasy brown paper bag. "I'm going to have to work straight through lunch anyway to finish these statements and billings."

"Yes, you'd better. We must not allow Levy Pants to fall behind in the struggle for the survival of the fittest."

Ignatius bit into his first sandwich, tearing it in half, and chewed contentedly for a while.

"I do hope that Miss Trixie does appear," he said after he had finished the first sandwich and emitted a series of belches which sounded as if they had disintegrated his digestive tract. "My valve will not tolerate luncheon meat, I'm afraid."

While he was tearing the filling of the second

131

sandwich from the bread with his teeth, Miss Trixie came in, her green celluloid visor facing the rear.

"Here she is," Ignatius said to the office manager through the big leaf of limp lettuce that was hanging from his mouth.

"Oh, yes," Mr. Gonzalez said weakly. "Miss Trixie."

"I imagined that the luncheon meat would activate her faculties. Over here, Mother Commerce."

Miss Trixie bumped into the statue of St. Anthony.

"I knew I had something on my mind all morning, Gloria," Miss Trixie said, taking the sandwich in her claws and going to her desk. Ignatius watched with fascination the elaborate process of gums, tongue, and lips that every piece of sandwich set into motion.

"You took a very long time to change," the office manager said to Miss Trixie, noting bitterly that her new ensemble was only a little more presentable than the robe and nightgown.

"Who?" Miss Trixie asked, sticking out a tongueful of masticated luncheon meat and bread.

"I said you took a long time to change."

"Me? I just left here."

"Will you please stop harassing her?" Ignatius demanded angrily.

"There was no need for the delay. She only lives down by the wharves somewhere," the office manager said and returned to his papers.

"Did you enjoy that?" Ignatius asked Miss Trixie when the last grimace of her lips had stopped.

Miss Trixie nodded and began industriously on a second sandwich. But when she had at last eaten half, she slumped back in her chair.

"Oh, I'm full, Gloria. That was delicious."

"Mr. Gonzalez, would you care for the bit of sandwich that Miss Trixie can not eat?"

"No, thank you."

"I wish that you would take it. Otherwise, the rats will storm us *en masse.*"

"Yes, Gomez, take this," Miss Trixie said, dropping the soggy half of uneaten sandwich on top of the papers on the office manager's desk.

"Now look what you've done, you old idiot!" Mr. Gonzalez screamed. "Damn Mrs. Levy. That's the statement for the bank."

"How dare you attack the spirit of the noble Mrs. Levy," Ignatius thundered. "I shall report you, sir."

"It took over an hour to prepare that statement. Look at what she's done."

"I want that Easter ham!" Miss Trixie snarled. "Where's my Thanksgiving turkey? I quit a wonderful job as cashier in a nickelodeon to come to work for this company. Now I guess I'll die in this office. I must say a worker gets shabby treatment around here. I'm retiring *right now.*"

"Why don't you go wash your hands?" Mr. Gonzalez said to her.

"That's a good idea, Gomez," Miss Trixie said and tacked off to the ladies' room.

Ignatius felt cheated. He had hoped for a scene. While the office manager began making a copy of the statement, Ignatius returned to the cross. First, however, he had to lift Miss Trixie, who had returned and was kneeling directly beneath it and praying in the spot where Ignatius had been standing to paint. Miss Trixie hovered about him, leaving only to seal some envelopes for Mr. Gonzalez, to visit the bathroom several times, and to catnap. The office manager made the only noise in the office with his typewriter and adding machine, both of which Ignatius found slightly distracting. By one-thirty the cross was almost finished. It lacked only the little gold leaf letters that spelled GOD AND COMMERCE which Ignatius had ready to apply across the bottom of the cross. After the motto was applied, Ignatius stood back and said to Miss Trixie, "It is complete."

"Oh, Gloria, that's beautiful," Miss Trixie said sincerely. "Look at this, Gomez."

"Isn't that fine," Mr. Gonzalez said, studying the cross with tired eyes.

"Now to the filing," Ignatius said busily. "Then off to the factory. I cannot tolerate social injustice."

"Yes, you must go to the factory while your valve is operating," the office manager said.

Ignatius went behind the filing cabinets, picked up the accumulated and unfiled material, and threw it in the wastebasket. Noticing that the office manager was sitting at his desk with his hand over his eyes, Ignatius pulled out the first drawer of the files, and, turning it over, dumped its alphabetical contents into the wastebasket, too.

Then he lumbered off to the factory door, thundering past Miss Trixie, who had fallen to her knees again before the cross.

III

Patrolman Mancuso had tried a little moonlighting in his effort to apprehend someone, anyone for the sergeant. After dropping off his aunt from the bowling alley, he had stopped in the bar on his own to see what he could turn up. What had turned up was these three terrifying girls who had struck him. He touched the bandage on his head as he entered the precinct to see the sergeant, who had summoned him.

"What happened to you, Mancuso?" the sergeant screamed when he saw the bandage.

"I fell down."

"That sounds like you. If you knew anything about your job, you'd be in bars tipping us off on people like those three girls we brought in last night."

"Yes, sir."

"I don't know what whore give you the tip on this Night of Joy, but our boys have been in there almost every night and they haven't turned up anything."

"Well, I thought . . ."

"Shut up. You gave us a phony lead. You know what we do to people give us a phony lead?"

"No."

"We put them in the rest room at the bus station."

"Yes, sir."

"You stay in the booths there eight hours a day until you bring somebody in."

"Okay."

"Don't say 'okay.' Say 'yes, sir.' Now get outta here and go look in your locker. You're a farmer today."

IV

Ignatius opened "The Journal of a Working Boy" to the first unused sheet of Blue Horse looseleaf filler, officiously snapping the point of his ballpoint pen forward. The point of the Levy Pants pen did not catch on the first snap and slipped back into the plastic cylinder. Ignatius snapped more vigorously, but again the point slid disobediently back out of sight. Cracking the pen furiously on the edge of his desk, Ignatius picked up

135

one of the Venus Medalist pencils lying on the floor. He probed the wax in his ears with the pencil and began to concentrate, listening to the sounds of his mother's preparations for an evening at the bowling alley. There were many staccato footfalls back and forth in the bathroom which meant, he knew, that his mother was attempting to accomplish several phases of her toilet at once. Then there were the noises that he had grown accustomed to over the years whenever his mother was preparing to leave the house: the plop of a hair brush falling into the toilet bowl, the sound of a box of powder hitting the floor, the sudden exclamations of confusion and chaos.

"Ouch!" his mother cried at one point.

Ignatius found the subdued and solitary din in the bathroom annoying and wished that she would finish. At last he heard the light click off. She knocked at his door.

"Ignatius, honey, I'm going."

"All right," Ignatius replied icily.

"Open the door, babe, and come kiss me goodbye."

"Mother, I am quite busy at the moment."

"Don't be like that, Ignatius. Open up."

"Run off with your friends, please."

"Aw, Ignatius."

"Must you distract me at every level. I am working on something with wonderful movie possibilities. Highly commercial."

Mrs. Reilly kicked at the door with her bowling shoes.

"Are you ruining that pair of absurd shoes that were bought with my hard-earned wages?"

"Huh? What's that, precious?"

Ignatius extracted the pencil from his ear and opened the door. His mother's maroon hair was fluffed high over her forehead; her cheekbones were red with rouge that had been spread nervously up to the eyeballs. One wild puff full of powder had whitened Mrs. Reilly's face, the front of her dress, and a few loose maroon wisps.

"Oh, my God," Ignatius said, "you have powder all over your dress, although that is probably one of Mrs. Battaglia's beauty hints."

"Why you always knocking Santa, Ignatius?"

"She appears to have been knocked a bit in her life already. Up rather than down. If she ever nears me, however, the direction will be reversed."

"Ignatius!"

"She also brings to mind the vulgarism 'knockers.'"

"Santa's a grammaw. You oughta be ashamed."

"Thank goodness Miss Annie's coarse cries restored peace the other night. Never in my life have I seen so shameless an orgy. And right in my very own kitchen. If that man were any sort of law enforcement officer, he would have arrested that 'aunt' right there on the spot."

"Don't knock Angelo, neither. He's got him a hard road, boy. Santa says he's been in the bathroom at the bus station all day."

"Oh, my God! Do I believe what I'm hearing? Please run along with your two cohorts from the Mafia and let me alone."

"Don't treat your poor momma like that."

"Poor? Did I hear poor? When the dollars are literally flowing into this home from my labors? And flowing out even more rapidly."

"Don't start that again, Ignatius. I only got twenty dollars out of you this week, and I almost had to get down on my knees and beg for it. Look at all them thing-a-ma-jigs you been buying. Look at that movie camera you brung home today."

"The movie camera will shortly be put to use. That harmonica was rather cheap."

"We never gonna pay off that man at this rate."

"That is hardly my problem. I don't drive."

"No, you don't care. You never cared for nothing, boy."

"I should have known that every time I open the door of my room I am literally opening a Pandora's Box. Doesn't Mrs. Battaglia want you to await her debauched nephew and her at the curb so that not one invaluable moment of bowling time will be lost?" Ignatius belched the gas of a dozen brownies trapped by his valve. "Grant me a little peace. Isn't it enough that I am harried all day long at work? I thought that I had adequately described to you the horrors which I must face daily."

"You know I appreciate you, babe," Mrs. Reilly sniffed. "Come on and gimme a little goodbye kiss like a good boy."

Ignatius bent down and lightly bussed her on the cheek.

"Oh, my God," he said, spitting out powder. "Now my mouth will feel gritty all night."

"I got too much powder on?"

138

"No, it's just fine. Aren't you an arthritic or something? How in the world can you bowl?"

"I think the exercise is helping me out. I'm feeling better."

A horn honked out on the street.

"Apparently your friend has escaped the bath-room," Ignatius snorted. "It's just like him to hang around a bus station. He probably likes to watch those Scenicruiser horrors arrive and depart. In his worldview the bus is apparently a good thing. That shows how retarded he is."

"I'll be in early, honey," Mrs. Reilly said, closing the miniature front door.

"I shall probably be misused by some intruder!" Ignatius screamed.

Bolting the door to his room, he grabbed an empty ink bottle and opened his shutters. He stuck his head out of the window and looked down the alley to where the little white Rambler was visible in the darkness at the curb. With all of his strength, he heaved the bottle and heard it hit the roof of the car with greater sound effects than he had expected it to.

"Hey!" he heard Santa Battaglia shout as he silently closed the shutters. Gloating, he opened his looseleaf folder again and picked up his Venus Medalist.

Dear Reader,
A great writer is the friend and benefactor of his readers.
                                                        —Macaulay

Another working day is ended, gentle reader. As I told you before, I have succeeded in laying a patina, as it were, over the turbulence and mania of our office. All non-essential activities in the office are slowly being curtailed. At the moment I am busily decorating our throbbing hive of white-collared bees (three). The analogy of the three bees brings to mind three *b*'s which describe most aptly my actions as an office worker: banish, benefit, beautify. There are also three *b*'s which describe most aptly the actions of our buffoon of an office manager: bait, beg, blight, blunder, bore, boss, bother, bungle, burden, buzz. (In this case, I am afraid that the list gets somewhat out of hand.) I have come to the conclusion that our office manager serves no purpose other than one of obfuscation and hindrance. Were it not for him, the other clerical worker (La Dama del Comercio) and I would be quite peaceful and content, attending to our duties in an atmosphere of mutual consideration. I am certain that his dictatorial methods are, in part, responsible for Miss T.'s desire to retire.

I can at last describe to you our factory. This afternoon, feeling fulfilled after having completed the cross (Yes! It is completed and gives our office a needed spiritual dimension.), I set out to visit the clank and whirr and hiss of the factory.

The scene which met my eyes was at once compelling and repelling. The original sweatshop has been preserved for posterity at Levy Pants. If only the Smithsonian Institution, that grab-bag of our nation's refuse, could somehow vacuum-seal the Levy Pants factory and transport it to the capital of the United States of America, each worker frozen in an attitude of labor, the visitors to that questionable museum would defecate into their garish tourist outfits. It is a scene which combines the worst of *Uncle Tom's Cabin* and Fritz Lang's *Metropolis*; it is mechanized Negro slavery; it represents the progress which the Negro has made from picking cotton to tailoring it. (Were they in the picking stage of their evolution, they would at least be in the healthful outdoors singing and eating watermelons [as they are, I believe, supposed to do when in groups al fresco].) My intense and deeply felt convictions concerning social injustice were aroused. My valve threw in a hearty response.

(In connection with the watermelons, I must say, lest some professional civil rights organization be offended, that I have never been an observer of American folk customs. I may be wrong. I would imagine that today people grasp for the cotton with one hand while the other hand presses a transistor radio to the sides of their heads so that it can spew bulletins about used cars and Sofstyle Hair Relaxer and Royal Crown Hair Dressing and Gallo wine about their eardrums, a filtered menthol cigarette dangling from their lips and threatening to set the entire cotton field ablaze. Although residing along the Mississippi River [This river is famed in atrocious song and verse; the most prevalent motif is one which attempts to make of the river an ersatz father figure. Actually, the Mississippi River is a treacherous and sinister body of water whose eddies and currents yearly claim many lives. I have never known anyone who would even venture to stick his toe in its polluted brown waters, which seethe with sewage, industrial waste, and deadly insecticides. Even the fish are dying. Therefore, the Mississippi as Father-God-Moses-Daddy-Phallus-Pops is an altogether false motif begun, I would imagine, by that dreary fraud, Mark Twain. This failure to make contact with reality is, however, characteristic of almost all of America's "art." Any connection between American art and American nature is purely coincidental, but this is only because the nation as a whole has no contact with reality. That is only one of the reasons why I have always been forced to exist on the fringes of its society, consigned to the Limbo reserved for those who do know reality when they see it.], I have never seen cotton growing and have no desire to do so. The only excursion in my life outside of New Orleans took me through the vortex to the whirlpool of despair: Baton Rouge. In some future install-ment, a flashback, I shall perhaps recount that pilgrimage through the swamps, a journey into the desert from which I returned broken physically, mentally, and spiritually. New Orleans is, on the other hand, a comfortable metropolis which has a certain apathy and stagnation which I find inof-fensive. At least its climate is mild; too, it is here in the Cres-cent City that I am assured of having a roof over my head and a Dr. Nut in my stomach, although certain sections of North Africa [Tangiers, etc.] have from time to time excited my interest. The voyage by boat, however, would probably ener-vate me, and I am certainly not perverse enough to attempt air travel even if I were able to afford it. The Greyhound Bus Line is sufficiently menacing to make me accept my status quo. I wish that those Scenicruisers would be discontinued; it would seem to me that their height violates some interstate highway statute regarding clearance in tunnels and so forth. Perhaps one of you, dear readers, with a legal turn of mind can dredge the appropriate clause from memory. Those things really must be removed. Simply knowing that they are hurtling somewhere on this dark night makes me most appre-hensive.)

141

The factory is a large, barn-like structure that houses bolts of fabric, cutting tables, massive sewing machines, and furnaces that provide the steam for pressing. The total effect is rather surreal, especially when one sees *Les Africains* moving about attending to their tasks in this mechanized setting. The irony involved caught my fancy, I must admit. Something from Joseph Conrad sprang to my mind, although I cannot seem to remember what it was at the time. Perhaps I likened myself to Kurtz in *The Heart of Darkness* when, far from the trading company offices in Europe, he was faced with the ultimate horror. I do remember imagining myself in a pith helmet and white linen jodpurs, my face enigmatic behind a veil of mosquito netting.

The furnaces keep the place rather warm and toasty on these chill days, but in the summer I suspect that the workers once again enjoy the climate of their forebears, the tropic heat somewhat magnified by those great coal-burning steam-producing contrivances. I understand that the factory is not working at capacity currently, and I did observe that only one of these devices was operating, burning coal and what looked like one of the cutting tables. Also, I saw only one pair of trousers actually completed during the time that I spent there, although the factory workers were shambling about clutching all sorts of scraps of cloth. One woman, I noticed, was pressing some baby's clothing and another seemed to be making remarkable progress with the sections of fuscia satin which she was joining together on one of the large sewing machines. She appeared to be fashioning a rather colorful but nonetheless rakish evening gown. I must say that I admired the efficiency with which she whipped the material back and forth under the massive electric needle. This woman was apparently a skilled worker, and I thought it doubly unfortunate that she was not lending her talents to the creation of a pair of Levy Pants . . . pants. There was obviously a morale problem in the factory.

I looked for Mr. Palermo, the foreman of the factory, who is, incidentally, normally only a few steps from the bottle, as the many contusions that he has sustained from falling down among the cutting tables and sewing machines can testify, with no success. He was probably quaffing a liquid lunch in one of the many taverns in the vicinity of our organization; there is a bar on every corner in the neighborhood of Levy Pants, an indication that salaries in the area are abysmally low. On particularly desperate blocks there are three or four bars at every intersection.

In my innocence, I suspected that the obscene jazz issuing forth from the loud speakers on the walls of the factory was at the root of the apathy which I was witnessing among the workers. The psyche can be bombarded only so much by these rhythms before it begins to crumble and atrophy. Therefore, I found and turned off the switch which controlled the music. This action on my part led to a rather loud and defiantly boorish roar of protest from the collective workers, who began to regard me with sullen eyes. So I turned the music on again, smiling broadly and waving amiably in an attempt to acknowledge my poor judgment and to win the workers' confidence. (Their huge white eyes were already labeling me a "Mister Charlie." I would have to struggle to show them my almost psychotic dedication to helping them.)

Obviously continual response to the music had developed within them an almost Pavlovian response to the noise, a response which they believed was pleasure. Having spent countless hours of my life watching those blighted children on television dancing to this sort of music, I knew the physical spasm which it was supposed to elicit, and I attempted my own conservative version of the same on the spot to further pacify the workers. I must admit that my body moved with surprising agility; I am not without an innate sense of rhythm; my ancestors must have been rather outstanding at jigging on the heath. Ignoring the eyes of the workers, I shuffled about beneath one of the loud speakers, twisting and shouting, mumbling insanely, "Go! Go! Do it, baby, do it! Hear me talkin' to ya. Wow!" I know that I had recovered my ground with them when several began pointing to me and laughing. I laughed back to demonstrate that I, too, shared their high spirits. *De Casibus Virorum Illustrium!* Of the Fall of Great Men! My downfall occurred. Literally. My considerable system, weakened by the gyrations (especially in the region of the knees), at last rebelled, and I plummeted to the floor in a senseless attempt at one of the more egregiously perverse steps which I had witnessed on the television so many times. The workers seemed rather concerned and helped me up most politely, smiling in the friendliest fashion. I realized then that I had no more to fear concerning my *faux pas* in turning off their music.

In spite of all to which they have been subjected, Negroes are nonetheless a rather pleasant folk for the most part. I really have had little to do with them, for I mingle with my peers or no one, and since I have no peers, I mingle with no one. Upon speaking with several of the workers, all of whom seemed eager to speak with me, I discovered that they received even less pay than Miss Trixie.

In a sense I have always felt something of a kinship with the colored race because its position is the same as mine: we both exist outside the inner realm of American society. Of course, my exile is voluntary. However, it is apparent that many of the Negroes wish to become active members of the American middle class. I can not imagine why. I must admit that this desire on their part leads me to question their value judgments. However, if they wish to join the bourgeoisie, it is really none of my business. They may seal their own doom. Personally, I would agitate quite adamantly if I suspected that anyone were attempting to help me upward toward the middle class. I would agitate against the bemused person who was attempting to help me upward, that is. The agitation would take the form of many protest marches complete with the traditional banners and posters, but these would say, "End the Middle Class," "The Middle Class Must Go." I am not above tossing a small Molotov cocktail or two, either. In addition, I would studiously avoid sitting near the middle class in lunch counters and on public transportation, maintaining the intrinsic honesty and grandeur of my being. If a middle-class white were suicidal enough to sit next to me, I imagine that I would beat him soundly about the head and shoulders with one great hand, tossing, quite deftly, one of my Molotov cocktails into a passing bus jammed with middle-class whites with the other hand. Whether my siege were to last a month or a year, I am certain that ultimately everyone would let me alone after the total carnage and destruction of property had been evaluated.

I do admire the terror which Negroes are able to inspire

in the hearts of some members of the white proletariat and only wish (This is a rather personal confession.) that I possessed the ability to similarly terrorize. The Negro terrorizes simply by being himself; I, however, must browbeat a bit in order to achieve the same end. Perhaps I should have been a Negro. I suspect that I would have been a rather large and terrifying one, continually pressing my ample thigh against the withered thighs of old white ladies in public conveyances a great deal and eliciting more than one shriek of panic. Then, too, if I were a Negro, I would not be pressured by my mother to find a good job, for no good jobs would be available. My mother herself, a worn old Negress, would be too broken by years of underpaid labor as a domestic to go out bowling at night. She and I could live most pleasantly in some moldy shack in the slums in a state of ambitionless peace, realizing contentedly that we were unwanted, that striving was meaningless.

However, I do not wish to witness the awful spectacle of the Negroes moving upward into the middle class. I consider this movement a great insult to their integrity as a people. But I am beginning to sound like the Beards and Parrigntons and will soon totally forget Levy Pants, the commercial muse for this particular effort. A project for the future could be a social history of the United States from my vantage point; if *The Journal of a Working Boy* meets with any success at the book stalls, I shall perhaps etch a likeness of our nation with my pen. Our nation demands the scrutiny of a completely disengaged observer like your Working Boy, and I already have in my files a rather formidable collection of notes and jottings that evaluate and lend a perspective to the contemporary scene.

We must hasten back on the wings of prose to the factory and its folk, who prompted my rather lengthy digression. As I was telling you, they had just lifted me from the floor, my performance and subsequent pratfall the sources of a great feeling of camaraderie. I thanked them cordially, they meanwhile inquiring in their seventeenth-century English accents about my condition most solicitously. I was uninjured, and since pride is a Deadly Sin which I feel I generally eschew, absolutely nothing was hurt.

I then questioned them about the factory, for this was the purpose behind my visit. They were rather eager to speak with me and seemed even most interested in me as a person. Apparently the dull hours among the cutting tables make a visitor doubly welcome. We chatted freely, although the workers were generally non-committal about their work. Actually, they seemed more interested in me than in anything else; I was not bothered by their attentions and parried all of their questions blithely until they at last grew rather personal. Some of them who had from time to time straggled into the office asked pointed questions about the cross and the attendant decorations; one intense lady asked permission (which, of course, was granted) to gather some of her confreres about the cross occasionally to sing spirituals. (I abhor spirituals and those deadly nineteenth-century Calvinist hymns, but I was willing to suffer having my eardrums assaulted if a chorus or two would make these workers happy.) When I questioned them about wages, I discovered that their average weekly pay envelope contained less than thirty ($30) dollars. It is my considered opinion that someone deserves more than that in the way of a wage for simply staying in a place like the factory for five days a week, especially when the factory is one like the Levy Pants factory in which the leaking roof threatens to collapse at any moment. And who knows? Those people might have much better things to do than to loiter about Levy Pants, such as composing jazz or creating new dances or doing whatever those things are that they do with such facility. No wonder there was such apathy in the factory. Still it was incredible that the disparity between the doldrums of the production line and the fevered hustle of the office could be housed within the same (Levy Pants) bosom. Were I one of the factory workers (and I would probably be a large and particularly terrifying one, as I said earlier), I would long before have stormed the office and demanded a decent wage.

Here I must make a note. While I was desultorily attending graduate school, I met in the coffee shop one day a Miss Myrna Minkoff, a young undergraduate, a loud, offensive maiden from the Bronx. This expert from the universe of the Grand Concourse was attracted to the table at which I was holding court by the singularity and magnetism of my being.

146

As the magnificence and originality of my worldview became explicit through conversation, the Minkoff minx began attacking me on all levels, even kicking me under the table rather vigorously at one point. I both fascinated and confused her; in short, I was too much for her. The parochialism of the ghettoes of Gotham had not prepared her for the uniqueness of Your Working Boy. Myrna, you see, believed that all humans living south and west of the Hudson River were illiterate cowboys or—even worse—White Protestants, a class of humans who as a group specialized in ignorance, cruelty, and torture. (I don't wish to especially defend White Protestants; I am not too fond of them myself.)

Soon Myrna's brutal social manner had driven my courtiers from the table, and we were left alone, all cold coffee and hot words. When I failed to agree with her braying and babbling, she told me that I was obviously anti-Semitic. Her logic was a combination of half-truths and clichés, her worldview a compound of misconceptions deriving from a history of our nation as written from the perspective of a subway tunnel. She dug into her large black valise and assaulted me (almost literally) with greasy copies of *Men and Masses* and *Now!* and *Broken Barricades* and *Surge* and *Revulsion* and various manifestos and pamphlets pertaining to organizations of which she was a most active member: Students for Liberty, Youth for Sex, The Black Muslims, Friends of Latvia, Children for Miscegenation, The White Citizens' Councils. Myrna was, you see, terribly *engaged* in her society; I, on the other hand, older and wiser, was terribly *dis-engaged*.

She had chiseled quite a bit of money from her father to go away to college to see what it was like "out there." Unfortunately, she found me. The trauma of our first meeting fed each other's masochism and led to an affair (platonic) of sorts. (Myrna was decidedly masochistic. She was only happy when a police dog was sinking its fangs into her black leotards or when she was being dragged feet first down stone steps from a Senate hearing.) I must admit that I always suspected Myrna of being interested in me sensually; my stringent attitude toward sex intrigued her; in a sense, I became another project of sorts. I did, however, succeed in thwarting her every attempt to assail the castle of my body and mind. Since Myrna and I confused most of the other students when we were apart, as a couple we were doubly confusing to the smiling Southern birdbrains who, for the most part, made up the student body. Campus rumor, I understand, linked us in the most unspeakably depraved intrigues.

Myrna's cure-all for everything from fallen arches to depression was sex. She promulgated this philosophy with disastrous effects to two Southern belles whom she took under her wing in order to renovate their backward minds. Heeding Myrna's counsel with the eager assistance of various young men, one of the simple lovelies suffered a nervous breakdown; the other attempted unsuccessfully to slash her wrists with a broken Coca-Cola bottle. Myrna's explanation was that the girls had been too reactionary to begin with, and with renewed vigor, she preached sex in every classroom and pizza parlor, almost getting herself raped by a janitor in the Social Studies building. Meanwhile, I tried to guide her toward the path of truth.

After several semesters Myrna disappeared from the college, saying in her offensive manner, "This place can't teach me anything I don't know." The black leotards, the matted mane of hair, the monstrous valise were all gone; the palmlined campus returned to its traditional lethargy and necking. I have seen that liberated doxy a few times since then, for, from time to time she embarks on an "inspection tour" of the South, stopping eventually in New Orleans to harangue me and to attempt to seduce me with the grim prison and chain and gang songs she strums on her guitar. Myrna is very sincere; unfortunately, she is also offensive.

When I saw her after her last "inspection tour" she was rather bedraggled. She had stopped throughout the rural South to teach Negroes folk songs she had learned at the Library of Congress. The Negroes, it seems, preferred more contemporary music and turned up their transistor radios loudly and defiantly whenever Myrna began one of her lugubrious dirges. Although the Negroes had tried to ignore her, the whites had shown great interest in her. Bands of crackers and rednecks had chased her from villages, slashed her tires, whipped her a bit about the arms. She had been hunted by bloodhounds, shocked by cattle prods, chewed by police dogs, peppered lightly with shotgun pellets. She had loved every minute of it, showing me quite proudly (and, I might add, suggestively) a fang mark on her upper thigh. My stunned and disbelieving eyes noted that on that occasion she was wearing dark stockings and not leotards. My blood, however, failed to rise.

We do correspond quite regularly, the usual theme of Myrna's correspondence tending to urge me to participate in lie-ins and wade-ins and sit-ins and such. Since, however, I do not eat at lunch counters and do not swim, I have ignored her advice. The subsidiary theme in the correspondence is one urging me to come to Manhattan so that she and I may raise our banner of twin confusion in that center of mechanized horrors. If I am ever really well, I may make the trip. At the moment that little musky Minkoff minx is probably in some tunnel far beneath the streets of the Bronx speeding in a subway train from a meeting on social protest to an orgy of folk singing or worse. Some day the authorities of our society will no doubt apprehend her for simply being herself. Incarceration will finally make her life meaningful and end her frustration.

A recent communication from her was bolder and more offensive than usual. She must be dealt with on her own level, and thus I thought of her as I surveyed the sub-standard conditions in the factory. Too long have I confined myself in Miltonic isolation and meditation. It is clearly time for me to step boldly into our society, not in the boring, passive manner of the Myrna Minkoff school of social action, but with great style and zest.

You will be witnesses to a certain courageous, daring, and aggressive decision on the part of the author, a decision which reveals a militancy, depth, and strength quite unexpected in so gentle a nature. Tomorrow I will describe in detail my answer to the Myrna Minkoffs of the world. The result may, incidentally, topple (all too literally) Mr. Gonzalez as a power within Levy Pants. That fiend must be dealt with. One of the more powerful civil rights organizations will no doubt cover me with laurels.

There is an almost unbearable pain needling my fingers as a result of these overabundant scribblings. I must lay down my pencil, my engine of truth, and bathe my crippled hands in some warm water. My intense devotion to the cause of justice has led to this lengthy diatribe, and I feel that my Levy circle-within-a-circle is zooming upward to new successes and heights.

Health note: Hands crippled, valve temporarily open (half-way)

Social note: Nothing today; Mother gone again, looking like a courtesan; one of her cohorts, you might like to know, has revealed his hopelessness by revealing a fetish for Greyhound buses.

I am going to pray to St. Martin de Porres, the patron saint of mulattoes, for our cause in the factory. Because he is also invoked against rats, he will perhaps aid us in the office, too.

> Until later,
> Gary, Your Militant Working Boy

V

Dr. Talc lit a Benson and Hedges, looking out of the window of his office in the Social Studies Building. Across the dark campus he saw some lights from the night classes in other buildings. All night he had been ransacking his desk for his notes on the British monarch of legend, notes hurriedly copied from a hundred-page survey of British history that he had once read in paperback. The lecture was to be given tomorrow, and it was now almost eight-thirty. As a lecturer Dr. Talc was renowned for the facile and sarcastic wit and easily digested generalizations that made him popular among the girl students and helped to conceal his lack of knowledge about almost everything in general and British history in particular.

But even Talc realized that his reputation for sophistication and glibness would not save him in the face of his being unable to remember absolutely anything about Lear and Arthur aside from the fact that the former had some children. He put his cigarette in the ashtray and began on the bottom drawer again. In the rear of the drawer there was a stack of old papers that he had not examined very thoroughly during his first search through the desk. Placing the papers in his lap, he thumbed through them one by one and found that they were, as he had imagined, principally unreturned essays that had accumulated over a period of more than five years. As he turned over one essay, his eye fell upon a rough, yellowed sheet of Big Chief tablet paper on which was printed with a red crayon:

Your total ignorance of that which you profess to teach merits the death penalty. I doubt whether you would know that St. Cassian of Imola was stabbed to death by his students with their styli. His death, a martyr's honorable one, made him a patron saint of teachers.

Pray to him, you deluded fool, you "anyone for tennis?" golf-playing, cocktail-quaffing pseudo-pedant, for you do indeed need a heavenly patron. Although your days are numbered, you will not die as a martyr—for you further no holy cause—but as the total ass which you really are.

ZORRO

A sword was drawn on the last line of the page.

"Oh, I wonder whatever happened to him," Talc said aloud.

s i x

Mattie's Ramble Inn was on a corner in the Carrollton section of the city where, after having run parallel for six or seven miles, St. Charles Avenue and the Mississippi River meet and the avenue ends. Here an angle is formed, the Avenue and its streetcar tracks on one side, the river and levee and railroad tracks on the other. Within this angle there is a separate little neighborhood. In the air there is always the heavy, cloying odor of the alcohol distillery on the river, an odor that becomes suffocating on hot summer afternoons when the breeze blows in from the river. The neighborhood grew haphazardly a century or so ago and today looks hardly urban at all. As the city's streets cross St. Charles Avenue and enter this neighborhood, they gradually change from asphalt to gravel. It is an old rural town that has even a few barns, an alienated and microcosmic village within a large city.

Mattie's Ramble Inn looked like all the buildings on its block; it was low, unpainted, imperfectly vertical. Mattie's rambled slightly to the right, tilting toward the railroad tracks and the river. Its façade was almost invulnerable, covered as it was with tin advertising posters for a variety of beers and cigarettes and soft drinks. Even the screen on the door advertised a brand of bread. Mattie's was a combination bar and grocery, the grocery aspect limited to a sparse selection of goods, soft drinks, bread, and canned foods for the most part. Beside the bar there was an ice chest that cooled a few pounds of pickled meat and sausage. And there was no Mattie; Mr. Watson, the quiet, tan, *café au lait* owner, had sole authority over the restricted merchandise.

"The problem come from not havin no vocation skill," Jones was saying to Mr. Watson. Jones was perched on a wooden stool, his legs bent under him like ice tongs ready to pick up the stool and boldly carry it away before Mr. Watson's old eyes. "If I had me some trainin I wouldn be moppin no old whore flo."

"Be good," Mr. Watson answered vaguely. "Be well behave with the lady."

"Wha? Ooo-wee. You don understan at all, man. I got a job workin with a *bird*. How you like workin with a bird?" Jones aimed some smoke over the bar. "I mean, I'm glad that girl gettin a chance. She been workin for that Lee mother a long time. She need a break. But I bet that bird be makin more money than me. Whoa!"

"Be nice, Jones."

"Whoa! Hey, you really been brainwash," Jones said. "You ain got nobody to come in and mop your flo. How come? Tell me that."

"Don't get yourself in no trouble."

"Hey! You soun just like the Lee mother. Too bad you two ain met. She love you. She say, 'Hey, boy, you the kinda fool oldtimey nigger I been lookin for all my life.' She say, 'Hey, you so sweet, how's about waxin my floor and paintin my wall? You so darlin, how's about scrubbin my tawlet and polishin my shoe?' And you be sayin, 'Yes, ma'm, yes, ma'm. I'm well behave.' And you be bustin your ass fallin off a chandelier you been dustin

153

and some other whore frien of her comin in so they can compare they price, and Lee star throwin some nickel at your feet and say, 'Hey boy, that sure a lousy show you puttin on. Han us back them nickel before we call a po-lice.' Ooo-wee."

"Didn that lady say she call a po-lice if you give her trouble?"

"She got me there. Hey! I think that Lee got some connection with the po-lice. She all the time tellin me about her frien on the force. She say she got such a high class place a po-lice never stick a foot in her door." Jones formed a thundercloud over the little bar. "She operatin *somethin* with that orphan crap, though. As soon as somebody like Lee say, 'Chariddy,' you know they somethin crooker in the air. And I know they somethin wron cause all of a sudden the Head Orphan stop showin up cause I'm axing plenty question. Shit! I like to fin out what goin on. I tire of bein caught in a trap payin me twenty dollar a week, workin with a bird as big as a eagle. I wanna get someplace, man. Whoa! I want me a air condition, some color TV, sit aroun drinkin somethin better than beer."

"You want another beer?"

Jones looked at the old man through his sunglasses and said, "You tryina sell me another beer, a poor color boy bustin his ass for twenny dollar a week? I think it about time you gimme a free beer with all the money you make sellin pickle meat and sof drink to po color peoples. You sen you boy to college with the money you been makin in here."

154

"He a schoolteacher now," Mr. Watson said proudly, opening a beer.

"Ain that fine. Whoa! I never go to school more than two year in my life. My momma out washing other people clothin, ain nobody talkin about school. I spen all my time rollin tire aroun the street. I'm rollin, momma washin, nobody learnin nothin. Shit! Who lookin for a tire roller to give them a job? I end up gainfully employ workin with a bird, got a boss probly sellin Spanish fly to orphan. Ooo-wee."

"Well, if conditions really bad . . ."

" 'Really bad'? Hey! I'm workin in modren slavery. If I quit, I get report for bein vagran. If I stay, I'm gainfully employ on a salary ain even startin to be a minimal wage."

"I tell you what you can do," Mr. Watson said confidentially; leaning over the bar and handing Jones the beer. The other man at the bar bent toward them to listen; he had been silently following their conversation for several minutes. "You try you a little sabotage. That's the only way you fight that kinda trap."

"Wha you mean 'sabotage'?"

"You know, man," Mr. Watson whispered. "Like the maid ain bein paid enough to throw too much pepper in the soup by accident. Like the parkin lot attendant takin too much crap skid on some oil and crash a car into the fence."

"Whoa!" Jones said. "Like the boy workin in the supermarket suddenly get slippery fingers and drop a dozen aigs on the floor cause he ain been pay overtime. Hey!"

"Now you got it."

"We really plannin *big* sabotage," the other man at the bar said, breaking his silence. "We havin a big demonstration where I work."

"Yeah?" Jones asked. "Where?"

"At Levy Pant. We got this big old white man

comin in the factory tellin us he like to drop a atom bum on top the company."

"It sound like you peoples havin more than sabotage," Jones said. "It sound like you havin a *war*."

"Be nice, be respectful," Mr. Watson told the stranger.

The man chuckled until his eyes filled with tears and he said, "This man say he prayin for the mulattas and the rats all over the world."

"Rats? Whoa! You peoples got a one-hunner-percen freak on your hand."

"He very smart," the man said defensively. "He very religious, too. He built him a big cross right in the office."

"Whoa!"

"He say, 'You peoples all be happier in the middle age. You peoples gotta get you a cannon and some arrows, drop a nuclear bum on top this place.'" The man laughed again. "We ain't got nothin better to do in that factory. He always interestin to listen to when he flappin his big moustache. He gonna lead us in a big demonstration he say make all the other demonstration look like a ladies' social."

"Yeah, and it sound like he gonna lead you peoples right into jail," Jones said, covering the bar with some more smoke. "He sound like a crazy white mother."

"He kinda strange," the man admitted. "But he work right in that office, and the manager in there, Mr. Gonzala, he think this guy pretty sharp. He let him do whatever he want. He even let him come back in the factory any time this guy want to. Plenty peoples ready to do demonstrate with him. He tell us he got permission from Mr. Levy hisself to have a demonstration, tell us Mr. Levy want us to demonstrate and get rid of

Gonzala. Who know? Maybe they raise our wage. That Mr. Gonzala afred of him already."

"Tell me, man, what this white savior cat look like?" Jones asked with interest.

"He big and fat, got him a huntin cap he wearin all the time."

Jones's eyes widened behind his glasses.

"This huntin cap green? He got him a *green* cap?"

"Yeah. How you know that?"

"Whoa!" Jones said. "You peoples in plenty trouble. A po-lice already lookin for that freak. He come in the Night of Joy one night, star tellin this Darlene gal about a bus."

"Well, whaddya know," the man said. "He tell us about a bus, too, tell us he go ridin into the har of darkness on a bus one time."

"He the same one. Stay away from that freak. He wanted by a police. You po color peoples all get your ass throwed in jail. Whoa!"

"Well, I gotta ax him about that," the man said. "I sure don wanna get led on no demonstration by a convic."

II

Mr. Gonzalez was at Levy Pants early, as usual. He symbolically lit his little heater and a filtered cigarette with the same match, lighting two torches that signaled the start of another working day. Then he applied his mind to his early morning meditations. Mr. Reilly had added a new touch to the office the day before, streamers of mauve, gray, and tan crepe paper looped from light bulb to light bulb across the ceiling. The cross and signs and streamers in the office reminded the office manager of Christmas decorations and made him feel slightly sentimental. Looking happily into Mr. Reilly's area, he noticed that the bean vines were growing so healthily that they had even begun to twine downward through the handles of the file drawers. Mr. Gonzalez wondered how the file clerk managed to do his filing without disturbing the tender shoots. Pondering this clerical riddle, he was surprised to see Mr. Reilly himself burst like a torpedo through the door.

"Good morning, sir," Ignatius said brusquely, his scarf-shawl flying horizontally in his wake like the flag of some mobilized Scottish clan. A cheap movie camera was slung over his shoulder and under his arm he had a bundle which appeared to be a rolled-up bed sheet.

"Well you certainly are early today, Mr. Reilly."

"What do you mean? I always arrive at this time."

"Oh, of course," Mr. Gonzalez said meekly.

"Do you believe that I am here early for some purpose?"

"No. I . . ."

"Speak up, sir. Why are you so strangely suspicious? Your eyes are literally flickering with paranoia."

"What, Mr. Reilly?"

"You heard what I said," Ignatius answered and lumbered through the door to the factory.

Mr. Gonzalez tried to compose himself again but was disturbed by what sounded like a cheer from the factory. Perhaps, he thought, one of the workers had become a father or won something in a raffle. So long as the factory workers let him alone, he was willing to extend the same courtesy to them. To him they were simply part of the physical plant of Levy Pants not connected with "the brain center." They were not his to worry about; they were under the drunken control of

Mr. Palermo. When he did find the proper courage, the office manager intended to approach Mr. Reilly in a most politic manner about the amount of time he was spending in the factory. However, Mr. Reilly had lately become somewhat distant and unapproachable, and Mr. Gonzalez dreaded the thought of a battle with him. His feet grew numb when he thought of one of those bear's paws landing squarely on the top of his head, driving him perhaps like a stake through the unpredictable flooring of the office.

Four of the male factory workers were embracing Ignatius around the Smithfield hams that were his thighs and, with considerable effort, were lifting him onto one of the cutting tables. Above the shoulders of his carriers Ignatius barked directions as if he were supervising the loading of the rarest and most precious of cargoes.

"Up and to the right, there!" he shouted down. "Up, up. Be careful. Slowly. Is your grip tight?"

"Yeah," one of the lifters answered.

"It feels rather loose. Please! I am deteriorating into a state of total anxiety."

The workers watched with interest as the lifters tottered back and forth under their burden.

"Now backward," Ignatius called nervously. "Backward until the table is directly beneath me."

"Don't you worry, Mr. R.," a lifter panted. "We aimin you right at that table."

"Apparently you are not," Ignatius replied, his body slamming into a post. "Oh, my God! My shoulder is dislocated."

159

A cry arose from the other workers.

"Hey, watch out with Mr. R.," someone screamed. "You men gonna bust his haid wide open."

"Please!" Ignatius cried. "Someone help! In another moment I shall probably be a broken heap."

"Look, Mr. R.," a lifter said breathlessly, "the table right behind us now."

"I shall probably be dumped into one of the furnaces before this misadventure terminates. I suspect that it would have been much wiser to address the group from floor level."

"Put your feets down, Mr. R. The table right under you."

"Slowly," Ignatius said, extending his big toe downward with great caution. "Well, so it is. All right. When I have steadied myself, you may release your hold upon my body."

Ignatius was at last vertically atop the long table, holding the bundled bed sheet over his pelvis to hide from his audience the fact that during the process of being lifted, he had become somewhat stimulated.

"Friends!" Ignatius said grandly and lifted the arm that was not holding the sheet. "At last the day is ours. I hope that you have all remembered to bring your engines of war." From the group around the cutting table there issued neither confirmation nor denial. "I mean the sticks and chains and clubs and so forth." Giggling in chorus, the workers waved some fence posts, broomsticks, bicycle chains, and bricks. "My God! You have really assembled a rather formidable and diffuse armory. The violence of our attack may surpass my expectations. However, the more definitive the blow, the more definitive the results. My cursory inspection of your arms, therefore, confirms my faith in the ultimate success of our crusade today. In our wake, we must leave a sacked and pillaged Levy Pants, we must fight fire with fire."

160

"What he say?" one worker asked another.

"We shall storm the office very shortly, thereby surprising the foe when his senses are still subject to the psychic mists of early morning."

"Hey, Mr. R., pardon me," a man called out from the crowd. "Somebody tell me you in trouble with a po-lice. Is that right?"

A wave of anxiety and uneasiness broke over the workers.

"What?" Ignatius screamed. "Where did you hear such slander. That is totally false. Some white supremacist, some upstate red-neck, perhaps even Gonzalez himself no doubt began that vile rumor. How dare you, sir. All of you must realize that our cause has many enemies."

While the workers were applauding him soundly, Ignatius wondered how that worker had learned of the mongoloid Mancuso's attempted arrest. Perhaps he had been standing in the crowd before the department store. That patrolman was the fly in everyone's ointment. However, the moment seemed to have been saved.

"Now this we will carry with us in the vanguard!" Ignatius shouted over the last sprinkled applause. He dramatically whipped from his pelvis the sheet, flapping it open. Among the yellow stains the word FORWARD was printed in high block letters in red crayon. Below this *Crusade for Moorish Dignity* was written in an intricate blue script.

"I wonder who been sleepin on that old thing," the intense woman with the spiritual bent, who was to be the leader of the choir, said. "Lord!"

Several other prospective rioters expressed the same curiosity in more explicitly physical terminology.

161

"Quiet now," Ignatius said, stomping one foot thunderously on the table. "Please! Two of the more statuesque women here will carry this banner between them as we march into the office."

"I ain puttin my hand on that," one woman answered.

"Quiet! Everyone!" Ignatius said furiously. "I am beginning to suspect that you people are not actually deserving of this cause. Apparently you are not prepared to make any of the ultimate sacrifices."

"How come we gotta take that old sheet with us?" someone asked. "I thought this suppose to be a demonstration dealin with wages."

"Sheet? What sheet!" Ignatius replied. "I am holding before you the proudest of banners, an identification of our purpose, a visualization of all that we seek." The workers studied the stains more intensely. "If you wish to simply rush into the office like cattle, you will have participated in nothing more than a riot. This banner alone gives form and credence to the agitation. There is a certain geometry involved in these things, a certain ritual which must be observed. Here, you two ladies standing there, take this between you and wave it thus with honor and pride, hands held high, et cetera."

The two women whom Ignatius indicated ambled slowly to the cutting table, gingerly took the banner with their thumbs and index fingers, and held it between them as if it were a leper's shroud.

"That looks even more impressive than I had imagined," Ignatius said.

"Don wave that thing around me, gal," someone said to the women, creating another ripple of giggles from the crowd.

Ignatius flipped his camera into action and aimed it

162

at the banner and the workers. "Will all of you please wave your sticks and stones again?" The workers complied merrily. Myrna would choke on her espresso when she saw this. "A bit more violently now. Brandish these weapons fiercely. Make faces. Scream. Perhaps some of you could jump up and down, if you don't mind."

They laughingly followed his directions, everyone, that is, but the two women who were sullenly holding the banner.

In the office Mr. Gonzalez was watching Miss Trixie bump into the door frame as she made her entrance for the day. At the same time he was wondering what the new and violent outburst from the factory meant.

Ignatius filmed the scene before him for a minute or two more, then he followed a post upward to the ceiling for what he imagined would be an interesting and rather recherché bit of cinematography suggesting aspiration. Envy would gnaw at Myrna's musky vitals. At the top of the post the camera focused upon several square feet of the rusted interior of the factory's roof. Then Ignatius handed the camera down to a worker and asked to be photographed. While the worker aimed the lens at him, Ignatius scowled and shook a fist, entertaining the workers greatly.

"All right now," he said benevolently when he had taken the camera back and flipped it off. "Let us control our riotous impulses for the moment and plan our stratagems. First, the two ladies here will precede us with the banner. Directly behind the banner comes the choir with some appropriate folk or religious melody. The lady in charge of the choir may choose the tune. Knowing nothing of your musical folk-ways, I shall leave the

163

selection to you, although I wish that there had been time enough to teach all of you the beauties of some madrigal. I will only suggest that you choose a somewhat forceful melody. The remainder of you will compose the warriors' battalion. I shall follow the entire ensemble with my camera in order to record this memorable occasion. At some future date all of us may realize some additional revenues from the rental of this film to student organizations and other similarly appalling societies.

"Please remember this. Our first approach will be a peaceful and rational one. As we enter the office, the two ladies will carry the banner to the office manager. The choir will then form about the cross. The battalion will remain in the background until needed. Because we are dealing with Gonzalez himself, I suspect that the battalion will be called upon in short order. If Gonzalez fails to respond to the emotion of this spectacle, I shall call, 'Attack!' That will be the signal for your onslaught. Are there any questions?"

Someone said, "This a lotta shit," but Ignatius ignored the voice. There was a happy hush in the factory, most of the workers eager for the change of pace. Mr. Palermo, the foreman, appeared drunkenly between two of the furnaces for a moment and then disappeared.

"Apparently the battle plan is clear," Ignatius said when no questions were forthcoming. "Will the two ladies with the banner please take their positions over there by the door? Now the choir please form behind them and then the battalion." The workers formed rapidly, smiling and sticking one another with their engines of war. "Fine! The choir may now begin singing."

The lady with the spiritual bent blew a pitchpipe and the choir members began singing lustily, "Oh,

Jesus, walk by my side,/ Then I always, always be satisfied."

"That really sounds rather stirring," Ignatius observed. Then he shouted, "Forward!"

The formation obeyed so rapidly that before Ignatius could call anything else, the banner had already passed through the factory and was rising up the stairs to the office.

"Halt!" Ignatius screamed. "Someone come help me off this table."

> Oh, Jesus, you be my friend
> Right, oh, yeah, right up till the end.
> You take my hand
> And I feel grand
> Knowing you walking
> Hearing me talking
> I ain't complaining
> Though maybe it's raining
> When I'm with Jesus.

"Stop!" Ignatius called frantically, watching the last of the battalion file through the door. "Come back in here immediately."

The door swung closed. He got down on his hands and knees and crawled to the edge of the table. Then he swung around and, after a long while spent in maneuvering his extremities, managed to sit on the edge of the table. Noticing that his feet were swinging only a few inches from the floor, he decided to risk the jump. As he pushed himself free of the table and landed on the floor, the camera slid from his shoulder and hit the cement with a hollow, cracking sound. Disemboweled, its film entrails spilled onto the floor. Ignatius picked it

165

up and flipped the switch that was supposed to set it in
motion, but nothing happened.

> Oh, Jesus, you pay my bail
> When they put me in that old jail.
> Oh, oh, you always giving
> A reason for living.

"What are those maniacs singing?" Ignatius asked
the empty factory while he tried to stuff foot upon foot
of film into his pocket.

> You never hurt me,
> You never, never, never desert me.
> I never sinning
> I always winning
> Now I got Jesus.

Ignatius, trailing unwound film, hustled to the door
and entered the office. The two women were stonily
displaying the back of the stained sheet to a confused
Mr. Gonzalez. Their eyes closed, the choir members
were chanting compulsively, lost in their melody. Ignatius pushed through the battalion loitering benignly on
the fringes of the scene toward the desk of the office
manager.

Miss Trixie saw him and asked, "What's happening, Gloria? What are all the factory people doing in
here?"

"Run while you're able, Miss Trixie," he told her
with great seriousness.

"Oh, Jesus, you give me peace/When you keeping away
them po-lice."

"I can't hear you," Miss Trixie cried, grabbing his arm. "Is this a minstrel show?"

"Go dangle your withered parts over the toilet!" Ignatius screamed savagely.

Miss Trixie shuffled away.

"Well?" Ignatius asked Mr. Gonzalez, rearranging the two ladies so that the office manager could see the lettering on the other side of the sheet.

"What does this mean?" Mr. Gonzalez asked, reading the banner.

"Do you refuse to help these people?"

"Help them?" the office manager asked in a frightened voice. "What are you talking about, Mr. Reilly?"

"I am talking about the sin against society of which you are guilty."

"What?" Mr. Gonzalez's lower lip quivered.

"Attack!" Ignatius cried to the battalion. "This man is totally without charity."

"You ain give him a chance to say nothin," observed one of the discontented women holding the sheet. "You let Mr. Gonzalez talk."

"Attack! Attack!" Ignatius cried again, even more furiously. His blue and yellow eyes protruded and flashed.

Someone halfheartedly whizzed a bicycle chain over the top of the file cabinets and knocked the bean plants to the floor.

"Now look what you've done," Ignatius said. "Who told you to knock those plants over?"

"You say, 'Attagg,' " the owner of the bicycle chain answered.

"Stop that at once," Ignatius bellowed at a man who was apathetically making a vertical slash in the DEPARTMENT OF RESEARCH AND REFERENCE—I.

REILLY, CUSTODIAN sign with a pen knife. "What do you people think you're doing?"

"Hey, you say, 'Attagg,'" several voices answered.

> In this lonesome place
> You give me grace
> Giving your light
> Through the long night.
> Oh, Jesus, you hearing my woe
> And I never, I never, never gonna let you go.

"Stop that awful song," Ignatius shouted at the choir. "Never has such egregious blasphemy fallen upon my ears."

The choir ceased its singing and looked hurt.

"I don't understand what you're doing," the office manager said to Ignatius.

"Oh, shut up your little pussymouth, you mongoloid."

"We goin back to the factory," the spokesman for the choir, the intense lady, said angrily to Ignatius. "You a bad man. I *believe* a police looking for you."

"Yeah," several voices agreed.

"Now wait a moment," Ignatius begged. "Someone must attack Gonzalez." He surveyed the warriors' battalion. "The man with the brick, come over here at once and knock him a bit about the head."

"I ain't hittin nobody with this," the man with the brick said. "You probly got a po-lice record a mile long."

The two women dropped the sheet disgustedly on the floor and followed the choir, which was already beginning to file through the door.

168

"Where do you people think you're going?" Ignatius cried, his voice choked with saliva and fury.

The warriors said nothing and began to follow the choir and the two standard bearers out of the office. Ignatius waddled swiftly behind the warriors straggling in the rear and grabbed one of them by the arm, but the man swatted at him as if he were a mosquito and said, "We got enough trouble without gettin throwed in jail."

"Come back in here! We're not finished. You can get Miss Trixie if you want," Ignatius cried frantically to the disappearing battalion, but the procession continued to move silently and determinedly farther down the stairs into the factory. Finally, the door swung closed on the last of the crusaders for Moorish dignity.

III

Patrolman Mancuso looked at his watch. He had been in the rest room a full eight hours. It was time to check his costume in at the precinct and go home. He had arrested no one all day and, in addition, he seemed to be catching a cold. It was chilly and damp in that booth. He sneezed and tried to open the door, but it wouldn't give. He shook it, fumbled with the lock, which appeared to be stuck. After a minute or so of rattling and pushing, he called, "Help!"

IV

"Ignatius! So you got yourself fired."

"Please, Mother, I am near the breaking point." Ignatius stuck the bottle of Dr. Nut under his moustache and drank noisily, making great sounds of sucking and gurgling. "If you are planning now to be a harpy, I shall certainly be pushed over the brink."

"A little job in a office and you can't hold it down. With all your education."

"I was hated and resented," Ignatius said, casting a hurt expression at the brown walls of the kitchen. He pulled his tongue from the mouth of the bottle with a thump and belched some Dr. Nut. "Ultimately it was all Myrna Minkoff's fault. You know how she makes trouble."

"Myrna Minkoff? Don't gimme that foolishness, Ignatius. That girl's in New York. I know you, boy. You musta really pulled some boo-boos at that Levy Pants."

"My excellence confused them."

"Gimme that paper, Ignatius. We gonna take a look at them want ads."

"Is that true?" Ignatius thundered. "Am I going to be thrown out again into the abyss? Apparently you have bowled all the charity out of your soul. I must have at least a week in bed, with service, before I shall again be whole."

"Speaking of bed, what happened to your sheet, boy?"

"I certainly wouldn't know. Perhaps it was stolen. I have warned you about intruders."

"You mean somebody broke into this house just to take one of your dirty sheets?"

"If you were a bit more conscientious about doing the laundry, the description of that sheet would be somewhat different."

"Okay, hand over the paper, Ignatius."

"Are you really going to attempt to read aloud? I doubt whether my system could bear that trauma at the moment. Anyway, I am looking at a very interesting article in the science column about mollusks."

Mrs. Reilly snatched the paper from her son, leaving two little scraps of it in his hands.

"Mother! Is this offensive display of ill manners one of the results of your association with those bowling Sicilians?"

"Shut up, Ignatius," his mother said, leafing compulsively toward the classified section of the newspaper. "Tomorrow morning you getting on that St. Charles trolley with the birds."

"Huh?" Ignatius asked absently. He was wondering what he could write to Myrna now. The film seemed to have been ruined, too. Explaining the disaster of the Crusade in a letter would be impossible. "What was that you said, mother of mine?"

"I said you gettin on that trolley with the birds," Mrs. Reilly screamed.

"That sounds appropriate."

"When you come home again, you gonna have you a job."

"Apparently Fortuna has decided upon another downward spin."

"What?"

"Nothing."

V

Mrs. Levy lay prone on the motorized exercising board, its several sections prodding her ample body gently, nudging and kneading her soft, white flesh like a loving baker. Winding her arms under the table, she held it tightly.

"Oh," she moaned softly and happily, nibbling on the section beneath her face.

"Turn that thing off," her husband's voice said somewhere behind her.

"What?" Mrs. Levy raised her head and looked dreamily around. "What are you doing here? I thought you were staying in town for the races."

"I changed my mind, if it's okay with you."

"Sure, it's okay with me. Do whatever you want. Don't let me tell you what to do. Have yourself a ball. See if I care."

"Pardon me. I'm sorry I tore you away from the board."

"Let's leave the board out of this, if you don't mind."

"Oh, I'm sorry if I insulted it."

"Just leave my board out of it. That's all I said. I'm trying to be nice. I don't start the arguments around here."

"Turn the damn thing on again and shut up. I'm going to take a shower."

"You see? You're very excited over nothing. Don't take all your guilt feelings out on me."

"What guilt feelings? What have I done?"

"You know what it is, Gus. You know how you've thrown your life away. A whole business down the drain. A chance to go nationwide. Your father's sweat and blood handed to you on a silver platter."

"Ugh."

"A growing concern failing."

"Listen, I have a headache from trying to save that business today. That's why I didn't go to the races."

After having fought with his father for almost thirty-five years, Mr. Levy had decided that he would spend the rest of his life trying not to be bothered. But he was bothered every day that he was at Levy's Lodge by his wife simply because she resented his not wanting to be bothered by Levy Pants. And in staying away from Levy Pants, he was bothered even more by the company because something was always going wrong there. It would all be simpler and less bothersome if he would have really operated Levy Pants and put in an eight hour day as manager. But just the name "Levy Pants" gave him heartburn. He associated it with his father.

"What did you do, Gus? Sign a few letters?"

"I fired somebody."

"Really? Big deal. Who? One of the furnace stokers?"

"You remember I told you about that big kook, the one that ass Gonzalez hired?"

"Oh. Him." Mrs. Levy rolled about on the exercising board.

"You should see what he did to that place. Paper streamers hanging from the ceiling. A big cross tacked up in the office. As soon as I walk in today, he comes up to me and starts complaining that somebody from the factory knocked his bean plants to the floor."

"Bean plants? He thought Levy Pants was a truck garden?"

"Who knows what went on in that head. He wants me to fire the one who knocked over his plants and this other guy he says cut up his sign. He says the factory workers are a bunch of rowdies who have no respect for him. He says they're out to get him. So I go back in the factory to find Palermo, who of course is not there, and what do I find? All those workers have bricks and chains lying all over the place. They're all very emotionally worked up, and they tell me this guy Reilly, that's the big slob, made them bring all that crap so they could attack the office and beat up Gonzalez."

"What?"

"He'd been telling them they were underpaid and overworked."

"I think he's right," Mrs. Levy said. "Just yesterday Susan and Sandra wrote something about that in their letter. Their little friends at college told them that, from what they'd said about their father, he sounded like a plantation owner living on slave labor. The girls were very excited. I meant to mention it to you, but I had so much trouble with that new hair designer that it slipped my mind. They want you to raise the salaries of those poor people or they won't come home again."

"Who do those two think they are?"

"They think they're your daughters, in case you forgot. All they want is to respect you. They said you have to improve conditions at Levy Pants if you want to see them again."

"What's their big interest in colored people all of a sudden? The young men gave out already?"

"Now you're attacking the girls again. You see what I mean? That's why I can't respect you either. If one of your daughters was a horse and the other a baseball player, you couldn't do enough for them."

"If one of them was a horse and the other a baseball player, we'd be better off, believe me. They could turn in a profit."

"I'm sorry," Mrs. Levy said, flipping the board on again. "I can't listen to any more of this. I'm too disillusioned already. I'll hardly be able to bring myself to write the girls about this."

Mr. Levy had seen his wife's letters to the girls,

174

emotional, irrational brainwashing editorials that could have made Patrick Henry out to be a Tory, that brought the girls home on holidays bristling with hostility against their father for the thousands of injustices he had committed against their mother. With him cast as a Klansman firing a young crusader, Mrs. Levy could really write a flaming broadside. The material at hand was too good.

"This guy was a real psycho," Mr. Levy said.

"To you character is a psychosis. Integrity is a complex. I've heard it all before."

"Look, I probably wouldn't have fired him if one of the factory workers hadn't told me he heard this kook is wanted by the police. That really made up my mind fast. I have enough trouble with that company without having a kooky police character working in there."

"Don't give me that. It's too typical. To somebody like you, crusaders and idealists are always beatniks and criminals. It's your defense against them. But thanks for telling me. It will add to the realism of the letter."

"I've never fired anybody in my life," Mr. Levy said. "But I can't keep somebody the police are looking for. *We* might get in trouble."

"Please." Mrs. Levy gestured warningly from her board. "That young idealist must be floundering somewhere at this very moment. It will break the girls' hearts, just as it's breaking mine. I'm a woman of great character and integrity and refinement. You've never appreciated that. I've been debased through my association with you. You've made everything seem so cheap, me included. I've become very hardened."

"So I ruined you too, huh?"

"I was a very warm and loving girl at one time with high hopes. The girls knew that. I thought you'd make

Levy Pants nationwide." Mrs. Levy's head bounced up and down, up and down. "Look. Now it's just a little run-down concern with a few outlets. Your daughters are disillusioned. I'm disillusioned. That young man you fired is disillusioned."

"You want me to kill myself?"

"You make your own decisions. You always have. I've just existed for your pleasure. I'm just another old sports car. Use me when you wish. I don't care."

"Oh, shut up. Nobody wants to use you for anything."

"You see that? You're always attacking. It's insecurity, guilt complexes, hostility. If you were proud of yourself and of the way you treat other people, you'd be pleasant. Just take Miss Trixie as another example. Look at what you've done to her."

"I've never done anything to that woman."

"That's just it. She's alone, afraid."

"She's almost dead."

"Since Susan and Sandra are gone, I feel a guilt complex myself. What am I doing? Where is my project? I am a woman of interests, ideals." Mrs. Levy sighed. "I feel so useless. You've caged me in with hundreds of material objects that don't satisfy the real me." Her bouncing eyes looked coldly at her husband. "Bring me Miss Trixie and I won't write that letter."

"What? I don't want that senile bag out here. Whatever happened to your bridge club? The last time you didn't write a letter you got a new dress. Settle for that. I'll buy you a ball gown."

"It's not enough that I've kept that woman active. She needs personal help."

"You've already used her as a guinea pig for that

correspondence course you took. Why not let her alone. Let Gonzalez retire her."

"Do that and you'll kill her. Then she'll really feel unwanted. You'll have a death on your hands."

"Oh, boy."

"When I think of my own mother. On the beach in San Juan every winter. A tan, a bikini. Dancing, swimming, laughing. Boy friends."

"She has heart failure every time a wave knocks her down. What she doesn't lose in the casinos she spends on the house doctor at the Caribe Hilton."

"You don't like my mother because she's on to you. She was right. I should have married a doctor, somebody with ideals." Mrs. Levy bounced sadly. "It really doesn't matter to me very much anymore. Suffering has only strengthened me."

"How much would you suffer if somebody pulled the wires out of that goddam exercising board?"

"I told you already," Mrs. Levy said angrily. "Leave the board out of this. Your hostility's getting the upper hand. Take my advice, Gus. Go see that analyst in the Medical Arts building, the one that helped Lenny pull his jewelry shop out of the red. He cured Lenny of that complex he had about selling rosaries. Lenny swears by that doctor. Now he's got some kind of exclusive agreement with a bunch of nuns who peddle the rosaries in about forty Catholic schools all over the city. The money's rolling in. Lenny's happy. The sisters are happy. The kids are happy."

"That sounds great."

"Lenny's put in a beautiful line of statues and religious accessories."

"I bet he's happy."

"He is. You should be the same. Go see that doctor

before it's too late, Gus. For the girls' sake you should be helped. I don't care."

"I'm sure you don't."

"You're a very mixed-up person. Sandra, person-ally, is much happier since she was psychoanalyzed. Some doctor at the college helped her out."

"I'm sure he did."

"Sandra may have a setback when she hears of what you did to that young activist. I know the girls will at last turn against you completely. They're warm and compassionate, just like I was before I was brutalized."

"Brutalized?"

"Please. Not another word of sarcasm." An aqua-marine-nailed gesture warned from the bouncing and undulating board. "Do I get Miss Trixie or do the girls get the letter?"

"You get Miss Trixie," Mr. Levy said finally. "You'll probably try to bounce her on that board and break her hip."

"Leave the board out of this!"

seven

PARADISE VENDORS, INCORPORATED, was housed in what had formerly been an automobile repair shop, the dark ground floor of an otherwise unoccupied commercial building on Poydras Street. The garage doors were usually open, giving the passerby an acrid nostrilful of boiling hot dogs and mustard and also of cement soaked over many years by automobile lubricants and motor oils that had dripped and drained from Harmons and Hupmobiles. The powerful stench of Paradise Vendors, Incorporated, sometimes led the overwhelmed and perplexed stroller to glance through the open door into the darkness of the garage. There his eye fell upon a fleet of large tin hot dogs mounted on bicycle tires. It was hardly an imposing vehicular collection. Several of the mobile hot dogs were badly dented. One crumpled frankfurter lay on its side, its one wheel horizontal above it, a traffic fatality.

Among the afternoon pedestrians who hurried past Paradise Vendors, Incorporated, one formidable figure waddled slowly along. It was Ignatius. Stopping before the narrow garage, he sniffed the fumes from Paradise with great sensory pleasure, the protruding hairs in his nostrils analyzing, cataloging, categorizing, and classifying the distinct odors of hot dog, mustard, and lubricant. Breathing deeply, he wondered whether he also detected the more delicate odor, the fragile scent of hot dog buns. He looked at the white-gloved hands of his Mickey Mouse wristwatch and noticed that he had eaten lunch only an hour before. Still the intriguing aromas were making him salivate actively.

He stepped into the garage and looked around. In a corner an old man was boiling hot dogs in a large institutional pot whose size dwarfed the gas range upon which it rested.

"Pardon me, sir," Ignatius called. "Do you retail here?"

The man's watering eyes turned toward the large visitor.

"What do you want?"

"I would like to buy one of your hot dogs. They smell rather tasty. I was wondering if I could buy just one."

"Sure."

"May I select my own?" Ignatius asked, peering down over the top of the pot. In the boiling water the frankfurters swished and lashed like artificially colored and magnified paramecia. Ignatius filled his lungs with the pungent, sour aroma. "I shall pretend that I am in a smart restaurant and that this is the lobster pond."

"Here, take this fork," the man said, handing Ignatius a bent and corroded semblance of a spear. "Try to keep your hands out of the water. It's like acid. Look what it's done to the fork."

"My," Ignatius said to the old man after having taken his first bite. "These are rather strong. What are the ingredients in these?"

"Rubber, cereal, tripe. Who knows? I wouldn't touch one of them myself."

"They're curiously appealing," Ignatius said,

clearing his throat. "I thought that the vibrissae about my nostrils detected something unique while I was outside."

Ignatius chewed with a blissful savagery, studying the scar on the man's nose and listening to his whistling.

"Do I hear a strain from Scarlatti?" Ignatius asked finally.

"I thought I was whistling 'Turkey in the Straw.' "

"I had hoped that you might be familiar with Scarlatti's work. He was the last of the musicians," Ignatius observed and resumed his furious attack upon the long hot dog. "With your apparent musical bent, you might apply yourself to something worthwhile."

Ignatius chewed while the man began his tuneless whistling again. Then he said, "I suspect that you imagine 'Turkey in the Straw' to be a valuable bit of Americana. Well, it is not. It is a discordant abomination."

"I can't see that it matters much."

"It matters a great deal, sir!" Ignatius screamed. "Veneration of such things as 'Turkey in the Straw' is at the very root of our current dilemma."

"Where the hell do you come from? Whadda you want?"

"What is your opinion of a society that considers 'Turkey in the Straw' to be one of the pillars, as it were, of its culture?"

"Who thinks that?" the old man asked worriedly.

"Everyone! Especially folk singers and third-grade teachers. Grimy undergraduates and grammar school-children are always chanting it like sorcerers." Ignatius belched. "I do believe that I shall have another of these savories."

After his fourth hot dog, Ignatius ran his

181

magnificent pink tongue around his lips and up over his moustache and said to the old man, "I cannot recently remember having been so totally satisfied. I was fortunate to find this place. Before me lies a day fraught with God knows what horrors. I am at the moment unemployed and have been launched upon a quest for work. However, I might as well have had the Grail set as my goal. I have been rocketing about the business district for a week now. Apparently I lack some particular perversion which today's employer is seeking."

"No luck, huh?"

"Well, during the week, I have answered only two ads. On some days I am completely enervated by the time I reach Canal Street. On these days I am doing well if I have enough spirit to straggle into a movie palace. Actually, I have seen every film that is playing downtown, and since they are all offensive enough to be held over indefinitely, next week looks particularly bleak."

The old man looked at Ignatius and then at the massive pot, the gas range, and the crumpled carts. He said, "I can hire you right here."

"Thank you very much," Ignatius said condescendingly. "However, I could not work here. This garage is particularly dank, and I'm susceptible to respiratory ailments among a variety of others."

"You wouldn't be working in here, son. I mean as a vendor."

"What?" Ignatius bellowed. "Out in the rain and snow all day long?"

"It don't snow here."

"It has on rare occasions. It probably would again as soon as I trudged out with one of these wagons. I would probably be found in some gutter, icicles dangling from all of my orifices, alley cats pawing over me to draw the warmth from my last breath. No, thank you, sir. I must go. I suspect that I have an appointment of some sort."

Ignatius looked absently at his little watch and saw that it had stopped again.

"Just for a little while," the old man begged. "Try it for a day. How's about it? I need vendors bad."

"A day?" Ignatius repeated disbelievingly. "A day? I can't waste a valuable day. I have places to go and people to see."

"Okay," the old man said firmly. "Then pay me the dollar you owe for them weenies."

"I am afraid that they will all have to be on the house. Or on the garage or whatever it is. My Miss Marple of a mother discovered a number of theater tickets stubs in my pockets last night and has given me only carfare today."

"I'll call in the police."

"Oh, my God!"

"Pay me! Pay me or I'll get the law."

The old man picked up the long fork and deftly placed its two rotting tongs at Ignatius' throat.

"You are puncturing my imported muffler," Ignatius screamed.

"Gimme your carfare."

"I can't walk all the way to Constantinople Street."

"Get a taxi. Somebody at your house can pay the driver when you get there."

"Do you seriously think that my mother will believe me if I tell her that an old man held me up with a fork and took my two nickels?"

"I'm not gonna be robbed again," the old man said, spraying Ignatius with saliva. "That's all that happens

183

to you in the hot dog trade. Hot dog vendors and gas station attendants always get it. Holdups, muggings. Nobody respects a hot dog vendor."

"That is patently untrue, sir. No one respects hot dog vendors more than I. They perform one of our society's few worthwhile services. The robbing of a hot dog vendor is a symbolic act. The theft is not prompted by avarice but rather by a desire to belittle the vendor."

"Shut your goddam fat lip and pay me."

"You are quite adamant for being so aged. However, I am not walking fifty blocks to my home. I would rather face death by rusty fork."

"Okay, buddy, now listen to me. I'll make a bargain with you. You go out and push one of these wagons for an hour, and we'll call it quits."

"Don't I need clearance from the Health Department or something? I mean, I might have something beneath my fingernails that is very debilitating to the human system. Incidentally, do you get all of your vendors this way? Your hiring practices are hardly in step with contemporary policy. I feel as if I've been shanghaied. I am too apprehensive to ask how you go about firing your employees."

"Just don't ever try to rob a hot dog man again."

"You've just made your point. Actually, you have made two of them, literally in my throat and muffler. I hope that you are prepared to compensate for the muffler. There are no more of its kind. It was made in a small factory in England that was destroyed by the Luftwaffe. At the time it was rumored that the Luftwaffe was directed to strike directly at the factory in order to destroy British morale, for the Germans had seen Churchill wrapped in a muffler of this sort in a confiscated newsreel. For all I know, this may be the same one that Churchill was wearing in that particular Movietone. Today their value is somewhere in the thousands. It can also be worn as a shawl. Look."

"Well," the old man said finally, after watching Ignatius employ the muffler as a cummerbund, a sash, a cloak, and a pair of kilts, a sling for a broken arm, and a kerchief, "you ain't gonna do too much damage to Paradise Vendors in one hour."

"If the alternatives are jail or a pierced Adam's apple, I shall happily push one of your carts. Though I can't predict how far I'll go."

"Don't get me wrong, son. I ain't a bad guy, but you can only take so much. I spent ten years trying to make Paradise Vendors a reputable organization, but that ain't easy. People look down on hot dog vendors. They think I operate a business for bums. I got trouble finding decent vendors. Then when I find some nice guy, he goes out and gets himself mugged by hoodlums. How come God had to make it so tough for you?"

"We must not question His ways," Ignatius said.

"Maybe not, but I still don't get it."

"The writings of Boethius may give you some insight."

"I read Father Keller and Billy Graham in the paper every single day."

"Oh, my God!" Ignatius spluttered. "No wonder you are so lost."

"Here," the old man said, opening a metal locker near the stove. "Put this on."

He took what looked like a white smock out of the locker and handed it to Ignatius.

"What is this?" Ignatius asked happily. "It looks like an academic gown."

Ignatius slipped it over his head. On top of his

185

overcoat, the smock made him look like a dinosaur egg about to hatch.

"Tie it at the waist with the belt."

"Of course not. These things are supposed to freely flow about the human form, although this one seems to provide little leeway. Are you sure that you don't have one in a larger size?

"Upon close scrutiny, I notice that this gown is rather yellow about the cuffs. I hope that these stains about the chest are ketchup rather than blood. The last wearer of this might have been stabbed by hoodlums."

"Here, put on this cap." The man gave Ignatius a little rectangle of white paper.

"I am certainly not wearing a paper cap. The one that I have is perfectly good and far more healthful."

"You can't wear a hunting cap. This is the Paradise vendor's uniform."

"I will not wear that paper cap! I am not going to die of pneumonia while playing this little game for you. Plunge the fork into my vital organs, if you wish. I will not wear that cap. Death before dishonor and disease."

"Okay, drop it," the old man sighed. "Come on and take this cart here."

"Do you think that I am going to be seen on the streets with that damaged abomination?" Ignatius asked furiously, smoothing the vendor's smock over his body. "Give me that shiny one with the white sidewall tires."

"Awright, awright." the old man said testily. He opened the lid on the little well in the cart and with a fork slowly began transferring hot dogs from the pot to the little well in the cart. "Now I give you a dozen hot dogs." He opened another lid in the top of the metal bun. "I'm putting a package of buns in here. Got that?"

186

He closed that lid and pulled upon a little side door cut in the shining red tin dog. "In here they got a little can of liquid heat keeps the hot dogs warm."

"My God," Ignatius said with some respect. "These carts are like Chinese puzzles. I suspect that I will continually be pulling at the wrong opening."

The old man opened still another lid cut in the rear of the hot dog.

"What's in there? A machine gun?"

"The mustard and ketchup's in here."

"Well, I shall give this a brave try, although I may sell someone the can of liquid heat before I get too far."

The old man rolled the cart to the door of the garage and said, "Okay, buddy, go ahead."

"Thank you so much," Ignatius replied and wheeled the big tin hot dog out onto the sidewalk. "I will be back promptly in an hour."

"Get off the sidewalk with that thing."

"I hope that you don't think I am going out into the traffic."

"You can get yourself arrested for pushing one of them things on the sidewalk."

"Good," Ignatius said. "If the police follow me, they might prevent a robbery."

Ignatius pushed slowly away from the headquarters of Paradise Vendors through the heavy pedestrian traffic that moved to either side of the big hot dog like waves on a ship's prow. This was a better way of passing time than seeing personnel managers, several of whom, Ignatius thought, had treated him rather viciously in the last few days. Since the movie houses were now off limits due to lack of funds, he would have had to drift, bored and aimless, around the business district until it seemed safe to return home. The people on the street looked at Ignatius, but no one bought. After he had gone half a block, he began calling, "Hot dogs! Hot dogs from Paradise!"

"Get in the street, pal," the old man cried somewhere behind him.

Ignatius turned the corner and parked the wagon against a building. Opening the various lids, he prepared a hot dog for himself and ravenously ate it. His mother had been in a violent mood all week, refusing to buy him any Dr. Nut, pounding on his door when he was trying to write, threatening to sell the house and move into an old folks' home. She described to Ignatius the courage of Patrolman Mancuso, who, against heavy odds, was *fighting* to retain his job, who *wanted* to work, who was making the best of his torture and exile in the bathroom at the bus station. Patrolman Mancuso's situation reminded Ignatius of the situation of Boethius when he was imprisoned by the emperor before being killed. To pacify his mother and to improve conditions at home, he had given her *The Consolation of Philosophy*, an English translation of the work that Boethius had written while unjustly imprisoned and had told her to give it to Patrolman Mancuso so that he might peruse it while sealed in his booth. "The book teaches us to accept that which we cannot change. It describes the plight of a just man in an unjust society. It is the very basis for medieval thought. No doubt it will aid your patrolman during his moments of crisis," Ignatius had said benevolently. "Yeah?" Mrs. Reilly had asked. "Aw, that's sweet, Ignatius. Poor Angelo'll be glad to get this." For about a day, at least, the present to Patrolman Mancuso had brought a temporary peace to life on Constantinople Street.

When he had finished the first hot dog, Ignatius

188

prepared and consumed another, contemplating other kindnesses that might postpone his having to go to work again. Fifteen minutes later, noticing that the supply of hot dogs in the little well was visibly diminishing, he decided in favor of abstinence for the moment. He began to push slowly down the street, calling again, "Hot dogs!"

George, who was wandering up Carondelet with an armload of packages wrapped in plain brown paper, heard the cry and went up to the gargantuan vendor.

"Hey, stop. Gimme one of these."

Ignatius looked sternly at the young boy who had placed himself in the wagon's path. His valve protested against the pimples, the surly face that seemed to hang from the long well-lubricated hair, the cigarette behind the ear, the aquamarine jacket, the delicate boots, the tight trousers that bulged offensively in the crotch in violation of all rules of theology and geometry.

"I am sorry," Ignatius snorted. "I have only a few frankfurters left, and I must save them. Please get out of my way."

"Save them? Who for?"

"That is none of your business, you waif. Why aren't you in school? Kindly stop molesting me. Anyway, I have no change."

"I got a quarter," the thin white lips sneered.

"I cannot sell you a frank, sir. Is that clear?"

"Whatsa matter with you, friend?"

"What's the matter with *me?* What's the matter with *you?* Are you unnatural enough to want a hot dog this early in the afternoon? My conscience will not let me sell you one. Just look at your loathsome complexion. You are a growing boy whose system needs to be surfeited with vegetables and orange juice and whole

189

wheat bread and spinach and such. I, for one, will not contribute to the debauchery of a minor."

"Whadda you talking about? Sell me one of them hot dogs. I'm hungry. I ain't had no lunch."

"No!" Ignatius screamed so furiously that the passersby stared. "Now get away from me before I run over you with this cart."

George pulled open the lid of the bun compartment and said, "Hey, you got plenty stuff in here. Fix me a weenie."

"Help!" Ignatius screamed, suddenly remembering the old man's warnings about robberies. "Someone is stealing my buns! Police!"

Ignatius backed up the cart and rammed it into George's crotch.

"Ouch! Watch out there, you nut."

"Help! Thief!"

"Shut up, for Christ's sake," George said and slammed the door. "You oughta be locked up, you big fruit. You know that?"

"What?" Ignatius screamed. "What impertinence was that?"

"You big crazy fruit," George snarled more loudly and slouched away, the taps on his heels scraping the sidewalk. "Who wants to eat anything your fruity hands touched?"

"How dare you scream obscenities at me. Someone grab that boy," Ignatius said wildly as George disappeared into the crowds of pedestrians farther down the street. "Someone with some decency grab that juvenile delinquent. That filthy little minor. Where is his respect? That little guttersnipe must be lashed until he collapses!"

A woman in the group around the mobile hot dog

said, "Ain't that awful? Where they get them hot dog vendors from?"

"Bums. They all bums," someone answered her.

"Wine is what it is. They all crazy from wine if you ast me. They shouldn't let people like him out on the street."

"Is my paranoia getting completely out of hand," Ignatius asked the group, "or are you mongoloids really talking about me?"

"Let him alone," someone said. "Look at them eyes."

"What's wrong with my eyes?" Ignatius asked viciously.

"Let's get outta here."

"Please do." Ignatius replied, his lips quivering, and prepared another hot dog to quiet his trembling nervous system. With shaking hands, he held the foot of red plastic and dough to his mouth and slipped it in two inches at a time. The active chewing massaged his throbbing head. When he had shoved in the last millimeter of crumb, he felt much calmer.

Grabbing the handle again, he shoved off up Carondelet Street, waddling slowly behind the cart. True to his promise to make it around the block, he turned again at the next corner and stopped by the worn granite walls of Gallier Hall to consume two more of the Paradise hot dogs before continuing on the last leg of his journey. When Ignatius turned the final corner and saw again the PARADISE VENDORS, INC., sign hanging out over the sidewalk of Poydras Street at an angle, he broke into a relatively brisk trot that brought him panting through the doors of the garage.

191

"Help!" Ignatius breathed pitifully, bumping the tin hot dog over the low cement sill of the garage.

"What happened, pal? I thought you was supposed to stay out a whole hour."

"We're both fortunate that I have returned at all. I am afraid that they have struck again."

"Who?"

"The syndicate. Whoever they are. Look at my hands." Ignatius shoved two paws into the man's face. "My entire nervous system is on the brink of revolt against me for subjecting it to such trauma. Ignore me if I suddenly go into a state of shock."

"What the hell happened?"

"A member of the vast teen-age underground besieged me on Carondelet Street."

"You was robbed?" the old man asked excitedly.

"Brutally. A large and rusty pistol was placed at my temples. Actually, was pressed directly upon a pressure point, causing the blood to stop circulating on the left side of my head for quite a while."

"On Carondelet Street at this time of day? Nobody stopped it?"

"Of course no one stopped it. People encourage this sort of thing. They probably derive some sort of pleasure from the spectacle of a poor and struggling vendor's being publicly humiliated. They probably respected the boy's initiative."

"What did he look like?"

"A thousand other youths. Pimples, pompadour, adenoids, the standard adolescent equipment. There might have been something else like a birthmark or trick knee. I really can't recall. After the pistol had been thrust against my head, I fainted from lack of circulation in the brain and from fright. While I was lying in a heap on the sidewalk, he apparently ransacked the wagon."

"How much money did he get?"

"Money? No money was stolen. After all, there was no money to steal, for I had not been able to vend even one of these delicacies. He stole the hot dogs.

"Yes. However, he apparently didn't take them all. When I had recovered, I checked the wagon. There are still one or two left, I think."

"I never heard of nothing like this."

"Perhaps he was very hungry. Perhaps some vitamin deficiency in his growing body was screaming for appeasement. The human desire for food and sex is relatively equal. If there are armed rapes, why should there not be armed hot dog thefts? I see nothing unusual in the matter."

"You're full of bullshit."

"I? The incident is sociologically valid. The blame rests upon our society. The youth, crazed by suggestive television programs and lascivious periodicals had apparently been consorting with some rather conventional adolescent females who refused to participate in his imaginative sexual program. His unfulfilled physical desires therefore sought sublimation in food. I, unfortunately, was the victim of all of this. We may thank God that this boy has turned to food for an outlet. Had he not, I might have been raped right there on the spot."

"He took all but four," the old man said, peering down into the well in the hot dog. "That son of a bitch, I wonder how he could carry all them hot dogs away."

"I really don't know," Ignatius said. Then he added indignantly, "I awaked to find the lid of the cart open. Of course no one would help me up. My white smock stamped me as a vendor, an untouchable."

"How about making another try?"

193

"What? In my present condition, do you seriously expect me to take to the streets again and hustle? My ten cents is going to be deposited in the hands of the St. Charles streetcar conductor. The remainder of the day I intend to spend in a hot tub trying to recapture some semblance of normality."

"Then how about coming back tomorrow, pal, and trying it again?" the old man asked hopefully. "I really need vendors."

Ignatius pondered the proposal for some time, scrutinizing the scar on the old man's nose and belching gassily. At least he would be working. That should satisfy his mother. The work offered little supervision and harassment. Ending his meditations with a clearing of the throat, he belched, "If I am functioning in the morning, I shall perhaps return. I cannot predict the hour at which I will arrive, but, more or less, I imagine that you can expect to see me."

"That's fine, son," the old man said. "Call me Mr. Clyde."

"I shall," Ignatius said and licked at a crumb that he had discovered in the corner of his mouth. "Incidentally, Mr. Clyde, I shall be wearing this smock home to prove to my mother that I am employed. You see, she drinks rather heavily, and she needs reassurance that money from my labors will be forthcoming in order that her supply of spirits won't be cut off. My life is a rather grim one. One day I shall perhaps describe it to you in detail. For the moment, however, you must know a thing or two about my valve."

"*Valve?*"

"Yes."

II

Jones was blindly running a sponge along the bar. Lana Lee had gone on a shopping trip, her first one in a long time, locking the cash register loudly and warningly before leaving. After he had wet the bar a little, Jones tossed the sponge back into the bucket, took a seat in a booth, and tried to look at the latest *Life* Darlene had given him. He lit a cigarette, but the cloud of smoke made the magazine even more invisible. The best reading light in the Night of Joy was the small one on the cash register, so Jones went over to the bar and flipped it on. He was just beginning a study in-depth of a cocktail party scene in a Seagram's V.O. advertisement when Lana Lee pushed into the bar.

"I thought I shouldn't leave you in here alone," she said, opening a bag and taking out a box of classroom chalk which she put in the cabinet under the bar. "What the hell are you doing with my cash register? Get back on my floor."

"I already finish on your flo. I turnin into a expert on flos. I think color cats got sweepin and moppin in they blood, it come natural. It sorta like eatin and breathin now to color peoples. I bet you give some little color baby one-year-old a broom in he han, he star sweepin his ass off. Whoa!"

Jones returned to the advertisement while Lana locked the cabinet again. Then she looked at the long tracks of dust on the floor that made it look as if Jones had plowed rather than mopped it. There were linear streaks of clean floor for the furrows, and linear streaks of dust, the hillocks. Although Lana did not know it, this was Jones's attempt at some subtle sabotage. He had some larger plans for the future.

"Hey, you there. Take a look at my goddam floor."

Jones reluctantly looked through his sunglasses and saw nothingness.

"Whoa! You got a fine flo. Ooo-wee. Everthin in the Night of Joy firs rate."

"You see all that crap?"

"For twenny dollar a week, you gotta expec a little crap. The crap star disappearin when the wage goin up aroun fifty or sigsty."

"I want performance when I put out money," Lana said angrily.

"Listen, you ever try livin on my kinda wage? You think color peoples get grossries and clothin at a specia price? What you thinkin about half the time you sittin up here playin with your penny? Whoa! Where I live, you know how peoples buy cigarette? Them peoples cain affor a whole pack, they buy they cigarette separate two cent apiece. You think a color mother got it easy? Shit. I ain foolin. I gettin pretty tire of bein vagran or tryina keep my ass alive on this kinda wage."

"Who took you off the streets and gave you a job when the cops was about to lock you up for vagrancy? You might think about that sometime when you're goofing off behind them goddam glasses."

"Goofin off? Shit. Goofin off ain cleanin up this mother-fuckin cathouse. They somebody in here sweepin and moppin up all the shit your po, stupor customer drippin on the flo. I feel sorry for them po peoples comin in here thinkin they gonna have theirself some fun, probly gettin knockout drop in they drink, catchin the clap off the ice cube. Whoa! And talkin about puttin out money it seem to me maybe you be puttin out a little more now that your orphan frien stop comin aroun. Since you cut out the chariddy, maybe you slip me some of the United Fun money."

Lana said nothing. She clipped the receipt for the box of chalk to her ledger book so that she could list it in the column of itemized deductions that always accompanied her income tax returns. She had already bought a used globe of the world. That, too, was stored in the cabinet. All she needed now was a book. When she saw George next, she would ask him to bring her one. He must have some kind of book left over from the days before he had dropped out of high school.

Lana had taken some time to assemble the little collection of props. While the plainclothesmen had been coming in at night, she had been too worried and preoccupied to attend to this project for George. There had been the major problem of Darlene, the vulnerable point in Lana's wall of protection against undercover policemen. But now, the plainclothesmen had gone away as suddenly as they had appeared. Lana had spotted each one as soon as he had entered, and with Darlene safely off the stools and practicing with her bird, the plainclothesmen had nothing to go on. Lana had seen to it that they were actively ignored by everyone. It took experience to be able to spot a cop. But a person who could spot a cop could also avoid a lot of trouble.

There were only two things to be settled. One was getting the book. If George wanted her to have a book, he could get it for her himself. Lana wasn't about to buy a book, even a used one. The other was getting Darlene back on the stools now that the plainclothesmen were gone. Having someone like Darlene on commission was better than having her on salary. And what Lana had seen Darlene do on the stage with the bird told her that, for the moment, the Night of Joy might do better if it decided not to cater to the animal trade.

"Where's Darlene?" Lana asked Jones. "I got a little message for her and that bird."

"She telephone and say she be in sometime this afternoon to do some more rehearsin," Jones said to the advertisement he was researching. "She say she takin her bird to the veternaria firs, she think it losin some of its feather."

"Yeah?"

Lana started to plan the ensemble with the globe, the chalk, and the book. If the thing had commercial possibilities, it should be done with a certain finesse and quality. She envisioned several arrangements that would combine grace and obscenity. There was no need to be too raw. After all, she was appealing to kids.

"Here we come," Darlene called happily from the door. She tripped into the bar in slacks and a pea jacket, carrying a covered birdcage.

"Well, don't plan to stay too long," Lana answered. "I got some news for you and your friend."

Darlene put the cage on the bar and uncovered a huge, scrofulous rose cockatoo that looked, like a used car, as if it had passed through the hands of many owners. The bird's crest dipped, and it cried horribly, "Awwk."

"Okay, get it out, Darlene. You go back to your stool starting tonight."

"Aw, Lana," Darlene moaned. "Whatsa matter? We been doing good in rehearsal. Just wait'll we iron out the kinks. This act is gonna be a boffo smash."

"To tell you the truth, Darlene, I'm afraid of you and that bird."

"Look, Lana." Darlene took off her pea jacket and showed the manager the tiny rings attached to the side of her slacks and blouse with safety pins. "You see these

198

things? That's what's gonna make the act smooth. I been practicing with it in my apartment. It's a new angle. He grabs at those rings with his beak and rips my clothes off. I mean, these rings is just for rehearsal. When I get my costume made, the rings are gonna be sewed on top of a hook and eye so when he grabs, the costume pops open. I'm telling you, Lana. It's gonna be a smash hit sensation."

"Listen, Darlene, it was safer when you just had that goddam thing flying around your head or whatever it did."

"But now it's gonna be a real part of the turn. It's gonna *pull* . . ."

"Yeah, and it might pull your tits off. All I need in this place is a goddam accident and a ambulance to drive away my customers and ruin my investment. Or maybe this bird gets it in his head to fly out in the audience and pull out somebody's eyes. No, to be frank, I don't trust you and a bird, Darlene. Safety first."

"Aw, Lana." Darlene was heartbroken. "Give us a chance. We just getting good."

"No. Beat it. Take that thing off my bar before it takes a shit." Lana threw the cover over the birdcage. "The you-know-whats are gone and you can go back to your stool."

"I think maybe I'll tell you-know-who about the you-know-whats and make you-know-who scared and quit."

Jones looked up from an advertisement and said, "If you peoples be talkin all this double-talk, I cain read. Whoa. Who the 'you-know-whats' and who 'you-know-who?' "

"Get off that stool, jailbait, and get on my floor."

"That bird been travelin to Night of Joy practicin

and tryin," Jones said from his cloud, smiling. "Shit. You gotta give it a chance, cain treat it like it's color peoples."

"That's right," Darlene agreed sincerely.

"Since we cuttin off the orphan chariddy and we not extendin it to the porter help, maybe we oughta give a little to a po, strugglin gal gotta hustle on commission. Hey!" Jones had seen the bird flap around on the stage while Darlene tried to dance. He had never seen a worse performance; Darlene and the bird qualified as legitimate sabotage. "Maybe it need a little polishin here and there, a little twistin and rockin, some more slippin and slidin, but I think that ack very good. Ooo-wee."

"You see that?" Darlene said to Lana. "Jones oughta know. Colored people got plenty rhythm."

"Whoa!"

"I don't wanna scare somebody with a story about some people."

"Oh, shut up, Darlene," Lana screamed.

Jones covered the two with some smoke and said, "I think Darlene and that there bird very unusual. Whoa! I think you be attractin plenny new peoples in this place. What other club got them a ball eagle on the stage?"

"You jerks think there's really a bird trade we could tap?" Lana asked.

"Hey! I sure they a bird trade. White peoples always got parrakeets and canayries they smoochin. Wait till them peoples fin out what kinda bird the Night of Joy offerin. You be havin a doorman in front this place. You be gettin the society trade. Whoa!" Jones created a dangerous-looking nimbus that seemed ready to burst. "Darlene and that bird jus gotta eye-rom out a few rough spot. Shit. The gal jus start-in in show biz. She need a break."

"That's right," Darlene said. "I'm just startin out in show biz. I need a break."

"Shut up, stupid. You think you can get that bird to strip you?"

"Yes, ma'm," Darlene said enthusiastically. "Suddenly it come to me. I was sitting in my apartment watching it play on its rings, and I said to myself, 'Darlene, how come you don't stick some rings on your clothes?'"

"Shut your moron up," Lana said. "Okay, let's see what it can do."

"Whoa! Now you talkin. All kinda mother be showin up to see this act."

III

"Santa, I hadda call you, honey."

"What's wrong, Irene babe?" Mrs. Battaglia's froggy baritone asked feelingly.

"It's Ignatius."

"What he's done now, sweetheart? Tell Santa."

"Wait a minute. Let me see if he's still in that tub." Mrs. Reilly listened apprehensively to the great liquid thrashings coming from the bathroom. One whalelike snort floated out into the hall through the peeling bathroom door. "It's okay. He's still in there. I can't lie to you, Santa. My heart's broke."

"Aw."

"Ignatius comes home about a hour ago dressed up like a butcher."

"Good. He's got him another job, that big fat bum."

201

"But not in a butcher shop, honey," Mrs. Reilly said, her voice heavy with grief. "He's a hot dog vendor."

"Aw, come on," Santa croaked. "A hot dog vendor? You mean out on the streets?"

"Out on the streets, honey, like a bum."

"Bum is right, girl. Even worst. Read the police notices in the paper sometimes. They all a bunch of vagrants."

"Ain't that awful!"

"Somebody oughta punch that boy in the nose."

"When he first comes in, Santa, he makes me guess what kinda job he's got. First, I guess, 'butcher,' you know?"

"Of course."

"So he says, very insolent, 'Guess again. You ain't even close.' I keep guessing for about five minutes until I can't think of no more jobs where you'd be wearing one of them white uniforms. Then he finally says, 'Wrong every time. I got me a job selling weenies.' I almost passed out, Santa, right on the kitchen floor. Wouldn't thata been fine, me with my head broke open on the linoleum?"

"He wouldn't care, not that one."

"Not him."

"Never in a million years."

"He don't care about his poor momma," Mrs. Reilly said. "With all his education, mind you. Selling weenies out on the street in the broad daylight."

"So what you told him, girl?"

"I didn't tell him nothing. By the time I got my mouth open, he runs off to the bathroom. He's still locked up in there splashing water all over the floor."

"Hold on a minute, Irene. I got one of my little

grandchirren over here for the day," Santa said and screamed at someone at her end of the line: "Get the hell away from that stove, Charmaine, and go play out on the banquette before I bust you right in the mouth."

A child's voice made some reply.

"Lord," Santa continued calmly to Mrs. Reilly. "Them kids is sweet, but sometimes I just don't know. Charmaine! Get the hell outside and go play on your bike before I come slap your face off. Hold the line, Irene."

Mrs. Reilly heard Santa put the telephone down. Then a child screamed, a door slammed, and Santa was back on the line.

"Christ, I tell you true, Irene, that child won't listen to nobody! I'm trying to cook her some spaghettis and daube, and she keeps on playing in my pot. I wish them sisters at her school would beat up on her a little. You know Angelo. You shoulda seen how them sisters beat up on him when he was a kid. One sister throwed him right into a blackboard. That's how come Angelo's such a sweet, considerate man today."

"The sisters loved Ignatius. He was such a darling child. He used to win all them little holy pictures for knowing his catechism."

"Them sisters shoulda knocked his head in."

"When he useta come home with all them little holy pictures," Mrs. Reilly sniffed, "I sure never thought then he'd end up selling weenies in the broad daylight." Mrs. Reilly coughed nervously and violently into the telephone. "But tell me, sweetheart, how Angelo's making out?"

"His wife Rita rings me up a little while ago to tell me she thinks he's coming down with pneumonia from being stuck in that toilet all the time. I tell you true,

Irene, that Angelo's getting as pale as a ghost. The cops sure don't treat that boy right. He loves the force. When he graduated from the cops' academy, you woulda thought he just made it outta the Ivory League. He was sure proud."

"Yeah, poor Angelo looks bad," Mrs. Reilly agreed. "He's got him a bad cough, that boy. Well, maybe he'll feel a little better after he reads that thing Ignatius give me to give him. Ignatius says it's inspirational literature."

"Yeah? I wouldn't trust no 'inspirational literature' I got from that Ignatius. It's prolly fulla dirty stories."

"Suppose somebody I know sees him with one of them wagons."

"Don't be ashamed, babe. It ain't your fault you got a brat on your hands," Santa grunted. "What you need is a man in that house, girl, to set that boy straight. I'm gonna find that nice old man ast about you."

"I don't want a nice old man. All I want is a nice child."

"Don't you worry. Just leave it to Santa. I'll fix you up. The man runs the fish market says he don't know the man's name. But I'll find out. As a matter of fact, I think I seen him walking down St. Ferdinand Street the other day."

"He ast about me?"

"Well, Irene, I mean I didn't get a chance to talk to him. I don't even know if it was the same man."

"You see that? That old man don't care neither."

"Don't talk like that, girl. I'll ask over by the beer parlor. I'll hang around Sunday mass. I'll find out his name."

"That old man don't care for me."

"Irene, they's no harm in meeting him."

"I got enough problems with Ignatius. It's the disgrace, Santa. Suppose Miss Annie, the next door lady, sees him with one of them wagons. She's awready about to get us put under a peace bond. She's all the time spying in that alley behind her shutters."

"You can't worry about people, Irene," Santa advised. "The people on my block got dirty mouths. If you can live down here in St. Ode of Cluny Parish, you can live anyplace. Vicious is the word, believe me. I got one woman on my block's gonna get a brick right in her face if she don't shut up about me. Somebody told me she's been calling me a 'merry widow.' But don't you worry. I'm gonna get her good. I think she's running with some man works at the shipyards, anyways. I think I'm gonna write her husband a little anonymous letter to straighten out that girl."

"I know what it is, sugar. Remember I lived down there on Dauphine when I was a girl. The anonymous letters my poppa useta get . . . about *me*. Vicious. I always thought my cousin, that poor spinster girl, was writing them."

"Which cousin was that?" Santa asked with interest. Irene Reilly's relatives always had gory biographies that were worth hearing.

"That was the one knocked a pot of berling water on her arm when she was a child. She was kinda scalded looking. You know what I mean? I always seen her writing away at the kitchen table at her momma's house. She was prolly writing about me. She was very jealous when Mr. Reilly started seeing me."

"That's the way it goes," Santa said. A scalded relative was a dull figure in Irene's dramatic gallery. Then she said hoarsely and cheerfully, "I'll have a little party with you and Angelo and his wife, if she'll come."

"Aw, that's sweet, Santa, but I don't feel much like a party these days."

"It'll do you good to shake yourself a little, girl. If I can find out about that old man, I'll invite him over too. You and him can dance."

"Well, if you see the old man, babe, tell him Miss Reilly said, 'Hello.' "

Behind the bathroom door Ignatius was lying passively in the tepid water pushing the plastic soap dish back and forth across the surface with one finger and listening now and then to his mother on the telephone. Occasionally he held the soap dish down until it filled with water and sank. Then he would feel for it on the bottom of the tub, empty it, and sail it again. His blue and yellow eyes rested on an unopened manila envelope on the top of the toilet. For quite a while Ignatius had been trying to decide whether or not he would open the envelope. The trauma of having found employment had affected his valve negatively, and he was waiting until the warm water in which he wallowed like a pink hippopotamus had a calming effect upon his system. Then he would attack the envelope. Paradise Vendors should prove to be a pleasant employer. He would spend his time parked somewhere by the river accumulating notes for the Journal. Mr. Clyde had a certain paternal quality that Ignatius liked; the old man, the scarred and wizened mogul of the frankfurter, would be a welcome new character in the Journal.

206

At last Ignatius felt relaxed enough and, raising his dripping hulk out of the water, picked up the envelope.

"Why must she use this sort of envelope?" he asked angrily, studying the little circle of a Planetarium Station, New York, postmark on the thick tan paper.

"The contents are probably written in marking pencil or worse."

He tore the envelope open, wetting the paper, and pulled out a folded poster that said in large letters:

LECTURE! LECTURE!

M. Minkoff speaks boldly about
*"Sex in Politics: Erotic Liberty
as a Weapon Against Reactionaries"*

8 p.m. Thursday, the 28th
Y.M.H.A. - Grand Concourse
Admission: $1.00 - OR - Sign M. Minkoff's Petition Which Aggressively Demands More and Better Sex for All and a Crash Program for Minorities! (The petition will be mailed to Washington.) Sign now and save America from sexual ignorance, chastity, and fear. Are you committed enough to help in this bold and crucial movement?

"Oh, my God!" Ignatius spurted through his dripping moustache. "Are they letting her speak in public now? What in the world does the title of this ludicrous lecture mean?" Ignatius read the poster again, viciously. "At any rate, I know that she will speak boldly, and in a perverse way I wish that I could hear that little minx babbling before an audience. This time she has outdone herself in offending taste and decency."

Following a handwritten arrow at the bottom of the poster and the word *over*, Ignatius complied and looked at the other side of the poster, where Myrna had written something:

Sirs:
What is wrong, Ignatius? I have not heard from you. Well, I don't really blame you for not writing. I guess I came on a

little strong in my last letter, but it was only because your paranoid fantasy disturbed me, rooted as it possibly was in your unhealthy attitude toward sex. You know that ever since I first met you I have directed pointed questions at you in order to clarify your sexual inclinations. My only desire was to aid you in finding your true self-expression and contentment through satisfying, natural orgasm. I respect your mind and I have always accepted your eccentric tendencies and that is why I want to see you reach the plateau of perfect mental-sexual balance. (A good, explosive orgasm would cleanse your being and bring you out of the shadows.) Just don't be angry at me about the letter.

I will explain this poster a little later in this letter because I imagine you are interested in knowing how this bold, dedicated lecture came about. First, though, I must tell you that the movie is off, so if you were planning to play the landlord, forget it. Basically, we had trouble with funds. I could not milk another drachma out of my father, so Leola, the Harlem find, got very hostile about salary (or lack of it) and finally dropped a remark or two that sounded a little anti-Semitic to me. Who needs a girl who isn't dedicated enough to work gratis in a project that would benefit her race? Samuel has decided to become a forest ranger in Montana because he is planning a dramatic allegory set in a dark woods (Ignorance and Custom) and he wants to get the feel of the forest. From what I know of Samuel, he will be a big flop as a ranger, but the allegory, I know, will be challenging and controversial, full of unpleasant truths. Wish him well. He is fantastic.

To get back to the lecture. At last it seems that I am finding a platform for my philosophy, etc. It all happened in a strange way. A few weeks ago I was at a party that some friends were giving for this very *real* boy who had just returned from Israel. He was unbelievable. I mean that.

208   Ignatius emitted a little Paradise gas.

For hours and hours he sang these folk songs he had picked up over there; really significant songs that proved my theory that music should basically be an instrument of social protest and expression. He kept us all in that apartment for hours and hours listening and asking for more. Later we all started talking—on many levels—and I let him know what was on my mind in general.

"Ho, hum," Ignatius yawned violently.

He said, "Why are you keeping all of this to yourself, Myrna? Why haven't you let the world in on this?" I told him that I often spoke in discussion groups and in my group therapy group. I also told him about these letters of mine to the editor that have been printed in *The New Democracy* and *Man and Masses* and *Now!*

"Get out of that tub, boy," Ignatius heard his mother scream outside the door of the bathroom.

"Why?" he asked. "Are you going to use it?"

"No."

"Then please go away."

"You been in there too long."

"Please! I am attempting to read a letter."

"A letter? Who wrote you a letter?"

"My dear friend, Miss Minkoff."

"The last thing you said was she got you fired outta Levy Pants."

"Well, she did. However, it might have been a favor in disguise. My new work may prove rather agreeable."

"Ain't that awful," Mrs. Reilly said sadly. "You get fired outta a two-bit clerk job in a factory and now you selling weenies in the streets. Well, I'll tell you one thing, Ignatius, you better not get fired by the weenie man. You know what Santa said?"

"I'm sure that it was rather perceptive and incisive, whatever it was. I would imagine that it is rather difficult to comprehend her assaults upon the Mother tongue."

"She said somebody oughta punch you right in the nose."

"Coming from her, that's rather literate."

"What that Myrna's doing now?" Mrs. Reilly asked suspiciously. "How come she's writing so much? She needed a good bath, that girl."

"Myrna's psyche is only capable of dealing with water in an oral context."

"What?"

"Will you please stop shrieking like a fishmonger and run along? Don't you have a bottle of muscatel baking in the oven? Now let me alone. I'm very nervous."

"Nervous? You been in that hot water over an hour."

"It's hardly hot anymore."

"Then get out the tub."

"Why is it so important to you that I leave this tub? Mother, I really don't understand you at all. Isn't there something that, as a housekeeper, you feel compelled to do at the moment? I noticed this morning that the lint in the hallway is forming into spheres almost as large as baseballs. Clean the house. Telephone for the correct time. Do something. Lie down and take a nap. You're looking rather peaked these days."

"Of course I am, boy. You breaking your poor momma's heart. What would you do if I dropped dead?"

210

"Well, I am not going to participate in this idiotic conversation. Carry on a monologue out there if you wish. Quietly. I must concentrate upon the new offenses that M. Minkoff has conceived in this letter."

"I can't take it no more, Ignatius. You gonna find me laying in the kitchen one of these days with a stroke. Just watch, boy. You gonna be all alone in the world. Then you gonna fall on your knees and pray to God for the way you treated your poor dear mother."

From the bathroom there came only silence. Mrs. Reilly waited for at least a splash of water or a rustle of paper, but the bathroom door might as well have been the door of a tomb. After a minute or two of fruitless waiting, she walked off down the hall toward the oven. When Ignatius heard the oven door creak open he returned to the letter.

He said, "With that voice and personality, you should be appearing before the people in prison." This guy was really amazing; in addition to his tough mind, he was a real *mensch*. He was so gentlemanly and thoughtful I could hardly believe it. (Especially after dealing with Samuel, who is dedicated and unafraid but all a little too loud and something of a clod.) I never met anybody so dedicated to fighting reactionary ideas and prejudice as this folk singer. His very best friend was a Negro abstractionist, he said, who made magnificent smears of protest and defiance across the canvas, sometimes slashing the canvas to shreds with a knife. He handed me this brilliant pamphlet that showed in detail how the Pope is trying to assemble a nuclear armory; it really opened my mind, and I forwarded it to the editor of *The New Democracy* to aid him in his battle against the Church. But this guy also had this big thing against WASPS. Like he hated them. I mean, this fellow was sharp.

The next day I got a telephone call from him. Would I lecture to this social action group he was going to form somewhere in Brooklyn Heights? I was overcome. In this world of dog eat dog, it is rare to find a friend . . . a really sincere friend . . . or so I thought. Well, to make my point as briefly as possible, I had learned the *hard* way that the lecture circuit is something like show business: the casting couch and that routine. Get what I mean?

"Do I believe this egregious offense against good taste that I am reading?" Ignatius asked the floating soap dish. "This girl is without shame entirely!"

Again I have been awakened to the fact that my body appeals to some people more than my mind.

"Ho hum," Ignatius sighed.

Personally, I feel like exposing this phony "folk singer" who I guess is preying on some other dedicated young girl liberal at this moment. Somebody I know said she heard this "folk singer" guy is really a Baptist from Alabama. Boy, what a fraud he was. So then I checked on this pamphlet he had given me and discovered that it was printed by the Klan. This will give you some idea of the ideological subtleties which we have to deal with today. It sounded like a good liberal pamphlet to me. Now I have had to humiliate myself by writing to the editor of *The New Democracy* to tell him that the pamphlet, although challenging, was written by the wrong people. Well, the WASPS struck back and got me this time. The incident reminded me of the time in Poe Park when this squirrel I was feeding turned out to really be a rat which at first glance could have passed for a squirrel any day. So live and learn. This phony gave me an idea. You can always learn something from crumbs. I decided to ask up here at the 'Y' if I could get the auditorium one night. After a while, they said o.k. Of course, the audience up here at the Bronx 'Y' will probably be a little parochial, but if I make good in the lecture, I might one day end up speaking down at the Lex. Ave. 'Y' where great thinkers like Norman Mailer and Seymour Krim are always airing their views. It won't hurt to try.

I hope that you are working on your personality problems, Ignatius. Is the paranoia getting any worse? The basis for the paranoia, I think, is the fact that you're always sealed up in that room and have become suspicious of the outside world. I don't know why you insisted on living way down there with the alligators. In spite of the complete overhaul that your mind is crying for, you have a brain that could really grow and flower here in N.Y. As it is, you are thwarting yourself and your mentality. The last time I saw you, when I was passing through from Mississippi, you were in pretty bad shape. You've probably regressed completely by now living in that substandard old house with only your mother for company. Aren't your natural impulses crying for release? A beautiful and meaningful love affair would transform you, Ignatius. I know it would. Great Oedipus bonds are encircling your brain and destroying you.

I don't imagine that your sociological or political ideas are getting any more progressive either. Have you abandoned your project to form a political party or nominate a candidate for president by divine right? I remember that when I finally met you and challenged your political apathy, you came up with this idea. I knew that it was a reactionary project, but it at least showed that you were developing some political consciousness. Please write to me about the matter. I am very concerned. We need a three-party system in this country, and I think that day by day the fascists are growing in strength. This Divine Right Party is the sort of fringe-group scheme that would syphon off a large part of the fascist support.

Well, let me stop. I hope the lecture is a success. You, especially, would benefit from its message. By the way, if you ever do activate the Divine Right movement, I can give you some help in organizing a chapter up here. Please get out of the house, Ignatius, and enter into the world around you. I am worried about your future. You have always been one of my most important projects and I am interested in hearing of your current mental condition, so *please* get out of the pillows and write.

M. Minkoff

Later, his puckered pink skin wrapped in the old flannel robe that a safety pin held around his hips, Ignatius sat at the desk in his room filling his fountain pen. In the hall his mother was speaking to someone else on the telephone saying, "And I used every last cent of the insurance money his poor old Grammaw Reilly left just to keep him in college. Ain't that awful? All that money down the drain." Ignatius belched and opened a drawer to search for the stationery that he believed he still had; there he found the yo-yo that he had bought from the Filipino who had been selling them in the neighborhood a few months ago. On one side of the yo-yo there was a palm tree which the Filipino had carved at Ignatius' request. Ignatius spun the yo-yo downward, but the string snapped and it rattled across the floor and under the bed where it landed on a pile of Big Chief tablets and old magazines. Removing the piece of string that hung from his finger, he dug into the drawer again and found a sheet of paper with a Levy Pants letterhead.

Beloved Myrna:

I have received your offensive communication. Do you seriously think that I am interested in your tawdry encounters with such sub-humans as folk singers? In every letter of yours I seem to find some reference to the sleaziness of your personal life. Please confine yourself to discussing issues and such; thereby you will at least avoid obscenity and offense. I did think, however, that the symbolism of the rat and squirrel or rat-squirrel or squirrel-rat was evocative and rather excellent.

On the dark night of that dubious lecture, the sole member of your audience will probably be some desperately lonely old male librarian who saw a light in the window of the lecture hall and hopefully came in to escape the cold and the horrors of his personal hell. There in the hall, his stooped figure sitting alone before the podium, your nasal voice echoing among the empty chairs and hammering boredom, confusion, and sexual reference deeper and deeper into the poor wretch's bald skull, confounded to the point of hysteria, he will doubtlessly exhibit himself, waving his crabbed organ like a club in despair against the grim sound that drones on and on over his head. If I were you, I would cancel the lecture immediately; I am certain that the 'Y' management would be only too glad to accept your withdrawal, especially if they have had a chance to see that tasteless poster which is now no doubt tacked to every telephone pole in the Bronx.

The comments upon my personal life were uncalled for and revealed a shocking lack of taste and decency.

Actually, my personal life has undergone a metamorphosis: I am currently connected in a most vital manner with the food merchandising industry, and therefore I doubt quite seriously whether I shall have much time in the future to correspond with you.

Busily,
Ignatius

eight

"LET HER ALONE," Mr. Levy said. "Look, she's trying to sleep."

"Let her alone?" Mrs. Levy propped up Miss Trixie on the yellow nylon couch. "Do you realize, Gus, that this is the tragedy of this poor woman's life. She's always been alone. She needs someone. She needs love."

"Ugh."

Mrs. Levy was a woman of interests and ideals. Over the years she had given herself freely to bridge, African violets, Susan and Sandra, golf, Miami, Fanny Hurst and Hemingway, correspondence courses, hairdressers, the sun, gourmet foods, ballroom dancing, and, in recent years, Miss Trixie. She had always had to settle for Miss Trixie at a distance, an unsatisfactory arrangement for carrying out the program outlined in the psychology correspondence course, the final examination of which she had failed resoundingly. The correspondence school had even refused to give her an F. But now that Mrs. Levy had played her card correctly in the game dealing with the firing of the young idealist, she had Miss Trixie in the wrinkled flesh, visor, sneakers, and all. Mr. Gonzalez had gladly given the assistant accountant an indefinite vacation.

"Miss Trixie," Mrs. Levy said sweetly. "Wake up."

Miss Trixie opened her eyes and wheezed, "Am I retired?"

"No, darling."

"What?" Miss Trixie snarled. "I thought I was retired!"

"Miss Trixie, you think that you're old and tired. This is very bad."

"Who?"

"You."

"Oh. I am. I am very tired."

"Don't you see?" Mrs. Levy asked. "It's all in your mind. You have this age psychosis. You're still a very attractive woman. You must say to yourself, 'I am still attractive. I am a very attractive woman.' "

Miss Trixie exhaled a grunting snore into Mrs. Levy's lacquered hair.

"Will you please let her alone, Dr. Freud?" Mr. Levy said angrily, looking up from a *Sports Illustrated.* "I almost wish Susan and Sandra were home so you could play with them. Whatever happened to your canasta circle?"

"Don't talk to me, you failure. How can I play canasta when there's a psycho in distress?"

"Psycho? The woman's senile. We had to stop at about thirty gas stations on the way over here. Finally I got tired of getting out of the car and showing her which was the Men's and which was the Women's, so I let her pick them herself. I worked out a system. The law of averages. I laid money on her and she came out about fifty-fifty."

"Don't tell me any more," Mrs. Levy cautioned. "Not another word. It's too typical. Permitting this anal compulsive to flounder like that."

"Isn't Lawrence Welk on?" Miss Trixie asked suddenly.

"No, dear. Relax."

"It *is* Saturday."

"He'll be on. Don't worry. Now tell me, what do you dream about."

"I can't remember at the moment."

"Try," Mrs. Levy said, making some sort of note on her date book with a rhinestoned automatic pencil. "You must try, Miss Trixie. Darling, your mind is warped. You're like a cripple."

"I may be old, but I'm not crippled," Miss Trixie said wildly.

"Look, you're exciting her, Florence Nightingale," Mr. Levy said. "With all you know about psychoanalysis, you're going to ruin whatever's left in that head of hers. All she wants is to retire and sleep."

"You've already wrecked your life. Don't do the same to hers. This case can't be retired. She must be made to feel wanted and needed and loved . . ."

"Turn on your goddam exercising board and let her take a nap!"

"I thought we agreed to let the board out of this."

"Let her alone. Let me alone. Go ride your exercycle."

"Quiet, please!" Miss Trixie croaked and rubbed her eyes.

"We must talk pleasantly in front of her," Mrs. Levy whispered. "Loud voices, arguing, will only make her more insecure."

218

"I'll buy that. Keep quiet. And get that senile bag out of my rumpus room."

"That's right. Think about yourself as usual. If your father could only see you today." Mrs. Levy's aqua lids rose in horror. "A motheaten playboy looking for kicks."

"Kicks?"

"Now you people shut up," Miss Trixie warned. "I must say it was a dark day when I was brought out here. It was much nicer in there with Gomez. Nice and quiet. If this is some sort of an April Fool, I don't think it's funny." She looked at Mr. Levy through rheumy eyes. "You're the bird that fired my friend Gloria. Poor Gloria. The kindest person ever worked in that office."

"Oh, no!" Mrs. Levy sighed. Then she turned on her husband. "So you only fired one person, is that right? What about this Gloria? One person treats Miss Trixie like a human being. One person is her friend. Do you know this? Do you care? Oh, no. Levy Pants might as well be on Mars for all you care. You walk in from the track one day and kick Gloria out."

"Gloria?" Mr. Levy asked. "I didn't fire any Gloria!"

"Yes, you did!" Miss Trixie piped. "I saw it with my very own eyes. Poor Gloria was the soul of kindness. I remember Gloria gave me socks and luncheon meat."

"Socks and luncheon meat?" Mr. Levy whistled through his teeth. "Oh, boy."

"That's right," Mrs. Levy shouted. "Make fun of this neglected creature. Just don't tell me whatever else you did at Levy Pants. I couldn't bear it. I won't tell the girls about Gloria. They wouldn't understand a heart like yours. They're too innocent."

"No, you'd better not try to tell them about Gloria," Mr. Levy said angrily. "Any more of this foolishness and you'll be down on the beach in San Juan with your mother, laughing, and swimming and dancing."

"Are you threatening me?"

"Now quiet!" Miss Trixie snarled more loudly. "I want to go back to Levy Pants right this very minute."

"You see that?" Mrs. Levy asked her husband. "You hear that desire to work. And you want to crush her by retiring her. Gus, please. Get help. You're going to end badly."

Miss Trixie was reaching for the bag of scraps that she had brought as luggage.

"Okay, Miss Trixie," Mr. Levy said as if he were summoning a pet cat. "Let's go get in the car."

"Thank goodness," Miss Trixie sighed.

"Take your hands off her!" Mrs. Levy screamed.

"I haven't even gotten up from my chair," her husband answered.

Mrs. Levy shoved Miss Trixie down on the couch again and said, "Now stay there. You need help."

"Not from you people," Miss Trixie wheezed. "Let me up."

"Let her up."

"Please." Mrs. Levy held up a warning hand, plump and ringed. "Don't worry about this neglected creature I've taken under my wing. Don't worry about me either. Forget your little daughters. Get in your sports car and ride. There's a regatta this afternoon. Look. You can see the sails from the picture window I had installed with your father's hard-earned money."

"I'll get even with you people," Miss Trixie was snarling on the couch. "Don't worry. You'll find out."

She tried to rise, but Mrs. Levy had pinned her to the yellow nylon.

II

His cold was getting worse and worse, and each cough caused a vague pain in his lungs that lingered on for moments after the cough had seared his throat and chest. Patrolman Mancuso wiped his mouth clean of saliva and tried to clear the phlegm from his throat. One afternoon he had had such a bad case of claustrophobia that he almost fainted in the booth. Now it seemed that he was ready to faint from the dizziness that the cold had induced. He leaned his head against the side of the booth for a moment and closed his eyes. Red and blue clouds floated across his eyelids. He had to capture some character and get out of that rest room before his ague got so bad that the sergeant had to carry him to and from the booth every day. He had always hoped to win honor on the force, but what honor was there in dying of pneumonia in a bus station rest room? Even his relatives would laugh. What would his children say to their friends at school?

Patrolman Mancuso looked at the tiles on the floor. They were out of focus. He felt panic. Then he stared at them more closely and saw that the haze was only the moisture that formed a gray film over almost every surface in the rest room. He looked again at *The Consolation of Philosophy*, which was opened on his lap, and turned a limp, damp page. The book was making him more depressed. The guy who wrote it was going to be tortured by the king. The preface had said so. Now all this time the guy was writing this thing, he was going to end up with something driven down into his head. Patrolman Mancuso felt sorry for the guy and felt obliged to read what he had written. So far he had only covered about twenty pages and was beginning to wonder whether this Boethius was something of a gambler. He was always talking about fate and odds and the wheel of fortune. Anyway, it wasn't the kind of book that exactly made you look up to the brighter side.

After a few sentences Patrolman Mancuso's mind began to wander. He looked out through the crack in the door of the booth, which he always left open an inch or two so that he could see who was using the urinals, the lavatories, and the paper-towel box. There at the lavatories was the same boy that Patrolman Mancuso had been seeing every day, it seemed. He watched the delicate boots moving back and forth from the lavatory to the paper-towel dispenser. The boy leaned against a lavatory and began drawing on the back of his hands with a ballpoint pen. There might be something in this, Patrolman Mancuso thought.

He opened the booth and went up to the boy. Coughing, he tried to say pleasantly, "What's that you're writing on your hand, pal?"

George looked at the monocle and the beard at his elbow and said, "Get the hell away from me before I kick your nuts in."

"Cawd the police," Patrolman Mancuso taunted.

"No," George answered. "Just get away. I ain't making trouble."

"You afred udda police?"

George wondered who this nut was. He was as bad as that hot dog vendor.

"Look, kookie, move it. I don't want no trouble with the cops."

"You dote?" Patrolman Mancuso asked happily.

"No, and neither does a screwball like you," George said, looking at the watering eye behind the monocle and the moistness at the mouth of the beard.

"You udder arrest," Patrolman Mancuso coughed.

"What? Boy, are you out of it."

"Patrolman Mancuso. Uddercover." A badge flashed in front of George's pimples. "Cubb alogg wid me."

"What the hell are you arresting me for? I'm just standing here," George protested nervously. "I ain't done nothing. What is this?"

"You udder suspiciudd."

"Suspicion of what?" George asked in panic.

"Aha!" Patrolman Mancuso slobbered. "You rilly afred."

He reached out to grab George by the arm and handcuff him, but George snatched *The Consolation of Philosophy* from under Patrolman Mancuso's arm and slammed it into the side of his head. Ignatius had bought a large, elegant, limited edition of the English translation, and all fifteen dollars of its price hit Patrolman Mancuso in the head with the force of a dictionary. Patrolman Mancuso bent over to pick up the monocle, which had fallen from his eye. When he straightened up again, he saw the boy scraping rapidly out of the door of the rest room with the book in his hand. He wanted to run after him, but his head was throbbing too badly. He returned to his booth to rest and grew even more depressed. What could he tell Mrs. Reilly about the book?

George opened the locker in the waiting room of the bus terminal as quickly as he could and took out the brown-paper packages he had stored. Without closing the locker door, he ran out onto Canal Street and jogged metallically toward the central business district, looking over his shoulder for the beard and monocle. There was no beard anywhere behind him.

This was really bad luck. That undercover agent

would be prowling the bus station all afternoon looking for him. And what about tomorrow? The bus station was no longer safe; it was off-limits.

"Damn Miss Lee," George said aloud, still walking as fast as he could. If she weren't so tight, this wouldn't have happened. She could have fired the jig, and he could have kept on picking up his packages at the old time, two o'clock. As it was, he had almost been arrested. And it was all because he had to go check the stuff in the bus station, all because he was stuck with the stuff now for two hours every afternoon. Where did you put stuff like that? You could get tired of carrying that stuff around all afternoon. Mother was home all the time, so you couldn't go around there with it.

"Tight bitch," George mumbled. He tucked the packages higher up under his arm and realized that he was also carrying the book he had taken from the undercover agent. Stealing from a cop. That was good, too. Miss Lee had asked him to bring her the book she needed. George looked at the title, *The Consolation of Philosophy*. Well, she had a book now.

III

Santa Battaglia tasted a spoonful of the potato salad, cleaned the spoon with her tongue, and placed the spoon neatly on a paper napkin next to the plate of salad. Sucking some pieces of parsley and onion from between her teeth, she said to the picture of her mother on the mantelpiece, "They gonna love that. Nobody makes a good potatis salad like Santa."

The parlor was almost ready for the party. On top of the old console radio there were two fifths of Early Times and a six-bottle carton of Seven-Up. The phonograph she had borrowed from her niece sat on the mopped linoleum in the center of the room, the cord rising to the chandelier where it was plugged in. Two giant-sized bags of potato chips rested in either corner of the red plush sofa. A fork stuck out of the open bottle of olives that she had placed on a tin tray on top of the covered and folded rollaway bed.

Santa grabbed the picture on the mantelpiece, a photograph of an ancient and hostile-looking woman in a black dress and black stockings standing in a dark alley paved with oyster shells.

"Poor momma," Santa said feelingly, giving the picture a loud, wet kiss. The grease on the glass that covered the photograph showed the frequency of these affectionate onslaughts. "You sure had it hard, kid." The little black coals of Sicilian eyes glared almost animatedly at Santa from the snapshot. "The only picture of you I got, momma, and you standing in a alley. Ain't that a shame."

Santa sighed at the unfairness of it all and slammed the picture down on the mantelpiece among the bowl of wax fruit and the bouquet of paper zinnias and the statue of the Virgin Mary and the figurine of the Infant of Prague. Then she went back to the kitchen to get some ice cubes and one of the kitchen chairs. After she had returned with the chair and a little picnic cooler of ice cubes, she arranged her best jelly glasses on the mantelpiece before her mother's picture. The proximity of the picture made her grab it and kiss it again, the ice cube in her mouth cracking against the glass.

"I say a prayer for you every day, babe," Santa told the snapshot incoherently, balancing the ice cube on her tongue. "You better believe they's a candle burning for you over in St. Ode's."

Someone knocked at the front shutters. In putting the picture down hurriedly, Santa tipped it over on its face.

"Irene!" Santa screamed when she opened the door and saw the hesitant Mrs. Reilly on the front steps and her nephew, Patrolman Mancuso, standing down on the banquette. "Come on in, sweetheart darling. You sure looking cute."

"Thanks, honey," Mrs. Reilly said. "Whoo! I forgot how long it takes to drive down here. Me and Angelo been in that car almost a hour."

"Id's the traffig is whad id is," Patrolman Mancuso offered.

"Listen to that cold," Santa said. "Aw, Angelo. You better tell them men at the precinct to take you out that toilet. Where's Rita?"

"She diddit feel like cubbig. She's got her a headache."

"Well, no wonder, locked up in that house with them kids all day long," Santa said. "Aw, she oughta get out, Angelo. What's wrong with that girl?"

"Nerbs," Angelo answered sadly. "She's got nerbous trouble."

"Nerves is terrible," Mrs. Reilly said. "You know what happened, Santa? Angelo lost the book Ignatius give him. Ain't that a shame. I don't mind about the book, but don't never tell Ignatius about it. We'll really have us a fight on our hands."

Mrs. Reilly put her finger to her lips to indicate that the book must forever be a secret.

226

"Well, gimme your coat, girl," Santa said eagerly, almost tearing Mrs. Reilly's old purple woolen topper off. She was determined that the ghost of Ignatius J.

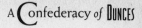

Reilly would not haunt her party as it had haunted so many evenings of bowling.

"You got you a nice place here, Santa," Mrs. Reilly said respectfully. "It's clean."

"Yeah, but I want to get me some new linoleum for the parlor. You ever used them paper curtains, honey? They don't look too bad. I seen some nice ones up by Maison Blanche."

"I bought some nice paper curtains for Ignatius' room once, but he tore them off the window and crumpled them up. He says they an abortion. Ain't that awful?"

"Everybody to his own taste," Santa observed quickly.

"Ignatius don't know I come here tonight. I told him I was going to a novena."

"Angelo, fix Irene here a nice drink. Take a little whiskey yourself, help out that cold. I got some cokes in the kitchen."

"Ignatius don't like novenas neither. I don't know what that boy likes. Personally, I'm getting kinda fed up on Ignatius, even if he is my own child."

"I fixed us a good potatis salad, girl. That old man tells me he likes a good potatis salad."

"You oughta see them big uniforms he's giving me to launder. And all the directions I get on how to wash them. He sounds like he's selling soap powder on the TV. Ignatius acts like he's really made good pushing that wagon around downtown."

"Look at Angelo, babe. He's fixing us a nice drink."

"You got any aspirins, honey?"

"Aw, Irene! What kinda party pooper I got on my hands? Take a drink. Wait till the old man comes. We gonna have us a nice time. Look, you and the old man can dance right in front the phonograph."

"Dance? I don't feel like dancing with no old man. Besides, my feet swole up this afternoon while I was ironing them uniforms."

"Irene, you can't disappoint him, girl. You shoulda seen his face when I invited him out in front the church. Poor old man. I bet nobody ast him out."

"He wanted to come, huh?"

"Wanted to come? He ast me should he wear a suit."

"And what you told him, honey?"

"Well, I said, 'Wear whatever you want, mister.'"

"Well, that's nice." Mrs. Reilly looked down at her green taffeta cocktail dress. "Ignatius ast me why I was wearing a cocktail dress to go to a novena. He's sitting in his room right now writing some foolishness. I says, 'What's that you writing now, boy?' And he say, 'I'm writing about being a weenie vendor.' Ain't that terrible? Who want to read a story like that? You know how much he brought home from that weenie place today? Four dollars. How I'm gonna pay off that man?"

"Look. Angelo fixed us a nice hi-ball."

Mrs. Reilly took a jelly glass from Angelo and drank half of it in two gulps.

"Where you got that nice high-fly from, darling?"

"What you mean?" Santa asked.

"That gramophone you got in the middle of the floor."

228

"That's my little niece's. She's precious. Just graduated outta St. Odo High and she's awready got her a good saleslady job."

"You see that?" Mrs. Reilly said excitedly. "I bet she's making better than Ignatius."

"Lord, Angelo," Santa said. "Stop that coughing. Go lay down in the back and rest up till the old man comes."

"Poor Angelo," Mrs. Reilly said after the patrolman had left the room. "He sure a sweet boy. You two sure been good friends to me. And to think we all met when he tried to arrest Ignatius."

"I wonder how come that old man ain't showed up yet."

"Maybe he's not coming, Santa." Mrs. Reilly finished her drink. "I'm gonna make me another one, if you don't mind, sugar. I got problems."

"Go ahead, babe. I'm gonna take your coat back in the kitchen and see how Angelo's making out. I sure got two happy people at my party so far. I hope that old man don't fall down and break his leg on the way over."

After Santa had left, Mrs. Reilly filled her glass with bourbon and added a jigger of Seven-Up. She picked up the spoon, tasted the potato salad, and, cleaning the spoon with her lips, put it back on the paper napkin. The family in the other half of Santa's double house was beginning to stage what sounded like a riot. Sipping her drink, Mrs. Reilly put her ear to the wall and tried to filter some meaning out of the loud shouting.

"Angelo's taking some cough medicine," Santa said as she returned to the parlor.

"You sure got you good walls in this building, babe," Mrs. Reilly said, unable to comprehend the gist of the argument on the other side of the wall. "I wish me and Ignatius lived here. Miss Annie wouldn't have nothing to complain about."

"Where's that old man?" Santa asked the front shutters.

"Maybe he ain't gonna come."

"Maybe he forgot."

"That's the way it is with old folks, honey."

"He ain't that *old*, Irene."

"How old is he?"

"Someplace in his late sixties, I guess."

"Well, that ain't too old. My poor old Tante Marguerite, the one I told you them kids beat up on to get fifty cents out her coin purse, she going on eighty." Mrs. Reilly finished her drink. "Maybe he went to see a nice picture show or something. Santa, you mind if I make me another drink."

"Irene! You gonna be on the floor, girl. I ain't gonna introduce no drunk to this nice old man."

"I'll make me a small one. I got nerves tonight."

Mrs. Reilly slopped a great deal of whiskey into her glass and sat down again, crushing one of the bags of potato chips.

"Oh, Lord, what I done now?"

"You just smashed them potato chips," Santa said a little angrily.

"Aw, they all crumbs now," Mrs. Reilly said, pulling the bag from beneath her. She studied the flattened cellophane. "Listen, Santa, what time you got? Ignatius says he's sure the burglars is striking tonight and for me to get in early."

"Oh, take it easy, Irene. You just got here."

"To tell you the truth, Santa, I don't think I want to meet this old man."

"Well, it's too late now."

"Yeah, but what me and this old man gonna do?" Mrs. Reilly asked apprehensively.

"Aw, relax, Irene. You making *me* nervous. I'm sorry I axt you over." Santa pulled Mrs. Reilly's drink

230

down from her lips for a moment. "Now listen to me.
You had arthritis very bad. The bowling's helping that
out. Right? You was stuck home with that crazy boy
every night until Santa come along. Right? Now listen
to Santa, precious. You don't wanna end up all alone
with that Ignatius on your hands. This old man looks
like he's got him a little money. He dresses neat. He
knows you from somewhere. He likes you." Santa
looked Mrs. Reilly in the eye. "This old man can pay
off your debt!"

"Yeah?" Mrs. Reilly hadn't thought of this before.
The old man suddenly became a little more attractive.
"He's clean?"

"Sure he's clean," Santa said angrily. "You think
I'm trying fix my friend up with a bum?"

Someone knocked lightly at the shutters on the
front door.

"Oh, I bet that's him," Santa said eagerly.

"Tell him I hadda go, honey."

"Go? Where you goint to, Irene? The man's right
by the front door."

"He is, huh?"

"Lemme go take a look."

Santa opened the door and pushed the shutters
outward.

"Hey, Mr. Robichaux," she said into the night to
someone whom Mrs. Reilly couldn't see. "We been
waiting for you. My friend Miss Reilly here's been wondering where you was. Come on in out the cold."

"Yeah, Miss Battaglia, I'm sorry I'm a little late, but
I had to take my little granchirren around the neighborhood. They raffling some rosaries for the sisters."

"I know," Santa said. "I bought a chance from a
little kid just the other day. They beautiful rosaries. A

lady I know won the outboard motor the sisters was raffling last year."

Mrs. Reilly sat frozen on the sofa staring into her drink as if she had just discovered a roach floating in it.

"Irene!" Santa cried. "What you doing, girl? Say 'hello' to Mr. Robichaux."

Mrs. Reilly looked up and recognized the old man whom Patrolman Mancuso had arrested in front of D. H. Holmes.

"Glad to meet you," Mrs. Reilly said to her drink.

"Maybe Miss Reilly don't remember," Mr. Robichaux told Santa, who was beaming happily, "But we met before."

"To think you two are old friends." Santa said happily. "It's sure a small world."

"Ay-yi-yi," Mrs. Reilly said, her voice choked with misery. "Eh, la la."

"You remember," Mr. Robichaux said to her. "It was downtown by Holmes. That policeman tried to take in your boy and he took me in instead."

Santa's eyes opened wide.

"Oh yeah," Mrs. Reilly said. "I think I remember now. A little."

"It wasn't your fault though, Miss Reilly. It's them police. They all a bunch of communiss."

"Not so loud," Mrs. Reilly cautioned. "They got thin walls in this building." She moved her elbow and knocked her empty glass off the arm of the sofa. "Oh, Lord. Santa, maybe you oughta go tell Angelo to run along. I can get me a taxi. Tell him he can run out the back way. It's easier for him. You know?"

"I see whatcha mean, honey." Santa turned to Mr. Robichaux. "Listen, when you seen my friend and me down by the bowling alley, you didn't see no man with us, huh?"

"You ladies was all alone."

"Wasn't that the night A. got himself arrested?" Mrs. Reilly whispered to Santa.

"Oh, yeah, Irene. You come by for me in that car of yours. You remember the fender came loose entirely right in front the bowling alley."

"I know. I got it in the backseat. Ignatius is the one made me wreck that car, he got me so nervous from the backseat."

"Aw, no," Mr. Robichaux said. "The one thing I can't stand is a poor loser or a bad sport."

"If somebody does me dirt," Santa continued, "I try to turn the other cheek. You know what I mean? That's the Christian way. Ain't that right, Irene?"

"That's right, darling," Mrs. Reilly agreed half-heartedly. "Santa, sweet, you got some nice aspirins?"

"Irene!" Santa said angrily. "You know, Mr. Robichaux, now suppose you saw that cop that took you in."

"I hope I never see him again," Mr. Robichaux said with emotion. "He's a dirty communiss. Them people want to set up a police state."

"Yeah, but just supposing. Wouldn't you forgive and forget?"

"Santa," Mrs. Reilly interrupted, "I think I'm gonna run in the kitchen and see if you got some nice aspirins."

"It was the disgrace," Mr. Robichaux said to Santa. "My whole family heard about it. The police called up my daughter."

"Aw, that ain't nothing," Santa said. "Everybody gets took in some time in they life. You see her?" Santa picked up the photograph lying face down on the mantelpiece and showed it to her two guests. "My poor dear momma. The police took her out the Lautenschlaeger Market four times for disturbing the peace." Santa paused to give the snapshot a moist kiss. "You think she cared? Not her."

"That's your momma?" Mrs. Reilly asked interestedly. "She had it hard, huh? Mothers got a hard road to travel, believe me."

"So, as I was saying," Santa continued, "I wouldn't feel bad about getting arrested. Policeman got them a hard line of work. Sometimes they make a mistake. They only human, after all."

"I always been a decent citizen," Mrs. Reilly said. "I wanna go wrench out my glass in the zink."

"Oh, go sit down, Irene. Lemme talk to Mr. Robichaux."

Mrs. Reilly went over to the old console radio and poured herself a glass of Early Times.

"I'll never forget that Patrolman Mancuso," Mr. Robichaux was saying.

"Mancuso?" Santa asked with great surprise. "I got plenty relatives with that very same name. As a matter of fact, one of them's on the force. As a matter of fact, he's here now."

"I think I hear Ignatius calling me. I better go."

"Calling you?" Santa asked. "Whadda you mean, Irene? Ignatius is six miles away uptown. Look, we ain't even give Mr. Robichaux a drink. Fix him a drink, kid, while I go get Angelo." Mrs. Reilly studied her drink furiously in the hope of turning up a roach or at least a fly. "Gimme that coat, Mr. Robichaux. Whatcha friends call you?"

"Claude."

"Claude, I'm Santa. And that there's Irene. Irene, say 'hello.' "

"Hello," Mrs. Reilly said automatically.

"You two make friends while I'm gone," Santa said and disappeared into the other room.

"How's that fine big boy of yours?" Mr. Robichaux asked to end the silence that had fallen.

"Who?"

"Your son."

"Oh, him. He's okay." Mrs. Reilly's mind flew back to Constantinople Street where she had left Ignatius writing in his room and mumbling something about Myrna Minkoff. Through the door, Mrs. Reilly had heard Ignatius saying to himself, "She must be lashed until she drops."

There was a long silence broken only by the violent sipping noises that Mrs. Reilly made on the rim of her glass.

"You want some nice potato chips?" Mrs. Reilly finally asked, for she found that the silence made her even more ill at ease.

"Yeah, I think I would."

"They right in the bag next to you." Mrs. Reilly watched Mr. Robichaux open the cellophane package. His face and his gray gabardine suit both seemed to be neat and freshly pressed. "Maybe Santa needs some help. Maybe she went and fell down."

"She just left the room a minute ago. She'll be back."

"These floors are dangerous," Mrs. Reilly observed, studying the shiny linoleum intently. "You could slip down and crack your skull wide open."

"You gotta be careful in life."

"Ain't that the truth. Me, I'm always careful."

"Me, too. It pays to be careful."

"It sure does. That's what Ignatius said just the other day," Mrs. Reilly lied. "He says to me, 'Momma, it sure pays to be careful, don't it?' And I says to him, 'That's right, son. Take care.'"

"That's good advice."

"I'm all the time giving Ignatius advice. You know? I'm always trying to help him out."

"I bet you a good momma. I seen you and that boy downtown plenty times, and I always thought what a fine-looking big boy he was. He kinda stands out, you know?"

"I try with him. I say, 'Be careful, son. Watch you don't slip down and crack your skull open or fracture a arm.'" Mrs. Reilly sucked at the ice cubes a bit. "Ignatius learned safety at my knee. He's always been grateful for that."

"That's good training, believe me."

"I tell Ignatius, I say, 'Take care when you cross the street, son.'"

"You gotta watch out in traffic, Irene. You don't mind if I call you by your first name, huh?"

"Feel free."

"Irene's a pretty name."

"You think so? Ignatius says he don't like it." Mrs. Reilly crossed herself and finished her drink. "I sure got a hard road, Mr. Robichaux. I don't mind telling you."

"Call me Claude."

"As God is my witness, I got a awful cross to bear. You wanna nice drink?"

"Yeah, thanks. Not too strong, though. I'm not a drinking man."

"Oh, Lord," Mrs. Reilly sniffed, filling two glasses

to the rim with whiskey. "When I think of all I take. Sometimes I could really have me a good cry."

With that, Mrs. Reilly burst into loud, wild tears.

"Aw, don't cry," Mr. Robichaux pleaded, completely confused by the tragic turn the evening was apparently taking.

"I gotta do something. I gotta call the authorities to come take that boy away," Mrs. Reilly sobbed. She paused to take a mouthful of Early Times. "Maybe they put him in a detention home or something."

"Ain't he thirty years old?"

"My heart's broke."

"Ain't he writing something?"

"Some foolishness nobody never gonna feel like reading. Now him and that Myrna writing insults to each other. Ignatius is telling me he's gonna get that girl good. Ain't that awful? Poor Myrna."

Mr. Robichaux, unable to think of anything to say, asked, "Why don't you get a priest to talk to your boy?"

"A priest?" Mrs. Reilly wept. "Ignatius won't listen to no priest. He calls the priest in our parish a heretic. They had a big fight when Ignatius' dog died." Mr. Robichaux could find no comment for that enigmatic statement. "It was awful. I thought I'd get throwed out the Church. I don't know where that boy gets his ideas from. It's a good thing his poor poppa's dead. He'd be breaking his poor father's heart with that weenie wagon."

"What weenie wagon?"

"He's out on the streets pushing a weenie wagon all over."

"Oh. He's got him a job now."

"A job?" Mrs. Reilly sobbed. "It's all over my neighborhood. The lady next door's been asking me a million questions. All Constantinople Street's talking about him. When I think of all the money I spent on that boy's education. You know, I thought chirren was supposed to comfort you in your old age. What kinda comfort Ignatius is giving me?"

"Maybe your boy went to school too long," Mr. Robichaux advised. "They got plenty communiss in them colleges."

"Yeah?" Mrs. Reilly asked with interest, dabbing at her eyes with the skirt of her green taffeta cocktail dress, unaware that she was showing Mr. Robichaux the wide runs in her stockings at the knee. "Maybe that's what's wrong with Ignatius. It's just like a communiss to treat his momma bad."

"Ax that boy what he thinks of democracy some time."

"I sure will," Mrs. Reilly said happily. Ignatius was just the type to be a communist. He even looked like one a little. "Maybe I can scare him."

"That boy shouldn't be giving you trouble. You got a very fine character. I admire that in a lady. When I recognized you down by the bowling alley with Miss Battaglia, I says to myself, 'I hope I can meet her some time.'"

"You said that?"

"I admired your integrity, standing up for that boy in front that dirty cop, especially if you got troubles with him at home. That takes courage."

"I wisht I woulda let Angelo take him away. None of this other stuff woulda happened. Ignatius woulda been locked up safe in jail."

"Who's Angelo?"

"There! I hadda go open my big mouth. What I said, Claude?"

"Something about Angelo."

"Lord, lemme go see if Santa's okay. Poor thing. Maybe she burnt herself on the stove. Santa's all the time getting herself burnt. She don't take care around the fire, you know."

"She woulda screamed if she was burnt."

"Not Santa. She's got plenty courage, that girl. You won't hear a word outta her. It's that strong Italian blood."

"Christ Awmight!" Mr. Robichaux screamed, jumping to his feet. "That's him!"

"What?" Mrs. Reilly asked in panic, and, looking around, saw Santa and Angelo standing in the doorway of the room. "You see, Santa. I knew this was gonna happen. Lord, my nerves is shot already. I shoulda stayed home."

"If you wasn't a dirty cop, I'd punch you right in the nose," Mr. Robichaux was screaming at Angelo.

"Aw, take it easy, Claude," Santa said calmly. "Angelo here didn't mean no harm."

"He ruint me, that communiss."

Patrolman Mancuso coughed violently and looked depressed. He wondered what terrible thing would happen to him next.

"Oh, Lord, I better go," Mrs. Reilly said despairingly. "The last thing I need is a fight. We'll be all over the newspaper. Ignatius'll really be happy then."

"How come you brought me here?" Mr. Robichaux asked Santa wildly. "What is this?"

"Santa, honey, you wanna call me a nice taxi?"

"Aw, shut up, Irene," Santa answered. "Now listen, Claude, Angelo says he's sorry he took you in."

"That don't mean nothing. It's too late to feel sorry. I was disgraced in front my granchirren."

"Don't be mad at Angelo," Mrs. Reilly pleaded. "It was all Ignatius' fault. He's my own flesh and blood, but he sure does look funny when he goes out. Angelo shoulda locked him up."

"That's right," Santa added. "Listen at what Irene's telling you, Claude. And watch out you don't step on my poor little niece's phonograpy."

"If Ignatius woulda been nice to Angelo, none of this woulda happened," Mrs. Reilly explained to her audience. "Just look at the cold poor Angelo's got. He's got him a hard road, Claude."

"You tell him, girl," Santa said. "Angelo got that cold on account of he took you in, Claude." Santa waved a stubby finger at Mr. Robichaux a little accusingly. "Now he's stuck in a toilet. Next thing they gonna kick him off the force."

Patrolman Mancuso coughed sadly.

"Maybe I got a little excited," Mr. Robichaux conceded.

"I shouldn't of toog you id," Angelo breathed. "I got nervous."

"It was all my fault," Mrs. Reilly said, "for trying to protect that Ignatius. I should of let you lock him away, Angelo." Mrs. Reilly turned her white, powdery face to Mr. Robichaux. "Mr. Robichaux, you don't know Ignatius. He makes trouble everyplace he goes."

"Somebody oughta punch that Ignatius in the nose," Santa said eagerly.

"Somebody oughta punch him in the mouth," Mrs. Reilly added.

"Somebody oughta beat up on that Ignatius," Santa said. "Now come on. Everybody make friends."

"Okay," Mr. Robichaux said. He took Angelo's blue-white hand and shook it limply.

"Ain't that nice," Mrs. Reilly said. "Come sit on the sofa, Claude, and Santa can play her precious little niece's high-fly."

While Santa put a Fats Domino record on the phonograph, Angelo, sniffling and looking a little confused, sat down on the kitchen chair across from Mrs. Reilly and Mr. Robichaux.

"Now ain't this nice," Mrs. Reilly screamed brightly over the deafening piano and bass. "Santa, honey, you wanna turn that down a little?"

The thumping rhythm decreased slightly in volume.

"Okay," Santa shouted at her guests. "Now everybody make friends while I go get us some plates for my good potatis salad. Hey, come on, Irene and Claude. Let's see you kids shake a leg."

The two little coal-black eyes scowled down at her from the mantelpiece as she stomped gaily out of the room. The three guests, drowned in the pounding beat of the phonograph, silently studied the rose-colored walls and the floral patterns on the linoleum. Then, suddenly, Mrs. Reilly screamed to the two gentleman, "You know what? Ignatius was running the water in the tub when I left, and I bet he forgot to turn it off." When no one answered, she added, "Mothers got a hard road."

nine

"WE GOT A COMPLAINT on you from the Board of Health, Reilly."

"Oh, is that all? From the expression on your face, I thought that you were having some sort of epileptic seizure," Ignatius said to Mr. Clyde through his mouthful of hot dog and bun, bumping his wagon into the garage. "I am afraid to guess what the complaint could be or how it could have originated. I assure you that I have been the very soul of cleanliness. My intimate habits are above reproach. Carrying no social diseases, I don't see what I could possibly transmit to your hot dogs that they do not already have. Look at these fingernails."

"Don't gimme none of your bullshit, you fat bum." Mr. Clyde ignored the paws that Ignatius had extended for inspection. "You only been on the job a few days. I got guys working for me for years never been in trouble with the Board."

"No doubt they're more foxy than I."

"They got this man was checking on you."

"Oh," Ignatius said calmly and paused to chew on the tip of the hot dog that was sticking from his mouth like a cigar butt. "So that's who that obvious appendage of officialdom was. He looked like an arm of the bureaucracy. You can always tell employees of the government by the total vacancy which occupies the space where most other people have faces."

"Shut up, you big slob. Did you pay for that weenie you eating?"

"Well, indirectly. You may subtract it from my miserable wage." Ignatius watched as Mr. Clyde jotted some numbers on a pad. "Tell me, what archaic sanitary taboo have I violated? I suspect that it's some falsification on the part of the inspector."

"The Board says they seen the vendor with Number Seven . . . that's you . . ."

"So it is. Thrice-blessed Seven! I'm guilty on that count. They've already pinned something on me. I imagined that Seven would ironically be an unlucky cart. I want another cart as soon as possible. Apparently I am pushing a jinx about the streets. I am certain that I can do better with some other wagon. A new cart, a new start."

"Will you listen to me?"

"Well, if I really must. I should perhaps warn you that I am about to faint from anxiety and general depression, though. The film I saw last night was especially grueling, a teen-age beach musical. I almost collapsed during the singing sequence on surfboard. In addition, I suffered through two nightmares last night, one involving a Scenicruiser bus. The other involved a girl of my acquaintance. It was rather brutal and obscene. If I described it to you, you would no doubt become frightened."

"They seen you picking a cat out the gutter on St. Joseph Street."

"Is that the best that they can do? What an absurd lie," Ignatius said and with a flip of his tongue pulled in the last visible portion of the hot dog.

"What was you doing on St. Joseph Street? That's all warehouses and wharfs out there. They's no people on St. Joseph. That's not even on our routes."

"Well, I didn't know that. I had only feebly shambled out there to rest a while. Occasionally a pedestrian happened along. Unfortunately for us, they did not seem to be in hot dog moods."

"So you *was* there? No wonder you not selling nothing. And I guess you was playing with that goddam cat."

"Now that you mention it, I do seem to remember a domesticated animal or two in the vicinity."

"So you was playing with the cat."

"No, I was not 'playing' with the cat. I only picked it up to fondle it a bit. It was a rather appealing calico. I offered it a hot dog. However, the cat refused to eat it. It was an animal with some taste and decency."

"You realize what a serious violation that is, you big ape?"

"No, I am afraid I don't," Ignatius said angrily. "It has apparently been taken for granted that the cat was unclean. How do we know that? Cats are notoriously sanitary, continuously licking at themselves when they suspect that there is the slightest cause for offense. That inspector must have some prejudice against cats. This cat hasn't been given a chance."

"We not talking about this cat!" Mr. Clyde said with such vehemence that Ignatius was able to see the purple veins swelling around the whitened scar on his nose. "We talking about you."

"Well, I certainly am clean. We've already discussed that. I just wanted to see that the cat got a fair hearing. Sir, am I going to be endlessly harassed? My nerves are nearing total decay already. When you

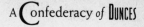

checked my fingernails a moment ago, I hope that you noticed the frightening vibration of my hands. I would hate to sue Paradise Vendors, Incorporated, to pay the psychiatrist's fees. Perhaps you do not know that I am not covered by any hospitalization plan. Paradise Vendors, of course, is too paleolithic to consider offering its workers such benefits. Actually, sir, I am growing quite dissatisfied with conditions at this disreputable firm."

"Why, what's wrong?" Mr. Clyde asked.

"Everything, I'm afraid. On top of that, I don't feel at all appreciated."

"Well, at least you show up every day. I'll give you that."

"That is only because I would be beaten senseless with a baked wine bottle if I dared stay at home. Opening the door of my home is like intruding into the den of a lioness. My mother is becoming increasingly abusive and vicious."

"You know, Reilly, I don't wanna fire you," Mr. Clyde said in a paternal tone. He had heard the sad tale of vendor Reilly: the drunken mother, the damages that had to be paid, the threat of penury for both son and mother, the mother's lascivious friends. "I'm gonna fix you up with a new route and give you another chance. I got some merchandising gimmicks maybe help you out."

"You may send a map of my new route to the mental ward at Charity Hospital. The solicitous nuns and psychiatrists there can help me decipher it between shock treatments."

"Now shut up."

"You see that? You've destroyed my initiative already," Ignatius belched. "Well, I do hope that you have selected a scenic route, preferably something in a park area where there are ample seating accommodations for sufferers from tired, stunned feet. When I rose this morning, my ankles gave way. Fortunately I grabbed for the bedpost in time. Otherwise, I would have landed on the floor in a broken heap. My tarsi are apparently about to throw in the towel completely."

Ignatius limped around Mr. Clyde to illustrate, his desert boots scuffing along the oily cement.

"Stop that, you big slob. You ain't crippled."

"Not completely as of yet. However, various small bones and ligaments are beginning to wave a white flag of surrender. My physical apparati seem to be preparing to announce a truce of some sort. My digestive system has almost ceased functioning altogether. Some tissue has perhaps grown over my pyloric valve, sealing it forever."

"I'm gonna put you down in the French Quarter."

"What?" Ignatius thundered. "Do you think that I am going to perambulate about in that sinkhole of vice? No, I am afraid that the Quarter is out of the question. My psyche would crumble in that atmosphere. Besides, the streets are very narrow and dangerous there. I could easily be struck down in traffic or be wedged against a building."

"Take it or leave it, you fat bastard. That's the last chance you get." Mr. Clyde's scar was beginning to whiten again.

"It is? Well, please don't have another seizure. You may tumble into that vat of franks and scald yourself. If you insist, I imagine that I shall have to trundle my franks down into Sodom and Gomorrah."

"Okay. Then it's settled. You come in tomorrow morning, we'll fix you up with some gimmicks."

"I can't promise you that many hot dogs will be

246

sold in the Quarter. I will probably be kept busy every moment protecting my honor against those fiends who live down there."

"You get mostly the tourist trade in the Quarter."

"That's even worse. Only degenerates go touring. Personally, I have been out of the city only once. By the way, have I ever told you about that particular pilgrimage to Baton Rouge? Outside the city limits there are many horrors."

"No. I don't wanna hear about it."

"Well, too bad for you. You might have gained some valuable insights from the traumatic tale of that trip. However, I am glad that you do not want to hear of it. The psychological and symbolic subtleties of the journey probably wouldn't be comprehended by a Paradise Vendors mentality. Fortunately, I've written it all down, and at some time in the future, the more alert among the reading public will benefit from my account of that abysmal sojourn into the swamps to the inner station of the ultimate horror."

"Now listen here, Reilly."

"In the account I struck upon an especially suitable simile in comparing the Scenicruiser bus to a loop-the-loop in a surrealistic amusement park."

"Now shut up!" Mr. Clyde screamed, waving his fork menacingly. "Let's go over your receipts for today. How much did you sell?"

"Oh, my God," Ignatius sighed. "I knew that we'd get to that sooner or later."

The two haggled over the profits for several minutes. Ignatius had actually spent the morning sitting at Eads Plaza watching the harbor traffic and jotting some notes about the history of shipping and Marco Polo in a Big Chief tablet. Between notes, he had contemplated

247

means of destroying Myrna Minkoff but had reached no satisfactory conclusion. His most promising scheme had involved getting a book on munitions from the library, constructing a bomb, and mailing it in plain paper to Myrna. Then he remembered that his library card had been revoked. The afternoon had been wasted on the cat; Ignatius had tried to trap the cat in the bun compartment and take it home for a pet. But it had escaped.

"It seems to me that you would be generous enough to give some sort of discount to your own employees," Ignatius said importantly after an audit of the day's receipts showed that, upon subtracting the cost of the hot dogs he had eaten, his take-home pay for the day was exactly a dollar and twenty-five cents. "After all, I am becoming your best customer."

Mr. Clyde stuck the fork in Vendor Reilly's muffler and ordered him out of the garage, threatening him with dismissal if he didn't show up early to begin working the French Quarter.

Ignatius flapped off to the trolley in a dark mood and rode uptown belching Paradise gas so violently that, although the car was crowded, no one would sit next to him.

When he walked into the kitchen, his mother greeted him by falling to her knees and saying, "Lord, tell me how come you sent me this terrible cross to bear? What I done, Lord? Tell me. Send me a sign. I been good."

"Stop that blasphemy this moment," Ignatius screamed. Mrs. Reilly was questioning the ceiling with her eyes, seeking an answer among the grease and cracks. "What a greeting I receive after a discouraging

248

day battling for my very existence on the streets of this savage town."

"What's them bo-bos on your hand?"

Ignatius looked at the scratches he had received in trying to persuade the cat to remain in the bun compartment.

"I had a rather apocalyptic battle with a starving prostitute," Ignatius belched. "Had it not been for my superior brawn, she would have sacked my wagon. Finally she limped away from the fray, her glad rags askew."

"Ignatius!" Mrs. Reilly cried tragically. "Every day it seems you getting worst and worst. What's happening to you?"

"Get your bottle out of the oven. It must be done by now."

Mrs. Reilly looked at her son slyly and asked, "Ignatius, you sure you not a communiss?"

"Oh, my God!" Ignatius bellowed. "Every day I am subjected to a McCarthyite witchhunt in this crumbling building. No! I told you before. I am not a fellow traveler. What in the world has put that into your head?"

"I read someplace in the paper where they got plenty communiss at college."

"Well, fortunately I didn't meet them. Had they crossed my path, they would have been beaten to within an inch of their lives. Do you think that I want to live in a communal society with people like that Battaglia acquaintance of yours, sweeping streets and breaking up rocks or whatever it is people are always doing in those blighted countries? What I want is a good, strong monarchy with a tasteful and decent king who has some

249

knowledge of theology and geometry and to cultivate a Rich Inner Life."

"A king? You want a king?"

"Oh, stop babbling at me."

"I never heard of nobody wanted a king."

"Please!" Ignatius pounded a paw into the oilcloth on the kitchen table. "Sweep the porch, visit Miss Annie, call the Battaglia bawd, practice with your bowling ball out in the alley. Let me alone! I am in a very bad cycle."

"What you mean, 'cycle'?"

"If you do not stop molesting me, I shall christen the prow of your broken Plymouth with the bottle of wine in the oven," Ignatius snorted.

"Fighting with some poor girl in the street," Mrs. Reilly said sadly. "Ain't that awful. And right in front a weenie wagon. Ignatius, I think you need help."

"Well, I am going to watch television," Ignatius said angrily. "The Yogi Bear program is coming on."

"Wait a minute, boy." Mrs. Reilly rose from the floor and pulled a small manila envelope out of a pocket in her sweater. "Here. This come for you today."

"Oh?" Ignatius asked with interest, seizing the little tan envelope. "I imagine that you have memorized its contents by now."

"You better stick your hands in the sink and wrench out them scratches."

"They can wait," Ignatius said. He ripped at the envelope. "M. Minkoff has apparently responded to my missive with a rather frantic urgency. I told her off quite viciously."

Mrs. Reilly sat down and crossed her legs, swinging her white socks and old black patent leather pumps sadly while her son's blue and yellow eyes scanned the unfolded Macy's bag on which the letter was written.

Sirs:
Well, at last I heard from you, Ignatius. And a sick, sick letter it was. I won't go into the "Levy Pants" letterhead on that stationery. It is probably your idea of an anti-Semitic prank. It's a good thing that I'm above attack on that level. I never thought that *you* would stoop so low. Live and learn.

Your comments about the lecture showed a very petty jealousy I didn't expect from someone who claims to be so broad and non-committed. Already the lecture is beginning to interest several dedicated people I know. One person who has promised to come (and bring several sharp friends, too) is a brilliant new contact I made during rush hour on the Jerome Avenue line. His name is Ongah, and he is an exchange student from Kenya who is writing a dissertation at N.Y.U. on the French symbolists of the 19th cent. Of course, you would not understand or like a brilliant and dedicated guy like Ongah. I could listen to him talk for hours. He is serious and does not come on with all of that pseudo stuff like you always did. What Ongah says is meaningful. Ongah is *real* and vital. He is virile and aggressive. He rips at reality and tears aside concealing veils.

"Oh, my God!" Ignatius slobbered. "The minx has been raped by a Mau-Mau."

"What's that?" Mrs. Reilly asked suspiciously.

"Go turn on the television set and warm it up," Ignatius said absently and returned to his furious reading of the letter.

He is not a bit like you, as you can imagine. He is also a musician and a sculptor and spends every minute in some real and meaningful activity, creating and sensing. His sculpture almost leaps out and grabs you, it is so filled with life and being.

At least your letter let me know that you are still alive, if you can call what you do 'living.' What were all these lies about being connected with the "food merchandising industry?" Is this some attack on my father's restaurant supply business? If so, that didn't get to me either because my father and I have been at ideological odds for years. Let's face it, Ignatius. Since I saw you last, you have done nothing but lie around rotting in your room. Your hostility to my lecture is a manifestation of your feelings of failure, nonaccomplishment, and mental (?) impotence.

"This liberal doxy must be impaled upon the member of a particularly large stallion," Ignatius mumbled furiously.

"What? What's that, boy?"

Ignatius, a very bad crack-up is on the way. You must do *something*. Even volunteer work at a hospital would snap you out of your apathy, and it would probably be non-taxing on your valve and other things. Get out of that womb-house for at least an hour a day. Take a walk, Ignatius. Look at the trees and birds. Realize that life is surging all around you. The valve closes because it thinks it is living in a dead organism. Open your heart, Ignatius, and you will open your valve.

If you are having any sex fantasies, describe them in detail in your next letter. I may be able to interpret their meaning for you and help you through this psycho-sexual crisis you are having. When I was at college, I told you many times that you would undergo a psychotic phase of this sort.

I thought you might be interested in knowing that I've just read in *Social Revulsion* that Louisiana has the highest illiteracy rate in the U.S. Come out from under the mess before it's too late. I really don't mind what you wrote about the lecture. I understand your condition, Ignatius. The members of my group therapy group are all following your case with interest (I have told it to them chapter by chapter beginning with the paranoid fantasy, adding certain background commentaries), and they are all rooting for you. If I were not so busy with the lecture, I would take off on a long-overdue inspection tour and come to see you personally. Hold on until we meet again.

M. Minkoff

Ignatius folded the letter violently; then he rolled the folded Macy's bag into a ball and heaved it into the garbage pail. Mrs. Reilly looked at her son's reddened face and asked, "What that girl wants? What she's doing nowadays?"

"Myrna is preparing to bray at some unfortunate Negro. In public."

"Ain't that awful. You sure pick up with fine friends, Ignatius. Them colored people already got it hard, boy. They got a hard road, too. Life's hard, Ignatius. You'll learn."

"Thank you very much," Ignatius said in a businesslike manner.

"You know that poor old colored lady sells them pralines in front the cemetery? Aw, Ignatius. I really feel sorry for her. The other day I seen her wearing a little cloth coat full of holes, and it was cold out. So I says to her, I says, 'Hey, honey, you gonna catch your death of cold wearing that little cloth coat full of holes.' And she says . . ."

"Please!" Ignatius shouted furiously. "I am not in the mood for a dialect story."

"Ignatius, listen to me. That lady's pitiful, yeah. She says, 'Oh, I don't mind the cold, sugar. I'm used to it.' Ain't that brave?" Mrs. Reilly looked emotionally at Ignatius for agreement but was treated only to a sneering moustache. "Ain't that something. So, you know what I done, Ignatius. I give her a quarter and I says,

253

'Here, darling, go buy you a trinket for your little granchirren.' "

"What?" Ignatius exploded. "So that is where our profits are going. While I am almost reduced to begging on the streets, you are flinging our money away at frauds. That woman's clothing is all a ruse. She has a wonderful, lucrative location at that cemetery. Doubtlessly she makes ten times more than I do."

"Ignatius! She's all broke down," Mrs. Reilly said sadly. "I wish you was as brave as she is."

"I see. Now I am being compared to a degenerate old female fraud. Worse, I am losing in the comparison. My own mother daring to malign me so." Ignatius thrust a paw onto the oilcloth. "Well, I have had enough of this. I'm going into the parlor to watch the Yogi Bear program. Between wine breaks, bring me a snack of some sort. My valve is screaming for appeasement."

"Shut up over there," Miss Annie screamed through her shutters as Ignatius gathered his smock about him and swept into the hall contemplating his most important problem: organizing a new assault against the minx's effrontery. The civil rights assault had failed because of defections in the ranks. There must be other assaults which could be launched in the fields of politics and sex. Preferably politics. The strategy deserved his full attention.

254

II

Lana Lee was on a barstool, her legs crossed in tan suede trousers, her muscular buttocks pinning the stool to the floor and commanding it to support her in perfectly vertical form. When she moved slightly, the great muscles of her nether cheeks rippled to life to prevent the stool from leaning and tottering even an inch. The muscles rippled around the cushion of the stool and grabbed it, holding it erect. Long years of practice and usage had made her rump an unusually versatile and dexterous thing.

Her body had always amazed her. She had received it free of charge, yet she had never bought anything that had helped her as much as that body had. At these rare moments when Lana Lee grew sentimental or even religious, she thanked God for His goodness in forming a body that was also a friend. She repaid the gift by giving it magnificent care, expert service and maintenance that was given with the emotionless precision of a mechanic.

Today was Darlene's first dress rehearsal. A few minutes earlier Darlene had arrived with a large dress box and disappeared backstage. Lana looked at Darlene's gadget on the stage. A carpenter had made a stand that looked like a hatrack but instead of hooks there were large rings attached to the top of the stand and three rings on chains hung from the top at different heights. What Lana had seen of the act so far was not promising, but Darlene said that the costuming would transform the performance into a thing of beauty. Lana couldn't complain all things considered, she was glad that she had let Darlene and Jones talk her into permitting Darlene to perform. She was getting the act cheap, and she had to admit that the bird was very good, a skilled and professional performer who almost made up for the act's human deficiencies. The other clubs along the street might get the tiger, chimp, and snake trade. The Night of Joy had the bird trade in the bag, and

255

Lana's peculiar knowledge of one aspect of humanity told her that the bird trade might indeed be very large.

"Okay, Lana, we're ready," Darlene called offstage.

Lana looked over at Jones, who was sweeping out the booths in a cloud of cigarette smoke and dust and said, "Put the record on."

"Sorry. Recor plain star at thirty a week. Whoa!"

"Put down that broom and get on that phonograph before I call up the precinct," Lana hollered at him.

"And you get off your stool and get on that phonograph before I call up the precinc and ax them po-lice mothers make a search for your orphan frien who disappear. Ooo-wee."

Lana studied Jones' face, but his eyes were invisible behind the smoke and dark glasses.

"What was that?" she asked finally.

"The only thing you ever be givin the orphan is siphlus. Whoa! Don gimme no shit about no motherfuckin record player. As soon as I crack open this orphan case, I callin a po-lice myself. I sick and tire of workin in this cathouse below the minimal wage and getting intimidatia all the time."

"Hey, kids, where's our music?" Darlene's voice called eagerly.

"What can you prove to the cops?" Lana asked Jones.

"Hey! Then they *is* somethin crooker with the orphans. Whoa! I knowed it all along. Well, if you ever plannin to call up a po-lice about me, I plannin to call up a po-lice about you. Phones at po-lice headquarters really be hummin. Ooo-wee. Now lemme in peace with my sweepin and moppin. Recor playin pretty advance for color peoples. I probably break your machine."

"I'd like to see a jailbait vagrant like you trying to

get the cops to believe you, especially when I tell them you been dipping into my cash register."

"What's happening?" Darlene inquired from behind the little curtain.

"The only thing I been dippin in around here is a mop bucket fulla dirty water."

"It's my word against yours. The police already got their eyes on you. All they need is to get the word about you from an old pal of theirs like me. Which one you think they'll believe?" Lana looked at Jones and saw that his silence had answered her question. "Now get on the phonograph."

Jones threw his broom into a booth and put on the record of *Stranger in Paradise*.

"Okay, everybody, here we come," Darlene called, bumping on stage with the cockatoo on her arm. She was wearing a low-cut orange satin evening dress, and at the peak of her upswept hair there was a large artificial orchid. She made several clumsily lascivious motions over toward the stand while the cockatoo swayed unsteadily on her arm. Holding onto the top of the stand with one hand, she made a grotesque pass at the pole with her pelvis and sighed, "Oh."

The cockatoo was placed in the lowest ring, and with beak and claw began to climb up to the next highest ring. Darlene bumped and ground around the pole in a sort of orgiastic frenzy until the bird was on a level with her waist. Then she offered the bird the ring sewed in the side of her gown. He grabbed at it with his beak and the gown popped open.

257

"Oh," Darlene sighed, bumping down to the edge of the little stage to show the audience the lingerie that showed through the opening. "Oh. Oh."

"Whoa!"

"Stop it, stop it," Lana screamed and, leaping from her stool, snapped off the phonograph.

"Hey, what's the matter?" Darlene asked in an offended voice.

"It stinks is what's the matter. For one thing, you're dressed up like a streetwalker. I want a nice, refined act in my club. I got a decent business, stupid."

"Whoa!"

"You look like a whore in that orange dress. And what's all these sounds you're making like a slut? You look like a drunk nympho passing out in a alley."

"But Lana . . ."

"The bird's okay. You stink." Lana stuck a cigarette between her coral lips and lit it. "We gotta rethink the whole act. You look like your motor's broke or something. I know this business. Stripping's an insult to a woman. The kinda creeps come in here don't wanna see a tramp get insulted."

"Hey!" Jones aimed his cloud at Lana Lee's. "I thought you say nice, refine peoples comin here at night."

"Shut up," Lana said. "Now listen, Darlene. Anybody can insult a tramp. These jerks wanna see a sweet, clean virgin get insulted and stripped. You gotta use your *head* for Chrissake, Darlene. You gotta be *pure*. I want you to be like a nice, refined girl who's surprised when the bird starts grabbing at your clothes."

"Who says I'm not refined?" Darlene asked angrily.

"Okay. You're refined. Then be refined on my stage. That's what gives a turn *drama*, goddammit."

"Ooo-wee. Night of Joy be winnin a Academy Awar with this ack. The bird get one, too."

"Get back on my floor."

"Right away, Scarla O'Horror."

"Wait a minute," Lana screamed in the best tradition of the director in a musical movie. She had always enjoyed the theatrical aspects of her profession: performing, posing, composing tableaux, directing acts. "That's it."

"That's what?" Darlene asked.

"An idea, moron," Lana answered, holding her cigarette before her lips and speaking through it as if it were a director's megaphone. "*Now* see this act. You're gonna be a southern belle type, a big sweet virgin from the Old South who's got this pet bird on the old plantation."

"Say, I like that," Darlene said enthusiastically.

"Of course you do. Now listen to me." Lana's mind began to whirl. This act could be her theatrical masterpiece. That bird had star quality. "We get you a big plantation dress, crinoline, lace. A big hat. A parasol. Very refined. Your hair's on your shoulders in curls. You're just coming in from a big ball where a lot of southern gentlemen were trying to feel you up over the fried chicken and hog jowls. But you cooled them all. Why? Because you're a lady, dammit. You come onstage. The ball's over, but you still got your honor. You got your little pet with you to tell it goodnight, and you say to it, 'There was plenty beaux at that ball, honey, but I still got my honor.' Then the goddam bird starts grabbing at your dress. You're shocked, you're surprised, you're innocent. But you're too refined to stop it. Got it?"

"That's great," Darlene said.

"That's drama," Lana corrected. "Okay, let's give it a try. Music, maestro."

"Whoa! Now we really back on the plantation."

Jones slid the needle across the first few grooves of the record. "I'm pretty stupor to open my mouth in this miser cathouse."

Darlene minced out on the stage, sashaying demurely, and making a rosebud of her mouth, said, "There sure was plenty balls at that beau, honey, but . . ."

"Stop!" Lana hollered.

"Give me a chance," Darlene pleaded. "It's my first time. I been practicing being an exotic, not a actress."

"You can't remember one simple line like that?"

"Darlene got Night of Joy nerves." Jones clouded the area in front of the stage. "It come from low wage and high intimidatia. The bird be gettin it, too, pretty soon, be snarlin and clawin and fallin off its stan. Whoa!"

"Darlene's your pal, huh? I see she's always passing you magazines," Lana said angrily. This Jones was really starting to get under her lotioned skin. "This act is mostly your idea, Jones. You sure you wanna see her get a chance on the stage?"

"Sure. Whoa! Somebody gotta get ahead in this place. Anyway, this ack got plenny class, bring in a lotta trade. I be gettin a raise. Hey!" Jones smiled a yellow crescent that opened the lower part of his face. "I got all my hope pin on that bird."

Lana had an idea that would help business and hurt Jones. She'd let him go too far already.

260

"Good," Lana said to him. "Now listen to me, Jones. You wanna help out Darlene here. You think this act is good, huh? I remember you said Darlene and the bird was gonna bring in so much business I'd need a doorman. Well, I got a doorman. You."

"Hey! I ain comin around here at night below the minimal wage."

"You're coming out on opening night," Lana said evenly. "You gonna be out front on the sidewalk. We're gonna rent you a costume. Real Old South doorman. You attract the people in here. Understand? I wanna see a full house for your pal and her bird."

"Shit. I quittin this motherfuckin bar. Maybe you gettin Scarla O'Horror and her ball eagle on the stage, but you ain gettin a fiel han out front, too."

"The precinct is gonna be gettin a certain report."

"Maybe they be gettin another orphan repor, too."

"I don't think so."

Jones knew that this was true. Finally, he said, "Okay. I be here on openin night. I bring in some peoples. I bring in some peoples shut down your place for good. I be bringin in peoples like that fat mother got him the green cap."

"I wonder where he went to," Darlene said.

"Shut up and lemme hear you say your lines," Lana hollered at her. "Your friend here wants to see you get ahead. He's gonna help you out, Darlene. Show him how good you are."

Darlene cleared her throat and enunciated carefully, "There sure was plenty beaux at the bowl, honey, but I still got me honor."

Lana grabbed Darlene and the bird off the stage and pushed them out into the alley. Jones listened to the loud sounds of argument and pleading coming from the alley and heard one plop of a slap land on someone's face.

261

He went behind the bar to get a glass of water and contemplated means of sabotage that could finish Lana Lee forever. Outside, the cockatoo was squawking and

Darlene was crying, "I ain't no actress, Lana. I already told you."

Looking down for a moment, Jones saw that Lana Lee had absentmindedly left the door open on the little cabinet under the bar. All afternoon she had been preoccupied with previewing Darlene's dress rehearsal. Jones knelt down and, for the first time in the Night of Joy, took off his sunglasses. At first his eyes had to adjust to the brighter but still dim light that revealed crusted dirt on the floor behind the bar. He looked into the little cabinet, and there he saw neatly stacked about ten packages wrapped in plain paper. Piled in the corner were a globe, a box of chalk, and a large, expensive-looking book.

He did not want to sabotage his discovery by taking anything from the cabinet. Lana Lee, with her hawk eyes and bloodhound nose, would notice that right away. He thought for a moment, then he took the pencil from the cash register and, running his hand down the side of the stacked packages, wrote as minutely as possible on the side of each package the address of the Night of Joy. Like a note in a bottle, the address might bring some reply, perhaps from a legitimate and professional saboteur. An address on a package wrapped in plain brown paper was as damaging as a fingerprint on a gun, Jones thought. It was something that shouldn't be there. He stacked the packages back carefully, straightening the pile to its original symmetry. Then he placed the pencil on the cash register and finished his water. He studied the door of the cabinet and decided that it was open at about the same angle at which he had found it.

He came from behind the bar and resumed his desultory sweeping just as Lana, Darlene, and the bird, looking like a small unruly mob, burst in from the alley. Darlene's orchid was hanging, and the bird's few feathers were ruffled. Lana Lee, though, was still well groomed and looked as though some cyclone had miraculously missed only her.

"Okay now, Darlene," Lana said, grabbing Darlene by the shoulders. "What the hell are you supposed to say?"

"Whoa! You sure a understandin director. If you be makin big movies, half the peoples in it be dead."

"Shut up and get on my floor," Lana said to Jones and shook Darlene a little. "Now say it right, stupid."

Darlene sighed hopelessly and said, "There sure was plenty bones at that ball, honey, but I still got my honor."

III

Patrolman Mancuso leaned against the sergeant's desk and wheezed, "You gotta tage me oud thad badroom. I can breed no more."

"What?" The sergeant looked at the wan figure before him, at the watery pink eyes behind the bifocals, at the dry lips through the white goatee. "What's wrong with you, Mancuso? Why can't you stand up like a man? Getting a cold. Men on the force don't catch cold. Men on the force are *strong.*"

Patrolman Mancuso coughed wetly into the goatee.

"You haven't picked up nobody out that bus station. Remember what I told you? You stay there until you bring me somebody."

"I'b getting pneumodia."

"Take some cold tablets. Get outta here and bring me somebody."

"My at says if I stay iddat badroom, I'b gudda die."

"Your aunt? A grown man like you's gotta listen to his aunt? Jesus. What kinda people you know, Mancuso? Old ladies who go sit in strip joints all alone, aunts. You probly belong to a ladies' sodality or something. *Stand up straight.*" The sergeant studied the miserable figure that was shaking with the aftereffects of a dangerous cough. He didn't want to be responsible for a death. It would be better to give Mancuso a probationary period and kick him off the force. "Okay. Don't go back to the bus station. Get out on the streets again and get some sunshine. But listen here. I'm giving you two weeks. If you don't bring in nobody by then, you're off the force. You understand me, Mancuso?"

Patrolman Mancuso nodded, sniffling.

"I'b gudda try. I'b gudda brig you subbody."

"Stop leaning over me," the sergeant screamed. "I don't wanna catch your cold. Stand up. Get outta here. Go take some pills and orange juice. Jesus."

"I'b gudda brig you subbody," Patrolman Mancuso wheezed again, this time even more unconvincingly than the first. Then he drifted off in his novel costume, the sergeant's ultimate practical joke on him. He was wearing a baseball cap and a Santa Claus outfit.

IV

264

Ignatius ignored his mother's pounding on his door and crying in the hall about the fifty cents in wages that he had brought home for the day's work. Sweeping the Big Chief tablets, yo-yo, and rubber glove from his desk, he opened the Journal and began to write:

Dear Reader,
A good book is the precious life-blood of a master-spirit, embalmed and treasured up on purpose for a life beyond.

—Milton

The perverted (and I suspect quite dangerous) mind of Clyde has devised still another means of belittling my rather invincible being. At first I thought that I might have found a surrogate father in the czar of sausage, the mogul of meat. But his resentment and jealousy of me are increasing daily; no doubt they will ultimately overwhelm him and destroy his mind. The grandeur of my physique, the complexity of my worldview, the decency and taste implicit in my carriage, the grace with which I function in the mire of today's world—all of these at once confuse and astound Clyde. Now he has relegated me to working in the French Quarter, an area which houses every vice that man has ever conceived in his wildest aberrations, including, I would imagine, several modern variants made possible through the wonders of science. The Quarter is not unlike, I would imagine, Soho and certain sections of North Africa. However, the residents of the French Quarter, blessed with American "Stick-to-it-tiveness" and "Know-how," are probably straining themselves at this moment to equal and surpass in variety and imagination the diversions enjoyed by the residents of those other world areas of human degradation.

Clearly an area like the French Quarter is not the proper environment for a clean-living, chaste, prudent, and impressionable young Working Boy. Did Edison, Ford, and Rockefeller have to struggle against such odds?

Clyde's fiendish mind has not stopped at so simple an abasement, however. Because I am allegedly handling what Clyde calls "the tourist trade," I have been caparisoned in a costume of sorts.

(Judging from the customers I have had on this first day with the new route, the "tourists" seem to be the same old vagrants I was selling to in the business district. In a stupor induced by Sterno, they have doubtlessly stumbled down into the Quarter and thus, to Clyde's senile mind, qualify as "tourists." I wonder whether Clyde has even had an opportunity to see the degenerates and wrecks and drifters who buy and apparently subsist on Paradise products. Between the other vendors—totally beaten and ailing itinerants whose names are something like Buddy, Pal, Sport, Top, Buck, and Ace—and my customers, I am apparently trapped in a limbo of lost souls. However, the simple fact that they have been resounding failures in our century does give them a certain spiritual quality. For all we know, they may be—these crushed wretches—the saints of our age: beautifully broken old Negroes with tan eyes; downtrodden drifters from wastelands in Texas and Oklahoma; ruined sharecroppers seeking a haven in rodent-infested urban rooming houses.

(Nevertheless, I do hope that in my dotage, I will not have to rely upon hot dogs for sustenance. The sale of my writings may bring some profit. If need be, I could always turn to the lecture circuit, following behind the ghastly M. Minkoff, whose offenses against taste and decency have already been described in detail to you readers, in order to clear away the boulders of ignorance and obscenity which she will have strewn among the various lecture halls of the nation. Perhaps, however, there will be some person of quality in her first audience who will wrest her from the podium and lash her a bit about her erogenous zones. In spite of whatever spiritual qualities it may possess, skid row is definitely substandard in the matter of physical comfort, and I seriously doubt whether my substantial and well-formed physique would easily adapt to sleeping in alleys. I would definitely tend to hang over park benches. Therefore, my size itself is a safeguard against my ever sinking too low within the structure of our civilization. [After all, I do not believe that one must necessarily scrape bottom, as it were, in order to view his society subjectively. Rather than moving vertically downward, one may move horizontally outward toward a point of sufficient detachment where a modicum of creature comforts are not necessarily precluded. I was there—on the very rim of our age—when my mother's cataclysmic intemperance, as you well know, catapulted me into the fever of contemporary existence. To be quite honest, I must say that since then things have been getting worse and worse. Conditions have deteriorated. Minkoff, my passionless flame, has turned upon me. Even my mother, the agent of my destruction, has begun to bite the hand that feeds her. My cycle is dipping lower and lower. Oh, Fortuna, you capricious sprite!] Personally, I have found that a lack of food and comfort, rather than ennobling the spirit, creates only anxiety within the human psyche and channels all of one's better impulses only toward the end of procuring something to eat. Even though I do have a Rich Inner Life, I must have some food and comfort also.)

But back to the matter at hand: Clyde's vengeance. The vendor who formerly had the Quarter route wore an improbable pirate's outfit, a Paradise Vendor's nod to New Orleans folklore and history, a Clydian attempt to link the hot dog with Creole legend. Clyde forced me to try it on in the garage. The costume, of course, had been made to fit the tubercular and underdeveloped frame of the former vendor, and no amount of pulling and pushing and inhaling and squeezing would get it onto my muscular body. Therefore, a compromise of sorts was made. About my cap I tied the red sateen pirate's scarf. I screwed the one golden earring, a large novelty store hoop of an earring, onto my left earlobe. I affixed the black plastic cutlass to the side of my white vendor's smock with a safety pin. Hardly an impressive pirate, you will say. However, when I studied myself in the mirror, I was forced to admit that I appeared rather fetching in a dramatic way. Brandishing the plastic cutlass at Clyde, I cried, "Walk the plank, Admiral!" This, I should have known, was too much for his literal and sausage-like mind. He grew most alarmed and proceeded to attack me with his spear-like fork. We lunged about in the garage like two swashbucklers in an especially inept historical film for several moments, fork and cutlass clicking against each other madly. Realizing that my plastic weapon was hardly a match for a long fork wielded by a maddened Methuselah, realizing that I was seeing Clyde at his *worst*, I tried to end our little duel. I called out pacifying words; I entreated; I finally surrendered. Still Clyde came, my pirate costume so great a success that it had apparently convinced him that we were back in the golden days of romantic old New Orleans when gentlemen decided matters of hot dog honor at twenty paces. It was then that a light dawned in my intricate mind. I know that Clyde was really trying to kill me. He would have the perfect excuse: self defense. I had played

267

right into his hands. Fortunately for me, I fell to the floor. I had backed into one of the carts, lost my always precarious balance, and had fallen down. Although I struck my head rather painfully against the cart, I cried pleasantly from the floor, "You win, sir." Then I silently paid homage to dear old Fortuna for snatching me from the jaws of death by rusty fork.

I quickly rolled my cart out of the garage and set out for the Quarter. Along the way, many pedestrians gave my semi-costume favorable notice. My cutlass slapping against my side, my earring dangling from my lobe, my red scarf shining in the sun brightly enough to attract a bull, I strode resolutely across town, thankful that I was still alive, armoring myself against the horrors that awaited me in the Quarter. Many a loud prayer rose from my chaste pink lips, some of thanks, some of supplication. I prayed to St. Mathurin, who is invoked for epilepsy and madness, to aid Mr. Clyde (Mathurin is, incidentally, also the patron saint of clowns). For myself, I sent a humble greeting to St. Medericus, the Hermit, who is invoked against intestinal disorders. Meditating upon the call from the grave which I had almost received, I began to think about my mother, for I have always wondered what her reaction would be were I to die in the cause of paying for her misdeeds. I can see her at the funeral, a shoddy, low-cost affair held in the basement of some dubious funeral parlor. Insane with grief, tears boiling from her reddened eyes, she would probably tear my corpse from the coffin, screaming drunkenly, "Don't take him! Why do the sweetest flowers wither and fall from the stem?" The funeral would probably degenerate into a circus, my mother constantly poking her fingers into the two holes dug in my neck by Mr. Clyde's rusty fork, crying an illiterate Grecian cry of curses and vengeance. There would be a certain amount of spectacle involved in the proceedings, I imagine. However, with my mother acting as director, the inherent tragedy would soon become melodrama. Snatching the white lily from my lifeless hands, she would break it in half and wail to the throng of mourners, well-wishers, celebrants, and sightseers, "As this lily was, so was Ignatius. Now they are both snatched and broken." As she threw the lily back into the coffin, her feeble aim would send it flying directly into my whitened face.

For my mother I sent a prayer flying to St. Zita of Lucca, who spent her life as a house servant and practiced many austerities, in the hope that she would aid my mother in fighting her alcoholism and nighttime roistering.

Strengthened by my interlude of worship, I listened to the cutlass slapping against my side. It seemed, like some weapon of morality, to be spurring me toward the Quarter, each plastic slap saying, "Take heart, Ignatius. Thou hast a terrible swift sword." I was beginning to feel rather like a Crusader.

At last I crossed Canal Street pretending to ignore the attention paid me by all whom I passed. The narrow streets of the Quarter awaited me. A vagrant petitioned for a hot dog. I waved him away and strode forth. Unfortunately, my feet could not keep pace with my soul. Below my ankles, the tissues were crying for rest and comfort, so I placed the wagon at the curb and seated myself. The balconies of the old buildings hung over my head like dark branches in an allegorical forest of evil. Symbolically, a Desire bus hurtled past me, its diesel exhaust almost strangling me. Closing my eyes for a moment to meditate and thereby draw strength, I must have fallen asleep, for I remember being rudely awakened by a policeman standing next to me prodding me in the ribs with the toe of his shoe. Some musk which my system generates must be especially appealing to the authorities of the government. Who else would be accosted by a policeman while innocently awaiting his mother before a department store? Who else would be spied upon and reported for picking a helpless stray of a kitten from a gutter? Like a bitch in heat, I seem to attract a coterie of policemen and sanitation officials. The world will someday get me on some ludicrous pretext; I simply await the day that they drag me to some air-conditioned dungeon and leave me there beneath the florescent lights and sound-proofed ceiling to pay the price for scorning all that they hold dear within their little latex hearts.

Rising to my full height—a spectacle in itself—I looked down upon the offending policeman and crushed him with a comment which, fortunately, he failed to understand. Then I wheeled the wagon farther into the Quarter. Because it was early afternoon, there were few people stirring on the streets. I guessed that the residents of the area were still in bed recovering from whatever indecent acts they had been performing the night before. Many no doubt required medical attention: a stitch or two here and there in a torn orifice or a broken genital. I could only imagine how many haggard and depraved eyes were regarding me hungrily from behind the closed shutters. I tried not to think about it. Already I was beginning to feel like an especially toothsome steak in a meat market. However, no one called enticingly from the shutters; those devious mentalities throbbing away in their dark apartments were apparently more subtle seducers. I thought that a note, at least, might flutter down. A frozen orange juice can came flying out of one of the windows and barely missed me. I stooped over and picked it up in order to inspect the empty tin cylinder for a communication of some sort, but only a viscous residue of concentrated juice trickled out on my hand. Was this some obscene message? While I was pondering the matter and staring up at the window from which the can had been hurled, an old vagrant approached the wagon and pleaded for a frankfurter. Grudgingly I sold him one, ruefully concluding that, as always, work was interfering at a crucial moment.

By now, of course, the window from which the can had been sent flying was closed. I rolled farther down the street, staring at the closed shutters for a sign of some sort. Wild laughter issued from more than one building as I passed. Apparently the deluded occupants therein were indulging in some obscene diversion which amused them. I tried to close my virgin ears to their horrid cackling.

A group of tourists wandered along the streets, their cameras poised, their glittering eyeglasses shining like sparklers. Noticing me, they paused and, in sharp Midwestern accents which assailed my delicate eardrums like the sounds of a wheat thresher (however unimaginably horrible that must sound), begged me to pose for a photograph. Pleased by their gracious attentions, I acquiesced. For minutes they snapped away as I obliged them with several artful poses. Standing before the wagon as if it were a pirate's vessel, I brandished my cutlass menacingly for one especially memorable pose, my other hand holding the prow of the tin hot dog. As a climax, I attempted to climb atop the wagon, but the solidity of my physique proved too taxing for that rather flimsy vehicle. It began to roll from beneath me, but the gentlemen in the group were kind enough to grab it and assist me down. At last this affable group bade me farewell. As they wandered down the street madly photographing everything in sight, I heard one kindly lady say, "Wasn't that sad? We should have given her something." Unfortunately, none of the others (doubtless right-wing conservatives all) responded to her plea for charity very favorably, thinking, no doubt, that a few cents cast my way would be a vote of confidence for the welfare state. "He would only go out and spend it on more liquor," one of the other women, a shriveled crone whose face bespoke WCTU affiliation, advised her friends with nasal wisdom and an abundance of harsh *r*'s. Apparently the others sided with the WCTU drab, for the group continued down the street.

I must admit that I would not have turned down an offering of some sort. A Working Boy can use every penny that he can get his ambitious and striving hands on. In addition, those photographs could earn those corn-belt clods a fortune in some photographic contest. For a moment, I considered running behind these tourists, but just then an improbable satire on a tourist, a wan little figure in Bermuda shorts panting under the weight of a monstrous apparatus with lenses that certainly must have been a CinemaScope camera, called out a greeting to me. Upon closer inspection, I noted that it was, of all people, Patrolman Mancuso. I, of course, ignored the Machiavel's faint mongoloid grin by pretending to tighten my earring. Apparently he has been released from his imprisonment in the rest room. "How you doing?" he persisted illiterately. "Where is my book?" I demanded terrifyingly. "I'm still reading it. It's very good," he answered in terror. "Profit by its lesson," I cautioned. "When you have completed it, I shall ask you to submit to me a written critique and analysis of its message to humanity!" With that order still ringing magnificently in the air, I strode proudly off down the street. Then, realizing that I had forgotten the wagon, I returned grandly to retrieve it. (That wagon is a terrible liability. I feel as if I am stuck with a retarded child who deserves constant attention. I feel like a hen sitting on one particularly large tin egg.)

Well, here it was almost two o'clock, and I had sold exactly one hot dog. Your Working Boy would have to bustle if success was to be his goal. The occupants of the French Quarter obviously did not place frankfurters high on their list of delicacies, and the tourists were not apparently coming to colorful and picturesque old N.O. to gorge themselves upon Paradise products. Clearly I am going to have what is known in our commercial terminology as a merchandising problem. The evil Clyde has in vengeance given me a route that is a "White Elephant," a term which he once applied to me during the course of one of our business conferences. Resentment and jealousy have again struck me down.

In addition, I must devise some means of handling M. Minkoff's latest effronteries. Perhaps the Quarter will provide me with some material: a crusade for taste and decency, for theology and geometry, perhaps.

Social note: A new film featuring my favorite female star, whose recent circus musical excess stunned and overwhelmed me, is opening shortly at one of the downtown movie palaces. I must somehow get to see it. Only my wagon stands in the way. Her new film is billed as a "sophisticated" comedy in which she must certainly reach new heights of perversion and blasphemy.

Health note: Astonishing weight increase, due no doubt to the anxiety which my dear mother's increasing unpleasantness is causing me. It is a truism of human nature, that people learn to hate those who help them. Thus, my mother has turned on me.

Suspendedly,
Lance, Your Besieged Working Boy

V

The lovely girl smiled hopefully at Dr. Talc and breathed, "I just love your course. I mean, it's grand."

"Oh, well," Talc replied delightedly. "That's very

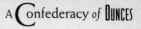

kind of you. I'm afraid the course is rather general . . ."

"Your approach to history is so vital, so contemporary, so refreshingly unorthodox."

"I do believe that we must cast aside some of the old forms and approaches." Talc's voice was important, pedantic. Should he invite this charming creature to have a drink with him? "History is, after all, an evolutionary thing."

"I *know*," the girl said, opening her eyes wide enough so that Talc could lose himself in their blueness for a moment or two.

"I only wish to interest my students. Let's face it. The average student is not interested in the history of Celtic Britain. For that matter, neither am I. That's why, even if I do admit it myself, I always sense a sort of rapport in my classes."

"I *know*." The girl brushed gracefully against Talc's expensive tweed sleeve in reaching for her purse. Talc tingled at her touch. This was the sort of girl who should be attending college, not ones like that dreadful Minkoff girl, that brutal and slovenly girl who had almost been raped by one of the janitors just outside of his office. Dr. Talc shuddered at the very thought of Miss Minkoff. In class she had insulted and challenged and vilified him at every turn, egging the Reilly monster to join in the attack. He would never forget those two; no one on the faculty ever would. They were like two Huns sweeping down on Rome. Dr. Talc idly wondered if they had married each other. Each certainly deserved the other. Perhaps they had both defected to Cuba. "Some of those historical characters are so dull."

"That's very true," Talc agreed, eager to join any campaign against the figures of English history, who had been the scourges of his existence for so many years. Simply keeping track of all of them gave him a headache. He paused to light a Benson and Hedges and cleared some of the phlegm of English history from his throat. "They all made so many foolish mistakes."

"I *know*." The girl looked into her compact mirror. Then her eyes hardened and her voice grew a little surly. "Well, I don't want to waste your time with all this historical chatter. I wanted to ask you what happened to that report that I handed in about two months ago. I mean, I'd like to get some idea of what kind of grade I'm going to get in this course."

"Oh, yes," Dr. Talc said vaguely. His hopeful bubble burst. Under their skins students were all alike. The lovely girl had turned into steely-eyed businesswoman checking, adding the profits of her grades. "You handed in a report, did you?"

"I most certainly did. It was in a yellow binder."

"Let me see if I can find it then." Dr. Talc got up and began to look through piles of various antique term papers, reports, and examinations on the top of the bookcase. As he was rearranging the stacks, an old sheet of wide-lined tablet paper folded into an airplane fell out of one binder and glided to the floor. Talc had not noticed the plane, only one of the many that had come sailing through his transom and window one semester a few years earlier. As it landed, the girl picked it up and, seeing that there was writing on the yellowed paper, unfolded the glider.

"Talc: You have been found guilty of misleading and perverting the young. I decree that you be hung by

274

your underdeveloped testicles until dead. ZORRO" The girl reread the red crayon message, and as Talc continued to press his search on top of the bookcase, she opened her purse, dropped in the airplane, and snapped the clasp.

ten

GUS LEVY WAS A NICE GUY. He was also a regular fellow. He had friends among promoters and trainers and coaches and managers across the country. At any arena or stadium or track Gus Levy could count on knowing at least one person connected with the place. He knew owners and ticket sellers and players. He even got a Christmas card every year from a peanut vendor who worked the parking lot across from Memorial Stadium in Baltimore. He was very well liked.

Levy's Lodge was where he went between seasons. He had no friends there. At Christmas the only sign of the season at Levy's Lodge, the only barometer of Yuletide spirit was the appearance of his daughters, who descended upon him from college with demands for additional money coupled with threats to disavow his paternity forever if he continued to mistreat their mother. For Christmas, Mrs. Levy always compiled not a gift list but rather a list of the injustices and brutalities she had suffered since August. The girls got this list in their stockings. The only gift Mrs. Levy asked of the girls was that they attack their father. Mrs. Levy loved Christmas.

Now Mr. Levy was waiting at the lodge for spring practice to begin. Gonzalez had his reservations to Florida and Arizona in order. But at Levy's Lodge it was like Christmas all over again, and what was going on in Levy's Lodge could have been postponed until he left for the practice camps, Mr. Levy thought.

Mrs. Levy had stretched Miss Trixie across his favorite couch, the yellow nylon one, and was rubbing skin cream into the old woman's face. Now and then Miss Trixie's tongue would flap out and sample a bit of cream from her upper lip.

"I'm getting nauseous from watching that," Mr. Levy said. "Can't you take her outside? It's a nice day."

"She likes this couch," Mrs. Levy answered. "Let her have some enjoyment. Why don't *you* go outside and wax your sports car?"

"Silence!" Miss Trixie snarled with the stupendous false teeth that Mrs. Levy had just bought her.

"Listen to that," Mr. Levy said. "She's really running this place."

"So she's asserting herself. Does that bother you? The teeth have given her a little self-confidence. Of course, you begrudge the woman even that. I'm beginning to understand why she's so insecure. I've found out that Gonzalez ignores her all day, makes her feel unwanted in about a hundred different ways. Subconsciously she hates Levy Pants."

"Who doesn't?" said Miss Trixie.

"Sad, sad," was all that Mr. Levy answered.

Miss Trixie grunted and some air whistled through her lips.

"Now let's cut this out," Mr. Levy said. "I've let you play a lot of ridiculous games around here. This one doesn't even make sense. If you want to open a funeral parlor, I'll set you up. But not in my rumpus room. Now wipe that goo off her face and let me drive

277

her back to town. Let me have some peace while I'm in this house."

"So. You're angry all of a sudden. At least you're having a normal response. That's unusual for you."

"Are you doing this just to make me angry? You can make me angry without all this. Now let her alone. All she wants is to retire. It's like torturing a dumb animal."

"I am a very attractive woman," Miss Trixie mumbled in her sleep.

"Listen to that!" Mrs. Levy cried happily. "And you want to throw her out in the snow? I'm just getting through to her. She's like a symbol of everything you haven't done."

Suddenly Miss Trixie leaped up, snarling, "Where's my eye-shade?"

"This is going to be good," Mr. Levy said. "Wait till she sinks those five-hundred-dollar teeth in you."

"Who took my eyeshade?" Miss Trixie demanded fiercely. "Where am I? Take your hands off me."

"Darling," Mrs. Levy began, but Miss Trixie had fallen asleep on her side, her creamed face smearing the couch.

"Look, Fairy Godmother, how much have you spent on this little game already? I'm not paying to have that couch re-covered."

"That's right. Spend all your money on the horses. Let this human flounder."

"You'd better take those teeth out of her mouth before she bites off her tongue. Then she'll really be stuck."

"Speaking of tongue, you should have heard all that she told me about Gloria this morning." Mrs. Levy made a gesture that indicated acceptance of injustice

278

and tragedy. "Gloria was the soul of kindness, the first person in years who took an interest in Miss Trixie. Then out of the blue you walk in and kick Gloria out of her life. I think it's given her a very bad trauma. The girls would love to know about Gloria. They'd ask you some questions, believe me."

"I bet they would. You know, I think you're really going out of your mind. There is *no* Gloria. If you keep on talking to your little protégé there, she's going to take you with her right into the twilight zone. When Susan and Sandra come home for Easter, they'll find you bouncing on that board with a paper bag full of rags in your arms."

"Oh, oh. I see. Mere guilt about this Gloria incident. Fighting, resentment. It's all going to end very badly, Gus. Please skip one of your tournaments and go see Lenny's doctor. The man works miracles, believe me."

"Then ask him to take Levy Pants off our hands. I talked to three realtors this week. Every one of them said it was the most unsalable property they'd ever seen."

"Gus, did I hear correctly? Did I hear you say something about selling your heritage?" Mrs. Levy screamed.

"Quiet!" Miss Trixie snarled. "I'll get you people. Wait and see. You'll get it. I'll get even."

"Oh, shut up," Mrs. Levy shouted at her and pressed her back to the couch, where she promptly dozed off.

"Well, one guy," Mr. Levy continued calmly, "this very aggressive-looking agent, gave me some hope. Like all the others, he said, 'Nobody wants a clothing factory today. The market's dead. Your place is

279

outmoded. Thousands for repairs and modernization. It's got a railroad switch line, but light goods like clothes are going by truck today, and the place is badly located for trucks. Across town from the highways. Southern garment business folding. Even the land's not worth much. The whole area is becoming a slum.' And on and on. But this one agent said maybe he could interest some supermarket chain in buying the factory for a store. Well, that sounded good. Then the hitch came in. There's no parking area around Levy Pants, the neighborhood's living median or something is too low to support a big market, and on and on again. He said the only hope was renting it out as a warehouse, but again warehouse revenues are not high and the place is badly located for a warehouse. Something about highways again. So don't worry. Levy Pants is still ours, like a chamberpot we inherited."

"A chamberpot? Your father's sweat and blood is a chamberpot? I see your motive. Destroy the last monument to your father's accomplishments."

"Levy Pants is a monument?"

"Why I ever wanted to work there I'll never know," Miss Trixie said angrily from among the pillows where Mrs. Levy had her pinioned. "Thank goodness poor Gloria got out of there in time."

"Pardon me, ladies," Mr. Levy said, whistling through his teeth. "You two can discuss Gloria alone."

He got up and went into the whirlpool bath. While the water swirled and jetted around him, he wondered how he might somehow be able to dump Levy Pants in the lap of some poor buyer. It must have some uses. A skating rink? A gym? A Negro cathedral? Then he wondered what would happen if he carried Mrs. Levy's exercising table to the seawall and dumped it into the

Gulf. He dried himself carefully, put on his terry-cloth robe, and went back into the rumpus room to get his dope sheet.

Miss Trixie was sitting up on the couch. Her face had been cleaned. Her mouth was an orange smear. Her weak eyes were accentuated by shadow. Mrs. Levy was adjusting a coiffed black wig over the old woman's thin hair.

"What in the world are you doing to me now?" Miss Trixie was wheezing at her benefactress. "You'll pay for this."

"Do you believe it?" Mrs. Levy asked her husband proudly, all traces of hostility gone from her voice. "Just look at that."

Mr. Levy couldn't believe it. Miss Trixie looked exactly like Mrs. Levy's mother.

II

In Mattie's Ramble Inn, Jones poured a glassful of beer and sank his long teeth into the foam.

"That Lee woman ain't treatin you right, Jones," Mr. Watson was telling him. "One thing I don like to see a colored man make fun of hisself for bein colored. That what she be doin with you fix up like a plantation darky."

"Whoa! Color cats got it har enough without peoples bustin out laughin cause they color. Shit. I make my mistake when I tell that Lee mother a po-lice tell me to get a job. I shoulda tell her them fair employmen peoples sendin me over, scare that gal a little."

"You better go to the po-lice and tell them you quittin at that place but you gonna fin you another job."

"Hey! I ain walkin in no precinc and flappin my mouth at no po-lice. Them po-lice take one look at me, throw my ass in jail. Whoa! Color peoples cain fin no job, but they sure can fin a openin in jail. Goin in jail the bes way you get you somethin to eat regular. But I rather starve *outside*. I rather mop a whore floor than go to jail and be making plenny license plate and rug and leather belt and shit. I jus was stupor enough to get my ass snatch up in a trap at that Night of Joy. I gotta figure this thing out myself."

"I still say you go to the po-lice and tell them you be between job a little while."

"Yeah. And maybe I be between job about fifdy year. I ain seen no peoples screamin for unskill color cats. Ooo-wee. Somebody like that Lee bastar know plenny po-lice. Otherwise that B-drinker, knockout drop cathouse be close down long ago. I ain takin no chance going to no Lee frien in the po-lice and sayin, 'Hey, man, I jus be vagran a little while.' He say, 'Okay, boy, you be servin jus a little while, too.' Whoa!"

"Well, how the sabotage comin along."

"Pretty poor. Lee make me work overtime on the floor the other day, she see the crap gettin a little thicker so pretty soon her poor, stupor customer be up to they ankle in dus. Shit. I tol you I wrote a address on one of her orphan package, so if she still distributin for the United Fun maybe we be gettin some answer on that. I sure like to see wha that address bringin in. Maybe it'll be bringin in a po-lice. Whoa!"

"It pretty clear you not gettin nowhere. Go talk to the po-lice, man. They understand your story."

"I *scare* of the po-lice, Watson. Ooo-wee. You be scare, too, if you was jus standin in Woolsworth and some po-lice drag you off. Especially when Lee probly goin roun the whirl with half the po-lice on the force. Whoa!" Jones sent up what looked like a cloud, a radio-active one which gradually sent some fallout down onto the bar and the cooler filled with pickled meat. "Say, whatever happen to that dumb mother was in here that day, the one workin for Levy Pant? You ever seen him aroun again?"

"The man talking about demonstratin?"

"Yeah, the cat got him that fat white freak for a leader, the one tellin them poor color peoples they suppose to drop a nucular bum on top they factory, kill theirselves and get what's left of their ass throwed in jail."

"I ain't seen him since."

"Shit. I like to fin out where that fat freak hidin out. Maybe I call up Levy Pant and ax for him. I like to drop him in the Night of Joy like a nucular bum. Seem like he the kin make that Lee mother shit in her drawer. Whoa! If I gonna be a doorman, I gonna be the mos sabotagin doorman ever guarded a plantation. Ooo-wee. The cotton fiel be burn to the groun before I'm through."

"Watch out, Jones. Don be gettin yourself in no trouble."

"Whoa!"

III

Ignatius was beginning to feel worse and worse. His valve seemed to be glued, and no amount of bouncing was opening it. Great belches ripped out of the gas pockets of his stomach and tore through his digestive tract. Some escaped noisily. Others, weaning belches, lodged in his chest and caused massive heartburn.

283

The physical cause for this health decline was, he knew, the too strenuous consuming of Paradise products. But there were other, subtler reasons. His mother was becoming increasingly bold and overtly antagonistic; it was becoming impossible to control her. Perhaps she had joined some fringe group of the far right wing that was making her belligerent and hostile. At any rate, she certainly had been carrying on a witch-hunt in the brown kitchen recently, asking him all sorts of questions concerning his political philosophy. Which was strange. His mother had always been notably apolitical, voting only for candidates who seemed to have been kind to their mothers. Mrs. Reilly had been solidly behind Franklin Roosevelt for four terms not because of the New Deal, but because his mother, Mrs. Sara Roosevelt, seemed to have been respected and well treated by her son. Mrs. Reilly had also voted for the Truman woman standing before her Victorian house in Independence, Missouri, and not specifically for Harry Truman. To Mrs. Reilly, Nixon and Kennedy had meant Hannah and Rose. Motherless candidates confused her, and in motherless elections she stayed at home. Ignatius could not understand her sudden, clumsy effort to protect the American Way against her son.

Then there was Myrna, who had been appearing to him in a series of dreams that was taking the form of the old Batman serials that he had seen at the Prytania as a child. One chapter followed the other. In one gruesome chapter, he had been standing on a subway platform, reincarnated as St. James, the Less, who was martyred by the Jews. Myrna appeared through a turnstile carrying a NON-VIOLENT CONGRESS FOR THE SEXUALLY NEEDY placard and began heckling him. "Jesus will come to the fore, skins or not," Ignatius-St. James

284

prophesied grandly. But Myrna, sneering, pushed him with the placard onto the tracks before the speeding subway train. He had awakened just as the train was about to crush him. The M. Minkoff dreams were getting worse than the old, terrifying Scenicruiser dreams in which Ignatius, magnificent on the upper deck, had ridden doomed buses over the rails of bridges and into collisions with jets taxiing along airport runways.

By night he was plagued by dreams and by day by the impossible route that Mr. Clyde had given him. No one in the French Quarter, it seemed, was interested in hot dogs. So his take-home pay was getting smaller, and his mother, in turn, was getting surlier. When and how would this vicious cycle end?

He had read in the morning paper that a ladies' art guild was having a hanging of its paintings in Pirate's Alley. Imagining that the paintings would be offensive enough to interest him for a while, he pushed his wagon up onto the flagstones of the Alley toward the variety of artwork dangling from the iron pickets of the fence behind the Cathedral. On the prow of the wagon, in an attempt to attract business among the Quarterites, Ignatius taped a sheet of Big Chief paper on which he had printed in crayon: TWELVE INCHES (12) OF PARADISE. So far no one had responded to its message.

The Alley was filled with well-dressed ladies in large hats. Ignatius pointed the prow of the wagon into the throng and pushed forward. A woman read the Big Chief statement and screamed, summoning her companions to draw aside from the ghastly apparition that had appeared at their art show.

"Hot dogs, ladies?" Ignatius asked pleasantly.

The ladies' eyes studied the sign, the earring, the scarf, the cutlass, and pleaded for him to move along.

Rain for their hanging would have been bad enough. But *this*.

"Hot dogs, hot dogs," Ignatius said a little angrily. "Savories from the hygienic Paradise kitchens."

He belched violently during the silence that followed. The ladies pretended to study the sky and the little garden behind the Cathedral.

Ignatius lumbered over to the picket fence, abandoning the hopeless cause espoused by the wagon, and viewed the oil paintings and pastels and watercolors strung there. Although the style of each varied in crudity, the subjects of the paintings were relatively similar: camellias floating in bowls of water, azaleas tortured into ambitious flower arrangements, magnolias that looked like white windmills. Ignatius scrutinized the offerings furiously for a while all by himself, for the ladies had stepped back from the fence and had formed what looked like a protective little grouping. The wagon, too, stood forlorn on the flagstones, several feet from the newest member of the art guild.

"Oh, my God!" Ignatius bellowed after he had promenaded up and down along the fence. "How dare you present such abortions to the public."

"Please move along, sir," a bold lady said.

"Magnolias don't look like that," Ignatius said, thrusting his cutlass at the offending pastel magnolia. "You ladies need a course in botany. And perhaps geometry, too."

286

"You don't *have* to look at our work," an offended voice said from the group, the voice of the lady who had drawn the magnolia in question.

"Yes, I do!" Ignatius screamed. "You ladies need a critic with some taste and decency. Good heavens!

Which one of you did this camellia? Speak up. The water in this bowl looks like motor oil."

"Let us alone," a shrill voice said.

"You women had better stop giving teas and brunches and settle down to the business of learning how to draw," Ignatius thundered. "First, you must learn how to handle a brush. I would suggest that you all get together and paint someone's house for a start."

"Go away."

"Had you 'artists' had a part in the decoration of the Sistine Chapel, it would have ended up looking like a particularly vulgar train terminal," Ignatius snorted.

"We don't intend to be insulted by a coarse vendor," a spokeswoman for the band of large hats said haughtily.

"I see!" Ignatius screamed. "So it is you people who slander the reputation of the hot dog vendor."

"He's mad."

"He's so common."

"So coarse."

"Don't encourage him."

"We don't want you here," the spokeswoman said tartly and simply.

"I should imagine not!" Ignatius was breathing heavily. "Apparently you are afraid of someone who has some contact with reality, who can truthfully describe to you the offenses which you have committed to canvas."

"Please leave," the spokeswoman ordered.

"I shall." Ignatius grabbed the handle of his cart and pushed off. "You women should all be on your knees begging forgiveness for what I have seen here on this fence."

"The city is certainly going down when *that's* out

on the streets," a woman said as Ignatius waddled off down the Alley.

Ignatius was surprised to feel a small rock bounce off the back of his head. Angrily, he shoved the wagon along the flagstones until he was near the end of the alley. There he parked the wagon in a little passageway so that it would be out of sight. His feet hurt, and while he was resting he didn't want anyone to bother him by asking for a hot dog. Even though business couldn't be worse, there were times when a person had to be true to himself and consider his welfare first. Much more of this vending and his feet would be bloody stumps.

Ignatius squatted uncomfortably on the side steps of the Cathedral. His recently increased weight and the bloating caused by the inoperative valve made any position other than standing or lying down somewhat awkward. Removing his boots, he began to inspect his great slabs of feet.

"Oh, dear," a voice said above Ignatius. "What am I seeing? I come out to see this dreadful, tacky art exhibit, and what do I find as Exhibit Number One? It's the ghost of Lafitte, the pirate. No. It's Fatty Arbuckle. Or is it Marie Dressler? Tell me soon or I'll die."

Ignatius looked up and saw the young man who had bought his mother's hat in the Night of Joy.

"Get away from me, you fop. Where is my mother's hat?"

"Oh, that," the young man sighed. "I'm afraid it was destroyed at a really wild gathering. Everyone dearly loved it."

"I'm sure that they did. I won't ask you just how it was desecrated."

"I wouldn't remember anyway. Too many martinis that night for little *moi.*"

"Oh, my God."

"What in God's name are you doing in that bizarre outfit? You look like Charles Laughton in drag as the Queen of the Gypsies. What *are* you supposed to be? I really want to know."

"Move along, you coxcomb," Ignatius belched, the gassy eructations echoing between the walls of the Alley. The women's art guild turned its hats toward the source of the volcanic sound. Ignatius glared at the young man's tawny velvet jacket and mauve cashmere sweater and the wave of blonde hair that fell over the forehead of his sharp, glittering face. "Get away from me before I strike you down."

"Oh, my goodness," the young man laughed in short, merry, childish breaths that made his downy jacket quiver. "You really are insane, aren't you?"

"How dare you!" Ignatius screamed. He unpinned his cutlass and began to strike the young man's calves with the plastic weapon. The young man giggled and danced about in front of Ignatius to avoid the thrusts, his lithe movements making him a difficult target. Finally he danced across the Alley and waved to Ignatius. Ignatius picked up one of his elephantine desert boots and flung it at the pirouetting figure.

"Oh," the young man squealed. He caught the shoe and threw it back at Ignatius, whom it hit squarely in the face.

"Oh, my God! I've been disfigured."

"Shut up."

"I can easily have you booked for assault."

289

"If I were you, I'd stay as far away from the police as possible. What do you think they'd say when they saw that outfit, Mary Marvel? And booking *me* with assault? Let's be a little realistic. I'm surprised that they're permitting you to go cruising at all in that for-tune-teller's ensemble." The young man clicked his lighter open, lit a Salem, and clicked it closed. "And with those bare feet and that toy sword? Are you kid-ding?"

"The police will believe anything I tell them."

"Get with it, please."

"You may be locked away for several years."

"Oh, you really are on the moon."

"Well, I certainly don't have to sit here listening to you," Ignatius said, putting on his suede boots.

"Oh!" the young man shrieked happily. "That look on your face. Like Bette Davis with indigestion."

"Don't talk to me, you degenerate. Go play with your little friends. I am certain that the Quarter is crawling with them."

"How is that dear mother of yours?"

"I don't want to hear her sainted name cross your decadent lips."

"Well, since it already has, is she all right? She's so sweet and dear, that woman, so unspoiled. You're very lucky."

"I will not discuss her with you."

"If that's the way you want to be, all right. I just hope that she doesn't know that you're flouncing around the streets like some sort of Hungarian Joan of Arc. That earring. It's so Magyar."

"If you want a costume like this, then buy one," Ignatius said. "Let me alone."

"I know that something like that couldn't be bought anywhere. Oh, but it would bring the house down at a party."

"I suspect that the parties you attend must be true visions of the apocalypse. I knew that our society was coming to this. In a few years, you and your friends will probably take over the country."

"Oh, we're planning to," the young man said with a bright smile. "We have connections in the highest places. You'd be surprised."

"No, I wouldn't. Hroswitha could have predicted this long ago."

"Who in the world is that?"

"A sibyl of a medieval nun. She has guided my life."

"Oh, you're truly fantastic," the young man said gleefully. "And although I didn't think it would be possible, you've gained weight. Where will you ever end? There's something so unbelievably tacky about your obesity."

Ignatius rose to his feet and stabbed the young man in the chest with his plastic cutlass.

"Take that, you offal," Ignatius cried, digging the cutlass into the cashmere sweater. The tip of the cutlass broke off and fell to the flagstone walk.

"Oh, dear," the young man shrieked. "You'll tear my sweater, you big crazy thing."

Down the Alley the women's art guild members were removing their paintings from the fence and folding their aluminum lawn chairs like Arabs in preparation for stealing away. Their annual outdoor exhibit had been ruined.

"I am the avenging sword of taste and decency," Ignatius was shouting. As he slashed at the sweater with his broken weapon, the ladies began to dash out the Royal Street end of the Alley. A few stragglers were snatching at their magnolias and camellias in panic.

"Why did I ever stop to talk to you, you maniac?"

291

the young man asked in a vicious and breathless whisper. "This is my very finest sweater."

"Whore!" Ignatius cried, scraping the cutlass across the young man's chest.

"Oh, isn't this horrible."

He tried to run away, but Ignatius had been holding his arm firmly with the hand that was not wielding the cutlass. Slipping a finger through Ignatius' hoop earring, the young man pulled downward, breathing to Ignatius, "Drop that sword."

"Good grief." Ignatius dropped the sword onto the flagstones. "I think that my ear is broken."

The young man released the earring.

"Now you've done it!" Ignatius slobbered. "You will rot in a federal prison for the remainder of your life."

"Just look at my sweater, you disgusting monster."

"Only the most flamboyant offal would be seen in a miscarriage like that. You must have some shame or at least some taste in dress."

"You awful creature. You huge *thing*."

"I will probably spend several years at the Eye, Ear, Nose, and Throat Hospital having this attended to," Ignatius said, fingering his ear. "You may expect to receive some rather staggering medical bills each month. My corps of attorneys will contact you in the morning wherever it is that you carry on your questionable activities. I shall warn them beforehand that they may expect to see and hear anything. They are all brilliant attorneys, pillars of the community, aristocratic Creole scholars whose knowledge of the more surreptitious forms of living is quite limited. They may even refuse to see you. A considerably lesser representative may be sent to call upon you, some junior partner whom they've taken in out of pity."

"You awful, terrible animal."

"However, to save you the anxiety of awaiting this phalanx of legal luminaries to arrive at your spider web of an apartment, I shall consent to accepting a settlement now, if you wish. Five or six dollars should suffice."

"My sweater cost me forty dollars," the young man said. He felt the worn portion that had been scraped by the cutlass. "Are you prepared to pay for it?"

"Of course not. Never become involved in an altercation with a pauper."

"I can easily sue you."

"Perhaps we should both drop the idea of legal recourse. For an event so auspicious as a courtroom trial, you would probably get completely carried away and appear in a tiara and evening gown. An old judge would grow quite confused. Both of us would doubtlessly be found guilty on some trumped up charge."

"You revolting beast."

"Why don't you run along and partake in some dubious recreation that appeals to you," Ignatius belched. "Look, there's a sailor drifting along Chartres Street. He looks rather lonely."

The young man glanced down to the Chartres Street end of the Alley.

"Oh, him," he said. "That's only Timmy."

"Timmy?" Ignatius asked angrily. "Do you know him?"

"Of course," the young man said in a voice heavy with boredom. "He's one of my dearest, *oldest* friends. He's not a sailor at all."

"What?" Ignatius thundered. "Do you mean that

he is impersonating a member of the armed forces of this country?"

"That's not all he impersonates."

"This is extremely serious." Ignatius frowned and the red sateen scarf rode down on his hunting cap. "Every soldier and sailor that we see could simply be some mad decadent in disguise. My God! We may all be trapped in some horrible conspiracy. I knew that something like this was going to happen. The United States is probably totally defenseless!"

The young man and the sailor waved at each other familiarly, and the sailor drifted out of sight around the front of the Cathedral. Following a few steps behind the sailor, Patrolman Mancuso appeared at the end of Pirate's Alley wearing a beret and goatee.

"Oh!" the young man shrieked gaily, watching Patrolman Mancuso stalking the sailor. "It's that marvelous policeman. Don't they know that everyone in the Quarter knows who he is?"

"Do you know him, too?" Ignatius asked guardedly. "He's a very dangerous man!"

"Everyone knows him. Thank goodness he's back again. We were beginning to wonder what had happened to him. We love him dearly. Oh, I simply wait to see what new disguise they put on him. You should have seen him a few weeks ago before he had disappeared, he was just too much in that cowboy outfit." The young man exploded in wild laughter. "He could hardly walk in these boots, his ankles kept giving way. Once he stopped me on Chartres when I was going truly mad with your mother's W.P.A. hat. Then he stopped me again on Dumaine and tried to start a conversation. That day he was wearing horn-rimmed glasses and a crew sweater, and he told me that he was a Princeton student down here on a vacation. He's just fabulous. I'm so glad the police have returned him to the people who truly appreciate him. I'm sure he was being wasted wherever he was recently. Oh, that accent of his. Some people like him best as the British tourist. That is choice. But I've always preferred his southern colonel. It's really a matter of taste, I guess. We've had him arrested twice for making indecent proposals. That's always wonderfully confusing to the police. I do hope that we haven't gotten him in too much trouble, for he's close to our hearts."

"He is thoroughly evil," Ignatius observed. Then he said, "I wonder how many of our 'military' are simply people like your friend, disguised tarts."

"Who knows? I wish they all were."

"Of course," Ignatius said in a thoughtful, serious voice, "this could be a worldwide deception." The red sateen scarf rode up and down. "The next war could turn out to be one massive orgy. Good grief. How many of the military leaders of the world may simply be deranged old sodomites acting out some fake fantasy role? Actually, this might be quite beneficial to the world. It could mean an end to war forever. This could be the key to lasting peace."

"It certainly could," the young man said pleasantly. "Peace at any price."

Two nerve ends in Ignatius' mind met and formed an immediate association. Perhaps he had found a means of assaulting the effrontery of M. Minkoff.

"The power-crazed leaders of the world would certainly be surprised to find that their military leaders and troops were only masquerading sodomites who were only too eager to meet the masquerading sodomite armies of other nations in order to have dances and balls and learn some foreign dance steps."

"Wouldn't that be wonderful? The government would pay us to travel. How divine. We would bring an end to world strife and renew people's hope and faith."

"Perhaps you are the hope for the future," Ignatius said, dramatically pounding one paw into the other. "There certainly doesn't seem to be anything else very promising on the horizon."

"We would also help to end the population explosion."

"Oh, my God!" The blue and yellow eyes flashed wildly. "Your method would probably be more satisfying and acceptable than the rather stringent birth control tactics which I have always advocated. I must dedicate some space to this in my writings. This subject deserves the attention of a profound thinker who has a certain perspective on the world's cultural development. I am certainly glad that you have given me this valuable new insight."

"Oh, what a fun day this has been. You're a gypsy. Timmy's a sailor. The marvelous policeman's an artist." The young man sighed. "It's just like Mardi Gras, and I feel so left out. I think I'll go home and throw something on."

"Wait just a moment," Ignatius said. He couldn't permit this opportunity to slip through his swollen fingers.

"I'll put on some clogs. I'm in my Ruby Keeler phase," the young man told Ignatius gaily. Then he began to sing, "'You go home and get your scanties, I'll go home and get my panties, and away we'll go. Oh-ho-ho. Off we're gonna shuffle, shuffle off to Buffalo-ho-ho . . .'"

296

"Stop that offensive performance," Ignatius ordered angrily. These people must be whipped into line.

The young man did a little soft shoe around Ignatius and said, "Ruby was such a darling. I watch her old movies on television religiously. 'And for just a silver quarter, we can tip the pullman porter, turn the lights down low, oh-ho-ho, off we're gonna shuffle, shuffle off to . . .'"

"Please be serious for a moment. Stop fluttering around here."

"*Moi?* Fluttering? What do you want, Gypsy Woman?"

"Have you people considered forming a political party and running a candidate?"

"Politics? Oh, Maid of Orleans. How dreary."

"This is very important!" Ignatius shouted worriedly. He would show Myrna how to inject sex into politics. "Although I had never considered it before, you may hold the key to the future."

"Well, what do you want to do about it, Eleanor Roosevelt?"

"You must start a party organization. Plans must be made."

"Oh, please," the young man sighed. "All this man's talk is making my mind reel."

"We may be able to save the world!" Ignatius bellowed in an orator's voice. "Good heavens. Why haven't I thought of this before?"

"This kind of conversation depresses me more than you could possibly imagine," the young man told him. "You're beginning to remind me of my father, and what could be more depressing than that?" The young man sighed. "I'm afraid I'll have to be running along. It's costume time."

297

"No!" Ignatius grabbed the lapel of the young man's jacket.

"Oh, my goodness," the young man breathed, putting his hand to his throat. "Now I'll be on pills all night."

"We must organize immediately."

"I can't tell you how much you're depressing me."

"There must be a large organizational meeting to kick off the campaign."

"Wouldn't that be something like a party?"

"Yes, in a way. However, it would have to express your purpose."

"Then it might be sort of fun. You can't imagine how drab, drab the parties have been lately."

"This is not to be a party, you ass."

"Oh, we'll be very serious."

"Good. Now listen to me. I must come to lecture to you people so that you will be set upon the correct path. I have a rather extensive knowledge of political organization."

"Marvelous. And you must wear that fantastic costume. I can assure you that you'll get everyone's undivided attention," the young man shrieked, covering his mouth with a hand. "Oh, my dear, what a wild gathering it could be."

"There is no time to be lost," Ignatius said sternly. "The apocalypse is near at hand."

"We'll have it next week at my place."

"You must have some red, white, and blue bunting," Ignatius advised. "Political meetings always have that."

"I'll have yards and yards of it. What a decorating job lies ahead. I'll have to get some close friends in to help me."

"Yes, do that," Ignatius said excitedly. "Begin organizing at every level."

"Oh, I never guessed that you would be such a fun person to know. You were so hostile in that dreadful, tacky bar."

"My being has many facets."

"You amaze me." The young man stared at Ignatius' outfit. "To think that they're letting you run around loose. In a way, I respect you."

"Thank you very much." Ignatius' voice was smooth, pleased. "Most fools don't comprehend my worldview at all."

"I wouldn't imagine so."

"I suspect that beneath your offensively and vulgarly effeminate façade there may be a soul of sorts. Have you read widely in Boethius?"

"Who? Oh, heavens no. I never even read newspapers."

"Then you must begin a reading program immediately so that you may understand the crises of our age," Ignatius said solemnly. "Begin with the late Romans, including Boethius, of course. Then you should dip rather extensively into early Medieval. You may skip the Renaissance and the Enlightenment. That is mostly dangerous propaganda. Now that I think of it, you had better skip the Romantics and the Victorians, too. For the contemporary period, you should study some selected comic books."

"You're fantastic."

"I recommend Batman especially, for he tends to transcend the abysmal society in which he's found himself. His morality is rather rigid, also. I rather respect Batman."

"Oh, look, there's Timmy again," the young man

299

said. The sailor was passing on Chartres Street in the opposite direction. "Doesn't he ever get tired of the same old route? Back and forth, back and forth. Look at him. It's winter and he's still wearing his summer whites. Of course he doesn't realize that he's a sitting duck for the shore patrol. You can't imagine how stupid and foolish that boy is."

"His face did appear rather clouded," Ignatius said. The artist in the beret and goatee passed Chartres, busily following the sailor by several feet. "Oh, my God! That ludicrous law officer will ruin everything. He's the fly in everyone's ointment. Perhaps you should run along and get the deranged sailor off the street. If the naval authorities apprehend him, they will discover that he is an imposter, and our political strategy will be undone. Spirit that clown away before he wrecks the most fiendish political coup in the history of western civilization."

"Oh!" the young man shrieked happily. "I'll go back and tell him about it. When he hears what he's almost done, he'll scream and faint."

"Now don't slacken in your preparations," Ignatius warned.

"I'll work myself to exhaustion," the young man said gaily. "Ward meetings, voter registration, pamphlets, committees. We'll start the kickoff rally around eightish. I'm on St. Peter Street, the yellow stucco building just off Royal. You can't miss it. Here's my card."

"Oh, my God!" Ignatius mumbled, looking at the austere little calling card. "You can't really be named Dorian Greene."

"Yes, isn't that wild?" Dorian asked languidly. "If I told you my real name, you'd never speak to me again.

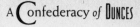

It's so common I could die just thinking of it. I was born on a wheat farm in Nebraska. You can take it from there."

"Well, at any rate, I am Ignatius J. Reilly."

"That isn't too dreadful. I sort of imagined you as a Horace or Humphrey or something like that. Well, don't fail us. Practice your speech. I guarantee a large crowd, everyone is almost dead from ennui and general depression, so they'll be fighting for invitations. Give me a tinkle and we'll iron out the exact date."

"Be sure to stress the importance of this historic conclave," Ignatius said. "We shall want no fly-by-nights in this core group."

"There may be a few costumes. That's what's so wonderful about New Orleans. You can masquerade and Mardi Gras all year round if you want to. Really, sometimes the Quarter is like one big costume ball. Sometimes I can't tell friend from foe. But if you oppose costumes, I'll tell everyone, although their little hearts will snap with disappointment. We haven't had a good party in months."

"I would not oppose a few tasteful and decent maskers," Ignatius said at last. "They may add the proper international atmosphere to the meeting. Politicians always seem to want to shake hands with mongoloids in ethnic and native costumes. Now that I think of it, you may encourage a costume or two. We do not want any female impersonators, however. I don't believe that politicians care to be seen with them particularly. They cause resentment among rural voters, I suspect."

301

"Now let me run along and find that silly Timmy. I'll frighten him to death."

"Beware of that Machiavel of a policeman. If he gets wind of the plot, we're lost."

"Oh, if I weren't so glad to see him back on the beat, I'd telephone the police and have him arrested immediately for soliciting. You don't know the wonderful expression that man used to get on his face when the squad car arrived to take him off. And the arresting officers. It was too priceless. But we'll all be so grateful to have him back. No one will dare mistreat him now. So long, Gypsy Mother."

Dorian skipped off down the alley to find the decadent mariner. Ignatius looked toward Royal Street and wondered what had happened to the women's art guild. He lumbered over to the passageway where his cart was hidden, prepared a hot dog, and prayed that some customers would happen along before the day was over. Sadly he realized how low Fortuna had spun his wheel. He had never imagined that he would one day be praying that people buy hot dogs from him. At least he had a magnificent new scheme ready for launching against M. Minkoff. The thought of the kickoff rally cheered him greatly. This time the minx would be totally confounded.

IV

It was all a matter of storage. From almost one to three every afternoon George was stuck with the packages. One afternoon he had gone to a movie, but even there in the dark watching a double bill of two nudist colony films he wasn't comfortable. He was afraid to put the packages down on an adjoining seat, especially in a theater like that one. Holding them in his lap, he was reminded of the burden throughout the three hours of tanned flesh that filled the screen. On the other days he had carried them around with him during boring wanderings through the business district and the Quarter. But by three o'clock he was so tired from the marathon of strolling that he hardly had the enthusiasm to negotiate his day's business; and in two hours of being carried, the wrapping on the packages got damp and started to break. If one of those packages broke open on the street, he could plan to spend the next few years in a juvenile detention home. Why had that undercover agent tried to arrest him in the rest room? He hadn't done a thing. That agent must have had some sort of detective ESP.

Finally George thought of a place that would at least guarantee him some rest and a chance to sit down, St. Louis Cathedral. He sat in one of the pews next to a bank of vigil lights and decorated his hands, his packages stacked beside him. When his hands were done, he picked a missal from the rack before him and looked through it, refreshing his dim knowledge of the mechanics of the Mass by studying the drawings of the celebrant as he moved through the devotions. The Mass was really very simple, George thought. Until it was time to leave he flipped back and forth through the missal. Then he gathered up his packages and went out onto Chartres Street.

A sailor leaning against a lamppost winked at him. George acknowledged the greeting with an obscene gesture of his tatooed hands and slouched off down the street. As he passed Pirate's Alley, he heard screaming. There in the Alley the crazy hot dog vendor was trying to stab a fairy with a plastic knife. That vendor was really far out. George paused for a second to look at the earring and scarf that were heaving and bobbing while

303

the fairy shrieked. That vendor probably didn't know what day it was or what month or even what year. He must have thought today was Mardi Gras.

Just in time George saw the rest room undercover agent coming down the street behind the sailor. He looked like a beatnik. George ran behind one of the arches of the ancient Spanish governmental building, the Cabildo, and dashed through the arcade out onto St. Peter Street, where he continued running until he reached Royal and headed uptown to the bus lines.

Now the undercover agent was prowling around the Cathedral. George had to give it to the cops. They were really on the ball. Christ. A guy didn't have a chance.

So his mind returned to the matter of storage. He was beginning to feel like some escaped convict hiding out from the cops. Where now? He climbed on an outbound Desire bus and pondered the matter while the bus swung around and headed out on Bourbon Street, passing by the Night of Joy. Lana Lee was out on the sidewalk giving the jig some directions about a poster he was putting up in the glass case on the front of the bar. The jig flipped a cigarette that would have set Miss Lee's hair on fire if it hadn't been aimed by a master marksman. As it was, the butt sailed over Miss Lee's head with about an inch to spare. These jigs were really getting smart. George would have to ride into one of their neighborhoods one of these nights and toss a few eggs. He and his friends hadn't done that in a long time, driving along in someone's souped-up car and splattering whatever jigs were stupid enough to be standing out on the sidewalk.

But back to the matter of storage. The bus crossed Elysian Fields before George came up with anything.

There it was. It had been before him all the time and he just hadn't realized it. He could have kicked himself in the shins with the stiletto toes of his flamenco boots. He saw a nice, roomy, weather-tight metal compartment, a mobile safety deposit box that no undercover agent in the world, however crafty, would think of opening, a safe vault operated by the biggest patsy in the world: the bun compartment in that oddball vendor's wagon.

eleven

"Aw, LOOK," SANTA SAID, holding the newspaper close to her eyes. "They got a cute picture show on in the neighborhood with little Debbie Reynolds."

"Aw, she's sweet," Mrs. Reilly said. "You like her, Claude?"

"Who's that?" Mr. Robichaux asked pleasantly.

"Little Debra Reynolds," Mrs. Reilly answered.

"I don't think I can place her. I don't go to the show much."

"She's darling," Santa said. "So petite. You ever seen her in that cute picture where she played Tammy, Irene?"

"Ain't that the picture where she went blind?"

"No, girl! You must be thinking of the wrong show."

"Oh, I know who I was thinking of, precious. I was thinking of June Wyman. She was sweet, too."

"Aw, she was good," Santa said. "I remember that picture where she played the dummy who got herself raped."

"Lord, I'm glad I didn't go see that show."

"Aw, it was wonderful, babe. Very dramatic. You know? The look on that poor dummy's face when she got raped. I'll never forget it."

"Anybody want more coffee?" Mr. Robichaux asked.

"Yeah, gimmee some there, Claude," Santa said, folding the newspaper and throwing it on top of the refrigerator. "I'm sure sorry Angelo couldn't make it. That poor boy. He told me he's gonna be working day and night on his own so he can bring somebody in. He's out someplace tonight, I guess. You oughta heard what his Rita been telling me. It seems Angelo went out an bought a lot of expensive clothes he can wear so maybe he can attract some character. Ain't that a shame. That just shows you how much that boy loves the force. If they was to kick him out, it'd break his heart. I sure hope he takes in some bum."

"Angelo's got him a hard road to travel," Mrs. Reilly said absently. She was thinking of the PEACE TO MEN OF GOOD WILL sign that Ignatius had tacked to the front of their house after he had come home from work. Miss Annie had immediately started an inquisition about that as soon as it had appeared, screaming questions through her shutters. "What you think about somebody wants peace, Claude?"

"That sounds like a communiss to me."

Mrs. Reilly's worst fears were realized.

"Who wants peace?" Santa asked.

"Ignatius got a sign up in front the house about peace."

"I mighta known," Santa said angrily. "First that boy wants a king, now he wants peace. I'm telling you, Irene. For your own good. That boy's gotta be put away."

"He ain't wearing no earring. I ask him and he says, 'I ain't wearing no earring, momma.'"

"Angelo don't lie."

"Maybe he just got him a small one."

"A earring's a earring to me. Ain't that right, Claude?"

"That's right," Claude answered Santa.

"Santa, honey, that's a sweet little Blessed Virgin you got on top that T.V.," Mrs. Reilly said to get them off the earring topic.

Everyone looked at the television set next to the refrigerator, and Santa said, "Ain't that nice, though? It's a little Our Lady of the Television. It's got a suction cup base so I don't knock it over when I'm banging around in the kitchen. I bought it by Lenny's."

"Lenny's got everything," Mrs. Reilly said. "It looks like it's made outta nice plastic, too, don't break."

"Well, how you kids liked that dinner?"

"It was delicious," Mr. Robichaux said.

"It was wonderful," Mrs. Reilly agreed. "I ain't had me a good meal in a long time."

"Aarff," Santa belched. "I think I put too much garlic in them stuffed eggplants, but I got a heavy hand with garlic. Even my granchirren tell me, they say, 'Hey, maw-maw, you sure got a heavy hand with garlic.'"

"Ain't that sweet," Mrs. Reilly said of the gourmet grandchildren.

"I thought the eggplants was fine," Mr. Robichaux said.

"I'm only happy when I'm scrubbing my floors and cooking my food," Santa told her guests. "I love to fix a big pot of meatballs or jumbalaya with shrimps."

"I like to cook," Mr. Robichaux said. "It helps out my daughter sometimes."

"I bet it does," Santa said. "A man who can cook is a big help around the house, believe me." She kicked

Mrs. Reilly under the table. "A woman's got a man that likes to cook is a lucky girl."

"You like to cook, Irene?" Mr. Robichaux asked.

"You talking to me, Claude?" Mrs. Reilly had been wondering what Ignatius looked like in an earring.

"Come back out the clouds, girl," Santa ordered. "Claude here was axing you if you like to cook."

"Yeah," Mrs. Reilly lied. "I like to cook okay. But sometimes it gets so hot in that kitchen, especially in the summer. You don't get no breezy out that alley. Ignatius likes to eat junk, anyways. You give Ignatius a few bottles of Dr. Nut and plenty bakery cakes, and he's satisfied."

"You oughta get you a letrit range," Mr. Robichaux said. "I bought my daughter one. It don't get hot like a gas stove."

"Where you getting all this money from, Claude?" Santa asked interestedly.

"I got me a nice pension from the railroad. I was with them for forty-five years, you know. They gimme a beautiful gold pin when I retired."

"Ain't that nice," Mrs. Reilly said. "You made good, huh, Claude?"

"Then," Mr. Robichaux said, "I got me a few little rental properties around my house. I was always putting a little of my salary aside to invest in properties. Property's a good investment."

"It sure is," Santa said, rolling her eyes wildly at Mrs. Reilly. "Now you well fixed, huh?"

"I'm pretty comfortable. But you know sometimes I get tired of living with my daughter and her husband. I mean, they're young. They got they own family. They are very nice to me, but I'd rather have my own home. You know what I mean?"

309

"If I was you," Mrs. Reilly said, "I'd stay where I was. If your little daughter don't mind having you around, you got you a nice setup. I wish I had me a nice child. Be grateful for what you got, Claude."

Santa ground the heel of her shoe into Mrs. Reilly's ankle.

"Ouch!" Mrs. Reilly cried.

"Lord, I'm sorry, babe. Me and my big feet. Big feet's always been my problem. They can hardly fit me down by the shoe store. That clerk sees me coming, and he says, 'Lord, here comes Miss Battaglia again. What I'm gonna do?'"

"Your feet ain't so big," Mrs. Reilly observed, looking under the kitchen table.

"I just got them squshed up in this little pair of shoes. You oughta see them things when I'm barefoot, girl."

"I got bum feet," Mrs. Reilly told the other two. Santa made a sign for Mrs. Reilly not to discuss her deficiencies, but Mrs. Reilly was not to be silenced. "Some days I can't hardly walk. I think they went bad when Ignatius was little and I useta have to carry him around. Lord but he was slow walking. Always falling down. He was sure heavy, too. Maybe that's how I got my arthuritis."

"Listen, you two," Santa said quickly so that Mrs. Reilly would not describe some new, horrible deficiency. "Why don't we go see that cute little Debbie Reynolds?"

310

"That would be nice," Mr. Robichaux said. "I never go to the show."

"You wanna go see a show?" Mrs. Reilly asked. "I don't know. My feet."

"Aw, come on, girl. Let's get out the house. It smells like garlic in here."

"I think Ignatius told me this movie ain't no good. He sees every picture that comes out, that boy."

"Irene!" Santa said angrily. "You all the time thinking of that boy, and with all the trouble he's giving you. You better wake up, babe. If you had any sense, you woulda had that boy locked away at Charity Hospital a long time ago. They'd turn a hose on him. They'd stick a letrit socket in that boy. They'd show that Ignatius. They'd make him behave himself."

"Yeah?" Mrs. Reilly asked with interest. "How much that cost?"

"It's all for free, Irene."

"Socialized medicine," Mr. Robichaux observed. "They probly got communiss and fellow travelers working in that place."

"They got nuns operating the place, Claude. Lord, where you all the time getting this communiss stuff from?"

"Maybe them sisters been fooled," Mr. Robichaux said.

"Ain't that awful," Mrs. Reilly said sadly. "Them poor sisters. Operating for a buncha communiss."

"I don't care who's operating the place." Santa said. "If it's free and they lock people away, Ignatius oughta be there."

"Once Ignatius started talking to them people, they'd maybe get mad and lock him up for good," Mrs. Reilly said, but she was thinking that even that alternative wasn't too unattractive. "Maybe he wouldn't listen to the doctors."

311

"They'd make him listen. They'd beat him in the

head, they'd lock him up in a straitjacket, they'd pump some water on him," Santa said a little too eagerly.

"You gotta think about yourself, Irene," Mr. Robichaux said. "That son of yours is gonna put you in your grave."

"That's it. You tell her, Claude."

"Well," Mrs. Reilly said, "We'll give Ignatius a chance. Maybe he'll make good yet."

"Selling weenies?" Santa asked. "Lord." She shook her head. "Well, lemme go dump these dishes in the zink. Come on, let's go see that precious Debbie Reynolds."

A few minutes later, after Santa had stopped in the parlor to kiss her mother goodbye, the three of them set out for the theater. The day had been a balmy day; a south wind had been blowing steadily from the Gulf. Now the evening was still warm. Heavy odors of Mediterranean cooking floated across the congested neighborhood from the opened kitchen windows in every apartment building and double house. Each resident seemed to be making some contribution, however small, to the general cacophony of dropping pots, booming television sets, arguing voices, screaming children, and slamming doors.

"St. Odo Parish is really at it tonight," Santa commented thoughtfully as the three slowly strolled down the narrow sidewalk between the curb and the steps of the double houses built in solid, straight rows down each block. The streetlights shone on the treeless stretches of asphalt and cement and continuous old slate roofs. "It's even worst in the summertime. Everybody's out on the streets till ten-eleven o'clock."

"Don't tell *me*, precious," Mrs. Reilly said as she hobbled dramatically between her friends. "Remember

I'm from Dauphine Street. We useta put the kitchen chairs out on the banquette and set there till midnight sometimes waiting for the house to cool off. And the things the people down here say! Lord."

"Vicious is what it is," Santa agreed. "Dirty mouths."

"Poor poppa," Mrs. Reilly said. "He was so poor. Then when he went and got his hand caught in that fanbelt, the people in the neighborhood had the nerve to say he musta been drunk. The anonymous letters we got about that. And my poor old Tante Boo-boo. Eighty years old. She was burning a candle for her poor departed husband and it fall off the night table and sets her mattress on fire. The people said she was smoking in bed."

"I believe people innocent until they proven guilty."

"That's the same way I feel, Claude," Mrs. Reilly said. "Just the other day I says to Ignatius, 'Ignatius, I think people innocent until they prove guilty.' "

"Irene!"

They crossed St. Claude Avenue during a lull in the heavy traffic and walked along the other side of the avenue under the neon lights. As they were passing a funeral parlor, Santa stopped to talk to one of the mourners standing out on the sidewalk.

"Say, Mister, who they got laid out in there?" she asked the man.

"They waking old lady Lopez," the man answered.

"You don't say. She the wife of that Lopez ran the little market over on Frenchman Street?"

"That's the one."

"Aw, I'm sorry to hear that," Santa said. "What she died from?"

"Heart trouble."

"Ain't that a shame," Mrs. Reilly said emotionally. "Poor girl."

"Well, if I was dressed," Santa told the man, "I'd go in and pay my respects. Me and my friends here just on our way to a picture show. Thank you."

As they walked along, Santa described to Mrs. Reilly the many sadnesses and tribulations that had comprised old lady Lopez's dismal existence. Finally Santa said, "I think I'll send her family a Mass."

"Lord," Mrs. Reilly said, overcome by old lady Lopez's biography, "I think I'll send a Mass, too, for the repose of that poor woman's soul."

"Irene!" Santa screamed. "You don't even know them people."

"Well, that's true," Mrs. Reilly agreed weakly.

When they arrived at the theater, there was some discussion between Santa and Mr. Robichaux over who was going to buy the tickets. Mrs. Reilly said that she would if she didn't have to meet a payment on Ignatius' trumpet before the week was out. Mr. Robichaux was adamant, though, and Santa at last let him have his way.

"After all," Santa said to him as he handed tickets to the two ladies, "you the one's got all the money."

She winked at Mrs. Reilly, whose mind had wandered again to that sign that Ignatius refused to explain to her. During most of the movie Mrs. Reilly thought about Ignatius' rapidly decreasing salary, the payment on the trumpet, the payment on the wrecked building, the earring, and the sign. Only Santa's happy exclamations of "Ain't she precious!" and "Just take a look at that cute dress she's got, Irene!" brought Mrs. Reilly back to what was happening on the screen. Then something else drew her from her meditations about her son and her problems, both of which were really the same thing. Mr. Robichaux's hand had gently covered and was now holding hers. Mrs. Reilly was too afraid to move. Why did movies always seem to make the men she had known—Mr. Reilly and Mr. Robichaux—amorous? She stared blindly at the screen, on which she saw not Debbie Reynolds cavorting in color but rather Jean Harlow taking a bath in black and white.

Mrs. Reilly was wondering if she could easily wrench her hand out of Mr. Robichaux's and bolt from the theater when Santa cried, "Just watch it, Irene, I betcha little Debbie's gonna have her a baby!"

"A what?" Mrs. Reilly screamed wildly, bursting into crazy, loud tears that didn't subside until the frightened Mr. Robichaux took her maroon head and placed it carefully on his shoulder.

II

Dear Reader,

Nature has sometimes made a fool; but a coxcomb is always of man's own making.

—Addison

As I was wearing the soles of my desert boots down to a mere sliver of crepe rubber on the old flagstone banquettes of the French Quarter in my fevered attempt to wrest a living from an unthinking and uncaring society, I was hailed by a cherished old acquaintance (deviate). After a few minutes of conversation in which I established most easily my moral superiority over this degenerate, I found myself pondering once more the crises of our times. My mentality, uncontrollable and wanton as always, whispered to me a scheme so magnificent and daring that I shrank from the very thought of what I was hearing. "Stop!" I cried imploringly to my godlike mind. "This is madness." But still I listened to the counsel of my brain. It was offering me the opportunity to Save the

315

World Through Degeneracy. There on the worn stones of the Quarter I enlisted the aid of this wilted flower of a human in gathering his associates in foppery together behind a banner of brotherhood.

Our first step will be to elect one of their number to some very high office—the presidency, if Fortuna spins us kindly. Then they will infiltrate the military. As soldiers, they will all be so continually busy in fraternizing with one another, tailoring their uniforms to fit like sausage skins, inventing new and varied battle dress, giving cocktail parties, etc., that they will never have time for battle. The one whom we finally make Chief of Staff will want only to attend to his fashionable wardrobe, a wardrobe which, alternately, will permit him to be either Chief of Staff or debutante, as the desire strikes him. In seeing the success of their unified fellows here, perverts around the world will also band together to capture the military in their respective countries. In those reactionary countries in which the deviates seem to be having some trouble in gaining control, we will send aid to them as rebels to help them in toppling their governments. When we have at last overthrown all existing governments, the world will enjoy not war but global orgies conducted with the utmost protocol and the most truly international spirit, for these people do transcend simple national differences. Their minds are on one goal; they are truly united; they think as one.

None of the pederasts in power, of course, will be practical enough to know about such devices as bombs; these nuclear weapons would lie rotting in their vaults somewhere. From time to time the Chief of Staff, the President, and so on, dressed in sequins and feathers, will entertain the leaders, i.e., the perverts, of all the other countries at balls and parties. Quarrels of any sort could easily be straightened out in the men's room of the redecorated United Nations. Ballets and Broadway musicals and entertainments of that sort will flourish everywhere and will probably make the common folk happier than did the grim, hostile, fascistic pronouncements of their former leaders.

Almost everyone else has had an opportunity to run the world. I cannot see why these people should not be given their chance. They have certainly been the underdog long enough. Their movement into power will be, in a sense, only a part of the global movement toward opportunity, justice, and equality for all. (For example, can you name one good, practicing transvestite in the Senate? No! These people have been without representation long enough. Their plight is a national, a global disgrace.)

Degeneracy, rather than signaling the downfall of a society, as it once did, will now signal peace for a troubled world. We must have new solutions to new problems.

I shall act as a sort of mentor and guide for the movement, my not inconsiderable knowledge of world history, economics, religion, and political strategy acting as a reservoir, as it were, from which these people can draw rules of operational procedure. Boethius himself played a somewhat similar role in degenerate Rome. As Chesterton has said of Boethius, "Thus he truly served as a guide, philosopher, and friend to many Christians; precisely because, while his own times were corrupt, his own culture was complete."

This time I shall really confound Myrna minx. The scheme is too breathtaking for the literal, liberal minx mind mired in a claustrophobic clutch of clichés. The Crusade for Moorish Dignity, my brilliant first attack upon the problems of our times, would have been a rather grand and decisive coup had it not been for the basically bourgeois worldview of the rather simple people who were members of the vanguard. This time, however, I shall be working with people who eschew the insipid philosophy of the middle class, people who are willing to assume controversial positions, to follow their cause, however unpopular it may be, however it may threaten the smugness of the middle class.

Does M. Minkoff want sex in politics? I shall give her sex in politics—and plenty of it! No doubt she will be too overcome to respond to the originality of my project. At the very least, she will seethe with envy. (That girl must be attended to. Such effrontery cannot go unchecked.)

A debate between Pragmatism and Morality rages in my brain. Is the glorious end, Peace, worth the awesome means, Degeneracy? Like two figures in the medieval Morality play, Pragmatism and Morality spar in the boxing ring of my brain. I cannot await the outcome of their furious debate: I am too

317

obsessed with Peace. (If any perceptive film producers are interested in buying the movie rights to this Journal, I might here make a note on the filming of this debate. A musical saw would provide excellent background accompaniment, and the hero's eyeball may be superimposed upon the debate scene in a most symbolic manner. Certainly some attractive new discovery could be found in a drugstore or a motel or in whatever den people are "discovered" to play the Working Boy. The film may be made in Spain, Italy, or some other interesting land which the cast may wish to see, such as North America.)

Sorry. Those of you who are interested in the latest bleak frankfurter news will find none. My mind is too preoccupied with the magnificence of this design. Now I must communicate with M. Minkoff and make some jottings for my lecture at the kickoff rally.

Social note: My truant mother is gone again, which is really rather fortunate. Her vigorous assaults and blistering attacks against my being are negatively affecting my valve. She said that she was going out to attend a Crowning of the May Queen at some church, but since it isn't May, I tend to doubt her veracity.

The "sophisticated comedy" featuring my number one female film favorite is opening at a downtown palace momentarily. Somehow I *must* be there on opening day. I can only imagine the film's latest horrors, its flaunting of vulgarity in the face of theology and geometry, taste and decency. (I do not understand this compulsion of mine for seeing movies; it almost seems as if movies are "in my blood.")

Health note: My stomach is getting out of bounds; the seams of my vendor's smock are creaking ominously.

Until later,

Tab, Your pacifist Working Boy

III

Mrs. Levy helped the renovated Miss Trixie up the steps and opened the door.

"This is Levy Pants!" Miss Trixie snarled.

"You're back again where you're wanted and needed, darling." Mrs. Levy spoke as if she were comforting a child. "And how you've been missed. Every day Mr. Gonzalez has been on the phone begging for you. Isn't it wonderful to know that you're so vital to a business?"

"I thought I was retired." The massive teeth snapped like a bear trap. "You people have tricked me!"

"Now are you happy?" Mr. Levy asked his wife. He was walking behind them carrying one of Miss Trixie's bags of scraps. "If she had a knife on her, I'd be taking you to the hospital right now."

"Listen to the fire in her voice," Mrs. Levy said. "So vigorous. It's unbelievable."

Miss Trixie tried to break away from Mrs. Levy as they entered the office, but her pumps did not give her the traction that she was used to with sneakers, and she only wobbled.

"She's *back?*" Mr. Gonzalez cried heartbrokenly.

"Can you believe your eyes?" Mrs. Levy asked him.

Mr. Gonzalez was forced to look at Miss Trixie, whose eyes were weak pools edged with blue shadow. Her lips had been extended in an orange line that almost reached her nostrils. Near the earrings a few gray wisps of hair escaped from beneath the black wig, which was slightly awry. The short skirt revealed withered, bowed legs and small feet that made the pumps look like snowshoes. Whole days of napping under a sunlamp had baked Miss Trixie to a golden brown.

"She certainly looks fit," Mr. Gonzalez said. His voice was false and he smiled a broken smile. "You've done her a wonderful service, Mrs. Levy."

"I am a very attractive woman," Miss Trixie babbled.

319

Mr. Gonzalez laughed nervously.

"Now listen here," Mrs. Levy said to him. "Part of this woman's trouble is that kind of attitude. Ridicule she doesn't need."

Mr. Gonzalez tried unsuccessfully to kiss Mrs. Levy's hand.

"I want you to make her feel wanted, Gonzalez. This woman still has a sharp mind. Give her work that will exercise those faculties of hers. Give her more authority. She desperately needs an active role in this business."

"Definitely," Mr. Gonzalez agreed. "I've said that myself all along. Haven't I, Miss Trixie."

"Who?" Miss Trixie snarled.

"I've always wanted you to assume more responsibility and authority," the office manager screamed. "Isn't that correct?"

"Oh, shut up, Gomez." Miss Trixie's teeth clattered like castanets. "Have you bought me that Easter ham yet? Answer me that."

"All right. You've had your fun. Let's go," Mr. Levy said to his wife. "Come on. I'm getting depressed."

"Just a moment," Mr. Gonzalez said. "I have some mail for you."

As the office manager went to his desk to get the mail, there was a crash in the rear of the office. Everyone, aside from Miss Trixie who had begun napping on her desk, turned around and looked in the filing department. There an extremely tall man with long black hair was picking up a file drawer that had fallen to the floor. He stuffed the filing roughly back into the drawer and slammed the drawer into its slot in the files.

"That's Mr. Zalatimo," Mr. Gonzalez whispered.

320

"He's only been with us for a few days, and I don't think he's going to work out. I don't think we'll want to include him in the Levy Pants plan."

Mr. Zalatimo looked confusedly at the filing cabinets and scratched himself. Then he opened another drawer and fumbled through its contents with one hand while the other scratched at his armpit through his threadbare knitted shirt.

"Would you care to meet him?" the office manager asked.

"No thanks," Mr. Levy said. "Where do you find the people that work in this place, Gonzalez? I never see people like this anywhere else."

"He looks like a gangster to me," Mrs. Levy said. "You don't keep any cash around here, do you?"

"I think Mr. Zalatimo's honest," the office manager whispered. "He only has trouble alphabeting." He handed Mr. Levy a sheaf of mail. "These are mostly confirmations on your hotel reservations for spring practice. There's a letter in there from Abelman. It's addressed to you and not the company, and it's marked personal, so I thought you'd better open it. It's been around for a few days."

"What does that crack want now?" Mr. Levy said angrily.

"Maybe he wonders what happened to a brilliant, growing concern," Mrs. Levy observed. "Maybe he wonders what happened since Leon Levy died. Maybe this Abelman has some words of advice to a playboy. Read it, Gus. It will be your work for Levy Pants for the week."

Mr. Levy looked at the envelope, on which "personal" had been written three times in red ballpoint.

He opened it and found a letter on which some attachment had been stapled.

Dear Gus Levy,
We were shocked and grievously injured to receive the attached letter. We have been a faithful outlet for your merchandise for thirty years and have heretofore always had the warmest affectionate feelings for your firm. Maybe you remember the wreath we sent when your father died for which we spared no expense.

This will be very short. After many nights without sleep, we have given the original letter to our lawyer, who is instigating a libel suit for $500,000. This may do a little to compensate for our hurt feelings.

Get a lawyer. We will see you in court like gentlemen. No more threats, please.

> Very best wishes,
> I. Abelman,
> Manager, Abelman's Dry Goods

Mr. Levy turned cold as he flipped the page and read the Thermofaxed copy of the letter to Abelman's. It was incredible. Who would go to the trouble of writing things like that? "Mr. I. Abelman, Mongoloid, Esq."; "Your total lack of contact with reality"; "your blighted worldview"; "you may feel the sting of the lash across your pitiful shoulders." Worst of all, the "Gus Levy" signature looked fairly authentic. Abelman must be kissing the original right now and smacking his lips. To somebody like Abelman that letter was like a savings bond, a blank draft on a bank.

"Who wrote this?" Mr. Levy demanded, giving the letter to Mr. Gonzalez.

"What is it, Gus? A problem? Are you having a problem? That's one of your problems. You never tell me your problems."

"Oh, my goodness!" Mr. Gonzalez squeaked. "This is horrible."

"Silence!" Miss Trixie snapped.

"What is it, Gus? Something you didn't handle correctly? Some authority you delegated to somebody else?"

"Yes, it's a problem. It's a problem that means we could lose the shirts off our backs."

"What?" Mrs. Levy grabbed the letters from Mr. Gonzalez. She read them and became a hag. Her lacquered curls turned into snakes. "Now you've done it. Anything to get back at your father, to ruin his business. I knew it was going to end like this."

"Oh, shut up. I never write the letters around here."

"Susan and Sandra will have to quit college. They'll be selling themselves to sailors and gangsters like that one there."

"Huh?" Mr. Zalatimo asked, sensing that he was being discussed.

"You're *sick*," Mrs. Levy shouted at her husband.

"Quiet!"

"And will I be any better off?" Mrs. Levy's aquamarine lids were trembling. "What will become of me? Already my life has been wrecked. What happens to me now? Prowling in garbage cans, following the fleet. My mother was right."

"Quiet!" Miss Trixie demanded, this time much more fiercely. "You people are the noisiest I've ever met."

Mrs. Levy had collapsed in a chair, sobbing something about going out to sell Avon products.

"What do you know about this, Gonzalez?" Mr.

Levy asked the office manager whose lips had turned white.

"I don't know a thing," Mr. Gonzalez piped. "It's the first time I've seen that letter."

"You write the correspondence around here."

"I didn't write *that*." His lips were quivering. "I wouldn't do something like that to Levy Pants!"

"No, I know you wouldn't." Mr. Levy tried to think. "Somebody really had it in for us."

Mr. Levy went over to the files, pushed the scratching Mr. Zalatimo aside, and opened the files in the A's. There was no Abelman folder. The drawer was completely empty. He opened several other drawers, but half of them were empty, too. What a way to begin fighting a libel suit.

"What do you people do with the filing?"

"I was wondering about that myself," Mr. Zalatimo said vaguely.

"Gonzalez, what was the name of that big kook you had working in here, the big fat one with the green cap?"

"Mr. Ignatius Reilly. He handled the letter to go out." Who had composed that awful thing?

"Hey," Jones's voice said over the telephone, "you people still got a fat mother with a green cap working there at Levy Pant? A big white guy got him a moustache?"

"No we don't," Mr. Gonzalez answered in a shrill voice and slammed the phone down.

"Who was that?" Mr. Levy asked.

"Oh, I don't know. Someone for Mr. Reilly." The office manager wiped his forehead with a handkerchief. "The one who tried to make the factory workers kill me."

"Reilly?" Miss Trixie said. "That wasn't Reilly, that was . . ."

"The young idealist?" Mrs. Levy sobbed. "Who wanted him?"

"I don't know," the office manager answered. "It sounded like a Negro voice to me."

"Well, I guess so," Mrs. Levy said. "He's out trying to help some other unfortunates right now. It's encouraging to know that his idealism is still intact."

Mr. Levy had been thinking of something, and he asked the office manager, "What was the name of that kook?"

"Reilly. Ignatius J. Reilly."

"It was?" Miss Trixie said with interest. "That's strange. I always thought it . . ."

"Miss Trixie, please," Mr. Levy said angrily. That Reilly blimp was working for the company at the time that that letter to Abelman was dated. "Do you think that that Reilly would write a letter like that?"

"Maybe," Mr. Gonzalez said. "I don't know. I had high hopes for him until he tried to get that worker to brain me."

"That's right," Mrs. Levy moaned. "Try to pin it on the young idealist. Put him away where his idealism won't bother you. People like the young idealist don't deal in underhanded things like that. Wait until Susan and Sandra hear about this." Mrs. Levy made a gesture that indicated that the girls would clearly go into a state of shock. "Negroes are calling here to get his counsel. You're about to frame him. I can't take much more of this, Gus. I can't, I can't!"

"Then do you want *me* to say I wrote that?"

"Of course not!" Mrs. Levy screamed at her

325

husband. "I'm supposed to end in the poorhouse? If the young idealist wrote it, he goes to jail for forgery."

"Say, what's going on?" Mr. Zalatimo asked. "Is this dump gonna close down or what? I mean, I'd like to know."

"Shut up, gangster," Mrs. Levy answered wildly, "before we pin it on you."

"Huh?"

"Will you keep quiet? You're getting everything confused," Mr. Levy said to his wife. Then he turned to the office manager. "Get me this Reilly's phone number."

Mr. Gonzalez awakened Miss Trixie and asked her for a phone book.

"*I* keep all of the phone books," Miss Trixie snapped. "And no one is going to use them."

"Then look up a Reilly on Constantinople Street for us."

"Well, all right, Gomez," Miss Trixie snarled. "Hold your horses." She took the three hoarded office telephone books out of some recess in her desk, and, studying the pages with a magnifying glass, gave them a number.

Mr. Levy dialed it and a voice answered, "Good morning. Regal Cleaners."

"Give me one of those phone books," Mr. Levy hollered.

"No," Miss Trixie rasped, slapping her hand down on the stack of books, guarding them with her newly enameled nails. "You'll only lose it. I'll find the right number. I must say you people are very impatient and excitable. Staying at your house took ten years off my life. Why can't you let poor Reilly alone? You already kicked him out over nothing."

Mr. Levy dialed the second number that she gave him. A woman who sounded slightly intoxicated answered and told him that Mr. Reilly wouldn't be home until late in the afternoon. Then she started crying, and Mr. Levy got depressed and thanked her and hung up.

"Well, he's not at home," Mr. Levy told the audience in the office.

"Mr. Reilly always seemed to have the best interests of Levy Pants at heart," the office manager said sadly. "Why he started that riot I'll never know."

"For one thing because he had a police record."

"When he came to apply, I certainly didn't think he was a police character." The office manager shook his head. "He seemed so refined."

Mr. Gonzalez watched Mr. Zalatimo probing his long index finger high into one of his nostrils. What would this one do? His feet tingled with fear.

The factory door banged open and one of the workers screamed, "Hey, Mr. Gonzalez, Mr. Palerma just burn his hand on one of them furnace door."

There were sounds of disorder in the factory. A man was cursing.

"Oh, my goodness," Mr. Gonzalez cried. "Quiet the workers. I'll be there in a minute."

"Come on," Mr. Levy said to his wife. "Let's get out of here. I'm getting heartburn."

"Just a moment." Mrs. Levy gestured to Mr. Gonzalez. "About Miss Trixie. I want you to give her a welcome every morning. Give her meaningful work to do. In the past her insecurity probably made her afraid of taking any responsible work. I think she's over that now. Basically she has a deep seated hatred of Levy Pants that I've analyzed as being rooted in fear. The insecurity and fear have led to hatred."

327

"Of course," the office manager said, half listening. The factory sounded bad.

"Go see about the factory, Gonzalez," Mr. Levy said. "I'll get in touch with Reilly."

"Yes, sir." Mr. Gonzalez made a deep bow to them and dashed out of the office.

"Okay." Mr. Levy was holding the door open. Just come near Levy Pants and you were subjected to all sorts of annoyances and depressing influences. You couldn't leave the place alone for a minute. Anyone who wanted to take it easy and not be bothered had better not have a company like Levy Pants. Gonzalez didn't even know what kind of mail was going out of the office. "Come on, Dr. Freud. Let's go."

"Look how calm you are. It doesn't matter to you that Abelman is about to sue our lives away if he can." The aquamarine lids trembled. "Aren't you going to get the idealist?"

"Some other time. I've had enough for one day."

"Meanwhile Abelman has Scotland Yard at our throats."

"He's not even home." Mr. Levy didn't feel like speaking with the crying woman again. "I'll call him tonight from the coast. There's nothing to worry about. They can't sue me for a half million for a letter I didn't write."

"Oh, no? I'm sure somebody like Abelman could. I can just see that lawyer he's got. Crippled from chasing ambulances. Mutilated from being caught in fires he's started for insurance money."

"Well, you'll take the bus back to the coast if you don't hurry up. I'm getting indigestion from this office."

"All right, all right. You can't spare a minute of

your wasted life for this woman, can you?" Mrs. Levy indicated the loudly snoring Miss Trixie. She shook Miss Trixie's shoulder. "I'm going, darling. Everything is going to be fine. I've spoken to Mr. Gonzalez and he's delighted to see you again."

"Quiet!" Miss Trixie ordered. Her teeth snapped menacingly.

"Come on before I have to take you to get a rabies shot," Mr. Levy said angrily and grabbed his wife through her fur coat.

"Just look at this place." A gloved hand gestured to the dingy office furniture, to the warped floors, to the crepe paper streamers still hanging from the days when I. J. Reilly was custodian of the files, to Mr. Zalatimo who was kicking at the wastebasket in alphabetical frustration. "Sad, sad. A business down the drain, unhappy young idealists stooping to forgery to get even."

"Get out of here, you people," Miss Trixie snarled, slapping her palm on the desk.

"Listen to the conviction in that voice," Mrs. Levy said proudly as her round, furry figure was being hauled through the door. "I've worked a miracle."

The door closed and Mr. Zalatimo came over to Miss Trixie, absently scratching himself. He tapped her on the shoulder and asked, "Say, lady, maybe you can help me out with this. What would you say comes first, *Willis* or *Williams?*"

Miss Trixie glared at him for a moment. Then she sank her teeth into his hand. In the factory Mr. Gonzalez heard Mr. Zalatimo's screaming. He didn't know whether to desert the seared Mr. Palermo and see what had happened or to stay in the factory, where the workers had begun dancing with one another under the loudspeakers. Levy Pants demanded a lot of a person.

329

In the sports car, as they drove through the salt marshes that led back to the coast, Mrs. Levy, pulling her blowing fur up closer around her neck said, "I'm establishing a Foundation."

"I see. Suppose Abelman's lawyer gets the money out of us."

"He won't. The young idealist is trapped," she said calmly. "A police record, inciting a riot. His character references will stink."

"Oh. Suddenly you agree that your young idealist is a criminal."

"He obviously was all alone."

"But you wanted to get your hands on Miss Trixie."

"That's right."

"Well, there will be no Foundation."

"Susan and Sandra will hate to know that your bum's attitude toward the world almost ruined them, that because you won't even take the time to supervise your own company, we have somebody suing us for half a million. The girls will really resent that. The least that you've always given them has been material comfort. Susan and Sandra will hate to know that they could have ended up as prostitutes or worse."

"They might at least have made some money at it. As it is, they're all for free."

"Please, Gus. Not another word. Even my brutalized spirit has some sensitivity left. I can't let you slander my girls like that." Mrs. Levy sighed contentedly. "This Abelman business is the most dangerous of all your mistakes and errors and evasions through the years. The girls' hair will curl when they read of it. Of course, I won't frighten them if you don't want me to."

"How much do you want for this Foundation?"

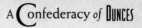

"I haven't decided yet. I've been composing the rules and regulations."

"May I ask what this Foundation is going to be called, Mrs. Guggenheim? The Susan and Sandra slush fund?"

"It will be called the Leon Levy Foundation, in honor of your father. I have to do something to honor your father's name for all that you haven't done to honor it. The awards will commemorate the memory of that great man."

"I see. In other words, you'll be tossing laurels at old men outstanding only for their unequaled meanness."

"Please, Gus." Mrs. Levy held up a gloved hand. "The girls have been thrilled by my reports on the Miss Trixie project. The Foundation will really give them faith in their name. I must do all I can to make up for your complete failure as a parent."

"Getting an award from the Leon Levy Foundation will be a public insult. Your hands will be really full of libel suits then, libel suits from the recipients. Forget it. Whatever happened to bridge? Other people are still playing it. Can't you go play golf at Lakewood anymore? Take some more dancing lessons. Take Miss Trixie with you."

"To be quite honest with you, Miss Trixie was beginning to bore me the last few days."

"So that's why the rejuvenation course ended all of a sudden."

"I've done all I can for that woman. Susan and Sandra are proud that I've tried to keep her active so long."

"Well, there will be no Leon Levy Foundation."

"Do you resent it? There's resentment in your

331

voice. I can hear it. There's hostility. Gus, for your own sake. That doctor in the Medical Arts building. Lenny's savior. Before it's too late. Now I'll have to watch over you every minute to see to it that you get in touch with that idealist criminal as soon as possible. I know you. You'll put it off, and Abelman will have a van out in front of Levy's Lodge taking everything away."

"Including your exercising board."

"I've already told you!" Mrs. Levy screamed. "Leave the board out of this!" She adjusted her ruffled furs. "Now get to that Reilly psycho before Abelman comes down here and starts taking the hub caps off this sports car. With somebody like that, Abelman has no case. Lenny's doctor can analyze Reilly, and the state will put him away someplace where he can't try to wreck people. Thank goodness Susan and Sandra won't know that they almost ended up selling roach tablets from door to door. Their hearts would break if they knew how carelessly their own father handled their welfare."

IV

George had set up his stakeout on Poydras Street across from the Paradise Vendors, Incorporated, garage. He had remembered the name on the wagon and looked up the address of the vending firm. All morning he had waited for the big vendor, who had never shown up. Perhaps he had been fired for stabbing the fairy in Pirate's Alley. At noon George had left his outpost and gone down to the Quarter to get the packages from Miss Lee. Now he was back on Poydras wondering whether the vendor was going to show. George had decided to try to be nice to him, to hand him a few dollars right away. Hot dog vendors must be poor. He'd appreciate a few bucks. This vendor was a perfect front man. He would never know what was coming off. He had a good education, though.

At last, sometime after one o'clock, a white smock billowed off the trolley and whipped into the garage. A few minutes later the oddball vendor wheeled his wagon out onto the sidewalk. He was still wearing the earring, scarf, and cutlass, George noticed. If he put them on in the garage, they must be part of his sales gimmick. You could tell by the way that he talked, though, that he had gone to school a long time. That was probably what was wrong with him. George had been wise enough to get out of school as soon as possible. He didn't want to end up like that guy.

George watched him push the wagon a few feet down the block, stop, and tape a piece of tablet paper to the front of his wagon. George would use psychology on him; he'd play up to the vendor's education. That and the money should make him rent out his bun compartment.

Then an old man stuck his head out of the garage, ran up behind the vendor, and struck him across the back with a long fork.

"Get moving, you ape," the old man shouted. "You're already late. It's already afternoon. Today you're gonna bring in a profit or else."

The vendor said something coolly and quietly. George couldn't understand it, but it lasted a long time.

"I don't care if your mother takes dope," the old man answered. "I don't wanna hear no more bullshit about that automobile accident and your dreams and your goddam girl friend. Now get outta here, you big baboon. I want five dollars minimum from you today."

333

With a push from the old man, the vendor rolled to the corner and disappeared onto St. Charles. After the old man returned to the garage, George slouched off in pursuit of the wagon.

Unaware that he was being trailed, Ignatius pushed his cart against the traffic down St. Charles toward the Quarter. He had stayed up so late the night before working on his lecture for the kickoff rally that he hadn't been able to move from his yellowed sheets until almost noon, and then it had only been his mother's violent pounding and screaming that had awakened him. Now that he was out on the streets, he had a problem. Today the sophisticated comedy was opening at the RKO Orpheum. He had been able to bleed ten cents out of his mother for carfare home, although she had even begrudged him that. Somehow he had to sell five or six hot dogs quickly, park the wagon somewhere, and get to that theater so that his disbelieving eyes could drink in every blasphemous technicolored moment.

Lost in speculation about means for raising the money, Ignatius did not notice that for quite some time his car had been traveling in a straight and unswerving line. When he attempted to pull closer to the curb, the cart would not incline to the right at all. Stopping, he saw that one of the bicycle tires had lodged in the groove of a streetcar track. He tried to bump the cart out of the groove; it was too heavy to be easily bounced. He bent and tried to lift the cart on one side. As he slipped his hands beneath the big tin bun, he heard through the light mist the grinding of an approaching streetcar. The hard little bumps appeared on his hands, and his valve, after wavering for a moment of frantic decision, slammed closed. Wildly Ignatius pulled upward on the tin bun. The bicycle tire shot up out of the tracks, rose upward, balanced for a second in the air, and then became horizontal as the cart turned over loudly on its other side. One of the little lids in the tin bun opened and deposited a few steaming hot dogs on the street.

"Oh, my God!" Ignatius mumbled to himself, watching the silhouette of the streetcar forming a half-block away. "What vicious trick is Fortuna playing on me now?"

Deserting the wreck, Ignatius lumbered down the tracks toward the streetcar, the white muu-muu of a uniform swishing around his ankles. The olive and copper trolley car ground slowly toward him, leisurely pitching and rocking. The motorman, seeing the huge, spherical, white figure panting in the center of the tracks, slid the car to a halt and opened one of the front windows.

"Pardon me, sir," the earring called up to him. "If you will wait a moment, I shall attempt to right my listing craft."

George saw his opportunity. He ran over to Ignatius and said cheerily, "Come on, prof, let's you and me get this off the street."

"Oh, my God!" Ignatius thundered. "My pubescent nemesis. What a promising day this appears to be. I am apparently to be run over by a streetcar and robbed simultaneously, thereby setting a Paradise record. Get away, you depraved urchin."

"You grab that end and I'll get this one."

The streetcar clanged at them.

"Oh, all right," Ignatius said finally. "Actually, I would be perfectly happy to let this ridiculous liability lie here on its side."

George took one end of the bun and said, "You better close that little door before more of them weenies falls out."

Ignatius kicked the little door closed, as if he were playing to win in a professional football game, neatly severing a protruding hot dog into two six-inch sections.

"Take it easy, prof. You gonna break your wagon."

"Shut up, you truant. I didn't ask you to make conversation."

"Okay," George said, shrugging. "I mean, I'm just tryna help you out."

"How could you possibly help me?" Ignatius bellowed, baring a tan fang or two. "Some authority of society is probably hot on the scent of your suffocating hair tonic right now. Where did you come from? Why are you following me?"

"Look, you want me to help you pick up this pile of junk?"

"Pile of junk? Are you talking about this Paradise vehicle?"

The streetcar clanged at them again.

"Come on," George said. "*Up.*"

"I hope you realize," Ignatius said as he breathlessly lifted the wagon, "that our association is only the result of an emergency."

The cart bounced back onto its two bicycle tires, the contents of the tin bun rattling against its sides.

"Okay, prof, there you go. Glad I could help you out."

336

"In case you haven't noticed, you waif, you are about to be hooked on the cowcatcher of that streetcar."

The streetcar rolled by them slowly so that the

conductor and motorman could study Ignatius' costume more closely.

George grabbed one of Ignatius' paws and stuck two dollars in it.

"Money?" Ignatius asked happily. "Thank God." He quickly pocketed the two bills. "I'd rather not ask the obscene motive for this. I'd like to think that you're attempting to make amends in your simple way for slandering me on my dismal first day with this ludicrous wagon."

"That's it, prof. You said it better than I ever could. You're a really educated guy."

"Oh?" Ignatius was very pleased. "There may be some hope for you yet. Hot dog?"

"No, thanks."

"Then pardon me while I have one. My system is petitioning for appeasement." Ignatius looked down into the well of his wagon. "My God, the hot dogs are quite disordered."

While Ignatius was slamming doors and plunging his paws down into the well, George said, "Now I helped you out, prof. Maybe you can do the same for me."

"Perhaps," Ignatius said disinterestedly, biting into the hot dog.

"You see these?" George indicated the brown paper packages he was carrying under his arms. "These are school supplies. Now this is my problem. I gotta pick them up from the distributor at lunchtime, but I can't deliver them to the schools until after school's closed. So I gotta carry them around for almost two hours. You understand? What I'm looking for is a place to put these things in the afternoon. Now I could meet you someplace about one and put them in your bun compartment and come get them out sometime before three."

"How bogus," Ignatius belched. "Do you seriously expect me to believe you? Delivering school supplies after the schools are closed?"

"I'll pay you a couple of bucks every day."

"You will?" Ignatius asked with interest. "Well, you will have to pay me a week's rent in advance. I don't deal in small sums."

George opened his wallet and gave Ignatius eight dollars.

"Here. With the two you already got, that makes ten for the week."

Ignatius happily pocketed the new bills and ripped one of the packages from George's arms, saying, "I must see what it is that I'm storing. You're probably selling goof balls to infants."

"Hey!" George shouted. "I can't deliver the stuff if it's opened."

"Too bad for you." Ignatius fended off the boy and tore off the brown wrapping. He saw a stack of what looked like postcards. "What are these? Visual aids for civics or some other equally stultifying high school subject?"

"Gimme that, you nut."

"Oh, my God!" Ignatius stared at what he saw. Once in high school someone had shown him a pornographic photograph, and he had collapsed against a water cooler, injuring his ear. This photograph was far superior. A nude woman was sitting on the edge of a desk next to a globe of the world. The suggested onanism with the piece of chalk intrigued Ignatius. Her face was hidden behind a large book. While George evaded indifferent slaps from the unoccupied paw, Ignatius scrutinized the title on the cover of the book: Anicius Manlius Severinus Boethius, *The Consolation of Philosophy*. "Do I believe what I am seeing? What brilliance. What taste. Good grief."

"Give that back," George pleaded.

"This one is *mine*," Ignatius gloated, pocketing the top card. He handed the torn package back to George and looked at the piece of torn wrapping between his fingers. There was an address on it. He pocketed that, too. "Where in the world did you get these? Who is this brilliant woman?"

"None of your business."

"I see. A secret operation." Ignatius thought of the address on the piece of paper. He would do his own investigating. Some destitute woman intellectual was doing anything for a dollar. Her worldview must be quite incisive, if her reading material were any guide. It could be that she was in the same situation as the Working Boy, a seer and philosopher cast into a hostile century by forces beyond her control. Ignatius must meet her. She might have some new and valuable insights. "Well, in spite of my misgivings, I shall make my cart available to you. However, you must watch the cart this afternoon. I have a rather urgent appointment."

"Hey, what is this? How long you gonna be?"

"About two hours."

"I gotta get uptown by three o'clock."

"Well, you shall be a little late this afternoon," Ignatius said angrily. "I am already lowering my standards by associating with you and fouling up my bun compartment. You should be glad that I haven't turned you in. I have on the police force a brilliant friend, a sly undercover agent, Patrolman Mancuso. He is just looking for the sort of break a case like yours would

339

offer. Fall to your knees and be grateful for my benevolence."

Mancuso? Wasn't that the name of the undercover agent who had stopped him in the rest room? George got very nervous.

"What does this undercover pal of yours look like?" George sneered in an attempt at bravery.

"He is small and elusive." Ignatius' voice was cunning. "He is given to many disguises. He is a veritable will-o'-the-wisp, scurrying here and there in his never-ending search for marauders. For a while he chose the covert of a bathroom but now is out on the streets where he remains at my beck and call every minute."

George's throat filled with something that choked him.

"This is a frame-up," he swallowed.

"That's enough from you, you guttersnipe. Encouraging the degeneration of some noble woman scholar," Ignatius barked. "You should be kissing the hem of my uniform in gratitude for my not advising Sherlock Mancuso of your evil goods. Meet me before the RKO Orpheum in two hours!"

Ignatius billowed grandly off down Common Street. George put his two packages in the bun compartment and sat down on the curb. This was really luck meeting a pal of Mancuso's. The big vendor really had him. He looked furiously at the wagon. Now he wasn't only stuck with the packages. He was stuck with a big hot dog wagon.

Ignatius tossed money at the cashier and literally lunged into the Orpheum, waddling down the aisle toward the footlights. His timing had been perfect. The second feature was just beginning. The boy with the magnificent photographs was definitely a find. Ignatius wondered if he could blackmail him into watching the wagon every afternoon. The urchin had certainly responded to his mention of a friend on the police force.

Ignatius snorted at the movie credits. All of the people involved in the film were equally unacceptable. A set designer, in particular, had appalled him too many times in the past. The heroine was even more offensive than she had been in the circus musical. In this film she was a bright young secretary whom an aged man of the world was trying to seduce. He flew her in a private jet to Bermuda and installed her in a suite. On their first night together she broke out in a rash just as the libertine was opening her bedroom door.

"Filth!" Ignatius shouted, spewing wet popcorn over several rows. "How dare she pretend to be a virgin. Look at her degenerate face. Rape her!"

"They sure got some funny people at matinees," a lady with a shopping bag said to her companion. "Just take a look at him. He's got on a earring."

Then there was a soft-focus love scene, and Ignatius began to lose control. He could feel the hysteria overtaking him. He tried to be silent, but he found that he couldn't.

"They're photographing them through several thicknesses of cheesecloth," he spluttered. "Oh, my God. Who can imagine how wrinkled and loathsome those two really are? I think I'm getting nauseated. Can't someone in the projection booth turn off the electricity? Please!"

He rattled his cutlass loudly against the side of his seat. An old usherette came down the aisle and tried to grab the cutlass from him, but Ignatius wrestled with her, and she slid to the carpet. She got up and hobbled away.

341

The heroine, believing her honor to be in question, had a series of paranoid fantasies in which she was lying on a bed with her libertine. The bed was pulled through the streets and floated across a swimming pool at the resort hotel.

"Good grief. Is this smut supposed to be comedy?" Ignatius demanded in the darkness. "I have not laughed once. My eyes can hardly believe this highly discolored garbage. That woman must be lashed until she drops. She is undermining our civilization. She is a Chinese Communist agent sent over to destroy us. Please! Someone with some decency get to the fuse box. Hundreds of people in this theater are being demoralized. If we're all lucky, the Orpheum may have forgotten to pay its electrical bill."

As the film ended Ignatius cried, "Under her All-American face she is really Toyko Rose!"

He wanted to stay for another showing, but he remembered the waif. Ignatius didn't want to ruin a good thing. He needed that boy. Weakly he climbed over the four empty popcorn boxes that had accumulated before his seat during the movie. He was completely enervated. His emotions were spent. Gasping, he staggered up the aisle and out onto the sunlit street. There, by the cab stand at the Roosevelt Hotel, George was keeping a surly watch over the wagon.

"Jesus," he sneered. "I thought you was never coming outta there. What kinda appointment you had? You just went to see a movie."

"Please," Ignatius sighed. "I've just been through trauma. Run along. I'll meet you at one sharp tomorrow at Canal and Royal."

"Okay, prof." George took his packages and started to slouch away. "Keep your mouth shut, huh?"

"We shall see," Ignatius said sternly.

He ate a hot dog with trembling hands and peeked down into his pocket at the photograph. From above the woman's figure looked even more matronly and reassuring. Some broken professor of Roman history? A ruined medievalist? If only she would have shown her face. There was an air of solitude, of detachment, of solitary sensual and scholarly pleasure that appealed to him greatly. He looked at the scrap of wrapping paper, at the crude, tiny address. Bourbon Street. The undone woman was in the hands of commercial exploiters. What a challenging character for the Journal. That particular work, Ignatius thought, was rather lacking in the sensual department. It needed a good injection of lip-smacking innuendo. Perhaps the confessions of this woman would perk it up a bit.

Ignatius rolled down into the Quarter and, for a wild and very fleeting moment, pondered an affair. How Myrna would gnaw at her espresso cup rim in envy. He would describe every lush moment with this scholarly woman. With her background and Boethian worldview, she would take a very stoic and fatalistic view of whatever sexual gaucheries and blunders he committed. She would be understanding. "Be kind," Ignatius would sigh to her. Myrna probably attacked sex with the vehemence and seriousness that she brought to social protest. How anguished she would be when Ignatius described his tender pleasures.

"Do I dare?" Ignatius asked himself, bumping the wagon absent-mindedly into a parked car. The handle sank into his stomach and he belched. He would not tell the woman how he came across her. First, he would discuss Boethius. She would be overwhelmed.

Ignatius found the address and said, "Oh, my God!

The poor woman is in the hands of fiends." He studied the facade of the Night of Joy and lumbered up to the poster in the glass case. He read:

ROBERTA E. LEE
presents

Harlett O'Hara,
the Virgin-ny Belle
(and pet!)

Who was Harlett O'Hara? Even more important, what kind of pet? Ignatius was intrigued. Afraid of attracting the wrath of the Nazi proprietress, he sat down uncomfortably on the curb and decided to wait.

Lana Lee was watching Darlene and the bird. They were almost ready to open. Now if only Darlene could get that line straight. She wandered away from the stage, gave Jones some additional directions about cleaning under the stools, and went to look out of the porthole of glass in the padded door. She'd seen enough of the act for one afternoon. The act was really pretty good in its own way. George was really bringing in the money with the new merchandise. Things were looking good. Too, Jones seemed to be broken in at last.

Lana pushed the door open and hollered out into the street, "Hey, you. Get off my curb, you character."

"Please," a rich voice answered from the street, pausing to think of some excuse. "I am only resting my rather broken feet."

"Go rest them someplace else. Get that crappy wagon away from in front my business."

"Let me assure you that I did not choose to collapse here before your gas chamber of a den. I did not return here of my own volition. My feet have simply ceased to function. I am paralyzed."

"Go get paralyzed down the block. All I need is you hanging around here again to ruin my investment. You look like a queer with that earring. People'll think this is a gay bar. Go on."

"People will never make that mistake. Without a doubt you operate the most dismal bar in the city. May I interest you in purchasing a hot dog?"

Darlene came to the door and said, "Well, look who it is. How's your poor momma?"

"Oh, my God," Ignatius bellowed. "Why did Fortuna lead me to this spot?"

"Hey, Jones," Lana Lee called. "Quit knocking that broom and come chase this character away."

"Sorry. Bouncer wage star at fifty dollar a week."

"You sure treat your poor momma cruel," Darlene said out the door.

"I don't imagine that either of you ladies has read Boethius," Ignatius sighed.

"Don't talk to him," Lana said to Darlene. "He's a fucking smart-aleck. Jones, I'll give you about two seconds to come out here before I get you picked up on a vagrancy rap along with this character. I'm getting fed up with smartasses in general."

"Goodness knows what storm trooper will descend upon me and beat me senseless," Ignatius observed coolly. "You can't frighten me. I've already had my trauma for the day."

"Ooo-wee!" Jones said when he looked out the door. "The green cap mother. In person. Live."

"I see that you've wisely decided to hire a particularly terrifying Negro to protect you against your enraged and cheated customers," the green cap mother said to Lana Lee.

"Hustle him off," Lana said to Jones.

"Whoa! How you hustle off a elephan?"

"Look at those dark glasses. No doubt his system is swimming in dope."

"Get the hell back in there," Lana said to Darlene, who was staring at Ignatius. She pushed Darlene and said to Jones, "Okay. Get him."

"Get out your razor and slash me," Ignatius said as Lana and Darlene went in. "Throw lye in my face. Stab me. You wouldn't realize, of course, that it was my interest in civil rights which led to my becoming a crippled vendor of franks. I lost a particularly successful position because of my stand on the racial question. My broken feet are the indirect result of my sensitive social conscience."

"Whoa! Levy Pant kick your ass out for tryina get all them po color people throwed in jail, huh?"

"How do you know about that?" Ignatius asked guardedly. "Were you involved in that particularly abortive coup?"

"No. I hear peoples talkin aroun."

"You did?" Ignatius asked interestedly. "No doubt they made some mention of my carriage and bearing. Thus, I am recognizable. I hardly suspected that I have become a legend. Perhaps I abandoned that movement too hastily." Ignatius was delighted. This was developing into a bright day after many bleak ones. "I have probably become a martyr of sorts." He belched. "Would you care for a hot dog? I extend the same courteous service to all colors and creeds. Paradise Vendors has been a pioneer in the field of public accommodations."

"How come a white cat like you, talkin so good, sellin weenies?"

"Please blow your smoke elsewhere. My respiratory system, unfortunately, is below par. I suspect that I am the result of particularly weak conception on the part of my father. His sperm was probably emitted in a rather offhand manner."

This was luck, Jones thought. The fat mother dropped out of the sky just when he needed him most.

"You mus be outa your min man. You oughta have you a good job, big Buick, all that shit. Whoa! Air condition, color TV . . ."

"I have a very pleasant occupation," Ignatius answered icily. "Outdoor work, no supervision. The only pressure is on the feet."

"If I go to college I wouldn be draggin no meat wagon aroun sellin peoples a lotta garbage and shit."

"Please! Paradise products are of the very highest quality." Ignatius rapped his cutlass against the curb. "Anyone employed by that dubious bar is not in a position to question another's occupation."

"Shit, you think I like the Night of Joy? Ooo-wee. I wanna get someplace. I like to get someplace good, be gainfully employ, make me a livin wage."

"Just as I suspected," Ignatius said angrily. "In other words, you want to become totally bourgeois. You people have all been brainwashed. I imagine that you'd like to become a success or something equally vile."

"Hey, now you gettin me. Whoa!"

"I really don't have the time to discuss the errors of your value judgments. However, I would like some information from you. Do you by any chance have a woman in that den who is given to reading?"

"Yeah. She all the time slippin me somethin to

read, tellin me I be improvin myself. She pretty decent."

"Oh, my God." The blue and yellow eyes flashed. "Is there any way that I can meet this paragon?"

Jones wondered what this was all about. He said, "Whoa! You wanna see her, you come around some night, see her dancin with her pet."

"Good grief. Don't tell me that she is this Harlett O'Hara."

"Yeah. She Harla O'Horror all right."

"Boethius plus a pet," Ignatius mumbled. "What a discovery."

"She be openin in a coupla three days, man. You oughta get your ass down here. This the very fines ack I ever seen. Whoa!"

"I can only imagine," Ignatius said respectfully. Some brilliant satire on the decadent Old South being cast before the unaware swine in the Night of Joy audience. Poor Harlett. "Tell me. What sort of pet does she have?"

"Hey! I cain tell you that, man. You gotta see for yourself. This ack a big surprise. Harla got somethin to say, too. This ain jus a reglar strip ack. Harla talkin."

Good heavens. Some incisive commentary which no one in her audiences could fully comprehend. He must see Harlett. They must communicate.

"There is one thing I would like to know, sir," Ignatius said. "Is the Nazi proprietress of this cesspool around here every night?"

"Who? Miss Lee? No." Jones smiled at himself. The sabotage was working too perfectly. The fat mother really wanted to come to the Night of Joy. "She say Harla O'Horror so perfec, she so fine, she don't havta be comin aroun at night to supervise. She say jus as soon Harla be openin, she leavin for a vacation in Califonia. Whoa!"

"What luck," Ignatius slobbered. "Well, *I* shall be here to see Miss O'Hara's act. You may secretly reserve a ringside table for me. I must see and hear everything she does."

"Ooo-wee. You be real welcome, man. Drag your ass over in a coupla days. We give you the fines service in the house."

"Jones, are you talking to that character or what?" Lana demanded from the door.

"Don't worry," Ignatius told her. "I'm leaving. Your henchman has terrified me completely. I shall never make the mistake of even passing by this vile pigsty."

"Good," Lana said and swung the door closed.

Ignatius gloated at Jones conspiratorially.

"Hey, listen," Jones said. "Before you be leavin, tell me somethin. Wha you think a color cat can do to stop bein vagran or employ below the minimal wage?"

"Please." Ignatius fumbled through his smock to find the curb and raise himself. "You can't possibly realize how confused you are. Your value judgments are all wrong. When you get to the top or wherever it is that you want to go, you'll have a nervous breakdown or worse. Do you know of any Negroes with ulcers? Of course not. Live contentedly in some hovel. Thank Fortuna that you have no Caucasian parent hounding you. Read Boethius."

"Who? Read wha?"

"Boethius will show you that striving is ultimately meaningless, that we must learn to accept. Ask Miss O'Hara about him."

"Listen. How you like bein vagran half the time?"

"Wonderful. I myself was a vagrant in happier, better days. If only I were in your shoes. I would stir from my room only once a month to fumble for my relief check in the mailbox. Realize your good fortune."

The fat mother was really a freak. The poor people at Levy Pants were lucky that they hadn't ended up in Angola.

"Well be sure you come aroun in a coupla nights." Jones blew a cloud at the earring. "Harla be doin her stuff."

"I shall be there with bells on," Ignatius said happily. How Myrna would gnash her teeth.

"Whoa!" Jones walked around to the front of the wagon and studied the sheet of Big Chief paper. "Look like somebody been playin tricks on you."

"That is only a merchandising gimmick."

"Ooo-wee. You better check it again."

Ignatius lumbered around to the prow and saw that the waif had decorated the TWELVE INCHES (12″) OF PARADISE sign with a variety of genitals.

"Oh, my God!" Ignatius ripped off the sheet covered with the ballpoint grafitti. "Have I been pushing this about?"

"I be out front lookin for you," Jones said. "Hey!"

Ignatius waved a happy paw and waddled off. At last he had a reason for earning money: Harlett O'Hara. He aimed the denuded prow of the wagon toward the Algiers ferry ramp, where the longshoremen gathered in the afternoons. Calling, entreating, he guided the wagon into the crowd of men and succeeded in selling all of his hot dogs, courteously and effusively squirting ketchup and mustard on his sold goods with all the energy of a fireman.

What a brilliant day. The signs from Fortuna were

more than promising. A surprised Mr. Clyde received cheery greetings and ten dollars from vendor Reilly, and Ignatius, his smock filled with bills from the waif and the mogul of frankfurters, billowed onto the trolley with a glad heart.

He entered the house and found his mother talking quietly on the telephone.

"I been thinking about what you said," Mrs. Reilly was whispering into the phone. "Maybe it ain't such a bad idea after all, babe. You know what I mean?"

"Of course it ain't," Santa answered. "Them people at Charity can let Ignatius take him a little rest. Claude ain't gonna want no Ignatius around, sweetheart."

"He likes me, huh?"

"Likes you? He called up this morning to ax me if I thought you was ever gonna remarry. Lord. I says, 'Well, Claude, you gotta pop the question.' Whoee. You two having a worldwin courtship if I ever seen one. That poor man's desperate from loneliness."

"He's sure considerate," Mrs. Reilly breathed into the mouthpiece. "But sometimes he makes me nervous with all them communiss."

"What in the world are you babbling about?" Ignatius thundered in the hall.

"Christ," Santa said. "It sound like that Ignatius come in."

"Ssh," Mrs. Reilly said into the phone.

"Well, listen, sweetheart. Once Claude gets married, he'll stop thinking about them communiss. His mind isn't occupied is what's wrong with him. You give him some loving."

"Santa!"

351

"Good grief," Ignatius spluttered. "Are you speaking with that Battaglia strumpet?"

"Shut up, boy."

"You better knock that Ignatius in the head," Santa said.

"I wish I was strong enough, sweetheart," Mrs. Reilly answered.

"Oh, Irene, I almost forgot to tell you. Angelo come around this morning for a cup of coffee. I hardly recognized him. You oughta seen him in that wool suit. He looked like Mrs. Astor's horse. Poor Angelo. He's sure trying hard. Now he's going to all the high-class bars, he says. He better get him some character."

"Ain't that awful," Mrs. Reilly said sadly. "What Angelo's gonna do if he gets himself kicked off the force? And him with three chirren to support."

"There are a few challenging openings at Paradise Vendors for men with initiative and good taste," Ignatius said.

"Listen at that nut," Santa said. "Aw, Irene. You better ring up the Charity, honey."

"We gonna give him another chance. Maybe he'll hit the jackpot."

"I don't know why I bother talking to you, girl," Santa sighed hoarsely. "I'll see you tonight then about seven. Claude says he's gonna come over here. Come pick us up and we'll take us a nice ride out to the lake for some of them good crabs. Whoo! You kids sure lucky you got me for a chaperone. You two need one, especially with that Claude around."

Santa guffawed in a voice huskier than usual and hung up.

"What in the world do you and that old bawd babble about?" Ignatius asked.

"Shut up!"

"Thank you. I see that things about here are as cheerful as ever."

"How much money you brought in today? A quarter?" Mrs. Reilly screamed. She leaped up and stuck her hand into one of the pockets of the smock and pulled out the brilliant photograph. "Ignatius!"

"Give that to me," Ignatius thundered. "How dare you besmirch that magnificent image with your vintner's hands."

Mrs. Reilly peeked at the photograph again and then closed her eyes. A tear crept out from beneath her closed eyelids. "I knew when you started selling them weenies you was gonna be hanging around with people like this."

"What do you mean, 'people like this'?" Ignatius asked angrily, pocketing the photograph. "This is a brilliant, misused woman. Speak of her with respect and reverence."

"I don't wanna speak at all," Mrs. Reilly sniffed, her lids still sealed. "Go sit in your room and write some more of your foolishness." The telephone rang. "That must be that Mr. Levy. He already rang up here twice today."

"Mr. Levy? What does that monster want?"

"He wouldn't tell me. Go on, crazy. Answer that. Pick up that phone."

"Well, I certainly don't want to speak with him," Ignatius thundered. He picked up the telephone, and in an assumed voice rich with Mayfair accents said, "Yus?"

"Mr. Reilly?" a man asked.

"Mr. Reilly is not here."

"This is Gus Levy." In the background, a woman's

voice was saying, "Let's see what you're going to say. Another chance down the drain, a psycho escaped."

"I'm terribly sorry," Ignatius enunciated. "Mr. Reilly was called out of town this afternoon on rather crucial business. Actually, he is at the state mental hospital in Mandeville. Since being so viciously dismissed by your concern, he has had to commute back and forth regularly from Mandeville. His ego is badly bruised. You may yet receive his psychiatrists' bills. They are rather staggering."

"He cracked up?"

"Violently and totally. We had something of a time with him here. The first time that he went to Mandeville, he had to be transported in an armored car. As you know, his physique is rather grand. This afternoon, however, he left in a state patrol ambulance."

"Can he have visitors at Mandeville?"

"Of course. Drive out to see him. Bring him some cookies."

Ignatius slammed the telephone down, pressed a quarter into the palm of his still sniffling, blinded mother, and waddled to his room. Before opening the door, he stopped to straighten the PEACE TO MEN OF GOOD WILL sign that he had tacked to the peeling wood.

All signs were pointing upward; his wheel was revolving skyward.

t w e l v e

THERE HAD BEEN a flurry of excitement. The wild blowing of the postman's whistle, the chugging postal truck out on Constantinople Street, his mother's excited screaming, Miss Annie's calling to the postman that his whistle had frightened her—all had interrupted Ignatius' dressing for the kickoff rally. He signed the postal delivery receipt and rushed back to his room, locking his door.

"What is it, boy?" Mrs. Reilly asked in the hall.

Ignatius looked at the AIR MAIL SPECIAL DELIVERY stamping on the manila envelope and at the little hand-written pleas, "Urgent" and "Rush."

"Oh, my goodness," he said happily. "The Minkoff minx must be beside herself."

He tore open the envelope and pulled out the letter.

Sirs:
Did you really send me this telegram, Ignatius?

MYRNA FORM PEACE PARTY CENTRAL COMMITTEE NORTHEASTERN ZONE AT ONCE STOP ORGANIZE AT EVERY LEVEL STOP RECRUIT SODOMITES ONLY STOP SEX IN POLITICS STOP DETAILS WILL FOLLOW STOP IGNATIUS NATIONAL CHAIRMAN STOP

What does this mean, Ignatius? Do you really want me to recruit fags? Who wants to be a registered Sodomite?

Ignatius, I am very worried. Are you hanging around with some queers? I could have guessed that this would happen. The paranoid fantasy of the arrest and accident was the first clue. Now the whole thing is out in the open. Your normal sexual outlets have been blocked for so long that now the sexual overflow is seeping out into the wrong channels. Since the fantasy, which was the beginning of it all, you have been undergoing a period of crisis which is culminating in overt sexual aberration. I could tell that you were going to flip sooner or later. Now it has happened. My group therapy group will really be depressed when they hear that your case has taken a turn for the worse. Please leave that decaying city and come north. Call me collect if you want to and we can talk over this problem of sexual orientation that you are having. You must have therapy soon or you will become a screaming queen.

"How dare she?" Ignatius bellowed.

Whatever happened to the Divine Right party? I had several people who were all ready to join. I don't know if they'll go for this Sodomite business, although I can see that we might use this Sodomite party to drain off the fringe-group fascists. Maybe we could split the right wing in half. Still I don't think this is a good idea at all. Suppose non-Sodomites want to join and we refuse. We will be accused of being prejudiced, and the whole thing will flop. The lecture was not exactly a success, I'm afraid. It went over all right—right over the people's heads. There were two or three middle aged people in the audience who tried to heckle me with these very hostile remarks, but a couple of my friends from the group therapy group challenged them hostility for hostility and finally drove those reactionaries out of the auditorium. Just as I suspected, I was a little too advanced for the neighborhood audience. Ongah did not show up, that crumb. As far as I'm concerned, they can send him back to Africa. I really thought that guy had something on the ball. Apparently he's very apathetic politically. He promised me he would be there, that schmuck. Ignatius, this Sodomite plan does not sound very practical at all. In addition, I think it is only a dangerous manifestation of your declining mental health. I don't know how I can tell my group therapy group about this weird development—however predictable it might have been. The group has been really pulling for you all along. Some are even identifying with you. If you go, they might go, too. I need immediate communication from you. Please call collect anytime after 6 P.M. I am very, very worried.

M. Minkoff

"She's totally confounded," Ignatius said happily. "Wait until she hears of my apocalyptic meeting with Miss O'Hara."

"Ignatius, what's that you got?"

"A communication from Myrna minx."

"What that girl wants?"

"She's threatening suicide unless I swear that my heart is hers alone."

"Ain't that awful. I bet you been telling that poor girl a lota lies. I know you, Ignatius."

Behind the door there were sounds of dressing; something that sounded like a piece of metal fell to the floor.

"Where you going to?" Mrs. Reilly asked the peeling paint.

"Please, Mother," a basso profundo voice answered. "I'm rather rushed. Stop bothering me, please."

"You might as well stay at home all day long for all the money you bringing in," Mrs. Reilly screamed at the door. "How I'm gonna meet the note I gotta pay that man?"

"I wish that you would let me alone. I am addressing a political meeting tonight, and I must organize my thoughts."

"A political meeting? Ignatius! Ain't that

wonderful. Maybe you'll make good in politics, boy. You got you a fine voice. What club, honey? The Crescent City Democrats? The Old Regulars?"

"The party is secret at the moment, I'm afraid."

"What kinda political party's a secret?" Mrs. Reilly asked suspiciously. "Are you gonna talk with a buncha communiss?"

"Ho hum."

"Somebody gimme some pamphlets on the communiss, boy. I been reading all about the communiss. Don't try to fool me, Ignatius."

"Yes, I saw one of those pamphlets in the hall this afternoon. You either dropped it there on purpose so that I could benefit from its message or you tossed it there accidentally during your regular afternoon wine orgy in the belief that it was a particularly elephantine bit of confetti. I imagine that your eyes have some trouble focusing at about two in the afternoon. Well, I read through the pamphlet. It's almost completely illiterate. Goodness knows where you get such garbage. Probably from the old woman who sells pralines at the cemetery. Well, I am not a communist, so let me alone."

"Ignatius, don't you think maybe you'd be happy if you went and took you a little rest at Charity?"

"Are you referring to the psychiatric ward by any chance?" Ignatius demanded in a rage. "Do you think that I am insane? Do you suppose that some stupid psychiatrist could even attempt to fathom the workings of my psyche?"

"You could just rest, honey. You could write some stuff in your little copybooks."

"They would try to make me into a moron who liked television and new cars and frozen food. Don't you understand? Psychiatry is worse than communism. I refuse to be brainwashed. I won't be a robot!"

"But, Ignatius, they help out a lot of people got problems."

"Do you think that I have a problem?" Ignatius bellowed. "The only problem that those people have anyway is that they don't like new cars and hair sprays. That's why they are put away. They make the other members of the society fearful. Every asylum in this nation is filled with poor souls who simply cannot stand lanolin, cellophane, plastic, television, and subdivisions."

"Ignatius, that ain't true. You remember old Mr. Becnel used to live down the block? They locked him up because he was running down the street naked."

"Of course he was running down the street naked. His skin could not bear any more of that dacron and nylon clothing that was clogging his pores. I've always considered Mr. Becnel one of the martyrs of our age. The poor man was badly victimized. Now run along to the front door and see if my taxi has arrived."

"Where you getting money for a taxi?"

"I keep a few pennies stuffed in my mattress," Ignatius answered. He had blackmailed another ten dollars out of the urchin, also forcing the waif to watch the wagon while he spent the afternoon at Loew's State watching a film about drag-racing teenagers. The guttersnipe was definitely a discovery, a gift sent by Fortuna to make amends for all of her bad spins. "Go peek through the shutters."

The door creaked open and Ignatius appeared in his pirate finery.

"Ignatius!"

"I thought that you might react like that.

Therefore I have kept all of this paraphernalia stashed at Paradise Vendors, Incorporated."

"Angelo was right," Mrs. Reilly cried. "You been out on the streets dressed up like a Mardi Gras all this time."

"A scarf here. A cutlass there. One or two deft and tasteful suggestions. That's all. The total effect is rather fetching."

"You can't go out like that," Mrs. Reilly hollered.

"Please. Not another hysterical scene. You'll dislodge all of the thoughts which are developing in my mind in connection with the lecture."

"Get back in that room, boy." Mrs. Reilly began beating Ignatius on the arms. "Get back in there, Ignatius. I ain't fooling this time, boy. You can't disgrace me like that."

"Good heavens! Mother, stop that. I'll be in no condition for my speech."

"What kinda speech you gonna make? Where you going to, Ignatius? Tell me, boy?" Mrs. Reilly slapped her son flatly in the face. "You ain't leaving this house, crazy."

"Oh, my God, Are you going mad? Get away from me this instant. I hope that you've noticed that scimitar dangling from my uniform."

A slap struck Ignatius in the nose: another landed on his right eye. He waddled down the hall, pushed the long shutters open, and ran out into the yard.

"Come back in this house," Mrs. Reilly screamed from the front door. "You ain't going no where, Ignatius."

"I dare you to come out in that shredded nightgown and get me!" Ignatius answered defiantly and stuck out his massive pink tongue.

"Get back in here, Ignatius."

"Hey, knock it off, you two," Miss Annie shouted from behind her front shutters. "My nerves is shot to hell."

"Take a look at Ignatius," Mrs. Reilly called to her. "Ain't that awful?"

Ignatius was waving to his mother from the brick sidewalk, his earring catching the rays of the streetlight.

"Ignatius, come in here like a good boy," Mrs. Reilly pleaded.

"I awready got me a headache from the goddam postman's whistle," Miss Annie threatened loudly. "I'm gonna ring up the cops in about one minute."

"Ignatius," shouted Mrs. Reilly, but it was too late. A taxi was cruising down the block. Ignatius flagged it down just as his mother, forgetting the disgrace of the shredded nightgown, ran down to the curb. Ignatius slammed the rear door right in his mother's maroon hair and barked an address at the driver. He stabbed at his mother's hands with the cutlass and ordered the driver to move along immediately. The taxi sped off, churning up some pebbles in the gutter that stung Mrs. Reilly's legs through the torn rayon gown. She watched the red taillights for a moment, then she ran back into the house to telephone Santa.

"Going to a costume party, pal?" the driver asked Ignatius as they turned onto St. Charles Avenue.

"Watch where you're going and speak when you're spoken to," Ignatius thundered.

During the ride the driver said nothing else, but Ignatius practiced his speech loudly in the back seat, rapping his cutlass against the front seat to emphasize certain key points.

At St. Peter Street he got out and first heard the

361

noise, dim yet frenetic singing and laughing coming from the three-story yellow stucco building. Some prosperous Frenchman had built the house in the late 1700s to house a menage of wife, children, and spinster *tantes*. The *tantes* had been stored up in the attic along with the other excess and unattractive furniture, and from the two little dormer windows in the roof they had seen what little of the world they believed existed outside of their own *monde* of slanderous gossip, needlework, and cyclical recitations of the rosary. But the hand of the professional decorator had exorcised whatever ghosts of the French bourgeoisie might still haunt the thick brick walls of the building. The exterior was painted a bright canary yellow; the gas jets in the reproduction brass lanterns mounted on either side of the carriageway flickered softly, their amber flames rippling in reflection on the black enamel of the gate and shutters. On the flagstone paving beneath both lanterns there were old plantation pots in which Spanish daggers grew and extended their sharply pointed stilettos.

Ignatius stood before the building regarding it with extreme distaste. His blue and yellow eyes denounced the resplendent façade. His nose rebelled against the very noticeable odor of fresh enamel. His ears shrank from the bedlam of singing, cackling, and giggling that was going on behind the closed black patent leather shutters.

Testily clearing his throat, he looked at the three brass doorbells and at the little white cards above each:

> Billy Truehard
> Raoul Frayle   - 3A
> Frieda Club
> Betty Bumper

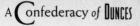

Liz Steele   - 2A
Dorian Greene   - 1A

He jabbed a finger into the bottom bell and waited. The frenzy behind the shutters abated very slightly. A door opened somewhere down the carriageway, and Dorian Greene came walking toward the gate.

"Oh, dear," he said when he saw who was out on the sidewalk. "Where in the world have you been? I'm afraid that the kickoff rally is fast getting out of hand. I have tried unsuccessfully once or twice to call the group to order, but apparently feelings are running rather high."

"I hope you've done nothing to dampen their morale," Ignatius said gravely, tapping his cutlass impatiently on the iron gate. He noticed somewhat angrily that Dorian was walking toward him a little unsteadily; this was not what he had expected.

"Oh, what a gathering," Dorian said as he opened the gate. "Everyone is simply letting his hair down."

Dorian did a rapid and uncoordinated pantomime to illustrate this.

"Oh, my God!" Ignatius said. "Stop that appalling obscenity."

"Several people will be completely ruined after this evening. There's going to be a mass exodus for Mexico City in the morning. But then Mexico City is so wonderfully wild."

"I certainly hope that no one has tried to inflict any warmongering resolutions upon the gathering."

"Oh, goodness, no."

"I'm relieved to hear that. Heaven knows what opposition we may have to face even at the outset. We may have some 'enemy within.' Word may have leaked out to the whole military combine of the nation and, for that matter, the world."

"Well, come along, Gypsy Queen, let's get inside."

As they walked down the carriageway, Ignatius said, "This building is repellingly flamboyant." He looked at the pastel lamps concealed behind the palms along the walls. "Who's responsible for this abortion?"

"I, of course, Magyar Maiden. I own the building."

"I should have known. May I ask where the money comes from to support this decadent whimsy of yours?"

"From my dear family out there in the wheat," Dorian sighed. "They send me large checks every month. In return I simply guarantee them that I'll stay out of Nebraska. I left there under something of a cloud, you see. All that wheat and those endless plains. I can't tell you how depressing it all was. Grant Wood romanticized it, if anything. I went East for college and then came here. Oh, New Orleans is such freedom."

"Well, at least we have a gathering place for our coup. Now that I've seen the place, however, I would have preferred your renting an American Legion hall or something equally appropriate. This place looks more like the setting for some perverted activity like a tea dance or a garden party."

"Do you know that a national home decorating magazine wants to do a four-page color spread on this building?" Dorian asked.

"If you had any sense, you would realize that that is the ultimate insult," Ignatius snorted.

364

"Oh, Girl with the Golden Earring, you are driving me out of my mind. Look, here's the door."

"Just a moment," Ignatius said cautiously. "What is that awful noise? It sounds as if someone's being sacrificed."

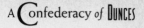

They stood in the pastel light of the carriageway listening. Somewhere in the patio a human was crying in distress.

"Oh, dear, what are they doing now?" Dorian's voice was impatient. "Those little fools. They never can behave themselves."

"I would suggest that we investigate," Ignatius said, his voice a conspiratorial whisper. "Some obsessed military officer may have slipped into the meeting incognito and may be trying to extricate our secrets from some faithful party member by means of torture. The dedicated military will stoop to anything. It could even be some foreign agent."

"Oh, what fun!" Dorian shrieked.

He and Ignatius tripped and waddled to the patio. There someone was crying for help in the slave quarters. The door of the slave quarters was slightly ajar, but Ignatius threw himself against it anyway, shattering several panes of glass.

"Oh, my God!" he screamed when he saw what was before him. "They've struck!"

He looked at the little sailor shackled and chained to the wall. It was Timmy.

"Do you see what you've done to my door?" Dorian was asking behind Ignatius.

"The enemy is among us," Ignatius said wildly. "Who tattled? Tell me. Someone is on to us."

"Oh, get me out of here," the little sailor pleaded. "It's awfully dark."

"You little fool," Dorian spat at the sailor. "Who chained you in here?"

"It was that terrible Billy and Raoul. They're so awful, those two. They brought me out here to show me how you're redecorating the slave quarters, and the next thing I knew they locked me in these dirty chains and ran back into the party."

The little sailor rattled his chains.

"I've just had this place redone," Dorian said to Ignatius. "Oh, my door."

"Where are those agents?" Ignatius demanded, unpinning his cutlass and waving it about. "We must apprehend them before they leave this building."

"Please get me out. I can't stand the dark."

"It's your fault that this door is broken," Dorian hissed at the deranged mariner. "Playing games with those two tramps from upstairs."

"He broke the door."

"What can you expect from him? Just look at him."

"Are you two deviates talking about me?" Ignatius asked angrily. "If you're going to get this excited about a door, I seriously doubt whether you'll survive for long in the vicious arena of politics."

"Oh, get me out of here. I'm going to *scream* if I stay in these tacky chains much longer."

"Oh, shut up, Nellie," Dorian snapped, slapping Timmy across his pink cheeks. "Get out of my house and go back on the streets where you belong."

"Oh!" the sailor cried. "What a terrible thing to say."

"Please," Ignatius cautioned. "The movement must not be sabotaged by internal strife."

"I did think that I had at least one friend left," the sailor said to Dorian. "I see I was wrong. Go ahead. Slap me again if it gives you so much pleasure."

"I wouldn't even touch you, you little tramp."

"I doubt whether any hack, under pressure, could pen such atrocious melodrama," Ignatius observed.

"Now stop all of this, you two degenerates. Exercise at least a little taste and decency."

"Slap me!" the sailor shrieked. "I know you're dying to do it. You'd love to hurt me, wouldn't you?"

"Apparently he won't settle down until you've agreed to inflict at least a little physical injury upon him," Ignatius told Dorian.

"I wouldn't put a finger on his stupid slut body."

"Well, we must do something to silence him. My valve can take only so much of this deranged mariner's neuroses. We shall have to politely drop him from the movement. He simply does not measure up. Anyone can smell that heavy musk of masochism which he exudes. It's stinking up the slave quarters at this very moment. In addition, he appears rather drunk."

"You hate me, too, you big monster," the sailor screamed at Ignatius.

Ignatius tapped Timmy soundly on the head with his cutlass, and the seafarer emitted a little moan.

"Goodness knows what debased fantasy he's having," Ignatius commented.

"Oh, hit him again," Dorian chirped happily. "What fun!"

"Please let me out of these awful chains," the sailor pleaded. "My sailor suit's getting all rusty."

While Dorian was unlocking the shackles with a key he took from over the door, Ignatius said, "You know, manacles and chains have functions in modern life which their fevered inventors must never have considered in an earlier and simpler age. If I were a suburban developer, I would attach at least one set to the walls of every new yellow brick ranch style and Cape Cod split level. When the suburbanites grew tired of television and Ping-Pong or whatever they do in their little homes, they could chain one another up for a while. Everyone would love it. Wives would say, 'My husband put me in chains last night. It was wonderful. Has your husband done that to you lately? And children would hurry eagerly home from school to their mothers who would be waiting to chain them. It would help the children to cultivate the imagination denied them by television and would appreciably cut down on the incidence of juvenile delinquency. When father came in from work, the whole family could grab him and chain him for being stupid enough to be working all day long to support them. Troublesome old relatives would be chained in the carport. Their hands would be released only once a month so they could sign over their Social Security checks. Manacles and chains could build a better life for all. I must give this some space in my notes and jottings."

"Oh, my dear," Dorian sighed. "Don't you ever shut up?"

"My arms *are* all rusty," Timmy said. "Just wait till I get my hands on that Billy and Raoul."

"Our little convention seems to be getting rather unwieldy," Ignatius said of the mad noises issuing from Dorian's apartment. "Apparently feeling about the issues is striking more than one nerve center."

"Oh, heavens, I'd rather not look," Dorian said, pushing the glass-paneled wisp of a French provincial door open.

Inside Ignatius saw a seething mass of people. Cigarette and cocktail glasses held like batons flew in the air directing the symphony of chatter, shrieking, singing, and laughing. From the bowels of a huge stereophonic phonograph the voice of Judy Garland was fighting its way through the din. A small band of young men, the only stationary ones in the room, stood before the phonograph as if it were an altar. "Divine!" "Fantastic!" "So human!" they were saying of the voice from their electric tabernacle.

His blue and yellow eyes traveled from this rite to the rest of the room, where the other guests were attacking one another with conversation. Herringbones and madras and lamb's wool and cashmere flashed past in a blur as hands and arms rent the air in a variety of graceful gestures. Fingernails, cuff links, pinky rings, teeth, eyes—all glittered. In the center of one knot of elegant guests a cowboy with a little riding crop flicked the crop at one of his fans, producing a response of exaggerated screaming and pleased giggling. In the center of another knot stood a lout in a black leather jacket who was teaching judo holds, to the great delight of his epicene students. "Oh, do teach me that," someone near the wrestler screamed after an elegant guest had been twisted into an obscene position and then thrown to the floor to land with a crash of cuff links and other, assorted jewelry.

"I only invited the better people," Dorian said to Ignatius.

"Good gracious," Ignatius spluttered. "I can see that we're going to have a great deal of trouble capturing the conservative rural red-neck Calvinist vote. We are going to have to rebuild our image along lines other than those I see here."

Timmy, who was watching the black leather lout twist and dump eager partners sighed, "How fun."

The room itself was what decorators would probably call *severe*. The walls and high ceilings were white, and the room itself was sparsely furnished with a few pieces of antique furniture. The only voluptuous element in the large room was the champagne-colored velvet drapes tied back with white ribbons. The two or three antique chairs had apparently been chosen for their bizarre design and not for their ability to seat anyone, for they were delicate suggestions, hints at furniture with cushions barely capable of accommodating a child. A human in such a room was expected not to rest or sit or even relax, but rather pose, thereby transforming himself into a human furnishing that would complement the decor as well as possible.

After Ignatius had studied the decor, he said to Dorian, "The only functional item in here is that phonograph, and that is obviously being misused. This is a room with no soul." He snorted loudly, in part over the room and in part over the fact that no one in the room had even noticed him, even though he complemented the decor as well as a neon sign would have. The participants in the kickoff rally seemed much more concerned about their own private fates this evening than they were about the fate of the world. "I notice that no one in this whitened sepulcher of a room has so much as even looked at us. They haven't even nodded to their host, whose liquor they are consuming and whose year-round air conditioning they are taxing with all of those overpowering colognes. I feel rather like an observer at a catfight."

"Don't worry about them. They've been simply dying for a good party for months. Come. You must see the decoration that I've made." He took Ignatius over to the mantelpiece and showed him a bud vase containing one red, one white, and one blue rose. "Isn't that wild? It's better than all of that tacky crepe paper. I did buy some crepe paper, but nothing that I could do with it satisfied me."

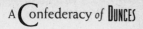

"This is a floral abortion," Ignatius commented irritably and tapped the vase with his cutlass. "Dyed flowers are unnatural and perverse and, I suspect, obscene also. I can see that I am going to have my hands full with you people."

"Oh, talk, talk, talk," Dorian moaned. "Then let's go into the kitchen. I want you to meet the ladies' auxiliary."

"Is that true? An auxiliary?" Ignatius asked greedily. "Well, I must compliment you upon your foresightedness."

They entered the kitchen where, except for two young men who were having an emotional argument in a corner, all was quiet. Seated at a table were three women drinking from beer cans. They regarded Ignatius squarely. The one who was crushing a beer can in her hand stopped and tossed the can into a potted plant next to the sink.

"Girls," Dorian said. The three beer girls raised a raucous Bronx cheer. "This is Ignatius Reilly, a new face."

"Put it there, Fats," the girl who had been crushing the can said. She grabbed Ignatius' paw and worked it over as if it, too, were a prospect for crushing.

"Oh, my God!" Ignatius screamed.

"That's Frieda," Dorian explained. "And they're Betty and Liz."

"How do you do," Ignatius said, slipping his hands into the pockets of his smock to prevent any further handshaking. "I'm sure that you'll be of invaluable help to our cause."

371

"Where did you pick him up?" Frieda asked Dorian while her two companions studied Ignatius and nudged each other.

"Mr. Greene and I met through my mother," Ignatius answered grandly for Dorian.

"No kidding," Frieda said, "Your mother must be a very interesting person."

"Hardly," Ignatius replied.

"Well, grab yourself a beer, Tubby," Frieda said. "I wish we had it in bottles. Betty here could open you one with her teeth. She's got teeth like an iron claw." Betty made an obscene gesture at Frieda. "And one of those days she's going to get them all knocked down her fucking throat."

Betty hit Frieda on the head with an empty can.

"You're asking for it," Frieda said, raising one of the kitchen chairs.

"Now stop it," Dorian spat. "If you three can't behave, you can just leave right now."

"Personally," Liz said, "we're getting very bored just sitting here in the kitchen."

"Yeah," Betty screamed. She grabbed a rung of the chair that Frieda was holding over her head, and she and Frieda began wrestling for possession of it. "How come we have to sit out here?"

"Put that chair down this minute," Dorian said.

"Yes, please," Ignatius added. He had retreated to a corner. "Someone will be injured."

"Like *you*," Liz said. She heaved an unopened beer can at Ignatius, who ducked.

"Good heavens!" Ignatius said. "I think I shall return to the other room."

"Beat it, bigass," Liz said to him. "You're using up all the air in here."

"Girls!" Dorian was screaming at the wrestling Frieda and Betty, whose T-shirts were growing damp.

They were huffing and heaving around the room with the chair, mashing each other against the wall and sink.

"Okay, cut it out," Liz screamed at her friends. "These people are going to think you're crude."

She picked up another chair and got between the two contestants. Then she slammed her chair down onto the one that Frieda and Betty were wrestling over, knocking the girls aside. The two chairs rattled and clattered to the floor.

"Who told you to butt in?" Frieda demanded of Liz, grabbing her by her cropped hair.

Dorian, stumbling over the chairs, tried to push the girls back to the table, snapping, "Now sit down there and be decent."

"This party stinks," Betty said, "Where's the action?"

"How come you invited us down here if all we're gonna do is sit here in this frigging kitchen?" Frieda demanded.

"You'll only start brawling in there. You know it. I thought it would be a neighborly thing to do to ask you down out of courtesy. I don't want any trouble. This is the nicest party we've had in months."

"Okay," Frieda growled. "We'll sit out here like ladies." The girls punched one another about the arms in agreement. "After all, we're only paying tenants. Go in there and be nice to that phony cowboy, the one that sounds like Jeanette MacDonald, the one that tried to bitch us on Chartres Street the other day."

"He's a very fine and friendly person," Dorian said. "I'm sure he didn't see you girls."

373

"He saw us all right," Betty said. "We copped him on the head."

"I'd like to kick his superior balls in," Liz said.

"Please," Ignatius said importantly. "All I see about me is strife. You must close ranks and present a unified front."

"What's with him?" Liz asked, opening the beer can she had thrown at Ignatius. A spray of foam shot out and wet Ignatius on his distended Paradise product stomach.

"Well, I've had enough of this," Ignatius said angrily.

"Good," Frieda said. "Shove off."

"The kitchen is our territory tonight," Betty said. "We decide who uses it."

"I certainly am interested in seeing the first sherry party that the auxiliary gives," Ignatius snorted and lumbered to the door. As he was exiting, an empty beer can struck the door frame near his earring. Dorian followed him out and closed the door. "I can't imagine how you decided to besmirch the movement by inviting those rowdies here."

"I had to," Dorian explained. "If you don't invite them to a party, they break in anyway. Then they're even worse. They're really fun girls when they're in a good mood, but they had some trouble with the police recently, and they're taking it out on everyone."

"They shall be dropped from the movement immediately!"

"Anything you say, Magyara," Dorian sighed. "I myself feel a little sorry for the girls. They used to live in California, where they had a grand time. Then there was an incident about assaulting a bodybuilder at Muscle Beach. They had been Indian arm wrestling with the boy, or so they say, and then it seems that things got out of hand. They literally had to flee southern California and dash across the desert in that magnificent

374

German automobile of theirs. I have given them sanctuary. In many respects they're wonderful tenants. They guard my building better than any watchdog could. They have loads of money that they get from some aging movie queen."

"Really?" Ignatius asked with interest. "Perhaps I was hasty about dropping them. Political movements must get their money from whatever source they can. The girls have, no doubt, a charm which their blue jeans and boots obscure." He looked over the seething mass of guests. "You must get these people quiet. We must bring them to order. There is crucial business at hand."

The cowboy, the phony bitch, was tickling an elegant guest with his riding crop. The black leather lout was pinning an ecstatic guest to the floor. Everywhere there were screams, sighs, shrieks. Lena Horne was now singing within the phonograph. "Clever," "Crisp," "Terribly cosmo," the group around the phonograph was saying reverently. The cowboy broke away from his aroused fans and began to synchronize his lips to the lyrics on the record, slinking around the floor like a chanteuse in boots and stetson. With a barrage of squeals, the guests gathered around him, leaving the black leather lout with no one to torture.

"You must stop all of this," Ignatius shouted to Dorian, who was winking at the cowboy. "Aside from the fact that I am witnessing a most egregious offense against taste and decency, I am also beginning to smother from the stench of glandular emissions and cologne."

375

"Oh, don't be so drab. They're just having fun."

"I am very sorry," Ignatius said in a businesslike tone. "I am here tonight on a mission of the utmost seriousness. There is a girl who must be attended to, a bold and forward minx of a trollop. Now turn off that offensive music and quiet these sodomites. We must get down to brass tacks."

"I thought you were going to be fun. If you're just going to be tacky and dreary, then you'd better leave."

"I shall not leave! No one can deter me. Peace! Peace! Peace!"

"Oh, dear. You *are* serious about this, aren't you?"

Ignatius broke away from Dorian and rushed across the room, pushing through the elegant guests, and un-plugged the phonograph. As he turned around, he was greeted by the guests' emasculated version of an Apache war cry.

"Beast." "Madman." "Is this what Dorian promised?" "That fantastic Lena." "The outfit—grotesque. And that earring. Oh, my." "That was my very favorite song." "Horrible." "How unbelievably gross." "So monstrously huge." "A bad, bad dream."

"Silence!" Ignatius bellowed over their enraged babbling. "I am here tonight my friends, to show you how you may save the world and bring peace."

"He's truly mad." "Dorian, what a bad joke." "Where in the world did he come from?" "Not even vaguely attractive." "Filthy." "Depressing." "Someone turn on that delicious record again."

"The challenge," Ignatius continued at full volume, "Is placed before you. Will you turn your singular talents to saving the world, or will you simply turn your backs on your fellow man?"

"Oh, how awful!" "Not at all amusing." "I'll have to leave if this tacky charade continues." "In such poor taste." "Someone turn on that record again. Dear, dear Lena." "Where is my coat?" "Let's go to a smart bar."

"Look, I've spilled my martini on my most priceless jacket." "Let's go to a smart bar."

"The world today is in a state of grave unrest," Ignatius screamed against the mewing and hissing. He paused for a moment to glance down in his pocket at some notes he had scribbled on a piece of Big Chief paper. Instead he pulled out the torn and dogeared photograph of Miss O'Hara. Several guests saw it and shrieked. "We must prevent the apocalypse. We must fight fire with fire. Therefore, I turn to you."

"Oh, what in heaven's name is he talking about?" "This is making me so depressed." "Those eyes, they're frightening." "Let's go to a smart bar." "Let's go to San Francisco."

"Silence, you perverts!" Ignatius cried. "Listen to me."

"Dorian," the cowboy pleaded in a lyric soprano. "Make him keep quiet. We were having such fun, such a grand, gay time. Oh, he's not even amusing."

"That's right," an extremely elegant guest, whose taut face was brown with suntan makeup, said, "He's truly awful. So depressing."

"Must we listen to all of this?" another guest asked, waving his cigarette as if it were a magic wand which would make Ignatius disappear. "Is this a trick of some kind, Dorian? You know that we dearly love parties with a motif, but *this*. I mean, I never even watch the news on television. I've been working all day in that shop, and I don't want to come to a party and have to hear all of this sort of thing. Let him talk later if he really has to. His remarks are in such terrible taste."

377

"So inappropriate," the black leather lout sighed, turning suddenly fey.

"All right," Dorian said. "Turn on the record. I

thought it might be fun." He looked at Ignatius, who was snorting loudly. "I'm afraid, my dears, that it turned out to be a terrible, terrible bomb."

"Wonderful." "Dorian's magnificent." "There's the plug." "I love Lena." "I truly think that this is her very best recording." "So smart. Those special lyrics." "I saw her in New York once. Magnificent." "Play *Gypsy* next. I adore Ethel." "Oh, good, it's coming on."

There Ignatius stood like the boy on the burning deck. The music rose from the tabernacle once again. Dorian fled to speak with a group of his guests, actively ignoring Ignatius, as was everyone else in the room. Ignatius felt as alone as he had felt on that dark day in high school when in a chemistry laboratory his experiment had exploded, burning his eyebrows off and frightening him. The shock and terror had made him wet his pants, and no one in the laboratory would notice him, not even the instructor, who hated him sincerely for similar explosions in the past. For the remainder of that day, as he walked soggily around the school, everyone had pretended that he was invisible. Ignatius, feeling just as invisible standing there in Dorian's living room, began feinting at some imaginary opponent with his cutlass to relieve his self-consciousness.

Many were now singing with the record. Two began dancing near the phonograph. The dancing spread like a forest fire, and soon the floor was filled with couples who swayed and dipped around the Gibraltar of a wallflower, Ignatius. As Dorian swept past in the arms of the cowboy, Ignatius tried futilely to attract his attention. He attempted even to stick the cowboy with his cutlass, but the two were a wily and elusive dance team.

378

Just as he was about to evanesce completely, Frieda, Liz, and Betty burst in from the kitchen.

"We couldn't take that kitchen any more," Frieda said to Ignatius. "After all, we're human beings, too." She gave Ignatius a light rabbit punch to the stomach. "Looks like you're left out, Fats."

"Just what do you mean?" Ignatius asked haughtily.

"Looks like your costume's not going over too well," Liz observed.

"Pardon me, ladies. I must leave."

"Hey, don't go, Tubby," Betty said. "Somebody'll ask you. They're just trying to bitch you. Don't give up the ship. They'd bitch their own mother."

At that moment, Timmy, who had slipped out to the slave quarters again to look for his missing charm bracelet and, he hoped, more games with the chains, appeared in the living room. He wandered over to Ignatius and asked wistfully, "Do you want to dance?"

"There. You see?" Frieda said to Ignatius.

"I want to see this," Liz shouted. "Let's see you two do the limbo. Come on. I'll get a broom we can use for the pole."

"Oh, my God!" Ignatius said. "Please. I don't dance."

"Oh, come on," Timmy said. "I can teach you. I love to dance. I'll lead."

"Go ahead, bigass," Betty threatened.

"No. It would be impossible. The cutlass, the smock. Someone would be injured. I came here to speak, not dance. I don't dance. I never dance. I have never danced in my life."

"Well, you're going to dance now," Frieda told him. "You don't want to hurt this sailor's feelings."

"I am not dancing!" Ignatius barked. "I have never danced, and I certainly am not going to begin with some drunken deviate."

"Oh, don't be so straight," Timmy sighed.

"I have always had a rather substandard sense of balance," Ignatius explained. "We will plunge to the floor a broken heap. This deranged mariner will be crippled or worse."

"Tubby looks like a troublemaker," Frieda said to her friends. "Right?"

With a wink from Frieda, the three girls attacked Ignatius. One wrapped a square leg around his; the other kicked him in the back of the knee; the third pushed him backward onto the cowboy, who was whirling in the vicinity. Ignatius steadied himself by grabbing the cowboy, who broke from Dorian's horrified grasp and toppled to the floor. As the cowboy landed, the needle jumped from the record and the music stopped. But in its place there began a chorus of shrieking and screaming from the guests.

"Oh, Dorian, get him out!" an elegant shrieked in panic.

There was a metallic crash of rings, bracelets, and cuff links as some of the guests pressed together in a corner.

"Hey, you knocked that bitch of a cowboy over like a tenpin," Frieda screamed admiringly at Ignatius, who was still flailing his arms to regain his balance.

"Nice work, Fats," Liz said.

380

"Let's aim him at somebody else," Betty said to her companions.

"What have you done, you huge beastly thing?" Dorian cried at Ignatius.

"This is an outrage," Ignatius was shouting. "I

have not only been ignored and vilified at this gathering. I have been viciously attacked within the walls of your cobweb of a home. I hope that you carry liability insurance. If not, you may well lose this flamboyant property once my legal advisors have attended to you."

Dorian was down on his knees, fanning the cowboy, whose lids were beginning to flutter.

"Make him leave, Dorian," the cowboy sobbed. "He almost *killed* me."

"I had thought you might be different and funny," Dorian hissed at Ignatius. "As it is, you have proved to be the most awful thing that has ever been in my house. From the moment that you broke the door, I should have realized that it would end like this. What did you do to this dear boy?"

"My trousers are *filthy*," the cowboy shrieked.

"I was savagely attacked and pushed onto that coxcomb cowpoke."

"Don't try to lie, Fats," Frieda said. "We saw the whole thing. He was jealous, Dorian. He wanted to dance with you."

"Awful." "Make him go." "Ruining the party." "So monstrous." "Dangerous." "Total loss."

"Get out!" Dorian cried.

"We'll handle him," Frieda said.

"All right," Ignatius said grandly as the three girls sank their stubby hands into his smock and started propelling him toward the door. "You have made your choice. Live in a world of war and bloodshed. When the bomb drops, do not come to me. I shall be in my shelter!"

"Can it," Betty said.

The three girls hustled Ignatius through the door and down the carriageway.

"Thank Fortuna I'm dissociating myself from this movement," Ignatius thundered. The girls had knocked the scarf down over one eye and he was having trouble seeing where he was going. "You distempered people hardly have voter appeal."

They pushed him through the gate and onto the sidewalk. The Spanish dagger plants at the gate pricked his calves painfully and he stumbled forward.

"Okay, buster," Frieda called through the gate as she closed it. "We're giving you a ten minutes head-start. Then we start combing the Quarter."

"We better not find your fat ass," Liz said.

"Shove off, Tubby," Betty added. "We haven't had a good fight in a long time. We're ready for one."

"Your movement is doomed," Ignatius slobbered after the girls, who were pushing one another down the carriageway. "Do you hear me? D-o-o-m-e-d. You know nothing about politics and voter persuasion. You will not carry a single ward in the nation. You won't even carry the Quarter!"

The door slammed and the girls were back in the party, which seemed to have regained its momentum. The music had started again, and Ignatius heard the squealing and shrieking growing louder than before. He knocked on the black shutters with his cutlass, screaming, "You will lose!" The tap and slide of many dancing feet answered his cry.

A man wearing a silk suit and a homburg came out of the shadow of an adjoining doorway for a moment to see whether the girls had gone. Then the man slipped back into the darkness, watching Ignatius, who was waddling back and forth before the building furiously.

Ignatius' valve responded to his emotions by plopping closed. His hands sympathized by sprouting a rich growth of tiny white bumps that itched maddeningly. What could he tell Myrna about the movement for peace now? Now, like the abortive Crusade for Moorish Dignity, he had another debacle on his itching hands. Fortuna, that vicious slut. The evening had hardly begun; he couldn't return to Constantinople Street and a variety of assaults from his mother, not now that his emotions had been stimulated toward a climax that had been snatched from his grasp. For almost a week he had been preoccupied with the kickoff rally, and now, ejected from the political arena by three dubious girls, he stood frustrated and furious on the damp flagstones of St. Peter Street.

Looking at his Mickey Mouse wristwatch which was, as usual, moribund, he wondered what time it was. Perhaps it was still early enough to see the first show at the Night of Joy. Perhaps Miss O'Hara had opened. If he and Myrna were not destined to joust on the field of political action, then it would have to be the field of sex. What a lance Miss O'Hara could be to hurl right between Myrna's offensive eyes. Ignatius looked at the photograph once more, salivating slightly. What kind of pet? The evening could still be wrenched from the jaws of failure.

Scratching one paw with the other, he decided that safety at least dictated his moving along. Those three savage girls might make good their threat. He billowed off down St. Peter toward Bourbon. The man in the silk suit and homburg came out of the shadow of the doorway and followed him. At Bourbon, Ignatius turned and began walking up toward Canal through the night's parade of tourists and Quarterites, among whom he did not look particularly strange. He shoved through the crowd on the narrow sidewalk, his hips swinging each way free and slamming people aside. When Myrna read of Miss O'Hara, she would spew espresso all over the letter in consternation.

As he crossed onto the Night of Joy's block, he heard the doped Negro calling, "Whoa! Come in, see Miss Harla O'Horror dancin with her pet. Guarantee one hunner percent real plantation dancin. Ever motherfuckin drink got a guarantee knockout drop. Whoa! Everbody guarantee to catch them some clap off they glass. Hey! Nobody never see nothin like Miss Harla O'Horror Old South pet dancin. Opening night tonight, maybe this be your one and only chance to catch this act. Ooo-wee."

Ignatius saw him through the crowd that was hurrying past the Night of Joy. Apparently no one was heeding the barker's plea. The barker himself had paused in his calling to emit a nimbus formation of smoke. He was wearing tails and a stovepipe hat that rested at an angle above his dark glasses, smiling through the smoke at the people who resisted his appeals.

"Hey! All you peoples draggin along here. Stop and come stick your ass on a Night of Joy stool," he started again. "Night of Joy got genuine color peoples workin below the minimal wage. Whoa! Guarantee plantation atmosphere, got cotton growin right on the stage right in front your eyeball, got a civil right worker gettin his ass beat up between show. Hey!"

"Is Miss O'Hara on yet?" Ignatius slobbered at the barker's elbow.

"Oo-wee!" The fat mother had arrived. In person. "Hey, man, how come you still warin that earrin and scarve? What you suppose to be anyway?"

"Please." Ignatius rattled his cutlass a bit. "I

haven't time to chat. I have no success pointers for you tonight, I'm afraid. Has Miss O'Hara begun?"

"She be startin in a few minute. You better get your ass in there and get you a ringside seat. I talk to the head waiter, he say he have a table all reserve for you."

"Is that true?" Ignatius asked eagerly. "The Nazi proprietress is gone, I hope."

"She jet away to California this afternoon, say Harla O'Horror so good she gonna go dip her ass in the ocean a while and stop worryin about her club."

"Wonderful, wonderful."

"Come on, man, get inside before the show start. Whoa! You don wanna miss one minute. Shit. Harla comin on in a few seconds, go get yourself right down by that motherfuckin stage, see ever goosebump on Miss O'Horror bum."

Jones propelled Ignatius rapidly through the padded door.

Ignatius stumbled into the Night of Joy with such momentum that his smock swirled around his ankles. Even in the darkness he noticed that the Night of Joy was somewhat dirtier than it had been on his previous visit. There was certainly enough dirt on the floor to permit a very limited cotton crop; but he saw no cotton. That must have been one of the Night of Joy's vicious come-ons. He looked about for the headwaiter and saw none, so he lumbered through the few old men scattered about at tables in the gloom and seated himself at a small table directly beneath the stage. His cap looked like a solitary green footlight. At this close range he could perhaps make some gesture to Miss O'Hara or whisper something about Boethius that would attract her attention. She would be overwhelmed when she realized that there was a kindred spirit in the audience.

385

Ignatius glanced about at the handful of empty-eyed men seated in the place. Miss O'Hara certainly had to cast her pearls before a dismal lot of swine, who looked like the type of vague, drawn old men who molested children at matinees.

A three-piece band in the wings of the tiny stage was beginning to thump through *You Are My Lucky Star*. At the moment the stage, which itself looked a bit dirty, was empty of orgiasts. Ignatius looked over at the bar to try to attract some sort of service and caught the eye of the bartender who had served his mother and him. The bartender pretended not to see him. Then Ignatius winked wildly at a woman leaning on the bar, a fortyish Latin who leered a terrifying response with a gold tooth or two. She pried herself loose from the bar before the bartender could stop her and came over to Ignatius, who was huddled against the stage as if it were a warm stove.

"You wanna dreenk, chico?"

Some halitosis filtered through his moustache. He ripped the scarf from his cap and shielded his nostrils with it.

"Thank you, yes," he said in a muffled voice. "A Dr. Nut, if you please. And be certain that it's frosty cold."

"I see what we have," the woman said enigmatically and clopped back to the bar in her straw sandals.

Ignatius watched her speak to the bartender in pantomime. They made a variety of gestures, most of which were directed at Ignatius. At least, Ignatius thought, he would be safe in this den if the sinewy girls were out prowling the Quarter. The bartender and the woman made some more signs; then she clopped back

386

to Ignatius with two bottles of champagne and two glasses.

"We no have Dr. Nut," she said and slammed the tray on the table. "*Mira*, you are owe twenty-four dollar for these champagne."

"This is an outrage!" He directed a few swipes of the cutlass at the woman. "Bring me a coke."

"No coke. No nawtheen. Only champagne." The woman took a seat at the table. "Come on, hawny. Open the champagne. I am very thirsty."

Again the breath wafted toward Ignatius, who pressed the scarf to his nose so tightly that he felt he would suffocate. He would catch some germ from this woman that would speed to his brain and transform him into a mongoloid. Misused Miss O'Hara. Trapped with subhuman women as co-workers. Of necessity, Miss O'Hara's Boethian detachment must be rather lofty. The Latin woman dropped the check in Ignatius' lap.

"Don't you dare touch me!" he bellowed through the scarf.

"*Ave Maria! Que pato!*" the woman said to herself. Then she said, "*Mira*, you are pay now, *maricon*. We throw you out on your big *culo*."

"Such grace," Ignatius mumbled. "Well, I did not come here to drink with you. Now get away from my table." He breathed deeply through the mouth. "And take your champagne with you."

"*Oye, loco*, you are . . ."

The woman's threat was submerged by the band, which emitted a debilitated fanfare of sorts. Lana Lee appeared on the stage in what looked like gold lamé overalls.

"Oh, my God!" Ignatius spluttered. The doped

387

Negro had tricked him. He wanted to bolt from the club, but realized that it would be wiser to wait until the woman had finished and left the stage. In a moment, he was crouched down against the side of the stage. Over his head, the Nazi proprietress was saying, "Welcome, ladies and genitals." It was so dreadful a beginning that Ignatius almost knocked over the table.

"You are pay me now," the woman was demanding, sticking her head under the table to find the face of her customer.

"Shut up, you slut," Ignatius hissed.

The band stumbled into a four-count version of *Sophisticated Lady*. The Nazi woman was screaming, "And now that pure Virgin-ny Belle, Miss Harlett O'Hara." An old man at one of the tables clapped feebly, and Ignatius peered over the rim of the stage and saw that the proprietress was gone. In her place stood a stand decorated with rings. What was Miss O'Hara up to?

Then Darlene swept onstage in a ball gown that trailed yards of nylon net. On her head was a monstrous picture hat and on her arm a monstrous bird. Someone else clapped.

"*Mira*, you are pay me now or else, *cabron*."

"There sure was plenty balls at that ball, but I still got my honor," Darlene said carefully to the bird.

"Oh, my God!" Ignatius bellowed, unable to remain silent any longer. "Is this cretin Harlett O'Hara?"

The cockatoo noticed him before Darlene did, for its beads of eyes had been focusing on Ignatius' hoop of a novelty earring ever since it had come onstage. When Ignatius bellowed, it flapped from Darlene's arm to the stage and squawking, hopping, dashed for Ignatius' head.

"Hey," Darlene cried. "It's the crazyman."

As Ignatius was about to dash from the club, the bird hopped from the stage to his shoulder. It sank its claws into his smock and snagged his earring with its beak.

"Good heavens!" Ignatius leaped up and beat at the bird with his itching paws. What avian menace had depraved Fortuna spun his way? The champagne bottles and the glasses shattered on the floor as he sprang and began staggering to the door.

"Come back here with my cockatoo," Darlene cried.

Lana Lee was on the stage now, screaming. The band had stopped. The few old male patrons moved out of the way of Ignatius, who was floundering around among the little tables making moose calls and beating at the mass of rose feathers welded to his ear and shoulder.

"How in the hell did that character get in here?" Lana Lee asked the confused septuagenarians in the audience. "Where's Jones? Somebody get me that Jones."

"Come here, you big crazyman," Darlene hollered. "On opening night. Why you hadda come here on opening night?"

"Good grief," Ignatius gasped, feeling for the door. In his wake he had left a trail of overturned tables. "How dare you fiends inflict a rabid bird upon your unsuspecting customers? You may expect to be sued in the morning."

"*Come!* You are owe twenty-four dollars to me. You are pay right now."

Ignatius knocked over another table as he and the cockatoo lurched forward. Then he felt the earring

389

loosening, and the cockatoo, the earring firmly in its beak, fell from his shoulder. Terrorized, Ignatius bounced out of the door just ahead of the Latin woman, who was waving the check with great determination.

"Whoa! Hey!"

Ignatius stumbled past Jones, who had never expected the sabotage to assume such dramatic proportions. Gasping, clutching his cemented valve, Ignatius continued forward onto the street and into the path of an oncoming Desire bus. He first heard the people on the sidewalk screaming. Then he heard the pounding tires and the crying brakes, and when he glanced up he was blinded by headlights a few feet from his eyes. The headlights swam and faded from his sight as he fainted.

He would have fallen directly before the bus if Jones hadn't leaped into the street and pulled at the white smock with his two large hands. Ignatius instead fell backward, and the bus, exhaling diesel exhaust, rumbled past an inch or two from his desert boots.

"Is he dead?" Lana Lee asked hopefully, studying the mound of white material lying in the street.

"I am hope not. He is owe twenty-four dollar, the *maricon*."

"Hey, wake up, man," Jones said, blowing some smoke over the inert figure.

The man in the silk suit and homburg stepped from an alleyway, where he had hidden himself when he saw Ignatius enter the Night of Joy. Ignatius' departure from the club had been so violent and rapid that the man had been too startled to act until now.

"Let me take a look at him," the man in the homburg said, bending over and listening to Ignatius' heart. A kettledrum of a thump told him that life still breathed within the yards of white smock. He held

Ignatius' wrist. The Mickey Mouse watch was smashed. "He's okay. He just passed out." The man cleared his throat and ordered weakly, "Everybody back. Give him air."

The street was filled with people and the bus had stopped a few yards down the street, blocking traffic. Suddenly it looked like Bourbon Street at Mardi Gras.

Through the darkness of his glasses Jones looked at the stranger. He looked familiar, like a well-dressed version of someone Jones had seen before. The weak eyes were most familiar. Jones remembered the same weak eyes on top of a red beard. Then he remembered the same eyes under a blue cap in the precinct on the day of the cashew nut incident. He said nothing. A policeman was a policeman. It was always best to ignore them unless they bothered you.

"Where he came from?" Darlene was asking the crowd. The rose cockatoo rested once again on her arm, the earring dangling from its beak like a golden worm. "What a opening night. What we gonna do, Lana?"

"Nothing," Lana said angrily. "Let that character lay there till the street sweeper comes around. Then let me get my hands on Jones."

"Whoa! Hey! That cat force his way in. We was fightin and grapplin, but that mother seem determine to get in the Night of Joy. I was ascare I be rippin this costume you rentin, you be havin to pay for it, Night of Joy be goin broke. Whoa!"

"Shut your smart mouth. I think I'm gonna have to call up all my pals at the precinct. You're fired. Darlene, too. I knew I shouldna let you get on my stage. Get that goddam bird off my sidewalk." Lana turned to the crowd. "Well, folks, now that you're all here, how's about coming into the Night of Joy? We got a class show."

"*Mira*, Lee." The Latin woman inflicted a little halitosis on Lana Lee. "Who is pay the twenty-four dollar for champagne?"

"You're fired, too, you dumb spic." Lana smiled. "Come on in folks, and enjoy a good drink made by our expert mixologists to your exact specifications."

The crowd, however, was craning at the white mound, which was wheezing loudly, and declined the invitation to elegance.

Lana Lee was about to go over and kick the mound into consciousness and get it out of her gutter when the man in the homburg said politely, "I'd like to use your telephone. Maybe I'd better call a ambulance."

Lana looked at the silk suit, the hat, the weak, insecure eyes. She could spot a safe one, a soft touch all right. A rich doctor? A lawyer? She might be able to turn this little fiasco into a profit.

"Sure," she whispered. "Look, you don't wanna waste your evening messing with that character laying in the street. He's some kinda bum. You look like you could use you some fun." She stepped around the white mountain of smock, which was wheezing and snorting volcanically. Somewhere in fantasyland Ignatius was dreaming of a terrified Myrna Minkoff being tried by a court of Taste and Decency and found wanting. A dreadful sentence was about to be pronounced, something guaranteeing physical injury to her person as penance for innumerable offences. Lana Lee got close to the man and reached into her gold lamé overalls. She squatted next to him and surreptitiously flashed the Boethian photograph cupped in her hand. "Take a look at this, baby. How'd you like to spend the evening with that?"

The man in the homburg turned his eyes from Ignatius' whitened face and looked at the woman, the book, the globe, the chalk. He cleared his throat once more and said, "I'm Patrolman Mancuso. Undercover agent. You're under arrest for soliciting and for possession of pornography."

Just then the three members of the defunct ladies' auxiliary, Frieda, Betty, and Liz, stomped into the crowd surrounding Ignatius.

thirteen

IGNATIUS OPENED HIS EYES and saw white floating above him. He had a headache and his ear was throbbing. Then his blue and yellow eyes focused slowly, and, through his headache, he realized that he was looking at a ceiling.

"So you finally woke up, boy," his mother's voice said near him. "Just take a look at this. Now we really ruined."

"Where am I?"

"Don't start acting smart with me, boy. Don't start with me, Ignatius. I'm warning you. I had enough. I mean it. How I'm gonna face people after this?"

Ignatius turned his head and looked about him. He was lying in a little cell formed by screens on either side. He saw a nurse pass by the foot of the bed.

"Good heavens! I'm in a hospital. Who is my doctor? I hope that you have been selfless enough to secure the services of a specialist. And a priest. Have one come. I'll see whether he's acceptable." Ignatius sprayed a little nervous saliva on the sheet that snow-capped the peak of his stomach. He touched his head and felt a bandage plastered over his headache. "Oh, my God! Don't be afraid to tell me, Mother. I can tell from the pain that it must be rather fatal."

"Shut up and take a look at this," Mrs. Reilly

almost shouted, throwing a newspaper on Ignatius' bandage.

"Nurse!"

Mrs. Reilly tore the newspaper from his face and slapped her hand over his moustache.

"Now shut up, crazy, and take a look at this here paper." Her voice was cracking. "We ruined."

Under the headline that said, WILD INCIDENT ON BOURBON STREET, Ignatius saw three photographs lined up together. On the right Darlene with her ball gown was holding the cockatoo and smiling a starlet's smile. On the left Lana Lee covered her face with her hands as she climbed into the rear seat of a squad car already filled with the three cropped heads of the members of the ladies' auxiliary of the Peace Party. Patrolman Mancuso, in a torn suit and a hat with a bent rim, purposefully held open the door of the car. In the center the doped Negro was grinning at what looked like a dead cow lying in the street. Ignatius scrutinized the center photograph through slitted eyes.

"Just look at that," he thundered. "What sort of clods does that newspaper employ on its photographic staff? My features are barely distinguishable."

"Read what it says underneath the pictures, boy." Mrs. Reilly stuck a finger into the newspaper as if she meant to lance the photograph. "Just read it, Ignatius. What you think people are saying on Constantinople Street? Go on, read that out loud to me, boy. A big brawl out on the street, dirty pictures, ladies of the evening. It's all there. Read it, boy."

"I'd rather not. It's probably full of falsification and smear. The yellow journalists doubtlessly suggested all sorts of lip-smacking innuendos." Nevertheless, Ignatius treated the story to a desultory reading.

"Do you mean to tell me that they claim that that wayward bus did not hit me?" he asked angrily. "The very first comment is a lie. Contact Public Service. We must sue."

"Shut up. Read the whole thing."

A stripper's bird had attacked a hot dog vendor wearing a costume. A. Mancuso, undercover, had arrested Lana Lee for soliciting and for possession of and posing for pornography. Burma Jones, porter, had led A. Mancuso to a cabinet under the bar where pornographic materials were discovered. A. Mancuso told reporters that he had been working on the case for some time, that he had already contacted one of the Lee woman's agents. Police suspect that the arrest of the Lee woman broke a citywide high school pornography distribution syndicate. Police found a list of schools in the bar. A. Mancuso said that the agent would be sought. While A. Mancuso was performing the arrest, three women, Club, Steele, and Bumper, emerged from the large crowd before the club and assaulted him. They were also booked. Ignatius Jacques Reilly, thirty, was removed to a hospital to be treated for shock.

"It's our bad luck they had a photographer hanging around doing nothing they could send out to take a picture of you laying in the street like a drunk bum." Mrs. Reilly began to sniffle. "I shoulda known something like this was gonna happen with your dirty pictures and running off dressed up like a Mardi Gras."

"I ran off into the most dismal night of my life," Ignatius sighed. "Fortuna was really spinning drunkenly last night. I doubt whether I can go much farther down." He belched. "May I ask what that cretin nemesis of a policeman was doing on the scene?"

"Last night after you run off I rung up Santa and

told her to get Angelo at the precinct and for him to go see what you was doing down on St. Peter Street. I heard you give a address to that taxi man."

"How clever."

"I thought you was going to a meeting with a buncha communiss. Was I wrong. Angelo says you was hanging around with some funny people."

"In other words, you were having me trailed," Ignatius screamed. "My own mother!"

"Attacked by a bird," Mrs. Reilly wept. "That hadda happen to you, Ignatius. Nobody never gets attacked by a bird."

"Where is that bus driver? He must be indicted immediately."

"You just fainted, stupid."

"Then why this bandage? I don't feel at all well. I must have damaged some vital part when I fell to the street."

"You just scraped your head a little. They's nothing wrong with you. They took Xrays."

"Have people been fooling with my body while I was unconscious? You might have had the good taste to stop them. Heaven knows where these salacious medical people have been probing." Ignatius now realized that in addition to the head and ear, an erection had been bothering him ever since he had awakened. It was demanding attention. "Would you mind leaving my booth for a moment while I inspect myself to see whether I've been mishandled? Five minutes should be sufficient."

397

"Look, Ignatius." Mrs. Reilly rose from the chair and grabbed Ignatius by the collar of the clownlike dotted pajamas that had been put on him. "Don't act smart with me or I'll slap your face off. Angelo told me all about it. A boy with your education bumming around with funny people down in the Quarter, going into a barroom to look for a lady of the evening." Mrs. Reilly cried anew. "We just lucky the whole thing's not in the paper. We'd have to move outta town."

"You're the one who introduced my innocent being to that den of a bar. Actually, it's all the fault of that dreadful girl, Myrna. She must be punished for her misdeeds."

"Myrna?" Mrs. Reilly sobbed. "She ain't even in town. I heard enough of your crazy stories already about how she got you fired outta Levy Pants. You can't do this to me no more. You're crazy, Ignatius. Even if I gotta say it, my own child's out his mind."

"You look rather haggard. Why don't you push someone aside and crawl into one of the beds around here and take a nap. Call again in about an hour."

"I been up all night. When Angelo rang me up and said you was in the hospital, I almost took a stroke. I almost fell down on the kitchen floor right on my head. I coulda split my skull wide open. Then I run into my room to get dressed and I sprain my ankle. I almost got in a wreck driving over here."

"Not another wreck," Ignatius gasped. "I would have to go to work in the salt mines this time."

"Here, stupid. Angelo says to give this to you."

Mrs. Reilly reached down next to her chair and picked from the floor the large volume of *The Consolation of Philosophy*. She aimed one of its corners at Ignatius' stomach.

"Awff," Ignatius gurgled.

"Angelo found it in that barroom last night," Mrs. Reilly said boldly. "Somebody stole it off him in the toilet."

398

"Oh, my God! This has all been arranged," Ignatius screamed, rattling the huge edition in his paws. "I see it all now. I told you long ago that that mongoloid Mancuso was our nemesis. Now he has struck his final blow. How innocent I was to lend him this book. How I've been duped." He closed his bloodshot eyes and slobbered incoherently for a moment. "Taken in by a Third Reich strumpet hiding her depraved face behind *my* very own book, the very basis of my worldview. Oh, Mother, if only you knew how cruelly I've been tricked by a conspiracy of subhumans. Ironically, the book of Fortuna is itself bad luck. Oh, Fortuna, you degenerate wanton!"

"Shut up," Mrs. Reilly shouted, her powdered face lined by anger. "You want the whole recovery ward coming in here? What you think Miss Annie's gonna say now? How I'm gonna face people, you stupid, crazy Ignatius? Now this hospital wants twenty dollars before I can take you outta here. The ambulance driver couldn't take you to the Charity like a nice man. No. He has to come dump you here in a pay hospital. Where you think I got twenty dollars? I gotta meet a note on your trumpet tomorrow. I gotta pay that man for his building."

"That is outrageous. You will certainly not pay twenty dollars. It is highway robbery. Now run along home and leave me here. It's rather peaceful. I may recover eventually. It's exactly what my psyche needs at the moment. When you have a chance, bring me some pencils and the looseleaf folder you'll find on my desk. I must record this trauma while it's still fresh in my mind. You have my permission to enter my room. Now, if you'll pardon me, I must rest."

"Rest? And pay another twenty dollars for another

day? Get up out that bed. I called up Claude. He's coming down here and pay your bill."

"Claude? Who in the world is Claude."

"A man I know."

"What has become of you?" Ignatius gasped. "Well, understand one thing right now. No strange man is going to pay my hospital bill. I shall stay here until honest money buys my freedom."

"Get up out that bed," Mrs. Reilly hollered. She snatched at the pajamas, but the body was sunken into the mattress like a meteor. "Get up before I smack your fat face off."

When he saw his mother's purse rising over his head, he sat up.

"Oh, my God! You're wearing your bowling shoes," Ignatius cast a pink and blue and yellow eye over the side of the bed down past his mother's hanging slip and drooping cotton stockings. "Only you would wear bowling shoes to your child's sick bed."

But his mother did not rise to the challenge. She had the determination, the superiority that comes with intense anger. Her eyes were steely, her lips thin and firm.

Everything was going wrong.

II

Mr. Clyde looked at the morning paper and fired Reilly. The big ape's career as a vendor was finished. Why was that baboon wearing his outfit when he was off duty? One ape like Reilly could demolish ten years of trying to build up a decent commercial name. Hot dog vendors had an image problem already without one of them passing out in the street by a whorehouse.

Mr. Clyde and the cauldron bubbled and boiled. If Reilly tried to show up at Paradise Vendors, Incorporated, again, he would really get it in the throat with the fork. But there were those smocks and that pirate gear. Reilly must have smuggled the pirate gimmicks out of the garage the afternoon before. He would have to contact the big ape after all, if only to tell him not to come around. You really couldn't expect to get your uniforms back from an animal like Reilly.

Mr. Clyde telephoned the number on Constantinople Street several times and got no answer. Maybe they had put him away somewhere. The big ape's mother must be dead drunk on the floor somewhere. Christ only knew what she was like. It must be quite a family.

III

Dr. Talc had been having a miserable week. Somehow the students had found one of those threats that that psychotic graduate student had flooded him with a few years before. How it got into their hands he didn't know. The results were already awful. An underground of rumors about the note was slowly spreading; he was becoming the butt of the campus. At a cocktail party one of his colleagues had finally explained to him the reason for the laughter and whispering that were disrupting his previously respectful classes.

That business in the note about "misleading and perverting the young" had been badly misunderstood and misinterpreted. He wondered if he might have to explain to the administration eventually. And that phrase "underdeveloped testicles." Dr. Talc cringed. Bringing the whole matter into the open might be the

401

best plan, but that would mean trying to find that former student, who was the sort who would deny all responsibility anyway. Perhaps he should simply try to describe what Mr. Reilly had been like. Dr. Talc saw again Mr. Reilly with his massive muffler and that awful girl anarchist with the valise who traveled around with Mr. Reilly and littered the campus with leaflets. Fortunately she hadn't stayed at the college too long, although that Reilly seemed as if he were planning to make himself a fixture on the campus like the palm trees and the benches.

Dr. Talc had had them both in separate classes one grim semester, during which they had disrupted his lectures with strange noises and impertinent, venomous questions that no one, aside from God, could possibly have answered. He shuddered. In spite of everything, he must reach Reilly and extract an explanation and confession. One look at Mr. Reilly and the students would understand that the note was the meaningless fantasy of a sick mind. He could even let the administration look at Mr. Reilly. The solution was, after all, really a physical one: producing Mr. Reilly in the abundant flesh.

Dr. Talc sipped the vodka and V-8 juice that he always had after a night of heavy social drinking and looked at his newspaper. At least the people in the Quarter were having rowdy fun. He sipped his drink and remembered the incident of Mr. Reilly's dumping all of those examination papers on the heads of that freshman demonstration beneath the windows of the faculty office building. The administration would remember it, too. He smiled complacently and looked at the paper again. The three photographs were hilarious. Common, bawdy people—at a distance—had always amused him. He read the article and choked, spitting liquid onto his smoking jacket.

How had Reilly ever sunk so low? He had been eccentric as a student, but now. . . . How much worse the rumors would be if it were discovered that the note had been written by a hot dog vendor. Reilly was the sort who would come to the campus with his wagon and try to sell hot dogs right before the Social Studies Building. He would deliberately turn the affair into a three-ring circus. It would be a disgraceful farce in which he, Talc, would become the clown.

Dr. Talc put down his paper and his glass and covered his face with his hands. He would have to live with that note. He would deny everything.

IV

Miss Annie looked at her morning newspaper and turned red. She had been wondering why it was so quiet over at the Reilly household this morning. Well, this was the last straw. Now the neighborhood was getting a bad name. She couldn't take it anymore. Those people had to move. She'd get the neighbors to sign a petition.

V

Patrolman Mancuso looked at the newspaper again. Then he held it to his chest and the flashbulb popped. He had brought his own Brownie Holiday camera to the precinct and asked the sergeant to photograph him against certain official backdrops: the sergeant's desk, the steps of the precinct, a squad car, a traffic patrolwoman whose specialty was school zone speeders.

When there was only one exposure left, Patrolman

Mancuso decided to combine two of the props for a dramatic finale. While the traffic patrolwoman, pretending to be Lana Lee, climbed into the rear of the squad car grimacing and shaking a vengeful fist, Patrolman Mancuso faced the camera with his newspaper and frowned sternly.

"Okay, Angelo, is that all?" the patrolwoman asked, eager to get to a nearby school before the morning speed zone hours ended.

"Thank you very much, Gladys," Patrolman Mancuso said. "My kids wanted to get some more pictures to show to they little friends."

"Well, sure," Gladys called, hurrying out of the precinct yard, her shoulder bag bursting with black speeding tickets. "I guess they got a right to be proud of they poppa. I'm glad I could help you out, honey. Anytime you want to take you some more pictures, just gimme the word."

The sergeant tossed the last flashbulb into a trash can and clamped his hand on Patrolman Mancuso's vertical shoulder.

"Single-handed you break up the city's most active high school pornography racket." He slapped his hand on the incline of Patrolman Mancuso's shoulder blade. "Mancuso, of all people, brings in a woman even our best plainclothesmen couldn't fool. Mancusco, I find out, has been working on this case on the q.t. Mancuso can identify one of her agents. Who's the person really been going out on his own all the time looking for characters like those three girls and trying to bring them in? Mancuso, that's who."

Patrolman Mancuso's olive skin flushed slightly, except in limited areas scratched by the Peace Party auxiliary. There it was simply red.

"Just luck," Patrolman Mancuso offered, clearing his throat of some invisible phlegm. "Somebody gimme a lead to the place. Then that Burma Jones told me to look in that cabinet under the bar."

"You staged a one-man raid, Angelo."

Angelo? He turned a spectrum of shades between orange and violet.

"I wouldn't be surprised if you was to get a promotion for this," the sergeant said. "You been a patrolman a pretty long time. And just a couple days ago I was thinking you was a horse's ass. How's about that? What do you say to that, Mancuso?"

Patrolman Mancuso cleared his throat very violently.

"Can I have my camera back?" he asked almost incoherently when his larynx was at last clear.

VI

Santa Battaglia held the newspaper up to her mother's picture and said, "How you like that, babe? How you like the way your grandson Angelo made good? You like that, darling?" She pointed to another photograph. "How you like poor Irene's crazy boy laying there in the gutter like a washed-up whale? Ain't that sad? That girl's gotta get that boy put away this time. You think any man's gonna marry Irene with that big bum laying around the house? Of course not."

Santa snatched at her mother's picture and gave it a moist smack. "Take it easy, babe. I'm praying for you."

405

VII

Claude Robichaux looked at the newspaper with a heavy heart as he rode the streetcar to the hospital. How could that big boy disgrace a fine, sweet woman like Irene? Already she was pale and tired from worrying about her son. Santa was right: that son of Irene's had to be treated before he brought any more disgrace to his wonderful mother.

This time it was only twenty dollars. Next time it might be much more. Even with a nice pension and some properties, a person couldn't afford a stepson like that.

But worst of all was the disgrace.

VIII

George was pasting the article in the Junior Achievement scrapbook that was one of his mementos from his last semester at school. He pasted it on an empty page between his biology drawing of the aorta of a duck and his civics project on the history of the Constitution. He had to give it to that Mancuso guy: he was really on the ball. George wondered if his name was on that list the cops had found in the cabinet. If it was, it might be a good idea to go visit his uncle who lived on the coast. Even then, they'd have his name. He really didn't have enough money to go anywhere. The best thing was to stay at home for a while. That Mancuso might spot him if he went downtown.

George's mother, vacuuming on the other side of the living room, hopefully watched her son work on his school scrapbook. Maybe he was getting interested in school again. She and his father didn't seem to be able to do anything with him. What chance did a boy without a high school education have nowadays? What could he do?

She turned off the vacuum cleaner and answered the doorbell. George was studying the photographs and wondering what that vendor had been doing at the Night of Joy. He couldn't have been some kind of police agent. Anyway, George hadn't told him where the pictures came from. There was something funny about the whole business.

"The police?" George heard his mother asking at the door. "You must have the wrong apartment."

George started for the kitchen before he realized that there was nowhere to go. The apartments in the housing project had only one door.

IX

Lana Lee tore the newspaper into shreds and then tore the shreds into smaller shreds. When the matron stopped by the cell to tell her to clean it up, one of the members of the ladies' auxiliary, all three of whom were sharing the cell, said to the matron, "Beat it. We're the ones living in this place. We like paper on the floor."

"Shove off," Liz added.

"Get lost," Betty said.

"I'll take care of this cell all right," the matron answered. "You four have been making noise ever since you come in last night."

"Get me out this goddam hole," Lana Lee screamed at the matron. "I can't take another minute with these three bats."

"Hey," Frieda said to her two apartment mates. "Doll doesn't like us."

"It's people like you been ruining the Quarter," Lana told Frieda.

"Shut up," Liz said to her.

"Can it, sweets," Betty said.

"Get me outta here," Lana screamed through the bars. "I just been through one fucking hell of a night with these three creeps. I got my rights. You can't stick me in here."

The matron smiled at her and walked away.

"Hey!" Lana screamed down the corridor. "Come back here."

"Take it easy, dearie," Frieda advised. "Quit rocking the boat. Now come on and show us those pictures of yourself you got hidden in your bra."

"Yeah," Liz said.

"Get out the snapshots, doll," Betty ordered. "We're tired of looking at these frigging walls."

The three girls lunged for Lana at the same time.

X

Dorian Green turned one of his severe calling cards over and printed on the reverse side: "Stunning apartment for rent. Apply at 1A." He stepped out onto the flagstone sidewalk and tacked the card to the bottom of one of the black patent leather shutters. The girls would be gone for quite a while this time. Police were always so adamant about second offenses. It was unfortunate that the girls had never been very sociable with their fellow residents in the Quarter; someone would certainly have pointed out that marvelous patrolman to them, and they would not have made the fatal mistake of attacking a member of the police force.

But the girls were so impulsive and aggressive.

Without them, Dorian felt that he and his building were completely unprotected. He took special care to lock his wrought iron gate securely. Then he returned to his apartment to finish the job of cleaning up the litter left from the kickoff rally. It had been the most fabulous party of his career: at the height of it Timmy had fallen from a chandelier and sprained his ankle.

Dorian picked up a cowboy boot from which a heel had been broken and dropped it into a wastebasket, wondering whether that impossible Ignatius J. Reilly were all right. Some people were simply too much to bear. Gypsy Queen's sweet mother must have been heartbroken over the dreadful newspaper publicity.

XI

Darlene cut her picture out of the paper and put it on the kitchen table. What an opening night. At least she had received a little publicity from it.

She picked up her Harlett O'Hara gown from the sofa and hung it in the closet while the cockatoo watched her and squawked a bit from its perch. Jones had certainly taken over when he found out that man was a cop, leading him right over to the cabinet under the bar. Now she and Jones were both out of a job. The Night of Joy was out of business. Lana Lee was out of circulation. That Lana. Posing for French pictures. Anything for a buck.

Darlene looked at the golden earring that the cockatoo had brought home. Lana had been right all along. That big crazyman was really the kiss of death. He sure treated his poor momma cruel. That poor lady.

Darlene sat down to ponder job possibilities. The cockatoo flapped and squawked until she stuck the novelty earring, its favorite toy, in its beak. Then the phone rang, and when she answered it, a man said, "Listen, you got some great publicity. Now I run a club in the five hundred block of Bourbon, and . . ."

XII

Jones spread the newspaper on the bar of Mattie's Ramble Inn and blew some smoke at it.

"Whoa!" he said to Mr. Watson. "You sure gimme a good idea with all this sabotage crap. Now I sabotage myself right back to bein a vagran. Hey!"

"It look like this sabotage go off like a nucular bum."

"That fat freak a guarantee one hunner percen nucular bum. Shit. Drop him on somebody, everybody gettin caught in the fallout, gettin their ass blowed up. Ooo-wee. Night of Joy really turn into a zoo las night. Firs we get a bird, then the fat mother come draggin along, then three cats look like they jus excape from gym. Shit. Everybody fightin and scratchin and screamin and that big fat freak layin in the gutter like he daid, peoples fightin and cussin and rollin all aroun that big cat pass out in the street. Look like a barroom fight in a western movie, look like a gang rumble. We got us a big crowd on Bourbon Street look like we could have us a football game. Po-lice drivin up draggin off that Lee Bastar. Hey! It turn out she don have no pal at the precinc anyways. Maybe they be haulin in some of them orphan she been sponsorin. Whoa! That paper sure sending out plenny mothers takin pictures and axin me all about wha happen. Who say a color cat cain get his picture on the front page? Ooo-wee! Whoa! I gonna be the mos famous vagran in the city. I tell that Patrolman

410

Mancusa, I say, 'Hey, now this cathouse shut down, how's about tellin your frien on the force I help you out so maybe they don star draggin my ass off for vagran?' Who wanna get stuck in Angola with Lana Lee? She was bad enough on the outside. Shit."

"You got any plan for gettin you a job, Jones?"

Jones blew a dark cloud, a storm warning, and said, "After the kinda job I jus had workin below the minimal wage, I really deserve a pay vacation. Ooo-wee. Where I gonna fin me another job? Too many color mothers draggin they ass aroun the street already. Whoa! Gettin your ass gainfully employ ain exactly the easies thing in the worl. I ain the only cat got him a problem. That Darlene gal ain gonna have no easy time gettin herself and that ball eagle gainfully employ. Peoples see wha happen the firs time she stick her ass on a stage, they be throwin water in her face if she be comin aroun lookin for work. See wha I mean? You drop somebody like that fat mother for sabotage, plenny innocen peoples like Darlene gettin theyselves screwed. Like Miss Lee all the time sayin, that fat freak ruin *everybody* inves'men. Darlene and her ball eagle probly starin at one another right now sayin, 'Whoa! We really boffo smash for openin night. Hey! We real openin *big*.' I plenny sorry that sabotage goin off in Darlene face, but when I see that big mother, I couldn resis. I knowed he make some kinda esplosion in that Night of Joy. Ooo-wee. He really go off. Hey!"

"You pretty lucky them po-lice didn't take you in, too, workin in that bar."

"That Patrolman Mancusa say he appreciate showin him that cabinet. He say, 'Us mothers on the force need peoples like you, help us out.' He say, 'Peoples like you be helpin me get ahead.' I say, 'Whoa! Be

411

sure and tell that to your frien at the precinc, they don star snatchin my ass for vagran.' He say, 'I sure will. Everybody at the precinc be appreciatin wha you done, man.' Now them po-lice mothers *appreciate* me. Hey! Maybe I be gettin some kinda awar. Whoa!" Jones aimed some smoke over Mr. Watson's tan head. "That Lee bastar really got her some snapshot of herself in that cabinet. Patrolman Mancusa starin at them pictures, his eyeballs about to fall out on the floor. He sayin, 'Whoa! Hey! Wow!' He sayin, 'Boy, I really be gettin ahead now.' I say to myself, 'Maybe some peoples be gettin ahead. Some other peoples be turnin vagran again. Some peoples ain gonna be gainfully employ below the minimal wage after tonight. Some peoples be draggin they ass all aroun town somewheres, be buyin me air condition, color TV.' Shit. Firs I'm a glorify broom expert, now I'm vagran."

"Things can always be worse off."

"Yeah. You can say that, man. You got you a little business, got you a son teachin school probly got him a bobby-cue set, Buick, air condition, TV. Whoa! I ain even got me a transmitter radio. Night of Joy salary keepin peoples below the air-condition level." Jones formed a philosophical cloud. "But you right in a way there, Watson. Things maybe be worse off. Maybe I be that fat mother. Whoa! Whatever gonna happen to somebody like that? Hey!"

XIII

Mr. Levy settled into the yellow nylon couch and unfolded his paper, which was delivered to the coast every morning at a higher subscription rate. Having the couch all to himself was wonderful, but the disappearance of Miss Trixie was not enough to brighten his spirits. He had spent a sleepless night. Mrs. Levy was on her exercising board treating her plumpness to some early morning bouncing. She was silent, occupied with some plans for the Foundation which she was writing on a sheet of paper held against the undulating front section of the board. Putting her pencil down for a moment, she reached down to select a cookie from the box on the floor. And the cookies were why Mr. Levy had spent a wakeful night. He and Mrs. Levy had driven out through the pines to see Mr. Reilly at Mandeville and had not only found he was not there but had also been treated very rudely by an authority of the place who had taken them for pranksters. Mrs. Levy had looked something like a prankster with her golden-white hair, her sunglasses with the blue lenses, the aquamarine mascara that made a ring around the blue lenses like a halo. Sitting there in the sports car before the main building at Mandeville with the huge box of Dutch cookies on her lap, she must have made the authority a little suspicious, Mr. Levy thought. But she had taken it all very calmly. Finding Mr. Reilly did not seem to bother Mrs. Levy particularly, it seemed. Her husband was beginning to sense that she did not especially want him to find Reilly, that somewhere in some corner of her mind she was hoping that Abelman would win the libel suit so that she could flaunt their resulting poverty in the face of Susan and Sandra as their father's ultimate failure. That woman had a devious mind that was only predictable when she scented an opportunity to vanquish her husband. Now he was beginning to wonder which side she was on, his or Abelman's.

413

He had asked Gonzalez to cancel his spring practice reservations. This Abelman case had to be cleared up. Mr. Levy straightened his newspaper and realized again that, were his digestive system able to take it, he should have given his time to supervising Levy Pants. Things like this would not happen; life could be peaceful. But just the name, just the three syllables of "Levy Pants," caused acid complications in his chest. Perhaps he should have changed the name. Perhaps he should have changed Gonzalez. The office manager was so loyal, though. He loved his thankless, low-salaried job. You couldn't just kick him out. Where would he find another job? Even more important, who would want to replace him? One good reason for keeping Levy Pants open was keeping Gonzalez employed. Mr. Levy tried, but he could think of no other reason for keeping the place open. Gonzalez might commit suicide if the factory were shut down. There was a human life to consider. Too, no one apparently wanted to buy the place.

Leon Levy could have named his monument "Levy Trousers." That wasn't too bad. Throughout his life, but especially when he was a child, Gus Levy had said, "Levy Pants," and had always received a standard reply, "He does?" When he was about twenty, he had mentioned to his father that a change of title might help their business, and his father had moaned, " 'Levy Pants' all of a sudden isn't good enough for you? The food you're eating is 'Levy Pants.' The car you're driving is 'Levy Pants.' *I* am 'Levy Pants.' This is gratitude? This is a child's devotion? Next I should change *my* name. Shut up, bum. Go play with the autos and the flappers. Already I got a Depression on my hands, I don't need smart advice from you. Better you should give with the advice to Hoover. You should go tell him to change his name to *Schlemiel*. Out of my office! Shut up!"

Gus Levy looked at the pictures and the article on the front page and whistled through his teeth, "Oh, boy."

"What is it, Gus? A problem? Are you having a problem? All night you were awake. I could hear the whirlpool bath going all night. You're going to have a crackup. Please go to Lenny's doctor before you become violent."

"I just found Mr. Reilly."

"I guess you're happy."

"Aren't you? Look, he's in the papers."

"Really? Bring it over here. I've always wondered about that young idealist. I guess he's received some civic award."

"Just the other day you were saying he was a psycho."

"If he was clever enough to send us over to Mandeville like two stooges, he's not that psycho. Even somebody like the idealist can play a joke on you."

Mrs. Levy looked at the two women, the bird, the grinning doorman.

"Where is he? I don't see any idealist." Mr. Levy indicated the stricken cow in the street. "That's him? In the gutter? This is tragic. Carousing, drunken, hopeless, already a bloated derelict. Mark him down in your book next to Miss Trixie and me as another life you've wrecked."

"A bird bit him on the ear or something crazy. Here, look at the bunch of police characters in these pictures. I told you he had a police record. Those people are his buddies. Strippers and pimps and pornographers."

"Once he was dedicated to idealistic causes. Now look at him. Don't worry. You'll pay for all of this

415

someday. In a few months, when Abelman has finished with you, you'll be out on the streets again with a wagon like your father. You'll learn what happens when you play games with somebody like Abelman, when you operate a business like a playboy. Susan and Sandra will go into shock when they find out they don't have a penny to their name. Will they give you the big go-by. Gus Levy, ex-father."

"Well, I'm going into town right now to speak with this Reilly. I'll get this crazy letter business straightened out."

"Ho ho. Gus Levy, detective. Don't make me laugh. You probably wrote that letter one day after you won at the track and felt good. I knew it would end like this."

"You know, I think you're actually looking forward to Abelman's libel suit. You actually want to see me ruined, even if you go down with me."

Mrs. Levy yawned and said, "Can I fight what you've been leading up to all your life? This really proves to the girls that what I've said about you all along was right. The more I think about Abelman's suit, the more I realize that the whole thing is inevitable, Gus. Thank goodness my mother has some money. I always knew I'd have to go back to her someday. She'll probably have to give up San Juan, though. You can't keep Susan and Sandra alive for peanuts."

"Oh, shut up."

"You're telling me to shut up?" Mrs. Levy bounced up and down, up and down. "I'm supposed to watch your smashup in silence? I have to make plans for myself and my daughters. I mean, life goes on, Gus. I can't end up on skid row with you. We can only be grateful that your father has left us. If he had lived to see Levy

Pants lost because of some practical joke, you'd really pay. Believe me. Leon Levy would have you run out of the country. That man had courage, determination. And whatever happens, the Leon Levy Foundation goes through. Even if Mother and I have to do without, I'm making those awards. I'm going to honor and reward people who have the kind of courage and bravery that I saw in your father. I won't let you drag his name down with you on your journey to skid row. After Abelman's finished, you'll be lucky to get hired as a water boy on one of those teams you love so much. Boy, will you have to work then, running around with a bucket and a sponge like a bum. But don't feel sorry for yourself. You had it coming."

Now Mr. Levy knew that his wife's strange logic made it necessary for him to be ruined. She wanted to see Abelman victorious; she would see in the victory some peculiar justification. Since his wife had read the letter from Abelman, her mind must have been working over the matter from every angle. Every minute that she was pedaling the exercycle or bouncing on the board, her system of logic was probably telling her more and more convincingly that Abelman must win the suit. It would be not only Abelman's victory, but hers, also. Every conversational and epistolary roadsign and guidepost that she had held up before the girls pointed to their father's final, terrible failure. Mrs. Levy couldn't afford to be disproved. She *needed* the $500 thousand libel suit. She wasn't even interested in his speaking with Reilly. The Abelman case had passed from a purely material and physical plane to an ideological and spiritual one where universal and cosmic forces decreed that Gus Levy must lose, that a childless and

417

desolate Gus Levy must wander endlessly with bucket and sponge.

"Well, I'm going after Reilly," Mr. Levy said finally.

"Such determination. I can hardly believe it. Don't worry, you won't be able to pin anything on the young idealist. He's too clever. He'll play another joke on you. Just watch. Another wild-goose chase. Back to Mandeville. This time they'll keep you there, a middle-aged man driving a little toy of a collegian's sports car."

"I'm going right to his house."

Mrs. Levy folded her Foundation notes and turned off her board, saying, "Well, if you're going to town, take me with you. I'm worried about Miss Trixie since Gonzalez reported that she bit that gangster's hand. I must see her. Her old hostility toward Levy Pants is out in the open again."

"Do you still want to play around with that senile bag? Haven't you tormented her enough already?"

"Even a little good deed you don't want me to do. Your type isn't even in the psychology books. You should at least go to Lenny's doctor for *his* sake. Once your case was in the psychiatric journals, they'd be inviting him to Vienna to speak. You'd make him a famous man just like that crippled girl or whoever it was put Freud on the map."

While Mrs. Levy was blinding herself with layers of aquamarine eyeshadow in preparation for her errand of mercy, he got the sports car out of the monumental three-car garage, built like a substantial rustic carriage house, and sat looking over the calm, rippling bay. Little darts of heartburn pricked about in his chest. Reilly had to make some kind of confession. Abelman's shysters could wipe him out; he couldn't give his wife the satisfaction of seeing that happen. If Reilly would confess to writing the letter, if somehow he could come out of this all right, he would change. He would vow to become a new person. He might even give the company a little supervision. It was only sensible and practical to supervise that place. A neglected Levy Pants was like a neglected child: it could turn out to be a delinquent, something that created all sorts of problems that a little nurture, a little care and feeding could prevent. The more you stayed away from Levy Pants, the more it plagued you. Levy Pants was like a congenital defect, an inherited curse.

"Everyone I know has a fine big sedan," Mrs. Levy said as she got into the little car. "Not you. No. You have to own a kid's car that costs more than a Cadillac and blows my hair all around."

To prove her point, a lacquered strand flew stiffly out in the breeze as they roared out onto the coast highway. Both were silent during the journey through the marshes. Mr. Levy nervously considered his future. Mrs. Levy contentedly considered hers, her aquamarine lashes flapping calmly in the wind. At last they roared into the city, Mr. Levy's speed increasing as he felt himself getting closer to the Reilly kook. Hanging around with that crowd in the Quarter. Goodness only knew what Reilly's personal life was like. One crazy incident after another, insanity upon insanity.

"I think I've finally analyzed your problem," Mrs. Levy said when they slowed down in the city traffic. "This wild driving was the clue. A light has dawned. Now I know why you've drifted, why you don't have any ambition, why you've thrown a business down the drain." Mrs. Levy paused for effect. "You have the death wish."

419

"For the last time today, shut up."

"Fighting, hostility, resentment," Mrs. Levy said happily. "It will all end very badly, Gus."

Because it was Saturday, Levy Pants had ceased its assaults upon the concept of free enterprise for the weekend. The Levys drove past the factory, which, open or closed, looked equally moribund from the street. Weak smoke of the type produced by burning leaves rose from one of the antennae of smokestacks. Mr. Levy pondered the smoke. Some worker must have left one of the cutting tables sticking in a furnace on Friday evening. Someone might even be in there burning leaves. Stranger things had happened. Mrs. Levy herself, during a ceramics phase, had once commandeered one of the furnaces for a kiln.

When they had passed the factory and Mrs. Levy had gazed at it and said, "Sad, sad," they turned along the river and stopped before a dazed-looking wooden apartment building across from the Desire Street wharf. A trail of scraps beckoned the passerby to climb the unpainted front steps toward some goal within the building.

"Don't take too long," Mrs. Levy said while she was going through the heaving and lifting process that was necessary to remove one's body from the sports car. She took with her the sampled box of Dutch cookies that had originally been intended for the patient at Mandeville. "I've just about had it with this project. Maybe she'll keep busy with the cookies and I won't have to try to make much conversation." She smiled at her husband. "Good luck with the idealist. Don't let him play another trick on you."

Mr. Levy sped off uptown. At a stoplight he looked at Reilly's address in the morning newspaper folded and

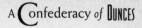

stored in the well between the bucket seats. He followed the river on Tchoupitoulas and turned at Constantinople, bouncing along in Constantinople's potholes until he found the miniature house. Could the huge kook live in such a dollhouse? How did he get in and out of the front door?

Mr. Levy climbed the steps and read the "Peace at Any Price" sign tacked to one of the porch posts and the "Peace to Men of Good Will" sign tacked to the front of the house. This was the place all right. Inside a telephone was ringing.

"They not home!" a woman screamed from behind a shutter next door. "They telephone's been ringing all morning."

The front shutters of the adjoining house opened and a harried-looking woman came out on the porch and rested her red elbows on her porch rail.

"Do you know where Mr. Reilly is?" Mr. Levy asked her.

"All I know is he's all over this morning's paper. Where he oughta be is in a asylum. My nerves is shot to hell. When I moved next door to them people, I was signing my death warrant."

"Does he live here alone? A woman answered the phone once when I called."

"That musta been his momma. Her nerves is shot, too. She musta went to get him out the hospital or wherever they got him."

"Do you know Mr. Reilly well?"

"Ever since he was a kid. His momma was sure proud of him. All the sisters at school loved him he was so precious. Look how he ended up, laying in a gutter. Well, they better start thinking about moving off my block. I can't take it no more. They'll really be arguing now."

"Let me ask you something. You know Mr. Reilly well. Do you think he's very irresponsible or maybe even dangerous?"

"What you want with him?" Miss Annie's bleary eyes narrowed. "He's in some other kinda trouble?"

"I'm Gus Levy. He used to work for me."

"Yeah? You don't say. That crazy Idnatius was sure proud of that job he had at that place. I useta hear him telling his momma how he was really making good. Yeah, he made good. A few weeks and he was fired. Well, if he worked for you, you really know him good."

Had that poor Reilly kook really been proud of Levy Pants? He had always said that he was. That was one good sign of his insanity.

"Tell me. Hasn't he been in trouble with the police? Doesn't he have some kind of police record?"

"His momma had a policeman coming around her. A regular undercover agent. But not that Idnatius. For one thing his momma likes her little nip. I don't see her drunk much lately, but for a while there she was really going good. One day I look out in the backyard and she had herself all tangled up in a wet sheet hanging off the line. Mister, it's already took ten years off my life living next to them people. Noise! Banjos and trumpets and screaming and hollering and the TV. Them Reillys oughta go move out in the country somewheres on a farm. Every day I gotta take six, seven aspirin." Miss Annie reached inside the neckline of her housedress to find some strap that had slipped from her shoulder. "Lemme tell you something. I gotta be fair. That Idnatius was okay until that big dog of his died. He had this big dog useta bark right under my window. That's when my nerves first started to go. Then the dog dies. Well, I think, now maybe I'll get me some peace and quiet. But no. Idnatius is got the dog laid out in his momma's front parlor with some flowers stuck in its paw. That's when him and his momma first started all that fighting. To tell you the truth, I think that's when she started drinking. So Idnatius goes over to the priest and ax him to come say something over the dog. Idnatius was planning on some kinda funeral. You know? The priest says no, of course, and I think that's when Idnatius left the Church. So big Idnatius puts on his own funeral. A big fat high school boy oughta know better. You see that cross?" Mr. Levy looked hopelessly at the rotting Celtic cross in the frontyard. "That where it all happened. He had about two dozen little kids standing around in that yard watching him. And Idnatius had on a big cape like Superman and they was candles burning all over. The whole time his momma was screaming out the front door for him to throw the dog in the garbage can and get in the house. Well, that's when things started going bad around here. Then Idnatius was at college for about ten years. His momma almost went broke. She even hadda sell the piana they had. Well, I didn't mind that. You oughta seen this girl he pickes up at college. I says to myself, 'Well, good. Maybe that Idnatius is gonna get married and move out.' Was I wrong. All they done is sit in his room. It seem like every night she and him was putting on a regular hootenanny. The things I useta hear through my window! 'Put down that skirt.' and 'Get off my bed.' And 'How dare you? I'm a virgin.' It was awful. I went on aspirins twenty-four hours a day. Well, that girl done left. I can't blame her. She musta been funny to hang around with him anyways." Miss Annie reached in the opposite direction for another strap. "Of all the houses in the city, how come I hadda move in here? Tell me that."

Mr. Levy could think of no reason for her having moved to this particular location. But the Ignatius Reilly story had made him depressed, and he wished he were away from Constantinople Street.

"Well," the woman rushed on, eager for the audience to hear her tale of suffering, "this stuff in the paper's the last straw. Look at the bad publicity the block's got now. If they start anything now, I'm gonna call up the police and get him put under a peace bond. I can't take it no more. My nerves is shot to hell. Even when that Idnatius takes a bath, it sounds like a flood's coming in my own house. I think all my pipes is busted. I'm too old. I had enough with them people." Miss Annie glanced over Mr. Levy's shoulder. "It's been nice talking to you, mister. So long."

She raced back into her house and slammed her shutters. Her sudden disappearance confused Mr. Levy as much as her strange biography of Mr. Reilly had. What a neighborhood. Levy's Lodge had always been a barrier against knowing people like this. Then Mr. Levy saw the old Plymouth trying to dock at the curb, scraping its hubcaps against its moorings before finally coming to rest. In the rear seat he saw the silhouette of the big kook. A woman with maroon hair climbed down from the driver's seat and called, "Okay, boy, get out that car!"

424

"Not until you clarify your relationship with that drooling old man," the silhouette answered. "I thought that we had escaped from that degenerate old fascist. Apparently I was wrong. All along you've been carrying on an affair with him behind my back. You probably planted him there in front of D. H. Holmes. Now that I think of it you probably planted that mongoloid Mancuso there, too, to start this vicious cycle whirling. How unsuspecting, how ingenuous I've been. For weeks now I've been the dupe of a conspiracy. It's all a plot!"

"Get down from that car!"

"You see?" Miss Annie said through her shutters. "They're at it again."

The rear car door swung rustily open and a bursting desert boot stepped down onto the running board. The kook's head was bandaged. He looked tired and pale.

"I will not stay under the same roof with a loose woman. I'm shocked and hurt. My own mother. No wonder you've turned on me so savagely. I suspect that you are using me as a scapegoat for your own feelings of guilt."

What a family, Mr. Levy thought. The mother did look like something of a floozie. He wondered why the undercover agent had wanted her.

"Shut up your dirty mouth," the woman was screaming. "All this over a fine, decent man like Claude."

"Fine man," Ignatius snorted. "I knew you'd end like this when you started traveling around with those degenerates."

Along the block a few people had come out on their steps. What a day this was going to be. Mr. Levy ran the risk of getting into a public scene with these wild people. His heartburn was spreading out to the limits of his chest.

425

The woman with the maroon hair had fallen to her knees and was asking the sky, "What I done wrong, God? Tell me, Lord. I been good."

"You're kneeling on Rex's grave!" Ignatius shouted. "Now tell me what you and that debauched McCarthyite have been doing? You probably belong to some secret political cell. No wonder I've been bombarded with those witchhunt pamphlets. No wonder I was trailed last night. Where is that Battaglia matchmaker. Where is she? She must be lashed. This whole thing is a coup against me, a vicious scheme to get me out of the way. My God! That bird was doubtlessly trained by a band of fascists. They'll try anything."

"Claude's been courting me," Mrs. Reilly said defiantly.

"What?" Ignatius thundered. "Do you mean to tell me that you have been permitting some old man to paw all over you?"

"Claude's a nice man. All he done is hold my hand a few times."

The blue and yellow eyes crossed in anger. The paws closed over the ears so that he would not have to listen to more.

"Goodness only knows what unmentionable desires that man has. Please don't tell me the whole truth. I would have a total breakdown."

"Shut up!" Miss Annie screamed from behind her shutters. "You people are living on borrowed time in this block."

"Claude ain't smart, but he's a nice man. He's good to his family and that's what counts. Santa says he likes the communiss because he's lonely. He ain't got nothing else to do. If he was to ax me to marry him this very minute, I'd say, 'Okay, Claude.' I would, Ignatius. I wouldn't haveta think twice about it. I got a right to have somebody treat me nice before I die. I got a right not to haveta worry about where my next dollar's coming from. When Claude and me went to get your clothes from that head nurse and she hands us over your wallet with almost thirty dollars in it, that was the last straw. All your craziness was bad enough, but keeping that money from your poor momma . . ."

"I needed the money for a purpose."

"For what? To hang around with dirty women?" Mrs. Reilly lifted herself laboriously from Rex's grave. "You ain't only crazy, Ignatius. You mean, too."

"Do you seriously think that Claude roué wants marriage?" Ignatius slobbered, changing the subject. "You'll be dragged from one reeking motel to another. You'll end up a suicide."

"I'll get married if I want to, boy. You can't stop me. Not now."

"That man is a dangerous radical," Ignatius said darkly. "Goodness knows what political and ideological horrors lurk in his mind. He'll torture you or worse."

"Just who the hell are *you* to try to tell me what to do, Ignatius?" Mrs. Reilly stared at her huffing son. She was disgusted and tired, disinterested in anything that Ignatius might have to say. "Claude is dumb. Okay. I'll grant you that. Claude is all the time worrying me about them communiss. Okay. Maybe he don't know nothing about politics. But I ain't worried about politics. I'm worried about dying half-way decent. Claude can be kind to a person, and that's more than you can do with all your politics and all your graduating smart. For everything nice I ever done for you, I just get kicked around. I want to be treated nice by somebody before I die. You learnt everything, Ignatius, except how to be a human being."

427

"It's not your fate to be well treated," Ignatius

cried. "You're an overt masochist. Nice treatment will confuse and destroy you."

"Go to hell, Ignatius. You broke my heart so many times I can't count them up no more."

"That man shall never enter this house while I am here. After he had grown tired of you, he would probably turn his warped attentions on *me*."

"What's that, crazy? Shut up your silly mouth. I'm fed up. I'll take care of you. You say you wanna take a rest? I can fix you up with a nice rest."

"When I think of my dear departed father barely cold in his grave," Ignatius murmured, pretending to wipe some moisture from his eyes.

"Mr. Reilly died twenty years ago."

"Twenty-*one*," Ignatius gloated. "So. You've forgotten your beloved husband."

"Pardon me," Mr. Levy said weakly. "May I speak with you, Mr. Reilly?"

"What?" Ignatius asked, noticing for the first time the man standing up on the porch.

"What you want with Ignatius?" Mrs. Reilly asked the man. Mr. Levy introduced himself. "Well, this is him in person. I hope you didn't believe that funny story he give you over the phone the other day. I was too tired to grab the phone out his hands."

"Can we all go in the house?" Mr. Levy asked. "I'd like to speak with him privately."

"It don't matter to me," Mrs. Reilly said disinterestedly. She looked down the block and saw her neighbors watching them. "The whole neighborhood knows everything now."

But she opened the front door and the three of them stepped into the tiny entrance hall. Mrs. Reilly put down the paper bag she was carrying that contained her son's scarf and cutlass, and asked, "What you want, Mr. Levy? Ignatius! Come back here and talk to this man."

"Mother, I must attend to my bowels. They are revolting against the trauma of the last twenty-four hours."

"Get out that bathroom, boy, and come back here. Now what you want with crazy, Mr. Levy?"

"Mr. Reilly, do you know anything about this?"

Ignatius looked at the two letters that Mr. Levy produced from his jacket and said, "Of course not. That is your signature. Leave this house immediately. Mother, this is the fiend who fired me so brutally."

"You didn't write this?"

"Mr. Gonzalez was extremely dictatorial. He would never permit me near a typewriter. Actually, he cuffed me once rather viciously when my eyes chanced to stray across some correspondence which he was composing in rather dreadful prose. If I was permitted to shine his cheap shoes, I was grateful. You know how possessive he is about that cesspool company of yours."

"I know. But he says he didn't write this."

"An obvious untruth. His every word is false. He speaks with a forked tongue!"

"This man wants to sue us for a lot of money."

"Ignatius done it," Mrs. Reilly interrupted a little rudely. "Whatever went wrong, Ignatius done it. He makes trouble everyplace he goes. Go on, Ignatius . Tell the man the truth. Go on, boy, before I knock you in the head."

429

"Mother, make this man leave," Ignatius cried, trying to push his mother against Mr. Levy.

"Mr. Reilly, this man wants to sue for $500 thousand. That could ruin me."

"Ain't that awful!" Mrs. Reilly exclaimed. "Ignatius, what you done this poor man?"

As Ignatius was about to discuss the circumspection of his behavior at Levy Pants, the telephone rang.

"Hello?" Mrs. Reilly said. "I'm his mother. Of course I'm sober." She glared at Ignatius. "He is? He did? What? Aw, no." She stared at her son, who was beginning to rasp one paw against the other. "Okay, mister, you'll get your stuff, all except the earring. The bird got that. Okay. Of course I can remember what you telling me. I ain't drunk!" Mrs. Reilly slammed down the telephone and turned on her son with, "That was the weenie man. You're fired."

"Thank God," Ignatius sighed. "I couldn't stand that cart again, I'm afraid."

"What you told him about me, boy? You told him I was a drunk?"

"Of course not. How ludicrous. I don't discuss you with people. No doubt he's spoken with you previously when you were under the influence. You've probably had a date with him for all I know, a drunken spree in several hot dog *boites*."

"You can't even peddle hot dogs in the streets. Was that man angry. He says you gave him more trouble than any vendor he ever had."

"He resented my worldview rather actively."

"Oh, shut up before I slap you again," Mrs. Reilly screamed. "Now tell Mr. Levy here the truth."

What a squalid homelife, Mr. Levy thought. This woman certainly treated her son dictatorially.

"Why, I am telling the truth," Ignatius said.

"Lemme see that letter, Mr. Levy."

"Don't show it to her. She reads rather dreadfully. She'll be confused for days."

Mrs. Reilly knocked Ignatius in the side of the head with her purse.

"Not again!" Ignatius cried.

"Don't hit him," Mr. Levy said. The kook's head was already bandaged. Outside of the prizefighting ring, violence made Mr. Levy ill. This Reilly kook was really pitiful. The mother ran around with some old man, drank, wanted the son out of the way. She was already on the police blotter. That dog was probably the only thing that the kook had ever really had in his life. Sometimes you have to see a person in his real environment to understand him. In his own way Reilly had been very interested in Levy Pants. Now Mr. Levy was sorry that he had fired Reilly. The kook had been proud of his job at the company. "Just let him alone, Mrs. Reilly. We'll get to the bottom of this."

"Help me, sir," Ignatius slobbered, grabbing histrionically at the lapels of Mr. Levy's sports jacket. "Fortuna only knows what she will do to me. I know too much of her sordid activities. I must be eliminated. Have you thought of speaking to that Trixie woman? She knows far more than you suspect."

"That's what my wife says, but I never believed her. After all, Miss Trixie is so old. I wouldn't think she could write a grocery list."

"Old?" Mrs. Reilly asked. "Ignatius! You told me Trixie was the name of some cute girl worked at Levy Pants. You told me you two liked each other. Now I find out she's a grammaw can't hardly write. Ignatius!"

It was sadder than Mr. Levy had thought at first. The poor kook had tried to make his mother think he had a girlfriend.

"Please," Ignatius whispered to Mr. Levy. "Come into my room. I must show you something."

431

"Don't believe a word Ignatius says," Mrs. Reilly called after them as her son dragged Mr. Levy through the door into the musty chamber.

"Just let him alone," Mr. Levy said to Mrs. Reilly somewhat firmly. This Reilly woman wouldn't even give her own child a chance. She was as bad as his wife. No wonder Reilly was such a wreck.

Then the door closed behind them and Mr. Levy suddenly began to feel nauseated. There was a scent of old tea leaves in the bedroom that reminded him of the teapot that Leon Levy had always had near his elbow, the delicately cracked china pot in whose bottom there was always a residue of boiled leaves. He went to the window and opened the shutter, but as he looked out his eyes met those of Miss Annie, who was staring back at him from between the blinds of her shutters. He turned from the window and watched Reilly thumbing through a loose-leaf folder.

"Here it is," Ignatius said. "These are some notes that I jotted while working for your company. They will prove that I loved Levy Pants even more than life itself, that my every waking hour was spent in contemplating means of helping your organization. And often at night I had visions. Phantoms of Levy Pants flitted gloriously across my slumbering psyche. I would never write a letter like that. I *loved* Levy Pants. Here. Read this, sir."

Mr. Levy took the loose-leaf folder and, where Reilly's fat forefinger indicated a line, he read, "Today our office was at last graced by the presence of our lord and master, Mr. G. Levy. To be quite honest, I found him rather casual and unconcerned." The forefinger skipped a line or two. "In time he will learn of my devotion to his firm, of my dedication. My example, in

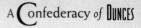

turn, may lead him to once again believe in Levy Pants." The guidepost of a forefinger indicated the next paragraph. "La Trixie still keeps her own counsel, thereby proving herself even wiser than I had thought. I suspect that this woman knows a great deal, that her apathy is a façade for her seeming resentment against Levy Pants. She grows most coherent when she speaks of retirement."

"There is your evidence, sir," Ignatius said, snatching the folder from Mr. Levy's hands. "Interrogate the Trixie jade. The senility is a guise. It is part of her defense against her work and the company. Actually, she hates Levy Pants for not retiring her. And who can blame her? Many times when we were alone, she would babble for hours about plans to 'get' Levy Pants. Her resentment surfaced in the form of vitriolic attacks upon your corporate structure."

Mr. Levy tried to assess the evidence. He knew that Reilly had really liked the company; he had seen it at the company, the woman next door had told him, he had just read it. Trixie, on the other hand, hated the company. Even though his wife and the kook claimed that the senility routine was a front, he doubted that she would be able to write a letter like that. But now he had to get out of the claustrophobic bedroom before he possibly got ill all over the tablets that covered the floor. When Mr. Reilly had been standing next to him pointing out the passages in the notebook, the scent had grown overpowering. He felt for the doorknob, but the Reilly kook threw himself against the door.

433

"You must believe me," he sighed. "The Trixie trollop had a fixation about a turkey or a ham. Or was it a roast? It was all rather fierce and confusing at times.

She swore vengeance in connection with not being retired at the proper age. She was filled with hostility."

Mr. Levy eased him aside and got out into the hall,
where the maroon-haired mother was waiting like a
doorman.

"Thank you, Mr. Reilly," Mr. Levy said. He had to
get out of that claustrophobic miniature of a heartbreak
house. "If I need you again, I'll call you."

"You'll need him again," Mrs. Reilly called as he
passed her and ran down the front steps. "Whatever it
is, Ignatius done it."

She called out something else, but Mr. Levy's roar
drowned out her voice. Blue smoke settled over the
stricken Plymouth, and he was gone.

"Now you done it," Mrs. Reilly was saying to Ignatius, her hands grasping the white smock. "Now we in
trouble for real, boy. You know what they can do you
for forgery? They can throw you in a federal prison.
That poor man's got a $500 thousand case on his hands.
Now you done it, Ignatius. Now you really in trouble."

"Please," Ignatius said weakly. His pale skin was
turning an off-white that shaded into gray. He felt
really ill now. His valve was executing several maneu-
vers that exceeded in originality and violence anything
it had done before. "I told you it would be like this
when I went out to work."

Mr. Levy picked the shortest route back to the Desire Street wharf. He sped out Napoleon to the Broad
overpass and got onto the expressway, fired by an emotion that was a distant but recognizable version of determination. If resentment had really driven Miss Trixie
to writing that letter, then Mrs. Levy was the person
responsible for the Abelman suit. Could Miss Trixie
write something as intelligible as that letter? Mr. Levy

hoped that she could. He drove through Miss Trixie's neighborhood quickly, flashing past the bars and the BOILED CRAWFISH and OYSTERS ON THE HALF SHELL signs that stuck out everywhere. At the apartment house he followed the trail of scraps up the stairs to a brown door. He knocked and Mrs. Levy opened it with, "Look who's back. The idealist's menace. Have you solved your case?"

"Maybe."

"Now you're talking like Gary Cooper. One word I get for an answer. Sheriff Gary Levy." She plucked at an offending aquamarine lash with her fingers. "Well, let's go. Trixie's gorging on the cookies. I'm getting nauseous."

Mr. Levy pushed past his wife into a scene he could never have imagined. Levy's Lodge had not prepared him for interiors like the one he had just seen on Constantinople Street—and for this one. Miss Trixie's apartment was decorated with scraps, with junk, with bits of metal, with cardboard boxes. Somewhere beneath it all there was furniture. The surface, however, the visible terrain, was a landscape of old clothes and crates and newspapers. There was a pass through the center of the mountain, a clearing among the litter, a narrow aisle of clear floor that led to a window where Miss Trixie was seated in a chair sampling the Dutch cookies. Mr. Levy walked down the aisle past the black wig that hung from atop a crate, the high pumps tossed on a pile of newspapers. The only aspect of the rejuvenation that Miss Trixie had apparently retained was the teeth; they gleamed between her thin lips as they knifed into the cookies.

435

"Suddenly you're very silent," Mrs. Levy observed. "What is it, Gus? Another mission ended in failure?"

"Miss Trixie," Mr. Levy screamed into her ears. "Did you write a letter to Abelman's Dry Goods?"

"Now you're scraping rock bottom," Mrs. Levy said. "The idealist fooled you again, I guess. You really fall for that Reilly's line."

"Miss Trixie!"

"What?" Miss Trixie snarled. "I must say you people know how to retire a person."

Mr. Levy handed her the letter. She picked a magnifying glass from the floor and studied the letters. The green visor cast a deadly color upon her face, upon the Dutch cookie crumbs that rimmed her thin lips. When she put down the magnifying glass, she wheezed happily, "You people in trouble now."

"But did you write that to Abelman? Mr. Reilly said you did."

"Who?"

"Mr. Reilly. The big man with the green cap who used to work at Levy Pants." Mr. Levy showed Miss Trixie the photographs in the morning paper. "That one there."

Miss Trixie applied her magnifying glass to the newspaper and said, "Oh, my goodness. So that's what happened to him." Poor Gloria. He seemed to be injured. "That's Mr. Reilly, is it?"

"Yes. You remember him, I guess. He says you wrote that letter."

"He did?" Gloria Reilly wouldn't lie. Not Gloria. True blue. Gloria had always been her friend. Miss Trixie tried hazily to recall. Perhaps she had written the letter. All sorts of things happened that she couldn't remember anymore. "Well, I guess I did. Yes. Now that you mention it, I guess I did write that. You people deserve it, too. You've driven me crazy these last few years. No retirement. No ham. Nothing. I must say I hope you lose everything you own."

"You wrote that?" Mrs. Levy asked. "After all I've done for you, you wrote something like that? A viper in our own bosom! You can kiss Levy Pants goodbye, traitor. Discarded? You'll get discarded!"

Miss Trixie smiled. That annoying woman was really getting excited. Gloria always had been her friend. Now the annoying woman would go to the poorhouse. Perhaps. But right now she was coming toward her, those aquamarine fingernails poised like talons. Miss Trixie started to scream.

"Let her alone," Mr. Levy said to his wife. "Well, well. Won't Susan and Sandra like to hear about this. Their mother tortures an old lady so much that the girls are in danger of losing all of their cardigans and culottes."

"So. Blame me," Mrs. Levy said wildly. "I stuck the paper in the typewriter. I helped her peck it out."

"Didn't you write that letter to get even with Levy Pants because you weren't retired?"

"Yes, yes," Miss Trixie said vaguely.

"To think I trusted you," Mrs. Levy spat at Miss Trixie. "Give me back those teeth."

Her husband blocked her grab for Miss Trixie's mouth.

"Quiet!" Miss Trixie snarled, all of her white fangs gleaming. "I can't even have a little peace in my own apartment."

"If it wasn't for your stupid, harebrained 'project' this woman would have been retired long ago," Mr. Levy said to his wife. "After all those years of predicting things, *you* turn out to be the one who almost threw Levy Pants down the drain."

437

"I see. You don't blame her. You blame a woman of standards and ideals. If a thief broke into Levy Pants, *I*'d be to blame. You need help, Gus. Badly."

"Yes, I do. And from Lenny's doctor, of all people."

"Wonderful, Gus."

"Quiet!"

"But you're the one who's going to call Lenny's doctor," Mr. Levy said to his wife. "I want you to get him to declare Miss Trixie senile and incompetent and to explain the motivation for writing the letter."

"This is your problem," Mrs. Levy answered angrily. "You call him."

"Susan and Sandra won't like to hear about their mother's little mistake."

"And blackmail, too."

"I've learned a few things from you. After all, we've been married for some time." Mr. Levy watched anger and anxiety play upon his wife's face. For once she had nothing to say. "The girls won't want to know that their dear mother was such a fool. Now plan to get Trixie over to Lenny's doctor. With her admission and any doctor's testimony, Abelman doesn't have an outside chance on this case. All you'd have to do is drag her into a courtroom and let a judge look at her."

"I'm a very attractive woman," Miss Trixie said automatically.

"Of course you are," Mr. Levy said, bending down next to her. "We're going to retire you, Miss Trixie. With a raise. You've had a lousy deal."

"Retirement?" Miss Trixie wheezed. "I must say this is unexpected. Thank goodness."

"You'll sign a statement that you wrote that letter, won't you?"

438

"Of course I will!" Miss Trixie cried. What a friend Gloria was. Gloria knew how to help her out. Gloria was smart. Thank goodness Gloria had remembered this magic letter. "I'll say anything you want me to."

"Everything is suddenly clear to me," Mrs. Levy's bitter voice said behind a pile of newspapers. "I'm blackmailed with my two darling girls. I'm pushed out of the way so that you can be a bigger playboy than ever. Now Levy Pants will be really down the drain. You think you have something on me."

"Oh, I do. And Levy Pants will be down the drain. But not because one of your games wrecked it." Mr. Levy looked over the two letters. "This Abelman business has made me think about a lot of things. How come nobody buys our pants. Because they stink. Because they're made from the same patterns my father used twenty years ago, the same fabrics. Because that old tyrant wouldn't change a thing in that plant. Because he destroyed whatever initiative I had."

"Your father was a brilliant man. Not another word of disrespect from you."

"Shut up. Trixie's oddball letter gave me an idea. From now on we make bermuda shorts only. Less trouble, higher profits on lower expenditures. I want a whole new line of wash and wear swatches from the mills. Levy Pants becomes Levy Shorts."

" 'Levy shorts.' That's rich. Don't make me laugh. You'll go broke in a year. Anything to obliterate the memory of your father. You can't run a business. You're a failure, a playboy, a racetrack tout."

"Quiet! I must say you people are a nuisance. If this is retirement, I'd rather be back at that Levy Pants." Miss Trixie raked at them with her cookie box. "Now get out of my house and mail me my check."

439
......

"I couldn't run Levy Pants. That's true. I think I can run Levy Shorts."

"Suddenly you're very smug," Mrs. Levy said in a voice that bordered on hysteria. Gus Levy operating a company? Gus Levy dominant? What could she say to Susan and Sandra? What could she say to Gus Levy? What would happen to her? "The Foundation goes down the drain, too, I guess."

"Of course not," Mr. Levy smiled inwardly. At last his wife was rudderless, trying to steer some sort of course on a sea of confusion, asking him for directions. "We'll make an award. What were they supposed to be for, meritorious service and bravery?"

"Yes," Mrs. Levy said humbly.

"Here. This is brave." He picked up the newspaper and pointed to the Negro who stood over the fallen idealist. "He gets the first award."

"What? A criminal with dark glasses? A Bourbon Street character? Please, Gus. Not this. Leon Levy is dead only a few years. Let him rest in peace."

"It's very practical, the kind of maneuver old Leon would have made himself. Most of our workers are Negroes. Good public relations. And I'll probably need more and better workers before long. This will make for a good employment climate."

"But not to *that*." Mrs. Levy sounded as if she were retching. "The awards are for *nice* people."

"Where's the idealism you're always coming on so strong for? I thought you had an interest in minority groups. At least you've always said so. Anyway, Reilly was worth saving. He led me to the real culprit."

"You can't live the rest of your life on spite."

"Who's living on spite? I'm doing some

constructive things at last. Miss Trixie, where's your telephone?"

"Who?" Miss Trixie was watching a freighter from Monrovia depart with a dockful of International Harvester tractors. "I don't have one. There's one at the grocery on the corner."

"Okay, Mrs. Levy. Go down to the grocery. Call Lenny's doctor and call the newspaper to find out if they know how we can reach Jones, but those people usually don't have telephones. Try the police, too. They might know. Give me the number. I'll call him personally."

Mrs. Levy stood staring at her husband, her colored lashes motionless.

"If you're going to the store, you can just get me that Easter ham," Miss Trixie rasped. "I want to see that ham right here in my home! I don't want any double talk this time. If you people want a confession from me, you'd better start paying off."

She snarled once at Mrs. Levy, flashing her teeth as if they were a symbol of something, a gesture of defiance.

"There," Mr. Levy said to his wife. "You have three reasons for going to the grocery now." He handed her a ten-dollar bill. "I'll wait for you here."

Mrs. Levy took the money and said to her husband, "I guess you're happy now. Now I'll be your maid. You'll hold this over my head like a sword. One little misjudgment and I suffer all this."

"One little misjudgment? A libel suit for half a million? What are you suffering? You're just going to the corner grocery."

Mrs. Levy turned and found her way along the aisle. The door slammed and, as if a weighty problem had been lifted from her, Miss Trixie fell into a juvenile slumber. Mr. Levy listened to her snoring and watched the Monrovian freighter moving out into the harbor and turning downstream toward the Gulf.

His mind grew calm for the first time in several days, and some of the events surrounding the letter began passing in review through his consciousness. He thought of the letter to Abelman, and then his mind was recalling another place where he had heard similar language. It was in the Reilly kook's yard just an hour ago. "She must be lashed." "Mongoloid Mancuso." So he had written it after all. Mr. Levy looked tenderly down at the little accused party snoring over her box of Dutch cookies. For everyone's sake, he thought, you will have to be declared incompetent and confess, Miss Trixie. You are being framed. Mr. Levy laughed out loud. Why had Miss Trixie confessed so sincerely?

"Silence!" Miss Trixie snarled, snapping awake.

That Reilly kook had really been worth saving after all. He had saved himself, Miss Trixie, and Mr. Levy, too, in his own kook way. Whoever Burma Jones was, he deserved a generous award . . . or reward. Offering him a job at the new Levy Shorts would be even better for public relations. An award and a job. With some good newspaper publicity to tie in with the opening of Levy Shorts. Was that a gimmick or wasn't it?

Mr. Levy watched the freighter cross the mouth of the Industrial Canal. Mrs. Levy would be on a ship soon, destination San Juan. She could visit her mother on the beach, laughing and singing and dancing. Mrs. Levy wouldn't really fit into the Levy Shorts plan.

f o u r t e e n

IGNATIUS SPENT THE DAY in his room napping fitfully and attacking his rubber glove during his frequent, anxious moments of consciousness. Throughout the afternoon the telephone in the hall had been ringing, each new ring making him more nervous and anxious. He lunged at the glove, deflowering it, stabbing it, conquering it. Like any celebrity, Ignatius had attracted his fans: His mother's jinxed relatives, neighbors, people Mrs. Reilly had not seen for years. They had all telephoned. At every ring Ignatius imagined that it was Mr. Levy calling back, but he always heard his mother say to the caller the lines that were becoming tearfully standard, "Ain't this awful? What I'm gonna do? Now our name is really ruint." When Ignatius could stand it no longer, he would billow out of his room in search of a Dr. Nut. If he chanced to meet his mother in the hall, she would not look at him but rather study the fleecy spheres of lint that drifted along the floor in her son's wake. There seemed to be nothing that he could say to her.

What would Mr. Levy do? Abelman, unfortunately, was apparently a rather petty person, a man too small to accept a little criticism, a hypersensitive molecule of a human. He had written to the wrong person; the militant and courageous broadside had been

443

delivered before the wrong audience. At this point his nervous system could not manage a court trial. He would break down completely before the judge. He wondered how long it would be before Mr. Levy descended upon him again. What senile conundrums was Miss Trixie babbling to Mr. Levy? An infuriated and confused Mr. Levy would return, this time determined to have him incarcerated at once. Now waiting for this return was like waiting for an execution. The dull headache persisted. The Dr. Nuts tasted like gall. Abelman certainly wanted a great deal of money; that sensitive plant of an Abelman must have been greatly offended. When the true author of the letter was discovered, what would Abelman demand in lieu of $500 thousand? A life?

The Dr. Nuts seemed only as an acid gurgling down into his intestine. He filled with gas, the sealed valve trapping it just as one pinches the mouth of a balloon. Great eructations rose from his throat and bounced upward toward the refuse-laden bowl of the milk glass chandelier. Once a person was asked to step into this brutal century, anything could happen. Everywhere there lurked pitfalls like Abelman, the insipid Crusaders for Moorish Dignity, the Mancuso cretin, Dorian Greene, newspaper reporters, stripteasers, birds, photography, juvenile delinquents, Nazi pornographers. And especially Myrna Minkoff. The musky minx must be dealt with. Somehow. Someday. She must pay. Whatever happened, he must attend to her even if the revenge took years and he had to stalk her through decades from one coffee shop to another, from one folk singing orgy to another, from subway train to pad to cotton field to demonstration. Ignatius invoked

444

an elaborate Elizabethan curse upon Myrna and, rolling over, frantically abused the glove once more.

How dare his mother contemplate a marriage. Only someone as simpleminded as she could be so disloyal. The aged fascist would conduct witchhunt after witchhunt until the formerly intact Ignatius J. Reilly was reduced to a fragmented and mumbling vegetable. The aged fascist would testify for Mr. Levy so that his future stepson would be locked away and he would be free to satisfy his warped and archaic desires upon the unsuspecting Irene Reilly, to perform his conservative practices upon Irene Reilly with free enterprise. Prostitutes were not protected by the Social Security and unemployment compensation systems. No doubt the Robichaux roué was thus attracted to them. Only Fortuna knew what he had learned at their hands.

Mrs. Reilly listened to the squeaking and belching emanating from her son's room and wondered whether, on top of everything else, he were having a fit. But she didn't want to look at Ignatius. Whenever she heard his door opening, she tried to run to her room to avoid him. Five hundred thousand dollars was a sum she could not even imagine. She could hardly imagine the punishment given someone who had done something bad enough to be worth five hundred thousand. If there were any cause for suspicion on Mr. Levy's part, there was none on hers. Ignatius had written whatever it was. Wouldn't this be fine? Ignatius in jail. There was only one way to save him. She carried the telephone as far down the hall as she could, and for the fourth time that day, she dialed Santa Battaglia's number.

"Lord, honey, you really worried," Santa said. "What happened now?"

"I'm afraid Ignatius is in worst trouble than just a

445

picture in the paper," Mrs. Reilly whispered. "I can't talk over the phone. Santa, you was right all along. Ignatius gotta go to the Charity."

"Well, at last. I been talking myself hoarse telling you that. Claude just rang up a little while ago. He says Ignatius made a big scene at the hospital when they met. Claude says he's ascared of Ignatius, he's so big."

"Ain't that awful. It was terrible in the hospital. I already told you how Ignatius started screaming. All them nurses and sick people. I coulda died. Claude ain't too angry, huh?"

"He ain't angry, but he don't like you being alone in that house. He ax me if maybe him and me shouldn't come over there and stay with you."

"Don't do that, babe," Mrs. Reilly said quickly.

"What kinda trouble Ignatius is in now?"

"I'll tell you later. Right now I can only say I been thinking about this Charity business all day, and I finally made up my mind. Now is the time. He's my own child, but we gotta get him treated for his own sake." Mrs. Reilly tried to think of the phrase that was always used in courtroom dramas on TV. "We gotta get him declared temporary insane."

"*Temporary?*" Santa scoffed.

"We gotta help out Ignatius before they come drag him off."

"Who's gonna drag him off?"

"It seem like he pulled a boo-boo when he was working at Levy Pants."

"Oh, Lord! Not something else. Irene! Hang up and call them people at the Charity right now, honey."

"No, listen. I don't wanna be here when they come, I mean, Ignatius is big. He might make trouble. I couldn't stand that. My nerves is bad enough now."

"Big is right. It'll be like capturing a wild elephant. Them people better have them a great big net," Santa said eagerly. "Irene, this is the best decision you ever made. I tell you what. I'll call up the Charity right now. You come over here. I'll get Claude to come over, too. He'll sure be glad to hear this. Whoo! You'll be sending out wedding invitations in about a week. You gonna have you some little properties before the year's out, sweetheart. You gonna have you a railroad pension."

It all sounded good to Mrs. Reilly, but she asked a little hesitantly, "What about them communiss?"

"Don't worry about them, darling. We'll get rid of them communiss. Claude's gonna be too busy fixing up that house of yours. He's gonna have his hands full turning Ignatius's room into a den."

Santa broke into some baritone peals of laughter.

"Miss Annie's gonna turn green when she sees this place fixed up."

"Then tell that woman, say, 'You go out and shake yourself a little. You'll get your house fixed up, too,'" Santa guffawed. "Now get off the line, babe, and get over here. I'm calling the Charity right now. Get out that house fast!"

Santa slammed the telephone down in Mrs. Reilly's ear.

Mrs. Reilly looked out the front shutters. It was very dark now, which was good. The neighbors would not see too much if they took Ignatius away during the night. She ran into the bathroom and powdered her face and the front of her dress, drew a surrealistic version of a mouth beneath her nose, and dashed into her bedroom to find a coat. When she got to the front door, she stopped. She couldn't say goodbye to Ignatius like this. He was her child.

447

She went up to his bedroom door and listened to the wildly twanging bedsprings as they reached a crescendo, as they built toward a finale worthy of Grieg's *In the Hall of the Mountain King*. She knocked, but there was no answer.

"Ignatius," she called sadly.

"What do you want?" a breathless voice asked at last.

"I'm going out, Ignatius. I wanted to say goodbye."

Ignatius did not answer.

"Ignatius, open up," Mrs. Reilly pleaded. "Come kiss me goodbye, honey."

"I don't feel at all well. I can hardly move."

"Come on, son."

The door opened slowly. Ignatius stuck his fat gray face into the hall. His mother's eyes watered when she saw the bandage.

"Now kiss me, honey. I'm sorry it all had to end like this."

"What do all of these lachrymose clichés mean?" Ignatius asked suspiciously. "Why are you suddenly pleasant? Don't you have some old man to meet somewhere?"

"You was right, Ignatius. You can't go to work. I shoulda known that. I shoulda tried to get that debt paid off some other way." A tear slid from Mrs. Reilly's eyes and washed a little trail of clean skin through the powder. "If that Mr. Levy calls, don't answer the phone. I'm gonna take care of you."

"Oh, my God!" Ignatius bellowed. "Now I'm really in trouble. Goodness knows what you're planning. Where are you going?"

"Stay inside and don't answer the phone."

"Why? What is this?" The bloodshot eyes flashed

with fright. "Who was that you were whispering to on the phone?"

"You won't have to worry about Mr. Levy, son. I'm gonna fix you up. Just remember your poor momma's got your welfare at heart."

"That's what I'm afraid of."

"Don't never be mad at me, honey," Mrs. Reilly said and, jumping up in her bowling shoes that she had not taken off since Angelo had telephoned her the night before, she embraced Ignatius and kissed him on his moustache.

She released him and ran to the front door, where she turned and called, "I'm sorry I run into that building, Ignatius. I love you."

The shutters slammed and she was gone.

"Come back," Ignatius thundered. He ripped at the shutters, but the old Plymouth, one of its front tires fenderless and exposed as if it were a stock car, was rumbling to life. "Come back, please. Mother!"

"Aw, shut up," Miss Annie hollered from somewhere in the darkness.

His mother had something up her sleeve, some clumsy plan, some scheme that would ruin him forever. Why had she insisted that he stay inside? She knew that he would not be going anywhere in his present condition. He found Santa Battaglia's number and dialed it. He must speak with his mother.

"This is Ignatius Reilly," he said when Santa had answered. "Is my mother coming down there tonight?"

"No, she ain't," Santa replied coldly. "I ain't spoke with your momma all day."

449

Ignatius hung up. Something was going on. He had heard his mother saying "Santa" over the telephone at least two or three times during the day. And that last telephone call, that whispered communication just before his mother had left. His mother only whispered to the Battaglia bawd and then it was only when they were exchanging secrets. At once Ignatius suspected the reason for his mother's emotional farewell, for its finality. She had already told him that the Battaglia matchmaker had advised a vacation for him in the psychiatric ward at Charity. Everything made sense. In a psychiatric ward he would not be liable to prosecution by Abelman and Levy, or whoever it was who would push the case. Perhaps both of them would sue him, Abelman for character defamation and Levy for forgery. To his mother's limited mind the psychiatric ward would seem an attractive alternative. It was just like her, with the very best of intentions, to have her child harnessed by a straitjacket and electrocuted by shock treatments. Of course, his mother might not be considering this at all. However, whenever dealing with her, it was always best to prepare for the worst. Wife of Bath Battaglia's lie was itself not very reassuring.

In the United States you are innocent until they prove you guilty. Perhaps Miss Trixie had confessed. Why hadn't Mr. Levy telephoned back? Ignatius would not be tossed into a mental clinic while, legally, he was still innocent of having written the letter. His mother, typically, had responded to Mr. Levy's visit in the most irrational and emotional manner possible. "I'm gonna take care of you." "I'm gonna fix you up." Yes, she would fix him up all right. A hose would be turned on him. Some cretin psychoanalyst would attempt to comprehend the singularity of his worldview. In frustration, the psychoanalyst would have him crammed into a cell three feet square. No. That was out of the question. Jail was preferable. There they only limited you physically.

450

In a mental ward they tampered with your soul and worldview and mind. He would never tolerate that. And his mother had been so apologetic about this mysterious protection she was going to give him. All signs pointed to Charity Hospital.

Oh, Fortuna, you wretch!

Now he was waddling around in the little house like a sitting duck. Whatever strong-arm men the hospital employed had their sights aimed directly at him. Ignatius Reilly, clay pigeon. His mother might only have gone to one of her bowling Bacchanalia. On the other hand, a barred truck might be speeding to Constantinople Street right now.

Escape. Escape.

Ignatius looked in his wallet. The thirty dollars was gone, apparently confiscated by his mother at the hospital. He looked at the clock. It was almost eight o'clock. Between napping and assaulting the glove, the afternoon and evening passed rather quickly. Ignatius searched his room, flinging Big Chief tablets around, mashing them underfoot, dragging them from beneath his bed. He came up with some scattered coins and went to work on the desk, where he found a few more. The total was sixty cents, a sum that limited and blocked escape routes. He could at least find a safe haven for the rest of the evening: the Prytania. After the theater had closed, he could pass along Constantinople Street to see whether his mother had come home.

There was a slipshod frenzy of dressing. The red flannel nightshirt sailed up and hung on the chandelier. He jammed his toes into the desert boots and leaped as well as he could into the tweed trousers, which he could hardly button at the waist. Shirt, cap, overcoat, Ignatius put them on blindly and ran into the hall, careening

451

against the narrow walls. He was just reaching for the front door when three loud knocks cracked against the shutters.

Mr. Levy returned? His valve sent out a distress signal that established communication with his hands. He scratched the bumps on his paws and peered through the shutters, expecting to see several hirsute brutes from the hospital.

There on the porch stood Myrna in a shapeless olive drab corduroy car coat. Her black hair was braided into a pigtail that twisted under one ear and fell on her breast. A guitar was slung over her shoulders.

Ignatius was about to burst through the shutters, splintering slats and latches, and wrap that one hemp-like pigtail around her throat until she turned blue. But reason won. He was not looking at Myrna; he was looking at an escape route. Fortuna had relented. She was not depraved enough to end this vicious cycle by throttling him in a straitjacket, by sealing him up in a cement block tomb lighted by fluorescent tubes. Fortuna wished to make amends. Somehow she had summoned and flushed Myrna minx from a subway tube, from some picket line, from the pungent bed of some Eurasian existentialist, from the hands of some epileptic Negro Buddhist, from the verbose midst of a group therapy session.

"Ignatius, are you in that dump?" Myrna demanded in her flat, direct, slightly hostile voice. She beat on the shutters again, squinting through her black-rimmed glasses. Myrna was not astigmatic; the lenses were clear glass; she wore the glasses to prove her dedication and intensity of purpose. Her dangling earring reflected the rays of the streetlight like tinkling glass Chinese ornaments. "Listen, I can tell there's somebody in there. I heard you stomping around in that hall. Open up these crummy shutters."

"Yes, yes, I'm here," Ignatius cried. He tore at the shutters and pushed them open. "Thank Fortuna you've come."

"Jesus. You look terrible. Like you're having a nervous breakdown or something. Why the bandage? Ignatius, what's the matter? Look how much weight you've gained. I've just been reading these pitiful signs out here on the porch. Boy, have you had it."

"I've gone through hell," Ignatius slobbered, pulling Myrna into the hall by the sleeve of her coat. "Why did you step out of my life, you minx? Your new hair-do is fascinating and cosmopolitan." He snatched at her pigtail and pressed it to his wet moustache, kissing it vigorously. "The scent of soot and carbon in your hair excites me with suggestions of glamorous Gotham. We must leave immediately. I must go flower in Manhattan."

"I knew something was wrong. But *this.* You are really in bad shape, Ig."

"Quickly. To a motel. My natural impulses are screaming for release. Do you have any money on you?"

"Don't put me on," Myrna said angrily. She grabbed the soggy pigtail from Ignatius' paws and threw it over her shoulder onto the guitar where it landed with a twang. "Look. Ignatius. I'm beat. I've been on the road since nine o'clock yesterday morning. As soon as I mailed you that letter about the Peace Party routine, I said to myself, 'Myrna. Listen. This guy needs more than just a letter. He needs your help. He's sinking fast. Are you dedicated enough to save a mind rotting right before your eyes? Are you committed enough to salvage the wreckage of that mentality?' I came out of the post office and got in my car and just started driving. All night. Straight. I mean, the more I thought about that wild Peace Party telegram, the more upset I got."

Apparently Myrna was very hard up for causes in Manhattan.

"I don't blame you," Ignatius cried. "Wasn't that telegram horrible? A deranged fantasy. I've been in the depths of depression for weeks. After all these years that I've stuck by my mother's side, she has decided to get married and wants me out of the way. We must leave. I can't stand this house another moment."

"What? Who'd marry *her*?"

"Thank God you understand. You can see how ludicrous and impossible everything has become."

"Where is she? I'd like to outline for that woman what she's done to you."

"She's out somewhere failing her blood test at the moment. I don't want to see her again."

"I guess not. You poor kid. What have you been doing, Ignatius? Just lying around in your room doping off?"

"Yes. For weeks, I've been immobilized by the neurotic apathy. Do you remember the fantasy letter about the arrest and the accident? I wrote that when my mother first met this debauched old man. It was then that my equilibrium started to fail. Since then, it's been a continuously downward movement culminating in the schizophrenia of the Peace Party. Those signs outside were just one physical manifestation of my inward torment. My psychotic desire for peace was no doubt a wishful attempt to end the hostilities which have been existing in this little house. I can only be grateful that you were perceptive enough to analyze my fantasy life as embodied in my letters. Thank goodness they were distress signals written in a code which you could understand."

"I can tell how inactive you've been from your weight."

"I've gained pounds lying continuously in bed, seeking surcease and sublimation in food. Now we must run. I must leave this house. It has terrible associations."

"I told you to get out of this place a long time ago. Come on, let's get you packed." Myrna's monotonous voice was growing enthusiastic. "This is fantastic. I knew you'd have to break away sooner or later to preserve your mental health."

"If only I had listened to you earlier, I wouldn't have had to go through this horror." Ignatius embraced Myrna and pressed her and her guitar flatly against the wall. He could see that she was beside herself with joy over finding a legitimate cause, a bona fide case history, a new movement. "There will be a place for you in heaven, my minx. Now we must dash."

He tried to drag her out the front door, but she said, "Don't you want to pack anything?"

"Oh, of course. There are all of my notes and jottings. We must never let them fall into the hands of my mother. She may make a fortune from them. It would be too ironic." They went into his room. "By the way, you should know that my mother is enjoying the questionable attentions of a fascist."

"Oh, no!"

"Yes. Look at this. You can imagine how they've been torturing me."

He handed Myrna one of the pamphlets that his

455

mother had slipped under the door of his room, *Is Your Neighbor Really an American?* Myrna read a note written in the margin of the cover: "Read this Irene. It is good. There is some questions at the end you can ask your boy."

"Oh, Ignatius!" Myrna moaned. "What has it been like?"

"Traumatic and dreadful. At the moment I think they're out somewhere lashing some moderate whom my mother overheard speaking in favor of the United Nations in the grocery this morning. She's been mumbling about the incident all day." Ignatius belched. "I've been through weeks of terror."

"It's so strange to find your mother gone. She used to be around here all the time." Myrna hung her guitar on a bedpost and stretched across the bed. "This room. We used to have a ball in here, exposing our minds and souls, composing anti-Talc manifestos. I guess that fraud is still hanging around that school."

"I would imagine so," Ignatius said absently. He wished that Myrna would get off the bed. Soon her mind would turn to exposing other things. Anyway, they had to get out of the house. He was in the closet, where he was looking for the overnight bag that his mother had bought for him for a disastrous one-day stay at a boys' camp when he was eleven. He pawed through a pile of yellowed drawers like a dog digging for a bone, throwing the drawers up behind him in an arc. "Perhaps you'd better rouse yourself, my little lily. There are tablets to be collected, notes to be gathered. You might look under the bed."

Myrna swung herself off the damp sheets, saying, "I've tried to describe you to my friends in the group therapy group, working away in this room, sealed off

from society. This strange medieval mind in its clois-
ter."

"No doubt they were intrigued," Ignatius murmured. Having found the bag, he was filling it with
some socks he found lying on the floor. "Soon they'll
be able to see me in the flesh."

"Just wait till they hear all that originality pouring
out of your head."

"Ho hum," Ignatius yawned. "Perhaps my mother
has done me a great favor by planning to remarry.
Those Oedipal bonds were beginning to overwhelm
me." He threw his yo-yo into the bag. "Apparently you
had safe passage through the South."

"I didn't have a moment to really stop along the
way. Almost thirty-six hours of drive, drive, drive."
Myrna was making piles of the Big Chief tablets. "I did
stop at a Negro diner last night, but they wouldn't serve
me. I think the guitar threw them off."

"That must have been it. They took you for some
red-neck hillbilly singer. I've had some experience with
those people. They're rather limited."

"I can't believe that I am *actually* taking you out of
this dungeon, this hole."

"It is unbelievable, isn't it? To think that I fought
your wisdom for years."

"We are going to have the most fantastic time in
New York. Honestly."

"I can't wait," Ignatius said, packing his scarf and
cutlass. "The Statue of Liberty, the Empire State
Building, the thrill of opening night on Broadway with
my favorite musicomedy stars. Gab sessions in the Village over espresso with challenging, contemporary
minds."

"You're coming to grips with yourself at last.

457

Really. I can hardly believe what I've heard in this shack tonight. We'll work on your problems. You're going into a whole new and vital phase. Your inactivity is over. I can tell. I can hear it. Just think of the great thought that is going to come streaming out of that head when we've finally cleared away all the cobwebs and taboos and crippling attachments."

"Goodness knows what will happen," Ignatius said disinterestedly. "We must leave. Now. I should warn you that my mother may return momentarily. If I see her again, I'll regress horribly. We must dash."

"Ignatius, you're jumping all over the place. Relax. The worst is over."

"No, it isn't," Ignatius said quickly. "My mother may return with her mob. You should see them. White supremacists, Protestants, or worse. Let me get my lute and trumpet. Are the tablets gathered together?"

"This stuff in here is fascinating," Myrna said, indicating the tablet through which she was flipping. "Gems of nihilism."

"That is merely a fragment of the whole."

"Aren't you even going to leave your mother some very bitter note, some articulate protest or something?"

"It would hardly be worthwhile. She'd be weeks in comprehending it." Ignatius cradled the lute and trumpet in one arm and the overnight bag in the other. "Please don't drop that looseleaf folder. It contains the Journal, a sociological fantasy on which I've been working. It is my most commercial effort. Wonderful film possibilities at the hands of a Walt Disney or a George Pal."

"Ignatius." Myrna stopped in the doorway, her arms laden with tablets, and moved her colorless lips for a moment before she spoke, as if she were formulating an address. Her tired, highway-drugged eyes searched Ignatius' face through the sparkling lenses. "This is a very meaningful moment. I feel as if I'm *saving* someone."

"You are, you are. Now we must flee. Please. We'll chat later." Ignatius pushed past her and lumbered down to the car, opening the rear door of the little Renault and climbing in among the placards and piles of pamphlets that covered the seat. The car smelled like a newsstand. "Hurry up! We don't have time to stage a *tableau-vivant* here before the house."

"I mean, are you really going to sit back there?" Myrna asked as she dropped her load of tablets through the rear door.

"Of course I am," Ignatius bellowed. "I am certainly not going to sit up in that deathtrap of a front seat for highway travel. Now get in this go-cart and get us out of here."

"Hold on. I left a lot of tablets behind," Myrna said and ran into the house, her guitar thumping against her side. She came down the steps with another load and stopped on the brick sidewalk, turning to look at the house. Ignatius could tell that she was attempting to *record* the scene: Eliza crossing the ice with a particularly large genius in her arms. Like Harriet Beecher Stowe, Myrna was still around to offend. At last, in response to Ignatius' cries, she came down to the car and threw the second load of tablets onto Ignatius' lap. "There are still some left under the bed, I think."

"Never mind about those!" Ignatius screamed. "Get in and start this thing. Oh, my God. Don't stick that guitar in my face like that. Why can't you just carry a purse like a decent young lady?"

"Go fall in a hole," Myrna said angrily. She slid

459

into the front seat and started the car. "Where do you want to spend the night?"

"Spend the night?" Ignatius thundered. "We're not spending the night anywhere. We must drive straight."

"Ignatius, I'm about to drop dead. I've been in this car since yesterday morning."

"Well, get across Lake Pontchartrain at least."

"Okay. We can take the causeway and stop in Mandeville."

"No!" Myrna would drive him right into the alerted arms of some psychiatrist. "We can't stop there. The water's polluted. They're having an epidemic."

"Yeah? Then I'll take the old bridge to Slidell."

"Yes. It's far safer anyway. Barges are always hurtling into that causeway. We'll plunge into the lake and drown." The Renault was dragging very low in the rear and accelerated slowly. "This car is rather small for my frame. Are you sure that you know how to get to New York? I seriously doubt whether I can survive more than a day or two in this fetal position."

"Hey, where are you two beatniks going?" Miss Annie's voice called faintly from behind her shutters. The Renault moved into the center of the street.

"Does that old bitch still live there?" Myrna asked.

"Shut up and get us out of here!"

"Are you going to bug me like this?" Myrna glared at the green cap in the rear-view mirror. "I mean, I'd like to know."

460

"Oh, my valve!" Ignatius gasped. "Please don't make a scene. My psyche will crumble entirely after the assaults it has recently received."

"I'm sorry. For a while it sounded like old times

with me playing chauffeur and you bugging me from the back seat."

"I certainly hope it isn't snowing up north. My system simply will not function under those conditions. And please watch out for Greyhound Scenicruisers along the way. They'll demolish a toy like this."

"Ignatius, all at once you're your old horrible self. All at once I think I'm making a very big mistake."

"A mistake? Of course not," Ignatius said sweetly. "But watch out for that ambulance. We don't want to begin our pilgrimage with an accident."

As the ambulance passed, Ignatius hunched over and saw "Charity Hospital" printed on its door. The rotating red light atop the ambulance splashed over the Renault for a brief moment as the vehicles passed each other. Ignatius felt insulted. He had expected a massive barred truck. They had underestimated him in sending out an old, well-used Cadillac ambulance. He would easily have been able to smash all of those windows. Then the glowing Cadillac fins were two blocks behind them and Myrna was turning onto St. Charles Avenue.

Now that Fortuna had saved him from one cycle, where would she spin him now? The new cycle would be so different from anything he had ever known.

Myrna prodded and shifted the Renault through the city traffic masterfully, weaving in and out of impossibly narrow lanes until they were clear of the last twinkling streetlight of the last swampy suburb. Then they were in darkness in the center of the salt marshes. Ignatius looked out at the highway marker that reflected their headlights. U.S. 11. The marker flew past. He rolled down the window an inch or two and breathed the salt air blowing in over the marshes from the Gulf.

461

As if the air were a purgative, his valve opened. He breathed again, this time more deeply. The dull headache was lifting.

He stared gratefully at the back of Myrna's head, at the pigtail that swung innocently at his knee. Gratefully. How ironic, Ignatius thought. Taking the pigtail in one of his paws, he pressed it warmly to his wet moustache.

ABOUT THE AUTHOR

JOHN KENNEDY TOOLE was born in New Orleans in 1937 and died in 1969. He received a master's degree in English from Columbia University and taught at Hunter College, the University of Southwestern Louisiana, and Dominican College in New Orleans.